NOTES AND QUERIES

HISTORICAL AND GENEALOGICAL

CHIEFLY RELATING TO

INTERIOR PENNSYLVANIA.

[REPRINT THIRD SERIES.]

EDITED BY

WILLIAM HENRY EGLE, M. D., M. A.

THIRD SERIES
IN THREE VOLUMES

VOLUME II

Baltimore
GENEALOGICAL PUBLISHING COMPANY
1970

Originally Published
Harrisburg, 1896

Reprinted with the cooperation of the
Pennsylvania State Library
Genealogical Publishing Company
Baltimore, 1970

Standard Book Number 0-8063-0406-5
Library of Congress Catalog Card Number 70-114834

Made in the United States of America

CONTENTS OF VOLUME TWO.

iv   *Contents.*

Contents.

Contents.

Contents. vii

Contents. ix

NOTES <u>AND</u> QUERIES.

HISTORICAL AND GENEALOGICAL.

NOTES AND QUERIES.—LXXXI.

RIFE.—Who can give us all the particulars of the following:
Joseph Rife died in 1820, leaving a wife Barbara, and children:

   i. Joseph, d. prior to his father, and left *Jacob* and *Joseph,* of
      Cumberland county, then under age.

   ii. Elizabeth, m. John Haldeman, of Centre county, Pa.

   iii. Jacob.

   iv. Esther, m. Casper Sharick, of Upper Canada.

   v. Abraham, d. shortly after his father, leaving a wife Nancy,
      and issue: *Polly,* m. Benjamin Longenecker, of Cum-
      berland county, *Joseph, Catharine,* and *Abraham.*

   vi. Nancy, m. Wendle Shelly.

   vii. Barbara, m. —— Mumma.

THE FAMILY OF SHUSTER.

On the 26th of October, 1767, there landed at Philadelphia, Province of Pennsylvania, from the boat "Britannia," Alex. Hardy,
Master, a mother—Mrs. Shuster—with a daughter and her three sons,
Adam, Peter and Lawrence. Whatever became of this daughter we
are unable to tell, and very little is known of Adam. He was undoubtedly under sixteen years of age when he came to the Province,
for his name does not appear amongst those males above sixteen who
arrived on the same ship. He, however, settled in New Jersey, where
he married Dorothy Hoover, and they had issue:

   i. David.

   ii. Peter.

  iii. Lawrence.
  iv. Mary.
   v. Dorothy.
  vi. Nancy.
  vii. Margaret.

We have no positive knowledge where the two remaining sons settled, nor in fact where the mother first located with her children, but, presume, from the following, they must have resided early at Middletown, in now Dauphin county: Peter Shuster, March 24, 1778, took the Oath of Allegiance before Joshua Elder, one of the justices of Lancaster county, Pa., and in the tax list for Middletown during the Revolution his name appears as a taxable. In the military line for 1786–1790 we find him as captain of a company in the Second battalion, commanded by Lieut. Col. Robert Clark. He resided and died at Middletown, where he kept store and followed his occupation, that of a tailor.

  I. Lawrence Shuster was born in Germany, April 19, 1749; came to America with his mother, sister and two brothers. Whether they all settled at Middletown, Pa., we are unable to find out, but for a while Lawrence resided there. His later years were spent in Gloucester county, N. J., where he died "second month, eighth day, and 1810 year," and is buried in the "Sandtown" grave-yard, Gloucester county, N. J. He married, in 1772, Mary Butterworth, daughter of Isaac Butterworth. She was born "10 month, 31 day, 1756 year,' and died "10 month, 30 day, 1831 year." They had issue, and as will be noticed by the manner in which the record was kept they were evidently Quakers in religion:

  2. *i. Jonathan*, b. 4th mo., 7th day, 1774; m. Elizabeth Spayd.
   ii. Mercy, b. 3d mo., 3d day, 1776; d. in Paulsborough, N. J.;
    m. Enos Fowler, a farmer; and had issue (surname
    Fowler): *Josiah, Mary, John, Isaac, Mercy, Aaron,* and *Enos.*
   iii. Christiana-D., b. 10th mo., 31st day, 1778; d. in Paulsborough, N. J., and buried in Friends' grave-yard,
    Woodbury, N. J.; m. John Packer; and had issue (surname Packer): *Jonathan, Lawrence, Hester-R., John,*
    Daniel, Christiana, and *Elizabeth.*
   iv. Adam, b. 1st mo., 2d day, 1781; d. at the age of three years
    by being " burned to death."
   v. Peter, b. 1st mo., 15th day, 1783; d. at the age of 23
    years and buried in grave-yard at Paulsborough, N. J.
   vi. Isaac, b. 3d mo., 27th day, 1785; died at his residence near
    Woodbury, N. J., aged 80 years; m., first, Mary Lamb;

and had issue: *Aaron,* and *Frederick;* m., secondly, Jane Cunnard.

  vii. *John-L.,* b. 6th mo., 20th day, 1787; died in Wilmington, Del.; was by occupation a blacksmith; m. Mary Dawson; and they had issue.

 viii. *Joseph,* b. 6th mo., 21st day, 1789; resided and died in Gloucester county, N. J., aged 72 years, and buried in the Woodbury, N. J., cemetery; m. Hannah Wood; and they had issue: *Constantine, William-W., Rebecca, Mary, Julia, James, Aaron, Clayton, Hannah, Sarah,* and *Deborah.*

   ix. *Benjamin-B.,* b. 7th mo., 13th day, 1791; resided and died near Thorawa, N. J.; m. Sarah Crim; and they had issue: *James, Mary, Adeline, Martha, Clayton, John,* and *Benjnmin.*

3. *x.* *Mary,* b. 7th mo., 4th day, 1793; m. Joel DeWalt.
4. *xi.* *Samuel,* b. 10th mo., 9th day, 1795; m. Caroline Horner.
   xii. *William,* b. 6th mo., 18th day, 1798; resided and died in Maryland; m. Rachael Steward; and they had issue: *Christian, Samuel, Elizabeth, William, Rachel,* and *Mary-Ann.*

  xiii. *George,* b. 3d mo., 8th day, 1800; d. s. p.

  xiv. *Aaron,* b. 12th mo., 28th day, 1801; resided and died near Thoroughfare, N. J.; m. Johanna Richards; and they had issue: *Charles, Silas, Joseph, Phœbe,* and *Johanna.*

5. *xv.* *Elizabeth,* b. 6th mo., 15th day, 1805; m. George Cattell.

II. JONATHAN SHUSTER (Lawrence), b. April 7, 1774; died in Middletown, Pa., about the year 1815; m. ELIZABETH SPAYD, daughter of Christian Spayd; she was born June 30, 1778; d. in Union county, O., October 11, 1854. They had issue:

   i. *Christian,* who moved to St. George, Del., in 1834; m. Mahala ——; and had issue: a daughter, m. Isaac Ubil; and another daughter, m. Daniel C. Welt, both residing in Delaware City, Del.

  ii. *Mary,* b. March 1, 1802, in Middletown; d. January 22, 1865, in Union county, Ohio; m. Feb. 4, 1817, Jacob Parthemore, son of Jacob Parthemore and Elizabeth Alleman; and had issue.

 iii. *Jonathan,* residing in Philadelphia; married Betsey, the widow of —— Lamb, and had issue.

6. *iv.* *Melchior,* b. May 10, 1810, in Middletown, Pa.; m. Sarah Davis.

    v. Peter, nothing can be learned of him.
    vi. Lawrence, there is no knowledge of him.

  III. MARY SHUSTER (Lawrence), b. July 4, 1793; d. July 26, 1845, in Licking Creek Valley, Juniata county, Pa., and buried in the Lutheran grave-yard, Mifflintown, Pa.; m. JOEL DEWALT, a native of Gloucester county, N. J., and who resided as above, and was engaged as a contractor on the State canal and a lumberman; he was b. Dec. 24, 1789; d. Dec. 2, 1863. They had issue (surname DeWalt):

    i. Eliza.
    ii. Joel.
    iii. Michael.
    iv. George.
    v. Christian.
    vi. John.
    vii. Mary-Jane.
    viii. Caroline.

  IV. SAMUEL SHUSTER (Lawrence), b. Oct. 9, 1795, in the vicinity of Mt. Holly, N. J.; d. June 2, 1876; m. Mar. 4, 1819, CAROLINE HORNER; d. June 2, 1876. They had issue:

    i. Joseph-Horner, b. Feb. 15, 1820; d. Oct. 15, 1821.
    ii. William-Morgan, b. Feb. 1, 1823.
    iii. Samuel, b. April 10, 1825; d. Sept. 5, 1829.
    iv. James, b. April 26, 1829; d. 1850, in Philadelphia.
    v. Mary-Horner, b. Dec. 6, 1832.
    vi. John-Lawrence, b. Dec. 6, 1835.
    vii. Henry-Clay, b. June 17, 1838.
    viii. Rosina, b. Oct. 11, 1840.

  V. ELIZABETH SHUSTER (Lawrence), b. 6th mo., 15th day, 1805; resided with her eldest son in Wenonah, N. J.; m., November 17, 1832, GEORGE CATTELL. They had issue (surname Cattell):

    i. William-S., b. Sept. 17, 1833; m., Jan. 14, 1858, M. J. McClure.
    ii. Hiram-B., b. Sept. 19, 1835; d. March 7, 1859.
    iii. D.-Cooper, b. Sept. 9, 1837; m., Jan. 10, 1861, Amanda Norris.
    iv. Sarah-Z., b. Aug. 12, 1839; m. Jan. 24, 1861, John Sheets; she d. Sept. 24, 1865.
    v. Mary-S., b. July 10, 1840; d. March 4, 1852.
    vi. Joseph-S., b. Feb. 28, 1842; m., Nov. 24, 1864, Anna Clark.

VI. MELCHIOR SHUSTER (Jonathan, Lawrence), b. May 10, 1810, in Middletown, Pa.; d. Mar. 12, 1876, in New Brighton, Pa.; m., Sept. 29, 1831, SARAH DAVIS, of Harrisburg; she resides at New Brighton, Beaver county, Pa. They had issue:

 i. Henry, b. July 29, 1832; m. May, 1857.
 ii. Mary, b. June 28, 1834; m. June 24, 1854.
 iii. Elizabeth, b. Feb. 12, 1837; d. Oct. 1, 1881.
 iv. Catharine, b. Oct. 23, 1839; m. April 14, 1865.
 v. Sarah, b. Oct. 18, 1841; d. June, 1872; m. Mar. 12, 1866.
 vi. Millie, b. June 19, 1843; m. April 17, 1879.
 vii. Lawrence, b. Nov. 19, 1846; m. Dec. 21, 1868.
 viii. George, b. Mar. 6, 1849; m. April 7, 1875.
 ix. Amanda, b. Sept. 27, 1851; m. Mar. 21, 1872.
 x. Emadton, b. Feb. 9, 1854; d. Feb. 4, 1875.
 xi. William, b. Mar. 11, 1858.   E. W. S. P.

BIOGRAPHICAL DATA.

[The following biographical notes are from the *Oracle of Dauphin* and the *Dauphin Guardian*.]

Marshall, John, Esq., an officer in the American army in the Revolution, d. in the town of Huntingdon, October 13, 1799. During his residence in that town for several years past he was a much respected citizen, a pleasant companion and kind neighbor. He filled several public trusts with promptitude and fidelity to the general satisfaction of all concerned.

Jordan, John, Esq., one of the associate judges of the Court of Common Pleas for Cumberland county, d. Thursday, Dec. 6, 1799.

Brooks, Benjamin, major Second U. S. regiment of artillery and engineers, an officer during the Revolution, d. at Upper Marlboro', Md., January 16, 1800.

Hoge, Jonathan, Esq., one of the associate judges for Cumberland county, d. on the 19th April, 1800, at his farm near Silvers Spring, in the 71st year of his age.

Elliott, William, Esq., d. at Lewistown, May, 1800, high sheriff of the county of Mifflin, and son of James Elliott, of Harrisburg.

Lahn, Jacob, late editor of the German paper printed at Lancaster, entitled *Americanische Staats bothe*, d. Jan. 13, 1801, in the 54th year of his age. Mr. L. was a native of Frankfort-on-the-Main, has resided in Lancaster upwards of twelve years, and has always preserved the character of an honest man and a good citizen.

Kittera, John Wilkes, late a member of the House of Representatives of the U. S., d. at Lancaster, June 6, 1801.

Stake, Capt. Jacob, d. at his residence on the York side of Wright's Ferry on June 25, 1801, in the 45th year of his age. He served as an officer with reputation and honor during the American Revolutionary war, and has since preserved the character of an excellent citizen.

Armstrong, Robert, of Cumberland county, died at Petersburg [Duncannon], October 8, 1801, aged 86 years.

Taylor, Abiah, representative from Chester county, d. at Lancaster, Thursday, Dec. 3, 1801.

Harris, Thomas, d. December 2, 1801, in Mifflin county, near town of Mifflin, aged 106 years.

Hiester, Mrs. Margaret, wife of Mr. John Hiester, of Reading, d. at Philadelphia, December 16, 1801, a daughter of John Fries, of that city.

Alexander, James, sergeant-at arms for the Senate of this State, d. at Lancaster, February 13, 1802.

Ettwein, Rev. John, Bishop of the Protestant Episcopal Church of Unitas Fratrum, or the United Brethren, died at Bethlehem, after an illness of four days, January 2, 1802, in his 85th year.

Moore, James, Esq., associate judge for Chester county, died suddenly, 31st March, 1802, in the 73d year of his age.

Porter, Edward, Esq., d. on August 7, 1802, in Warrior Mark township, Huntingdon county.

Jacks, James, d. at Lancaster, September 6, 1802, in the 63d year of his age.

Scull, Mrs. Susanna, d. Wednesday evening, September 22, 1802, at Reading, in her 60th year.

Clymer, Mrs. Mary, wife of Daniel Clymer, Esq., d. in Caernarvon township, Berks county, Tuesday, December 7, 1802.

Potter, Mrs., consort of Robert Porter, d. at Lewistown, Mifflin county, Dec. 15, 1802.

Carpenter, Jacob, Esq., late Treasurer of the Commonwealth of Pennsylvania, d. on February 18, 1803, of a consumption, in the borough of Lancaster, in the 36th year of his age.

Nesbitt, Dr. James, d. at Huntingdon, on Wednesday, February 23, 1803, in the 34th year of his age.

Young, Dr. Benjamin, d. at Northumberland, March 23, 1803, aged 34 years.

Douglass, John, d. at Carlisle, April 29, 1803, aged 71 years.

Wilson, William, Esq., a member of the Legislature of this State, d. at his plantation in Lycoming county, June 1, 1803, aged 45 years, and about the same time Mrs. Wilson, consort of the above-mentioned gentleman. They are both interred in one grave.

Simpson, Mrs. Ann, wife of John Simpson, Esq., of Sunbury, d. at that place August 25, 1803. Her remains were interred in the Presbyterian burying ground at Sunbury.

Humphreys, John, Esq., of Northumberland town, d. Sept. 1, 1803.

Heinitsh, Charles F., d. at Lancaster, Sept. 3, 1803, aged 66 years.

Simon, Joseph, d. at Lancaster, January 24, 1804, aged 92 years.

Briggs, David, innkeeper, d. at Silvers Spring, Cumberland county, Jan. 31, 1804, aged 59 years.

NOTES AND QUERIES.—LXXXII.

" AMERICAN PATRIOT."—This was the title of a newspaper published in Harrisburg in 1812 and 13. Are any copies of it in existence? The editor was Alexander Hamilton. Who was he?

CHRONOLOGY OF THE ANTHRACITE COAL TRADE.

1768.—Anthracite coal first used in Wyoming Valley by Obadiah Gore, blacksmith.

1775-6.—Several boat loads of anthracite coal were sent from Wyoming down the Susquehanna, and thence hauled to Carlisle barracks, to manufacture arms for the Government.

1790.—Coal first known in Schuylkill county.

1794.—Blacksmiths used it in Schuylkill county.

1808.—Used in grates by Judge Fell, of Wilkes-Barre.

1812.—Col. George Shoemaker hauled nine wagon loads of coal from Pottsville to Philadelphia, and was obliged to give away the coal.

1814.—Charles Miner sent an ark load, twenty-four tons, of coal from Mauch Chunk, via the Lehigh and Delaware, to Philadelphia.

1815.—Schuylkill navigation commenced.

1820.—Three hundred and sixty-five tons of coal shipped by the Lehigh canal.

The following show the first shipments of anthracite coal over the several avenues to market:

1822.—The Schuylkill canal shipped fourteen hundred and eighty tons.

1829—The Lehigh and Susquehanna railroad shipped one thousand tons.

1833—The Union canal shipped thirty-five hundred tons.

1834.—The North Branch canal shipped thirty-nine hundred and twenty-three tons.

1834—The Lykens Valley railroad shipped forty-one hundred and eighty tons.

The first railroad in the United States to carry anthracite coal was the Lehigh Navigation Company's gravity railroad, in 1820. Then the Schuylkill county branch roads to the canal, in 1822, and third was the Lehigh and Susquehanna railroad; next and fourth in order, and first in Dauphin county, was the Lykens Valley railroad.

MIDDLETOWN PATRIOTISM.

During the war of 1812 companies were raised in Dauphin county by volunteering and by draft, and a large number of the citizens of Middletown and vicinity entered the service. Many of them were attached to Capt. Peter Snyder's company, which was in the Second regiment commanded by Colonel Richter. Among those enrolled were Christian Spayd, Joshua Heppich, John Wolf, Michael Cassel, Michael Hemperley, David Ettele, George Johntz, Daniel Bollinger, Jacob Bollinger, John Conrad, George Critson, George Remley, Wm. Strouse, Lawrence Elberti, John Snyder. Christian Spayd became brigade inspector, and Joshua Heppich was a corporal.

A military company was formed some years afterwards of which Dr. Mercer Brown was captain, who was succeeded by Joseph Ross.

The Swatara Guards, commanded by John Blattenberger, had within its ranks many of the young men of the town. Captain Blattenberger took great pride in maintaining the standard of the company and it had an excellent reputation for discipline.

A rifle company was organized about the same time, and most of its members were crack shots. A target, representing Benedict Arnold, of life size, was used by the companies in their trials of skill, and bore evidence that as marksmen they were not to be despised. This target was in existence a few years ago.

The Mexican war attracted a number of the young men to the volunteer army, who served until peace was declared.

The Swatara Infantry Company was organized about 1851, and existed some eight years. Capt. Henry Smith was in command the greater part of that time.

During the Civil war, 1861–65, Middletown and immediate vicinity furnished three companies of volunteers, besides many soldiers who were attached to different regiments. SWATARA.

THE MILL-DAM TROUBLES OF 1793 AND 1794.

[The following documents relate to this transaction, in which our ancestors showed far more patriotism than that which actuates the citizens of to-day. It forms a portion of the history of our town which deserves perpetuating.]

May 6th, A. D. 1794.

At the meeting of the committee appointed on the 5th Instant at the House of Reitzel to wait on the Landis's to treat with them for the purchase of their Mills, Land, and appurtenances near the Borough of Harrisburg, the said committee propose to allow them the sum of Twenty-five hundred pounds to be paid in the following manner, to wit:

In one month from this date (including the monies due to
the Heirs of Mr. Harris Dec'd, ... £1,500
On the 1st of May, 1795, with int., ... 500
On the 1st of May, 1796, with ditto, ... 500
                                                          —————
                                                          £2,500
The Interest will amt to, ... 90

The two last installments to be secured by the Title remaining (if required) in the hands of the Landis's, until all the money is paid and possession of the property to be delivered to the Borough, or their representatives, on the payment of the first money.

An answer will be expected on or before Friday next, and a Final conclusion of the business on the part of the Borough will then take place.

[Copy Delivered to the Landis's.]

Conveyance—Peter, John and Abraham Landis and their wives, of their Mills, &c., near Harrisburgh, to Stacy Potts, et als for the use of the Borough of Harrisburgh.

THIS INDENTURE made the twenty-ninth Day of April, in the year of our Lord one thousand seven hundred and ninety-five, Between Peter Landis and Eva his wife of the Township of Londonderry, John Landis and Catharine his wife of Londonderry Township, and

Abraham Landis and Barbara his wife of Paxtang Township, all of the county of Dauphin and State of Pennsylvania, of the one part, and Stacy Potts, Moses Gillmor, William Graydon, Jacob Bucher, John Kean, John Dentzel and Alexander Berryhill, all of the Borough of Harrisburgh in the county aforesaid (a committee chosen at a public meeting of the inhabitants of the said Borough at the Court Room on the seventh day of April instant, for certain purposes and cloathed with certain powers expressed in the minutes and proceedings of the said public meeting) for and on behalf of the said Borough of the other part;

WHEREAS, John Harris, late of Harrisburgh, aforesaid deceased, on the 16th day of April, 1790, covenanted and agreed with the said Peter, John and Abraham Landis, their heirs and assigns, for a mill seat, the privileges of a dam and mill race, three acres of ground and sundry other advantages, as in and by the said contract at large may appear;

And whereas, The said Abraham Landis purchased a small piece of Land from Gen'l John A. Hanna in addition to the premises contracted for with the said John Harris, Deceased;

Now, *This Indenture Witnesseth,* That the said Peter Landis and Eva his wife, John Landis and Catharine his wife, and Abraham Landis and Barbara his wife for and in consideration of the sum of twenty-six hundred and thirty-three pounds four shillings and six pence, to them or some of them in hand well and truly paid and secured to be paid by the said Stacy Potts, Moses Gillmor, William Graydon, Jacob Bucher, John Kean, John Dentzel and Alexander Berryhill, at and before the ensealing and delivery hereof, the receipt and payment whereof is hereby confessed and acknowledged, *have* and each of them *hath* Granted, Bargained, Sold, Aliened, Released, and Confirmed, and by these presents *Do* and each of them *doth* Grant, Bargain, Sell, Alien, Release and Confirm unto the said Stacy Potts, Moses Gillmor, William Graydon, Jacob Bucher, John Kean, John Dentzel, and Alexander Berryhill, their Heirs and Assigns, for the use of the Borough aforesaid, all those the aforementioned and above described premises, property, privileges and advantages.

———

Inventory of the moveables, &c., contained in the Mill House Sold by the Landises to the Borough of Harrisburgh, Apl. 29th, 1795.

In the Garret—
    The hoisting Tackle compleat with the necessary ropes. 2 panes Glass broke or cracked.

In the third Story—
  One Bolting chest containing a sup. fine cloth.   22 Ditto.

In the second Story—
  1 Rolling screen and Tackle compleat with a Fan, &c.
  1 small common screen & Frame.
  1 Packing chest with a pr. loose hinges.   68 Ditto.

In the First Story—
  3 Pr. Bur. millstones, except nether stone on the East side of which
    is common, size Beginning at the east side, feet 4:1—4:3—4:0.
  1 p. chopping stones, 3:16.
  2 Bolting chests and 2 cloths—1 country, the other midling.
  1 Hoisting Cask, Iron Hoops, & Bolting Geers compleat for all the
    Bolting Chests.
  1 Bound Box for sifting in.
  4 Hoops, 4 Hoppers, 4 Stands, 4 Shoes & 4 Damzels.
  7 Step Ladders on the Lower Floor & 6 above.
  3 Water wheels and all the Running Geers compleat for 4 Pr. Stones.
  4 Chopping Chests.
  1 Large Bolting Chest brush.
  2 Meal rakes.   21 Ditto.
  Lights Glass, 113 broke or cracked.
  Property examined & taken, parties present.   Witness our hands,
Apl. 29th, 1795.

> STACY POTTS,
> MOSES GILLMOR,
> W. GRAYDON,
> J. BUCHER,
> J. KEAN,
> J. DENTZEL,
> ALEX. BERRYHILL,
> ABRAHAM LANDIS.

NOTES AND QUERIES.—LXXXIII.

WHITE.—We have before us an "Indenture" of the date of 4th
March, 1771, between Hugh White and Margaret, his wife, William
White and Agnes, his wife, of Allen township, Cumberland county,
and Rowland McDonald, of the same locality, for 200 acres of land
on Yellow Breeches creek.   Were these of the family who afterwards
settled in Northumberland now Lycoming county?

HUNTER—McDANIEL—SAWYERS.

Through the kindness of Mr. McDaniel, of New Cumberland, we are placed in possession of the following information :

The will of MARY HUNTER, widow, dated the 17th of August, 1786, in which year she died. The children mentioned in this will are as follows :

 i. Ephraim, d. unm., in Cumberland county.

 ii. Joseph, was first lieutenant in the Second battalion, York county associators, commissioned July 5, 1777; d. in Cumberland county ; a son rose to be a general in the Rebellion.

 iii. Margaret, m. Josias McDaniel.

 iv. Jean, m. James Sawyers.

 v. Elsy, m. —— Hodge.

 vi. Mary, m. —— Colter.

 vii. ——, m. Allen Hays. Mrs. Hays d. at Harrisburg, Sunday, May 24, 1807. Mr. Hays was a clock and watch-maker.

MARGARET HUNTER, m. April 14, 1774, by Rev. John Steel, at John Trindel's, JOSIAS McDANIEL. Their children were (surname Mc-Daniel):

 i. John, b. Sept. 28, 1776; baptized by Rev. John Hodge.

 ii. Mary, b. August 30, 1779; d. aged 77; unm.

 iii. Elizabeth, b. August 16, 1783; d. aged 21 years.

 iv. James-Hunter, b. April 9, 1790 ; m. and had issue:

  1. *Josiah-Sawyer.*

  2. *Margaret*, m. Joseph Sunday.

  3. *Mary*, m. Melchoir Mash.

JEAN HUNTER married Capt. James Sawyers. He was born about 1753, and died at the age of 82 years, at Harrisburg, where he lived many years, and quite prominent in the early history of the town. He was a soldier of the Revolution and was buried with military honors.

LYKENS VALLEY COAL DEVELOPMENT.

In addition to what was stated in the last number of *Notes and Queries* in relation to the coal trade, we have the following from the pen of Prof. P. W. Scheafer, of Pottsville, a native of Dauphin county.

The Wiconisco Coal company (named after Wiconisco creek, in the northeastern portion of the county), was organized in 1831, composed of six members—Simon Gratz, Samuel Richards, George H. Thompson, Charles Rockland Thompson, all of Philadelphia, and Henry Schriner and Henry Sheafer, both of Dauphin county. They began work at opening their mines by drifts in the gap at Bear Creek, and sold coal in the vicinity in 1832. The first miners were three Englishmen—James Todoff, John Brown, and William Hall, who came from Schuylkill county.

The Lykens Valley railroad was located by Mr. Ashwin, an English civil engineer, and extended from the mines in Bear Gap, sixteen miles, to the Susquehanna river, along the north foot of Berry's mountain. This road was constructed under the direction of John Paul, civil engineer, Henry Sheafer, superintendent, and Simon Sallade, director. The road was completed and began transporting coal in 1834 by horse power, on a flat strip rail. A number of ark loads of coal were shipped from Millersburg in March and April, 1834. Then the coal cars were boated across the Susquehanna, from the terminus of the railroad at Millersburg to Mt. Patrick, on the opposite side of the canal, in Perry county. This site was formerly owned by Peter Ritner, brother of Governor Ritner. Here the Lykens Valley company had a set of schutes on the Pennsylvania canal, where they shipped their coal to market. The first boat load of Lykens Valley coal was sent on Saturday, April 19, 1834, by boat "76," forty-three tons, Capt. C. France, consigned to Thomas Baldridge, Columbia, Pa.

Shipments continued in this manner until 1845, when the railroad was worn out, and abandoned until 1848. Then a portion of the railroad was re-graded, and all laid with a new "T" rail. The Wiconisco canal was built and shipments resumed in 1848, and have continued ever since. Up to and including 1858, the total shipment of coal from the Lykens Valley mines, from the beginning, amounted to eight hundred and forty-eight thousand seven hundred and eighty-one tons, and the grand total shipments on the Susquehanna were three millions two hundred and thirty-four thousand seven hundred and eighty-one tons, which included shipments of coal by the Union canal, and other avenues, as follows:

The Shamokin railroad was opened in 1839.

The Dauphin and Susquehanna in 1854.

The Trevorton railroad in 1855.

At this early day of the coal trade, this portion of the country was wild and seemed far removed in the woods. Lykens Valley is the broad expanse, three to five miles in width, of fertile red shale soil between the Mahantongo mountain on the north and Berry's mountain on the south, with the Susquehanna river as its boundary on the west. Its eastern portion is a distance of twelve miles from the river, and is sub-divided into two smaller valleys, the main or northern one extending some ten miles east to the valley of the Mahanoy creek. The south portion is named after its early settler, Williams, who built a grist mill near Williamstown, also named after him.

RECORDS OF FETTERHOFF CHURCH.

[Two miles northeast of the town of Halifax is Fetterhoff's church, under the control of the Reformed and Lutheran congregations. The following transcripts from the tombstones in the grave-yard attached to the church have been kindly forwarded us.]

Bowman, Daniel, b. Nov. 20, 1831; d. May 1, 1880.
Bowman, Elizabeth, *wf.* of H., b. Dec. 3, 1792; d. July 22, 1864.
Bowman, Henry, b. Oct. 1, 1791; d. Jan. 30, 1857.
Bowman, John, b. March 21, 1785; d. June 19, 1839.
Bressler, Rev. N. E., d. March 8, 1877, aged 55 years.
Countryman, John, b. Jan. 5, 1805; d. Aug. 2, 1868.
Countryman, Leonard, b. March 11, 1788; d. Jan. 14, 1851.
Countryman, Maria Magdalena, *wf.* of L., b. Dec. 2, 1784; d. Feb. 7, 1840.
Crosson, Hannah, *wf.* of J., b. Feb. 9, 1797; d. Jan. 24, 1881.
Crosson, Jacob, b. March 19, 1784; d. Nov. 25, 1871.
Dunkel, Anna Mary, *wf.* of J., b. Sept. 11, 1790; d. June 4, 1870.
Dunkel, George, b. Dec. 20, 1790; d. Nov. 11, 1846.
Dunkel, Jacob, b. Sept. 13, 1787; d. Sept. 3, 1849.
Enders, Conrad, b. May 18, 1788; d. Dec. 5, 1874.
Enders, Elizabeth, *wf.* of C., b. April 25, 1794; d. Sept. 20, 1849.
Enders, John, b. March 11, 1774; d. June 25, 1835.
Enders, Margaret, *wf.* of Philip, b. Nov. 26, 1813; d. Oct. 30, 1870.
Fetterhoff, Catharine, *wf.* of John and *dau.* of John Hain, b. June 18, 1791; d. Dec. 6, 1862.
Fetterhoff, Eve, *wf.* of Philip, b. June 27, 1792; d. Jan. 1, 1839.
Fetterhoff, Frederick, d. July 16, 1837, aged 72 years.
Fetterhoff, George, b. May 3, 1795; d. Aug. 3, 1863.
Fetterhoff, John, *s.* of Frederick, b. Oct. 2, 1790; d. June 27, 1829.
Fetterhoff, Col. Philip, b. Sept. 2, 1788; d. Sept. 4, 1833.
Fetterhoff, Susannah, *wf.* of Fred., b. June 25, 1765; d. June 28, 1834.
Forney, Michael, b. May 31, 1809; d. Feb. 24, 1881.

Forney, Salome, *wf.* of P., b. April 8, 1810; d. Dec. 22, 1875.
Forney, Simon, b. June 27, 1817; d. April 11, 1869.
Forney, Susan, *wf.* of M., b. May 19, 1817; d. May 1, 1877.
Forney, Peter, b. April 7, 1807; d. Dec. 14, 1866.
Fronk, David, b. Oct. 19, 1799; d. May 22, 1873.
Fronk, Frederick, b. May 17, 1804; d. May 25, 1867.
Hoke, Elizabeth, *wf.* of J., b. April 12, 1790; d. Nov. 27, 1857.
Hoke, John, b. Nov. 25, 1786; d. June 19, 1856.
Hetrick, Catharine, *w.* of Michael, b. Nov. 1, 1791; d. Mar. 7, 1865.
Hemping, Elizabeth, *wf.* of Rev. J., b. Jan. 8, 1792; d. March 15, 1860.
Hemping, Rev. Johann N., b. July 4, 1778; d. March 12, 1855.
Killinger, Jacob, b. Nov. 3, 1809; d. April 2, 1876.
Killinger, Maria, *wf.* of J., b. Oct. 25, 1808; d. July 23, 1876.
Keiter, Anna Barbara, *wf.* of Gerhardt, b. Feb. 2, 1782; d. Oct. 10, 1814.
Keiter, Anna Mary, *wf.* of J., b. Oct. 16, 1811; d. March 10, 1874.
Keiter, Benjamin, b. Feb. 14, 1775; d. Feb. 24, 1867.
Keiter, Dorothy, *wf.* of P., b. April 4, 1776; d. August 2, 1876.
Keiter, Elizabeth *w.* of John, d. June 14, 1833; aged 64 years.
Keiter, Elizabeth, *wf.* of Joseph, b. Oct. 14, 1811; d. Oct. 23, 1879.
Keiter, Elizabeth, *wf.* of Peter, Sr., b. March 13, 1783; d. Feb. 16, 1849.
Keiter, Gerhardt, b. Sept. 6, 1768; d. March 1, 1855.
Keiter, John, b. Nov. 22, 1763; d. Dec. 16, 1843.
Keiter, John, b. April 1, 1803; d. April 1, 1848.
Keiter, Joseph, b. Aug. 29, 1807; d. Feb. 14, 1863.
Keiter, Mary, *w.* of Gerhardt, b. Sept. 8, 1812; d. Oct. 8, 1876.
Keiter, Peter, b. Dec. 16, 1765; d. Aug. 10, 1850.
Keiter, Peter, b. April 16, 1817; d. June 24, 1878.
Laudermilch, Adam, b. Jan. 6, 1787; d. July 8, 1841.
Laudermilch, Christina, *wf.* of John J., b. March 20, 1801; d. Dec. 10, 1875.
Laudermilch, John J., b. Dec. 11, 1791; d. Nov. 3, 1864.
Laudermilch, Mary, *wf.* of A., b. April 9, 1796; d. May 5, 1863.
Lentz, Catharine, *wf.* of G. M.; d. Sept. 27, 1846; aged 79 years.
Lentz, George M., b. Nov. 3, 1757; d. Dec. 22, 1822.
Lodge, Mary, *wf.* of W., b. Sept. 11, 1805; d. April 19, 1860.
Lodge, William, d. Aug. 22, 1841; aged 45 years.
Martin, Catharine, wife of W., b. April 9, 1795; d. Jan. 7, 1852.
Martin, William, b. April 13, 1793; d. March 20, 1869.
Matchett, Magdalena, *w.* of Geo., b. Feb. 25, 1816; d. May 3, 1872.
Matter, Christopher, b. May 5, 1816; d. Oct. 12, 1843.

Moyer, Catharine (Wagner), *w.* of H., b. Feb. 29, 1795; d. March 5, 1866.
Moyer, Henry, a soldier of 1812, b. Jan. 27, 1787; d. Jan. 27, 1875.
Noblet, Mary Ann, wife of John, b. Sept. 8, 1793; d. March 10, 1878.
Novinger, Hannah, wife of I., b. Dec. 24, 1804; d. April 2, 1875.
Novinger, Isaac, b. July 27, 1796; d. March 24, 1858.
Reisch, Amey, *wf.* of Peter, b. Nov. 17, 1793; d. March 26, 1857.
Reisch, Peter, b. June, 1795; d. Oct. 5, 1836.
Rineberger, Catharine, *wf.* of H., b. Dec. 28, 1813; d. Aug. 26, 1879.
Rineberger, Henry, b. March 1, 1801; d. March 10, 1881.
Rutter, George, b. Sept. 16, 1764; d. Oct. 14, 1834.
Rutter, Isaac, b. Dec. 2, 1798; d. Oct. 15, 1821.
Rutter, Joel W., b. July 14, 1812; d. April 9, 1847.
Rutter, Margaret, *wf.* of Geo., b. Sept. 15, 1771; d. Dec. 25, 1852.
Seiler, Charles, b. June 4, 1807; d. Feb. 6, 1869.
Seller, Barbara, *wf.* of Jacob, *dau.* of Jacob Frawitz, b. Oct. 10, 1815; d. July, 1855.
Seller, Jacob, b. Aug. 26, 1813; d. March 1, 1842.
Sheaffer, Catharine, *wf.* of J., b. 1774; d. Aug. 27, 1852.
Sheaffer, John, b. 1782; d. June 25, 1827.
Sheesley, Christopher, b. June 11, 1798; d. June 13, 1867.
Sheesley, Lydia (Gilbert), *wf.* of C., b. June 23, 1802; d. April 24, 1863.
Shepley, John, b. May 25, 1782; d. June 10, 1866.
Shepley, Susannah, *wf.* of J., b. Feb. 24, 1789; d. April 28, 1845.
Shott, Philip, b. Feb. 25, 1791; d. June 1, 1854.
Shottler, —— b. Jan. 30, 1800; d. Feb. 27, 1853.
Smith, Isaac, d. Aug. 13, 1834; aged 61 years.
Smith, Susan, *wf.* of I., d. March, 1830; aged 59 years.
Straw, Mary, *wf.* of N., b. Jan. 16, 1764; d. May 15, 1818.
Straw, Nicholas, b. Aug. 8, 1769; d. May 26, 1845.
Uhrich, Christian, b. May 14, 1798; d. Aug. 12, 1859.
Uhrich, Valentine, d. Jan. 1, 1873; aged 75 years.
Ummel, Christian, b. March 17, 1809; d. July 11, 1880.
Ummel, Molley, *w.* of I. and *d.* of Jacob Bauman, b. Sept. 12, 1775; d. in her 56th year.
Ummel, Isaac, b. June 12, 1772; d. May 30, 1839.
Whitman, Sarah, *w.* of Samuel, b. Mar. 16, 1815; d. Sept. 26, 1868.
Wilt, Catharine, *w.* of Michael, b. Mar. 17, 1781; d. June 21, 1867.
Wilvert, Adam, b. Dec. 30, 1796; d. Feb. 6, 1875.
Wilvert, Julia, *w.* of A., b. Feb. 13, 1800; d. April 12, 1862.
Zimmerman, Anna M., *w.* of C., b. Nov. 10, 1776; d. Oct. 28, 1855.
Zimmerman, Christian, b. Dec. 19, 1772; d. Jan. 27, 1837.
Zimmerman, Christian, b. Oct. 25, 1799; d. July 15, 1868.

NOTES AND QUERIES.—LXXXIV.

OLD ASSESSMENT LISTS.

WEST END OF DERRY, 1751.

	s.	d.
Allison, John,	2	6
Armstrong, Robert,	2	6
Boo, Randall,	2	6
Boman, Thos.,	3	6
Bratchy, Robt.,	1	6
Black, Hugh,	3	0
Black, Thomas,	4	6
Black, David,	4	6
Breeden, William,	2	6
Blackburn, William,	2	6
Blackburn, Widow,	2	6
Brand, Martin,	4	6
Candor, Joseph,	5	0
Clark, James,	5	0
Chambers, James,	4	0
Carithers, Hugh,	2	6
Chambers, Robt.,	4	6
Cample, David,	2	0
Carithers, Robert,	2	6
Chambers, Arther, the man on David Walker place,	4	6
Callwell, David,	2	0
Clanninger, Valintin,	4	0
Down, Patrick,	1	6
Drennan, William,	2	0
Fley, Alexd.,	1	0
Hall, Thomas,	3	6
Harris, John,	4	0
Hour, Michael,	2	6
Irland, James,	3	6
Jenan, Jacob,	1	6
Keer, John,	7	0
Long, James,	4	0
Leard, John,	4	0
Lockerd, Andrew,	1	0
McKee, James	6	0

	s.	d.
Morrison, Andrew,	4	0
McNear, David,	4	0
Mitchel, William,	1	6
Nelie, Charles,	1	0
Nicom, John,	2	0
Patterson, Moses,	2	0
Ramse, Rob't,	3	0
Russell, Jas.,	3	0
Robinson, Alex'dr,	2	6
Russell, James,	3	0
Semple, James,	8	6
Show, James,	5	0
Saddeler, Christian,	2	0
Starrit, William,	2	0
Singer, John,	1	6
Tise, John,	1	0
Thomson, John,	4	1
Vanlier, John,	3	0
Wiley, James,	1	0
Wilson, Moses,	4	0
Welsh, John,	1	0

Freemen.

	s.	d.
Harris, James,	6	0
Island, William,	6	0
Leard, Hugh,	6	0
Poar, William,	6	0

JAMES RUSSELL, *Collector.*

THE HERSHEY FAMILY.

[From our note book we glean the following relating to a large family now resident in Dauphin county. From two or three sources we have been promised information, but there has been no fulfillment. If any person can furnish us with additions to this meager data, we will be under obligations—and in due time endeavor to properly arrange the same.]

I. ANDREW HERSHEY, b. 1702, in Switzerland; removed early in life with his parents to the Palatinate. In the year 1719 he and his brother Benjamin sailed for America and settled in Lancaster county, Pa. His brother Christian followed in 1739; and all three were

chosen ministers in the Mennonite Church. Andrew Hershey died
in 1792, aged ninety years. There was issue:

    i. Christian, b. 1734; d. January, 1783; m. Elizabeth Hiest-
        and, daughter of Abraham Hiestand, of Hempfield,
        Lancaster county, Pa.
2. *ii. Andrew,* b. 1736, m., first Magdalena Baughman; secondly,
        Maria Acker.
    iii. John.
    iv. Benjamin, d. prior to 1780; and had *Elizabeth,* m. Henry
        Landis, *Benjamin,* and *Mary.*
    v. Jacob, resided in Hempfield township; d. prior to 1767, at
        which time his children, *Maria* and *Ann,* were above
        fourteen years but not of age.
    vi. Abraham.
    vii. Isaac.
   viii. Henry.
    ix. Catharine.
    x. Maria.
    xi. Odti.

II. ANDREW HERSHEY (Andrew), b. 1736, in Lancaster county, Pa.;
d. July 16, 1806; was twice married; m. MAGDALENA BAUGHMAN, d.
prior to 1763; daughter of Michael Baughman; and had issue:

    i. Catharine, b. 1760.

He m., secondly, MARIA ACKER, b. September 26, 1743; d. September 13, 1831. They had issue:

    ii. Anna, b. February 28, 1762.
    iii. Jacob, b. October 2, 1765.
    iv. Maria, b. May 23, 1768.
3. *v. Andrew,* b. September 14, 1770; m. Esther Kauffman.
    vi. Henry, b. December 19, 1772.
    vii. Elizabeth, b. Dec. 5, 1775.
   viii. John, b. March 31, 1783.

III. ANDREW HERSHEY (Andrew, Andrew), b. September 14, 1770;
d. August 1, 1835; m. ESTHER KAUFFMAN, b. May 31, 1770; d. March
3, 1829. They had issue:

    i. Christian, b. December 22, 1796; d. September 5, 1834.
    ii. Anna, b. July 15, 1799.
    iii. Andrew, b. January 15, 1802.
    iv. Maria, b. December 9, 1804.
    v. Catharine, b. January 15, 1809.
    vi. Esther, b. Sept. 11, 1811.
    vii. Barbara, b. December 9, 1814.

viii. Elizabeth, b. December 9, 1814.
ix. John, b. March 14, 1815.
x. Magdalena, b. March 20, 1821.

In addition to the foregoing, which evidently refers to one branch of the family, we have the following:

BENEDICT HERSHEY died prior to 1763, leaving a wife Judith, and children:

i. Jacob.
ii. Barbara.
iii. Andrew.
iv. Peter.
v. John.
vi. Esther.

ANDREW HERSHEY, of Londonderry township, Dauphin county, died in 1792, leaving a wife, and children:

i. Benjamin.
ii. Henry.
iii. Christian, of Manor township, Lancaster county.
iv. Andrew, of Donegal township, Lancaster county.
v. John, wf. Magdalena ———.

THE FALLING STARS OF 1833 AT DAUPHIN.

The 13th of November, 1833, has been signalized as the period of the greatest meteoric shower—an exhibition of natural fireworks that was long remembered by those who witnessed it. The scene in the vicinity of Dauphin in this county is stated to have been " grand, awful, and sublime," and to the ignorant and superstitious citizens the phenomena was overwhelming and terrific. It literally rained stars. Never before or since did such a countless number of meteors fall from the empyrean in so short a space of time. Most of them were globular in shape, but many in their rapid motion left behind a luminous trail, and these imaginations of the credulous very readily transformed into so many fiery serpents. It is almost impossible to conceive the horror of mind which seized upon some people, even where the phenomena were explained by the better informed. Many of the bold, as well as timid citizens, yielding alike to apprehension, gave over all as lost, and rushing frantically to the old " Hill Church," passed the exciting period in prayer and lamentation. It was astonishing to behold how many became suddenly devout who were never devout before. Yet, generally speaking, the fit of devotion was of no longer duration than the phenomena. Old and intelligent citizens like Col. James Gayman, William Wilson and Robert Simmons used their efforts to quiet the fears of the ignorant and frightened. The radiating space of the stars was not exactly in the zenith, but a little below S. S. E. of it. Some of the meteors were so bright as to throw a strong light on the whole sky, and attract attention even when behind a person. Sometimes a long track of light was left in the sky and remained for more than a minute. The very great number and rapidity of motion of these meteors could be compared to a large shower of hail. One appeared to be as large as a man's fist, and was of great brilliance. The stream of light that remained in some cases seemed to be a straight line, and assumed first a snake-like form, and then doubled together. The east was ruddy and the morning star very bright when seen in the morning a quarter past five. They were not always regular in their emission, but there was not a moment when several were not visible. It seemed as if there were several great discharges every minute. At a quarter past six, when the sun was nearly up, their light was very faint, but it appeared as if the number was only apparently diminished by being lost in the light of the morning. The shooting stars, as they were erroneously termed, were first seen at eleven o'clock on the night of the 12th, and continued to increase until five the next morning, when the view which the heavens presented was grand beyond description. Ten thousand little meteors might be observed at a time igniting, falling perpendicularly for a short distance, and then disappearing to be supplied by others. Not a cloud was visible, not a breath of air perceptible. The luminous trail which each meteor left behind as it moved gave the heavens almost the appearance of a solid mass of flame. The scene continued until their light was eclipsed by the morning dawn, when the superstitious recovered in a degree their senses.

NOTES AND QUERIES.—LXXXV.

THE TOWN OF DAUPHIN.—A correspondent sends us the following notes relating to the town of Dauphin, originally named Port Lyon, then Greensburg, and when it became a post town, its present name :

The oldest houses in the town are those of the Winn heirs, built nearly three quarters of a century ago; of Peter Snyder, on Erie street, formerly owned by Mr. Garlicher; of Elias Fertig, formerly the property of George Myers; of the heirs of William J. Robinson;

and of Wm. Bell's estate, built by Mr. Ormes. The first store was kept by Peter Miller, on Erie street, now the property of Mrs. Cogley. The first tavern was the stone hotel, "Dauphin House," recently kept by Charles Rodearmel. This was built by Innis and Richard Green, who kept it. The first physician was Dr. Means, whose successor was Dr. Heck, still living at Heckton, two miles below town. The first postmaster was Benjamin Stees, about 1832, who kept the office at his hotel. His successors have been Thomas Milliken, Sr., R. G. Hetzel, Henry Sponsler, Jeremiah Frame, and Jefferson Clark, who was appointed in the spring of 1861. The first blacksmith was Isaac Bell; wagon-maker, John Gepford, and cabinet-maker, George Myers. The earliest teacher now remembered was Mr. Park.

OUR EARLY SETTLERS.

Tax List, East End of Derry, 1751.

	s.	d.
Allen, Thomas,	2	0
Boyd, Wm.,	3	0
Boyd, Robert,	3	0
Cample, James,	9	0
Colp, John,	3	6
Connoy, Charles,	1	6
Clinn, David,	1	0
Clark, Charles,	3	0
Cample, John,	4	0
Cooper, Dison,	2	6
Cochran, John,	1	0
Coughan, Christian,	1	6
Dinie, Leaneard,	4	0
Daugherty, Neal,	1	0
Duncan, James,	4	0
Duncan, John,	4	0
Esby, George,	5	0
Foster, James,	4	0
Fallopo, Fottie,	2	6
Foster, John,	3	6
Foster, Robert,	2	6
Foster, David,	4	0
Galbreath, James, Esq.,	9	6
Goarly, John,	1	0

	s.	d.
Haine, Fogal,	1	0
Hover, Michael,	3	0
Hall, Hugh,	6	0
Hays, Hugh,	7	6
Hays, Patrick,	6	0
Hays, William,	4	0
Hemple, Anthoney,	1	0
Hays, John,	3	0
Jonson, David,	2	6
Ketrim, Harris,	4	0
Keer, John,	3	0
Kelly, Patrick,	2	6
Kingre, John,	4	6
Logan, Thomas,	4	0
Longnecker, Jacob,	1	6
McCord, John,	2	0
McCord, David,	1	0
Miller, James,	3	0
Mitchell, David,	5	0
McColoch, John,	1	0
Make, Thomas,	0	6
More, Andrew,	4	0
McClire, Robert,	2	6
McQuin,	6	0
McCallister, Neal,	5	0
Miller, George,	2	6
McCallister, John,	3	6
Maben, John,	6	0
McCleland, John,	2	0
Mordah, Robert,	3	0
McDonnall, Duncan,	1	6
McClan, Widow,	3	0
Miller, Hugh,	2	6
McColouh, John,	1	0
Miller, William,	3	0
Moar, John,	3	0
Nai Hamer, Adam,	2	0
Over, John,	6	0
Pinogel, John,	6	0
Palmar, Hannas,	2	0
Peters, Hendry,	2	6

Page 24 — *Notes and Queries.*

	s.	d.
Potts, Moses,	3	0
Robinson, William,	1	0
Row, Vandall,	1	6
Rutherford, Thomas,	4	6
Rea, Willm.,	4	0
Ree, John,	4	0
Rife, Jacob,	1	6
Rowan, Andrew,	2	0
Syers, Wm.,	6	0
Shank, David,	1	0
Snider, Criste,	4	0
Sloan, Widow,	3	0
Strean, John,	2	0
Sailer, Jacob,	1	0
Siglee, Aullbright,	3	6
Tylor, David,	5	0
Willson, James,	4	6
Walker, James,	5	0
Walker, John,	4	6
Walker, Hendry,	6	0
Walker, Archbald,	4	0
Willison, William,	4	6
White, Joseph,	1	0
Willison, Thomas,	3	0
Willison, James.	2	6
Wisan, John,	1	6

Freemen.

	s.	d.
Freeman, Thomas,	6	0
Hover, John,	6	0
Huston, Willm.,	6	0
Mordoch, John,	6	0
Rea, David,	6	0

JOHN HAYS, *Collector.*

THE BAUMS OF DERRY.

I. ADAM BAUM, a native of the Palatinate, emigrated to America about 1760, and settled in Derry township, Lancaster now Dauphin county, Pa., where he died in December, 1785; m. VERONICA ———; both are buried in the family grave-yard, on the Horseshoe turnpike, two miles east of Hummelstown. They had issue, among others:

2.   *i. Michael,* b. 1757 ; m. Margaret Ebersole.
3.   *ii. Daniel,* b. January 30, 1759 ; m. Catharine Fishburn.
    iii. John, b. 1761 ; d. and left a son, *John.*

II. MICHAEL BAUM (Adam), b. 1757, in Derry township, Dauphin county, Pa.; d. in 1796; m. MARGARET EBERSOLE ; his widow subsequently married John Miller. They had issue:
4.   *i. Daniel,* b. April 9, 1783 ; m. Mary Hummel.
5.   *ii. Abraham,* b. 1785; m. Elizabeth Eshleman.
    iii. John, b. 1787; d. April, 1839 ; m. Nancy ———.
    iv. Ann, b. 1789.
    v. Freny, b. 1791; m. Isaac Snavely.
    vi. Mary, b. 1793; m. Felix Burkholder; removed to Ohio.

III. DANIEL BAUM (Adam), b. January 30, 1759; d. December 30, 1839; was an ingenious mechanic, learned gunsmith with his father, and during the war of the Revolution was noted for his rifles which he manufactured for the patriot army.   He m. CATHARINE FISHBURN. They had issue:
6.   *i. Michael,* m. Nancy Sheller.
    ii. Barbara, m. Thomas Fox.
7.   *iii. John,* b. March 9, 1794; m. Rebecca Zimmerman.

IV. DANIEL BAUM (Michael, Adam), b. April 7, 1783; d. Dec. 4, 1857 ; m. MARY HUMMEL, b. March 13, 1789; d. Nov. 23, 1862; dau. of David Hummel and Mary Toot.   They had issue:
    i. Mary-Ann, m. Samuel Murray.
    ii. Lena.
    iii. Sarah, d. unm.
    iv. Susan, m. Levi Jones.
    v. Catharine, m. Edward Magee, of Newark, N. J.
    vi. Adam-Hummel.
    vii. Caroline, m. John Yordy, of Lebanon.
    viii. David-Hummel.
    ix. Amanda, d. s. p.

V. ABRAHAM BAUM (Michael, Adam), m. ELIZABETH ESHLEMAN. They had issue:
    i. Mary, m., first, Abraham Fackler, secondly, John Gerhart.
    ii. John, m. Elizabeth Metz.
    iii. Michael, m. a dau. of Philip Michael, of Dauphin county.
    iv. Catharine, m. Benjamin Miller.
    v. Susan.
    vi. Isaac, m. Barbara Baer.

vii. Elizabeth, m. John Baum.
viii. Abraham.

VI. MICHAEL BAUM (Daniel, Adam), d. March, 1831; m. NANCY SHELLER. They had issue:
    i. John, d. s. p.
    ii. Daniel, m. and removed to the west.

VII. JOHN BAUM (Daniel, Adam), b. March 9, 1794; d. October 8, 1826; m. REBECCA ZIMMERMAN. They had issue:
    i. Catharine, m. John Abel.
    ii. Maria, m. Jacob Hamaker.
    iii. Eliza, d. s. p.
    iv. Margaret, d. s. p.
    v. Mary, m. —— Gill, of Lebanon county.
    vi. Louisa, m. Franklin Scott.

NOTES AND QUERIES.—LXXXVI.

THE ORIGINATOR OF CHEAP POSTAGE.—A correspondent writes us from Kingston, Roane county, Tennessee, to this effect: "Between the years 1854 and 1855, the Historical Society of Pennsylvania, or the Philosophical Society of Philadelphia, passed a series of resolutions declaring that Samuel Martin, of Campbell's Station, Knox county, East Tennessee, was the originator of the system of cheap postage. Mr. Martin died in September, 1856, and his dwelling was burned about the same period, with all his papers. His family are anxious to know if a copy of those resolutions can be secured." Can anyone answer this query?

COL. JAMES BURD.

In an article recently published relating to Col. James Burd, of "Tinian," there is a quotation from a letter of March 30, 1756, that "Patterson's fort was attacked yesterday," and "several shots were heard towards Mr. Burd's fort." Following the quotation there is this comment: "He (Col. James Burd) must have been at Augusta, and (Capt. James) Patterson, his lieutenant, at Pomfret (Castle), about a dozen miles northwest of him. Patterson afterwards married one of Burd's daughters."

It would be difficult to crowd into the same space a larger number of errors. Ft. Augusta was at Sunbury, and Pomfret Castle at Richfield. Pomfret was therefore southwest of Augusta. The distance on an air line is twenty miles, and by the route then traveled thirty miles. There was, however, no Augusta at that date. It was not even ordered to be built by the Governor until June 12, 1756, and hence Burd "must" not have been there in March previous. Burd then had charge of Granville, though sometimes absent, for on April 19, 1756, he was at Carlisle, expecting to go to Granville the next day.

It was George, the youngest son of Capt. James Patterson, that married a daughter of Col. James Burd, and many of their descendants live at Pottsville to this day. James Patterson was married to Mary Stewart, and he died in Mexico in 1771, where he is on the assessment lists regularly back as far as 1763—the first one ever taken west of the Tuscarora mountain. He got his patent for his land there in 1755.

It has been shown that Patterson's fort and Pomfret Castle are not the same. "Patterson's fort" was his own block-house at Mexico. "Burd's fort" was Fort Granville, at Lewistown. This is evident from the Pennsylvania Archives, where the same attack is described. "The Indians appeared on the hill opposite to Patterson's fort and fired six guns, a bullet from one of which struck the guard-house." On the same night those in the fort "heard firing supposed to be at Fort Granville or the fort at Tuscarora (Bigham's), and imagine it taken." The Indians captured Hugh Mitcheltree, living on the Juniata river near Patterson's fort, and "the same party fired on Pomfret Castle" during their retreat. This is probably the firing that they mistook for an attack on Granville or on Bigham's fort.

The order of March 28, 1756, to the commander of each fort to send a guard of thirteen men with the paymaster from fort to fort, in a foot note in Pennsylvania Archives, vol. II., p. 603, is to the effect that the letter sent to Colonel Burd, at Granville, ordered him that on leaving his fort the escort was to go with Salter to "Pomfret Castle or Patterson's fort." This expression has probably led to the error in the Archives (Article on Forts), that the two names designated the same place. The phrase might mean a place called "Pomfret Castle or Patterson's fort," and it may mean, and in this case does mean, that the escort was to go either "to Pomfret Castle or Patterson's fort," as the case might be, for it was uncertain at which place the soldiers might be, and the one could be passed on the way to the other, and it is unlikely that Pomfret Castle ever was finished, for when Augusta was ordered they no longer had need for the castle.

THE FAMILY OF AGNEW.

From the " List of the first settlers on the Manor of Maske," I learn that my great-great grandfather, James Agnew, settled on that Manor in May, 1741, and as my great-grandfather was born January 29, 1738, he must have been three years old when his father went there. I find by my family record that he was born in Lancaster county, Pa. This important fact I had overlooked, and from the fact that they were identified with the Marsh Creek country from its first settlement, I had supposed that was the place of his birth. It is now established that he was a child when the family went there. The " List " contains the name of Samuel Agnew as having settled in Marsh Creek at the same time as James Agnew. This confirms a tradition that our great-great grandfather had a brother Samuel, and there is said to be yet another who settled in New Jersey. From the record in my possession I send you the following:

JAMES AGNEW, born July 31, 1711; died October 2, 1770; married MARTHA ———, his first wife, and had two children:

"*i. John*, born March 4, 1732; married twice; d. childless; was a judge, and resided at Carlisle, Pa.

ii. Janet, b. August 22, 1735; m. Abram Scott, and had several children.

James Agnew m., the second time, REBECCA SCOTT, fourth child of Abraham Scott. She was born Dec. 17, 1707, and died Dec. 22, 1789. There were born unto them nine children, viz:

　　i. Samuel.
　　ii. Martha.
　　iii. James.
　　iv. David.
　　v. Margaret.
　　vi. Rebecca.
　　vii. Sarah.
　　viii. Abram.
　　ix. Ann.

ABRAHAM SCOTT had six children, viz:

　　i. Ann.
　　ii. Samuel.
　　iii. Jonas.
　　vi. Rebecca.
　　v. Alexander.
　　vi. Grace.

ARTHUR PATTERSON, b. in 1696; m., in 1724, ANN SCOTT. She was born in 1698 or 1699; d. May, 1792, aged 93 years. There was born to them nine children, viz:

 i. Catharine, died young.
 ii. Samuel, m. Martha Agnew.
 iii. Elizabeth.
 iv. James, m. Margaret Agnew.
 v. Eleanor.
 vi. Jane.
 vii. Rebecca.
 viii. William.
 ix. Arthur.

From the above it seems that Arthur Patterson and James Agnew were both sons-in-law of Abraham Scott.   SAMUEL A. AGNEW.
Bethany, Lee county, Miss.

[The date of warrant of survey in very few instances denote date of settlement. The latter frequently was from five to ten years previous. At the time when Samuel Agnew was born the Marsh creek settlement was in Lancaster county.]

HARRISBURG IMPRINTS.

[In the early months of 1792 Harrisburg was an infant town, but several printers were enterprising enough to forsee future profits in the lines of their avocation, so a press was set up and it is possible a newspaper was issued at once. It is, however, certain, that in October of that year the *Oracle* of Dauphin was issued. The proprietors of it had excellent fonts of type and were trained and capable workmen. Their first imprint in book form, was an expensive work in two volumes, issued in 1802. With the increase of population and the patronage of the State, in the next twenty years, a great many printing offices were established, from whence issued a profusion of miscellaneous works. Excluding the State printing, we find the following imprints before 1840, in books generally very well printed and bound.—A. B. H.]

Abridgement of the Laws of the United States, by William Graydon, Esq., printed by John Wyeth, 1802: Price $4.50: 850 pps., 2 vols. [This was a standard reference work for many years.]

Adventures in a Castle, an original story written by a citizen of Philadelphia: Harrisburg, Jacob Elder, 1806.

Reflections on Courtship and Marriage in Two Letters to a friend. Harrisburg: Printed by John Wyeth: 1803.

Essays on Faith and Repentance. By Thomas Scott, D. D, Rector of Aston Sanford, Bucks, and chaplain to the Lock Hospital, London ; author of the Commentary on the Bible, &c., &c. Harrisburgh : Printed and sold by W. Gillmor. 1812. 24 mo. pp. 316.

Geistliche Lieder, von Bernhard Henrich Sasse, einem Hausmann in Kirchlengern nebst Einem Anhang, bestehend aus geist-und trostreichen Leidern von verschiedenen Dichtern. Harrisburg : Gedruckt und zu haben bey C. Gleim, 1814. 48 mo. p. vi., 128.

A sermon preached in Harrisburg before both houses of the *legislature* of Pennsylvania on the 12th of January, 1815, the day of the late General Fast, by Henry R. Wilson, A. M., pastor of the church of Silvers Spring. "Cry aloud and spare not," &c., Isaiah. Harrisburg. Printed by James Peacock, 1815.

A Serious Call to a Devout and Holy Life, adapted to the state and condition of all orders of Christians, by William Law, A. M. From the fifteenth London edition. "Behold I come quickly and my reward is with me." Rev. 22 : 12. Harrisburg, printed and sold by William Gillmor, 1816.

The Alphabet of Thought, or Elements of Metaphysical Science : By a Lady [Mrs. Dunlop Harris, Bellefonte,] Harrisburg, Hugh Hamilton, 1825.

To the Public: The answer to a rule entered on the 28th July, 1821, viz : Lawrence D. Franks, &c., by John Adams Fisher. Harrisburg, John S. Wiestling, 1827.

Jacob Wrestling with God, and Prevailing ; or a Lecture concerning the necessity and efficacy of Faith and Prayer. By Thomas Taylor. [John xvi., 24.] First American edition published by James McGregor. Harrisburg. Printed by Francis Wyeth, 1830. 24mo. pp. 138.

Constitution of the Harrisburg Beneficial Society, founded 1829. Harrisburg, D. K. Callender, 1833.

Repository of Sacred Music, by John Wyeth. Harrisburg, John Wyeth, 1826. [Printed] 1834.

Discourses on the Depravity of the Human Family, particularly applied to this nation and these times ; under the Divine Master, by John Landis, sacred historical painter, author of "the Messiah," and the "Soul's Aid," &c., 2d Cor., chap. 13, verse 5th. Harrisburg, by Rich. S. Elliott & Co., 1839.

[On a fly leaf of this copy is this distich addressed "to the author:"

In t'other words except hard blows,
No water will wash your stains out,
Horace will pluck you by the nose,
And Hornet will beat your brains out.

D. S.   Harrisburg, 1839.]

The Social Lyrist: A collection of Sentimental, Patriotic, and Pious Songs, set to music, arranged for one, two, or three voices. By J. H. Hickok. Harrisburg, Pa.; Published by W. Orville Hickok, 1840. 32mo. p. 144.

The United States Constitutional Manual being a comprehensive compendium of the system of government of the country, &c., in the form of questions and answers, designed for academies, schools, and readers in general. By Mordecai McKinney. Harrisburg, Hickok & Cantine, 1845.

NOTES AND QUERIES.—LXXXVII.

OBERLANDER.—George Oberlander, a son of Frederick Oberlander, d. in 1816, leaving his estate to his aunt, Mary Gilliard; his uncle, Conrad Seebaugh, and Aunt Barbara Jamison. Can any one at Middletown give us a record of the Oberlander family, or tell us somewhat concerning them?

CAMPBELL.—Margaret Campbell, widow, of West Hanover, died in December, 1813. Her children were:

  i. Jane, m. David McCreight.
  ii. Margaret.
  iii. James, who had a daughter *Margaret.*
  iv. William, whose daughter *Margaret* m. a Snodgrass.
Information is desired as to these families.

OUR EARLY SETTLERS.

For the year 1755 we have the returns for the East and West Ends of Derry which are herewith given, followed by that of the South End of East side of Derry in 1757 and the West End of Derry in 1759. These are valuable as they give us the names of those who were among the earliest settlers.

West End of Derry—1755.

Armstrong, Robt.,	Greap, John,	Ramsey, Robert,
Bradshaw, Robt.,	Gensel, Frederick,	Russel, James, Jr.,
Bredy, William,	Hall, Thomas,	Russel, James,
Blackny, Anthony,	Hepsher, Wolry,	Starratt, William,
Black, Hugh,	Huber, Michael,	Shaw, James,
Black, Thomas,	Heart, Henry,	Sample, Widow,

Bever, George,
Baum, Adam,
Brand, Martin,
Camble, David,
Cander, Joseph,
Cander, James,
Caruthers, Robert,
Campbel, Moses,
Cook, John,
Chambers, James,
Caruthers, Hugh,
Caruthers, James,
Crocket, John,
Dalker, Adam,
Dornnan, Wm.,
Fleming, John,
Frey, George,
Flenshabouch, Melchar,
Groseles, Peter,

Ireland, James,
Karr, John,
Karr, Thomas,
Kinter, Peter,
Lard, John,
Lard, Mathew,
Morrow, Lewis,
Magill, Lawrence,
Martin, Edward,
McKee, Robert,
McCee, Widow,
McCormag, Alex.,
Nelson, James,
Newcommer, Francis,
Paterson, Moses,
Parks, Thomas,
Pennelton, John,
Pennelton, Isaac,
Reed, Samuel,

Soop, Stofel,
Spangler, Peter,
Singer, John,
Spencer, William,
Taylor, Robert,
Thompson, Wilson,
Tyce, John,
Vanlear, John,
Vance, Handel,
Wilson, Robert,
Walker, Robert,
Wilson, Mathew,
Wagner, Adam,
Wilson, Moses,
Wiseler, Conrad,
Walker, Samuel,
Wetberry, George,
Wiry, Anthony,
Walker, James.

Freemen.

Bowman, John,
Clark, John,
Finton, James,
James, John,

McCormack, Sam'l,
McCleery, William,
Queen, Edward,
Queen, Cornelius,

Rannex, Alex.,
Sherger, George Philip,
Snoddy, James,
Vanlear, James.

ROBERT CARUTHERS,
Collector.

REV. RICHARD McALLISTER.

SKETCH OF A NOTED DAUPHIN COUNTY METHODIST.

[In 1854, this sketch was prepared by the Rev. Dr. Holdich, of the Baltimore Conference, and we reproduce it here, because it is the bright record of a worthy native Pennsylvanian.]

Many pleasing facts connected with the early history of Methodism are, no doubt, embalmed in the memories of its older ministers. They delight to relate them as illustrations of the work of God in its origin and early progress, and they generally interest, and not unfrequently edify their hearers. One such incident is in my possession, and I communicate it for the reader's entertainment, and perchance instruction.

Within the bounds of the Philadelphia and Baltimore Conferences, many yet remember the devoted Richard McAllister. I knew him well. It is more than thirty years ago that I had the privilege of forming his acquaintance. Nearly three years I lived in his father's house, and the incidents I shall relate I received directly from the family or himself.

Archibald McAllister, Esq., the father of Richard, was a man of note in his neighborhood. He had been an officer in the Revolutionary army, and had something of the military in his character. To a genial warmth of feeling, ease and cordiality of manner, and real kindness of heart, he added a considerable share of self-will. He was easily excited, but his passion soon died away, and left him subject to the kindest feelings.

His residence was at Fort Hunter, on the east bank of the Susquehanna river, six miles above Harrisburg, where he owned a handsome property, which still remains in the family. It is a romantic region. On the one side the majestic Susquehanna rolls its ceaseless tide of waters, which, chafed and irritated by the numerous rocks against which they perpetually beat in their passage, send forth a constant murmur, amounting in damp weather even to a roar. Some distance above the house, the river breaks through a spur of the Blue mountains and makes a rapid descent, forming what are called Hunter's Falls. The channel of the river, though the stream is a mile wide, is very narrow, and is navigable for rafts and arks only a few weeks in the year; that is, in the freshets of spring and fall. The farm is surrounded by mountain ridges, green and well-wooded to the top. The entire scenery is beautifully picturesque and wild. The road from Fort Hunter to Clark's Ferry was one of the most romantic that I ever saw. In some spots it was truly sublime, the towering mountains rising abruptly from the water's edge. I say was; for the Pennsylvania canal, made since that day, has very much changed its character. But it is wildly grand still; and no doubt many a voyager on the canal has felt his mind elevated to sublimity as, passing between the mountain base and the noble river, he has seen the immense masses of rock jutting out high above his head, threatening to fall upon him and crush him and his frail craft at once.

It was but a few years before I resided there that Methodism had been introduced into that neighborhood. I found two members of Mr. McAllister's family (nieces) members of the Methodist Church, and also a daughter, but she was married and had removed to the State of New York. Richard had already commenced his ministry. It is of this fact in his history that I am about to speak.

When the Methodist ministers first came into his neighborhood Mr. McAllister was strongly opposed to them. Nevertheless, he at length yielded so far as to allow them to establish meetings on his property, his tenants and work people and servants forming a considerable part of the congregation. At length his oldest daughter and youngest son united with this flock, at that time so feebly and lightly esteemed in the circle of his acquaintance. This was far from being agreeable to the father's wishes; but he was not implacable nor unreasonable. In fact he found that these people were not as he at first supposed, "setters forth of strange gods," but only "preached unto them Jesus and the resurrection." A decided change in his views took place, so that he at length gave land upon his estate to build a church and contributed a large part toward the expense. Many still remember the old Fishing Creek church, on what was then, and for many years afterward, Dauphin Circuit. An unostentatious church, to be sure, it was, nestling there in the valley, with the mountain streamlet gurgling by its side; yet to many souls is that little church dear, for it was radiant with more than worldly charms. To many it was a gate of heaven.

Yet was Mr. McAllister still far from possessing a sanctified or Christian spirit. This was a great grief to his eminently pious and devoted children. Indeed, he barely endured their Christian life, and often gave painful evidence of his want of sympathy with them. It happened one day when he and Richard were engaged in their rural affairs on some part of the premises distant from the dwelling, that Mr. McAllister, under a provocation, gave way to a burst of temper, accompanied with a profane expression, for which Richard reproved him. This so offended the father that he struck him, and ordered him instantly to leave his house. Richard took him at his word; went home, packed up a few things in his handkerchief, and, with his bundle on his arm, kissed his mother and departed, no one knew whither.

When his father came in the first thing that he did was to inquire for Richard. When Mrs. McAllister, who was a most superior woman, as well as affectionate mother, related what occurred, the father was struck dumb, not dreaming that what he had said in his haste would be literally taken. He loved his son, and thought with agony of his situation. It was the depth of winter. He had gone on foot, slenderly provided, as he knew he must be, without funds, without letters, a small supply of clothing, and but indifferently prepared to buffet with the world. He immediately ordered every horse from his stables, and sent a rider in every direction in search of the wanderer. But it was in vain. The river was frozen over, and Richard, unseen by the family, had crossed on the ice, and taken the road direct for Baltimore, where he had few acquaintances, if any, but where he had learned that the Methodist Church was strong and influential, and where he hoped to find or make friends. The journey came near to having a fatal termination. The ground was covered with snow, the road on that side of the river running up a wild valley but thinly settled, was not well broken, and walking was very laborious. Richard having traveled on foot most of the day, became completely exhausted. Providentially, a gentleman who knew him overtook him on the road, and seeing his pitiable condition, dismounted and gave him the use of his horse, until they reached a place of accommodation. Thus assisted he finally reached Baltimore in safety. After what was thought a suitable delay, a friend communicated the place of Richard's residence to his father, who immediately sent another son to bring him home, giving him every assurance of the utmost indulgence in his religious views and habits. After this, for some time, he walked his Christian path without hinderance or molestation.

Sometime after this—I do not know exactly how long—Richard felt that a dispensation of the gospel was committed to him; and having obtained permission, he began to pray and exhort in social meetings, greatly to the satisfaction of his Christian friends and the church.

Mr. McAllister thought Richard not at all fitted by education for the work of the ministry. His two elder sons, intended for professional life, were liberally educated; the two younger, being intended for rural pursuits, received only good substantial English instruction. To undertake the responsible work of the ministry, with so slender an amount of intellectual culture, the father thought preposterous in the extreme. He was willing to send him to college and prepare him for the ministry in a branch of the church possessing better opportunities for eligible situations; but this did not meet Richard's views. He was a Methodist. He was impatient to begin his work. His brethren and the officiary of the church saw that he had native talents—sound judgment, clear views of theology, and especially a correct knowledge of the way of salvation—and they saw him fitted in their view for immediate usefulness, and holding out great promise for the future. They were as earnest as Richard was that he should lose no time in commencing his ministry.

It was drawing toward the close of the conference year, and Richard was particularly anxious to obtain his recommendation from the Quarterly Conference and be admitted into the ensuing Annual Conference in April; the father was equally anxious to prevent it. They both had a secret motive for this solicitude—and yet scarcely secret either, since each knew what was passing in the other's mind. The fact was, Mr. McAllister's eldest son, George Washington, afterward well known as Col. McAllister, who on completing his education, and gone to Georgia, had married and become wealthy, was expected with his family to spend the summer at his father's house. He was a very superior man, of high accomplishments, finished education, and of noble, honorable, elevated sentiments and bearing.

Richard feared as much as his father hoped from the influence of this highly cultivated but worldly brother. However, Washington arrived, and Richard was yet at home. His father had utterly refused to supply him with a horse and the necessary equipments for an itinerant minister. Richard feared the worst from the combined influence of father and brother. The father soon communicated his views to Washington, and according to expectation, quite secured him on his own side. Washington had no idea that Richard should expose himself and disgrace the family by attempting what he considered him inadequate to perform.

It so chanced some little time after this, that Richard, who had already received a local preacher's license, and officiated occasionally in the neighborhood, had an appointment in the church on his father's estate. The father, hearing of it, told Washington that it would be an excellent opportunity for him to hear and judge for himself, when he had no doubt he would soon put an end to this preaching mania. All things being thus arranged, Washington placed himself in the congregation. Those who were present related to me the facts. Richard, instead of quailing before the keen eye that was so scrutinizingly bent upon him, only called more fervently upon his God, and threw himself upon his gracious aid. He was nerved to uncommon vigor. The opening services passed off without anything marked. After taking his text, the preacher soon began to show that he was not the novice that his brother had supposed. He handled his subject with skill, his ideas flowed freely, his language was correct and sufficiently copious, and after a time there began to breathe through his words a holy influence, a sacred power that touched the heart. Washington was first surprised, then astonished, at length amazed, until, forgetting where he was, as his hands rested on the back of the seat before him, he gradually and unconsciously rose upon his feet, his nether jaw dropped down, and thus standing up in the midst of the congregation with his mouth half open he listened in breathless attention to the sermon. As soon as the services were ended he returned to the house. The father was waiting to learn the issue. "Well, Washington, what do you think of this preaching now?"

"Father," was the calm and serious reply, "if ever a man was called to preach the gospel Richard is, and he ought to preach, and if you will not give him a horse and saddlebags I will."

"O!" said the father, for his resistance was all gone, "if he must have a horse and saddlebags, I suppose I am the most suitable person to buy them for him."

Richard had no more trouble. He ran a brief but bright career. He was appointed first to the city of Philadelphia, I think, by the presiding elder; he then traveled for a short season with one of the bishops, by whom he was appointed to Baltimore to fill a vacancy, and thus became attached to the Baltimore conference. After traveling a few years, while stationed a second time in Baltimore he married a daughter of Colonel Barry, of that city, and the same year took the yellow fever, from the effects of which he never fully recovered. He filled one or two appointments afterward, but his health utterly failing, he went to the South for change of climate, and died in great peace and Christian triumph at the house of his brother in Georgia, who subsequently became a pious man and died the death of the righteous.

Thus rose, and shone, and set "a bright particular star" in Methodism. He was not a meteor. His light was mild, gentle, and constant; a "burning and a shining light" he was, and by the brightness of his example many were guided into the way of peace. As "he that winneth souls is wise," and "they that be wise shall shine as the brightness of the firmament, and they that turn many to righteousness, as the stars forever and ever," so shall many in the last day, while they admire and approve his choice, bless God that they were ever permitted to know that devoted and exemplary minister of Christ, Richard McAllister.

NOTES AND QUERIES.—LXXXVIII.

AN OLD MAP.—On an old map of the date of 1645, we find the Susquehanna laid down with branches as follows, from the mouth upwards:

1. S k a h a d o w r i.
2. A r a t u m q u a t.
3. C h e n e g a i d e.
4. C a n o h a g a.
5. J u r a g e n.
6. G o d o c o r a r e n.
7. S i o n a s s i.
8. J u r a g e n.
9. S e a w o n d a o n a.

On another of ten years later are these:
1. C o n e w a g o.
2. S w a h a d o w r a.
3. G a n a d a g u e h e t.
4. E n w a g a.
5. A r a t u m q u a t.
6. C h e n e g a i d e.
7. C a n a h a g o.
8. J u r a g e n.
9. G o d o c a r a r e n.
10. S i o n a s s i.
11. S e a w o n d a o n a.
12. J u r a g e n.

Who can give us the names of the present streams.

OUR EARLY SETTLERS.

EAST END OF DERRY, 1755.

Albright, Jacob,
Armstrong, Robert,
Brown, Adam,
Black, Hugh,
Black, Thomas,
Breading, William,
Breadshaw, Robert,
Baker, Dawalt,
Bare, George.
Brand, Martin,
Bronck, Jacob,
Bomback, George,
Camble, David,
Cook, John,
Crockens. John,
Camble, Moses,
Cander, Joseph,
Carithers, James,
Catts, Jacob,
Carber, Henry,
Chambers, James,
Clark, James,
Corithers, Robert,
Corithers, Hugh,

Drening, William,
Etter, David,
Fleming, John,
Glassbloss, Peter,
Hart, Henry,
Hall, Thomas,
Hershaw, Andrew,
Irland, James,
Kinder, Deter,
Karr, John,
Laird, Mathew,
Laird, John,
Magill, Lawrence,
Morrow, Samuel,
McCobb, William,
Martin, Edward,
McCay, James,
Newcomer, Francis,
Patterson, Moses,
Penilton, John,
Pennelton, Isaac,
Park, Thomas,
Pearsh, Peter,
Pidle, Macks,

Russell, James,
Ramsey, Robert,
Russell, James,
Spencer, William,
Sterrett, William,
Sample. James,
Shoop, Stophel,
Singer, John,
Spangler, Peter,
Shaw, James,
Talker, Adam,
Talker, Robert,
Thompson, William,
Tyce, John,
Vanlear, John,
Wiley, James,
Walker, James,
Wilson, Samuel,
Wilson, Mathew,
Wagner, Adam,
Wiry, Andrew,
Willson, Robert,
Were, John,
Weetaberger, George,

Freemen.

Bready, Robert,
Bowman. John,
Carr, Thomas,
Clark, John,

Findleer, James,
Finley, William,
Harris, James,
McKee, Robert,

McCormag, James,
McClay, William,
Snody, James.

ADAM BAUM, *Col.*

BURGESSES BOROUGH OF HARRISBURG.—1791-1860.

[We have endeavored to prepare a complete list of all the burgesses of the borough of Harrisburg from the year of its incorporation. However, there are quite a number of gaps which we would like to fill. If any of our readers can do so, we will be under obligations. Under the original charter there were two chief burgesses and four assistants. This continued until about the year 1808, when the charter was so amended as to make one chief burgess and one assistant burgess. After that period the first person named after the date was the chief, the second the assistant burgess. The list is a valuable one.]

1791—George Hoyer, Adam Boyd.
1792—Adam Boyd, John Luther. Assistants—Moses Gilmor, Henry Beader, William Glass, John Hocker.
1793—John Luther, Adam Boyd. Assistants—William Glass, John Hocker, Moses Gilmor, Henry Beader.
1794—Conrad Bombaugh, Alexander Berryhill. Assistants—Samuel Hill, Andrew Krause, Samuel Berryhill, Jacob Bucher.
1795—[Not to be found.]
1796—Christian Kunkel, William Graydon.
1797—William Graydon, James Sayers.
1798—Michael Kapp, Stacy Potts. Assistants—Henry Bruner, John Gillum, John Shoch, George Whitehill.
1799—Stacy Potts, Andrew Mitchell. Assistants—Peter Bricker, Conrad Fahnestock, Adam Ebert, Andrew Krause.
1800—[Not to be found.]
1801—Stacy Potts, George Peffer. Assistant Burgesses—John Hise, Obed Fahnestock, Moses Gilmor, Samuel Weir.
1802—[Not to be found.]
1803—George Peffer, Samuel Berryhill.
1804, 1805, and 1806—[Not to be found.]
1807—Abraham Bombaugh, George Youse. Assistants—John Mytinger, Matthias Hutman, Michael Krehl, Jacob Boas.
1808—William Graydon, Moses Gillmor.
1809—William Graydon, Moses Gillmor.
1810—Joshua Elder, John Wyeth.
1811-1816—[Not to be found.]
1816—William Wallace, Robert Harris.
1817—Benjamin Kurtz, John Horter.
1818—Hugh Hamilton, George Ziegler.
1819 and 1820—[Not to be found.]

1821—Obed Fahnestock, John Horter.
1822—Obed Fahnestock, William Murray.
1823—Frederick Kekler, John Downey.
1824—John Capp, Abraham Oves.
1825—William Graydon, Peter Brua.
1826—George Beatty, John Brooks.
1827—George Beatty, John Brooks.
1828—John Brooks, Abraham Bombaugh.
1829—Abraham Bombaugh, William Allison.
1830—Abraham Bombaugh, William Graydon.
1831—Abraham Bombaugh, Jacob Ziegler.
1832—Joel Baily, Hugh Hamilton.
1833—Christian Seiler, Mordecai McKinney.
1834—Valentine Hummel, Mordecai McKinney.
1835—Geo. Beatty, Frederick Heisely.
1836—Christian Seiler, Jacob Shoemaker.
1837—Christian Seiler, Samuel Pool.
1838—Christian Seiler, William Kline.
1839—William Kline, Robert Harris.
1840—Hugh McIlvaine, E. L. Orth.
1841—George Beatty, John B. Thompson.
1842—Charles F. Muench, David Harris.
1843—Charles F. Muench, Jacob Baab.
1845—William Kline, Robert H. Morton.
1846—Henry Chritzman, John Hiney.
1847—Henry Chritzman, David Harris.
1848—David Harris, Cyrus J. Rees.
1853—William Kline, John Knepley.
1854—William Kline, Thomas W. Buffington.
1855—J. Martin Lutz, Ebenezer Ward.
1858—Daniel E. Wilt, John B. Tomlinson.
1859—John B. Tomlinson, Henry Beader.
1860—Councilman-at-large—William H. Kepner.

NOTES AND QUERIES.—LXXXIX.

OLD RESIDENTS.—From the *Oracle of Dauphin* we glean the following deaths:

Rachel Wallace, wife of Gen. James Wallace, of Hanover, d. February 15, 1823.

Gen. James Wallace, d. Dec. 17, 1823.

Margaret Carson, wife of John Carson, dec'd, d. March 2, 1823, aged 63 years.
David Ritchey, of Hanover, d. April 23, 1823, aged 71 years.
Dr. Samuel Wiestling, d. April 22. 1823, aged 63 years.
Maj. John Barnett, d. May 13, 1823, aged 72 years.
Christian Kunkel, d. Sept. 8, 1823, aged 67 years.
Capt. Samuel Finney, of Hanover, d. Dec. 5, 1823, aged 68 years.
James Dixon, Esq., d. Jan. 20, 1824.
Jacob Henning, Sr., d. Feb. 23, 1824, aged 88 years.

TRANSCRIPTIONS FROM U. B. GRAVE-YARD, MIDDLETOWN.—The following are the only records of this burying ground :
Campbell, Joseph, d. Oct. 20, 1845, aged 82 years.
Campbell, Isabella, *wf.* of J., d. March 16, 1842, aged 72 years.
Lehman, Anna, *wf.* of Christian, b. July 25, 1784; d. Sept. 13, 1854.
Lehman, Martin, b. Oct. 19, 1805 ; d. Mar. 31, 1844.
Lehman, Susan S., *wf.* of Henry, b. May 12, 1817 ; d. May 1, 1852.
Metzgar, Jonas, b. Sept. 29, 1775 ; d. Jan. 4, 1856.
Rodfong, Eliza, *wf.* of George, b. Jan. 13, 1813 ; d. Dec. 4, 1841.

THE DAYS OF NEGRO SLAVERY.—The following paper comes to us from the West.   Who was Mary Smith ?

" PAXTANG, *October the 14th, 1780.*

" In pursuance of the act of the Assembly for the gradual Abolition of Slavery, Mary Smith, Gloverist, of Paxtang Township, in Lancaster County, Do hereby Enter with the Clark of the Sessions of said County the following Person, a Sleave during her life, viz : Shusanah, a Negro Wench about twenty-two years of age and owned by me.   MARY SMITH.
" To John Hubley, Esq'r, Clrak of the Sessions of Lancaster County."

OFFICERS BOROUGH OF HARRISBURG.—1817–1860.

Borough Treasurers.

1817—1818, Moses Gillmor.
1818—1821, John Brooks.
1821—1839, Michael Keller.
1839—1850, Christian Seiler.
1850—1852, Jacob Seiler.
1858—1860, Adam K. Fahnestock.

Clerks of the Borough.

1817—1819, John Kean.
1819—1821, James Alricks.
1821—1823, John Downey.
1823—1829, Warum Holbrook.
1829—1837, James Montgomery.
1837—1840, John Houser.
1840—1845, George J. Shoemaker.
1845—1846, Henry Peffer.
1846—1847, Abram Edwards, Jr.
1847—1860, David Harris.

THE MILITIA IN THE REVOLUTION.

If any of our readers are under the impression that the militia, the minute men, of the Revolution, saw but little dangerous service, let them read the following :

To the Justices of the Orphans' Court for the County of Lancaster:

Whereas, a certain Peter Boal, of the Fourth Batt'n of Lancaster County Militia, some time in July last went to Northumberland county against the Indians, under the command of Capt'n James Collier, and unfortunately was Dangerously wounded, having his Scull fractured, his Leg & thigh bones broke, & scalp'd at the same Time by the Indians, nigh Wallace's Fort, on the West Branch of the Susquehannah, and in this deplorable condition was sent to the home of his father in Paxtang township who applied to Dr. —— near Jonestown who has nearly cured the wounds, in as much that the patient is able to walk with a little assistance, & is desirous of returning home, but the Doctor refused letting him go until his Bill is paid, which is impossible for the Patient to do, & his father thinks it hard for him to pay, as he's an old man having a large family to support, & in low circumstances, especially as his son is become a cripple & in the publick service. Your worships are therefore requested to order Payment to the Surgeon and Relief to the Patient if you think it consistent with your authority and agreeable to the laws of the State ; as the above are Facts. Certified the 4th Day of February, 1779, by

JOSHUA ELDER,
Sub-Lieut. of Lanc'r County Militia.
JAMES COLLIER,
Captain.
J. WORK,
Capt. 3d B. Lanc. M.

Indorsed on the foregoing paper is the following:

At an Orphans' Court held 5th, Feb'y, 1779, Before Emanuel Carpenter, Michael Hubley and Henry Slaymaker, Esquires.

The Court upon Consideration of the within representation, do order and adjudge that the within named Peter Boal, do receive a pension of twenty-five shillings & three pence pr. month during his Life or disability of getting a Livelyhood, and that the same Pension begin from & after the twentieth Day of Septem'r last, and the Lieutenant of the County of Lancaster is ordered to pay the same agreeably to Law.

THE MILITIA OF 1812–14.

ROLL OF CAPT. SHELL'S COMPANY OF THE SECOND BATTALION, NINETY-EIGHTH REGIMENT, FIRST BRIGADE.

[It is doubtful if any of the members of the following militia company are alive in this year of grace, 1885. Many of them, however, are remembered by our older citizens, especially Maj. John Shell. These, no doubt, are full of the reminiscences of the long ago, and of the festive and hilarious days of the battalions, which semi-annually took place in the neighborhood of Linglestown or Gilchrist's. In the list herewith given will be recognized the rames of many whose descendants yet reside in our county, while others have passed out and founded new homes in the lands beyond the Ohio and Mississippi. The numbers to the names are the ages in 1814.—P.]

Captain.
John Shell, 23.
Lieutenant.
Adam Shope, 18.
Ensign.
Alex. Hanna, 27.
Privates—First Class.
John Snyder, 25,
Jacob Hoover, 25,
Jacob Holtzstein, 35,
Joseph Snyder, 20,
John Kieffer, 25,
William Millisen, 24,
Daniel Shoop, 36,
William Orth, 18.
Second Class.
John Walborn, 23,
Emanuel Cassel, 39,
Andrew Miller, 30,
John Wilson, 26,

John Shaffer, 36,
Jacob Shaffer, 37,
James Duncan, 20,
Bob Synny, 20,
Jacob Shoop, 35,
Joseph Keiffer, 25,
Samuel Schwartz, 26,
Henry Snyder, 23,
Henry Light, 23,
Daniel Shell, 20,
Jacob Cassel, 20.
Third Class.
John Carson, 32,
Andrew Harrof, 26,
John Staufer, 21,
John Zimmerman, 21,
Jacob Ebersole, 25,
John Ewing, 25,
Gearls Gamberly, 33.

Fourth Class.
William Aspy, 38,
Wm. Poorman, 33,
Christ Coffman, 31,
George Cayney, 33,
Joseph Light, 20,
Jacob Pack, 30,
S. Rutherford, 44,
George Witzal, 26,
Jacob Snyder, 20,
Abram Miller, 20.
Fifth Class.
Jacob Cassel, 30,
John Albert, 41,
Christian Buck, 25,
George Shetz, 33,
John Rickert, 24,
Christian Hoover, 27,
David Boys, 30,
Jacob Early, 30,

——— Hawk, 18,
John Rickert, 24,
Christian Hoover, 23,
John Hamberly, 27,
Jacob Horning, 34,
Frederick Richert, 21,
Henry Hiesey. 20,
S. Newcommer, 27,
Thomas Jones, 21.
Sixth Class.
Wm. Rutherford, 38,
John Richey, 38,
Deter Weaver, 28,
Paniel Smith, 21,

Wm. Anderson, 30,
Daniel Page, 23,
Jacob Reickert, 25,
John Hefelfinger, 21,
Peter Hefelfinger, 20.
Seventh Class.
Philip Hoover, 24,
John Hised, 23,
Stopel Shoop, 33,
Frederick Shoop, 28,
Samuel Hoover, 20,
William Ewing, 18,
John Prame, 38,

Jacob Millisen, 36,
Windel Minnit, 31,
Joseph Eversole, 23,
Conrad Peck, 23,
Peter Shetz, 26,
Peter Stall, 44,
Thomas Reed, 28,
David Mader, 28,
John Miller, 22,
Frederick Rudy, 39,
Jacob Martin, 40,
George Hains, 26,
John Moyer, 20.

NOTES AND QUERIES.—XC.

WOLTZ FAMILY.—A correspondent at Fredericksburg Va., and an editor of distinguished ability in the Old Dominion, writes us in regard to this family. He says: "I have long been anxious to learn more of that branch of our family which resided in Pennsylvania and Maryland. It has been my misfortune when I attempted to trace any of them to find that they were not where I expected them. In your *Notes and Queries*, it is stated that Mary Wolz, who married J. B. McKennan, "is still living, a widow, at Brownsville, Pa." I wrote to Mrs. McK. but my letter was returned, the name not being recognized by the postmaster. I have never learned of but one family of our name that came to this country from Germany. The Virginia branch of the Woltz family have been conspicious only for their quiet and retiring dispositions. I never heard of but one of the name who joined the Confederate army. But two have ever figured in public affairs. Dr. Louis Woltz, of Carroll county, has served one or two terms in the Legislature.   J. W. W.

STILWELL FAMILY.—A correspondent from Western Pennsylvania writes: "Have you the name of John Stilwell, who removed with his family from Staten Island, New York. and settled in Tuscarora Valley, this State, and was attainted in 1778. If you know aught of his history I will be pleased to hear. From his daughter, Rachel Stilwell, descended Hon. A. T. Goshorn. of Cincinnati, who was Director General of the Centennial Exhibition in 1876. From his son, John Stilwell, descended Hon. Thomas Stilwell, of Indiana. From his son, William Stilwell, descended the writer of these notes. The name originally was Cooke. During the reign of Charles I., Nicholas, John and Jasper Cooke, brothers, fled from England to Holland. In 1638 they emigrated to America under the name of Stilwell. Nicholas Stilwell was the first English settler on Manhattan Island, and it was he who built the stone house, which the "Sons of Liberty" took at the breaking out of the Revolutionary war. Nicholas Stilwell was the common ancestor of the family. His brother John returned to England and assuming his original name was arrested and executed with some other persons by order of Charles II. in 1660 for the death of his father. Maj. General Harrison was his cousin.

M. S.

CAPT. LAZARUS STEWART.

[Shortly before his death the Hon. Stewart Pearce, of Wilkes-Barre, sent us the following information concerning the descendants of the brave Lazarus Stewart. It is of much interest.]

"Enclosed I send you all I know about Captain Stewart's descendants. Respecting himself see Annals of Luzerne county. The date of his death in that book is wrong. He was born in 1733, and married Martha Espy, whose father lived in Lancaster, now Dauphin county. I do not know the date of his children's birth or death.

Their son JAMES STEWART m. HANNAH JAMESON, whose children were *Martha*, m. Abram Tolles; *Francis*, m. Benjamin A. Bidlack; *Abigail*, m. Abraham Thomas, she is still living, 84 years of age; *Caroline*, m. Rev. Morgan Sherman; *Lazarus*, and *Mary*, who both died single. My father, Rev. Marmaduke Pearce, m. James Stewart's widow and had three children, *Stewart*, *Cromwell*, and *John*. My father named me in honor of my mother's first husband.

ELIZABETH STEWART m. ALEXANDER JAMESON, whose children were *William*, who m. Margaret Henry; *Robert*, who d. unmarried; *Minerva*, who m. Dr. A. B. Wilson; *Elizabeth*, who m. Rev. Francis Macartney; *Martha*, who d. recently, unmarried.

JOSIAH STEWART, m. MERCY CHAPMAN, removed to Western New York at an early day, but I have not been able to trace him out. He had two daughters, one named *Hannah*, the name of the other I do not know.

MARY STEWART m. Rev. ANDREW GRAY. Mr. Gray was b. in county Down, Ireland, Jan. 1, 1757; d. Aug. 13, 1839. He lived in Paxtang and came to Wyoming, and settled in Hanover, where he preached. He was a Presbyterian. He removed to Western New York, was a missionary several years among the Seneca Indians, and finally settled at Dansville,

Livingston county, N. Y. His children were *James*, m. Rebecca Roberts; *Margaret*, m. Richard Gillespie; *Jane*, m. Daniel Gallatin; *William*, d. unmarried; *Andrew*, left home young and was never heard from; *Maria*, m. James Jack; *Martha*, d. unmarried; *Elizabeth*, m. Robert Perine. I received this information respecting Gray's family from Mrs. Jane Knappenburg, a daughter of Martha Gray Gillespie. Mrs. K. resides at Dansville, N. Y.

PRISCILLA STEWART, m. JOSEPH AVERY RATHBUN, who also settled in Western New York. Their children were *John, Lazarus, Joseph.* They all married and have descendants at or near Almond, N. Y.

MARGARET STEWART, m. JAMES CAMPBELL. They both lived and died in Hanover township, Luzerne county. Their children were *James-S.*, who died unmarried; *Martha*, who m. James S. Lee; *Mary*, who m. Jameson Harvey; *Peggy*, who m. James Dilley.

There are several descendants—Lees, Harveys and Dilleys—residing in the valley.

MARTHA STEWART, d. unmarried.

I advertised in Western New York papers for information respecting the Grays, Rathbuns and Josiah Stewart. They all have descendants living there now, but I could not find out anything about Josiah Stewart's family any further than what I have stated. I hope the above information will be satisfactory.

LETTERS OF JOHN HARRIS.

[We are indebted to Rev. J. A. Murray, D. D., of Carlisle, for copies of the letters which follow. They were all addressed to Col. Robert Magaw, of Carlisle.]

PAXTANG, *Aug't 30th, 1769.*

SIR: By the Post I Send you a Letter from Mr. Maclay With Some Bills Inclosed, Wch. he Requested might goe by a safe hand to you. I Expect Woods' money by the Election without fail, & if the Cash is not pd. by that time, Please to Let the Sherrif Take the Necessary Steps to have it By Next Court, & Hutten's & McGills Debts Take Every Law Method to Discover as Quick as you can. I expect youl not fail & youl

Oblige Sir Your Most Obdt &
Most Humble Servant,

JOHN HARRIS.

P. S. Please to give the Post a Receipt for what he may Deliver you from me on accot. of Mr. Maclay.

PAXTANG, *March 27th, 1784.*

SIR: I am just returned from Philada. Inclosed is the act of Assembly for the consideration of the people ab't my town. I miss'd Two votes only of gett'g the law Inacted at this Sessions, on acco't of the Constitution ab't the law laying over for consideration, &c., till the next meeting of the house, w'ch my enemys and fr'ds made use of. I carry'd every thing else with ease, and makes no doubt of Having the county. I am, sir, yr. most Humble Servant,

JOHN HARRIS.

P. S.—The trustees of yr. Colledge is to meet at Carlisle the 6th day of April next. Sr. yrs., &c. J. H.

———

PAXTANG, *May 28th, 1784.*

SIR: Be pleas'd to send me by son Robert the cash Gahig owes me on acco't of John Beard's Estate, with any other cash in y'r hands of mine. If any collected yet please to let him know. If the Judges will Return this way from Sunbury, I shall be glad to see you here next week, if it suits y'r conveniency to spend a day on the Bank and partake of some Rock fish, having a little other Business with you. If you don't goe to N. Thumberl'd Court pr'haps it may suit you; please to let Bobby know. I am, sir, y'r most humble servant,

JOHN HARRIS.

———

HARRISBURG, *Oct. 14th, 1786.*

Sir: We Carry'd every Member of Assembly in this County, the Sheriff & Commissioner, has therefore gave our antagonists a mortal defeat. Please to send me by the Bearer, Mr. George Page, a White Sword Belt for my son Robert, as abt. 20 or near 30 young men have agreed with the Lebanon Troop of Light horse men yesterday, to meet them at Lebanon on next Saturday to choose the officers, therefore our men will equip themselves by next Friday (If Possible). The Lebanon Gentlemen, with Colo'l Cloninger, paid us a visit, & were Compleatly Equipt, abt. 12 file of them, Behaved with the greatest decorum, spent abt. 24 hours with us and returned yesterday. It's expected that the greatest unanimity will hereafter take place in future (in this county) and party spirit decrease. If you please to take the trouble to provide the Sword Belt, if to be got, shall be obliged to you. Underneath is a list of our Ticket that carry'd. I expect a few

lines from you with a list of yr. members; & York county, If you have
heard from them. I am sir, yours most respectfully,

JOHN HARRIS.

Robert Clarke, ⎫
Jacob Mylye, ⎬Assemblymen.
John Carson, ⎭
   Sheriffs, Kelker and Berryhill.
   Commissioner, Capt'n. James Wilson, only one to be chose or we
cou'd carry'd them.   J. H.
   P. S.—We are well pleas'd at our election for this year, and the
prospects of uniting all parties in a few years, or Perhaps less time.

J. H.

————

HARRISBURG, *Jany 24th, 1787.*

   SIR: I saw Mr. William Miller, of Juniata, here yesterday, and he
s'd he p'd Mr. Starit, a deputy of Mr. Postle's, y'r late sherif, long
since my money. Please to inquire & let Mr. Postle know I expect
it. Also please to inform him that I am told that a certain John
Carver has p'd a considerable debt to him, or my Attorney. I expect
he will please to inquire at the office how that is, and forw'd my
money safe. If he don't come here soon, wch he wrote me he wou'd
on a visit (& other business), please to push McGahey's estate for my
debt, & get my money as soon as the law will admit. I have made
free to trouble you to receive & forward to Baltimore some letters for
me to my son, David Harris, and Mr. Crocket. I hope they are sent
safe (ere this arrives). If any letters from them come to y'r care, be
pleased to forw'd them by safe conveyances only, as my s'd son has
wrote me several letters from France, & other parts of Europe, & will
contrive to write frequently till his return. I depend on your particular care of them, if any should happen to arrive. I am, sir, your
most humble serv't,   JOHN HARRIS.

————◄•►•————

NOTES AND QUERIES—XCI.

————

DEATH OF SOME WORTHIES.—From one of our note books we ex-
tract the following:
   William Murray, d. June 1, 1823, at Washington, Pa. He was an
early merchant at Harrisburg, and a man of prominence.
   John Horter, d. Nov. 26, 1823, aged 47 years. His father, John
Valentine Horter, was an early settler at Harrisburg.
   William Denning, d. Nov. 22, 1823, aged 40 years.

John Frazer, d. March 6, 1824. He came from Lancaster upon the removal of the seat of government to Harrisburg, holding a position under the Snyder administration.

John Mytinger, Oct. 19, 1822.

Maj. John Irwin, Nov. 23, 1822.

Col. Frederick Hubley, Dec. 28, 1822.

Samuel Bryan, Jan. 11, 1823.

REVOLUTIONARY PENSIONERS.

[In the year 1800 the following Revolutionary Pensioners were living in Lebanon county. The figures annexed were the ages of the respective individuals.]

In Lebanon Borough—George Hess, 79.

In Swatara Township—Peter Witmoyer, 80; Anna Barbara Yeagley, 78; Peter Sailor, 77; John Shalley, 79; Jacob Herim, 74; John Bickel, 88; Valentine Shouffler, 88; Martin Meily, 68; George Heilman, 81.

In East Hanover Township—Thomas Kopenhaver, 80; John Hetrich, 77; Jacob Decker, 84; Philip Witmeyer, 80; John Garberich, 81; James Stewart, 83.

In Londonderry Township—Jacob Lentz, 81; Adam Trist, 80; Jacob Keaner, 80; Andrew Robeson, 81.

In Heidelberg Township—George Wolf, 79; Margaret Leob, 79; Elizabeth Derr, 81.

In Lebanon Township—Andrew Hoover, 75; Dilman Doup, 81; Mary Weaver, 75.

In Bethel Township—Catharine Walborn, 85.

In Jackson Township—Mary Bainny, 75; Rebecca Bowers, 74; John Smith, 86.

IN THE REVOLUTION.

The following memoranda we find on a paper in our possession. They may be of historic value, as items of less import have proved to be:

" Richard Rogers, commander of an armed vessel taken by Capt. Barry, & Jno. Draper, another officer of said vessel, being brought to this city [Philadelphia] as Prisoners, were agreed to be enlarged on their separately signing the following parole, which they did accordingly

" I, ——, being a Prisoner in the United Colonies of America, do upon the Honor of a Gent'n promise that I will not go into or near any Seaport Town, nor farther than Six Miles distant from Lebanon in Lancaster County, my present place of Residence, without permission of the Continental Congress or of the Committee of Safety of Penn'a, and that I will carry on no political correspondence whatever on the subject of the dispute between Great Britain or these Colonies so long as I remain a prisoner."

" *Ordered,* That Doct'r Rush & Dr. Duffield be appointed to Receive all Medicines belonging this Province, and to deliver the same in such proportions to the different Battalions & other armaments of this Province as they, or this Board [Penn'a Board of War] shall think proper, giving & taking Receipts for what they receive and deliver."

LEBANON, *May 21, 1776.*

SR : I make Bold to Request the favoure of you To Send Me the new Association Paper for my Batalion. I cannot make my Batalion In Readiness to Return the same to the Commissioner for want of the same, & In so Doing you will oblige
Your Humb. Ser't,
PHILIP GREENAWALT.

N. B.—I desire that you will let me No Whether We shall chuse another Committeeman in the place of Dehaas, & likewise to let me No about chusing three men to Disarm the Non-Associators in the said Township.
To Mr. Jasper Yeats, Esq.

JOHN MARTIN MACK'S JOURNAL

OF A VISIT TO ONONDAGA.—I.

INTRODUCTION.—On the 17th of July, 1749, at an interview between Bishops A. G. Spangenberg, J. C. F. Cammerhoff and John M. von Watteville, and Rev. Nathaniel Seidel, of the Moravian Church, and the sachems of the Six Nations, held in the parsonage of the Moravian Church, in Philadelphia, permission was given to the Moravians to send a deputation to Onondaga in the following year to arrange preliminaries for the commencement of missionary enterprises in their country. In the summer of 1750 Bishop Cammerhoff and David Zeisberger visited Onondaga and applied to the Council for permission for at least two missionaries to reside there in order to learn the language. This was granted. Owing to the troubles between England and France, it was not until the summer of 1752 that Zeisberger and Carl Godfrey Rundt were appointed to take up their residence in Onondaga, and Mack was to accompany them, take part in the negotiations, and then return to Bethlehem to report the result to the mission board. The journal which Mack kept was originally written in German, a translation of which is now given to the reader.

John Martin Mack, for many years employed in the Indian mission of his church, was born in Leysingen, Wurtemberg, April 13, 1715. Twenty years later he was sent to Georgia, and in 1740 left for Pennsylvania, where he assisted in the building of Nazareth and Bethlehem. In March, 1742, he was appointed assistant missionary in the Indian mission in New York and Connecticut, and six months later was married to Jeannette Rau, who resided in the "Oblong," New York. Her knowledge of the Mohawk and Delaware languages rendered her an efficient assistant to her husband and the mission. She died at Gnadenhutten, on the Mahoning, December 15, 1749. In April, 1746, Mack commenced the mission at Gnadenhutten, the field of his labors until the autumn of 1755. During this interval he annually visited the Indian villages of the West Branch of the Susquehanna. In 1753 he was married to Anna Rebstock. For the Moravian Indians, who were sojourning in Bethlehem in 1757, he commenced the building of Nain, near that place. "Here," he states in his autobiography, "I made my most trying experiences as a missionary, enduring not only temporal privations, but harrassed also by constant anxiety for the welfare of my charge. I commenced the work with misgivings, as the project of settling the Indians so far down in the Province was viewed with displeasure by whites and savages." In 1761, he was appointed superintendent of the mission in the Danish West Indies. While on a visit to Bethlehem in 1770 he was consecrated a bishop. Died on Santa Croix, January 9, 1784.

J. W. JORDAN.

THE JOURNAL.

Wednesday, July 26.—In the evening, after the service, we set out from Bethlehem with the blessing of the congregation. We felt an attachment to our dear brethren and sisters. The watch-words (1) were, "And I shall put my Spirit in you, and you shall live." Christian Seidel (2) and Gottlieb (3) accompanied us to Christian's Spring (4) where we arrived after midnight.

Thursday, July 27.—Towards noon we left Christian's Spring. Bro

Moyer (5) went with us to the Delaware, and then returned with many hearty salutations from us. We continued on our journey with cheerful minds and happy thoughts. Our bundles, although not heavy, made us perspire very much, it being very warm all day.

Saturday, July 29.—At ten o'clock in the forenoon we reached Brunswick and called on Mr. Schuyler (6) who was very glad to see us. We gave him a letter from Bro. Joseph (7), and he willingly offered to assist us in any way in his power, furnished us with a pass (8) and also a letter of recommendation to the Mayor of New York (9). At his request we related about the visit of the Indians who recently visited Bethlehem from Wyomick (10), which interested him very much. At noon we set out for Elizabethtown, as there were no boats here that left soon for New York.

Sunday, July 30.—At Elizabethtown we found a boat bound for New York, where we arrived late in the afternoon, and were given a hearty welcome by our brethren and sisters (11).

Wednesday, August 2.—This day especially, as also the foregoing, we provided ourselves with necessaries for our journey, being cheerfully assisted by our brethren. We observed and felt that they take great interest in Indian affairs (12).

Thursday, August 3.—This morning we bade farewell to our brethren, and at 8 o'clock went with our things on board the sloop which is to take us to Albany. We set sail immediately. The captain's name is Egbert Egbertse (13), a Low Dutchman by birth, who showed us much civility, offering us his private cabin. We sailed to-day upwards of twenty miles.

Friday, August 4.—To-day we sailed past the Highlands, the wind light all day.

Saturday, August 5.—Fair winds all day. The captain continues his kindness towards us, and he has not asked us who we are, which is otherwise not the way of the Low Dutch in this country. 'Tis probable he knows that we belong to the brethren. At noon we arrived off Cornelius Beekman's, where Bro. Martin left us to go on to Rhinebeck (14) to buy a horse, and then to follow us by land to Albany. In the afternoon Bro. Martin arrived at Christian Feuhrer's (15), who returned yesterday from Pachgatgoch (16), to which place he and Jacob Maull (17) had accompanied Bro. Senseman (18) and wife. Bro. David and Rundt arrived at Albany about 11 o'clock at night and remained on the sloop until morning.

Sunday, August 6.—To-day Bro. Martin visited in Rhinebeck. Bro. David and Rundt lodged with the Captain. In the afternoon they went to hear Dominie Freylinghausen (19) preach.

Monday, August 7.—Christian Fuehrer and Jacob Maull endeavored to buy a horse for our journey, Bro. Mack being sick all day.

Tuesday, August 8.—Bro. Martin was obliged to keep his bed all day. A horse was purchased this afternoon.

Wednesday, August 9.—This morning Bro. Martin set out from Rhinebeck, and on

Thursday, August 10, rejoined his brethren in Albany.

Friday, August 11.—Early this morning we made preparations for continuing our journey, and left Albany at 10 o'clock. In the evening we reached Schenectady (20) where we remained over night.

Saturday, August 12.—We came this afternoon to William's Fort (21), a Maqua town, where many Indians live, who were baptized by a minister of the Church of England by the name of Ogilby (22). We found but few at home. Conrad Weiser's son (23) resided here last summer to learn their language. We remained here but a short time and then proceeded some miles further and came to a Low Dutchman's, where we had very good lodgings.

Sunday, August 13.—We were obliged to rest all day, and called to mind the great festival which is to-day celebrated in all our congregations.

Monday, August 14.—We started on our journey again in good spirits. In the afternoon we left the Low Dutch settlements (24), and continued through a severe thunder storm to within eight miles of Canajoharie, and lodged with a German. The watch words for to-day were: "As one whom his mother comforteth, so will I comfort you," was a blessing to us.

Tuesday, August 15.—We set out early in the morning, but found the walking difficult owing to the rain of yesterday, and at 8 o'clock reached Canajoharie (25), a Maqua Indian town, where Bro. David and Post were arrested seven years ago and carried to prison in New York (26). Bro. David showed us the house in which they then lodged. Very few Indians were to be seen, but we learned subsequently that they were in the castle (27), which was built during the last war—half a mile from the town. We also heard that a minister preached (28) to them in English through an interpreter. We did not remain here long, but continued for eight miles through the woods until noon, when we came to the Great Falls, where the settlements again commence.

In the afternoon we crossed the river, which was much swollen by the rain. Here we met about one hundred Indians, mostly from Anajot (29) and Cayuga (30), who live at present in these parts and dig roots (31) which are very good in all kinds of sickness. The Indians sell them to the people in the neighborhood or exchange them for goods with the traders who come from Albany. Towards evening we left the river and lodged with an Irishman who has a German wife. We had not been here long before five Oneida Indians arrived and stayed all night. Bro. David talked with them a long time.

Wednesday, August 16.—Early this morning we continued our journey, and about 10 o'clock reached the last house between here and Onondaga, where we found many Indians. From here our path lies altogether through the woods. The man who lives here is a German and was quite civil to us. His people were very anxious to know whither we were going and the object of our visit to Onondaga. The Indians, too, asked us the same questions, whereupon Bro. David informed them. After being here half an hour the Indians we met yesterday arrived, and with them the chiefs of the Oneida. They talked with us, too, and we felt that something more than usual would take place here, but we knew not what. We were told that a large party of Indians were near the river drinking, where we must cross, it being impossible to cross anywhere else nearby, owing to the mountains on both sides of the river. We finally determined to remain and await events.

Notes.

1. The custom of issuing each year "watch words" or a "text book," consisting of a selection of verses from the Bible for each day, with appropriate collects taken from the hymn book, has prevailed in the Moravian Church since the year 1731.

2. Came to America in 1751. In 1756 he was employed in the ministry among the Moravians in North Carolina. Died 1759.

3. Gottlieb Pezold from Saxony, came to Philadelphia in 1742. In 1748 he was ordained a Deacon. Died at Lititz, Pa., April 1, 1742. It is stated in his memoir that he was present at Conrad Weiser's in August, 1742, when Zinzendorf ratified the treaty with the Six Nations.

4. A Moravian settlement, 9 miles N.N.W. from Bethlehem, named after the son of Count Zinzendorf. It was commenced in 1749.

5. John Moyer came to America in 1743. A daughter married Godfrey Haga, a wealthy merchant of Philadelphia, who left a large estate to the Moravian Church.

6. Dirk Schuyler, an alderman of New Brunswick, is enrolled in Registers of the Moravian Church in New York and vicinity prior to 1746. His house was always open for the entertainment of Moravian evangelists.

7. Bishop A. G. Spangenberg, as early as 1746, had substituted the Hebrew name Joseph for its latin equivalent, Augustus, one of his given names.

8. To whom it may concern: Y^e bearer hereof, David Zeisberger, a Deacon of ye Church of Unitas Fratrum, or United Brethren, and Gottfried Rundt, his companion, being personally known to me, both of Bethlehem, in ye county of Northampton and Province of Pennsylvania, having signified to me ye intention of traveling through ye Jerseys and ye Government of New York, up to ye Indian settlements, on these lawful occasions; All magistrates and others, through whose jurisdiction the said David Zeisberger and Gottfried Rundt may have occasion to pass and repass, are hereby requested to permit them to quietly proceed on their journey, they behaving themselves well. Given under my hand and ye seal of New Brunswick, this ye 17th day of July, 1752.   DIRK SCHUYLER, [SEAL.]
Alderman.

9. WHEREAS, Messrs. Martin Mack, David Zeisberger, and Gottfried Rundt, ye Bearers hereof, are inclined to travel to and about ye City and County of Albany upon these lawful occasions; These are therefore to desire all Persons to suffer them, the above Mack, David Zeisberger, and Gottfried Rundt to pass and repass, they behaving themselves according to law.   Given under my hand and seal, ye 21st day of July, 1752.   ED. HOLLAND, [SEAL]
Mayor of ye City of New York.

10. On July 20, 1752, there arrived at Bethlehem a deputation of Nanticokes and Shawanese from Wyoming via Gnadenhutten—57 of the former and 24 of the latter.   Fifty-five of the Moravian Indians of the Gnadenhutten Mission accompanied them.   On Monday, July 24, Bishop Spangenberg gave them an audience, when a covenant was made between them and the Moravians, and an invitation extended to the missionaries to visit their towns and preach the Gospel.

11. The Moravian congregation in New York was organized by Bishop John von Watteville, December 27, 1748, and a meeting-house built in 1751, on Fair street (now Fulton).   At the date of this Journal there was no pastor settled there.

12. Bethlehem, Monday, June 8, 1752.   "Issued 1½ yds. of Strouwater for a waistcoat for D. Zeisberger to go to Onondaga with Rundt." June 15, "issued 1¼ yds. Shallow and 1 yd. Linen for David Zeisberger, 5s. 1d."   July 31, "Bro. H. Van Vleck must be credited for cash paid to Martin Mack and comrades to buy a horse, and for traveling expenses to

Onondaga, ... £20		
1 piece ⅛ Gailic, 1 piece ditto, ...	5	11
1 doz. cap Knives, 3 doz. Thimbles, ...	7	9
6 pieces Gartering, 1 doz. Scissors, ...	16	3
4 lbs. Gunpowder, Shot, Flints and 2 Indian Blankets, . .	1 18	9
1400 Wampum (Black), 1500 ditto (White), ...	4 13	6
1 File, Comb, Knife, Fish Hooks, ...	3	11
5 Looking Glasses, Ink Pot, Ink, ...	4	10
Tobacco, 1 piece Silk Ferret, ...	1 6	4
New York currency, ... £43 2		4
Deduct 1-6 per £, ... 3 4		8
Pennsylvania currency, ... £39 17		8

13. A descendant of one of the first settlers of Albany. At this date about forty large sloops were engaged in trade between New York and Albany.

14. A German settlement on the east bank of the Hudson, opposite to Esopus, about 80 miles from New York, within Henry Beekman's Patent, in Duchess county.

15. A Palatine, father of Valentine Fuehrer, ferryman, and subsequently landlord of the Crown Inn, Bethlehem.

16. A Moravian Indian Mission, S. W. from Kent, in Connecticut. In 1859 the Moravian Historical Society erected a monument on its site to the memory of two of its former missionaries.

17. Jacob Maull was one of the Palatines who immigrated to New York in 1710, and is enrolled in a list of the freeholders of Duchess county in 1740. The Moravian missionaries in passing through Rhinebeck made the acquaintance of a number of the residents of the town.

18. Joachim and Ann Senseman came to Philadelphia with the first Moravian colony, June 7, 1742. While acting as steward and stewardess of the Indian Mission at Gnadenhutten, on the Mahoning, the latter was murdered when the mission house was destroyed by the so-called French Indians. He died in Jamaica, W. I., whither he had gone as missionary.

19. Theodorus Freylinghausen came to Albany in 1746, and was installed pastor of the Dutch Reformed Church. In October of 1759 he sailed from New York for Holland, from whence he never returned.

20. At the date of this Journal it was a village of about 250 houses, and was inhabited principally by descendants of the old Dutch settlers. It was incorporated as a city in 1798.

21. In the year 1756 this post on the Mohawk river was destroyed by General Webb on his famous flight from Wood Creek. The present city of Rome is built on the site.

22. Rev. John Ogilvie was a native of New York and a graduate of Yale College. Being a Dutch scholar he was appointed to the Mohawk mission in 1748. Subsequently he succeeded Rev. Henry Barclay as rector of Trinity church, New York. Died Nov. 26, 1774.

23. Samuel Weiser.

24. These settlements were scattered along the Mohawk river, and numbered from thirty to one hundred families in each.

25. Situated on the right bank of the Mohawk river is the town of Danube, Herkimer county, eight miles east of Little Falls. This was the upper or third Mohawk castle, where Soiengarahta, or King Hendrick resided. In Indian *Ga-na-jo-hi-e*, " signifying " a kettle-shaped hole in the rock," or " the pot that washes itself." This name refers to a deep hole worn in the rock by action of the water at the falls on Canajoharie creek, about one mile from its confluence with the Mohawk. Nearly opposite this point, on the north side of the Mohawk, and about two miles back from the river, was the Indian town of "Canajorha," visited by Greenkalgh. It appears that the town was removed afterwards to a point east of the present village of Fort Plain, on the south side of the river, where it is called " Canajohie " by Morgan, and afterwards to the site of the present town of Danube, where Zeisberger and Christian Frederick Post visited in 1745. James Burnside and Leonhard Schnell (Moravians), who visited the neighborhood in the spring of 1747, reported " that the Germans, numbering about 2,000, lived in three distinct settlements—at Canajoharie, at the Falls, and at Stone Arabia (now Palatine), and that a schoolmaster read from a ' postelle' on the church on Sunday." There is no place in New York so mixed up as Canajoharie—no less than *six locations* are entitled to it and *double* that number claim it.

26. In 1745 these two Moravian missionaries, being desirous of improving themselves in the Mohawk tongue, were, while on their way to the Indian towns arrested because they had no passes, and also unjustly accused of being in sympathy with the French. They were released April 10.

27. This fort was built of upright pickets joined together with lintels. Small cannon were in position on each bastion. Five or six families of Mohawks lived outside of the fort.

28. John Christopher Hartwick, the founder of the Hartwick Seminary. He was born in Saxe-Gotha in 1714, and was sent to America to take charge of some Palatine congregation in New York. He died in 1796.

29. An Oneida town located on the headwaters of Sucker creek, a tributary of Oriskany creek, in the southeast corner of the town Vernon, in Oneida county. It was the chief town called Onnejoust by the French, and was destroyed by Vaudreuil in Frontenac's expedition in 1696. It is marked on Sauthier's map of 1679 as "Old Oneida Castle," and was visited and described in 1677 by Greenkalgh, at which time "it was newly settled." In 1700 it was also visited by Colonel Romer, and appears on the map made to accompany his report, the original of whicn is now in the British museum.

30. The chief town and capital of the Cayuga tribe, situated near the east shore of Cayuga lake, in the town of Ledyard, and on the south bank of Great Gully Creek, 7 miles south of the present village of Cayuga. Bishops Cammerhoff and Zeisberger spent a day here in 1750, and describe it as "a beautiful village nestling among the trees on the shore of the lake, distinguished by its roomy and substantial houses."

31. Kalondaggouh, the Indian name for Ginseng.

NOTES AND QUERIES.—XCII.

JOHN MARTIN MACK'S JOURNAL

OF A VISIT TO ONONDAGA IN 1752.—II.

In the afternoon a chief came to us and inquired our business in Onondaga. Bro. David told him the whole object, but he did not seem satisfied and left us. During the evening the chief of the Oneidas and a Seneca came and began by saying that we were going to Onondaga, and then asked us our business there. Bro. David replied: "Two years ago Gallichwis (32) and he visited Onondaga, and made a proposition to the Council, which he believed they must have heard, as one of the chiefs of the Oneida Nation was present. They appeared, however, as if they had not heard a syllable of it. Bro. David then related the principal heads thereof, when they asked who had sent us, "T'girhitontie (33) and his Brethren," was the reply. Then a chief spoke as follows: "We two years ago heard much of the Brethren from a man whose name we will not now mention, and he advised us to beware of them. He told us all manner of bad things of you, and if any of you ever came to see us, we should send you home. Therefore we are unwilling that you should go any further, and that to-morrow morning you must turn back and return to whence you came." We did all we could to remove their wicked suspicions and accusations, but it was to no purpose. They were very bitter and told us several times: " Don't you take it upon yourselves to go any further, for if you do you will see what will come of it ; for we have heard no good of you and have been charged not to let you go any further, therefore you shall go back to-morrow !" The Oneida chief who was present at the Council two years ago was not with them. They were continually repeating : " We have been warned of the Brethren, and have been told that they have no occasion to learn our language, as other persons are appointed for that purpose." Being convinced that it would be imprudent for us to proceed on our journey without their consent, we requested the chiefs to meet again to-morrow, and we would hold a council with them, to which they consented and left us.

The Germans in the house overheard the greater part of the conversation and observed how much the Indians were prejudiced against us. One of them remarked: "It will be impossible for you to go on to Onondaga, for if you do, you will endanger your lives. Nine years ago there were also two persons who had a mind to go to Onondaga to learn the language, but the Indians sent them back, and if they had gone there they would have been killed." Probably they referred to Bros. Anton and Pyrlaeus (34). We spent the greater part of the night in prayer.

Thursday, August 17.—The four Oneida chiefs met this morning with twenty of their nation, and a chief of the Tuscaroras. When we went to them they bid us be seated, whereupon a chief arose and said : " The reason why we have so many of our people present is that they may also hear your matters." We replied : " We like it, we are glad to see that our matters will be treated publicly—every one may hear them." Bro. David was then called upon to speak concerning the object of our journey : " Ye brethren of the Oneidas ! We are come a great way, sent to you by your Brother T'girhitontie and his brethren, for no other reason and end but because they love you. Not that we seek your lands, as so many of you think, for after you are better acquainted with us, you find also, that as we speak to-day so we will speak always—ten, twenty, thirty years hence. Therefore it grieves us that you don't know us better." All listened with great attention. A chief inquired whether we had a belt of wampum to the council, to which Bro. David replied that we had not, but some strings of wampum. These were handed to them and explained according to the instructions given us at Bethlehem.

We sat with them upwards of an hour discoursing on our matter ;s when after a short consultation among themselves, the chief arose and said: "Ye Brethren! We have heard your matters and see that there is in them nothing bad, but that your words are good ; therefore you may go on to Onondaga, and lay your proposals before the Council. This we chiefs say to you, ye may go in peace and we are glad that we have heard of your affair." Bro. David replied : "We are also pleased that we have had an opportunity to lay our matters before your chiefs and your people, as the covenant we made with the Six Nations, also concerns you." The chiefs were quite orderly, and at parting called us "their Brethren," and also told us their names, being Huyenjot, Hatchtachguosde, T'gawio, Onontio, Guntantie, Kontartie, Satiunganichnarontie, Ognico, Iagotisgenogechtie and Iagothonto, the speaker. They also informed us that on our way up we must pass through several towns, among the number two Tuscarora towns, where we should tell the chiefs that the Oneidas were aware of our going to Onondaga. At the last town a chief would accompany us there to hear our proposals. Suggesting that two of their chiefs should go with us, they replied that it was not necessary, for they had listened to and knew our message already, and you may appeal thereto if you are asked about us. We observed, however, that they sent out messengers, and soon after learned that they were sent to the Cayuga and Seneca country to summon the chiefs to Onondaga to listen to the message of the Brethren.

When we returned to our landlord we found him anxiously waiting to hear how our matter would turn out. "How is it," said he, "must you go back?" "Good friend," we replied, "we go to Onondaga." "Aye! I never would have thought that the Indians would have given you permission for they were so much against it last night, and I have never yet seen Indians change their minds as soon." We bade him farewell and set out on our journey, going through the forest. Praises be to the Lamb for faithfully guiding us! The watchwords of to-day comforted us: "They shall come and declare his righteousness." We found the forest very thick and the ground in many places marshy. By nightfall we reached a fine creek by the side of which we refreshed ourselves, and after a happy devotional service slept under the trees.

Friday, August 18.—Having rested comfortably, we set forward early this morning, the watchwords for the day being, " The Lord will be with them." At noon we met an old Seneca who informed us that he had been appointed by a messenger to accompany us to Onondaga. In the afternoon it rained in torrents. Two hours before sundown we reached Anajot, where, finding only a few women at home, we continued on to Ganatisgoa (35), a Tuscarora town, where we found about thirty houses, large and regularly built, with a wide street through the middle. We secured lodgings in a hut, where we were joined by two old Senecas, who had been hunting not far from hence, and were also on their way to Onondaga.

Saturday, August 19.—The watchword to-day : " The people shall take them and bring them to their place," was a promise that was fulfilled in us. In the morning the Tuscarora chief, who lives here, called to see us and told us that yesterday he had received an account of the matters we had to lay before the Council from the Oneidas. Being lame and unable to attend the Council, he requested us to tell him of our matters, which we did, to his great satisfaction. The Senecas started with us. Before noon we came to a few huts occupied by some Tuscaroras, and in the afternoon to a town of the same tribe. The Senecas remained here all night and told that they would overtake us the next morning. We went on a little further and camped in a cold, dark woods. Just as we were seating ourselves around the fire, which we had made, there began such a crackling and rattling over our heads that we were at a loss to know in what direction to run, and there fell a huge tree close by our fire. We thanked our Saviour for his protection over us, and before going to sleep we had a happy " singing-hour " (36) together.

Sunday, August 20.—We were stirring betimes this morning, and by 8 o'clock were joined by the Senecas who told us that they had had bad lodgings, that the Indians were nearly all drunk in the town, and some had almost killed one another. At noon we were met by some Indians from Onondaga. We then came to a place where many posts were standing, from which we concluded that a town must have stood there formerly. The old Seneca told Bro. David that when he was a child of eight years of age Onondaga stood on this spot, but was burned by the French (37). In the afternoon between 4 and 5 o'clock with the watchwords—" And it shall come to pass, if they will diligently learn the ways of my people, then shall they be built in the midst of my people," we arrived at Onondaga. We were taken to the hut of a chief who was absent, and did not return until evening. Several chiefs hearing of our arrival came to visit us. We also learned that some of the chiefs were in Canada and would not return until autumn.

Monday, August 21.—Many visitors called on us this morning, among the number a very old chief who told us that the Council would meet during the day, and would listen to what we had to lay before them. In the afternoon we met the Council but found only Onondagas present. To them we related the object of our visit and gave them one string of wampum after another. When we concluded, the wampum was returned to us by a chief, who said : " We

only had a mind to hear, what you had to offer; we will let all to
the Cayugas and Senecas that are called hither, come, and then you
shall declare your matter publicly that they may also hear it"—
which was according to our desire.   Then a servant laid an affair
relating to the Catawbas before the Council.   First of all he laid an
instrument, which they use in the time of war, at the feet of the
chiefs, declaring at the same time that the Catawbas would not fain
have full peace with the Six Nations.   Next he laid down a pass
which the Catawbas had brought from the Governor of Charleston
(38), sealed with the King's seal.   This they handed to Bro. Zeisberger to read to them.   The contents of it were to this purport: The
Governor desired the Six Nations to be willing to make peace with
the Catawbas, assuring them that the Catawbas would faithfully keep
to it.   He also set before them the harm that arises from their being
at war; that both were only weakened thereby, and yet they are
children of the same land.   The Governor in every article called the
Six Nations "Brethren."   In conclusion, he assured the Six Nations
that the Catawbas were true friends of the English.   The chiefs then
asked us what we thought of the matter, to which we replied: "It is
good, we find nothing bad."   They appeared satisfied with our opinion, and from their conversation it is probable a peace will soon be
concluded (39).   All night long it was very noisy, as many of the
Indians were drunk.

Tuesday, August 22.—We were awakened early this morning by
many drunken men and women coming into our hut, but when they
commenced to fight among themselves, we thought it prudent to
withdraw and passed part of the day in the woods.   In the afternoon
one of the Seneca chiefs visited us, from whom we learned that they
thought of leaving for their town to-morrow, whereupon Bro. David
went to the Onondaga chief.   He began to make excuses that he had
been unable to call the Council together to-day, owing to so many
Indians being drunk, but hoped to do so in the morning.   Then Bro.
David said: "I have heard that the Senecas who are here will leave
to-morrow, which we shall not like.   We would rather that they hear
our matters."   The chief then promised to speak to the Senecas.
After dark the chief came and told us that the chief of the Cayugas
had arrived, for whom the Council had waited, and that the Senecas
would also remain to attend the Council.

NOTES.

32. The name means a "good message," and was given to Bishop
J. C. F. Cammerhoff by Shikellimy while on a visit to Bethlehem in
April of 1748.   It was the name of an Oneida chief living at Anajot.

33. The name given to Bishop Spangenberg, signifying "a row of standing trees." *From Spangenberg's Notes of Travel to Onondaga in 1745,* under date of June 10, he has recorded: "It rained all day. Our course was due north, and after traveling ten miles it changed to northeast following the narrow valley of Diadachton (Lycoming) creek. The wilderness here was almost impassible, so dense was the forest and so tangled the undergrowth. In the evening we came to a salt lick which is frequented by elk. Here we encamped. Our guides, Shikellimy and his son Andrew, and Andrew Montour, saw good enough to give us Indian names in lieu of our own, which they stated they could remember and pronounce only with difficulty. They named Bro. Spangenberg *T'girhitonti* and Bro. Zeisberger *Anonsseracheri.* When Indians name the whites they usually name them after connections of their own." The site of this encampment was probably in Lewis township, Lycoming county, Pa.

34. Rev. John C. Pyrlaeus and Anton Seyffert, the former the well-known Mohawk scholar. "Together, we (Pyrlaeus) now visited the other Mohawk castles and resolved to go on to Onondaga. On arriving at the last white settlement on our way thither, we met a sachem of the Six Nations, who, on learning our purpose, opposed its execution, first by using dissuasion and then by threatening violence. Thus foiled we returned to Canajoharie and afterwards set out for Bethlehem." This was in the early part of September, 1743.

35. Noted on Guy Johnson's "Maps of the Country of the Six Nations," 1771. Located six miles south of Oneida Castle, in the town of Stockbridge, on Oneida creek.

36. A short devotional service consisting entirely of singing hymns selected for particular occasions. These meetings were also held in the congregations. In these days of grace they are called "Service of Song," without Moravian circles.

37. Located about one mile south of the present village of Jamesville, in lot No. 3, in town of Lafayette, Onondaga county. It was first settled about 1680, and burned by the Onondagas on the approach of Frontenac in 1696. Abandoned about 1720, when they settled about five miles further west in Onondaga Valley, south of Syracuse.

38. James Glenn, Governor of South Carolina.

39. In the summer of 1750 Conrad Weiser was sent to Onondaga to bring about a treaty of peace between the Catawbas and the Six Nations, between whom great enmity had existed for many years owning to an act of treachery on the part of the former. Peace was finally declared after Zeisberger and Rundt left Onondaga.

NOTES AND QUERIES.—XCIII.

BISHOFF.—Paul Bishoff, a native of Germany, came to America in 1753, landing in Philadelphia. He had two brothers who went to Virginia and Tennessee. Paul's son John, settled near Berrysburg now Dauphin county, where he married Maria Bonawitz. Their only son, Peter Bishoff, married Eve Wert. What other information is there extant concerning this family ?   B.

McCANN—EBBCKA.—George McCann, a native of county Donegal, Ireland, came to America about the year 1785. He located in Dauphin county, Pa., near Middletown, at the base of Round Top, facing the pike where it crosses on Swatara hill, where he became a land owner, married and had issue : *Michael*, m. Sarah Ebbcka, *George, John, Daniel, Mary, Ann, Catharine, Cecilia,* and *Elizabeth.* Michael McCann's daughter, Sarah Ellen, m. James Dougherty, whose daughter, Sarah E., m. Henry Ulrich.

John Frederick Ebbcka, born on the Weser, Germany, came to America towards the close of the last century. He located in Londonderry township, Dauphin county, having previously married in the Tulpehocken settlement in Berks county. He had issue : *Charles* and *Sarah.* He was a gentleman of considerable culture, taught school, English and German. He was considerable of an artist, as numerous signs which graced the front of the old taverns from Middletown to Lancaster bore ample testimony.   H. A. G.

JOHN MARTIN MACK'S JOURNAL

OF A VISIT TO ONONDAGA IN 1752.—III.

[With this number we conclude the very interesting Journal of Bishop Mack.]

Wednesday, August 23.—In the afternoon a chief came to inform us that at noon the Council would meet in the hut where we lodged, which it did. There were about thirty present, among whom were four Senecas, the Cayuga chief, the rest belonging to Onondaga. We were placed next to the Cayuga chief, as Bro. David understood their language best, to whom he told the object of our visit and explained the strings of wampum. Then he desired the Council to attend, and taking the first string of wampum he sang in the Indian manner the names of all our brethren, mentioning at the same time Bro. Johanan (40) as a great and mighty man. "These men" he continued, "are sent by Bro. Johanan, T'girhitontie (41), T'garihontie (42), Anuntschi (43), and the rest of the Brethren on this side and the other side of the Great Water, to bring good words to the Six Nations. They know that the chiefs of the Aquanoschioni will take all in good part. Then the string of wampum was hung on a pole with the usual "Juheh!" of all present.

The second string of wampum was then taken up. "Gallichwio," (44) he continued, " had ' gone home,' and that the Brethren would let the Six Nations know how dear he was to us, that we loved him much and them also, that he loved the Indians very much, that we were unwilling to part with him, but we knew that he was gone to God, whom he loved much, and therefore we did not grieve (45). That we would liked to have brought the message sooner, but several of our chiefs had gone over the Great Water." This string was also hung on the pole and the Council sung "Juheh!"

The third string was then held up and he sang as follows: " That T'girhitontie, Anuntschi, and Anonsacharie (46), who was present, had returned from over the Great Waters and brought salutations T'garihontie (47) and Johanan his father."

Our message being ended we delivered our presents to the Cayuga chief when he announced: "T'girhitontie, Anuntschi, and his Brethren had sent presents. These were two pieces of linen, each 22 yards, some thread, and tobacco. Being a present they were laid upon a blanket. They conferred together, when two servants took the presents and divided them in three parts. Then a chief arose, gave one part to the Cayugas, another to the Senecas, and the third to the Onondagas, which was sub-divided, one part for Upper and one for Lower Onondaga. Our strings of wampum were divided in the same manner, whereupon the whole was confirmed with a loud "Juheh!" We were then informed that the chiefs would meet and consider our message, and that they would give us an answer to-day. They then took leave, shaking hands with us all.

About four o'clock the Council again assembled. We were again requested to sit aside of the Cayuga chief, after which he took a string of wampum in his hand and lifted it aloft, saying, "We have heard and understood that our Bro. T'girhitontie, Anuntschi, and Gallichwio, with those over the Great Water, among whom there is a great man, who has the affairs of the Brethren in hand, send good words to the Aquanoschioni. Brethren we have heard and under-

stand all.   We are glad and thankful they have sent Ganachgagregat
(48), Anouseracheri, and the white brother (49) [Rundt].   It rejoices
us to hear that thou and thy Brethren are well and sit in peace by
your fires."   Then he handed to us the string of wampum.

Taking up the second string he continued: " T'girhitontie, thou
and thy Brethren and those of the Great Water inform us that our
and your brother, Gallichwio, went home a year ago.   Now Bro.
T'girhitontie! the Aquanunschioni say to thee, use thy best endeavors
to find us such another person among thy Brethren, for we know
that Gallichwio truly loved the Aquanunschioni, in whose heart was
no guile."   This was confirmed by the whole Council with a " Juheh!"
The string of wampum was then handed to us.

With a third string in his hand he continued : " Bro. T'girhitontie
thou has let us know that together with other Brethren thou hast
been over the Great Water and art now come back, and hast brought
salutations from our Bro. T'garihiontie and his father Johanan.   Thou
must salute them from us, the united Six Nations.   Bro. T'girhitontie
thou hast also assured us that the brotherhood betwix us and you
stand fast, and you hold it fast.   We also hold it fast.   [Here the
speaker locked his hands together and lifted them up, showing how
firmly they kept the covenant.]   Thus minded were all the chiefs of
the Six Nations," which was confirmed by all present.   Then the
string was delivered to us.

Next he related that Bro. Gallichwio two years ago made a proposition for two Brethren to live among them in order to learn their
language, "And as thou, Bro. T'girhitontie and thy Brethren have
again taken this matter in hand, we think wisely, and have sent Bro.
Anouseracheri and his white brother whose name we do not know
(Rundt).   We are pleased and think a good work is set on foot thereby.   It shall be as you desire, as all the chiefs are of the same mind.
The two Brethren shall live a couple of years among us and learn
the language that we may tell one another the thoughts of our hearts.
Then they may go to the Cayugas and reside there some months and
also to the Senecas."   When he concluded a string of wampum was
handed to us and the whole matter was confirmed with three
" Juheh!" in which we joined.   It was suggested that the two Brethren should visit the houses in the town, and whenever they have the
opportunity, to converse with the Indians.   When the Council meets
they may attend so as to learn the ways and manners of the Indians
in propounding any matter, that when the Brethren have a message
for them, they may know how to deliver it.   The chiefs inquired
where we wished the two Brethren to live while they reside in

Onondaga? We replied: " We have not thought much about it but leave it to them and take their advice." " It is well," said they, " for we have not considered about it, but will do so soon and give you an answer before Ganachragregat goes away." They also spoke of the maintenance of the Brethren, and said: " If the Brethren will frequently visit the houses they will be supplied with victuals, but especial care shall be taken of them where they lodge." When all was concluded the servants brought in two kettles of boiled Indian corn, when we ate socially together.

We have thus far been very well and happy, and have not seen on any one a dark look nor heard a contrary word. They have acted towards us in a brotherly manner, and even the children are quite free with us. We wished that our Brethren who are engaged in the work among the Heathen could have been present at the Council. The watchwords and texts have been uncommonly suitable.

Thursday, August 24.—This morning we were visited by several Indians from the next town, five miles distant from here (50). Some of them were present at the Council. The women were friendly, invited us to come to their town and gave us apples (51). Our friends, the Seneca chiefs, returned home to-day. Their names are: Thagachtatie, Julchcotanne, Ataneckenni, Thojanorie; the Cayugas: Giottononannie. The names of the Onondaga chiefs are: Otschinochiatha, "the Thick;" Ganatschiagajio (53), and where we lodged, Garachguntie. In Lower Onondaga are these chiefs: Zargonna, Ganochronia, and the Tuscarora, Thequalischki.

Friday, August 25.—Our matters being so far advanced, we consulted together about the return of Bro. Mack to Bethlehem. The head chief sent for us, as he had something further to speak about. When we entered his hut he bade us sit down, and asked if Gangachragregat would leave to-day. We told him that he would and that we would accompany him to Anajot and then return. He then said: " Very well, we have spoken together concerning the residence for the two Brethren, and as soon as they return they may select a house to their own mind, for the doors of all stand open. They have full liberty to go where they will and live where they please." We thanked him and then retired. In the afternoon we visited the chiefs and many of the Indians in their huts, and the chief with whom we lived ordered some food prepared for us.

Two hours before sun-down Bro. Mack set out for Bethlehem, with Bro. David and Rundt who go part of the way. When we had walked six miles we came to a fine creek (54), by which we camped for the night. Bro. David caught eight fine trout, which we ate for our supper. Before retiring for the night we kept a happy "singing hour"—the watchword for the day being—" The people that do know their God, shall be strong and do exploits."

Saturday, August 26.—This morning we started early hoping to reach Anajot, which is 45 miles from Onondaga, by dusk. The chief there called us into his hut and treated us to squashes and pumpkins. After finishing our meal, we continued on our journey, passing several houses and meeting some Indians. Two hours before night we reached Ganatisgoa, the second Tuscarora town, but found most of the Indians from home in quest of roots. At evening we came near to Anajot, but as we wished to be alone together, we selected an agreeable spot and remained there all night. We kept a blessed Lord's Supper together and then retired to rest.

Sunday, August 27.—Having rested well we arose early and sang some verses. After passing through Anajot, we came to a hill about a quarter of a mile beyond where we rested. Here we must part! We sang some verses, wept like children and blessed one another— so we parted. Bro. David and Rundt on their return will visit in Anajot and the Tuscarora towns. My eyes all day long were not very dry and I cannot express what I felt at parting with my two Brethren. By night I reached Kash's.

Monday, August 28.—To-day I remained here (Kash's) and visited the Oneidas who live hereabouts. Some of the chiefs were very friendly, gave me something to eat and asked why I left my companions. When I informed them, they gave me to understand by friendly looks their satisfaction.

Tuesday, August 29.—This morning I left Kash's and went down the Maqua country. Towards night I passed through Canajoharie and came

Wednesday, August 30,—To William's fort. Here I learned that Conrad Weiser's son had returned to learn the Indian language. I would have visited him but he was not at home.

Thursday, August 31.—To-day I passed through Schenectady to Albany and came

Sunday, September 3,—To my father-in law (55), with whom I remained two days.

Wednesday, September 6.—I reached Pachgatgoch, where I met Bro. Senseman and his wife. The Indian brethren and sisters, when they heard of my arrival, came running to see their old Martin once more among them (56). I remained six days with them and kept many meetings.

Wednesday, September 13.—This morning I set out for Bethlehem.

Saturday, September 23.—Between 10 and 11 o'clock this morning I reached Bethlehem well and happy and was received by my Brethren right heartily. I thanked my dear Saviour for all the grace and protection he had shown me and my brethren on our journey and for my safe return home. Glory be to the Lamb (57)!

NOTES.

40. Count Zinzendorf. Under what circumstances or on what occasion he received this name from the Indians is not determined.

41. Bishop Spangenberg.

42. Bishop J. von Watteville, who was adopted into the Six Nations.

43. It is a Seneca word signifying "the head," and name given to Nathaniel Seidel by Shikellimy in April of 1748.

44. Bishop J. C. F. Cammerhoff, who was so named by Shikellimy.

45. Cammerhoff died in April of 1751.

46. David Zeisberger. He was so named by Shikellimy in June of 1745.

47. Bishop von Watteville, who was a son-in-law of Zinzendorf's. Nathaniel Seidel and David Zeisberger returned from Europe in September and Spangenberg in December of 1751.

48. John Martin Mack. It is a Cayuga word meaning "one who heads a troop," and was given to Mack at Bethlehem by Shikellimy in April of 1748.

49. While a resident of the town, he was adopted into the tribe of the Tortoise receiving the name of Thaneraquechta.

50. Teatachtonti, south of Onondaga.

51. They had extensive orchards.

52. Probably the same as Otsinonghyatta, who attended the Council at Fort Johnson in 1757.

53. Probably same as Canatsyagaya, who attended the Fort Johnson Council in 1757.

54. Butternut creek in the present country of Onondaga.

55. John Rau, a Palatine farmer, in the "Oblong." Mack married his daughter Jeannette, September 14, 1742. She died at Gnadenhutten, on the Mahoning, December 15, 1742. Rau died June 2, 1768, and is buried in the grave-yard of the English meeting-house.

56. Mack was stationed here as assistant missionary in 1743.

57. Zeisberger and Rundt returned to Bethlehem in December, of 1752. "Wednesday, January 31, 1753, Bro. Van Vleck must have credit for cash which he paid on account of Zeisberger & Rundt to Captain Egbertse at Albany, which they borrowed of the latter on their return from Onondaga, £2, N. Y. currency."

NOTES AND QUERIES.—XCIV.

PRICES IN 1808.—In that year, judging by the following quotations, the currency was mixed:
Wheat, 14 shillings per bushel.
Buckwheat, 7s. 6d. per bushel.
Flour, $4.25 per barrel.
Rye, 53 cents per bushel.
Oats, 2s. 6d. or $33\frac{1}{3}$ cents per bushel.
Beef, 3 pence per pound.

AN OLD TIME LETTER.

[The original of the following letter from James Tilghman, Secretary of the Proprietaries Land Office, in 1770, to John Lukens, the Surveyor, is in our possession. It is worth preserving.]

Sept'r, 7th, 1770.

MR. LUKENS: I request you will, as soon as you arrive at Fort Augusta, get the best intelligence you can of the actions of the N. Englanders on the West Branch, especially of their dispossessing any of our People there by Violence, and have a Deposition or two taken of the particulars before Capt. Hunter and sent down to the Governor; and I shall be obliged if you'd make inquiry if possession be taken of my Land by those People. I remain,

Y'r most h'ble Serv't,

JAMES TILGHMAN.

Pray get particular information if you can of any transactions wherein Major Durkee is concerned.

Pray make it known to any purchasers under Wallis' Patents in the New Purchase before the purchase made, that those patents are fraudulent & good for nothing.

When at Fort Augusta be pleas'd to look about the Forks for a proper Situation for a Town, whether directly at the Forks or a small distance up either Branch.

If you go near my Land at Chillesquaqua or Loyal Sock, I shall be obliged to you to take a look at it.

PERSONAL RECOLLECTIONS OF DR. DAVID SHOPE.

A correspondent sends us the following relating to Dr. David Shope, one of the earliest practitioners of medicine at Hummelstown, who died in December, 1842 :

Dr. Shope was a man of fine appearance, nearly six feet in height, with fair complexion, a keen grey eye, broad forehead, and hair of a light brown. He was a close observer of nature, and a man of no ordinary accomplishments. Although a gentleman of correct habits, he was an excellent sportsman, an expert with the rifle or fishing rod. Fox hunting in his day was a favorite pastime, and one of his fellow-practitioners, Dr. William Henderson, kept a small pack of hounds, and many a fine chase was indulged in by these M. D.'s, the late David Earnest, Joe Spidler, the dog fancier and tailor of the village, accompanied by other lovers of the chase who lived in the neighborhood at that day.

As an angler, Dr. Shope carried the palm. The first pike of the season were shot in the meadow on the west bank of the Swatara, near Earnest and Shearer's bridge, at the Harrisburg turnpike, when the stream had slightly risen, and the pickerel came out from under their icy beds to sun themselves in the open pools. While other fishermen sat patiently for hours waiting for "bites," on the Derry side of the Swatara, that skillful Waltonian would lift the finest pickerel out of their native element on the Swatara and Hanover township boundaries of the creek, along the deep water formed by the slope-walls of the Union canal.

The writer has known patient fishermen to spend two or three hours in the early part of the day or evening, with rod and line and tempting bait, endeavoring to lure the huge snapping turtles from the muddy bottom of the Swatara, and invariably succeeded in landing "a whopper," much to the wonderment and envy of other anglers who prided themselves on their piscatory accomplishments.

Dr. Shope was well versed in natural history, and was clever with the pencil as a sketcher whenever inclination led him to pass a leisure hour in that way.

The Doctor was the successor in medicine of Dr. Benjamin Ryner Rice, whose property on Main street, Hummelstown, he purchased, and most of whose practice he retained after that gentleman removed to Hamburg, Berks county, this State. As a "regular," Dr. Shope was a successful practitioner. His contemporaries were Dr. William Henderson, of Hummelstown, Dr. William Simonton, of Hanover, and Dr. John A. Shuster, of the homœopathic school. He was a deep thinker, a devout student, and a man of fine conversational powers. He was of an easy, kind, lenient disposition, and consequently did not amass a fortune, leaving but little worldly goods when he died, in the very prime of life. He was unmarried. A. H. B.

OUR EARLY SETTLERS.

SOUTH END OF EAST SIDE OF DERRY, 1757.

John Chestnut,
John McAllister,
John McQueen,
John Hall,
Moses Potts,
Robert Allison,
David Wray,
Jacob Martin,
Abraham Reiner,
Samuel Moore,
Archibald Walker,
Christy Snyder,
John Wray,
Joseph White,
Neal McAllister,
Hugh Hall,
Wendel Bon,
Philip Reiner,
Patrick Hays,
Robert Hays,
John Hays,
David Johnson,
Rev'd John Roan,
Wm. Robison,
James Willson,
Robert Mordach,

Hugh Hays,
Jacob Leamen,
Philip Fishburn,
Daniel Taylor,
Widow Sloan,
Robert Boyd,
John McCord,
David McCord,
John Campbell,
Felty Delabach,
Peter Delabach,
Andrew Roan,
Jacob Longnecker,
Jacob Starratt,
William Boyd,
Thomas Logan,
Christian Swikley,
John Meabing,
John Meabing, Jr.,
Patrick Kelley,
Widow Duncan,
John Duncan,
Lambard Shelley,
Widdow Foster,
Joseph Berryhill,

David Foster,
Andrew Moore,
And. Burckholder,
Michael Bittner,
Michael Tanner,
Niclous Evert,
William Moore,
James Mitchell,
William Miller,
John Espy,
Robert McLery,
Hans Carmony,
Jacob Groves,
James Foster,
John Logan,
John Moore,
Josiah McQueen,
George Kelley,
Widdow McAllister,
Robert Foster,
John McQueen,
Wm. McCord,
John Craig,
Joseph Crain,
Robert Mordach.

Freemen.

Francis Bishopp,
John McQueen,
John Carson,
Wm. McCord,

John Mordach,
Thomas Kennedy,
Robert Kennedy,

John McClure,
Michael McGerety,
Mich. Tanner's Son.

GENEALOGICAL NOTES.

ZENT.

Jacob Zent, of West Hanover, d. in 1809, leaving children as follows:

> *i. Elizabeth,* m. Valentine King, and had a daughter *Susanna.*

 ii. John.
iii. Phœbe (*Pevey*), m. Christian Kish.
 iv. Mary, m. Abraham Houser.
  v. Catharine, m. John Snyder.
 vi. Susanna, m. Jacob Moyer.
vii. Jacob.

MILLER.

SUSANNA MILLER, widow of Daniel Miller, of Londonderry, d. January, 1811, leaving children:
  i. Mary.
 ii. Abraham.
iii. Peter.
 iv. Daniel.
  v. Susanna, m. Frederick Hoover.

MEYRICK.

SAMUEL MEYRICK, "Doctor of Physick," of Middletown, d. June, 1811. He directed his wife and son to continue "the apothecary shop." The children were:
  i. Samuel.
 ii. Ruth.
iii. Esther.

BORDNER.

JOHN BORDNER, of Lykens, d. June, 1812, leaving a wife Susanna, and children as follows.
  i. Peter.
 ii. Anna, m. Adam Heller.
iii. Susanna.
 iv. Elizabeth.

WETHERHOLD.

SUSANNA WETHERHOLD, widow, of Harrisburg, d. July, 1812, leaving children as follows:
  i. Margaret, m ―――― Barnett.
 ii. Elizabeth, m. ―――― Wingert, and had *Charles* and *John.*
iii. John, of Hummelstown, m., and had *Elizabeth,* m. Peter Snyder, *Charles,* and *Susanna.*
 iv. George.

REEL.

PHILIP REEL, of Paxtang, d. July, 1812, leaving a wife Catharine, and children as follows:

  i. Peter.
  ii. Mary.
  iii. Jacob.
  iv. Sarah.
  v. Catharine.
  vi. Benjamin.

HARRISON.

SARAH HARRISON, widow, of East Hanover, d. September, 1806, leaving children as follows:

  i. Elizabeth, m. —— Martin.
  ii. Sarah.
  iii. Jean.
  iv. Mary.
  v. John.

SHOPE.

BERNARD SHOPE, of Paxtang township, d. August, 1813, leaving issue as follows:

  i. Barbara, m. Henry Michael.
  ii. Julianna, m. George Silsel.
  iii. Jacob.
  iv. Margaret.
  v. Mary.
  vi. Christiana.
  vii. Magdalena.
  viii. Adam.
  ix. Bernhart.
  x. Eve, deceased.

NOTES AND QUERIES.—XCV.

MONTGOMERY.—David Montgomery, of Lower Paxtang, d. in January, 1805, the executors of his estate being Thomas Bennett and James Montgomery. Mr. Bennett's wife was a Montgomery. What was the relationship existing between the former and his executors?

PURCHASES FROM THE INDIANS IN PENNSYLVANIA PRIOR TO THE COMING OF PENN.

1621.—First settlement on Delaware river by and under West India Company.

July 15, 1630.—Director General and Council of Manhattan purchase of Indians 8 large miles from Cape Hinlopen, along Delaware Bay, and landwards half a mile—[a large mile was equal to 4 English miles.]

May 5, 1631—They made another purchase of Indians at Cape May 4 miles on the coast, and 4 miles on the bay.

1633.—Arent Corssen purchased a tract of land on the Schuylkill, on which a fort was erected called Beversrede.

1638.—The Swedes, early after their arrival, purchased all the lands from Cape Henlopen to Santickan, Trenton Falls.

March 27, 1642.—New Haven people purchased large tracts of land.

Sept. 25, 1646.—Hudde purchased land from savages, 1 Dutch mile (4 English) north of Fort Nassau, present site of Philadelphia.

April 27, 1648.—Hudde's purchase confirmed by savages.

May 23, 1649.—Peter Stuyvesant writes to Hudde expressing surprise at the bold enterprises of the Swedes in purchasing the lands all about Fort Nassau and on the Schuylkill.

July 19, 1651.—Indian chiefs confirm title to Stuyvesant of all lands ever sold or presented to the Swedes.

June 17, 1664.—Indians confirmed title to Swedes at a meeting held in Printz Hall on Tinnicum Island.

Oct. 3, 1675.—A purchase is made in the name of Edmund Andros for the Duke of York from the true sachems and lawful Indian proprietors of all that tract of land on west side of Delaware, at a creek next to the Cold Spring, somewhat above Mattincum Island, about 8 or 9 miles below the falls, and as far above said falls; also, all the islands in Delaware river.

In 1677 Andros made numerous grants of land out of the territory embraced in above purchases on the Delaware, the Schuylkill and the Neshaminy.

July 20, 1680.—Indians sell John Moll lands about Christiana creek and the islands.

Charter to Wm. Penn for Province of Pennsylvania granted by Charles II., March 4, 1681.

Penn sends William Markham, his cousin, over as Deputy Governor of his Province, by commission being dated 20 April, 1681.

1682.—The first purchase of lands made for Wm. Penn was made by treaty between Deputy Governor Markham and the Indians, of lands near Neshaminy, within the bounds of the former purchases hereinbefore referred to. The deed was dated 15th July, 1682. William Penn arrived at the 'town of New Castle, Del., from England, 27th Oct., 1682, more than three months after the treaty. He embarked on the ship Welcome, Capt. Robert Greenway, master, 11th Sept., 1682. At a monthly meeting held 8th of 9th mo., 1682, Gov. Wm. Penn and Friends met about half a mile from Shackamaxon, and established the city of Philadelphia.

HISTORICAL NUGGETS.

Extract from a letter dated Wheeling, November 12, 1789: "The spirit of emigration to the western regions rages more than ever; upwards of 3,000 persons are encamped near this place, some of whom have been here ever since July last; they are detained on account of the high freshets in the river, want of boats, provisions, &c. Their situation is truly deplorable, as this part of the country is thinly settled. This large body of people with their horses and cattle, have raised the price of provisions to an alarming height, which has induced many of them who are able, to return, while others are spending their little all in expectation to see the waters fall."

Extract from a letter dated Pittsburgh, Feb. 12, 1817.—"Possibly you may think it strange that I have not written you before this, but the sequel of my letter will furnish you with an explanation. . . . * On the whole we have had a prosperous journey and have enjoyed our usual health since we have been hence. On our arrival, however, we found the City full of Yankee Horses and Chariots selling at auction through the streets. As my wagon would live without eating I thought I had better let it stand by a while than to give it to the Crier for selling. But to my astonishment the emigrants continued to flock in from the northward in troops till about the first of January, and kept the City glutted with Horses and Carriages, so you see I have been completely frustrated in my expectation of raising money from my team. This is the fifth week since the rivers have been passable on the ice, a thing scarcely known in the annals of this Country."

MARRIAGES.—On Thursday last, by the Rev. Mr. Newcomb, Mr. John Conrad Winebiddle to Miss Olive Newton, daughter of Mr. B. B. Newton, of this city.—*Pittsburgh Gazette, June 18, 1818.*

Married, on Thursday, the 1st instant, by the Right Rev. Bishop White, William Wilkins, Esq., of Pittsburgh, to Miss Matilda Dallas, daughter of the late A. J. Dallas, Esq., of Philadelphia.—*Ib. Oct. 13, 1818.*

On Tuesday evening, the 20th inst., by the Rev. Mr. Stockton, Mr. David Pride to Miss Matilda Erwin, both of this city.

On Thursday evening last, by the Rev. Mr. Newcomb, Mr. Charles Plumb to Miss Hannah H. Skelton, and Mr. Gilbert McKown to Miss Anna Maria W. Skelton, of this city.—*Ib. Oct. 29, 1818.*

At Philadelphia, on Friday evening, the 4th ult., by the Rev. Mr. Janeway, Dr. Charles Lewis, of Virginia, to Miss Mary Irvine, daughter of the late Gen. William Irvine.

At Washington (Pa.), on Thursday evening, 31st ult., by the Rev. Mr. Brown, Mr. David Acheson to Miss Mary Wilson, daughter of John Wilson, Esq., all of that place.

On the 16th ult., at the seat of Stephen Lowry, Esq., Queen Anne's county, Maryland, Mr. Thomas Collins, of this place, to Miss Sarah Lowry, daughter of Mr. Lowry.—*Pittsburgh Commonwealth, Nov. 16, 1805.*

In Maryland, Hon. Uriah Forrest to Miss Plater.—*American Museum, Nov., 1789.*

At Waynesborough, William Richardson Atlee, Esq., to Miss Wayne.

In Franklin county, Dr. Wm. M. Magaw to Miss McDowell.—*Ib. Nov., 1790.*

In Philadelphia, Colonel Hodgdon to Miss Hodges.

At Acton, the Rev. Elisha Riggs to Miss Jane Atlee.

At Pittsburgh, Mr. John Irwin to Miss Susan Parker.—*Ib. Dec., 1790.*

In Philadelphia, Col. Williams to Miss Betsey Hulings.—*Ib. May, 1792.*

GENEALOGICAL NOTES.

CLARK.

Walter Clark, of Londonderry township, d. in August, 1813, leaving a wife Mary, and children as follows:

   i. Ann.
   ii. Sarah.
   iii. Mary.
   iv. Charles.

> *v. William,* his wife Eleanor d. March 13, 1829, in the 51st
> year of her age.
> *vi. James.*

In addition bequests were made to his nephew, Walter Johnson
and Walter Clark.

———

KOCH.

DAVID KOCH, of Lower Paxtang, d. in November, 1813. He left
his estate to his mother, Eva Koch, and his sisters as follows:
> *i. Magdalena.*
> *ii. Jane.*
> *iii. Catharine.*
> *iv. Eva.*

———

FOX.

PETER FOX, of Lower Paxtang, d. in May, 1814, leaving a wife
Anna, and the following children:
> *i. Henry.*
> *ii. Peter.*
> *iii. Anna.*

———

HOFFMAN.

JOHN HOFFMAN, of Lykens township, d. July, 1814, leaving a wife
Elizabeth, and children:
> *i. John.*
> *ii. Daniel.*
> *iii. Jacob.*
> *iv. Jonas.*

———

NISLEY.

ESTHER NISLEY, widow of Jacob Nisley, of Derry township, d. in
December, 1814. The children mentioned in her will were:
> *i. Martin,* d. prior, leaving three children.
> *ii. Freeny,* m. Joseph Bosler.
> *iii. Barbara,* m. Jacob Hershey.

———

SHENK.

MICHAEL SHENK, of Londonderry, d. April, 1815, leaving a wife
Veronica, and children as follows:

 i. John.
 ii. Christian.
 iii. Michael.
 iv. Catharine, m. Christian Longenecker.
 v. Anna.
 vi. [*a dau.*], dec'd, m. Abraham Martin, and had a son *Michael.*

SMITH.

 JACOB SMITH, of West Hanover, d. July, 1815, leaving a wife Margaret, and children as follows:
 i. Elizabeth, m. —— Ziegler.
 ii. Hannah, m. Henry Balsbaugh.
 iii. Abraham.
 iv. David.
 v. Daniel.
 vi. Jacob, dec'd.
 vii. John, dec'd, leaving a son Samuel.

McCLURE.

 JAMES McCLURE, of West Hanover, d. September, 1815, unm.; leaving a mother and brothers and sisters as follows:
 i. Martha, m. —— Wilson, and had three children.
 ii. William, m., and had *James.*
 iii. Frances.
 iv. Isabel, m. James Cathcart.
 v. John.
 vi. Mary, m. —— Snodgrass.
 vii. Andrew.
 viii. Stewart.

CATHCART.

 JAMES CATHCART, of West Hanover, died in May, 1815, leaving a wife Isabella, daughter of James McClure, of West Hanover, and children as follows:
 i. Sarah.
 ii. Isabel.
 iii. Mary.

JONES.

 ISAAC JONES, of Halifax, d. January, 1816, leaving children as follows:

     i. Jacob.
     ii. John.
     iii. George.

MATTER.

JOHN MATTER, Jr., son of Michael Matter, of Upper Paxtang township, d. in February, 1816, leaving a wife Anna Mary, and children as follows:
     i. Simon.
     ii. Anna-Mary.
     iii. Elizabeth.

COL. HENRY BOUQUET.

[Through the courtesy of the Swiss Consul at Philadelphia, R. Koradi, Esq., we have the following facts relating to the gallant and brave Bouquet, who stemmed the tide of Indian war in 1764, and dictated his own terms to the red savages in their homes on the Muskingum. The information was procured at our request. We give it as in the original translation.]

Extract from the Cantonal Archives of the Canton of Vaud at Lausanne, tendered to the prefect of Rolle, concerning the searches after General Henry Bouquet and his family relations by the Chief of the Department of Public Instruction.

The searches made in the Cantonal Archives, to find some notes on the family and the biography of Henry Bouquet, of Rolle, have not brought to light great results. His certificate of birth could not be found in the civil State registers of the community of Rolle, but in a parochial register, kept by the minister, an entry is found, as follows: List of those, whom I have examined with a view to participate in the holy communion, March 25th, 1735, of Rolle:

1. Louis Alexander Roncier, my nephew, aged 18 years.
2. Henry Bouquet, aged 16 years.

As Henry Bouquet is said to have been born in the year 1719, this entry, No. 2 is undoubtedly meant for him. From divers other documents it also appears, that the Bouquet family were citizens of Rolle, and that one of its members was a member of the city council of that town. Entries, concerning the family of Bouquet, are found as follows:

Bouquet, Louis, General Quartermaster and Lieutenant Colonel in the Regiment Stuerler in the service of the Netherlands, renounces his citizenship of Rolle on the 14th of April, 1750, and is discharged from his duties as a citizen on the 8th of October, 1750.

Madeleine, oldest daughter of Ferdinand Rolas, baptized May 16th, 1645, wife of Bartholomew Bouquet, son of Peter Bouquet, hotelkeeper at the Tete Noire, left Elizabeth and Jacquette Bouquet. (This is from the family of Rolas, widow of Savoy, established in Rolle since 1549.)

In the history of the Canton of Vaud by Verdeil, vol. iii., page 96 and following, there appears:

Henry Louis Bouquet of Rolle, the oldest of seven brothers entered the service of Holland in 1736 and afterwards passed into the service of Piedmont in the Swiss Regiment Roguin, where he distinguished himself in the office of aide-major in the war sustained by the King of Sardinia against the combined armies of France and Spain.

The accounts, which Bouquet gave to his former compagnons in Holland having come to the knowledge of the Prince of Orange, the latter called him to the command of a company of his guard. Bouquet profited of his leisure hours in the garrison, to study the military and the mathematical sciences and entered into connection with the most distinguished persons of Holland, among others with his countryman Allamand of Lausanne, Professor of Physick and Rector of the University of Leyden.

Lord Middleton engaged him to accompany him in his travels, for scientific purposes, in France, Belgium, Germany and Italy; studying with him the celebrated battlefields of these countries.

In 1754 the English Government confided to him and to his companion and fellow countryman Haldimand of Yoerdon (also in the Canton of Vaud) the organization of a brigade, named the Royal-American, into which he drew several other fellow-citizens of the Canton of Vaud, among whom Du Tes of Moudon and Vullgamot of Lausanne.

After having participated in the war in Canada, Bouquet was charged to reduce the hostile Indian tribes of Canada. He disengaged Fort Pitt, which was by them invested, and afterwards was placed by Lord Gage at the head of a corps of 6,000 men, when by a series of fights he succeeded to regain the security of the country of the Ohio and to force the Indians to peace. In the beginning of 1765 he re-entered Philadelphia, where the assembly of representants of Pennsylvania voted to him the following address:

In assembly of January 15th, 1765, the representants of the free men of Pennsylvania to the Hon. Henry Bouquet, chevalier commanding in chief of the forces of Great Britain in the American provinces.

SIR: The representants of the free men of Pennsylvania having been informed of your intention to embark for England, and considering the services which you have rendered to His Majesty and to the Colonies in the course of our last wars with the French and with the savage Indians, by the signal victories which you have gained over the savages at Bushy Run in the month of August, 1763, which next to God were due to your gallantry and high capacities in command, assisted by the bravery of your officers, and your soldiers (your small army), crowned at last by your late march into the country of the savage nations, by which you have spread terror among them and become the founder of a honorable peace and the restorer from captivity of more than 200 of our Christian brethren—these eminent services, and the regards which you constantly observed for the civil rights of His Majesty's subjects, impose to all free men a just tribute of gratitude.

Therefore the representants of the free men of Pennsylvania, in the name of the whole people of the province, thank you for your eminent services.   By order of the chamber,

JOSEPH FOX, *Speaker.*

Bouquet was nominated brigadier general and died in the same year 1765.

The writer says, that about the career in America of our compatriot he would not know where to find a more accurate and more detailed information in his native country than the one he has cited.

Bouquet left a pamphlet, "A historical record of the expedition against the Indians of the Ohio, commanded by Sir Henry Bouquet, which was translated into French and published at Amsterdam in 1769, which, however, could not be found in the libraries at Rolle or Lausanne.

The writer expresses his regrets that he had not sufficient time to find out and call on such persons who might be in possession yet of documents concerning the family Bouquet, of which several members have served with distinction in foreign counties, particularly in Holland, where among others one of the uncles was engineer officer. (I suppose the party mentioned here is Louis Bouquet, named before, who expatriated himself on account of his attachment to the service of Holland and perhaps the same party who is named in the general's will, in case his father should be dead.)

NOTES AND QUERIES.—XCVI.

THE FAMILY OF STEELE.

WILLIAM STEELE, SR., settled along " Puddle Dock " run, a small branch of Conawingo creek, in Drumore township, Lancaster county, about one mile and a-half east of Chestnut Level, and along a public road laid out in 1737, which led from Caleb Pennel's turning mill, on the north side of Peter's creek, via James King's mill, on Conawingo creek, to a public road leading from Mt. Pleasant to Lancaster. Prior to this date, as the road is described as running by " William Steele's farm," he took up two hundred acres and established a tannery, probably as early as 1730-5. Mr. Steele was a stalwart Presbyterian and patriot. In 1756 he commanded a company of Associators, John Evans being his lieutenant and James McNeely his ensign.

The Revolutionary war found the old man full of military ardor, although by reason of his advanced years, and the infirmities of old age, he was incapable of enduring the fatigues and hardships of an active campaign. When the first battle-cry was heard, he sent four *stalwart sons* in defence of the Colonies to fight for their independence and release the people from the thraldom of a tyrannical King and his corrupt Parliament. Some of his sons were maimed for life, and carried British bullets in their bodies to their graves. He did not live to see his country free, nor were his stalwart sons, whom he sent to battle and were in the tented field, with their armor buckled on ready for the bugle's blast, which was to call them into action, present when he died in 1780. His wife Rachel, and his two daughters, and some friends were the only persons with him in his last hours. His children were :

  i. Archibald.
  ii. Ann, m. Thomas Jordan.
  iii. William.
  iv. Rachel, m. Jacob Bailey, son of Robert B., of Sadsbury
      township.
  v. John.
  vi. James.

During the war an incident occurred, which came very near causing a tragedy. After the death of Mr. Steele his widow Rachel lived alone, or without any male protector about the house, when she was visited by a neighbor, probably a Quaker, who was opposed to all wars, and especially to the war of the Revolution, who commenced to upbraid her for allowing her sons to go to war instead of following the quiet pursuits of a country life. Mrs. Steele replied with great spirit, and ordered her unwelcome guest from the house, and it is said that the craven struck her with his fist. Whether the last was true or not, it was so reported in the neighborhood. When her sons came from the army they heard what was said in the neighborhood, that a tory had gone into their mother's house and struck her. One of these sons, James or John, immediately took down his rifle from its resting place, and started to wreak condign punishment upon him. He went to the man's residence or met him on his way thither, and accused him of the offense of which the neighbors reported to him. Whether he refused to apologize or added another insult to the indignity offered his mother was never known, for he shot him down. The tradition is that he died from the wound received; but it is more than probable that he left the neighborhood and was lost sight of.

Their son William resided and owned the old homestead, and his son William Washington Steele, who was a justice for many years, came to own it.

Capt. John Long, of Drumore, married a daughter of Mr. Steele, probably the second husband of his daughter Ann.

SAMUEL EVANS.

THE KELLYS OF LONDONDERRY.

I. PATRICK KELLY, b. 1709, in the north of Ireland; d. June 27, 1769, in Londonderry township, then Lancaster county, Pa; came to America in 1734, and took up a large tract of land in the Swatara region, where he lived and died; his wife RACHEL, b. in 1708, in Province of Ulster, Ireland; d. August 5, 1782, in Londonderry, and with her husband buried in old Derry church grave-yard. They left issue:

    i. Rachel, b. 1735; m. William Forster.

2. *ii. George*, b. 1737; m., and had issue.

    iii. Anne, b. 1739; d. prior to 1806; m. —— Patrick; and left *Mary*, m. Thomas Nicholson.

3. *iv. John*, b. February, 1741; m. Sarah Polk.

    v. Patrick, b. April 28, 1743; d. October 28, 1826, in Londonderry; unm.

    vi. Thomas, b. 1747; of whom we have no further record.

4. *vii. James*, b. 1749; m. Elizabeth Forster.

5. *viii. Mary*, b. 1751; m. John Duncan.

II. GEORGE KELLY (Patrick), b. 1737, in Londonderry township; d. prior to 1806, and left issue:

    i. Andrew.

    ii. Thomas.

    iii. Rachel, d. prior to 1806; m. James Snodgrass; and left *Sarah, Mary, Margaret, Rosina, Rachel, Elizabeth, William, George, James,* and *Thomas.*

III. JOHN KELLY (Patrick), b. February, 1741, in Londonderry township, Lancaster, now Dauphin county, Pa.; d. February 8, 1832, in Buffalo Valley. After the Indian purchase of 1768, he settled in the Buffalo Valley, enduring all the hardships of pioneer life. At the age of twenty-seven he was a captain and major on the frontiers, and at the outset of the Revolution was ready for the conflict; he was a member of the Convention of July 15, 1776, and subsequently entered the army, having previously assisted in organizing the Associators, being appointed major in Col. James Potter's battalion. After the battle of Princeton, when Cornwallis by a forced march arrived at Stony Brook, General Washington sent an order to Colonel Potter to destroy the bridge at Worth's Mills in sight of the advancing British. Colonel Potter ordered Major Kelly to make a detail for that purpose, but the latter said he would not order another to do what some might say he was afraid to do himself; he took a detachment and went to work. The enemy opened upon him a heavy fire of round shot; before all the logs were cut off, several balls struck the log on which he stood, and it breaking down sooner than he expected, he was precipitated into the stream; his party moved off, not expecting him to escape. By great exertions he reached the shore, through the high water and floating timbers, and followed the troops. Encumbered as he was with his wet and frozen clothes, he succeeded in making prisoner an armed British scout, and took him into camp. During the summer of 1777, Colonel Kelly commanded on the frontier, and continued in that service almost to the close of the Revolution. The record of his adventures during those troublesome times reads like a romance. Colonel Kelly was appointed agent for confiscated estates May 6, 1778, and in 1780 was chosen to the Assembly. He was one of the magistrates of Northumberland county from August 2, 1783, for upwards of twenty years. He married SARAH POLK, daughter of James Polk, of the Valley, d. Jan. 2, 1831. They had issue:

    i. James, removed to Penn's Valley, and died there; was father of James K. Kelley, U. S. Senator from Oregon, 1872–1878.

    ii. John, removed to Penn's Valley.

 iii. William, m. a daughter of Archibald Allison, of Centre county, and died there January 27, 1830.

 iv. Andrew, b. 1783; d. September 24, 1786; unm.

 v. Samuel, removed to Armstrong county, Pa.

 vi. Elizabeth, m. Simeon Howe.

 vii. Maria, d. Jan., 1861; m. John Campbell, of Lewisburg.

 viii. Robert, b. 1798; d. April 12, 1865.

 ix. Joseph, b. 1793; d. March 2, 1860.

 x. David-H., b. 1803; d. Feb. 11, 1875; was county commissioner of Union county.

IV. JAMES KELLY (Patrick), b. 1781, in Londonderry township, Lancaster, now Dauphin co., Pa.; d. February 10, 1813; m. ELIZABETH FORSTER, daughter of James Forster and Elizabeth Moore; b. 1759, in Londonderry township; d. September 7, 1822, in Londonderry, and with her husband buried in old Derry church grave-yard. They had issue, but we have not been able to secure their names.

V. MARY KELLY (Patrick), b. 1751; d. prior to 1816; m. JOHN DUNCAN. They had issue:

 i. Samuel.

 ii. William.

 iii. Battana.

 iv. Mary.

 v. Rachel, dec'd; m. William Smith, and left *Mary* and *Rachel.*

 vi. Margaret, m. Hugh Dempsey.

 vii. James, m., and left *James, John, Andrew,* and *Elizabeth.*

 viii. Thomas.

 ix. David.

 x. Rebecca, m. William Elliott.

NOTES AND QUERIES.—XCVII.

NAIL MANUFACTORY.—In 1793 Benjamin Duncan, of Middle Paxtang township, manufactured nails, his residence being six miles from Harrisburg and four miles from Hummelstown.

DUNLOP.—John Dunlap or Dunlop, a soldier of the Revolution, was killed in service during the campaign of 1777. His widow resided in Harrisburg in 1795. What is known concerning this family?

A CASE OF OFFENSIVE PARTISANSHIP EIGHTY YEARS AGO.

[The following is worth reproducing at this time. John Wyeth, editor of the *Oracle of Dauphin*, was postmaster at Harrisburg, having filled that office about ten years. The course pursued by his paper was no doubt considered offensive by the postmaster-general, and that official sent Mr. Wyeth the following remarkable notice:]

GENERAL POST OFFICE, *Jan. 27, 1802.*

SIR:—Believing that the printer of a newspaper is not the most proper person to discharge the duties of a postmaster, owing to jealousies which will exist, and also believe that the public interest will be promoted by the appointment of a new postmaster at Harrisburg, I have appointed Mr. John Wright, of Harrisburgh, postmaster at that place, to whom on receipt of this, you will please to deliver all the Post office property in your possession. It is necessary for you to close your accounts with the general Post office. Accept sir, my thanks for all the faithful services you have rendered while in office. With esteem and respect.

GIDEON GRANGER.

John Wyeth, Esq., Harrisburg, in Penn.

To this, in his issue of March 1st, Mr. Wyeth took occasion to say:

☞The public are informed that the Post Office which has been held for a number of years past by the Editor of this paper is now transferred into the hands of Mr. Wright. Mr. Jefferson's Postmaster General, Gideon Granger, having in the plenitude of his sagacity, discovered that a "printer of a newspaper is more susceptible to perjury and mal-conduct in transacting the duties required in that department, than any other profession, notwithstanding a difference of opinion hitherto held by predecessors as experienced and nearly as respectable as citizen Gideon. But whether this disgraceful stigma fixed on all newspaper printers by the Postmaster General, arises from his intimacy with Duane and other printers belonging to his sect, must remain a secret in the breast of the exalted man. Be this as it will, the ex-postmaster is happy to inform his customers and friends that he has ANOTHER office at present not at the disposal of Mr. Granger, in which he will be happy to receive their commands.

March 1, 1802. THE EDITOR.

OUR EARLY SETTLERS.

West End of Derry—1759.

Jacob Albracht,
Christly Allman,
Robert Armstrong,
William Britan,
Robert Bratsha,
George Bombaugh,
George Beaver,
Anthony Blessing,
Widow Black,
Martin Brown,
Adam Baum,
Widow Blackburn,
John Crocket,
Moses Campbell,
Widow Chambers,
James Carothers,
Robert Carothers,
Joseph Cander,
James Clark,
William Dreanon,
Adam Dalker,
David Ettlee,
George Fry,
John Fleming,
Peter Groselos,
Jebel Hall,

David Hunter,
Michael Hover,
James Ireland,
John Kerr,
Peter Kender,
John Lighter,
John Laird,
Matthew Laird,
Robert McKee,
Samuel Murray,
Archibald Montgomery,
Edward McConnell,
William McComb,
Lewis Murray,
Robert Nelson,
Francis Newcomer,
Thomas Parks,
Philip Parthemer,
Petter Bentz,
John Porterfield,
Samuel Reed,
James Russell,
James Russell, Jr.,
John Rutherford,
Ann Semple,
William Sterrett,

Peter Spangler,
Mark Spangler,
William Spencer,
Matthias Stall,
Stople Shoop,
James Shaw,
John Tice,
Robert Taylor,
John VanLear,
John Vance,
Widow Wiley,
John Willson,
Robert Walker,
Matthew Willson,
Adam Waggener,
Geo. Wetsenberger,
Conrad Wolfly,
Anthony Weirick,
Moses Willson,
Samuel McCormick,
Samuel Parker,
Thomas Kerr,
Samuel Clarke,
Philip Shaker,
John Bowman.

Freemen.

Henry Taylor,
James Vanlear,

Edward Queen,

Cornelius Queen.

Joseph Cander, *Collector.*

DEATH OF GEN. JAMES POTTER, 1789.

The exact date of the death of Gen. James Potter, who was a prominent officer in the Revolutionary war, could not heretofore be ascertained after diligent inquiry. He was injured at the raising of a barn on one of his farms in Penn's Valley (now Centre county), in the autumn of 1789, and on the 27th of October, 1789, no doubt soon after the accident, executed his will. Soon after he was taken in a bed on a wagon to Franklin county for medical treatment, and died at the residence of his son-in-law, Capt. James Poe, near the present village of Marion. He was buried in Brown's Mill graveyard, near by, in Antrim township, Franklin county, and no head or foot stone marks his grave.

A number of receipts have turned up lately, but the only one indicating the proximate date of his death, is one signed by Patrick Campbell, as follows:

November 28th, 1789.

Captain Woods bought of Patrick Campbell,

36 sq's of mourning goods, 3s., ...	£5. 2s.0d.
3 " red cloth, 3s.9d., ...	1.10s.0d.
18 pounds of cheese, 7d., ...	10s.6d.

£7. 2s.6d.

The bill is receipted to Capt. James Poe, "being for funeral expenses for Genl. James Potter, deceased." Patrick Campbell was a Chambersburg merchant. (McCauley's Hist., page 76).

Another receipt for five pounds, eight shillings and two pence, "for General Potter's funeral expenses," is signed by Samuel Purviance, who, according to Mr. McCauley, was a merchant in Chambersburg as early as 1786. A receipt for "the sum of two pounds five shillings, it being for making a coffin for the corpse of James Potter, deceased," is signed by Alexander Dunlap and Joseph Keys. Reduced to Pennsylvania currency this would be six dollars. Another receipt for one pound, eight shillings and ten pence, "funeral charges for James Potter, deceased," is signed by Robert McCulloh.

Five physicians attended General Potter in his last illness. Of the reputation and eminence of four of them history and tradition has preserved a record. The fifth, whose bill is made out in elegant script, I have never heard of.

"General James Potter to Richard Pindell. To medicine, consultation and attendance, £8., 12s. 9d. Errors excepted.

R. PINDELL."

To this bill, which would be in the currency of Pennsylvania $23, is appended a receipt signed by Dr. Robert Johnston, which would indicate that Dr. Pindell was not a resident of the neighborhood.

There was a prominent Virginia family of that name, and Dr. Pindell may have been a Hagerstown or Maryland physician.

Dr. William Magaw's bill reads: "Nov., 1789. To a visit, 10 shillings; 2oz. extract Saturn, 4 shillings—14 shillings." This prescription being two ounces of lead water, discloses the nature of General Potter's ailment—a sprain—which corresponds with the traditionary accounts of his injury. Dr. William Magaw was a surgeon of the First Pennsylvania regiment (Col. James Chambers), of the Continental line. When General Lafayette was wounded in the battle of

Brandywine, Sept. 11, 1777, Dr. Magaw dressed his leg. At the time of General Potter's death Dr. Magaw resided at Mercersburg. He built and resided in the large stone mansion in Mercersburg, which, when I was in college there in 1846–8, was owned and occupied by the late Dr. McDowell. Dr. Magaw had a son, Col. William Magaw, mentioned by the late Mr. McCauley in his History of Franklin county, page 97, as the inventor of straw paper. Col. William Magaw went to Meadville, Pa., in the employ of his uncle, Samuel B. Magaw, as early as 1808, and from thence was transferred to Detroit, where he volunteered in the ranks at the time of Hull's surrender, August 16, 1812; but returned to Meadville where he established manufactures of potash, &c.

The old surgeon went from Mercersburg to Meadville to spend the remainder of his days with his son. In the latter part of May, 1825, General Lafayette, when making his famous tour through the United States, passed through Meadville. Dr. Magaw, who was then in his 81st year, called upon the General and taking him by the hand said: "General, do you know me?" "I cannot recall your name," said Lafayette, "but you are the surgeon who dressed my wound at the battle of Brandywine." The old surgeon felt very happy over the recognition. Dr. Magaw died in Meadville, May 21, 1829, aged 85 years. Another son, Dr. Jesse Magaw, married a sister of President James Buchanan. Dr. Jesse Magaw was a graduate of Dickinson College, and died young. I once came across his tombstone in some grave-yard near Mercersburg. Col. Wm. Magaw has two sons and a daughter still living at Meadville. To the eldest, Leon C. Magaw, I am indebted for information in relation to his father and grandfather.

Another physician who attended General Potter was Dr. Robert Johnston. Mr. McCauley gives a short notice of him on page 121, too short for that of so remarkable a man. He served as a surgeon and surgeon-in-chief all through the Revolutionary war, from the St. Lawrence river to Savannah, Georgia. It was he that volunteered and was sent in by General Greene to the suffering American prisoners at Charleston. In examining Gen. Wm. Irvine's papers some time since, I noticed that when war with the French Directory became imminent in 1798, and General Irvine was selected to command the Pennsylvania quota, he chose Dr. Robert Johnston for his surgeon general. Dr. Johnston was major general of the Seventh division of Pennsylvania militia in 1807, and died Nov. 28, 1808, and is buried in the Johnston grave-yard on the Witmer farm near Greencastle.

Dr. J. McClelland's bill for medical attendance on General Potter was £9. Dr. McClelland's reputation was very great, and the tradition in the Potter family in Centre county is that General Potter went to

Franklin county especially to secure Dr. McClelland's services. Dr. Mc-Clelland was the father of the late Wm. McClelland, Esq., of Chambersburg.

Dr. William Crawford charges, Nov. 12, 1789, to a visit, £1 15s. "Consultation on your case with Dr. Pindell and Magaw, £1 15s. Total, £3 10s. Dr. Crawford lived on Marsh Creek, Adams county, and was a member of Congress from 1809 to 1817, and died in 1823. Poore's Congressional Directory has a short biographical sketch of Dr. Crawford. JOHN BLAIR LINN.

NOTES AND QUERIES.—XCVIII.

MANOR OF ANTOLHOUGH.—In the list of manors given with the "Historical Map of Pennsylvania," published by the Historical Society, the manor of Antolhough, or Antolhea, as occasionally written, was thought to be the same as the manor of Little Swatara, now embraced in Schuylkill county. I find that the former manor was included in what is now Bethel and Tulpehocken townships, Lebanon county, and adjoined Freame's manor, both being south of the "North Mountain."

AN OLD TIME LETTER.

[The following letter was written by James Trotter to afterwards Col. James Burd. Who was James Trotter? The Luna was probably a club with which both were associated. The letter is interesting.]

Philad'd, 22 May, 1753.

DEAR JAMIE:

Tho' I have not had the pleasure of hearing in particular from you, yet it gives me pleasure to hear of your & family's welfare. It's true, I have been to blame in not writing you long e'er now, which I hope you will not impute to disregard or neglect; it has wholly proceeded from hurry or absence from Town, which has been pretty much my case for sometime past. I need not tell you the difficulty in finishing affairs in my way. I shall be obliged at last to leave more debts than I choose. My departure from Europe will be determined by the arrival of Cap. Ritchie who I look for every hour & don't think I shall stay many days after, as I intend for Scotia. Should be glad of your command to your friends as no doubt they will be anxious to hear from you.

If I come out here I propose remaining until next spring, as I shall scarcely go home for some time. Our Luna society is now reduced to a small number. Brey, Smith and Wallace gone to London; Smith to Jamaica; Lardner to his Iron Works. Few as we are, when Cynthia calls together we pass our moments agreeably, wishing health and prosperity to all our members that can't be with us. Pray, if the hurry of a country life will permit, write me how you are reconciled to it, with any observations you have made since settling there. There's no news in town worth remarking. The Lunas increase in town, as well with you, of which we wish you and Sister Sally joy. My kind love to her, and I shall be glad on my return to find you and her settled here. I must now beg leave to retire, as I am going about an important business, viz: dunning, the most disagreeable of all employments. So wishing you all happiness and prosperity,

I am, with great regard,

Your af't Luna & friend,

JAMES TROTTER.

To James Burd at Shippensburg, per favor of Mr. Magraw.

IN THE FRENCH AND INDIAN WAR.

[For the following roll of the company of Capt. James Patterson, we are indebted to our friend, 'Squire Evans, of Columbia, who found it among the Patterson papers. It is one of the few muster rolls of the ranging companies on the frontiers during the French and Indian war of which we have any knowledge. Of the names (some of which, however, are not distinguishable), we recognize early settlers in this locality.]

A ROLL OF CAPTAIN PATTERSON'S COMPANY AT FORT HUNTER THE 3D DAY OF FEBRUARY, 1758.

Men's Names.	Times of Enlistment.	Terms of Enlistment.
1 James Ferguson, serg.,	March 3, 1757,	1 yr.
2 John Ferguson, serg.,	March 3, 1757,	1 yr.
3 David Kidd, corporal,	June 11, 1757,	3 yrs.
4 Edward Yeats,	Feb. 21, 1757,	1 yr.
5 Samuel Dean,	Feb. 26, 1757,	1 yr.
6 Abel Pearson,	Mar. 23, 1757,	1 yr.
7 Jacob Pearson,	Mar. 23, 1757,	1 yr.
8 Fargus Highlands,	June 18, 1757,	3 yrs.
9 Charles McNeely,	July 28, 1757,	3 yrs.
10 John Sturgis, drummer,	July 28, 1757,	3 yrs.

11 Robert Mack,	Nov.	2, 1757,	3 yrs.
12 William Poor,	Nov.	26, 1757,	3 yrs.
13 James Brown,	Nov.	27, 1757,	3 yrs.
14 John Shields,*	Nov.	27, 1757,	3 yrs.
15 Richard Hogans,	Dec.	1, 1757,	3 yrs.
16 William Wattson,	Dec.	1, 1757,	3 yrs.
17 Alexander Fisher,	Dec.	1, 1757,	3 yrs.
18 Samuel Devinny,	Dec.	1, 1757,	3 yrs.
19 Alexander McMullin,	Dec.	1, 1757,	3 yrs.
20 Michael Gallagher,	Dec.	1, 1757,	3 yrs.
21 Thomas James,	Dec.	1, 1757,	3 yrs.
22 Peter Gillespie,	Dec.	20, 1757,	3 yrs.
23 George Barclay,	Dec.	20, 1757,	3 yrs.
24 Benjamin Endsworth,	Dec.	26, 1757,	3 yrs.
25 Michael Carney,	Dec.	26, 1757,	3 yrs.
26 John Kelliah,	Dec.	23, 1757,	3 yrs.
27 John Ayres,	Dec.	26, 1757,	3 yrs.
28 John Mitcheltree,	Dec.	26, 1757,	3 yrs.
29 Samuel Grily,	Dec.	27, 1757,	3 yrs.
30 Samuel Wayser,	Dec.	28, 1757,	3 yrs.
31 Edward Kelley,	Dec.	29, 1757,	3 yrs.
32 Daniel McDaniel,	Dec.	31, 1757,	3 yrs.
33 James Armstrong,	Jan.	1, 1758,	3 yrs.
34 Miles McCullough,	Jan.	1, 1758,	3 yrs.
35 Ezekiel McAdoe,	Jan.	1, 1758,	3 yrs.
36 John Winslow,	Jan.	1, 1758,	3 yrs.
37 John McCotter,	Jan.	2, 1758,	3 yrs.
38 Andrew Sears,	Jan.	5, 1758,	3 yrs.
39 Andrew McCauley,	Jan.	6, 1758,	3 yrs.
40 Wm. Bean, corporal,	Jan.	6, 1758,	3 yrs.
41 Daniel Martin,	Jan.	8, 1758,	3 yrs.
42 William McAlevy,	Jan.	10, 1758,	3 yrs.
43 John McDaniel,	Jan.	13, 1758,	3 yrs.
44 Thomas Tibbon,	Jan.	14, 1758,	3 yrs.
45 Joseph Pearson,	Jan.	18, 1758,	3 yrs.
46 James Armstrong,	Jan.	27, 1758,	3 yrs.
47 John Doyle,	Feb.	1, 1758,	3 yrs.

Pr. JAMES PATTERSON.

* Deserted 1st January.

RELATING TO THE WHISKEY INSURRECTION.—I.

[The Pennsylvania Archives, 2d series, Vol. IV., page 82, gives Judge Wilson's letter to President Washington, informing him that "from the evidence which has been laid before me, I hereby notify to you that in the counties of Washington and Allegheny, in Pennsylvania, laws of the United States are opposed, and the execution thereof obstructed by combinations too powerful to be suppressed by the ordinary course of judicial proceedings or by the powers vested in the marshal of that district." The evidence laid before Judge Wilson has never been published; it is as follows.—ISAAC CRAIG.]

PITTSBURGH, *July ye 18th, 1794.*

DEAR SIR : The blow is struck, which determines that the Revenue law cannot be carried into execution in this country, until government changes their system, and adds considerable force to the means already adopted. From an easy and convenient situation in life, I am in a few hours reduced to difficulties and distress ; however, I will enter on the detail of transactions, not doubting the justice of Government to reimburse my losses.

Prior to the arrival of the Marshal, I had information that the malcontents were meditating an attack on my house, and consequently I made such arrangements for defense as was in my power with my small family of domestics. He arrived here on Saturday, the 12th instant, having served his subpœnas in Fayette county, without great difficulty. On Tuesday, the 15th, being a stranger, unacquainted in the country, I went with him to serve four in this county ; the people assembled about us in considerable numbers ; were very ill-natured and finally fired, but without doing any mischief. We returned, the Marshal having done his duty. On Wednesday morning, the 16th, about daylight, my servants having just gone out to their employments, I discovered my house was surrounded with men, supposed about 100, sixty of whom were armed, the others with sticks and clubs ; tho' alone, being well provided with arms and ammunition, I determined to defend myself to the last, knowing that extreme insult would be the consequence of falling into their hands. An action accordingly commenced, and to make good the old adage, "that victory is not always to ye strong," after a firing of 25 minutes, I obliged them to retire, having wounded at least five of them, one or two supposed dangerously—they did me no other damage firing about 50 balls into my house. Mrs. Neville (1), a young lady, and little girl (2), the only companions of my danger, narrowly escaping.

Thus irritated, I expected they might return. I applied to Major Butler, commandant in Pittsburgh, for some assistance ; he sent me twelve men. I also made application to the Judges of our Court, the Generals of Militia and the Sheriff of the County, but had no hopes of assistance from these quarters. Thus circumstanced I had certain information about ten o'clock yesterday that a large party were again advancing. I immediately wrote to my friends to come to my assistance ; a very few of them attempted it, but were too late (3). About five o'clock 500 men, in regular order properly appointed, made their appearance ; but feeling the inequality of opposition, I quitted the house privately, leaving a friend, aided by the twelve soldiers, to capitulate for the property. My servants, rendered timid by their numbers, had disappeared. Several Flags and Messages pass'd between the parties ; but the assailant's not offering Terms sufficiently implicative of safety, an engagement once more commenced. The numbers in the house were reduced to twelve, who kept up a smart fire about one hour, which was returned many hundred fold from without, when they were obliged to surrender.· During the skirmish they had fired the barn, stable and different outhouses, and immediately on the surrender a large and well finished dwelling house, with all its appurtenances, shared the same fate, the fences all destroyed, and the whole crop of grain consumed. What was yesterday an elegant and highly cultivated farm with every convenience, is now a melancholy waste. The party in the house had three badly wounded, all soldiers in the U. S. service. The loss without is not ascertained, one of their leaders fell (4), an old officer and a man of respectability, and we know of some wounded.

I am retired to Pittsburgh with my family, without a single particle of clothing, furniture, or any kind of personal property, save what we have on our backs. I write this on the spur of the occasion, expecting to be more succinct in my next. I do not think my loss less than £3,000. [Here the letter is torn and some words are wanting.] and believes of four fine horses belonging to gentlemen who either came in or sent in ammunition to my assistance—three of which were wantonly shot, and the fourth burnt in the barn.

The Marshal has not escaped some share in the business, but will detail his own account.

I will only add that neither of those expeditions were undertaken privately or in disguise—they came publicly forward, composed of, and commanded by the best people in the country, among whom were several magistrates and [a word torn out by the wafer] officers.

I've the honor to be, Sir,

Your Obt. Servt.,

Tench Coxe Esq'r.   JOHN NEVILLE.

———

Philad'a ss.

The 2d Augt., 1794, before me the Subscriber President of the Court of Common Pleas of the first District, came George Clymer, of the City of Philad'a., and deposeth & saith that he has seen John Neville, of Washington county, Esqr., Inspector of the Survey No. 4, & District of Pennsylvania, frequently write, and is well acquainted with his hand writing, and that the subscription of the above Letter is of the hand writing of the said John Neville, Esqr., and further saith not.

Sworn before me,   GEO. CLYMER (7).

James Biddle.

PHILADELPHIA, *August 13, 1794.*

SIR: In consequence of an arrangement of the Secretary at War, who is absent, your letter of the 3d instant has been communicated to me.

It is satisfactory to receive exact intelligence of the movements of the insurgents.

Your care of the interests confided to you is in every event depended upon, according to circumstances. The keeping the arms and stores out of the hands of the insurgents is a matter of great importance. *It is hoped that you will personally in the worst issue of things find safety in the Fort.*

The friends of government may depend that it will not be wanting to its duty and interest upon this occasion. And can there be any doubt of the sufficiency of its means?

With much esteem,

I am, Sir,

Your obedient servant,

ALEXANDER HAMILTON.

Isaac Craig, Esq'r, D. Q. M. G., Pittsburgh.

———

WAR DEPARTMENT, *August 25, 1794.*

SIR: Your letter of the 17th instant, to the Secretary at War, has been received and duly attended to.

The suggestions respecting additional measures of defense have been considered, but the danger of the means falling into the hands of the insurgents appear at present an objection.

It is hoped that everything at Pittsburgh, or which shall come there, not necessary for the Post itself, has been forwarded down the river, and will continue to be so as long and as fast as it can be done with safety.

The friends of government at Pittsburgh ought to rally their confidence, and if necessary to manifest it by Acts. They cannot surely doubt the power of the U. States to uphold the authority of the laws, and they may be assured that the necessity of doing it towards preserving the very existence of Government so directly attacked, will dictate & produce a most vigorous and persevering effort; in which the known good sense and love of order of the great body of the people and all the information hitherto received of their sentiments & feelings with regard to the present emergency, authorize a full expectation of their hearty co-operation. With esteem,

I am, Sir,

Your most obedient servant,

ALEXANDER HAMILTON,

Isaac Craig, Esquire, D. Q. M. G.   *For the Sec'y at War.*

NOTES TO THE FOREGOING.

1. Mrs. Neville's maiden name was Winifred Oldham. Her six brothers were all officers in the Virginia Line in the Revolutionary war, one of whom yielded up his life in the cause of his country in the battle of Eutaw Springs, another at St. Clair's defeat. Her sister was the wife of Maj. Abraham Kirkpatrick, as brave a man as ever drew a sword.

2. The "little girl" was Harriet Craig, daughter of Major Craig, and granddaughter of General Neville, then a little more than eight and a half years old. I have often heard her tell the story of this attack on the house; her grandfather made her lie down on the parlor floor, and her grandmother and the young lady, whose name I have forgotten, loaded the guns as fast as General Neville discharged them.

3. Col. Presley Neville, the Inspector's son, Maj. Isaac Craig, his son-in-law, David Lenox, the U. S. Marshal, Ensign Sample, and a son of John Ormsby attempted to go to the Inspector's assistance, but arrived after the Insurgents had surrounded the house, and were taken prisoners.

4. James McFarlane, who served as a lieutenant through the Revolutionary war; at this time he had a mill on Mingo creek. Brackenridge in his *Incidents of the Insurrection, i., p. 17,* says: "James Lang, of Brownsville, formerly of Philadelphia, was on his way to Pittsburgh, and halted some time, and conversed with McFarlane, and used much endeavor to dissuade from the act. McFarlane fairly owned that, on reflection, he had become sensible for the rashness of it, but that they had gone too far to retreat. That was, I presume, he could not find a reasonable pretense of receding; and could not, with a good grace, draw off, after having used activity in exciting the people.

5. For an interesting sketch of Gen. John Neville, see first volume of *Pennsylvania Genealogies*, by Dr. Egle, recently published, under families of "Neville and Craig," p. 478.

6. Tench Coxe, at this period, was commissioner of the Revenue.

7. George Clymer was the supervisor of the Revenue.

NOTES AND QUERIES.—XCIX.

RELATING TO THE WHISKEY INSURRECTION.—II.

PHILADELPHIA, *August 25th, 1794.*

DEAR SIR: Mr. Baird (1) has been so obliging as to call and inform me that he sitts off early to-morrow morning, which gives me the opportunity to thank you for your attentions to me while in your quarter. Believe me I have felt very sincerely for the situation of you and your immediate connections. Your fortitude has been equal to the trial, and I hope the day is not far distant when you will be fully compensated in every way. Our friend Presley has not yet made his appearance among us. We, however, have had the pleasure to hear of his being on the road. The General I have just parted with, and he no doubt will inform you more particularly as to the circumstances which have occasioned his delay. I beg you to present my best respects to Mrs. Craig, to both the Mrs. Nevilles, and to assure them that I sympathize with them; at the same time assure them that there are virtuous men enough left to do ample justice to the virtuous part of the community among whom their husbands have the first rank.

I sent my portmanteau from Marietta by return of Crawford's sergeant, has it reached you? If so, send it forward at your convenience. One of my horses I found at Lancaster, the other I am told is with you, he had a very sore back and as it would be attended with trouble and expense in sending him down I think you had better sell him for what he will bring; he was an excellent Carriage Horse and when in my possession perfectly sound.

Things look with you as I expected, but you may expect to see *better days* and this I shall be happy to contribute to all in my power. Tell my friend Butler (2) that I should have wrote him *now* to thank him very kindly for his attention and support as well as for the attention of Mrs. Butler, but that I really had not time; this shall be done by letter in a few days, but I expect to do it in person *before many months.*

Dear Sir, Your Obliged Servant,

D. LENOX (3).

Major Isaac Craig.

PHILA., *Sept. 12th, 1794.*

DEAR MAJOR:

My anxiety to hear from Pittsburgh can only be equalled by my uneasiness on account of my family. The Commissioners arrived yesterday, but have nothing decisive with them—the post arrived last night, not a single letter from any one to us band of Exiles (4). What can be the reason of this? Surely we have some friends behind us.

We are told that yesterday was the day when the general sense of the country was to be taken on the important question of *Peace* or *War.* What has been determined? Did reason, prudence, and good sense prevail? or was the triumph in favor of violence and intrigue? Shall we meet returning Peace or be involved in the horrors and difficulties of a War? If an accommodation takes place all is well, if not, Government is surely roused, and a very few days will show ten or twelve thousand men on their march. Dreadful alternative!

In what temper are the Pittsburghers? I have heard that they determined to associate to preserve a neutrality, if not to support the Government—if I was sure this was the case I would immediately join them and partake of their fortunes.

If an accommodation does not take place, will they then not attack Fort Fayette? In this case, what will become of the town and what will be the situation of our families? Pray endeavor to guard against contingencies.

The Troops of Jersey are embodied and now about to march—they are encamped at Trenton. Governor Mifflin pitches his Marquee on the opposite bank of the Schuylkill to-morrow, and will march in a few days; the Marylanders are ready; the Virginians under General Morgan are, I suppose, now ready also. Every class and denomination in the country of whatever party reprobate the conduct of those Enemies of Peace and good order, and every man seems determined to assist in crushing so unjustifiable an opposition.

How is my mother, and how Mrs. Craig and the children? We are all well (I mean the Exiles) and receive from the hospitality, attention and politeness of the Philadelphians, as well as the officers of the federal government, a compensation in some measure for the unmeritted indignity intended us by our Countrymen.

How is Col. Butler, his family, Capt. Howe and the other officers? I shall never forget the attention of those gentlemen.

I am happy to say that government thinks highly of them, and approves every part of their conduct.

My love to my mother, Mrs. Craig, and Mrs. Kirkpatrick.

Yours,

Major Isaac Craig, Pittsburgh.   PRESLEY NEVILLE.

BRADFORD, *21st Oct., 1794.*

DEAR MAJOR: We shall, I believe, move from this place to-morrow morning, perhaps the Glade road will be our route. We have nothing new in this quarter, all the accounts we receive in this place is that peace is established in every quarter in your country. I sincerely wish it had been the case three months ago, I might now have had some shelter for my poor distressed family. Last night Judge Peters had Herman Husbands and a certain Filson storekeeper in the Glades brought to town and safely lodged in jail; it is generally thought it will go hard with them. The Judge and Attorney General marches with the army. What will be the consequence when we arrive over the mountains I know not.

Presley came here last night, from Cumberland, with the President and the Commander in Chief (Governor Lee (5). He will return to the left column on Braddock's road to-morrow or the next day, at farthest.

Wednesday Morning. The Troops are just ready to march, and four of the Insurgents, taken at this place, or at least in the Country, Old Husbands among them, are starting off for the jail in Philadelphia, under the command of 12 Light Horse and an officer; 10 or 12 more are bound over to the District Court to be tried in this County, their offences being less criminal.

Yours affectionately,

Major Craig.   JOHN NEVILLE.

DIER SIR: After my respects to you I heer that you have a rit in the hands of the Sherriff for mee, which I cold wich had not been the Case, as I am willing to Setle my proportion of your loss that happened that unfortunate day of the burning with out having my name Cauld in A public Cort to under goe the rede Cule of a Lawyer, or to be an object of Contempt for the Publick to gase uppon, as every man of Sence and feelings of humanity must no to be the Case to under goe A tryall of Such a nature. Such a tryall I wish to Evade if possibell, as the Law of Conviction has taken Place in my one brest to gide mee to do right; I therefore trust that when you receve these lines that you will feel for my Situation, and stay the prosedings against mee, and right mee an answer by the bearer, and I will come amediately to See you. When you reflect and look back how you wass used your self I must Confess that if an Eye is to go for an Eye and a tooth for a tooth that such a favor is not due to mee from you but what is past Cannot bee recauld, or if It Could I Can Assure you my hand would bee Clear of Such a peece of bisiness again, and it never would have been in that had I not have been imposed uppon by others. I started from home Several times lately to see you on that Subject but Still met Some person or other that advised mee not to goe Every time for Sertain reasons that had weight with mee as the bearer Mr. Bartley can tell you.

      Sir, I am yours With respect,

                              JOHN BALDWIN.

To General John Nevell.

———

                                UNITED STATES, ⎱
                          Pennsylvania District. ⎰

    Stephen Ross, of Shirtee Creek, Fayette township, being duly sworn deposeth and saith that about the middle of Sept'r, (after the Amnisty was signed,) in the mill of James Ewing, Esq'r., of same Township, this deponent & Samuel Ewing (son of James Ewing) had a conversation together when said Samuel said he was of opinion the Excise Law would not go on again in this Country. On the Deponent replying he thought the Office would again be opened, Ewing asked who he thought would conduct the Excise. He said he had no doubt General Neville. Ewing rejoined that General Neville would not be so hardy as to attempt it again. if he did he (Ewing) was certain the people would kill him, and for his own part he would not stop to go and help do it

    Pittsburg, Nov'r. 19, 1794.   STEPHEN ROSS.
Sworn 19 Nov'r, 1794.
    RICHARD PETERS.

PENNSYLVANIA VS. SAMUEL EWING.

    Charged before Judge Peters & bound over to me on the within affid't to be bound over to the peace and good behavior for twelve months to all men and especially to Gen'l John Nevill.

    Samuel Ewing, of Fayette Township, Allegheny Co'y, Tent in 1000 Dollars.

    Presley Neville, of Pittsburgh Township, Allegheny Co'y, Tent in 500 Dollars. Cond'n as above.

      Cape 22d Nov'r, 1794.

           Before   ALEXANDER ADDISON.

———

           HEAD QUARTERS, *Jan'y 22d, 1794.*

DEAR SIR:

    When we consider the violent proceedings which heretofore prevailed in this country, and that by them not only the laws were opposed, but the persons and property of the peaceable citizen sacrificed, it must afford the friends of order and good government the sincerest pleasure to find the inhabitants of all descriptions coming forward with unequivocal marks of a returning sense of duty. Amongst other proofs of this kind I have the pleasure to inform you, that there appears a willingness in the people to enter into voluntary contributions for the purpose of indemnifying those persons who may have sustained damages during the late commotions. James Marshall, Wm. Hays, John Baldwin and Daniel Hamilton have waited upon me for an estimate of such losses; but not being possessed of information sufficient to ascertain them, have at their request written to you upon the subject. You will therefore please transmit me an estimate of the damages sustained by the several sufferers, that a design so just and praiseworthy may be put into execution. As it may happen that some individuals may not be willing to contribute their share, the above gentlemen wish that the sufferers would empower such persons as may be elected by the people, to bring suits in their names, and also to nominate their attornies, that prosecutions may be carried on without their being at any expense. I am, Sir, with respect,

Your Humble Servant,

DAN'L MORGAN (6).

NOTES TO THE FOREGOING.

1. James Baird; in consequence of mail having been robbed by the Insurgents, he had been sent to Philadelphia by the officers of the government at Pittsburgh, with dispatches. The following is from the *History of Pittsburgh, p. 248:* "So general was the combined influence of actual disaffection upon one portion of the community, and dread of violence of the turbulent among the others, that the writer has often heard Major Craig say, that out of the family connection of General Neville, and out of the *employees* of the Government, James Baird, a blacksmith, and James Robinson, the father of Wm. Robinson, Jr., were the only persons in Pittsburgh on whom reliance could be placed under all circumstances."

2. Col. Thomas Butler commanding Fort Fayette.

3. David Lenox was the United States Marshal.

4. The Exiles were Gen. John Gibson, James Brison, Edward Day, Major Kirkpatrick and Col. Presley Neville.

5. The Commander-in-Chief was Henry Lee, Governor of Virginia; not Gen. Thomas S. Lee, of Maryland, as is stated in the very erroneous account of "The Nation's First Rebellion," in the *Magazine of American History* for October.

6. One of the persons most active as a leader in the western oppo-sition to the laws is said to have written to General Morgan, of Vir-ginia, that the moment he should set foot upon Pennsylvania at the head of his troops, certain relations of his in the disaffected counties should be put to death. He answered that he was not to be deterred from his duty by any such unmanly threats; but if they offered those relations the slightest insult, he would hang every Insurgent he caught on the first tree."—*Dunlap's American Daily Advertiser, of Sept. 12, 1794.*

General Morgan's daughter was the wife of Col. Presley Neville.

THOMAS EWING.

Very unexpectedly I came across some items of interest concerning the Ewings and Mrs. Ewing, *nee* Patterson, which throw some light upon their antecedents. The reader of *Notes and Queries* will recol-lect that James Patterson, the Indian trader, died in October, 1735, leaving a son James and three daughters—Susanna, one name not known, and Rebecca, who m. George Polson. Mrs. Patterson m. Thomas Ewing in the year 1736. In looking over the appraisement of Ewing's personal estate I find it dated September 14, 1741, and the amount £1,422 : 13 : 1.

He left children, whose names appear in the following order in a subsequent division of the personal estate:

     i. James, m. Patience Wright, ... £331 3 9
    ii. William, d. single, ... £115 11 10
   iii. Samuel, d. single, ... £115 11 10
    iv. John, ... £115 11 10

In 1744 Susanna (Connolly), *nee* Ewing, Gordon Howard, and James Wright (son of John Wright, Esq.), were appointed guardians of Ewing's children, as they also were of James Patterson's children.

In May, 1745, Mrs. Connolly resigned, and Samuel Blunston, Esq., took her place. Blunston died in 1746, and in September, 1753, Rev. George Craig, James Wright, and William Hamilton were ap-pointed guardians over John Ewing's estate, and on the same day Wright and Craig were appointed guardians over John Connolly, son of Susanna and John Connolly, and on March 29, 1755, James Ewing, being then about nineteen years of age, came into court and chose Richard Thompson, Esq., and James Wright his guardians. Thompson took Hamilton's place.

Dr. Zackry, of Philadelphia, attended Mr. Ewing in his last sick-ness.

It seems that Mrs. Ewing, when she was appointed one of the guardians of her children, took the entire charge of the estate. She was cited to file an account, which she did, when she resigned. In her account she takes credit for £50, set apart for the support of her mother, Susanna Howard, who probably resided with her. Gordon Howard was doubtless the brother of Mrs. Ewing. She also took credit for £7 paid to the support of Donegal church and school. Thomas Ewing died intestate, but I infer that he agreed to support Mrs. Ewing's mother, and also give the same amount to Donegal church, as both sums seemed to have been named in "bonds." Gordon Howard and Andrew Mays went on Mrs. Ewing's administrator's bond.

I have no means to fix the exact date when Thomas Ewing came to Lancaster county. Mr. Patterson settled in Conestoga Manor in 1715, and Gordon Howard settled in Donegal along the Paxtang and Conestoga road in 1720, upon land now owned by H. Hershey, about two and one-half miles west of Mount Joy.

Mr. Ewing may have been a relative of one or both of these families. He commenced buying real estate in 1734 adjoining James Patterson's land. In 1736, '37, '39 he purchased several hundred acres at the mouth of Chickies creek, four hundred acres on the Quitapohilla at or near Lebanon, and three hundred acres in Hempfield township. He was unquestionably a person of large means and probably an officer of distinction in the British army. He was elected to the Legislature in 1738 and 1739. The following are a few of the articles named in the appraisement of his personal effects:

Personal apparel, ...	£100
Riding horse, bridle, saddle and watch, ...	30
Silver tankard and 4 silver spoons, ...	14
Deer skins, ...	10
3 guns, 1 sword and pistol, ...	3 10 0
Dressed hemp, ...	70
Bonds, ...	832 16 9
2 negro men, ...	80
Boy and girl, ...	20
2 negro women, ...	65
Horses, cattle and sheep, ...	148 8 0

Gen. James Ewing and Capt. John Ewing, his brother, doubtless inherited a taste for a military life from their father.

Susanna Connolly died in Lancaster borough in May, 1752, and left personal estate amounting to £2,309 : 11 : 0. Among her personal effects were:

A gold ring, a pair of gold buttons, £3 : 10.
4 silver table spoons, £4.
6 silver tea spoons, £1 : 7.
Copper coffee pot.
She gave a silver spoon to her son John Connolly.
The Howards were a very prominent and wealthy family. It will be some satisfaction to the Chambers, of Chambersburg, and the Pattersons, of Juniata Valley, to know who their maternal ancestor was.   SAMUEL EVANS.
Columbia, Pa.

NOTES AND QUERIES.—C.

CRUDE COAL OIL EIGHTY-FOUR YEARS AGO went by the name of " Seneca French Creek Oil, or Indian Oil," and from an advertisement in the *Oracle of Dauphin* for August 16, 1802, it is thus recommended : " Its use has the greatest efficacy in all asthmas, consumptions, dropsies, or any internal complaint. In external cases, it is of equal service, such as mortifications, bruises, strains, backache, or rheumatism." This potent remedy was " to be had of Samuel B. Davis, book-binder, next door to Mr. Jacob Henning's tavern, Harrisburg." Henning's tavern was located in Mulberry street near Second—then the business street, next to Front street, of the town. How times change ?

A MASONIC FUNERAL IN 1802.

For the benefit of our Masonic friends we republish the following from the *Oracle of Dauphin* for August 16, 1802 :

" MASONIC BURIAL.—Died on the 8th inst., at the town of Lisburn, in Cumberland county, in the 31st year of his age, after a short illness, Mr. Samuel Bunting,—whose amiable disposition left a numerous circle of acquaintances and friends to lament his unexpected end. This young gentleman belonging to the ancient and honorable order of free and accepted Masons; all the brethren of that and the neighboring towns met, according to notice, under the warrant of Lodge No. 21, to pay his remains their sincere and last tribute of affection and esteem. The concourse was numerous and respectable; and with great solemnity, order and harmony, peculiar to the proceedings of that Mystic institution, the burying took place on the following day at high noon, when a short, but pertinent, oration was delivered by brother James Ph. Puglia. The text was, "Blessed are those who die in the Lord." After a laconic review of the happy situation of our first parent in his primitive state of innocence, and the miseries into which he sunk after he committed sin, the attention of the congregation was pathetically called to the weakness of the human constitution, the shortness and uncertainty of life, and the inconstancy of worldly affairs. He impressed on the audience the pious and sound idea that all projects and expectations of man in this transient valley of tears prove by experience to be, in the end, nothing but vanity; and that the steady practice of virtue and morality is the only solid acquisition and consoling credentials that a soul passing to immortality can bring along, to approach with confidence the presence of its Supreme Maker. After the usual ceremonies of the Masonic order, the brethren committed the corpse into its earthly abode and filled up the grave. The whole concluded with a short prayer and the lodge retired in procession with equal solemnity to their place of meeting."

The author of this panegyric was no doubt Mr. Puglia. He was a man of ability but exceedingly vain. Who was Samuel Bunting?

ABOUT HARRISBURG.

Towards the latter years of his life, the late Hermanus Alricks, Esq., was much interested in the early history of our town and county. His knowledge of early land titles gave him a fund of information, and he prepared quite a number of historical articles of value. The following is worthy of a permanent place in *Notes and Queries:*

John Harris the *first* acquired title to the original site of this city in 1733. His title embraced two adjoining tracts of land at Harris' Ferry, in Paxtang, one of which, containing about 400 acres, he held by warrant in his own name, the boundary of which began at the ravine near Front and Walnut streets, and ran across the upper end of the Market Square, out through Hamilton's brickyard, to a corner north of the Hummelstown turnpike near Vernon street, thence toward the poor house, crossing the turnpike near its intersection with the old Hanover road, to a corner on lands now, I think, of Joshua Elder, and from that to the river a short distance below Hoffer's mill. This tract was devised to John Harris the *second*, who laid out Harrisburg in 1785.

The other tract, which contained 300 acres, John Harris the first obtained by purchase, and it extended from Front and Walnut up to the line of what is now Herr street, and ran along the line of that street to a point a few perches east of the canal; thence by a line past the lower gate of the cemetery to a stump in the field of Mr. Sales, north of the Jonestown road; thence easterly to the corner of the other tract near Vernon street. This tract was devised to some other of the family of John Harris the first; but before John Harris, the younger, laid out the town he purchased the land fronting on the river, between Walnut street and South street, and then his northern line of South street was run out easterly to the said corner in the field of Mr. Sales.

William Maclay, who was son-in-law of John Harris, the younger, purchased that part of the tract which had belonged to John Harris the first, extending from South street to Herr street, upon part of which all the public buildings stand, except the arsenal. Mr. Maclay, soon after the town was laid out, built the stone house at Front and South streets. John Harris, after the town was laid out, gave that part of the public hill lying south of South street to the State. On this part the old log school house stood, at the intersection of Walnut and Third streets, fronting on Walnut, and which was taken down about thirty years ago. It was for many years the only school house in the town, and there are persons now living in this city who went to school there in the last century. The highest part of the public ground was in front of the arsenal. At the end of Locust street, opposite the residence of Mr. Barnitz, there was, as late as 1820, a flight of wide steps, perhaps fifteen in number, to enable people to reach the first plateau, then the ground rose rapidly toward the arsenal. Where the present board walk is the cutting must have been twelve to fifteen feet. The earth dug off was used in filling up State street between Second and Third. At an early day nearly all the traveling from the town up the country was done from Walnut up Front street. The crossing of a gully in Second street near Cranberry alley was bad, and Second street was not opened above South until 1812 or '14. In 1820 there were but four or five houses between South street and Pottstown above Herr street, and one of these was Maclay's stone house, and one the old "ferry house," yet standing near the water house. The Land Office and Treasury Office were built in 1812–13, and the Legislature came here I think in December, 1813, and sat in the old Court House until December, 1822. The State House was begun in 1819 and finished in 1822.

The land lying along the river above the land of the first John

Harris—that is, above Herr street—extending to the lower line of John Reel's farm was reserved by the Penns. It extended back from the river to Miller's school house, on the high grounds, and included the Asylum. It embraced about twelve hundred acres. Before the Revolution the Penn family divided the reservation into three tracts of four hundred acres each, and granted the lower one to Thomas Simpson, the next one to Thomas Forster, and the upper one to Thomas McKee.   A.
1870.

NOTES AND QUERIES—CI.

B. FRANK CHANDLER.—Few persons in our city knew the late B. Frank Chandler, Esq., so well as to appreciate his great worth. By those who had occasion within the past twenty-five years to make researches among the archives of the State, he will be greatly missed. He had informed himself of the existence of all papers and documents having an historic interest, and his directions and suggestions were of value to all having occasion to consult them. Although a native of Chester county, almost his whole life was spent in Harrisburg, where he died April 29, 1886, in the 66th year of his age. When men like B. Frank Chandler pass from off the stage of life there is a vacancy which is not easily filled. He left behind him a memory which is fragrant of manly worth and esteem, a devoted friend and a sincere Christian. Peace to his ashes.

PRICES ONE HUNDRED AND TWENTY YEARS AGO.

The following bill may interest our readers, as showing the wholesale prices of dry goods in 1766. Where was McCord's store?

PHILADELPHIA, *15th Nov'r, 1766.*

Mr. Wm. McCord
        Bought of White & Caldwell:

1 p's. 9:8 white Irish sheeting, 79 yds. @ 2:3, ...	8	17	9
2 p's. yd. wd. linen check 34½ ells 2:5, ...	4	3	2½
1 p's. blue Durant, ...	3	10	0
1 p's. black do	3	8	0
1 p's. brown Shallon, ...	3	5	0
1 p's. striped Camblett, ...	2	14	0

1 p's. sprig Osnaburg, 106 ells, 18,	. . . .	7	19	0
1 p's. yd. wd. Irish linen, 26 yds. 3:1,	. . . .	4	0	2
1 p's. finer Irish linen, 26, 3:9,	. . . .	4	17	6
1 groce narrow worsted binding for cloths,	. . . . . .		12	6
1 groce bird eye gartering,	. . . .	1	0	0
1 dz. women's clock'd worsted hose,	. . . .	1	18	0
1 dz. men's grey worsted hose, No. 6,	. . . .	1	18	0
1 dz. finer grey worsted hose, No. 7,	. . . .	2	4	0
6 ℔. Tailor's col'd thread, 5:6,	. . . .	1	14	0
2 packets No. 12 pins, 5:6,	. . . .		11	0
1 gro. set sleeve buttons, No. 1,	. . . .		7	0
1 gro.　　 do.　　　 2,	. . . .		8	0
½ gro.　　 do.　　　 3,	. . . .		4	6
½ p's. beaver coating, 15 yds., 6:1,	. . . .	4	11	3
1 black trunk to pack in,	. . . .		15	0

£58 17 0¼

PAXTANG OR LOUTHER MANOR.—I.

To those who are truly interested in the early and reliable history of Pennsylvania, it is a matter of regret that we have not had collected together a full and correct account of the several manors that were in the Province, their locality and limits, and which were so many tracts of land set apart exclusively for the Proprietary, and not immediately offered for sale. It is also a matter of regret that so much misapprehension and misrepresentation prevail on this subject. We know that there were *two* manors within the bounds of what is now Cumberland county, as we have some papers of an early date that clearly show it, and yet we have never heard of any excepting that of *Louther* or Paxtang (as it was first called), and it is to be regretted that an error has obtained currency in regard to it. Hence, at the suggestion of some friends we furnish the following facts :

Within less than ten years the statement has been repeatedly published that the Louther Manor extended *eleven miles* west of the Susquehanna river, whereas we believe that it did not extend much more than about one-third of that distance, or only *four* miles instead of " eleven."

We do not know what authority existed for making such a statement in the first instance, as it certainly contradicts Rupp's statement, made on the very credible authority of Col. R. M. Crain, in regard to the same matter—and his statement of 1846 must have been then known—and it also clearly contradicts the specific details of the original survey, than which better authority cannot be cited. The proof of this we will now give.

We have an old paper in our collection with this endorsement:— " 26th Decem'r 1764. Warrant for the Resurvey of the manor of Lowther, Cumberland County. Returned, &c., May 16, 1765. Quantity 7551 acres, &c." It has the signature of John Penn, and is addressed to John Lukens, Esq., Surveyor General. (He was S. G. under the Provincial Government.) It also bears the testimony of Daniel Brodhead, Surveyor General, of April, 1793, as being " a true copy of the original." (He was S. G. under the State Government.) This warrant is a long one and abounds in interesting statements relative to the Indians, but we will give only so much of it as recites the specified limits of the manor in question, which, by the way, was first laid out in 1736 by the Deputy Surveyor of Lancaster county. It may also be here added, that the land included in Louther Manor was part of the territory acquired by Treaty from the Five Nations, at Philadelphia, Oct. 11, 1736, and it was the *second* of the *six* Treaties with said Indians for the acquisition of their lands. We now faithfully copy from the aforesaid valid authority the proper limits of the manor : " On the West side of the Susquehannah River opposite to John Harris's Ferry and bounded to the Eastward by the said River, to the Northward by Conodagwinet Creek, to the Southward by the Yellow Breeches Creek, and to the Westward by a line drawn North a little Westerly from the said Yellow Breeches to Conodagwinet Creeks aforesaid, containing Seven thousand five hundred and seven Acres or upwards," &c. These boundaries correspond with those given in Rupp's History, page 356, where he says : " The manor on Conodoguinette was, as will appear from the following, kindly furnished by R. M. Crain, Esq., surveyed and divided, and sold by the proprietors to those first named after the No. and acres. *This manor embraced all the land between the Conodoguinette and Yellow Breeches Creek, extending as far west as the road leading from the Conodoguinette to the Yellow Breeches, past the Stone Church or Frieden's Kirch, and immediately below Shiremanstown.*" Just here it may be proper to remark, that Colonel Crain, who died in 1852, is represented as " more thoroughly acquainted with the business of the Land Office than any other man in Pennsylvania," and served for the greater part of half a century as Deputy Secretary in that office. (Men of Mark of Cumberland Valley, p. 96.) We also know from the same authority, as well as old papers in our possession, that the Manor of Louther was " surveyed at an early date." Again, in 1765, it was surveyed by John Armstrong and divided into eight and twenty portions, and in 1767 it was re-surveyed by John Lukens. As stated, it was divided into twenty-eight "Tracts or Plantations," varying in size, but the aggregate number of acres in them all is about equal to the whole manor as originally surveyed. The writer has in his possession several of the old papers indicating the No. of the Tract, and the name of the original purchaser. These papers bear date of 1772, '73, and '74. When Rupp published his history of Cumberland county, nearly forty years ago, only No. 4, No. 12, and part of No. 17—but three of the twenty-eight—were owned by any of the heirs or representatives of the original purchasers; and, on this point, the writer cannot say what is the fact at present.

Now, in turning to the Atlas of Cumberland county, carefully prepared from actual surveys, and published in 1872, we have a plan of the county, having a scale of distances (three miles to the inch), and from this plan we have here very carefully traced so much as includes the entire Louther Manor, as embraced between the creeks and within four miles from the river, as well as the land within "eleven miles" of it, as indicated by the western extension and termination of each creek. The manor proper incloses about the eastern half of Lower Allen, about the southern half of East Pennsboro', and the southeast corner of Hampden townships, containing the quantity of land given in the early survey. J. A. MURRAY.

NOTES AND QUERIES.—CII.

WOLTZ (*N. & Q. xc.*)—It was George or Samuel Woltz, the silversmith, who lived in Hagerstown. His relatives in Brownsville have old family silver with his initials stamped thereon. He had George or Samuel, who married Catharine Bowman, sister of Jacob Bowman, of Hagerstown, Md. Mr. Bowman moved to Brownsville, Pa., in 1787. After Mr. Woltz's death at Hagerstown, his widow, with her two children, George and Mary, moved to Brownsville to be near her brother. George, the eldest child, died young, of typhoid fever. Mary married Jacob Bowman McKennan, brother of Hon. Wm. McKennan, and son of Hon. Thomas McKean Thompson McKennan, LL. D., Secretary of the Interior under President Fillmore. Mr. J. B. McKennan was a prominent business man in Brownsville. He was associated with me for some years as a vestryman of my church at B. He died about 1878. His cousin, Jacob Bowman McKennan, also lived in Brownsville, and was warden of my church. To distinguish them one was known as Jacob B. McKennan, and the other, who married Mary Woltz, was known as J. Bowman McKennan. Mrs. McK. still lives in Brownsville, an invalid. It must have been the postmaster's clerk who returned the letter to your correspondent. If he will write to Mr. Nelson B. Bowman, of Brownsville, he will give him other facts, but in that case he had better enclose a stamped envelope, and not mention the name of the writer.

HORACE EDWIN HAYDEN.

A NEGLECTED GRAVE-YARD.

Some fifteen days since, returning from a professional visit in Cumberland county, we were shown the location of an old neglected graveyard. It belonged to the Presbyterians, but what its extent is not now determined, owing to the constant encroachments of the adjoining farm. It is located two miles west of Harrisburg at the junction of the Carlisle Ferry road and the State road to Gettysburg. But one tombstone was found entire. On it was the folowing:

In memory of | Robert Patterson | Who was born the 4th | Day of March 1744 | and Deceased the 30th | of September 1792 | Aged 48 Years Six | Months and 25 Days.

On a small foot stone were the letters M. G. This was evidently a Galbraith, as it is stated that as late as twenty-five years ago there were quite a number of stones containing the name Galbraith. Now what have become of them? Buried out of sight, one by one, so that in due time not a sign of this abode of the early settlers of the locality may be seen, and the resting place of the old pioneers be included in the cultivated land adjoining. Such is the greed and cupidity of the present generation. What is Carlisle Presbytery doing towards the reclaiming and preserving these ancestral graves? These are its legacy, and let it look well to the heritage. Since writing the foregoing we have received in reply to some inquiries the following:

"I would have replied sooner but wanted to see several old people. Neither my father nor his sister know when it was started. They moved on the farm in 1807; it was then an old burying place. After 1820 very few persons were buried there—not many after my grandfather bought the place, in 1807. I recollect several tomb-stones with names—I believe only two, Magdalena Galbraith and Robert Patterson, and it appears to me one with ——— Hendricks' name, one which was walled around, although I may be wrong; and Patterson's grave had a wall around it. I think the latter the case."

PAXTANG OR LOUTHER MANOR.—II.

On an average Louther Manor could not have embraced more than an area of about three miles between the creeks and four miles west of the river, as such an area would inclose twelve square miles, or 7,680 acres, and which is really between one and two hundred acres more than was actually contained in the manor.

As something worthy of notice, on the plan or map it will be observed that the entire land embraced within the true limits of the Louther Manor is the most compact or the very narrowest between the two creeks, forming of itself a desirable reservation, and from the western boundary of the manor, where it touches the creeks, *each creek begins suddenly to diverge or incline outwardly more and more.* So that, if the manor, as has been repeatedly alleged, really extended eleven miles west of the Susquehanna, it would necessarily have to embrace a vastly larger extent of territory than it really contained, or than the actual survey gives it, and nearer 30,000 acres than "between seven and eight thousand." In addition to the ground that was only and truthfully in it, if it extended westward the distance now claimed of "eleven miles," it would have to embrace, besides the half of East Pennsboro', the entire townships of Upper and Lower Allen, nearly half of Hampden, a very large part of the large township of Silvers Spring, about half of Monroe, and a slice of Middlesex, and in Silvers Spring and Monroe townships, the extreme distance between the two creeks is about ten miles.

Therefore, to declare as a matter of clear and veritable history that "the Proprietaries laid off between seven and eight thousand acres of land, *extending eleven miles from the river,* and between the Conedoguinet and Yellow Breeches creek, for a manor on which settlements were forbidden," seems to the writer somewhat unfortunate.

Of course we can imagine a narrow strip of land as actually extending eleven miles from the river, and as between the two creeks, and as embracing the given number of acres, "between seven and eight thousand." But in this case such a stretch of imagination is certainly not allowable. Because the proper and naturally permanent boundaries of the Manor, as detailed in the early survey, are: The *river* on the east side, with a well-known *creek* on the north side and a no less well-known *creek* on the south side, and then on the west side "by a line drawn *from* the said Yellow Breeches *to* Conodagwinet creeks aforesaid." And the quantity of land specified in the old surveys as existing within those clearly defined limits—that of 7,507 acres, or that of 7,551 acres, and which quantity does fully exist therein—could not possibly have extended farther westward than "the road leading from the Conodoguinette to the Yellow Breeches, past the Stone Church, and immediately below Shiremanstown." We can also easily understand, as both creeks are very crooked, that, by following their devious courses westward from the mouth of each, for the distance of about eleven miles, it might probably lead to the

Manor of Louther.*

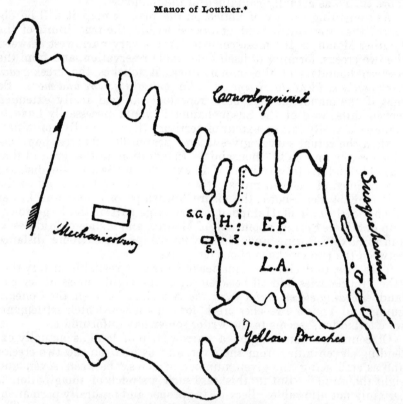

*EXPLANATION OF THE MAP.

[The initial letters within the limits of the Manor indicate portions of Hampden, East Pennsboro', and Lower Allen townships; the other initials indicate the Stone Church and Shiremanstown; the western boundary of the Manor is "the road leading from the Conodoguinette to the Yellow Breeches, past the Stone Church or Frieden's Kirch, and immediately below Shiremanstown," about four miles from the river; and the two creeks extend westward about "eleven miles," to show what would be the greatly increased quantity of land embraced in the Manor if it really extended that distance from the river.]

point on each creek where touches the line drawn by the old survey from the one creeek to the other, as the termini of the western limit of the Manor, and this doubtless was the way in which the survey was originally made, to ascertain the acreage of it. But *the line constituting the western boundary of the Manor*, and which is really its true extent from the river, is, as we believe and maintain, only four miles from the river, in popular and intelligible parlance, and no more than four miles. And to assert that it "extended eleven miles west of the river" is alike incorrect and misleading. We do not believe that one person in a thousand, in hearing or reading such a statement, would suppose that the distance thus given referred to and meant the length so far of the serpentine or the incurve-recurved course of the creeks! Just as reasonable would it be to assert that Lower Allen township (part of which forms the southern portion of the Manor), whose eastern boundary is the Susquehanna, extends *twenty-five* miles west of said river, because its southern boundary is the meandering course of the Yellow Breeches for about that distance! When, in fact, the true length or extent of the township from the river is not more than one-fourth of said distance, or about six miles instead of about twenty-five. Likewise, according to the same common sense method of speaking and understanding, the territory of Louther Manor, in its extent from the river to its western boundary, reached but four miles, and not "eleven."

It is generally understood that the first white people came over the Susquehanna about 1723. They were chiefly Scotch-Irish, to whom the Donegal Presbytery sent a supply as early as 1734. But it was not until two years afterwards that the Manor of Louther was laid out. Was not the land embraced in it previously settled, in part, if not wholly? Is it not reasonable to suppose that the first settlers would move warily as well as bravely into a country belonging to the Indians, and be careful not to leave a side belt of unoccupied land between them and their eastern friends? Was not even then squatter sovereignty, with its pre-emptive privileges, practically observed? And while the settlers were willing in due time to purchase the land which they had commenced to improve, yet it was not an easy matter to dispossess them—because they had settled upon it, and claimed their rights as colonists who had been desired to come to the country, and who, as a hearty and combative frontier people, formed a desirable cordon of defense between the savages and the more eastern settlers. (The Penn and Logan Correspondence, Watson's Annals, &c.)

As evidence that the land subsequently contained in Louther Manor had been very early settled by the whites, we will be excused in giving the following additional matter.

It has been said that about 1722 the Delaware Indians moved to the branches of the Ohio, and that in 1725 the Shawanese, who had been the predominating aborigines of our valley, gradually followed them. Afterwards French emissaries tried to alienate them from the English. Consequently the Pennsylvania authorities became alarmed and appointed three persons to visit them and persuade them to return. The following letter, addressed to one of the three, contains inducement to return, and also the evidence of an early settlement by the whites on the west side of the river.

PESHTANK,* *Nov. ye 19th, 1731.*

FRIEND PETER CHARTIERE: This is to Acquaint Thee that By the Comisioners' and the Governour's order We are now Going over Susquehanna, To Lay out a Tract of Land between Conegogwainet & The Shaawna Creeks five or six miles back from the River, in order to accommodate the Shaawna Indians or such others as may see fit to Settle there, To Defend them from Incroachments. And we have also orders to Dispossess all Persons Settled on that side of the River, That Those woods may Remain free to ye Indians for Planting & Hunting, And We Desire thee to Communicate this to the Indians who Live About Allegening. We conclude

Thy Assured Ff'ds,

JOHN WRIGHT,
TOBIAS HENDRICKS,
SAM'L BLUNSTON.

This enterprise failed. The Indians did not return. But the letter shows that the "Tract of Land" mentioned in it is the same about which we have been writing; that white persons were settled on it as early as 1723; and that timberland or "woods" really existed there. As the Indians did not accept the offer to come back, about five years afterwards the Manor was there laid out.

It may be of some pertinent interest just here to add, that two of the three persons selected to visit the Indians who had gone westward were James Le Tort and Peter Chartier. The former was a Frenchman and Indian trader, who had his cabin not far from where Carlisle is, and after whom the town spring is named. The other was the son of Martin Chartier, also a Frenchman, who lived among the Shawanese. His son, Peter (who was appointed an Indian trader by the Lancaster court), married a Shawanese squaw, and lived at the mouth of the Yellow Breeches creek, which was then known as the *Shawanee* creek, presumably because occupied by them; but it was

---

* The same as Paxtang, Peixtan, Paxton, &c., where Harrisburg now is.

J. A. M.

also called the *Callapasscinck,* with reference to its curvatures, and this name, according to Heckewelder, is a Delaware Indian word. Not only is the name of one of these Frenchmen perpetuated among us by the Letort spring, but the name of the other is also perpetuated in Western Pennsylvania by Chartier creek. The other negotiator was Edmund Cartlidge, a prominent Indian trader, whose name occurs in the Colonial Records and Pennsylvania Archives, and who, in his correspondence with Governor Gordon relative to this business, reports more favorably of Chartier than of Le Tort, though the former at last went over to the French, and the latter has been regarded as a person of better character. (Pennsylvania Archives, vol. i., pp. 299, 328. Historical Register, vol. ii., p. 250. Memoirs of Charlotte Chambers, by her grandson, Lewis H. Gerrard, p. 12, and also Chambersburg in the Colony and in the Revolution, by the same writer, p. 12, &c.)

The foregoing statement we respectfully submit to the candid judgment of those who may be interested in the matter. We know that to err is human; and if it should appear hereafter that our statement is faulty or inaccurate, we shall be glad to revise it, as our sole object is to give the truth and nothing but the truth.   J. A. MURRAY.
Carlisle, 1885.

P. S.—We have also some old documents, written and printed, that indicate the existence of such Proprietary Reservation as "Eden Manor," which embraced a few thousand acres of land in the northwestern portion of what is now Cumberland county. In one of the papers—bearing date of 1746, and signed by "Wm. Parsons, Surveyor General," under the Provincial Government—there is a plan of the manor, an oblong square, which contains a section of the creek and some of its tributaries. The distances are given, and the number of acres.   J. A. M.

NOTES AND QUERIES.—CIII.

A NEW STATE.—On the 20th of November, 1782, a bill was reported in the General Assembly, entitled, "An act to prevent the erecting of any new and independent State within the limits of this Commonwealth," and read the first time. On the 27th of November it passed second reading and on the 1st of December read the third time, and passed finally. On the day following, December 2, 1782, it was signed by the Speaker. Now what was the occasion of the hasty passage of this act. Can any of our readers inform us?

HISTORY OF THE WAR OF 1812-14.

We are indebted to Rev. Horace E. Hayden for a copy of the following advertisement:

"Proposal by Samuel White, of Adams county, Penn'a (a Prisoner in the Late War), for publishing by subscription an account of the American Troops under the command of Colonels Fenton and Campbell, crossing the Lake from Erie to Long Point in May, 1814, and the occurrences that took place. Also, the crossing of the Niagara by the troops under the command of Generals Gaines, Brown, Scott, and Porter, on the third of July, 1814, the taking of Fort Erie, the battle of Chippewa, and the imprisonment of Colonel Bull, Major Galloway, and the author (then a captain), by the savages; their treatment—the murder of Colonel Bull by the Indians and the cause—the treatment of American prisoners of war by the British, and also a historical account of the Canadas, from Fort Erie to York and Kingston, in Upper Canada; Montreal and Quebec in Lower Canada, and Halifax in Nova Scotia.

"The undersigned, members of the Perseverance Lodge, at Harrisburg, are personally acquainted with Gen. Samuel White, and have every confidence in his integrity and veracity. Having lost a valuable estate, from his absence in the service of his country during the late war, he is endeavoring to raise a small sum for the maintenance of his family, by publishing a history of the events which transpired under his notice. It is hoped *every brother* will aid the author in his undertaking by subscribing for, at least, one copy of the work.

(Signed)
                                 SIMON CAMERON,
                                   JOEL BAILEY,
                                   HENRY CHRITZMAN,
                                   N. B. WOOD,
                                   HENRY BEADER,
                                   JOHN A. STEHLEY.

"*Harrisburg, Penn'a., Jan., 1829.*"

"CONDITIONS—This interesting work will be handsomely printed in pamphlet form, on good paper, and contain upwards of one hundred pages, at the low price of fifty cents per copy, payable on delivery. A considerable number of subscribers being already obtained, the work will shortly be put to press and finished without delay."

RECORDS OF THE SCOTCH-IRISH.

Our Scotch-Irish maternal ancestors were a remarkable people; they were certainly not as selfish as the "lords of creation." Whilst the latter claimed the privilege of marrying two or three times, and more frequently after the first, to a widow, they often inserted a clause in their wills depriving their widows of the enjoyment of the "homestead in case they remarried." In looking over the records I find that but little attention was given to dying requests of this kind. It will be remembered that SUSANNA HOWARD m., first, JAMES PATTERSON, by whom she had issue (surname Patterson):

    i. James.
    ii. Susanna.
    iii. Sarah.
    iv. Rebecca.
    v. Thomas.

She m., secondly, THOMAS EWING, by whom she had issue (surname Ewing):

    vi. James.
    vii. William.
    viii. Samuel.
    ix. John.

She m., thirdly, JOHN CONNOLLY; and had issue (surname Connolly):

    x. Dr. *John.*

Let us take two or three more cases by way of illustration.

ROBERT McFARLAND settled along Little Chickies creek, in Donegal township, Lancaster county, about one mile south of Mount Joy borough, in the year 1720. Hugh White adjoined on the north, on the south Andrew Mays, and on the west the Works. Mr. McFarland's family were grown up, some of whom were married at the time he made his settlement, or soon afterwards. His wife Janet survived him. They had issue:

    i. John.
    ii. James. He was the joint owner with his father of the mansion farm containing about 300 acres. James d. in 1752, and left no issue. His wife, Margaret, survived him. His property went to James, son of his brother John, who was 20 years of age at this time. He also gave legacies to Robert, son of his brother John and also to his brothers Joseph and Robert. His wife, Mar-

garet, and his brother-in-law, William Greer, were his executors.

iii. *Robert*, m. Esther Dunn, of Donegal, in 1748, by Lutheran minister in Lancaster. He owned a farm adjoining
his father's and another one further down Chickies
creek, which he sold to Jacob Heistand. He also became sole owner of his father's plantation, containing
two hundred and eighty-six acres, which he sold to
Thomas Clingan, June 20, 1757. He was then living
in Bedford county, Va.

iv. *Rachel*, m. John Wilkins, Indian trader, in 1731 or 2,
by whom she had :

1. *Rachel*, m. Matthew Laird, who resided along Big
Chickies creek in Hempfield township.

2. *John*, b. in 1733 ; m., 1st, Mary ; 2d, Catharine.
John Wilkins, Jr., became owner of several hun-
dred acres of his father's estate, situated in
Mount Joy township, on the north side of the
Paxtang and Conestoga road, now owned by the
Nisleys, about two miles west of Mount Joy.
This land adjoined Gordon Howard, Samuel
Smith and John Wilson. In 1761 he moved to
Carlisle and became a storekeeper. John Wilson,
who owned part of the Wilson tract, also moved
to Carlisle, where he carried on carpentering.
Colonel Wilkins moved to Pittsburgh, and was
the ancestor of that branch of the family in that
place.

3. *Rebecca*, m. Thomas Anderson (blacksmith), son
of the Rev. James Anderson, of Donegal.

4. *Mary*, m. William Poor.

5. *Jean*, m. John Kirkpatrick.

John Wilkins Sr., d. in 1741, and in 1742 his widow,
Rachel, m. John Ramsey, an uncle of Dr. Ramsey, the
historian, and a distinguished general of the Revolution. Mr. Ramsey died in the winter of 1746–47, and
on April 16, 1751, she was married to Gordon Howard
by the Lutheran minister in Lancaster. In 1755 she
was again a widow, and resided until her death with
Joseph Howard, son of Gordon Howard, upon his
mansion farm, now owned by J. Hershey. She became
involved in a law suit with Joseph Howard about one
of the Wilkins farms, but lost her case.

v. Joseph.

vi. Rebecca, the youngest daughter of Robert McFarland, Sr., m. Andrew Mays, who owned a farm on the south side of her father's. He died in 1754 and left:

    1. *James.*

    2. *Mary.*

    3. *Rachel.*

    4. *Rebeckah.*

    5. *Margaret.*

    6. *Susanna.*

Mr. Mays in his will provided for his widow, but expressly said that she could not enjoy his mansion if she again married. In 1755 she married Samuel McElhenny, and changed her place of abode.

DUNCAN McFARLAND was old enough to be a brother of Robert of Donegal. He died in 1769 and left a widow Mary, and children as follows:

    i. Thomas.

    ii. [*A dau.*], m. Robt. Willson.

    iii. [*A dau.*], m. Samuel Hamilton.

    iv. [*A dau.*], m. Edward Knight.

    v. John.

James Hamilton and Wm. Reed were the witnesses to his will. This family resided near Pequea creek, in Strasburg township, Lancaster county.

DANIEL McFARLAND was also old enough to be a brother of Robert. He died in July, 1752, and left a widow Jean, and children:

    i. William.

    ii. Margaret.

He devised a sum to his grandson, James Chesnut. He resided in the lower end of Lancaster county, and must have been well advanced in years when he died.

GORDON HOWARD settled in Donegal in 1720, or at least was a large landholder in that year. He resided on the farm now owned by I. Hershey, about two miles northeast from Donegal meeting house. At this time he had a large family of grown up children. His sister, Susanna, m. James Patterson, the Indian trader, the year that Mr. Howard came to Donegal. He, too, was an Indian trader, and a very prominent person. He m. RACHEL McFARLAND in 1751. His children were then married and had families. He left issue:

    i. Thomas, who owned a farm adjoining Donegal meeting house.

   ii. Joseph, m. Rebecca ——— ; died in 1777, and left issue :
      1. *James.*
      2. *Thomas.*
      3. *Joseph.*
      4. *John.*
      5. *David.*
      6. *Martha.*
      7. *Mary.*
  iii. John, d. in 1778 ; m. Ann ——— ; and left issue :
      1. *Martha.*
      2. *David.*
      3. *Mary.*
      4. *Thomas.*
      5. *Joseph.*
      6. *John.*
  iv. William, d. prior to 1766.
   v. Robert, m. Sarah ——— ; he sold his land to John Eby
     in 1763.
  vi. Rebecca, d. 1764; m. James Allison; d. 1762; and left issue :
      1. *James,* who became owner of the mansion farm of
        300 a., a short distance north of General Cameron's
        Donegal farm.
      2. *Ann,* m. ——— Defrance ; and had issue : *James,*
        and *John.*
      3. *Janet,* m. William Watt.
      4. *Margaret,* m. ——— Bowman.
      5. *Sarah.*
      6. *Rebecca.*
  vii. [A dau.], m. Samuel Allison.
 viii. Martha, m. George Erwin, a shopkeeper in York, Pa.
  ix. Susanna, m. Charles McClure, and moved to Mecklenburg,
     N. C., prior to 1766.

    The McFarlands of Cumberland, Centre, and Mifflin counties doubtless belong to the families who settled along Chickies creek. They intermarried with the Howards also. I hope to hear from that branch of the family who settled in Bedford county, Va. The McFarlands and Howards left Donegal prior to the Revolution. I find that Thomas Ewing's farm in Dauphin county was located along the Swatara at the mouth of the Quitopahilla. Gen. James Ewing and Capt. John Ewing sold this farm to Andrew Hershey, from whom the Dauphin county branch came from.   SAMUEL EVANS.
   Columbia, Pa.

NOTES AND QUERIES.—CIV.

TWO INTERESTING LETTERS.

[The following letter would show that Colonel Burd, of Tinian, was in the Jamaica trade prior to the French and Indian war. It may furnish a clue to some other points in his very interesting history.]

[*John Swift to James Burd.*]

PHILAD'A, *July 26, 1751.*

MR. JAMES BURD—*Dear Sir:* When you arrive in Jamaica please to dispose of my 36 Barrels of Flower, and if you have an opportunity Ship the net proceeds in heavy Pistoles to Mr. John White of Croydon, in Surry (near London) for my account. If there should be no opportunity to London, I then leave it to your discretion either to ship the Pistoles to me here, or to purchase any produce of the Island that you imagine will answer in this place. God bless you, my good wishes will always attend you wherever you go; because I am
Your Humble Serv't,
JOHN SWIFT.

Endorsement on back of original letter:
To James Burd, 'Merch't on Board the Sloop Charming Nancy; or in his absence to Messrs. Minot & Hatton, Merch'ts in Kingston, Jamaica.

[*John Harris to James Burd.*]

PAXTANG, *March 19th, 1771.*

SIR: The Bearer, Philip Craft, is Beginning to take in Subscription in Order to see if a sufficient number of Subscribers can be got in Order to Encourage him to ride a post for 1 year like that ——— rode. Please to speak to Captain Green or any you Please to subscribe. He proposes to carry a paper for Every Person for a year once a week for a dollar. Two papers 10s a year, which I think Reasonable. I put 15s to my name as an Encouragement. I would have been at Widow Martin's, but a Number of Persons came here that I can't get away at Present. I am, sir, with the Greatest Regrets, your most obed't and Humble Servant. JOHN HARRIS.

JOURNAL OF LIEUTENANT KERN IN 1758.

[The following report was probably made to Capt. James Patterson, who was in command at Fort Hunter, or to Col. James Burd in command at Fort Augusta, to whose command Captain Patterson belonged. This Journal belongs to the Patterson papers.—s. e.]

JOURNAL OF MY JOURNEY FROM READING TO FORKS OF DELAWARE
AND BACK TO FORT HUNTER, VIZ:

January 23d, 1758.—I left Reading and on ye 24th I arrived at Oyty block house; Lieut. James Handshaw commanded. I mustered the company at the same place; 23 men are stationed at Mr. Depoyes and 29 men at the block house. They have 100 weight powder, 200 lbs. lead and 4 months Provision. Mr. Denane commissary. I delivered Lieut. Handshaw and Ensign Hughes there commission. The companys are in good order.

25th.—I arrived at the block house where Lieut. Jacob Shnyder, with 24 men of Lieut. Engle's company. I mustered them, and are in good order and a good place for Fortification. I have delivered Mr. Shnyder his commission. The same day I arrived at Fort Leashaw where Lieut. Engel was stationed. I mustered that company and was not satisfied because I did not bring him a Captain's Commission. His men are not in good order; are 55 men in number.

26th.—I arrived at Fort Allen. I delivered Capt. Arnd and Lieut. Conradt there commissions and mustered the companys. Them men are in good order. This fort is of no service to the country.

27th.—I arrived at the block house of Allemengel, where Lieut. Henry Guyger commands 13 men, but he being absence. The men are in good order. The same day I arrived at Mr. Eberetz where Capt. Weatherholtz commands 43. I mustered the company. They are in good order and fine soldiers.

I gave Lieut. Weatherholtz your order. I arrived at Fort Williams where Capt. Jacob Morgan commands.

January 29th.—I mustered Capt. Morgan's company, being 53 men and are in good order. This fort is of little service to the country.

January 30th.—I arrived at Fort Henry where Capt. Samuel Wyser at present commands. Capt. Busse's and Capt. Wyser's are stationed here except 17 men of Capt. Wyser's men are at Fort Sweetara. Them men are in good order. The two companies are completed.

January 31st.—I staid at Fort Henry.

February 1st.—I arrived at Fort Sweetara, where Lieut. Philip Marsloff and Ensign Martin are stationed.

February 2d.— I gave them their discharge, agreeable to your order and ordered Capt. Lieut. Samuel Allen to take the command. Them men are not in good order. The same day I whent to Crawford's.

Feb. 3.—I arrived at Fort Hunter.

Feb. 4.—I mustered that company. They have no ammunission.

Feb. 5.—I arrived at Lancaster. A true coppie of my Journall.

JACOB KERN.

IN THE FRENCH AND INDIAN WAR.

[The letter which follows was written to Governor Morris, of Pennsylvania, at the outset of the Indian war following Braddock's defeat. We are anxious to know why John Harris sent the young men mentioned " to the Ohio " to fetch scalps," and by what authority.]

HEIDELBERG, BERKS Co., *Dec. 22, 1755.*

HONORED SIR: Last night I arrived from John Harris's Ferry, and herewith inform you that I did not reach my house in Heidelberg till the 14th inst. I sat out on the 16th for Harris's Ferry, where I found no Indian but the Old Belt and another Sinecker, called commonly " Broken Thigh," a lame man.

Their young men, about six or seven in number, being sent out by John Harris, to fetch scalps from Ohio, but stopt at Aughwick by Mr. Croghan. I sent for Thomas McKee, John Carson, and Samuel Hunter to John Harris's, to consult with them how to send your Honor's message to the Indians on the West Branch of the Susquehanna. They recommended one Hugh Crawford to me, on whom I prevailed to go to Aughwick with the message, and from there send Indians to the W. Branch of the Susquehanna with it; and if the Indians thought it advisable, to go with them and coı duct them down the river, either himself or James Patterson, who is to go along with him to Aughwick.

I had two old Indians in council with me. They received the message from me and Hugh Crawford ; the wampum I gave and necessaries for them, and the written invitation from me, in presence of the above named gentlemen. I hope he will go through with it.

Upon my arrival at John Harris's, I gave a string of wampum to the two old Indians above mentioned, requesting them to look upon me as a public messenger from their Brother Onas, and desired them in his behalf to let me know all that they knew about this war, and who it was that murdered Onas' people? And for what reason?

Next morning they made answer to the following purport:

BROTHER: We are very glad to see you here once more at these troublesome times. We look upon you here as our Brother Onas' messenger as we always did. The author of the murder of the people of Pennsylvania is Onontio; he employs his children for that purpose, and they come to this river (Susquehanna) to murder. We are sorry to tell you that they have prevailed upon our cousins, the Delawares, living about half way from Shamokin to *Schantowano* (Wayomack) in a town called *Nescopeckon*. Those Indians have given their town (in defiance of us their uncles) to Onontio's children as a place of their rendezvous, and had undertaken to join and guide them the way to the English. That thereupon the Shickalamys and others of the Six Nations, fled towards the Six Nation country. That a report was spread among the 'Delawares, on that river, that the Pennsylvanians were coming with thousands to destroy the Indians on Susquehannah, which had occasioned the Six Nation Indians before named to fly, because they would not fight against their Brethren, nor against the Indians, and that everything was in a great confusion. Honored Sir,

Your most obedient
And humble servant,

CONRAD WEISER.

P. S.—Your Honor will have heard by this time that the Paxton people took an enemy Indian on the other side of the Narrows, above Samuel Hunter's, and brought him down to Carson's house, where they examined him. The Indian begged his life and promised to tell all he knew to-morrow morning, but (shocking to me) they shot him in the midst of them, scalped him, and threw his body into the river.

The Old Belt told me, that as a child of Onontio, he deserved to be killed; but that he would have been very glad if they had delivered him up to the Governor, in order to be examined stricter and better.

Yours, &c.,

CONRAD WEISER.

To Gov. Morris.

NOTES AND QUERIES.—CV.

GENEALOGICAL NOTES.

JOB.

JACOB JOB, d. prior to 1763, and had issue:
    i. Andrew, d. s. p.
    ii. Jeremiah.
    iii. Sarah, m. Jonathan White, of Chester county.
    iv. Samuel, resided in Leacock township, Lancaster county.
    v. Mary.

JOHNSTON.

GAWIN JOHNSTON, d. prior to 1769, for at that time his widow Mary had become the wife of Henry McKinney. Johnston left the following children:
    i. James.
    ii. Margaret, m. Francis Johnston.
    iii. Alexander.
    iv. Jennett.

KUPPER.

JOHN GEORGE KUPPER, of Upper Paxtang, d. prior to 1780, leaving a wife Elizabeth, and children:
    i. Adam.
    ii. Anna-Maria.
    iii. Jacob.
    iv. Catharine.
    v. Elizabeth.
    vi. Maudlina.
The first two were above fourteen years of age, the others under.

LECRON.

DANIEL LECRON, d. prior to 1770, leaving a wife Maria Margaret, and issue:
    i. John.
    ii. Matthias.
    iii. Andrew.

    iv. Maria-Susanna.
    v. Susanna.
    vi. Dorothea.

—

MAXWELL.

ROBERT MAXWELL, d. prior to March, 1761, for at that date his widow Catharine was the wife of James Porterfield. He left issue:
    i. James.
    ii. Samuel.
    iii. Robert.
    iv. Margaret.
    v. Joseph.
    vi. Thomas.
    vii. Francis.

LEHMAN FAMILY.

[A correspondent handed us the following letter shortly after its receipt. The writer, a resident of Wayne county, O., is still living at the age of ninety-six years. (Mr. L. d. July 14, 1886.) The orthography is as in the original, and when it is taken into consideration that the writer had reached the age of ninety-four years when the letter was penned, apart from its interesting information, it is a remarkable one.]

My father's name was Martin Lehman a native of Germany where he was born January 1, 1744. His parents emigrated to America in 1746, locating on some land in Berks county, where the son was brought up, learning the trade of a carpenter. After Martin Lehman's marriage he purchased a small tract of land near what is now Pinegrove, Schuylkill county. Here he built a log cabin, cut out doors and windows and removed there with his wife. The place was surrounded by wild beasts, and during the absence of Mr. Lehman, his wife would frequently rise from her bed and shoot from a rifle at the wolves to drive them away. Deer and other game were plentiful and supplied their table. Much of the time Mr. Lehman was employed building cabins in Lykens Valley.

The soil, however, not being very productive, in the year 1796 he removed to Lancaster county on a farm belonging to James Patterson who was then in his minority and under the guardianship of his brother Arthur. This farm lies on Little Chickies creek one half a mile east of the town of Mount Joy. Here he resided for a number of years cultivating the farm on shares; in the meanwhile the elder members of his family coming to mature age left their home and sought occupation elsewhere.

Catharine Lehman, the eldest of the family, married Jacob Heistand, son of Peter Heistand. There were three others in the Heistand family, Elizabeth, John, and Peter. The grist mill was given to Peter, the farm to the other three, but John died young, unmarried. Jacob and his wife had one daughter, and she became the wife of Christian Heistand, whose farm lies adjoining the village of Landisville, seven miles west of the city of Lancaster, on the pike to Harrisburg. Here they resided long enough to raise a family of ten children to mature age. These children all remained in that and the adjoining counties, except John, the eldest, who went to California and died there. Four are dead, and six survive of the descendants of Catharine.

Brother Henry Lehman married Margaret Oberlin. They had six children, to wit: *Mary, David, Catharine, Sarah, John,* and *Elizabeth.* Mary married George Johns, and had two children, when he died. Her second husband was William Beck and they had four children. She is now a widow. Two of her sons are preachers of the Gospel, and one lives in Nevada. The second of Henry's children, David, married Susan Bitner, and their children were *Sarah, Jacob, Christian, Elizabeth, Harriet, Mary, David, Henry, Daniel,* and *Simon.* Henry's daughter Catharine married Benjamin Brubaker, and they had six sons and six daughters, of whom only *David* and *Peter* survive of the sons, and the daughters, *Leah, Sarah,* and *Fanny.* Henry's daughter Sarah married S. Zimmerman and they had six sons and five daughters of whom only *Jacob, David, Fanny, Sarah,* and *Martha* are living. The fifth member of Henry's family was John, who married Elizabeth Storet. They had five sons and three daughters, of whom *John, Daniel,* and *Catharine* are dead—*Joseph, Henry, David,* and *Margaret* surviving their parents. Henry's daughter Elizabeth married David Switzer. They raised a family of nine children: *Henry-R., Annie, John, Sarah, Harriet, Mary-Ann, Elizabeth, David,* and *Philena,* all now living except *Mary-Ann.*

The third member of father's family was Christian Lehman. Brother Christian's family were not long lived. He, himself, did not quite reach three score and ten. Henry R. is the only survivor. Whether Martin left any male issue I know not.

Brother George comes in fourth. He married M. Stohler. They had three children, *Henry, Catharine* and *C.-Ann.* George died on the 10th of September, 1816, at the age of thirty-five. His son Henry married Miss Hannah, and they had four daughters and three sons, all living. They reside in Philadelphia. The eldest daughter, Caroline, married Trimble and lives in Iowa. The names of the children are *Louis, George, Alfred,* and *Caroline,* all married, and *Amanda* and *Emma,* single.

Mary, the fifth of father's family, married Adam Smith, and their children were *Christian, Martin, Henry, Abraham, Nancy, Fanny,* and *Catharine.* *Nancy,* the eldest, married Benjamin Leib, and they had five sons and three daughters: *Daniel, Adam, William, Christian, Samuel, Sarah, Eliza,* and *Mary.* Fanny, the second daughter of sister Mary, married Levi Strayer, and their children were *Fanny, Mary, Catharine, John,* and *Samuel,* all living except John.

Martin, the sixth of father's family, married Miss Martin. They had four daughters and three sons, *John, Henry, Daniel, Fanny, Catharine, Martha,* and *Eliza,* all living except Eliza and Henry. Fanny lives in Shippensville, Clarion county, Pa., Martha in Lancaster county, and Catharine in Progress, Dauphin county. The parents are dead.

We will now speak of John, the seventh child, the youngest, and the only survivor. He was born the 14th of August, 1790. In 1812 he married Christina Smith and they had one son and three daughters. He moved to Ohio in the spring of 1823. His wife died shortly after and lies buried in Wooster, Wayne county. I married a second time, and we had twelve children, swelling my family record to seventeen. Of these only nine survive. *Benjamin,* the oldest, now about seventy-one, lives in San Buenaventura, Ventura county, Cal. *Cyrus E.,* the youngest, forty years old, resides in San Bernardino county, California. *John H. Lehman* and *Martin B. Lehman* live in Lebanon, St. Clair county, Illinois. *Ephraim, George,* and *Maria,* married Al. Miller, live in Wayne county, O. *Sarah,* married to Frome, lives in Wooster. *Caroline* married Dr. Foltz, reside in Akron, Ohio. All have issue except Cyrus.

Having traced the genealogy of the Lehman family over one hundred and fifty years, I shall not venture to go farther back. I need offer no apology. My writing shows the difficulty under which I attempt to write, having no command of my right side and arm since I had that stroke of palsy as also my sight fails me very much, but by exercising patience you may pick up something you can read.

Respectfully,

Dec. 24th, 1884.   JOHN LEHMAN.

I will say a little more concerning Brother Christian's sons, Henry R. and Daniel. I stated that Daniel had three sons; but he had five, *John, Christian, Franklin, Cameron,* and *William.* Henry's wife died May 7, 1850, aged 34 years. Her maiden name was Susan Strayer. Their son Aaron lives in Wooster, O.; he married Julia Geitgey.

The names of father's brothers were Michael, Ludwick, Frederick, and John—his sisters were Maria, and one married a Mr. Wallick, but I have forgotten her name. Michael and Ludwick died in Lancaster county, Pa. Frederick died in York county.

In another handwriting is the following recapitulation:

MARTIN LEHMAN, b. December 30, 1744; d. September 13, 1801. Frederica C., his wife, b. March 4, 1751; d. September 8, 1822; both buried in Manheim, Lancaster county, Pa. Their children were:

    i. Catharine, b. November 23, 1773; d. June 17, 1844; m. Jacob Hiestand, b. November 12, 1767; d. June 27, 1834; both buried in Mount Joy.

    ii. Henry, b. December 19, 1775; d. June 13, 1847; m. Margaret Oberlin; both buried at Salem church, Salem township, Wayne county, O.

    iii. Christian, b. May 28, 1778; d. August 9, 1847; m. Nancy ———; buried in Middletown, Dauphin county, Pa.

    iv. George, b. June 11, 1781; d. September 10, 1819; buried in Manheim, Pa.; m. M. Stohler, b. August 19, 1787; d. December 19, 1881; buried at Des Moines, Iowa.

    v. Mary, b. March 25, 1784; d. December 16, 1860; buried at Salem church; m. Adam Leister, d. April, 1823; buried in old Lutheran grave-yard, Middletown, Pa.

    vi. Martin, b. August 8, 1787; d. April 14, 1863; m. ——— Martin, b. January 24, 1789; d. October 25, 1861; buried in Napiersville, Dupage county, Ill.

    vii. John, b. August 14, 1790; (the writer of this letter), m. first, Christina Smith, b. January 24, 1790; d. July 13, 1823; buried at Wooster, O.; m., secondly, Nancy ———, b. May 25, 1802; d. August 28, 1867; buried at Salem church, Wayne county, O.

NOTES AND QUERIES.—CVI.

BEULA.—Coming across this name a few days since, we were reminded of the fact that among the towns in Pennsylvania which sprung up like mushrooms and then vanished away, at the beginning of the century, was that of Beula in the "Cambria Settlement on the Waters of the Conemaugh and Blacklick creek," as the advertisements then set forth. Beula was located in the midst of the "Garden of Pennsylvania," but alas for the town which had such a short-lived existence, that "Garden" was not in Cambria county."

CENSUS OF PITTSBURGH IN SEPTEMBER, 1810.—A Mss. in our possession, with the foregoing endorsement by Judge Jasper Yeates, is as follows:

There are 283 brick houses, places of worship, court houses, &c., included. Stables, kitchens, and other back buildings excepted.
 473 frame and log houses, excepted as above.
 11 stone, the jail included, backbuildings excepted as above.

———

 767 total houses in Pittsburgh.
 2424 white males of all ages.
 2132 white females of all ages.
 184 both sexes, free blacks.

———

 4740 total souls in Pittsburgh.

————

BRITISH PRISONERS AT YORK, 1781.

[The following memorial of the date of December, 1781, was directed to the Supreme Executive Council of the State and to General Lincoln, of the Continental forces. What action, if any, was ever taken in regard to the memorial we know not, but presume Daniel Brubaker was remunerated for his losses.]

To the Honorable Major General Lincoln, Minister of War of the United States of America: The Memorial and Petition of David Brubaker, of Lancaster Co., in the State of Pennsylvania, Most Humbly Sheweth:

That your Memorial is justly entitled to & possessed of a certain Plantation & Tract of Land situate near York Town, in the County of York, in the State aforesaid, containing 280 Acres for which he paid £1200 specie.

That upon the late Removal of Part of the British Convention Prisoners from the Borough of Lancaster, the Plantation aforesaid then in the Possession of a Tenant was pitched upon for the Reception of such Prisoners as should be removed to York County.

That above 100 Acres thereof being already cleared, the persons employed constructing the Stockades & Huts for the Prisoners & Guards have made use of large quantities of wood growing on the said Plantation, & have already cleared 30 Acres of wood land thereon, so that the Plantation aforesaid is considerably impaired in value.

That the Guards have used & destroyed almost all the Rails on the Plantation, utterly depriving the Tenant of the Indian Corn thereon, & the benefit of the Pasturage of his Meadows.

Your Memorialist has no View in this State of the Facts to insinuate anything to the Disadvantage of Col. Wood, who has the care of the Prisoners. The Grievances of which he complains being out of Col. Wood's Power to remedy, & which he has seen with Concern and Regret. A Participation of the Common Burthens of Government must be the lot of every Man in Society. But the imposition of greater Duties or more Hardships on an Individual than he is justly subjected to, is evidently subversive of the Rights of Freedom of such Individual, and it is humbly hoped will not be countenanced either by Congress or your Honour.

Your Memorialist does not flatter himself with a Removal of the Prisoners from his Plantation at this Inclement Season of the Year; he feels that for a time he must submit to the Inconvenience; yet he humbly requests that immediate orders may be given to the Officers Commanding the Guard over the said Prisoners for the Time being, to prevent all further Waste or Destruction of his Timber or other Property on the said Plantation, or that such other effectual steps may be taken for the Prevention of such damages as may be consistent with the Wisdom and Justice of Congress or the known good character of your Honour.

And your Petitioners as in Duty bound will ever pray, etc.

GENEALOGICAL NOTES.

FERTIG.

MICHAEL FERTIG, of Middle Paxtang, d. prior to 1800, leaving a wife Mary, and children as follows:

i. Michael.
ii. John.
iii. Zachariah.
iv. Peter.
v. Adam.
vi. Elizabeth, m. Jacob Bogner.

HAMILTON.

WILLIAM HAMILTON, d. in 1782, having made his will Sept. 17, 1778. In this he mentions his wife Jean, and the following children:

 i. Hugh.
 ii. William.
 iii. John.
 iv. Robert.
 v. Ann, m. James Wallace.
 vi. James, " now in the army."
 vii. Nancy, m. Thomas Wade.
The executor of the estate was his son Hugh.

McCullough.

Archibald McCullough, of West Hanover, d. prior to 1792, leaving a wife Agnes, and issue :
 i. Archibald.
 ii. John.
 iii. William.

Miller.

Jacob Miller, of Middle Paxtang, d. prior to 1801, leaving a wife Susanna, and issue:
 i. Jacob, m. Margaret ———.
 ii. Daniel, m. Gertroot [Gertrude] ———.
 iii. John.
 iv. Adam, m. Mary ———; reside in Harrisburg.
 v. Susanna, m. Hervey Creek.
 vi. Margaret, m. Joseph Cogley.
 vii. Elizabeth, m. Philip Ettinger.

McQueen.

John McQueen, of Derry, d. prior to 1750.   His children were:
 i. David, d. prior and left issue :
  1. *Jane,* m. John Bayley, of Donegal.
  2. *Mary,* m. James Anderson, of Donegal.
 ii. Josiah.
 iii. Robert.

McClure.

I. John McClure, of Hanover, d. prior to 1763, leaving a wife Margery, and issue:
 i. James, m. Margaret ———.
 ii. William.
 iii. Jane.
 iv. Ann.

II. WILLIAM McCLURE, of Paxtang, d. prior to 1763; m. MARGARET
WRIGHT, daughter of Robert Wright. They had issue:

  i. Captain *Robert.*
  ii. Rebecca, m. Peter Sturgeon.
  iii. Mary, m. Samuel Russell.
  iv. Sarah, m. David Riddle.
  v. Margaret, m. James Crain.
  vi. Jean.

-------------◄●►-------------

IN THE FRENCH AND INDIAN WAR.

[The following account is from a paper in Col. James Burd's handwriting. Endorsed on the back is "Acc't of Disbursements in View-
ing & Laying out the Road leading to ye Ohio, 1755." This was the
so-called "Braddock's Road." It will be noticed that two Armstrongs
are mentioned, Joseph and John. Who was Joseph Armstrong?]

Acco't of Disbursements by George Croghan, John Armstrong,
  James Burd, William Buchannan, & Adam Hoops, Hewing and
  laying out the Roads to Youghiogains & the camp at Wills Creek:

	£	s.	d.
1755, March—			
To our expenses at Francis Campbell's at Shippensburg at our meeting to settle the time to sett upon the service,	1	13	7
April 1st—			
To our expenses at Anthony Thompson's when we were going out,	2	10	7
To provisions purchased of Allen McLean the commissary at the camp,	4	17	6
To George McSwain, one of the Blaisers for 6 days' work,	0	18	0
To John Enlos, Pilott,	1	7	0
To our expenses at Anthony Thompson's on our return,	1	5	0
To one Carrying horse from Anthony Thompson's 25 days 2s per day,	2	10	0
To three of Geo. Croghan's 25 days at 2s per day,	7	10	0
To two men 25 days at 2s 6d per day for driving ye horses,	6	5	0
To 10 Galls of Rum at 6s 9d per Gall.,	3	7	6
To 10 Galls of whisky at 3s per Gal.,	1	10	0
To 69 ℔ of Gammons,	1	11	7
To 16 ℔ of chees,	0	6	3

To 6 ℔ of Butter, ...	0	2	6
To 259 ℔ of flour, ...	1	10	0
To 2 ℔ of sugar, ...	0	1	3
To 1 ℔ of poudder, ...	0	3	0
To 2 ℔ of lead, ...	0	1	0
To 2 Caggs for the Rum & Whisky, ...	0	5	0
To 3 days of a man which turned back, ...	0	7	1
To 2 days of a horse that was lost & afterwards found, .	0	1	0
To Mr. Hoops, Expenses coming from ye camp, ...	0	10	0
To John Pollock, Pilott, ...	2	10	0
To two men for Blaising 25 days at 2s 6d per day, . . .	6	5	0
To two horses 25 days at 2s per day, ...	5	0	0
To Mr. Buchanan's Expenses to Caneogeg, ...	0	3	6
To Sundrys bought of John Smith for the Journey, . .	0	16	6
To 19½ ℔ of loaf sugar at 1s 6d per ℔, ...	1	9	3
To one man for Blaising 2 days at 3s per day, ...	0	6	0
To whisky for ye hands at ye camp, ...	0	2	6
To a small cagg bought at the Camp, ...	0	2	6
To 6 ℔ 7 oz. loaf suger bt. at ye camp at 2s per ℔., . . .	0	16	0
To 3 Gall's of Rum bt. of Jos. Simons at ye camp, . . .	1	4	0
To our Expenses at Collier's Tavern, Maryland, ...	0	9	6
To 2 men for 3 days Blaising, ...	0	15	0
To John Walker for whisky, ...	0	7	6
To expenses at Mrs. Tusty's, ...	0	4	8
To Mr. Buchannan's Expenses coming home, ...	0	3	2
To cash for sundry small articles, ...	0	2	7
To John Walker, Pilott, ...	1	7	0
To one Blaiser, ...	1	0	0
To our expenses at Mrs. Tusty's, ...	1	0	0
To Sundrys per J. Armstrong's acc't, ...	2	10	9
To J. Armstrong's Expenses to Carlisle, ...	0	3	4
To Dolton sent Express upon the arrivall of ye Commiss'r to Mr. Croghan to ye camp, ...	2	12	9
To 2 chain carriers 28 days at 2s 6d per day, ...	6	10	
To our Expenses at Carlisle in settling the acco'ts & making out the Returns, ...	1	9	5
	£76	2	10
The Commiss'rs Expenses viz: George Croghan, Adam Hoops, Joseph Armstrong and James Burd, upon our Return from the viewing ye roads omitted when this account was made to ye Governor, ...	11	16	6

John Armstrong has been out on this service, ... 28 days
James Burd, ... 28 days
William Buchannan, ... 25 do
George Croghan, ... 25 do
Adam Hoops, ... 25 do

NOTES AND QUERIES.—CVII.

COBEA.—Capt. Samuel Cobea, of the Revolutionary army, resided on Marsh creek, in York county, in 1787. What is known of his subsequent history. How was he related to Capt. John Cobea, of the Second regiment of the Pennsylvania Line?

McFARLAND.—Col. James McFarland died in Mifflin county, November 16, 1830, at an advanced age. He was an early settler in Kishacoquillas Valley, and represented Mifflin county in the Legislature. We have examined the recent "History of Mifflin county," but find no mention made of him—not even in the list of representatives. And yet few men in the Juniata region were more prominent in public affairs than Colonel McFarland.

GENEALOGICAL NOTES.

BARTLETT.

JOHN BARTLETT, d. prior to August, 1761, leaving sisters as follows:
    i. Rachel, m. William Mills.
    ii. Mary, m. Matthew Chambers.
    iii. Bathsheba, m. John Baily.
    iv. Rebecca.
    v. Martha.
What is known of these families?

BARCLAY.

WILLIAM BARCLAY, d. prior to 1761, at that time his widow Esther being the wife of ——— McIntire. William Barclay's children were:
    i. John.
    ii. Hugh.

  iii. Stephen.
  iv. Joseph.
  v. Mary.
  vi. Margaret.
  vii. Martha.
  viii. Esther.

————

CRAIG.

 JOHN CRAIG, d. prior to September, 1760, and left issue:
  i. Sarah, m. David Allen.
  ii. Mary.
  iii. Isabel.
  iv. John.

————

FOSTER.

 DAVID FOSTER, of Derry, d. prior to 1765, leaving a wife Catharine, and children as follows:
  i. John, d. in 1765, leaving a wife and children, as follows:
   1. *David*, b. 1750.
   2. *Catharine*, b. 1752.
   3. *Margaret*, b. 1755.
   4. *John*, b. 1757.
  ii. Robert.
  iii. David.
  iv. Joseph.
  v. William.
  vi. Anne.
  vii. James.
  viii. Mary.

————

GILLILAND.

 HUGH GILLILAND, d. prior to 1751, leaving a wife Anna, and children:
  i. Robert.
  ii. Mary.
  iii. Eleanor.

 These were above fourteen years of age, and chose their uncle, John Gilliland, their guardian.
  iv. Ann.
  v. Elizabeth.
  vi. Agnes.
  vii. Hugh.

GEIGER.

CHRISTIAN GEIGER, of Warwick township, Lancaster county, d. prior to 1779, leaving issue:

    i. George.
    ii. William, d. prior to 1779; and left issue.
    iii. Elizabeth, m. Peter Leib.
    iv. Margaret, m. John Bender.
    v. Anna-Maria, m. George Unger.
    vi. Christina, m. Michael Wyland.

A WHITE SAVAGE.

[The following deposition concerning the unprovoked murder of two Indians by a white savage, which occurred in Western Pennsylvania prior to the Revolution, comes to us from New York. Perchance our friends, Isaac Craig or William M. Darlington, Esqs., can give us some information as to the facts here presented. If true, it is a piece of cruelty which puts to shame that of the savage red men.]

Bedford, ss :

Richard Brown, being duly sworn according to Law, deposeth and Saith that Mathey Haley, an Indentred Servant, belonging to him, the said Brown, had been run away for some time, that he went in pursuit of him, and came up with him near Redstone Fort about Two Months after he went off; that as he was bringing him home the said Mathew Haley made the following Declaration, falling upon his knees at the time of doing it:

I have done a very bad action to you, but I have done much worse since I have been away from you. I have killed Two Indians. This Deponent charged him with telling lies, threatened to beat him, and asked him what he could intend by such a Story; but he the s'd Haley persisted in the same Declaration, making solemn protestations of the truth of it, saying also that if he must be hanged for it he could not help it, for it lay so heavy on his Conscience he could not conceal it. This Deponent then asked him how he did it and what could induce him to it. Haley answered, that after he had escaped from Andrew McConnell he overtook the Two Indians that had taken him up, and brought him into Colonel Croghan in company with another Indian Man and Woman, that they received him kindly, gave him a Tomhawk, and a pair of new Mocosons and promised that they would not take him to the White People again, that the third Indian man the Morning after he (Haley) joined them gave

him a Bridle and told him he must go with the other two and steal
horses from the White People, that they traveled that day to the
Kittanning, where the Indians burnt the doors of a house to get the
Locks and Hinges; that next day they traveled into the Woods and
towards evening they killed a Bear and a Deer; that next day they
encamped and made a Fire and cut the deer into small, thin pieces
and stuck them upon small sticks around the Fire to barbecue; that
one of the Indians stayed by the Fire to cook the kettle and take care
of the meat, and that the other Indian and he, the said Haley, went
some distance off to strip Bark to make cover for their sleeping place;
that the Indian had cut a Tree round at the upper part, and he the
said Haley was cutting it at the Lower part, when the Indian got a
kind of Handspike to force the Bark off with, and when he was employed about that and stooping to it, he the said Haley struck his
Tomhawk into his head and repeated the Blow a great many times
'till he was quite dead and the Blood spurted all over his Arm and
the Tomhawk, so that he was afraid to return to the fire where the
other Indian was lest he should discover it; but to conceal as well as
he possibly could, he thrust his Arm and Tomhawk into a Roll of
Bark they had taken from a small Tree, and carried it in that manner
to the Fire, that he laid the Bark down behind, the Indian was then
stirring some Flour in a tin Cup over the Kettles, that the Indian
looked round, smiled and made some signs of Approbation at the
Bark he had brought, and turned about again to mind his Cooking;
that then he the said Haley Drew the Tomhawk out of the Bark and
struck it into the head of this Indian also and repeated the blow 'till
he was motionless; that he was immediately seized with such Fear
that he could not stay there, but that he took a Tomhawk, Two
Powder horns, a Rifle Gun, Two Blankets and a Britch Cloth, a Brass
Kettle and a tin Cup, and hid the other Gun and Tomhawk and some
other things in a hollow Chestnut Tree about half way between
where the Indians lay, (which was about the distance of 150 yards
apart): that he tied up what things he chose to take in one of the
Blankets and then set off and traveled Eight Days without seeing
the face of a living Person and at last fell in upon one John Miller,
who lives about five miles from Fort Pitt up the Allegheny River;
that Miller's people concealed him two days, for which he gave them
the Kettle, the tin Cup and the Britchcloth; that he grew tired of
carrying the rest of the things and threw them away, all but a Gun,
a Powder horn, and a blanket of which he made Leggins.

These Circumstances induced the Deponent to believe there might
be some truth in what he told; he therefore left him the said Haley
in the Care of another person, and went down to Fort Pitt to acquaint

Coll. Croghan and enquire if there was any account of the murder there; there had been no Complaint made of it at that time, and Coll. Croghan did not believe it; but he this Deponent had still some suspicion that it was true; he therefore went to John Miller's where Haley said he had left the things, to see if that part of his story was right and took Andrew McConnell along with him; that McConnell asked Miller if he had seen anything of Brown's Servant, for that his master was come and that he (McConnell) was like to suffer by his having escaped from him; Miller and his wife both denied then having seen him, but said that Capt. Montour had told them that he had gone up the Allegheny and that the Indians who brought him in were but a little way before him. McConnell told them that he was sure Montour had not told them so, for he had spoke with Montour himself, on which this Deponent s'd to Mrs. Miller, I know who told you so, it was my servant himself when he returned to your house, and left a Brass Kettle, a tin cup and a Britch cloth with you; but Miller and his wife solemnly denied it and offered to take a Voluntary Oath (reaching to a Bible at the same time) that they knew nothing about him; that then this deponent told them that he knew certainly that he had been at his house and had left the things mentioned; but that if they would give them up he would take no further notice of them, but if they would not he would prosecute them to the full extent of the Law, on which they immediately produced and delivered them. And further this Deponent saith, that the Gun which Haley carried off from him this Deponent he Haley had given to an Indian Man, and that Coll. Croghan got it again for him, and that Haley had a Rifle when he took him up which is the same he now delivers with him and that the Kettle and Tin Cup are the same he got from John Miller, which he owned Haley had left with him.

 (Signed)   RICHARD BROWN.
Sworn and subscribed before me the 7th of September, 1771.
 (Signed)   AR. ST. CLAIR.

NOTES AND QUERIES.—CVIII.

ALLISON.—Richard Allison, of Lancaster county, removed to the Juniata Valley prior to the Revolution. Of his children, Mary m. John Allison, son of John Allison, probably a cousin; a daughter m. James Sterrett, and they are the ancestors of the Sterrett family of Kishacoquillas Valley; and John, who was a ruling elder in Donegal Presbyterian church and served as a justice of the common pleas court for Lancaster county. What is known concerning the descendants of these families?

INTERESTING CORRESPONDENCE.

The following letter from Major Jasper Ewing, then on military duty at Fort Pitt, now Pittsburgh, to his uncle, Judge Jasper Yeates, has never been published. It is valuable in connection with the history of Western Pennsylvania.

FORT PITT, *Aug. 26, 1777.*

HOND. SIR: Scarce a day passes without some Instance of Savage Barbarity. Nothing but an Expedition in their Country will induce them to listen to Reason. Every Preparation is making for it & the only obstruction that we shall meet with is want of Flour. The General proposes to engage the men for 6 months from the first day of September next & has made a demand of 1,500 men from the Colony of Virginia. The remainder is to be taken from the Counties of Westmoreland and Bedford.

Among all the numerous Tribes of Indians the Delawares are the only Nation firm to our interests. They left a Family here as Hostages for their Friendship & Seem in every way heartily attached to us. Present my duty to Aunt, & Love to all the Children, & am, Sir,

Your much hon'd Nephew,

J. EWING.

Jasper Yeates, Esq., per favor of Col. Steele.

GENEALOGICAL NOTES.

GINGRICH.

JOHN GINGRICH, of Warwick township, d. prior to 1772; his wife Barbara prior to 1785. They had issue:

    i. Christian.
    ii. David.
    iii. Emanuel.
    iv. Josephine, m. David Forney.
    v. Henry.
    vi. Jonathan.
    vii. George.
    viii. Elizabeth, m. Leonard Smith.
    ix. Benjamin.

From which branch does the Dauphin county family spring?

GRAHAM.

SAMUEL GRAHAM, of Hanover, d. prior to 1772, leaving a wife and children as follows :
    i. William, b. 1741.
    ii. Mary, b. 1743.
    iii. Jane, b. 1745.
    iv. Martha, b. 1747.
    v. Ann, b. 1750.
    vi. Samuel, b. 1752.
    vii. John, b. 1754.

HOWER.

CHRISTOPHER HOWER, of Paxtang; d. prior to 1784, for at that date his widow was the wife of Franz Peter Lorentz. The Hower children were :
    i. John.
    ii. Catharine.
    iii. Jacob.
    iv. Susanna.

MEESE.

PHILIP MEESE, d. prior to 1762, leaving a wife Louisa, and children as follows :
    i. George.
    ii. Christian.
    iii. Barbara.
    iv. Casper.
    v. Philip.
    vi. Paul.
    vii. Balzer.

STEDMAN.

RICHARD STEDMAN, d. prior to 1776, leaving issue :
    i. John.
    ii. Sarah, m. John Cox.
    iii. Ann, m. Samuel Brown.
    iv. James.
    vi. Esther.
    vii. Susanna.
    viii. Benjamin.

SNODGRASS.

WILLIAM SNODGRASS, d. prior to 1763, leaving a wife Sarah, and children as follows:
    i. Robert.
    ii. Samuel.
    iii. James.
    iv. Sarah.

STEWART.

JOHN STEWART, of Hanover, d. prior to 1763, leaving a wife Frances, and children as follows:
    i. William.
    ii. Mary.
    iii. Lazarus.
    iv. Jane.
    v. George.
    vi. James.
    vii. John.

TWEED.

ROBERT TWEED d. prior to 1771, leaving a wife Agnes, and the following children:
    i. John.
    ii. Robert.
    iii. Margaret, m. James Galbraith.
    iv. James.
    v. Archibald.
    vi. Joseph.
    vii. William.
    viii. Elizabeth.

TATE.

JOSEPH TATE, of Donegal, d, prior to 1779, leaving a wife Margaret, and children as follows:
    i. Matthew.
    ii. Jane, m. James Anderson.
    iii. Adam.
    iv. John.
    v. Margaret, m. David McQueen.
    vi. Sarah.
    vii. Benjamin.

WILLSON.

I. JOSEPH WILLSON, of Hanover, d. prior to 1769. His children then living were:
  i. James.
  ii. William.
  iii. Hugh.
  iv. Rosanna, m. ——— McAllister.
  v. Jane, m. John Walker, of Derry.

II. WILLIAM WILLSON, of Paxtang, d. prior to 1762, leaving a wife Eleanor, and children as follows:
  i. John.
  ii. Jane.
  iii. Martha.

The executors of the estate were Thomas Rutherford and John Willson.

TROUBLES OF EARLY SETTLERS IN YORK COUNTY.—I.

[The following facts in relation to the early settlements west of the Susquehanna are from 'Squire Evans, of Columbia. They are of great interest and value, and embrace information not heretofore in print.]

Prior to 1727 the Penns gave no patent for land west of the Susquehanna river, until finding that the Proprietary of Maryland determined to fortify his claim to all the land west of the river, and as far up as the mouth of the Codorus creek by throwing his Roman Catholic subjects into the rich valleys, and maintain the occupation of the land thus violently obtained by force of arms. The Penns, in anticipating this manoeuvre, first had the land surveyed as a manor in 1722, with the consent of the Indians, who had not then relinquished or sold their right, in the hope that this movement would prevent settlers from moving upon the land. In this both parties were disappointed, for in 1727 several families moved from the lower part of Chester county into "Conojohela Valley" (four miles below Wrightsville). These, it seems, maltreated and abused the Indians most outrageously, when the Proprietaries of Pennsylvania had them ejected; and James Patterson, an Indian trader, who resided in Conestoga Manor, was given permission to occupy a portion of this land for a pasture for his pack horses.

Finding, however, that the Marylanders intended to occupy this section, the Penns decided to promote settlements west of the river; but instead of encouraging the Scotch-Irish Presbyterians to settle there, they sent some Quakers and non-resident Germans, who were not the kind of settlers to resist the encroachments upon their land by the Roman Catholics of Maryland, who rode "ruff-shod" over them. Had permission been given to the Scotch-Irish of then Donegal to settle upon this land a somewhat different reception would have been accorded the Maryland outlaws.

In March, 1732, Thomas Cresap was sent up in advance, by the Maryland authorities, and made a settlement three miles and a half below John Hendricks. On the 29th day of January, 1733, John Hendricks and a few others made a feeble effort to get Cresap away. On the 5th day of February, 1733, Robert Gordon, Esq., one of the justices of the Provincial Court of Maryland, issued a warrant for the arrest of the parties supposed to have been concerned in the attack upon Cresap.

On the 19th day of February, 1733, Robert Gordon directed the following missive to the high sheriff of Anne Arundel county:

"MARYLAND, *ss:*

"*To Mr. Nicholas Manubbin, High Sheriff of Anne Arundel county:*

"Herewith I send you the bodies of John Hindrek and Joshua Minshall, Brought before me by the Sheriff of Baltimore County, as being accessorys in the riot committed upon Thomas Crissop, of Baltimore county, on the night of the 29th day of January last, Commanding you to take them into custodie and them safe keep till they be further examined and for so doing this shall be your warrant. Given under my hand and seal this 19th day of Feb'ry, 1733.

"ROBERT GORDON."

The foregoing was followed by a precept from the Provincial Council of Maryland, especially directed against Joshua Minshall as the principal offender:

"MARYLAND, *ss:*

"Whereas, it appears to us the subscribers, members of his Ld. pps. Honourable Council met in council at the city of Annapolis the 21st of February, 1733, that Joshua Minshall hath fomented divers Riots and Disturbances, and frequently disparaged the title to the Right Honourable the Lord Proprietary of Maryland to the said Province; and hath given out threatening & menacing speeches that he would shoot his Lordship or any person who should dare to act by virtue of any authority derived from his Lordship against the Peace.

These are therefore in his Lordship's name to will and require you to take into your custody the body of him the said Minshall and him safely to keep until he shall be discharged by due course of law, for which this shall be your sufficient warrant. Dated at Annapolis this 21st day of February, A. D. 1733.

SAM'L OGLE,
W. P. WARD,
BENJ. TASKER,
PHILIP LEE,
EDW'D JENINGS.

"*To Mr. Nicholas Manubbin, High Sheriff of Anne Arundel County.*"

Minshall and Hendricks hurriedly sent forward the following letter to Pennsylvania:

" ANNAPOLIS, *Feb. ye 22d, 1733–4.*

" HONOURABLE PROPRIETOR:

" Wee, your Tenants, Joshua Minshall and John Hendricks both of Langkester county, now lyeing in the Goall of Annapolis, being brought down by a Provinciall warrant and Strictly examined before Governour and Councell, the orders is wee are to be close confined until such time as we have a Delivery by a Due course of law. Wee are but Strangers here and as we have Endeavoured to stand and maintain your rights wee humbly begg your Honour will be pleased to send us a line with your candid advice which way to proceed or behave, for wee are here amongst our Enemys and noe friend to depend upon in any manner of respect but Intirely like unto soe many lost Sheep amongst a parcell of ravenous Wolfs.

" We have proceeded to the uttermost of our judgments, and does not intend to proceed farther until such time as wee hear from your Honour which we take to be our Protector in that which is just. Wee hear send you our Committments to satisfy your Honour how and after what manner we are detained here.

" The Messenger being just agoeing of that wee had noe time to write any more, but with Sincerity do subscribe our selves your Honours most true and Loyall Tenants.

" JOSHUA MINSHALL,
" JOHN HENDRICKS."

This letter was probably sent to the Governor of Pennsylvania by a messenger through Samuel Blunston at Wright's Ferry, who sent remittances and answered Minshall's letter. They again wrote, this time to Blunston:

" ANNAPOLIS, *March ye 10, 1733-34.*

" FRIEND SAMUEL: This comes to accqt thee yt all are in good health and is in close confinement; still we could have Beale enough but those yt would Beale us is afraid to give any offense to the government, wee are advised to pet. ym but are not willing to submit to ym or any of their laws without further advice. We have had no letters as yett butt what wee received from thee. In our last to thee wee mentioned yt wee sent to our Proprietor but we are Dubious of our letters being Delivered, for the Bearer being a liver here and their being soe deceitfull that we scarce know how to behave or yett express our words. Wee endeavour to be as frugall as may be but the place being so extravagant yt for one maile a day are obbliged to pay three shillings. Such a place you never see. Wee cannot believe but they use us soe oute of perfect Spite and malice. ffriend Onions being now in towne told us what wee had a mind to write he would give it a safe passage. Wee desire thee would write to us by his man and he will directly send it to us, for he comes back the same week, which will be as speedy a passage as thee can have. The confinement is very disagreeable. Wee are nineteen days here. Wee are informed yt wee shall have noe hearing until the Provincial court meets which will be in May next. Wee are afraid the warm weather with close Confinement will prejudice our healths being so many in number that wee scarce have room to stirr; having noe more to add att present wee conclude with our love to thee and all our friends and neighbours in generall.

" Written in the Goall of Unhappiness and Delivered to friend Onions.　　　　　　　　　　　　" JOSHUA MINSHALL,
　　　　　　　　　　　　　　　　　　　　　　" JOHN HENDRICKS."
" *To Samuel Blunston.*"

NOTES AND QUERIES.—CIX.

THE ELDER JEFFERSON.—The following brief notice of the death of the elder Jefferson is from the *Telegraph* of August 7, 1832:

" Died on Saturday last [August 4th] in this borough, Joseph Jefferson, Sen., known for many years as one of the greatest comedians in America, aged 62 years.

THE ADMISSION OF MISSOURI.—From a letter written by Gen. James Wallace, then a member of Congress, to the wife of Col. Robert Clark, we have the following data concerning the proposed admission of Missouri as a State:

" As to the affairs of the nation there is little doing in our body at present. The bill for the Missouri to be admitted as a new State into the Union is now discussing in the Senate. The friends of slave-holding have got the bill coupled with the Province of Maine, in the view to introduce slavery in the State of Missouri. They will doubt-less be able to attain their object and some are of opinion in our house also; but I hope they will be disappointed, unless the Governor of the Universe sees fit to punish us for our many national iniquities, I hope we will not be saddled with so great a curse. The members of the slave-holding States are using every strategem for the spread of slavery. The members from Pennsylvania will give a unanimous vote excepting Mr. Baldwin, of Pittsburgh. He will, it is expected, vote for spreading the evil of slavery."

INDIAN NAMES GIVEN MISSIONARIES.

Contribution to Aboriginal Philology.

The following paper was prepared by the Rev. John C. Pyrlæus, the well-known missionary among the Indians, and Mohawk scholar. It is written partly in German and partly in English.

Tgirhitontie (a row of trees) was the name given to Bishop A. G. Spangenberg. He received it on his journey to Onondaga, in 1745, and it was the name of an old chief of the tribe of the Bear. (Och-quaeri.)

Anousseraeheri (on the pumpkin) was the name given to the Rev. David Zeisberger, on the same journey. It belongs to the tribe of the Turtle. (Anawaragoa.)

Hajingonis (one who spins tobacco or makes twists) was the name given to Rev. Joseph Shebosch, on the same journey.

Tganniatarecheo (between two seas) was the name given to Rev. John C. Pyrlæus, in the year 1748, and belongs to the tribe of the Wolf. (Oquaeho.)

Gallichwio (a good message) was the name given to Bishop J. C. F. Cammerhoff, at Bethlehem, April 15, 1748, as the assistant of Tgir-hitontie, (Spangenberg.) It was the name of a chief of the Oneidas in Anajot of the tribe of the Turtle.

Ganachragejat (the first man or leader of a company). This name was given to the Rev. Martin Mack, April 15, 1748. It belongs to the tribe of the Turtle.

Anuntschi (the head) was the name given to Bishop Nathaniel Seidel, and belongs to the tribe of the Turtle.

Tgarihontie (a messenger) was the name given to Bishop John von Watteville on the occasion of the renewal of the treaty with the Five Nations in Philadelphia, July 6, 1749, Bishops Spangenberg, Cammerhoff, and Seidel being present. This name, too, belongs to the tribe of the Turtle.

Z'higochgoharo was the name given to Rev. C. H. Rauch, in Shamoko; and

Rachwistoni, to Anton Schmidt.

Ziguras was the name of Conrad Weiser, until July, 1743, when he received another in Onondaga, namely *Tharochiawacu.*

Gannerachtaeheri (on the leaves) was the name given to Richard Peters, secretary in Philadelphia.

Ganagaratochqua was the name given to Conrad Weiser's brother-in-law, Brandt, who kept a tavern at Fort Hunter.

In reference to Conrad Weiser there is the following note:

"Conrad Weiser came to America with his parents, in the reign of Queen Anne. His father was a blacksmith and lived on the Mohawk river, near the Mohawk Indians. He sent his son Conrad to reside with an Indian named Tajuajanont, in order that he might learn the Indian language. Conrad distinguished himself amongst the Indians to such a degree that he obtained great influence over them, and, in his twenty-sixth year, was adopted into the family of the Turtles, which is considered the most noble."

The following note in English is also interesting:

"At a treaty held at Lancaster with the Six Nations and the Governor of Pennsylvania, and the deputies from Maryland and Virginia, because they got it by conquest; for they conquered the Indian nations living on Cohongoronta or Cohongoruton (Susquehanna or Potomac rivers) and on the back part of the great mountains of Virginia, the Ganajaehsaehrohne.

Gachnawasrohne, (N. B.—These are *Canai.*)

Tohoairoehrohne, and

Gannutskinoehrohne."

The last page contains the following in German:

"The Nantikok or Sganiateratichrohne method of numbering:

Killi—one.

Filli—two.

Sabo—three.

Nano—four.

Turo—five.

Woro—six.

Wollango—seven.
Hecki—eight.
Collengo—nine.
Ta—ten.

"The Nantikoks (as they call themselves) passed by Shamoko on the 21st of May, 1741, on their way from Maryland in ten canoes.

"The Mohigans call the Nantikoks '*Otajachgo*,' from *Tajachquan*, which means a tree bridge across the river, probably because the Nantikoks do not like to go into the water, but are accustomed to cut down trees as a pathway across streams."   JOHN W. JORDAN.

THE CUMBERLAND VALLEY.

GENEALOGICAL NOTES OF EARLY SETTLERS.

DUNWOODY [DINWIDDIE.]

THOMAS DUNWOODY, of Peters township, d. July, 1782, leaving a wife Agnes, and children :
    i. James.
    ii. Ann.
    iii. Sarah.
    iv. Agnes.

A brother probably, Samuel Dunwoody, was executor.

STEEL.

The Rev. JOHN STEEL, of Carlisle, d. May, 1779, leaving issue:
    i. Lydia, m. Robert Sample.
    ii. John.
    iii. Elzabeth, m. —— McKinley.
    iv. Margaret.
    v. Mary.
    vi. Sarah.
    vii. Robert.
    viii. Andrew.
    ix. Jean, deceased, m. and had *Andrew* and *Steel* McLean.

BEATTY.

I. JOHN BEATTY, of Rye township, d. in October, 1790, leaving a wife Margaret, and children:
    i. Andrew.
    ii. John, of Greenwood, d. February, 1795.

    iii. James.
    iv. Robert.
     v. Elizabeth, m. ——— Marshall.
    vi. Alexander.
    vii. Samuel.
    viii. Joseph.
    ix. William.

II. SAMUEL BEATTY, ensign in the Second regiment, U. S. A., made his will September 24, 1791, at "Miami River, fifty miles from the mouth." It was probated at Carlisle February 11, 1794, Alexander Beatty being administrator. What is known of this officer?

ELLIOTT.

JAMES ELLIOTT d. at Carlisle in 1795. The legatees named in his will are given in full. He states that he is "from near Maguire's Bridge, County Fermanagh, Ireland."
Wife Mary, now in Ireland.
Brother John's son William, now in Ireland.
Cousins James Brownlie, William, Nancy, and Archibald Elliott, all of Ireland.
William Lyon, of Carlisle.
Samuel Weakley, sisters of whom are married to David McCurdy, John Dillon, David King, Nathaniel Gillespie, and Stephen Groves.
William, Thomas, Edward, Robert, and Nathaniel Weakley.
Widow Arthurs, of Carlisle, and her daughter Elizabeth.
Brother John Elliott.
James Elliott, of Middleton, Cumberland county.
Sidney Johnston, of Carlisle.
Sidney Case, of Chamberstown.
Margaret Elliott, of Middleton.
Samuel Liggatt, of Cumberland county.
William Ferguson, of Hamilton township.
William Brotherton.
John Elliott, of county Fermanagh, Ireland.
What is known of this testator, and how related to the legatees?

WHITESIDES.

JAMES WHITESIDES, of Carlisle, d. prior to 1761, as in December o that year his widow was the wife of John Giles. The children were
     i. John.
    ii. Samuel.
    iii. William.

    iv. James.
     v. Ayles, m. Thomas McGee.
    vi. Margaret.
    vii. Elizabeth.
    viii. Ann.
Ralph Whitesides was one of the executors.

BUCHANAN.

ANDREW BUCHANAN, d. in April, 1774, leaving issue:
    i. William.
    ii. John.
    iii. Catharine, m. Moses Boyd.
    iv. Jean, m. James Gilkison.
    v. Sarah.
    vi. Mary.

THE EFFECT OF WASHINGTON'S DEATH.

The following letters are interesting so far as they show the feeling of the people of America upon the death of him, who "was first in war, first in peace, and first in the hearts of his countrymen." The first is from Gen. Samuel Dale, then a member of the Assembly from Northumberland county; as to the writer of the second letter, which wholly relates to "G. W.," we have no information.

[Samuel Dale to Col. Robert Clark.]

LANCASTER, *January 7th, 1800.*

DEAR SIR: This day, by order of General Hand, all shops are closed—workmen of every kind are to refrain from all manner of occupations, and the day to be observed as a day of mourning and deep humiliation. A solemn procession is to take place at the hour of 12 in memory of our late celebrated General George Washington; both Houses are requested to attend.

We are not likely to agree in the mode or manner of electing our Electors; the Senate have passed a bill for the purpose, dividing the State into districts; the House of Representatives negatived the bill and in their turn they have sent us a bill to elect in one general election. On Monday next we are to take their bill in like manner. If so, the matter rests with the Governor to issue his proclamation to the sheriffs of the several counties directing them to hold an election agreeable to the former laws. On this ground there may be some reason to conclude that Congress may dispute the validity of our election.

The accounts from Hamburg are not favorable; several of their most famous trading houses have shut up. I am informed that Baltimore and perhaps New York will suffer amazingly through their failure.

We are not able to aacertain what is the fate of the Duke of York, he must have fled, or is a French prisoner by this time. Field Marshal Suwarrow is a fugitive in the mountains of Italy. After his defeat we hear little of him; he had an opportunity of flying, and he has made use of it.

Our Governor in answer to the address presented to him from the citizens of Philadelphia, enumerated all the several grades of opponents to Republicanism. The classing old tories, apostate old whigs and office hunters in one group have roused the indignation and resentment of our Federal gentry to the utmost degree.

In the House of Representatives, on the answer to the Governor's address which he presented to both houses on his being sworn into office, they divided nearly equal, and a warm debate, ensued. In the course of the debate, a Mr. Blair from Huntingdon county moved a substitute of the most inflammatory nature, heaping abuse on the Governor for the several answers to addresses. The Republicans are most numerous in the House of Representatives, therefore the Answer was agreed to and the substitute was rejected.

I am, dear sir, with every sentiment of respect, your friend and Humble Servant, SAMUEL DALE.

To Coll. Robert Clark, Chillisquaque.

[*John Hutchison to Andrew Hutchison.*]

HARRISBURG, *Feb. 22d, 1800.*
Saturday Morning.

DEAR SIR: I wrote you by Mr. James Storey, of Warrior Run, which probably may not have come to your hand before you receive this. I shall make no apologies for obtruding this upon you, but inform you that this is a fast day or day of mourning with us, as I expect it is with you. Mr. Snowden is to preach a sermon this afternoon, suitable to the occasion, which I intend to hear. Whether he will deify G. Washington, I know not, but from the eulogiums pronounced by several of the public panegyrists who have, in different parts of the U. S. become very vociferous in his praises, and from the great number of funeral processions with which he has been honoured since his decease, we have reason to fear that numbers of people think there is something divine in him. I think it was very proper for the Congress to manifest their concern and grief by going in mourning, especially as they represented the whole nation ; but the various processions, I apprehend, could have no meaning in them, unless those who projected them were impressed with the belief that G. W. is omnipresent; for what else can be inferred from the carrying an empty coffin, than that they supposed he was in it and knew of the honor done him by his obsequious admirers? It must be acknowledged that greater honours should be done to his memory than any of his contemporaries; but an enlightened nation ought, while they pay him every tribute of respect, compatible with the principles of Christianity, to avoid any ceremonies that savour in the least of heathenism. The first Jupiter of the heathens was nothing more than an eminent and illustrious king of the Island of Crete, until his deification by those who looked upon him as a divinity after his death. Other heathen nations imitated the Cretans, by paying divine honours to their deceased kings, and therefore every nation had its Jupiters. The inferior Deities originated in similar ways until their numbers increased to thousands. And, if Americans proceed in this manner, they may, in a few centuries have a multiplicity of gods as well as the heathen who were ignorant of the true God. General Washington has rendered his character conspicuous by his great, prudent and wise procedure, and his achievements will transmit his name unsullied to the latest generation, without any divine honours.

I am, with respect, your affectionate brother.

JOHN HUTCHISON.

Mr. Andrew Hutchison, Washington, honoured by Col. Clark.

TROUBLES OF EARLY SETTLERS IN YORK COUNTY.—II.

Minshall and Hendricks wrote a letter to Thomas Penn of a similar import but after they jointly signed the letter, the following was added:

" I thought proper to add something further as concerning my committment. Some time last July, to the best of my memory the second day of the same Instant I was Committed by Crissop and Remained a prisoner during seven or eight days and now being taken by one Guinn and my name not being mentioned in the Warrant; this same Guinn is a man of ill repute, he has been whipt and pillowed in Seycill County; if such as them are fitt persons to be putt in any office to disturb Honest men from the welfare of their families itt seems strange to me and I doe belive will doe soe to all men yt hears of itt; but however as for what we wrongfully Suffer by these Kind of people wee shall entirely committ yt to thee who is a better judge in those affairs then wee can pretend to bee. Soe to Conclude wee subscribe as before. JOSHUA MINSHALL."

" *To Thos. Penn.*"

"ANNAPOLIS GOAL, *May ye 6th, 1734.*

"HONOURABLE PROPRIETOR: Upon the 5th of this Instant Thomas Crissop came down here to the Governour with a full Packett relating to him yt there is Daily a number of Scotch-Irish which lyes in Ambush for him to the quantity of one hundred and fifty, lyeing about Fences, soe yt he dare not bide att home for fear of his life. This wee had from his owne mouth, for he came to the Goal Door Semingly with great friendship to us, but wee imagined he came on some other Design which wee found to be as we supposed, for he Endeavoured to pick what he could from us, but we regarded not what he said, but told him as he had before disturbed us yt he had no business to disturb us here as wee were in custody; he told us yt he had more business here than wee had; wee then replied and told him if he had his desserts yt this place was fitter for him or there were a worse place to be gott; he then finding wee would not aquest to his desire he went off in great anger and is still in town. Upon ye last of Aprill there was to men committed to New Castle County goal owne Thomas Rothwell and Jarred Rothwell, both brothers; the crime is because they will not submit themselves to be in the jurisdiction of Baltimore; when they were taken by eleven men with arms. They bound them hand and foot for all noe resistance made by them in the least—I believe James Steel will inform thee about their Land; having noe more to add at present wee conclude with our best respects to thee.   JOHN HENDRICKS &
                                            JOSHUA MINSHALL."

"ANNAPOLIS GOEL, *May ye 8th, 1734.*

"HONOURABLE PROPRIETORS: Soon after wee written the other letter of ann older date, wee were informed yt the Governour has sent letters to England, Upon ye acc't of what complaint he had from Crissop against us, as concerning this affair, but finding this Secrett of theirs outt, which they seem to keep very private but wee finding it outt by chance, we thought proper to acqt thee with; itt all from thy Respectfull tenants.   JOHN HENDRICKS,
                                            JOSHUA MINSHALL.

"Had wee been butt at Liberty, wee could inspect into more of their Spitefull proceedings, but being close confined wee have no opportunity to learn much, but what wee have by some friends yt comes Downe from our Neighbouring Parts yt has some dealings in Towne."

"Anoples gayl *ye 20 of ye 12 mo 1733.*

"Ffrd Samuel Blunston :

"These are to let thee know we were comited to prison ye 19 day of this instant by Robert Gordon; and John Hendricks is very bad with a fever and Stitches; he lise at one Peter Overs, so not in preson with mee, yet I am in a nasty stinking lousey hole, and they will not take paper money, so am like to suffer. The Governour and counsel are to sit this weke and then wee shall be examined. I have not got a copy of the warrant not yet, nor mitemus. I don my indever but am put of; I have got an extreme could; I make a shift yet to hold up; yet pray remember my kind louf to my wife and frend; hasten her up; I hope to see her in a littel time; so no more att present but kind love to all my frends in general from your friend to home.   Joshua Minshall.

"For Samuel Blunston, living in the county of Lancaster, township of Hempfield, with speed there."

This letter was evidently the first one written and it should take precedence of the others. Although it is dated 12 mo., 1734, it refers to February, 1734, as that was the 12 mo. in the Quaker calendar, March being the first. His Quaker teaching did not entirely prevent him from giving expression to his Irish indignation. It will be seen, therefore, that Minshall's arrest was made January 31, 1734.

I infer from the following letter that both Minshall and Hendricks were liberated on or before August, 1734:

"*August ye 23rd, 1734.*

"Most esteemed Friend :

"It is with no small trouble I am obliged to intimate this to thee, to let thee understand that att this very instant of time came here Thomas Crisop with seven men of the Marylanders with force of arms & took of my canno before I was aware of theyr cuming; and had not my family cum on them unawares they had laid hands on my Flat and would a taken it away, only they were prevented, the finding there was a good many people and some of the neighbors standing present at the time. Also some boards of mine they took with them; and Crisop swore in a months time he wo'd have possession of all and that the land properly belonged to him, also a man that works for me that lives by my Doore. Crisop gave him warning that he must lease the little house he was in and if he did not lease the house immediately he wo'd send all his family to prison. All that I want is to know how I shall manage in this affair in case they cum again to be trublusum or to take anything away belonging to me. I expect thee will favor me with an answer being what offer from thy friend.   John Hendrix.

"Crisop also said that he thought he might take away the Flat as well, as his neighbor Right was Devouring to take away the Ferry. The Bearer Abraham Harr was present when the came all in arms and saw how the acted.

"*To Thos. Penn.*"

Probably through the influence of Hendricks' wife, he joined the Marylander, and assisted them in various ways to drive out the German settlers. Hendricks was a carpenter and first settled in Conestoga Manor. He belonged to the Society of Friends, and was given permission to settle on the west side of the river in 1729, with the hope that he would be a valuable acquisition to the interest of the Penns. He must have been a coward, and was overawed by the aggressive force of the Marylanders, and supposed that the Penns would lose possession of all the land west of the river. Mrs. Hendricks was probably a sister of Nathan Worley, the surveyor. In order to get rid of Hendricks and his wife, Sam'l Blunston bought his land, but was forced to throw Hendricks into jail for drunkenness, &c., and had to use force to eject Mrs. Hendricks. This was in the early part of the year 1736. The family removed to Maryland and probably left the Quakers. Blunston sold his farm to Samuel Taylor, who married a daughter of John Wright about the year 1745.

Joshua Minshall was the son of Thomas and Martha Minshall, who resided in Lancashire, England. On the 25th day of July, 1715, their son John brought a certificate from Hartshaw Monthly Meeting in Lancashire to Chester Monthly Meeting in Pennsylvania. On the 14th day of August, 1718, "John Minshall of the Borrough of Chester, Cordwainer," was married to Hannah Saunders of the same place, at Chester Monthly Meeting. Joshua Minshall is the first witness to his brother John's marriage. He removed to Sadsbury, Chester county, and died there in 1736, leaving a daughter Martha. His widow Hannah married William Boyd, son of John Boyd, who came from Ballynacree, Ireland, in 1736.

It is probable that the Minshalls worked for the Barbers in Chester, who were all Cordwainers. Joshua probably came to the Susquehanna in 1726 with Robert Barber, whose daughter he married. The Minshalls were Irish Quakers. Joshua must have been sorely tried when he languished in the jail at Annapolis, and forgot to use plain and mild language. He died a few years after his imprisonment. Thomas Doyle, a tavern keeper in Lancaster borough, was his executor. Doyle's daughter who lived with Minshall was one of the legatees. It is probable that Doyle was a Quaker. He was quite wealthy and on very intimate terms with Minshall.

NOTES AND QUERIES.—CX

THE CUMBERLAND VALLEY.

Genealogical Notes of Early Settlers.

KILGORE.

JAMES KILGORE, of Newton township, d. in September, 1771, leaving a wife Elizabeth, and issue:

 i. Hugh.
 ii. Benjamin.
 iii. Joseph.
 iv. Patrick.
 v. David.
 vi. Mary.
 vii. Oliver.
 viii. Ezekiel, d. April, 1775.
 ix. John.
 x. Jonathan.
 xi. William.
 xii. Jesse.
 xiii. Robert.

ALLISON.

I. JAMES ALLISON, of Newton township, d. in March, 1770, leaving a wife Elizabeth, and issue:

 i. John.
 ii. Isabella.
 iii. Robert.
 iv. Elizabeth.

In his will he mentions his brother, Andrew, of county Tyrone, Ireland.

II. WILLIAM ALLISON, of Antrim township, d. January, 1779, leaving a wife Catharine, and issue:

 i. William.
 ii. John.
 iii. Patrick.
 iv. Agnes, m. Robt. McCrea, and had *William.*
 v. Robert.

  vi. Catharine, m. James Hendricks. He also mentions his
   grandson William Allison, nephew John Allison, and
   brother Robert Allison.

HULING.

 MARCUS HULING, SR., of Greenwood township, Cumberland county,
now Perry county, d. September, 1788, leaving issue:
  i. Marcus.
  ii. Mary, m. ——— Stewart.
  iii. Samuel.
  iv. James.
  v. Thomas.

STEWART.

 I. ARTHUR STEWART, d. July, 1750, leaving a wife Dinah, and
children:
  i. Thomas.
  ii. Arthur.

 II. ANDREW STEWART, d. April, 1754, leaving a wife and children:
  i. Moses.
  ii. Hugh.
  iii. Eliza.

 III. ROBERT STEWART, of West Pennsboro', Cumberland county,
d. March, 1785, leaving a wife Elizabeth. He mentions in his will
his grandchildren, Rachel, Elizabeth, Mary, and Moses Starr.

WALLACE.

 JOHN WALLACE, of Hopewell township, d. February, 1770, leaving
a wife Margaret, and children:
  i. William.
  ii. Ann.

THOMAS.

 GEORGE THOMAS, of Hopewell, died September, 1777, leaving issue:
  i. William.
  ii. John.
  iii. Alexander.
  iv. Thomas.
  v. Sarah, m. George Wright.

REMINISCENCES OF OLD TIMES.

THE STAGE COACHES.

Peter Pancake, who died in 1860, at an advanced age, was one of the early stage drivers in Harrisburg. He delighted in telling of his experience in staging, when turnpikes were unknown, especially west of Lancaster (the one from Philadelphia being made at an early day to Lancaster). The stage had straight bodies, with three seats, hung on the old time braces; trunks were little used then, leather saddle bags instead, containing the travelers wardrobes, these being hung over the sides or placed on the floor. Only two horses were used to draw the coach. Mr. P. said that in the spring when the roads were bad and the mud deep, it would take from the time of starting which was four o'clock in the morning until ten o'clock at night, to go from Harrisburg to Lancaster, or from Lancaster to Harrisburg. He said he had frequently stalled in the streets of Lancaster, the mud being almost up to the axle; he said it was more like wagoning than staging.

Elizabethtown was the dining place, being midway. On one occasion the passengers were all of the legal fraternity going to Lancaster to attend the Supreme Court. While Mr. Pancake was eating his dinner (having to change his horses while the passengers dined), Judge ———, I have forgotten his name, took the driver's place and drove away, leaving the driver behind, as a joke, while Mr. P. had to run after to overtake the stage.

The direct and only road to Lancaster previous to the making of the turnpike was what is now Second street extended below Paxtang street, west of the canal bank, called the mill road to what is at present the Lochiel mill. The writer will state a circumstance which occurred at this old stone mill. Peter Pancake's father-in-law, Mr. Mahan, lived as a tenant and farmer of the now Lochiel farm, General Cameron's. Peter had married Miss Mahan contrary to the wishes of her father. The former went to the mill soon after the marriage, when the father-in-law came with a loaded gun to shoot him. The late Robert Dickey was there also, and to prevent the shooting, inserted slyly a cask nail into the touchhole of the lock, which prevented the gun from discharging and Peter of being shot. Mr. Pancake was quite poor when he married, commencing housekeeping with only two old chairs and two knives and forks. These they retained during their lives as mementoes. But by industry and economy they accumulated considerable, and at their decease left the Mahan family in good circumstances.

THE NEWSPAPERS.

All the newspapers published outside of Philadelphia were weekly papers, filled entirely with political articles, and advertisements, which were scattered over the third and fourth pages. The first page was appropriated to foreign news which came in sailing packet ships and other copied news which occurred sometime previous. There was no local news of any kind, except occasionally a marriage or death notice. It was not surprising, for politics engrossed the minds of the people above all other subjects except religion, which was too often a secondary matter. Men's minds were so absorbed and excited that they would bet nearly all they possessed on the result, and if they unfortunately were on the minority side, became impoverished. Even the women were excited on party issues, causing many good friends to become enemies, or else cease to associate as good friends. Such was the influence excited by the newspapers in former years.

These lines were written after having examined a copy of the *Democratic Union* of October 4, 1848, published by Messrs. McKinley & Lescure. There is not one line of local matter in that issue of the paper from borough or county; nothing but politics, politics, for the reader, who was left in ignorance of matters perhaps of interest which transpired during the previous week. The files of all the newspapers published since the formation of the borough are just as remiss in noticing local matters occurring around them. Had simply the erection of the three-story brick residences, and other improvements which were made from time to time been noticed it would be of great satisfaction in later years. We leave any one to state by examining former files of the papers published in Harrisburg, when the attention to local news occurring in and near the town was commenced. In a few county seats the newspaper was truly a home newspaper giving its patrons weekly the local events; such a paper was the *Village Record* of West Chester, and a few others.   A. BURNETT.

FISHER FAMILY OF MIDDLETOWN.

The *Journal* of the 2d gives us the following account of a family re-union, which we transfer to *Notes and Queries* as a portion of the county's history.

On the 21st ult. [June, 1886], the members of that branch of the Fisher family which still retains a portion of the ancestral acres, were reunited at " Pineford farm," the old homestead, to celebrate the sixty-eighth birthday of their mother. They came from widely separated homes—one from Emporia, Kan.; one from Philadelphia; one from Rahway, N. J.; one from Swarthmore, Pa.; one from Sac and Fox agency, Indian Territory ; two are located in Ida county, Iowa, and one lives with his mother on the farm.

There are comparatively few families in this State who have held estates so long.

John Fisher, the founder of the family in this country, came from England with Wm. Penn, in the ship Welcome in 1682. His grandson John Fisher conveyed to his son George a tract of land containing eleven hundred acres purchased by him from the Penns, the original deed of which is in the possession of Hon. Rob't J. Fisher, of York, Pa.

In 1752 he (George Fisher) settled on this land, and in 1755 (thirty years before Harrisburg was laid out) founded the town of Middletown on the site of an old Indian village. The town was so called on account of its being located half way between Lancaster and Carlisle. On his death the property was left to his son George, who, being but ten years of age, was taken to Philadelphia, where he afterwards studied law with his guardian, Isaiah Pemberton.

In 1814 he laid out the town of Portsmouth (now a part of Middletown). He also owned a large body of land now included in the city of Harrisburg, which he afterwards disposed of, under the impression that Middletown would be the State capital.

His second wife was Ann Shippen Jones, daughter of the then mayor of Philadelphia, and granddaughter of charter mayor, Edward Shippen, the first mayor of Philadelphia. One of his sons, Edward Fisher, father of the children who were thus temporarily reunited, retained the old homestead, and a portion of the patrimonial acres. Mrs. Hannah Fisher, whose birthday was here commemorated, is the last member of the family bearing the name, now residing in Dauphin county.   c. h. h.

In connection with the above perhaps a slight sketch of Middletown, taken from a work presented to me by my father in 1844, may not prove uninteresting. [Rupp's History of Dauphin, &c.]

" Middletown, with its near neighbor Portsmouth, takes the second rank in the county (to Harrisburg), and as a town is the most ancient. It occupies the high ground about half a mile from the confluence of the Swatara with the Susquehanna; Portsmouth is on the plain immediately at the mouth, ten miles below Harrisburg. Middletown was laid out by George Fisher, Esq., in 1755."

" The proprietor being a Friend, several of this denomination from Philadelphia, and the lower counties followed him ; and these, with some Scotch and Irish merchants formed the first inhabitants of the village, who enjoyed, up to the period of the Revolution, a very extensive and lucrative trade with the natives and others who settled on the Susquehanna and Juniata, and also with the western traders. Several of the Scotch and Irish merchants entered the army, whence few returned. During the war a commissary department was established here, when the small boats for General Sullivan's army were built, and his troops supplied with provisions and military stores for his expedition against the Six Nations."

"After the war trade again revived, and flourished extensively until 1796, after which it gradually declined. Until then, the mouth of the Swatara was considered the termination of the navigation of the Susquehanna and its tributary streams. Below this it was believed to be impracticable, on account of the numerous and dangerous falls and cataracts impending its beds. In 1796 an enterprising German miller named Kreider, from the neighborhood of Huntingdon, appeared in the Swatara with the first ark ever built in those waters, fully freighted with flour, with which he safely descended to Baltimore. His success becoming known throughout the interior, many arks were constructed, and the next year numbers of them, fully freighted, arrived at tide water. The enterprise of John Kreider thus diverted the trade of this place to Baltimore, where it principally centered, until the Union canal was completed in 1827, when it was again arrested at its old port. It would probably have so continued, if the Pennsylvania canal had not been finished to Columbia by which the principal obstruction in the river (the Conewago falls), was completely obviated. Middletown again declined. A large trade, however, in lumber and other articles of domestic produce, is still intercepted here, supplying the valleys of the Swatara, Quitopahilla, Tulpehocken, and Schuylkill. It may fairly be presumed from the local advantages enjoyed by this town that it is destined ere long to become one of much importance."

NOTES AND QUERIES.—CXI.

HEAVY WEIGHTED HEROES.—Recently we came across the following which is worthy of preservation in *Notes and Queries*:

Weight of several officers of the Revolutionary army, August 19, 1788—weighed on the scales at West Point: General Washington, 209 pounds; General Lincoln, 224; General Knox, 280; General Huntingdon, 182; General Greaton, 166; Colonel Swift, 219; Colonel Michael Jackson, 252; Colonel Henry Jackson, 238; Lieutenant Colonel Huntingdon, 212; Lieutenant Colonel Cobb, 182; Lieutenant Colonel Humphreys, 221.

"SHIN-PLASTER"—The term "shin-plaster" was applied derisively to the small paper currency which was plentiful after the war of 1812–1814 and especially during the financial crisis of 1838. Bartlett says that it was in use during the Revolutionary war, and was applied to the Continental- currency, which was decreasing in value every day; so that, when it became utterly worthless, an old soldier who had been paid off with it, and who could not get rid of it, very philosophically made use of it as plasters for a wounded leg. This suggestion we consider as an invention—got up to account for the use of the phrase in the absence of any known reason for its original adoption.

COLONIAL OR PROVINCIAL.—Many of our writers, especially newspaper historians, use the term Colonial to the events in Pennsylvania under the Proprietary Government. Prior to the purchase by William Penn, it was the *Colony on the Delaware*, afterwards the *Province of Pennsylvania.* New Jersey, Maryland, and Pennsylvania were Provinces, while Massachusetts, New York, Virginia and others were always Colonies until they declared their independence. The Governor of a Colony was appointed by the Crown—those of the Province by the Proprietary. Perchance the use of this term Colonial as to Pennsylvania arose from the fact that Mr. Hazard, who edited them, misnamed our Provincial Records, Colonial records. He ought to have known better.

AN OLD TURNPIKE ORDER has been sent us, a copy of which is herewith given. There is no date, but we presume it must be at least fifty if not sixty years old :

"THE SPRUCE CREEK AND WATER STREET TURNPIKE COMPANY, HUNTINGDON COUNTY, PENN.

('Copy of an order issued to gatekeepers.)
'RESOLVED, That the maximum burden to be drawn on the Spruce Creek and Water Street turnpike be six thousand pounds, and any person attempting to haul a greater load than above specified will not be allowed to pass through said turnpike or gates.
(Signed,) 'SAMUEL WIGTON, *Secretary.*
'By order of the Board of Managers.

(Instructions to gatekeepers.)
'You are hereby required to enforce above resolutions strictly, as civilly and courteously as possible. But if assaulted, or attempt to force through the gate without your consent, defend yourself and your

office in the best manner possible. Knock down horse or driver with a club, or any other way necessary, and you will be fully sustained by the company.

(Signed,)   'JOHN S. ISETT, *President.*' "

MINSHALL, ATKINSON, DOYLE, AND KITTERA.

In *Notes and Queries* (*No. cix*), it is stated that Joshua Minshall married a daughter of Robert Barber. Several years have passed since that article was written, and I have ascertained that Joshua Minshall married the daughter of Stephen Atkinson, who built a fulling mill on the east side of the Conestoga about the year 1713. It was located a mile or two south of the present city of Lancaster. Minshall was a Quaker and it was his son Thomas Minshall who married Robert Barber's daughter. It is quite probable that Atkinson and his wife were Scotch-Irish.

Although Thomas Minshall was reared a Quaker, and became an active member of that society, he could not altogether restrain a natural taste for a military life. He raised a company of volunteers in York county, and marched at their head to join Forbes' army at Fort Bedford in 1758. There was so much pressure brought to bear against this movement of his, by the Wrights and Barbers at the Susquehanna, that he resigned his command and returned to his farm near the present town of Wrightsville. A few years before the Revolutionary war he sold his land and removed to Middletown, on the Swatara. He married a second time, a Mrs. Young, of Middletown.

Thomas Doyle (hatter), of Lancaster, also married a daughter of Stephen Atkinson. His son, Thomas Doyle, was a lieutenant and captain in the First and Third regiments of the Penn'a Line of the Revolution. He was wounded and became a pensioner. He was stationed at Fort Washington (Cincinnati), where he died about 1802 or 1803.

John Doyle, brother of Thomas, was also a lieutenant and captain in the Revolutionary army. He commanded an independent company, and was stationed at Lancaster and York. He was promoted, and marched with the Pennsylvania troops to Virginia in June, 1781, and was wounded July 6, 1781. These brothers became prominent, and evidently inherited a taste for military life.

The Hon. John Wilkes Kittera, who was an officer in the Revolutionary army, and a member of Congress for ten years from the Lancaster district, married a sister of Capt. Thomas Doyle. Mr. Kittera was a very successful lawyer, and had an extensive and profitable practice. The large fortunes made during the Revolution in the manufacture of iron led him to embark extensively in that business. He owned several thousand acres of land and the furnace at the mouth of Codorus creek in York county. He also owned the ore lands on Chestnut Hill in Lancaster county, which afterwards came into possession of the Grubbs as did also the furnace, &c. He lived elegantly and entertained a great deal of company, when he was a member of Congress. His wife was a very attractive and accomplished lady. His furnace and land speculations proved disastrous, and when Mr. Kittera died, in 1802 or 1803, his estate was bankrupt. Mrs. Kittera was disappointed, for she supposed that her husband was a rich man, and returned to Lancaster from Philadelphia, whither he had removed when he was appointed U. S. District Attorney by the elder Adams. Few ladies of culture, and position in society, held by Mrs. K., could have withstood the shock of so sudden a reverse. She was equal to the emergency. She sold many fine dresses and her jewelry, and took her son and two daughters to Philadelphia, where she opened a small store. Her son was sent to college, and afterwards became an eminent lawyer in Philadelphia. Her daughters received a good education, and became the heads of prominent families. Mrs. Kittera accumulated a large fortune by her own exertions, and lived to enjoy it in ease and comfort.

There have been no descendants of the Atkinsons and Doyles or Kitteras in Lancaster county for eighty or more years.

Samuel Reed also married a daughter of Stephen Atkinson. He was a prominent citizen, and probably lived in Martick township.

Columbia, Pa. SAMUEL EVANS.

THE "WALKING PURCHASE."

[In the Editor's *History of Pennsylvania,* page 443, is given an account of the famous "Indian Walk" on the 19th of September, 1737, to which the following paper has reference. This "walk" was no doubt the cause of jealousies and heart-burnings among the Indians, which eventually broke out in loud complaints of injustice and atrocious acts of savage vengeance.]

REMINISCENCES OF SOLOMON JENNINGS, ONE OF THE "THREE WALKERS."

John Hyder, in his deposition concerning the day and a half day's walk, made before Governor Denny in March, of 1757, tells us that Solomon Jennings "went no further with the walkers, about 10 or 11 of the clock, of the first day; that then and there he fell back, keep-

Notes and Queries.

ing, however, in the company of the curious crowd that was following in the wake of the contestants, as far as the Indian ford on Lehigh " (Ysselstein's Ford), at which point he bade them adieu and
turned home.   Jennings' home at this time was on a tract of 200
acres of land, situate on the south bank of the West Branch of Delaware or Lehigh, upwards of a mile west by south from the present
borough of Bethlehem.   This land was a portion of a great tract of
5,000 acres, which John, Thomas, and Richard Penn had ordered by
a warrant, (dated at London, 18 March, 1732,) issued to the Surveyor
General of the Province, to be laid out for the proper use of Thomas
Penn, and his heirs.   Thomas Penn, by his assignment endorsed on
the aforesaid warrant of the same date, granted and assigned over
the said warrant, and 5,000 acres of land to Joseph Turner and his
heirs, who by his assignment endorsed on said warrant, and dated 10
Sept., 1735, made over the same to William Allen, of Philadelphia,
whereupon there was surveyed to the said Allen the before-mentioned
tract of 200 acres, then situate in Bucks county, but now in Salisbury township, Lehigh county.

The precise time at which Jennings got possession of this tract and
entered it, we have failed to satisfactorily ascertain.   In the deed for
it made by the attorneys of William Allen to the executors of Solomon Jennings, in May of 1773, it is indefinitely stated that " Whereas
Sol. Jennings in his life time did agree with said Allen to purchase
the said tract and did pay £131 11s—a part of the consideration
money, &c."   It may have been (and probably the supposition is
correct) that Jennings occupied it in the spring of 1736, the following
item extracted from the " Pennsylvania Journals 1765–1769," vol. v.,
of " The Penn Papers " pointing to that year.

"August 2, 1765.   John Jennings (a son of Solomon) Dr. For 28
years of Quit-rent on 200 acres of land surveyed to his Father, per
warrant of 5th March, 1736, £11 13s 4d sterling.   He is to pay *no
purchase money, the Proprietors having given his Father this Land in
recompense for his services.*"*

When the Moravians came into the Forks of the Delaware (to the
Whitefield tract, Nazareth, in the spring of 1740), and founded Bethlehem in the spring of 1741, Solomon Jennings was one of their
nearest neighbors in that then sparsely settled portion of Bucks county.

---

* Solomon Jennings in his life-time paid William Allen £131 11s. on the land.
After his death in February of 1757, his executors paid Allen " £50, also a part
of consideration money ;" and in May of 1764, the same parties paid into the
hands of John Allen and Joseph Turner, William Allen's attorney, "a further
payment of £229 14s., it being the *remainder* of the consideration money ;" whereupon a deed was given.

Between the peace-loving brotherhood and the sturdy yeoman there were never other than friendly relations during the sixteen years of their intercourse. Jennings also found a ready market for his surplus produce at Bethlehem, and from its shops he soon learned that he could have nearly all the wants of his household satisfactorily and expeditiously supplied. Jennings, furthermore, was accustomed to call upon the Moravian clergymen, at Bethlehem, whenever a clergyman's services were needed. The Rev. Abraham Reinke, of Bethlehem, in a private record of his official acts, records, under date of 14th November, 1745, the baptism of an infant daughter of Solomon Jennings. The act he adds, was performed in the father's house, and the babe was named Judith. A Rachael Jennings (an older daughter) is mentioned as occasionally coming to Bethlehem about this same time and earlier.

From this time forward until the erection of Northampton county, in 1752, we find no notices of the discomfited walker having aught of interest, except that he frequently served as a juryman on roads at different and at remote points of Upper Bucks, occasionally as arbitrator or assessor in neighborly disagreements—circumstances which would seem to show that he was a man of some repute in the community in which he moved. Nevertheless he was illiterate, always making his mark (it was So) instead of affixing his name to documents that legally required his signature.

In October of 1755 Jennings was elected one of the County Commissioners of Northampton county, and being unable to write, made an X in place of signing his name on taking the oath of office.*

In November of 1775 the French Indians, as is well known, began to lay waste the borders of the Province. Upper Northampton (now Monroe) suffered severely in the month of December. The affair at Hoeths, and the affair at Brodheads (by Stroudsburg), struck consternation into the settlers and called for the interference of the military. The Province sent troops to the scene of the savage inroads, and the inhabitants also organized for defense. Of such a company of volunteers Solomon Jennings was captain, passing through Nazareth en route for transmontane Northampton, on the 14th of December. We have learned nothing further of his military career. "Last night," i. e. on the night of 15th and 16th of February, 1757, writes a Moravian recorder, "our good old neighbor, Solomon Jennings died, after a short illness." This item will wipe out from the page of history the gratuitous assertion that Jennings died a few years or shortly after the consummation of the walk in consequence of over-exertion in

---

* Henry's History of the Lehigh Valley.

that contest. The Rev. Abraham Reinke, furthermore, conducted the funeral service at the decedent's house, in the presence of a large concourse of yeomanry, and the remains of the historic walker were interred in the family grave-yard near by—the afternoon of February 17th.

Jennings left a widow, Eleanor by name, and two sons, John and Josiah. In his last will and testament he appointed these two sons and Nicholas Scull, his executors. In addition to 200 acres of land cited above, he was at the time of his death possessed of a tract of 164 acres, lying contiguous. After the death of his widow in the early spring of 1764 (she was buried by the side of her husband), his executors pursuant to the tenor of his will " advertised the above lands in the public newspapers upwards of three months for public sale," whereupon they and the tenements upon them were openly sold to Jacob Geisinger, of Saucon township, Northampton county, he being the highest bidder. The consideration was £1,500, and the deed bears date of 21 June, 1764. Thus the Jennings property passed into the hands of the Geisingers, and is held by them to the present day.

Of Solomon Jennings' family we know that his son John figures rather prominently in Provincial history. In the autumn of 1756 " he set up for the Sheriff's office," being then, according to William Parsons, of Easton, " a sober, well-behaved young man, much the fittest of the candidates, having had some experience of the office." But he was defeated. He was elected sheriff of Northampton, however, in 1762, and again in 1768, approving himself an efficient officer, and a man of good metal, too, which was severely tried in the course of the conflict between the authorities of the Province and the Connecticut men of the Wyoming Valley. He was well disposed towards the Moravians, and did them good service as sheriff in that critical time of their Indian Mission, which followed the Pontiac war. He was then residing on a farm nearly opposite his father's old place, on the right bank of the Lehigh. Of his subsequent career I have no knowledge. Nor can I adduce aught concerning his younger brother Josiah. What became of Rachel and Judith Jennings? Henry, in his History of the Lehigh Valley, states that Nicholas Scull was a son-in-law of Solomon Jennings. Which one of the daughters did he marry?

Jacob Geisinger, on taking possession of the Jenning's plantation, occupied the old house, a massive two-story limestone house, 70x30 feet, with heavy gambrel roof, surmounted with dormer windows. It was unquestionably the second dwelling erected by the " old Walker," and its Silesian style of architecture would have us conclude it was built after the model of the large Moravian houses at Bethlehem, probably about 1750. This house the writer remembers. Its heavy roofs and flaring gables embowered in trees on the loveliest flat in the Lehigh Valley—thrown in strong relief against the mountain side, always impressed one with somewhat of wonderment—its huge proportions and sombre cast of countenance being so decidedly out of keeping with the smiling landscape that encircled it. In the autumn of 1855, this old square-shouldered pile was demolished and on its site stands the substantial brick residence of Mr. Robert Yost, a son-in-law of Jacob Geisinger, a grandson of old Jacob Geisinger.

Jacob Geisinger (2d) told the writer that during the war for Independence, while the Continental Hospital in part occupied the House for Single Men at Bethlehem, invalid soldiers were quartered at his grandfather's, and that some of these on dying were buried in the adjacent fields; that in 1788 (his father, George Geisinger, then occupied the premises), the house was one day entered by masked robbers and plundered; and that about 1841 the graves of Solomon Jennings and his wife sank, in consequence of the coffins having decayed and fallen together. Finally in rehearsing the traditions respecting old Solomon that had been preserved in the family, he related that he was a man of powerful frame and great muscular strength, being able to carry four three-bushel bags of wheat from the threshing floor to the granary on the attic of the house, carrying one bag upon each shoulder—one thrown across these in front, and one in like manner behind. JOHN W. JORDAN.

NOTES AND QUERIES.—CXII.

THE FATHER OF THADDEUS STEVENS.—Were it not for the fact that a falsehood oft repeated and uncontradicted eventually becomes quoted as an historic fact, we would willingly pass by a statement going the rounds of the newspaper press relating to the father of the great "commoner." The New York *Tribune* is credited with this remarkable data:

"The father of Thaddeus Stevens was a soldier in the Mexican war, where he came under the notice of Gen. Winfield Scott. He was made a sergeant and detailed for duty about the General's headquarters. General Scott had a high regard for him, and when he was killed in battle, wrote a letter to Mrs. Stevens, speaking in tender terms for an old soldier and of the affection that he felt for the sergeant. As Thaddeus grew up his mother often mentioned this letter to him, but it was not until after he left home that she discovered it among his father's relics and sent it to him by the hand of the relative who told me this incident. When he received it he was affected to tears, the only time his relative had ever seen him weep."

Of just such stuff are most of the so-called *historical* references by our modern newspaper correspondents. It is the merest twaddle; but the life of an earnest antiquary is too short to correct every such perversion of history. But to the case in point. Thaddeus Stevens was born in 1792, his father about the year 1760, so that at the time of the war with Mexico, say 1847, he would have been at least 87 years of age—a pretty old sergeant. The facts are that Mr. Stevens was left an orphan at an early age, long prior to the war with England, 1812–14. How such statements can find place in reliable newspapers we are at a loss to imagine, unless, in the rage for sensation, assertions are taken for facts, by thoughtless or ignorant-of-history editors, who appear to fill the chairs of the leading newspapers of our great cities.

"DOUGHFACES."—H. J. asks, "why were certain politicians called 'doughfaces' before the war of the Rebellion? I think the term was applied as a sneer by the Abolitionists to the other party. I suppose that the meaning was that the 'doughfaces' would not vote the same way as the Abolitionists did. I have heard of men with noses of wax who might be led by others, and I have even heard of men of putty and of straw. But a 'doughface' would seem to have been a term invented by a baker, or a term which came out of the kitchen." [Strange as it may appear, this term, which the Abolitionists used very effectively, was invented by the champion of slaveholders, John Randolph, of Roanoke, as early as 1820, and was applied to the allies of the South among Northern Democrats. Randolph was willing to avail himself of the treason; but he despised the traitors. Speaking of them he said: "I knew that these men would give way. They were scared at their own doughfaces. Yes, they were scared at their own doughfaces. We had them; and, if we had wanted more, we could have had them." Twenty years after the New York *Tribune* almost re-echoed this sentiment: "The truth is that while the Southerners need and are willing to pay for the services of the doughfaces, they dislike their persons and despise their discourse." During the same campaign the word "doughface" was applied in the South to those men of their own section who were not willing to aver their strong devotion to slavery. Thus said a writer of the time: "There are Southern as well as Northern doughfaces. Men looking to the spoils care not for principles, whether they are of the North or of the South."]

RECORDS OF BINDNAGLE CHURCH.—I.

To the descendants of the early German families there is no spot in our section of country around which cluster more hallowed and interesting associations than Bindnagle's Lutheran and Reformed church. After a ride of about three miles from Palmyra, Lebanon county, Pa., on the line of the Philadelphia and Reading railroad, over a pleasant way across the "gravel hills" northward, we approach the above church on the banks of the Big Swatara below the mouth of the Quitopahilla creek. The country round about was first settled by the aristocratic "blue stockings," who worshiped at Derry and Hanover churches. The tract upon which Bindnagle church stands was patented October 26, 1753, in a lot of one hundred and fifty acres. The following paper is of interest:

John Pinogle surveyed by Wm. Galbraith 12th October, 1753. Beg'g at ——; thence by the church land N. 52° E. 34 p. to a dogwood; by l'd of Jas. Ewing N. 80° E. 61 p. to a ——; by Con'd Vishong S. 38° E. 24 p. to —— S. 47° E. 90 p. to a post; S. 10° E. 24 p. —— S. W. 26 p.; thence by Anthony Hemperly S. 82° west 36 p. to ——; N. 67° W. 20 p. to a Spautz; & N. 43° W. 11 p. to a chestnut oak by Albright Siegely N. 80° W. 210 p. to —— on the bank of Swatara creek up the same N. 43° E. 56 p. N. 57° E. 72 p. to a chestnut by the church land S. 60° E. 14 p. to the beginning.

I do certify the above to be a true copy as transcribed from the field book of Wm. Galbraith of John Pinogle's survey now in Londonderry township, Dauphin county, Pa.   BERTRAM GALBRAITH.
9th August, 1802.

The ground for a church and burial place and school house was deeded by "Hans Bindnagle," January 16, 1753, to George Berger, Michael Bolz, Wilhelm Strober, and Christopher Suesz for a Lutheran congregation, on the banks of the Swatara creek, in Derry township, in Lancaster county, Province of Pennsylvania. The first church was built about this time and was constructed of logs, which stood to the northeast of the present structure. This was built in 1803, and is a two-story brick building with entrances upon the north (which leads to the grave-yard), east (which is the entrance from the public road), and the south (which leads from the garden or school teachers' garden patch). The present edifice retains its original interior appearance, with its old style pulpit, some eight or ten feet above the floor and shaped like a "saur kraut" stand, with the back of it, about twelve feet square, against the wall. As an ornament, carved from wood, above the pulpit, is an oval-shaped sounding board, and underneath this a painting of the Saviour; while on either side of the pulpit, on this carved ornamentation are the paintings of ———. The pews are divided into four sections with very straight backs and high; one aisle runs from the south to the north door, and the pews to the left as you enter the south door face from right to left. In the vacant space in front of the pulpit and in center of the sections of pews above mentioned, is the altar, box-shaped, surrounded by a railing. The pews to the right of the aisle are in two sections. A gallery surrounds on three sides. There is a steeple on the church from which a fine toned bell echoes its silver strains up and down the Swatara and across the hills and valleys, until its sounds are caught up by its offspring, Shell's church to the north, Palmyra church to the south; and its sister denomination " Old Derry," snuffs from the breezes that summons, although its parishioners are no more. On the northeast is Sherk's U. B. meeting-house, now the oldest in this section of the State of that denomination who statedly meet and worship in their progressive manner to bring the erring to Christ; yet they send back to old Bindnagle not the sweet music of the old bell but their praises and hosannas.

Last year the church was, through the Early family, who were among the *early* worshipers there, rescued from the possession of the bats and wasps, who renovated it by placing a new slate roof on it, repairing the brick and wood work and repainting the interior. This seemed to give a new impetus to the staid old parishioners, and now they not only have a church building handsome in appearance, but one which will stand until Dauphin celebrates its second centennial. Much praise is due William Early and Daniel Seacrist (whose mother was an Early), and also D. S. Early, of Harrisburg (whose father, grandfather, and great-grandfather lie buried in the old grave-yard), for substantial aid in this undertaking. On entering the east door we were confronted with a large limestone weighing nearly a ton, from the native hills thereabouts, upon which is cut D. S. Early, 1885."

The minister's gown used in former times is on exhibition in' the church, while the communion set is a very ancient one. The collection bags are still preserved. These were made of some black material fastened to a pole about ten feet long, and at the end of the pole to which the bag was attached is also to be found the bell which was rung when the member was sleeping, or neglected to drop his contribution. We are not now able to give the names of the preachers who administered statedly to these people, but hope to do so some time in the future.

In 1787 the following subscribed the amounts opposite their names to the schoolmaster (no doubt preacher) to bettering Bindnagle's church:

A list of persons for the schoolmaster who promise to give something towards bettering the Bindnagle's church:

	£	s.	d.
John Early,	0	7	6
Andrew Keifer,	0	7	6
Michael Zimmerman,	0	5	0
John Zimmerman,	0	2	6
John Early, Jr.,	0	5	0
Henry Zigler,			
Joseph Carmany,	0	7	6
Christian Bomberger,	0	2	0
Wilhelm Early,			
Adam Dieninger,			
Frederick Bickel,	0	5	0
Adam Dieninger, Jr.,			
Anthony Hemperly,			
John Schnuck, Sr.,			
Michael Eli,			
Jacob Kissner,	0	2	6
Jacob Veish,	0	5	0
John Sharp,			
Charles Sprecker,	0	2	6
John Schnuck, Jr.,			

Sealed, signed and delivered in presence of us,

CHRISTIAN FREDERICK WAGMAN,
JOHN MARTIN GORN,
FREDERICK WILLIAM HAGER.

We translate the following from the parish record of deaths and burials, to be followed by the baptismal and marriage records:

ANNA ELIZABETH RAMBERGER, b. May 19, 1714, in Bergwangen; dau. of John Lenhart and Margaret Ziegler. Sponsors at her bap., John Michael Werner and wife Regina. She m., first, January 3, 1736, John George Ziegler and was blessed with two children, one son living; m., secondly, Dec. 3, 1743, John Lenhardt Lang (Long), and God blessed her with eight children, of whom three are living; m., thirdly, in 1759, Christian Ramberger, and was blessed with one son, who is living. She d. Sept. 11, 1794, at the age of 80 years, 4 months and 6 days, and leaves twenty-three grandchildren and three great-grand-children.

John Welsh, b. Oct. 2, 1792, son of Christian Welsh; sponsors at bap., John Goutz and wife; d. Oct. 29, 1794, of summer complaint.

Elizabeth New (Nye), b. Aug. 13, 1793; daughter of John Nicholas Nye and wife Eve Catharine; sponsors at bap., John Adam Biel and Mary Elizabeth Fernsler; d. July 14, 1795, of fever.

John Frederick Bickel, b. Oct. 5, 1723, at Wassenbach, Germany; son of George Bickel and wife Ann Mary; sponsors at bap., John Michael Miller and Mary Margareth Raucher (Rauch); m., first, Catharine Dorothea Miller, lived with her 45 years, 3 months, and had issue, seven children. He m., secondly, Nov., 1788, Elizabeth Berger. This matrimony was not blessed with any issue; died Aug. 12, 1795, of liver complaint.

Catharine Gramer (possibly Kramer), b. May 31, 1795, dau. of Adam Gramer and wife Barbara; sponsor at bap., Barbara Bieles; d., aged 4 mo., 18 ds.

Johannes Oehrley (Early), b. Jan. 9, 1724, in Jensingen, Kingdom of Wurtemburg, Germany; son of Thomas Oehrley and wife Margaretta; sponsors at bap., Geo. Spitz and Anna Catharine Algayer, confirmed in the Lutheran faith; emigrated to America, 1750; m., first, 1752, Susanna Brumach (possibly Brumbach). She d. 1753, in Reading, Pa. They were blessed with one child, a son. He m., secondly, 1755, the widow Regina Sichler (possibly Zigler), and God blessed them with nine children, of whom are living three sons and two daughters. He d. October 21, 1796, at 8 o'clock p. m., of *short of breath* [asthma], possibly also typhoid fever; he leaves sixteen grandchildren [of whom the father of D. S. Early, of this city, was one.] Text, Psalm li. 13.

Barbara Hauk, b. June 26, 1745, in Earl township, Conestoga [Lancaster county]; dau. of Lenhart Fesler and wife Margaret; baptized and confirmed in Lutheran church; m., February, 1773, Philip Hauk and God blessed her with seven children, of whom five are yet living, four sons and one daughter; d. October 21, 1796, of typhoid fever.

PARTY NAMES.

[We give the following for what it is worth. Several of the names given were sectional nicknames, not generally applied, and therefore not strictly party names. There is one party that was and is of considerable account which is omitted altogether—namely, the Anti-Federalist, afterward the Republican and then the Democratic party This party, about 1838 and afterwards, was called by the Whigs "the

Locofoco party." In Pennsylvania there were beside, just after the Revolution, Constitutionalists and Anti-Constitutionalists, and at a later period a third party, nicknamed "Tertium Quids," or "Quids." There were also in this State for many years the Old School and the New School Democrats, who were bitterly opposed to each other. There was no political party in this country before the Revolution. During the Revolution there were Whigs and Tories. We never heard of a Nova Scotia Cowboy's party in American politics. "Cowboys" during the Revolution were marauders who hung upon the skirts of the Continental and British armies, and robbed the unprotected people without reference to their political opinions. The term is now used for the same class of individuals in the Far West.]

"1773, Nova Scotia Cowboys; 1789, Federalists and Black Cockades; 1808, Anti-Jeffersonians, Improvement Men, Federalists; 1811, British Bank Men; 1812, Peace and Submission party; 1813, Blue Lights; 1814, Hartford Conventionists; 1816, Washington Society Men; 1818, No Party Men; 1820, Federal Republicans; 1825, National Republicans; 1828, Anti-Mason; 1834, Anti-Masonic Whigs; 1836, Conservatives; 1837, Independent Democratic Whigs; 1840, Log Cabin, Hard Cider Whigs; 1843, Native American Whigs; 1844, Coon Party; 1845, Whig party; 1846, Mexican War party; 1847, Anti-War party; 1848, Rough and Ready party; 1852, Fuss and Feathers party; 1853, American party; 1854, American Black Republican party; 1855, Know Nothing party; 1856, National People's party; 1858, Anti-Lecompton People's party; 1868, National Union Republican party; since 1878, the Prohibition and Labor and Greenback parties."

NOTES AND QUERIES.—CXIII.

ORIGIN OF THE NAME "UNITED BRETHREN."—The origin of the name of this worthy Christian denomination is said to date from one of the earliest meetings held by the founder, Rev. Philip William Otterbein, in 1766. During a meeting held at Isaac Long's in Lancaster county, at which he was assisted by Rev. Boehm, the latter delivered a remarkably effective sermon. At its conclusion Otterbein arose and embraced him, exclaiming, "We are Brethren." The first annual conference was held in Otterbein chapel, in the city of Baltimore, in 1789, which was the first church built by the society.

BRICKS FROM ENGLAND.—Every now and then when reference is made to some old historic mansion, we are informed that the bricks were brought from England. This is in keeping with much of our traditionary history and is simply ridiculous. Before Philadelphia was founded, bricks were made within twenty miles of that metropolis—and why, if this was the case, should bricks be imported from England at a period when there was a demand for the shipping of freight. One or two houses in this locality, notably the Carson house, now the residence of Col. L. N. Ott, it is stated—were built of these English bricks." As bricks—good bricks—were made at Middletown before the erection of these dwellings, it is more than probable that the early settlers on the Swatara manufactured those *English* bricks.

NICK-NAMES FOR STATES.—In answer to a query sent us, we give the following as the appellations to certain States, without entering into an explanation as to the origin of the nick name:

Pennsylvania—Keystone State.
Virginia—Old Dominion.
Massachusetts—Bay State.
Delaware—Blue Hen's Chickens.
Maine—Border State.
Rhode Island—Little Rhody.
New York—Empire State.
New Hampshire—Granite State.
Vermont—Green Mountain.
Connecticut—Nutmeg.
North Carolina—Old North.
Ohio—Buckeye.
South Carolina—Palmetto.
Kentucky—Corn-cracker.
Missouri—Puke.
Indiana—Hoosier.
Illinois—Sucker.
Iowa—Hawkeye.
Michigan—Wolverine.
Wisconsin—Badger.
Texas—Lone Star.
California—Golden.
Colorado—Centennial.

Who can furnish us with those of the other States, and the origin of the same?

MIDDLETOWN AND HARRISBURG IN 1797.

[In the July number of the *Pennsylvania Magazine of History and Biography* is an interesting journal of the Moravian missionary, Heckewelder, who, in company with William Henry, John Rothrock and Christian Clewell, made a visit to Gnadenhutten, on the Muskingum, in the summer of 1797. They passed through Middletown and Harrisburg on the way westward, and on their return, through the latter place. We copy that portion which relates to this locality.]

[*April 23d.*] "Arrived at a seasonable hour in Middletown, where we remained over night. Middletown is an attractive village, having the Susquehanna on the west side and on the east the Big Swatara creek, which flows into it about a mile below the village. The square and the cross streets are in good condition, and the streets running north and south are mostly built up. The houses are built of limestone or brick—the majority, however, are frame or log houses.

"On the morning of the 24th we made an early start, and notwithstanding the rain, had good roads to Chambers' Ferry, where we took breakfast and then crossed the Susquehanna. A half hour is necessary to cross this beautiful river, and while doing so we had a fine view of Harrisburg, situated on the river about 2½ miles on the north of us. The country from Middletown to the ferry is very pleasing and exhibits some fine farms."

*   *   *   *   *   *   *   *

[*July 17th.*] "On the next day, after we had our saddles and various other things repaired, we started from Carlisle at 11 o'clock, crossed the Susquehanna and reached Harrisburg, where we spent the night with Mr. Ott. This town has many fine houses, and its situation is advantageous to trade, but is not very healthy on account of the marshy bottoms on Paxtang creek which flows near the town. On the 18th we left Harrisburg at sunrise, arrived in good time at Hummelstown and breakfasted with Mr. Fox. From here we passed through Palmstown and Millerstown to Lebanon."

[The Mr. Ott with whom our travelers spent the night at Harrisburg, on their return from the Ohio country was Nicholas Ott, Sr., who kept the ferry house corner Vine and Paxton streets. He died in January, 1800. His widow, Mary, and son, Nicholas, kept the inn for a number of years. Nicholas Ott, the younger, died suddenly about ten miles east of Womelsdorf, on the 5th of November, 1832, buried there, but subsequently disinterred and brought to Harrisburg, where he was again buried on the 13th. His age was fifty years. His wife Margaret had previously deceased in April, 1823, aged thirty-six years. Of their daughters, Eliza Kissecker m. Jacob Dock, of Philadelphia, and Maria m. Jacob Baker, of Louisiana. Of their sons, George is yet living, residing with his widowed sister, Mrs. Baker, near New Orleans; David Kissecker lives in Lycoming county, this State, while Leander N. is our very worthy citizen, member of the Dauphin county bar, residing in Susquehanna township. . . . Mr. Fox, of Hummelstown, was John Fox, Sr., who died May 11, 1816, at Hummelstown, at an advanced age. He was the ancestor of the family in that locality, and in the early history of the county of Dauphin was a leading and representative man.]

CAPT. JOHN SIMPSON'S NEIGHBORS, 1776.

[I have before me an account book of my grandfather, John Simpson, opened Jan. 1st, 1776, to which many names and accounts appear to have been transferred from an older book. As these names may be of use to you in your historical researches, I have transcribed them below,—J. S. A.]

Thomas Sturgeon,
John Murray,
John Bell, Jr.,
Thomas Gallagher,
Thomas Forster,
John Cochran,
Charles Stewart,
John Finlay,
Robt. Armstrong, Jr.,
Richard Johnson,
Alexr. Givens,
Henry Miers,
John Ryen,
John Colligan,
Jacob Hyman,
Samuel Cochran,
Patrick Marlin,
Robert Smith,
Hugh Stephen,
John Garber,
James Smith,

Robt. McGill,
Moses Lockart,
William Smith,
Peter Brown,
Robt. Montgomery,
Martin Fridlay,
Joseph Brown,
George Gartner,
David Allison,
John Clark,
James Murray,
John Bell, Sr.,
Isaac Bell,
Peter Corbett,
Samuel Pogue,
John Elder,
Cornelius Frey,
Robt. Armstrong, Sr.,
John Meetch,
Michael Yincal,
Adam Miers,

Robt. McCord,
John Tice,
Joseph Colligan,
Alexander Galley,
Patrick Sufferin,
John Bolland,
John Moore,
Andrew Stephen,
William Ayres,
John Gowdy,
Robt. Gowdy,
John Brown,
William Boyer,
Jacob Tinturf,
John Cramer,
Peter Fridlay,
Daniel Barton,
Lodwick Minsker,
Martha Simpson,
John McFadion.

Other names occur later as follows:

George Bell, 1783.
William Forster, 1784.
Stephen Forster, 1787.
Arthur Bell, 1786.
Andrew Bell, 1782.
Peter Sturgeon, 1783.
Casper Dull, 1784.

James Watt, 1783.
William Clark, 1786.
John Wright, 1785.
Barefoot Brunson, 1783.
William Foulk, 1783.
Laughlin McNeil, 1787.
John Thomas, 1784.

John Ayres, 1784.
Adam Cressman, 1786.
Patrick Lafferty, 1778.
Thomas Kennedy, 1786.
John Duncan, 1784.
George Strow, 1784.

In November, 1783, is the following charge :

" To a hoop for a shaft, wt. 13½ lb., laying a gudgeon—his iron—dressing the N—t and making a band for a shaft—his iron, £1 7s 3d." This is against " *John Garber* " who, I suppose, was the owner of the mill where the election was held 8th July, 1776. There are many " gaps " in the charges in the accounts. Few charges are made in the year 1776 ; 1777 is almost wholly wanting; a few are found in January to March, 1778; 1779 is almost blank; 1780 and 1781 ditto. From March, 1783, entries are regular for 12 or 15 years. These " gaps " indicate his absence from his shop (he was a blacksmith), and he was probably oftener in the Continental Army than I have any account of.

RECORDS OF BINDNAGLE CHURCH.—II.

ELIZABETH FERNSLER, d. March 10, 1797, aged 8 weeks, 3 days ; text, Romans viii. 18.

JOHN SICHLER, b. July 18, 1793, son of John Sichler and wife, Susanna; sponsor at bap., Christian Oehrley and wife Catharine; d. Aug. 23, 1797, of dysentery.

CHARLOTTE GRUBER, b. June 5, 1795 ; dau. of Ludwig Gruber ; d. Sept. 12, 1797, of dysentery.

ROSINE WILHELM, dau. of Abraham Wilhelm ; d. 1798, of small pox, aged 12 years.

MARGARET SPRECHER, b. Jan. 29, 1791; dau. of George Sprecher; d. April 14, 1798, of small pox.

HENRY NYE, b. July 22, 1797 ; son of Peter Nye; sponsor, John Snoke; d. April 17, 1798, of small pox.

GEORGE DEININGER, b. Nov. 1, 1790; son of Michael Deininger; d. April 25, 1798, of small pox.

DAVID DEININGER, b. Feb. 17, 1797, son of Michael Deininger ; d. May 21, 1798, of small pox.

ELIZABETH BAUMAN, b. Aug. 7, 1796 ; dau. of Jacob and Catharine Bauman ; sponsors, Michael Zeller and Anna Mary Wilen; d. May 14, 1798, of small pox.

GEORGE KILLINGER, b. Dec. 12, 1794, son of Peter Killinger; sponsors, Thomas Oehrley and wife; burned to death May 14, 1798.

JOHN PALM, b. July 25, 1713, at the cloister of Heilbron, in the kingdom of Wurtemberg, Germany. He was baptized and confirmed in the Lutheran church ; m., first, in Germany and was blessed with one son ; emigrated to America in 1749 ; m., secondly, Salome Fenger and was blessed with eight children; she d. in 1764. He m., thirdly, widow Elizabeth Kleim and with her he was blessed with

one child.   He d. April 25, 1799, and was the founder of the village
of " Palmstettle." [Palmyra, Leb. Co., Pa.]
    ROSINE HEMPERLY, b. March 3, 1764; m., 1787, Michael Palm;
d. April 25, 1799, in child-birth, leaving issue seven children.
    BARBARA DEININGER, b. 1723, at Aichholz, near Halle, Wurtem-
berg, Germany; emigrated to America with her parents in her eighth
year; d. in 1800, aged 76 years and 7 months, of inflammation of the
bowels.
    JOHN HICKS, b. Aug. 18, 1799; sponsor, John Romich; d. aged
11 m.
    NICHOLAS NYE, b. June 6, 1742, in Germany; emigrated to Amer-
ica with his parents in his eighth year; m., in 1770, Eve Rudisil,
lived with her 30 years and was blessed with six sons and six daughters, of whom nine are living; d. Nov., 1800, of suffering on his
breast connected with a cough; his sickness was of long duration.
    JOHN MALVIER (Maulfair), b. Dec. 23, 1796, son of John and Mar-
garet Maulfair; sponsors at bap., Conrad Meyer and wife; d. of headache, aged four years less five days.
    EVE CATHARINE ZIEGLER, b. Aug. 10, 1781; dau. of Peter and
Anna Maria Jetter (possibly Etter); d. June 1, 1800.
    JOHN ZIEGLER, d. Nov. 2, 1800.
    MARY BARTO, b. Aug., 1763; dau. of Jacob Schumacher; m., first,
Henry Rauch; m., secondly, Anthony Barto.
    JOHN FUCHS (Fox), b. 1769; son of Peter Fox; m., 1793, Susanna
Vollmer (Walmer); d. March, 1801.
    CATHARINE DOLL, b. March 13, 1772; m., March 7, 1789, Lenhart
Doll; sponsor at bap., John Cassell; d. July 11, 1801.
    HENRY KISSNER, b. April 26, 1772; d. Dec., 1801.
    HENRY LANART, (?) b. 1743; d. Dec., 1801.
    ADAM KRAMER, b. 1767; m., 1793, Barbara Biel; d. May, 1802.
    JOHN NICHOLAS GOETZ, b. June 22, 1736; emigrated to America in
1775; son of Jacob and Appolonia Goetz; m., March, 1775, Barbara
Mechlin; d. aged 66 years, 7 months and 10 days.
    EVE EMMET, (?) b. May 19, 1784; d. of Andrew and Elizabeth Em-
met; d. aged 19 years, 2 months and 6 days.
    CHRISTIAN OEHRLEY (Early), b. Jan. 13, 1754; son of John and
Susannah Early; m., 1779, Elizabeth Killinger; God blessed them
with fourteen children; d. aged 49 years, 7 months and 10 days.
    ANN MARY LAUDERMILCH, b. 1739, at Muehlbach; dau. of Michael
Nest; m., in her 26th year, Jacob Laudermilch; she was a widow 32
years, d. 1803.
    JACOB KIEFER, b. May 6, 1717, at Gersdorf, Alsace, France; m.,
first, in Germany, and lived in matrimony nine years, when he emi-

grated to America in 1750; m., secondly, Catharine Altman; he d. August, 1804.

SUSAN FERNSLER, b. October 14, 1771; dau. of Joseph Carmany; m., 1791, Peter Fernsler; d. in confinement, aged 32 years and 5 months.

ANNA BARBARA GOETZ, b. December 25, 1737, at Goshenhoppen; dau. of Thomas Kohr; m., first, Peter Mechlin, and was blessed with 3 children; he d. in 1766; m., secondly, in 1774, Nicholas Goetz; d. aged 66 years, 8 months and 19 days.

WILLIAM NYE, b. Aug. 19, 1746, in Germany; son of Adam and Elizabeth Nye; m., April 18, 1769, Julianna Fernsler. He d. Jan., 1805.

JOHN ADAM DEININGER, b. April 23, 1722, in the kingdom of Wurtemburg, Germany; emigrated to America in the year 1732; baptized and confirmed in the Lutheran faith in his 26th year; he m. Rosina Diller; she d. in 1780, leaving him eight children. He m., secondly, Widow Elizabeth Nest; d. aged 89 years, 10 months, less 7 days.

DOROTHEA SPRECHER, b. Aug. 5, 1726, in Mertzweiler, Baurischen Pfalz, Germany; dau. of —— Schalles; emigrated to America in her 14th year; confirmed in the Lutheran faith at the age of twenty years; m., first, in 1747, William Blecher; m., secondly, in 1759, Jacob Sprecher; d. aged 78 years, 7 months and 12 days.

ADAM REDIG, (?) b. March 17, 1790, son of Adam Redig; sponsor at bap., Adam Weber and wife; d. Sept., 1805.

ELIZABETH RIES, b. July 21, 1773; dau. of Jacob Witzs (?); m. Daniel Ries; d. Mar., 1802.

MARIA JULIANNA HEMPERLY, b. Feb. 16, 1729, in Durlach, Baden, Germany; dau. of Michael and Eve Gassele (?); emigrated to America in her youth; m., first, Jacob Bauman; m., secondly, Antony Hemperly; d. Sept. 1, 1802.

MICHAEL ZIMMERMAN, b. May 1, 1725, in Durlach, Baden, Germany; son of John Michael and Mary Zimmerman; he emigrated to America in his 25th year; m., March 15, 1750, Eve Koenig, with whom he lived for 55 years, and was blessed with eight children. He was one of the first members and establishers of the German Lutheran church on the banks of the Swatara, below the mouth of the Quitopahilla creek. He served almost constantly in the church councils. After a long illness he died April 1, 1805.

EVE CARMANY, b. Oct. 16, 1738, in the kingdom of Wurtemberg, Germany; emigrated to America in her youth with her parents; dau. of Andrew and Eve Frey; m., in her 20th year, Joseph Carmany, and was blessed with ten children; she d. May 21, 1805.

MICHAEL DEININGER, b. Nov. 18, 1763, son of John Adam and Rosine Deininger; m., first, April 21, 1778, Anna May Killinger, she d. Oct., 1802; m., secondly, Eve Nye. He d. at the age of 41 years, 8 months, and 8 days.

JACOB BIELY, b. Feb. 20, 1803; son of Adam and Elizabeth Biely; d. aged 2 years, 8 months and 10 ʼdays.

DANIEL HUFNAGLE, b. Aug. 12, 1803; son of Daniel Hufnagle; d. aged 3 years, 3 months and 3 days.

CONRAD WOERTH, b. at Woelstein, Germany; d. Nov. 17, 1824.

ᴷ BENJAMIN OEHRLEY (Early), d. May 5, 1827, at Gettysburg, while attending the Theological Seminary; buried at Bindnagle's May 8, 1827.

GOTTFRIED WEBER, d. May 9, 1827.

EVE CHRISTINA CARMANY, b. March 12, 1785; d. Aug. 15, 1841.

ELIZABETH LEVY, b. March 1, 1768; m., 1784, Jacob Levy; d. Jan. 31, 1842.

MARGARET PEW (widow), b. Nov. 1767; d. March 27, 1843.

ELIZABETH RICKERT (widow), b. 1767; d. Sept. 22, 1843.

ADAM BIELY, b. 1763; d. Nov. 6. 1843.

JACOB LENTZ, b. June 7, 1759; m. Elizabeth Urich; was a soldier in the Revolutionary war; d. March 23, 1845.

ANNA BARBARA SCHEURER, b. Nov. 21, 1784, in Dauphin county, Pa.; d. Aug. 26, 1847.

MARGARET THOMAS, b. Dec. 8, 1759, in Hanover township; dau. of Jacob Sprecher; d. Oct. 28, 1847.

EVE SCHNOOK (Snoke), b. Jan. 26, 1794; dau. of John Snoke; d. March 3, 1848.

MARIA BARBARA GUNDRUM, b. July 25, 1781; dau. of John Gundrum; d. March 22, 1848.

WIDOW HURST, b. Jan. 17, 1780; dau. of Gebhardt Zeible; lived with John Hurst in matrimony 44 years; d. March 28, 1848.

MARGARET NYE, b. March 12, 1772; dau. of Nicholas Nye; baptized and confirmed a member of the Lutheran church; was the mother of two illegitimate children; d. Feb. 20, 1849.

ANNA MARIA ZIMMERMAN, b. May 24, 1770; dau. of Peter Yoeter; m., July 11, 1792, Gottfried Zimmerman; d. Feb. 8, 1849.

SUSANNA ELIZABETH MEYER, b. Nov. 9, 1776, in Heidelberg township, Lebanon county, Pa.; dau. of Henry Schrack; m. Henry Meyer; she d. Oct. 20, 1849.

JACOB LONG, b. July 17, 1791; son of Martin Long; d. Nov. 23, 1849.

CHRISTINA DEININGER, b. Sept. 19, 1764; dau. of Michael Fernsler; m. Adam Deininger; d. Jan. 3, 1850.

GEORGE HEMPERLEY, b. Sept. 20, 1797; son of Antony Hemperley; m. Anna M. Yingst, d. April 23, 1850.

NOTES AND QUERIES.—CXIV.

THE LAST ELDER OF OLD DERRY.

Death of David Mitchell, at Piqua, O.

We have recently received the following memorial of David Mitchell, Esq., of Piqua, O., by his pastor, Rev. A. N. Carson, of that place. In addition to the facts here given, it may be stated that the ancestors of David Mitchell were early settlers in Derry, and among the tombstones in the old grave-yard may be found quite a number of the family—perchance four or five generations. The subject of the sketch was an elder in the church there from 1823 to his removal in 1839, and for three terms represented Lebanon county in the Legislature, from 1831 to 1834, his residence being a little over the line in Londonderry township, that county. He was the last survivor, not only of that band of Presbyterians who worshipped on Spring Creek, but also, at the time of his decease, the oldest surviving member of the Legislature of 1831. Here is the tribute to a good and worthy man:

David Mitchell was born in Dauphin, now Lebanon county, Pa., January 30, 1792; died at the residence of his son-in-law, Henry Muchmore, on High street, Piqua, O., May 11, 1886, aged 94 years, 4 months and 11 days. At the age of about 23 years he was married to Mary Porter, near his old home, with whom he lived for more than 64 years. He at once went to the home of his parents after his marriage and made it his duty to care for them in their declining years as well as to provide for his own growing family. He commenced his home as a Christian man, and for 80 years never failed in his devotions to Christ and his church. In April, 1839, he, with his family, moved to what was then called the small village of Piqua, and in the spring of 1852 moved into the town, and has since resided in this city, interested in its growth and development all these years. And now, after 64 years of married life, 94 years of earthly existence past, as the buds of spring were opening with new life and beauty, this aged man of God fell asleep in Jesus and has gone to his reward. Six of the twelve children born to him remained to bury the father as they buried the mother at the age of 85 years. Father Mitchell was more than an ordinary man, three times representing his county in the Legislature in the State of Pennsylvania, and serving the Master as a humble, devout follower for eighty years, the Presbyterian church in its highest office (that of ruling elder) for seventy years— not always active, having for some years laid off the active duties of the office because of the infirmities of age. Few men were better posted in God's word and in the work of the church. A close student of the Bible up to his very last sickness, and always watching for his church paper, the *Herald and Presbyter*, eagerly reading to remember everything in it, even to the advertisements, saying, "these are legitimate or they would not occur in my church paper." It is a great treat to read many of the scrap books which he has filled up during the last twenty-five years of his life in which he gives his experience as God's child, always recording a new consecration of himself to his Master and his service on each of his birthdays for the last twenty-five. In like manner he recorded his impressions of the sermons he had heard and of the prayer-meetings attended, frequently making an outline of the sermons followed by a comment or criticism, speaking tenderly of his pastors and uttering the deepest sympathy with them in their work. May God bless his memory to his church and his family and raise up many more to take his place!   C.

THE IRVINE FAMILY.

As preliminary to a genealogy of the Irvine family, we give the following, which we find floating through the newspaper press:

The Irvine family of Pennsylvania were men of large brain, fine physique, imposing presence and distinguished gallantry and bravery. Gen. Irvine McDowell derived his first name from that family. William Irvine was born in County Fermanagh, near Enniskillen, 1740; was appointed a surgeon in the British Navy. In 1763 he emigrated to America and settled in Carlisle, Pa., where he pursued his profession with great success and distinction until 1774, when he took a conspicuous part in the politics of Cumberland county, from which he was appointed one of its representatives in the provincial convention which sat in Philadelphia in 1774. In January, 1776, he was appointed colonel of the Sixth battalion, afterwards the Seventh regiment of the Pennsylvania Line.

On the 8th of March, 1782, he was ordered to Fort Pitt, in the Western Department, for which post he immediately marched with the Second Pennsylvania regiment to protect the northwestern frontier, then threatened with British and Indian invasions. He was also engaged in allaying the troubles between the citizens of Pennsylvania and Virginia arising out of the disputed boundaries between those States. These great duties were performed with ability and integrity.

In 1794 he was appointed with Andrew Ellicott to lay out the towns of Erie, Warren, Waterford, and Franklin, in which service they were accompanied by a military escort under his command, as the Indians were then averse to the cession of that part of Pennsylvania. He was a member of the convention to form a Constitution for the State of Pennsylvania, and was appointed Commander-in-Chief of the Pennsylvania troops to suppress the whiskey rebellion, and commissioned with Chief Justice McKean to treat with the insurgents.

About nine miles north from Enniskillen, on the banks of Lough Eine, lies the little village of Irvinestown, of about 1,300 inhabitants, by some barbarously named Loutherstown. Some thirty years ago, John Irvine, a justice of the peace and deputy lieutenant of the county of Fermanagh, lived here at the family seat, named Rockfield. Among the physicians and surgeons of the village was Gerrard Irvine, and among its merchants was William Irvine. This was the house and these were the Irish representatives of the great American general and statesman, William Irvine. Far away, west from this ancestral house, in Warren county, lies the village of Irvine, named after Gen. William Irvine, where his grandson, William A. Irvine, now resides, the worthy representative of one of the most illustrious families of the United States, who takes an honest pride in his forefathers and in the old green sod from which they came.

General Irvine married Anne Callender, daughter of Robert Callender, of Middlesex, near Carlisle, in Pennsylvania, who was an extensive Indian trader, and who commanded with much credit a Pennsylvania company at Braddock's defeat. One of his sons, Callender Irvine, born at Carlisle, 1774, was president of the Hibernia Society of Philadelphia, and of the State Society of the Cincinnati. Elizabeth Irvine married Dr. Reynolds, a United Irishman of '98, who came to this country and practiced medicine successfully in Philadelphia. But there was more of American glory in this family. Two of General Irvine's brothers served their adopted country whom I must notice briefly.

Andrew Irvine was a brave soldier—a captain in the Revolution. He was a brother of the foregoing and of Matthew Irvine. Matthew was the younger brother of Gen. William Irvine, and was born in Ireland, and came out to this country when a boy. On the way over he had a misunderstanding with the son of the captain, who was older and stronger. They had a fight, in which it was said Matthew did not come off second best. The young pugilists met in after life when both had become well-known citizens and made friends. Matthew studied medicine at Carlisle and Philadelphia under his brother and Dr. Rush. From his brother he willingly imbibed enthusiasm in the cause of the colonies against England, and left his studies to join General Washington at Boston.

WARRANTS TO EARLY SETTLERS.

[From our note book we glean the following relating to some of the early settlers. The dates given are those of warrants unless otherwise noted.]

RACHEL WILKINS, widow, October 27, 1742, land situate at Yellow Breeches creek on the west side of the Sasquahannah river, in the county of Lancaster, settled since the 13th of November, 1735.

HUGH HAYES, March 14, 1737, surveyed 20th August, 1742, 253 acres situate in Derry township, Lanncaster county, adjoining lands of Patrick Hayes, Wm. Morrison and William Hayes.

JAMES BEATTY, November 11, 1742, 124 acres " on Yellow Breeches creek, in Pennsborough township, Lancaster county."

JAMES STEWART, December 5, 1738, land in Hanover township, Lancaster county, " by the side of Swahatawro creek," adjoining John Murray.

THOMAS WILLSON, April 8, 1738, surveyed 12th November, 1742, 120 acres in Derry township adjoining William Morrison, Moses Wilson, John Carr and Patrick Hayes.

DAVID CURRY, April 8, 1741, land " on Latimore's creek in the county of Lancaster, on the west side of the Sasquahannah river."

JAMES ARMSTRONG, November 26, 1736, survey returned 14th December, 1742, for 204 acres " in the township of Pextang, county of Lancaster," adjoining James Alcorn, Andrew Picken, Simon Edgell, Robert Chambers and Proprietary's land.

ANDREW HUME, January 25, 1737, survey returned January 25, 1743, for 160 acres in Hanover township, in the county of Lancaster, adjoining William Watson, James Greenlie, John Wilson and James Clark.

JOHN MAYBIN, February 22, 1741, survey returned February 15, 1743, for 236 acres in Derry township, Lancaster county, adjoining Andrew Robinson, William Hays and James Hays.

JAMES SILVERS, October 30, 1735, " on Conedagwanet creek, by a limestone barren."

JOHN STUMP, April 1, 1743, 115 acres " on the main branch of Tulpehoccon creek."

DAVID FOSTER, February 25, 1741, survey returned May 26, 1743, for 115 acres on Conewago creek, in Derry township, adjoining William Smith, John Foster, and David Foster, Jr.

ALEXANDER MCCULLOUGH, December 20, 1742, survey returned September 14, 1743, for 240 acres, in Hanover township, Lancaster county, adjoining William Barnett, James Clark, Thomas Ludington, Matthew Galt, William Cunningham, and John Gilliland.

SIMON EDGELL, March 27, 1738, survey returned August 2, 1743, in favor of his widow, Rebecca Edgell, for 338 acres of land in Paxtang township, Lancaster county, " by the side of Sasquahannah river," adjoining Robert Chambers, James Armstrong, Andrew Pickens, and Josiah Hughes.

MOSES DICKEY, of Fallowfield township, Chester county, May 31, 1742, for 219 acres in Paxtang township, Lancaster county, adjoining Thomas Mayes, Thomas Morrison, John Carson, Thomas McArthur, and John Forster.

DANIEL SLEGLE, March 11, 1740, for land "on Conewago creek, west of ye Sasquahannah."

ROBERT WALLACE, February 7, 1738, survey returned December 3, 1743, for 200 acres in Hanover township, Lancaster county, " by the side of Suataro creek," adjoining James Harris and Hugh Wilson.

WILLIAM RICHEY, May 7, 1737, survey returned December 14, 1743, for 210 acres in Paxtang township, Lancaster county, " by the side of Sasquahannah river," adjoining Thomas Morrison and Thomas Renick.

JOHN TODD, November 29, 1742, survey returned February 6, 1744, for 210 acres in Derry township, Lancaster county, " by Sasquahannah river at the mouth of Conewago creek."

JOHN FORSTER, January 20, 1737, survey returned July 28, 1744, for 321 acres in Paxtang township, adjoining Joseph Kelso, Arthur Forster and William Armstrong.

JAMES GALBRAITH, March 13, 1737, surveyed February 28, 1744, for 187 acres on Spring creek, in Derry township, Lancaster county, adjoining James Campbell and Sarah Graham.

NOTES AND QUERIES.—CXV.

PENNSYLVANIA ANTE-REVOLUTIONARY CURRENCY.

Before the Revolution, as was natural with British colonies, the money accounts of the business of the people were conducted in pounds, shillings and pence. The Colonists did not coin money, and whenever they were in financial straits they were compelled to issue paper money of various kinds. A pound sterling of Pennsylvania currency ought to have represented a pound sterling of English currency. But at a very early period there seems to have been invented an ideal Pennsylvania currency which was different from the British standard of coinage. Thus in 1672, before Penn came, a Boston shilling was ordered to pass for a shilling; and a piece of eight, a Spanish or Mexican dollar—the modern dollar—at six shillings, for debt and purchases. In 1682 the Assembly enacted a law ordering that every old English shilling should pass for fifteen pence, and every piece of English money in a like proportion. This act established a difference between Pennsylvania and the English money, so that a pound sterling of British money was worth more than a pound sterling of Pennsylvania money. A British guinea was made to pass at twenty-seven shillings, and other coins at a like advance. In 1693 King William and Mary abrogated the law fixing the value of the English shilling at fifteen pence Pennsylvania money. In the same year the Assembly passed another law to adopt the Mexican, Peruvian, Spanish, and French rate of money in the province. In 1698 another act was passed upon the same subject of foreign money. There was an act passed in 1700 to settle a rate of money or coin which was repealed in 1703. Another act was passed in 1709 (which was repealed) to ascertain the rates of money. There were frequent controversies between the Assembly and the Crown in regard to passing laws. The Assembly would pass a law, and it would be repealed in England—sometimes several years after it had been put in operation. And then the Assembly would pass the same law, or something very near like it, and it would go immediately into operation, but would be repealed months or years afterward, the statute having in the meanwhile been enforced in Pennsylvania. In addition, there was a sort of tacit agreement among the people to carry out many laws which had been repealed in England, by consent, as if they were still in effect; and this could be easily done in reference to currency or money. For this reason it is difficult, and according to our idea almost impossible, to ascertain the difference between a pound sterling of English money and a pound sterling of Pennsylvania money in 1706. If it went at the rate of twelve pence Pennsylvania money to fifteen pence British money, the latter was worth, in the pound sterling, sixty pence more than the former.

THE STORY OF "LUKE HOLLAND."

[The following anecdote is given by the Rev. Mr. Heckewelder in his "Historical account of the Indians," to exemplify their sagacity as well as veracity. We must confess that we are inclined to the opinion that that God-fearing missionary was imposed upon by "Holland" and that the entire story is a myth. It is true that not all Indians were bad Indians, but the good were very, very few.]

In the beginning of the summer of the year 1755, a most atrocious and shocking murder was unexpectedly committed by a party of Indians, on fourteen white settlers within five or six miles of Shamokin. The surviving whites, in their rage, determined to take their revenge by murdering a Delaware Indian who happened to be in those parts, and was far from thinking himself in danger. He was a great friend to the whites, was loved and esteemed by them, and in testimony of their regard had received from them the name of Luke Holland, by which he was generally known. This Indian, satisfied that his nation was incapable of committing such a foul murder in a time of profound peace, told the enraged settlers that he was sure that the Delawares were not in any manner concerned in it, and that it was the act of some wicked Mingoes or Iroquois, whose custom it was to involve other nations in wars with each other by clandestinely committing murders, so that they might be laid to the charge of others than themselves. But all his representations were vain; he could not convince exasperated men whose minds were fully bent upon revenge. At last, he offered that if they would give him a party to accompany him, he would go with them in quest of the murderers, and was sure he could discover them by the prints of their feet and other marks well known to him, by which he would convince them that the real perpetrators of the crime belonged to the Six Nations. His proposal was accepted, he marched at the head of a party of whites and led them into the tracks. They soon found themselves in the most rocky parts of the mountain, where not one of those who accompanied him was able to discover a single track, nor would they believe that ever a man had trodden on this ground, as they had to jump over a number of crevices between the rocks, and in some instances to crawl over them. Now they began to believe that the Indian had led them across those rugged mountains in order to give the enemy time to escape, and threatened him with instant death the moment they should be fully convinced of the fraud. The Indian true to his promise would take pains to make them perceive that an enemy had passed along the place through which he was leading them; here he would show them that the moss on the rock had been trodden down by the weight of a human foot, then it had been torn and dragged forward from its place; further he would point out to them that pebbles or small stones on the rocks had been removed from their beds by the foot hitting against them, that dry sticks by being trodden upon were broken, and even that in a particular place an Indian's blanket had dragged over the rocks and removed or loosened the leaves lying there, so that they lay no more flat, as in other places; all which the Indian could perceive as he walked along, without ever stopping. At last arriving at the foot of the mountain on soft ground, where the tracks were deep, he found out the enemy were eight in number, and from the freshness of the foot prints, he concluded that they must be encamped at no great distance. This proved to be the exact truth; for after gaining the eminence on the other side of the valley the Indians were seen encamped, some having already lain down to sleep, while others were drawing off their *leggings* for the same purpose, and the scalps they had taken were hanging up to dry. "See!" said Luke Holland to his astonished companions, "there is the enemy! not of my nation, but Mingoes, as I truly tell you. They are in our power; in less than half an hour they will all be fast asleep. We need not fire a gun, but go up and tomahawk them. We are nearly two to one and need apprehend no danger. Come on, and you will now have your revenge!" But the whites, overcome with fear, did not choose to follow the Indian's advice, and urged him to take them back by the nearest and best way, which he did, and when they arrived at home late at night, they reported the number of the Iroquois to have been so great that they durst not venture to attack them.

RECORDS OF BINDNAGLE CHURCH.—III.

Family of Michael Kitzsch.

MICHAEL KITZSCH, b. Oct. 30, 1732; bap. Dec. 4, 1732; sponsors at bap., Michael Pfrantz and wife; m., June 3, 1755, Elizabeth ———. Their children were:

    i. Elizabeth, b. Nov. 30, 1757; bap. Dec., 1757; sponsors, George Wolf and Maria Berger.

    ii. George-Michael, b. July 7, 1760; bap. 1760; sponsors, Michael Weiss and wife.

    iii. Catharine, b. Aug. 14, 1764; bap. Aug. 19, 1764; sponsors, George Wolf and wife Barbara.

    iv. John, b. Jan. 19, 1767; bap. Feb. 2, 1767; sponsors, John Early and wife Regina.

    v. John-Jacob, b. Aug. 13, 1769; bap. Aug. 27, 1769; sponsors, John Early and wife Regina.

    vi. Regina, b. Feb. 26, 1772; bap. March 1, 1772; sponsors, John Early and wife.

    vii. [A dau.], b. Jan. 8, 1777; bap. Jan. 26, 1777; sponsors, John Shrod and wife Anna Maria.

Family of George Henrich Ziegler.

The family of GEORGE HENRICH ZIEGLER and his wife Augusta
Dorothea were:

 i. Eve-Catharine, b. Jan. 17, 1767; bap. Feb. 17, 1767;
sponsors, John Snoke and Hannah Zimmerman (both
single).

 ii. George-Henry, b. Dec. 19, 1768; sponsors, John Snoke and
Hannah Zimmerman.

 iii. John, b. Aug. 6, 1770; sponsors, John Snoke and Hannah Zimmerman.

 iv. Christian, b. Dec. 1, 1773; sponsor, John Snoke, Sr., and
wife Catharine.

 v. Magdalena, b. Jan. 12, 1776; sponsors, Andrew Brown (?)
and wife Magdalena.

 vi. Lena-Christiana, b. Nov. 15, 1779; bap. Nov. 21, 1779;
sponsors, John Snoke and wife Margaretta.

Family of Ernst Frederick Personn (?).

ERNST FREDERICK PERSONN, b. Aug. 12, 1726; bap. Aug. 21, 1726;
m., May 21, 1763, under his Royal Highness the King of Prussia,
ANNA MARIA HECKER (?). Their children are:

 i. Jacob-Emanuel, b. March 18, 1764; sponsors, Jacob Brown
and wife.

 ii. Maria-Barbara, b. Aug. 9, 1766; sponsors, George Ober-
meyer and wife.

Family of Michael Zimmerman.

The children of MICHAEL ZIMMERMAN and his wife, EVA KOENIG,
were:

 i. Hannah, b. June 15, 1752; bap. June 25, 1752; sponsors,
Wilhelm Staver and wife Margaretta.

 ii. Johannes, b. April 11, 1756; bap. April 19, 1756; sponsors, John Early and wife Regina.

 iii. Johann-Adam, b. Oct. 26, 1757; bap. Oct. 26, 1757; sponsors, John Early and wife Regina.

 iv. Eva-Katharina, b. May 9, 1761; bap. May 20, 1761; sponsors, John Early and wife Regina.

 v. Godfried, b. Oct. 5, 1763; bap. Oct. 20, 1763; sponsors, John
Early and wife Regina.

 vi. Maria-Elizabeth, b. Aug. 11, 1767; bap. Oct. 16, 1769; sponsors, Matthew Hess and wife Maria Elizabeth.

Family of John Schieble.

The children of JOHN SCHIEBLE and wife Eva were:
  i. *Conrad*, b. May 1, 1773; bap. June 4, 1774; sponsors, Martin Beidner (?) and wife Maria Elizabeth.
  ii. *Christian*, b. Feb. 1, 1775; bap. June 4, 1775; sponsors, John Early and wife Regina.

Family of Antonius Hemperley.

The children of ANTONIUS HEMPERLEY and his wife Julianna were:
  i. *Maria*, b. Jan. 26, 1761; bap. Feb. 10, 1761; sponsors, Anthony Blessing and wife.
  ii. *Rosina*, b. May 3, 1764; bap. May 10, 1764; sponsors, Frederick Hummel and wife.
  iii. *Eva*, b. Oct. 2, 1765; bap. Oct. 15. 1765; sponsors, Anthony Blessing and wife.
  iv. *George*, b. July 15, 1767; bap. July 19, 1767; sponsors, George Wolf and wife.
  v. *Anthony*, b. Oct. 21, 1768; bap. Nov. 7, 1768; sponsors, Anthony Blessing and wife.
  vi. *Catharine*, b. March 13, 1772; sponsors, John Cassell and wife.

Family of Theobolt Schautz.

The child of THEOBOLT SCHAUTZ and his wife Margaret were:
  i. *Margaret*, b. June 20, 1782; bap. Sept. 29, 1782; sponsor, Margaret Thielmann.

Family of John Zimmerman.

The child of JOHN ZIMMERMAN and his wife Anna Maria:
  i. *Johannes*, b. Oct. 17, 1767; bap. Nov. 8, 1767; sponsors, John Weber and Hannah Zimmerman.

Family of John Straw.

The child of JOHN STRAW and his wife Catharine Elizabeth:
  i. *Catharine-Elizabeth*, b. Sept. 23, 1782; bap. Sept. 29, 1782; sponsors, Peter Straw or Stroh and Rebecca Karnechi (?)

Family of Johannes Senior (?).

The child of JOHANNES SENIOR and wife Lena:
  i. *John-George*, b. Feb. 29, 1783; bap. Aug. 13, 1783; sponsors, George Walmer and wife.

THE ENDERS FAMILY.

A copy of the circular of the "Enders Monumental Association" has been placed in our hands. The objects are so worthy and honorable that we take the liberty of making these extracts: "The object of this association shall be to erect a monument over the grave of Capt. Philip Christian Enders and his wife, Anna Appolonia Degen, who lie buried in Armstrong Valley, Dauphin county, Pa., on lands of their grandson, Daniel Enders; secure the preservation and keep sacred the last resting place of the old pioneer and his worthy helpmate; to gather and preserve genealogical records, biographical sketches and all other matter of salient interest connected with their descendants, and create and foster among a common kinship, closer association and more fraternal spirit. . . . . The regular members shall consist of the descendants of Philip Christian Enders in connection with those who have or may become associated with the former through marrage. . . . . . We here take occasion to say that Dr. L. Jay Enders, the secretary of the association, has been engaged the past few years in collecting and compiling the genealogy of the descendants all of which will soon be published in a book entitled "Philip Christian Enders and His Descendants." Some of the relatives have not yet furnished their biographies or family records, and as it is the desire of the compiler to make the promised work as complete and interesting as possible we earnestly request that those who have not yet done so forward the desired information to the secretary without delay."

With the circular are given the following sketch and record of descendants:

I. PHILIP CHRISTIAN ENDERS, b. July 22, 1740, in Braunsigweiler, District of Zugenheim, Nassau, Germany; d. February 26, 1809, in Halifax township, Dauphin county, Pa. After completing his education he entered the military service of his sovereign, William Heinrich, Prince of Nassau, participating in numerous battles of the "Seven Years' War." For gallantry and other soldierly qualities he was promoted to a captaincy in the Royal cavalry. He subsequently resigned his commission, and on May 13, 1764, married ANNA DEGEN, daughter of Conrad Degen, of Sippertsfield, Nassau. A few months later he came to America, accompanied by his bride. His first settlement was in Philadelphia, and later in this part of then Lancaster county. In 1788 he purchased a tract of over 1,300 acres of land in Upper Paxtang township. On this he permanently located, and here

his last years peacefully passed away. He was one of the founders of
Fetterhoff church, erected the first saw mill in the valley, taught the
first school, and bore a leading part in many other enterprises. In
1796 his wife and eldest son, John Philip, died and were buried a few
rods from the cabin of the old settler. Thirteen years later the husband and father was laid by their side. He lived a long, useful and
honored life, and his descendants have cause to thank God that their
ancestor deserves their reverence, respect and gratitude. His children were:

      i. John-Henry, b. 1765; d. s. p.
2.   *ii. John-Philip,* b. April 26, 1766; m. Elizabeth ————.
    iii. Margaret, b. April 21, 1768; d. s. p.
3. *iv. Ann-Elizabeth,* b. Dec. 15, 1769; m., first, Adam Kreeger;
      secondly, John Shoener.
    , v. [*A son*], b. July, 1771; d. s. p.
4. *vi. George-Michael,* b. July 12, 1772; m. Elizabeth Crum.
   vii. John-George, b. March 11, 1774; d. 1825 in Dauphin
      county; m. Catharine Bowman, and left a large family.
  viii. [*A son*], b. April, 1776; d. s. p.
5. *ix. Margaret-Martha* (called Eva Margaret in her father's
      will), b. Jan. 24, 1778; m. Isaac Baughman.
    x. Christiana, b. July 24, 1779; m. John Miller, and their
      numerous descendants are scattered over many States.
   xi. Susannah, b. Feb. 12, 1781; d. s. p.
  xii. Catharine, b. March 25, 1783; d. in 1844; m. Peter Phil-
      lips; a number of their children live in Bellville, O.;
      he was a soldier in the war of 1812–14; removed to
      Ohio in 1839, but after the death of his wife returned
      to Pennsylvania, where he died October 2, 1860.
  xiii. [*A son*], b. Jan. 11, 1785; d. s. p.
  xiv. John-Conrad (twin), b. Jan. 11, 1785; d. Dec. 5, 1874; he
      inherited the old homestead which is now in the pos-
      session of his youngest son, Daniel, and on which farm
      the proposed monument is to be erected.

  II. JOHN PHILIP ENDERS (Philip-Christian), b. April 26, 1766, in
Philadelphia; d. October, 1794, in Dauphin county; m. ELIZABETH
————; and had children:
6.   *i. Philip,* b. August 15, 1790; m. Anna Hummel.
   ii. Susanna, b. June 25, 1791; m. Leonard Peters; of their
      descendants, nearly all reside in Pennsylvania.
  iii. John, b. August 25, 1792; went West when young, and
      all trace of him lost.

III. ANNA ELIZABETH ENDERS (Philip-Christian), b. December 15, 1769, in Lancaster county, Pa.; d. in Crawford county, O., many years ago; m., first, ADAM KREEGER, a tailor by trade, who died in Cumberland county, Pa.; and there was issue (surname Kreeger):

 i. John, d. in 1878, s. p.; was a minister in the Church of God.

 ii. Jacob, d. April 7, 1850, in Galion, O.; m. Anna Campbell, and had issue, besides four children d. in infancy (surname Kreeger):

  1. *Sarah-Jane*, b. Jan. 22. 1828; m. John Hindman.
  2. *Elizabeth-F.*, b. Sept. 7, 1829; m. Milton Penders; reside in Indiana.
  3. *Jacob-C.*, b. May 21, 1833; resides in New Orleans.
  4. *Jeremiah-W.*, b. April 11, 1838; m. Prudence Love reside in Indiana.
  5. *Mary-A.*, b. April 7, 1842; m. William Angle.
  6. *Benjamin-F.*, b. April 22, 1843; m. Sarah A. Scott; reside in Galion, O.
  7. *Joseph-R.*, b. Jan 15, 1845; married.
  8. *Amanda-J.*, b. Jan. 11, 1847; m. John Warden .

 iii. Margaret, m. Michael Watson.
 iv. Elizabeth, m. John Rose.

Mrs. Kreeger afterwards m. John Shoener, a clock maker; they emigrated to Ohio, where they both deceased; no children.

IV. GEORGE MICHAEL (Philip-Christian), b. July 12, 1772; d. October, 1831, in Dauphin county, Pa.; m. ELIZABETH CRUM, and had issue:

 i. Jacob, d. March 16, 1857, s. p.
 ii. Elizabeth, b. Oct. 25, 1799; m. Christian Zimmerman, and had eleven children.
 iii. Catharine, m. Michael Hummel; had one son.
 iv. Sarah, b. Feb. 18, 1810; m. Frederick Eberween; resided in Winterset, Iowa.
 v. William, b. April 28, 1812; m., and resided in Harrisburg.

VI. MARGARET MARTHA ENDERS (Philip-Christian), b. January 24, 1778; d. March 29, 1864, in Ohio; m. ISAAC BAUGHMAN, d. July 25, 1869, in Knox county, O., whence he emigrated with his family in 1848; was a miller by trade. They had issue (surname Baughman):

 i. John, b. June 3, 1802; d. near Chambersburg, Pa.; m., and had a large family.

 ii. Samuel, b. Jan. 30, 1804 ; a son, *Jeremiah*, resides at Fort
  Wayne, Ind.
 iii. Elizabeth, b. Jan. 28. 1807 ; m. John Ventling, and had
  seven children.
 iv. Margaret, b. March 4, 1809 ; m. ——— Reed ; resided at
  Mt. Vernon, O.
 v. Sarah, b. Feb. 5, 1811 ; m. Peter Hoke.
 vi. Mary, b. June 21, 1812 ; m. Rev. Solomon McHenry ; had
  seven children.
 vii. Catharine, b. March 29, 1814 ; m. ——— Wingert, and
  had six children.
 viii. Isaac, b. July 5, 1817 ; d. Jan. 15, 1883 ; m., and left
  three children.
 ix. Rosanna, b. March 14, 1818 ; resided at Chambersburg, Pa.
 x. William-C., b. March 15, 1822 ; was a miller ; m. Frances
  Wingert, and had twelve children.

VI. PHILIP ENDERS (John-Philip, Philip-Christian), b. August 15,
1790 ; d. 1874, in Genesee county, Mich.; removed to Erie county,
N. Y., in 1827, and shortly after to Genesee county, Mich.; m. Anna
Hummel, and there was issue:

 i. Sarah, m. William Myers.
 ii. Lucy, m. Benjamin Ineasly.
 iii. Samuel, m. Nancy Rhodes.
 iv. Jeremiah, m., and resides in Australia.
 v. George-W., m., and resides in Genesee county, Mich.
 vi. Elizabeth, m. B. Brosius.
 vii. Norman, a farmer, living in Genesee county, Mich.
 viii. Mary-A., m. Abraham Mastin.
 ix. Harry-H., m., and resides in Michigan.
 x. Martha, d. in infancy.
 xi. Almeda, d. in infancy.
 xii. Frauhlin, d. s. p.

NOTES AND QUERIES.—CXVI.

THE FIRST NEWSPAPER west of the Susquehanna was *Kline's Carlisle
Gazette*, which commenced publication in August, 1785. The title of
this paper is omitted in the list given in the Centennial number of
the *Pittsburgh Gazette*. It antedated the latter paper one year. A
file running from 1787 to 1817 is in possession of the Dauphin County
Historical Society, and is of great value for reference.

DURING THE REVOLUTION.

[We accidentally came across a slip of paper of the Revolutionary era which contains the following bill of fare for the soldiers of Independence—at least when there was a supply. Many and many a time the day's rations did not equal one-fourth of that here given. The trials and sufferings of our ancestors in the war for freedom were very great. Had the soldiers of the Rebellion been compelled to live on as slim diet as they of Valley Forge, there would have been open revolt. Libby Prison and Andersonville were not much worse. But to the rations prescribed, yet seldom given in full:

RATIONS ESTABLISHED IN THE CONTINENTAL ARMY BEFORE BOSTON.

1 lb. Beef, or ¾ lb. Pork, or 1 lb. Salt Fish per day.

1 lb. Bread or Flour per day.

3 Pints of Pease or Beans per Week, or Vegetables equivalent at the Rate of 6s. per Bush. for Pease and Beans.

1 pint of Milk per Day, or at the Rate of one penny per Pint.

½ a pint Rice, or one Pint of Indian meal per man per week.

1 Quart of Spruce Beer or Cyder per man per Day, or 9 Gall's molasses for Comp'y of 100 Men per week.

3 lbs. Candles to 100 Men per Week for Guards, &c.

24 lbs. Soft Soap, or 8 lbs. Hard Soap for 100 men per Week.

Of the above there is drawn by a

Major Gen'l,	15 [Rations]
Brig. Gen'l,	12 "
Colonel,	6 "
Lt. Colonel,	5 "
Major,	4 "
Captain,	3 "
Subaltern,	2 "
Staff,	2 "

STEPHEN BRULÉ.

THE FIRST WHITE MAN WHO DESCENDED THE SUSQUEHANNA.

[We are indebted to John Gilmary Shea, LL. D., for the following reference to Stephen Brule, the first white man who crossed from Lake Ontario to the head waters of the Susquehanna, descended the North Branch to within a few miles of Shamokin, and furnished the Jesuit fathers with the earliest information we have of the Aborigines in that section.]

Stephen Brule, whose eulogy of the country of the Neuters led Father de la Roche Daillon to visit them, had, we must infer, already been in that part of the country, and been struck by its advantages. He came over at a very early age and was employed by Champlain from about 1610 and perhaps earlier. He was one of the first explorers, proceeding to the Huron country and acquiring their language was to serve as interpreter. (Laverdiere's Champlain, vi., pp. 244, 266.) As early as September 8, 1615, when Champlain was preparing to join the Hurons in their expedition against the Entouohonorons, in Central New York, Stephen Brule set out with a party of twelve Hurons from Upper Canada for the towns of the Carantouannais, allies of the Hurons, living on the Susquehanna, and evidently forming part of the Confederacy known as the Andastes, (Ib. [1615] p. 35) to secure their co-operation against the enemy.

He crossed from Lake Ontario apparently to the Susquehanna, defeated a small Iroquois party and entered the Carantouannais town in triumph. The force marched too slowly to join Champlain, and Brule returned to their country where he wintered. He descended their river (the Susquehanna), visiting the neighboring tribes, meeting several who complained about the harshness of the Dutch. At last he started to rejoin his countrymen, but his party was attacked and scattered by the Iroquois and Brule losing his way entered an Iroquois village. He tried to convince them that he was not of the same nation of whites who had just been attacking them, but they fell upon him, tore out his nails and beard and began to burn him in different parts of the body. He was far from being an exemplary character, but wore an Agnus Dei, and when the Indians went to tear this from his neck he threatened them with the vengeance of heaven. Just then a terrible thunder storm came up, his tormentors fled and the chief released him. After he had spent some time with them they escorted him four days' journey and he made his way to the Atinouaentans, the Huron tribe occupying the peninsula between Nattawassaga and Matchedash bays on Lake Huron (Laverdiere's Champlain, 1619, pp. 134–140, 1615, p. 26; Sagard, Histoire du Canada, p. 466).

He found Champlain in 1618 and made his report to him. It was apparently on this return march that he passed through the territory of the Neuters, as it would be his safest course. We find him in Quebec in 1623, when he was sent to meet and bring down the Hurons coming to trade. He returned with them, leading a very dissolute life among the Indians (as Segard complained). (Laverdiere's Champlain, 1624, p. 81.) When Kirk took Quebec he went over to the English, and was sent up to the Hurons in their interest in 1629, notwithstanding the bitter reproaches of Champlain. (Ib. 1632, p· 267.) Segard, writing in 1636, states that, provoked at his conduct, the Hurons put him to death and devoured him. (Segard, Histoire du Canada, p. 466, Rejeune Relation, 1633, p. 34.) The latter fact is not mentioned by the Jesuites. From this remark of Father Brebeuf (Relation, 1635, p. 28), it would seem that he met his death at the very town, Toanchain, whence Father de la Roche wrote. It was about a mile from Thunder Bay. (Laverdiere's Champlain, 1619, p. 27.)

Such was the fate of the man who was the first to cross from Lake Ontario to the Susquehanna, and pass from the villages of the Iroquois through the Neutral territory to the shores of Lake Huron.

THE CUMBERLAND VALLEY.

GENEALOGICAL NOTES OF EARLY SETTLERS.

DUNCAN.

THOMAS DUNCAN d. January, 1776, leaving a wife Jean, and children:

   i. William.
   ii. John.
   iii. Stephen.
   iv. David.
   v. Samuel.
   vi. Daniel.

HOLLIDAY.

JOHN HOLLIDAY, of Peters township, d. in March, 1770, leaving a wife and children:

   i. William.
   ii. Samuel, d. prior to his father.
   iii. John.
   iv. Adam.
   v. Joseph.
   vi. Agnes, m., and d. prior to her father.
   vii. Mary, m., and d. prior to 1770.
   viii. Frances.

MURRAY.

JAMES MURRAY d. in December, 1757, leaving a wife Jennett, and children :

　　i. John.
　　ii. James.
　　iii. William.

SEMPLE.

JOHN SEMPLE, of East Pennsboro', d. February 1758, leaving the following children :

　　i. John.
　　ii. James.
　　iii. David.
　　iv. Robert.
　　.v. Samuel.

The witnesses to the will were John and Thomas McCormick and Jonathan Hoge.

RENINGER.

CONRAD RENINGER, of Allen township, d. March, 1798, leaving a wife Margaret, and children :

　　i. Martin.
　　ii. George.
　　iii. Margaret, m. Thomas Miller.
　　iv. Catharine.
　　v. Elizabeth, m. Simon Benege.
　　vi. Martha, m. Henry Rothroff.
　　vii. Mary, m. John Thomas.

LOUDON.

JAMES LOUDON, of Tyrone township, d. prior to 1785, leaving children :

　　i. Archibald.
　　ii. John.
　　iii. Margaret.
　　iv. Matthew.
　　v. Elizabeth, above 14 years in 1785.
　　vi. Christian, under 14 years in 1785.

CHAMBERS.

WILLIAM CHAMBERS d. August, 1762, leaving a wife Jean, and children as follows, all minors:

    i. John.
    ii. William.
   iii. Mary.
   iv. George.

POTTER.

  JOHN POTTER d. in April, 1761, leaving a wife Martha and children:
    i. James, was Gen. James Potter, of the Revolution.
   ii. Samuel.
  iii. Thomas.
  iv. Margaretta.
    v. Anna.
   vi. Catharine.
  vii. Mary.
 viii. Hannah.
   ix. Isabella.

PEEBLES.

  WILLIAM PEEBLES, of Newton township, d. November, 1778, leaving children:
    i. John.
   ii. Elizabeth.
  iii. Robert.
They were all under fourteen years of age. Their uncles, Robert and Matthew Peebles, were appointed guardian over their estate.

DICKSON.

  JOHN DICKSON d. prior to June, 1761, leaving children as follows:
    i. James.
   ii. William.
  iii. Robert.
  iv. John.
    v. Margaret.
   vi. Samuel.
  vii. Joseph.
 viii. David.

DUNNING.

  JOHN DUNNING d. prior to March, 1778, leaving a wife Margery, and children as follows:

>   *i. Robert,* b. 1760.
>   *ii. William,* b. 1763.
>   *iii. John,* b. 1765.
>   *iv. Ezekiel,* b. 1767.
>   *v. Mark,* b. 1770.

BUCHANAN.

WILLIAM BUCHANAN d. in 1758, leaving a wife Margaret, and children as follows:

>   *i. William.*
>   *ii. John.*
>   *iii. Catharine,* m. Moses Boyd.
>   *iv. Jean,* m. James Gilkeson.
>   *v. Sarah.*
>   *vi. Mary.*

WALKER.

WILLIAM WALKER d. prior to August, 1768, leaving a wife Mary, and children.

>   *i. John.*
>   *ii. Thomas.*
>   *iii. William.*
>   *iv. Samuel.*

NOTES AND QUERIES.—CXVII.

SHEARMAN'S VALLEY.—When was this name changed to Sherman's Valley? In going over the files of the *Carlisle Gazette* from 1787 to 1817 we find the original spelling in all references and in official advertisements—so named for one of the original settlers, Jacob Shearman.

THE OPPOSITION TO THE FORMATION OF DAUPHIN COUNTY.

On the 20th of March, 1784, Christopher Kucher, Christopher Wegman and Col. John Philip DeHaas, in behalf of themselves and others residing in and near the town of Lebanon, in the county of Lancaster, sent in a memorial to the General Assembly praying that the bill for erecting part of the county of Lancaster into a separate county may not be enacted into a law at the present time.

The next day, March 22, "Proposals from John Harris" were read, containing the offer of a free ferry on the river Susquehanna, with a convenient landing place on his land, reserving only to himself, his family and their descendants the right of passing and repassing at the said ferry free from all charges whatever.

On the 23d of March the act for the erection of the county of Dauphin was taken up on third reading, yeas 28, nays 30—negatived. Among the nays were all the members from Lancaster county, including Brown and Orth, while Col. Jacob Cooke was absent. William Maclay, who then represented Northumberland county in the Assembly, voted in favor. The next day he asked leave of absence during the remainder of the session.

At the third session of the Assembly on the 9th of August, 1784, many petitions and remonstrances were presented, most of them, however, stating that if the town of Lebanon was selected as the county town, they were perfectly willing a new county should be formed.

On the 14th of August petitions were read to the effect "that the boundaries of the said new county may be as follows, viz: By a line extending from the mouth of Conewago creek to the Middle Spring thereof in the South Mountains, and along said mountains to the line of Berks county, and that the place to be assigned for holding the courts of justice may be in the most central part thereof." These were laid on the table, as also were sundry petitions "that the town of Middletown be fixed as the place for holding the courts of justice."

On the 16th of August, a letter from Joseph Montgomery and Jonathan Hoge, Esquires, was read setting forth that "they have viewed and surveyed the tract of land allotted by John Harris for a town, and found the same healthy and convenient, and enclosing a draught thereof for the perusal of this House."

On the same day a large number of petitions from the inhabitants of Cumberland and Northumberland counties in favor of the new county; while a petition was read from the inhabitants of Berks county remonstrating against the same, "so far as relates to fixing the place of holding the courts of justice at Harris' Ferry, and praying the town of Lebanon may be assigned for that purpose."

On motion to take up the bill on third reading the yeas were 23, nays 33, Messrs. Orth and Brown, members residing within the limits of the proposed new county, being among the latter.

At the next General Assembly early the subject was once more taken in hand, with the result we are all familiar.

RECORDS OF BINDNAGLE CHURCH.—IV.

Family of Christian Snoke.

CHRISTIAN SNOKE, b. Aug. 18, 1740; bap. Aug. 30, 1740; sponsors, Christian Kreysheller and Catharine Bergner. His children were:

 i. Catharine, b. Feb. 1, 1765; bap. February 21, 1765; sponsors, Jacob Walz and Susan Beyer.

 ii. Elizabeth, b. May 11, 1766; bap. May 26, 1766; sponsors, Frederick Fensler and Elizabeth Beyer.

 iii. Eva-Catharine, b. Oct. 10, 1767; bap. Oct. 11, 1767; sponsors, John Snoke and wife Anna Catharine.

 iv. Susan-Margaret, b. Jan. 13, 1769; bap. Jan. 25, 1769; sponsors, John Snoke and Susan Margaret Baeyer (?).

 v. Anna-Christiana, b. Aug. 20, 1770; bap. Sept. 2, 1770; sponsors, Christian Fox and wife.

Family of John Early.

JOHN EARLY was born Jan. 9, 1724; sponsors at bap., Eberhardt Mathias and wife Jacobina Regina; his wife was Susan Christiana, and their children were:

 i. John, b. July 31, 1757; sponsors at bap., Albrecht Siegel and wife Eva Elizabeth.

 ii. John-William, b. Aug. 10, 1763; sponsors at bap., Michael Zimmerman and wife Eve.

 iii. Thomas, b. Nov. 4, 1767; sponsors at bap., Michael Heicks (?) and wife Elizabeth.

 iv. Catharine, b. July 7, 1772; sponsors at bap., George Peters and wife Catharine.

 v. Anna-Margaretta, b. Feb. 29, 1779; sponsors at bap., Christopher Ernst and wife Anna Margaretta.

Family of Joseph Carmony.

The children of JOSEPH CARMONY and wife Eve were:

 i. Anna-Margaret, b. May 15, 1759; bap. June 17, 1759; sponsors, Frederick and Margaret Morell.

 ii. Julianna, b. Dec. 8, 1761; bap. Dec. 17, 1761; sponsors, John and Julianna Carmony.

 iii. Catharine-Elizabeth, b. Mar. 28, 1765; bap. April 10, 1765; sponsors, Frederick and Catharine Dietzel.

 iv. John, b. July 2, 1768; bap. July 10, 1768; sponsors Jacob and Margaret Neushue (?).

v. Susan, b. Oct. 16, 1771; bap. Oct. 22, 1771; sponsors, Conrad and Susan Neushue.
vi. Joseph, b. Oct. 8, 1773; bap. Oct. 12, 1773; sponsors, John and Regina Early.
vii. Adam, b. April 1, 1775; bap. April 25, 1775; sponsors, Adam and Rosina Deininger.
viii. Jacob, b. Jan. 14, 1777; bap. Jan. 26, 1777; sponsors, Jacob Reisch and wife.
ix. George, b. Jan. 4, 1782; bap. Jan. 19, 1782; sponsors, Jacob Kinzel and wife.
xi. Anthony, b. Dec. 31, 1786; bap. Feb. 11, 1787; sponsors, Anthony Hemperley and wife Julianna.

Family of William Nye.

The children of WILLIAM and JULIANNA NYE were:
i. Maria-Barbara, b. June 8, 1770; bap. June 17, 1770; sponsors, John and Maria Barbara Peters.
ii. Catharine, b. March 5, 1772; bap. March 29, 1772; sponsors, John and Eve Catharine Nicholous.
iii. Henry, b. Nov. 6, 1773; bap. Nov. 6, 1773; sponsors, Daniel Beil and wife Barbara.
iv. Maria-Christiana, b. Aug. 20, 1775; bap. Sept. 6, 1775; sponsors, Michael Maulfair and Maria Elizabeth Nye.
v. Elizabeth, b. May 13, 1777; bap. May 17, 1777; sponsors, John Nye and Catharine Fernsler.
vi. John, b. Oct. 3, 1779; bap. Oct. 17, 1779; sponsors, John Nye and Catharine Schultz.
vii. Anna-Maria, b. Dec. 6, 1781; bap. Jan. 2, 1782; sponsors, John Adam Nye and wife Veronica Barbara.
viii. John Frederick, b. Nov. 15, 1783; bap. Dec. 10, 1783; sponsors, Henry Fernsler and wife Julianna.

Family of Andrew Vogel.

The children of ANDREW and LENA MARIA VOGEL were:
i. Andrew, b. Jan. 3, 1770; bap. Jan. 11, 1770; sponsors, Martin Long and Johanna Zimmerman.
ii. Elizabeth, b. Oct. 20, 1772; bap. Oct. 27, 1772; sponsors, Christian Bomberger and wife Elizabeth.

Family of John Wolf Kisner.

The child of JOHN WOLF KISNER and his wife Sabina was:
i. John, b. Nov. 6, 1778; bap. Oct. 31, 1779; sponsors, Martin and Mary Elizabeth Bindnagle.

Family of John Schaefer.

The child of JOHN SCHAEFER and his wife Barbara was :
   i. Eve-Catharine, b. Oct. 21, 1779; bap. Oct. 31, 1779; sponsors, George Wolf and wife Barbara.

Family of John Hershereder.

The children of JOHN HERSHEREDER and wife Lena Barbara were :
   i. Maria-Catharine, b. Nov. 19, 1774; bap. Dec. 17, 1774; sponsors, Jacob Bruner and wife.
  ii. John, b. Jan. 11, 1776; bap. Jan. 29, 1776; sponsors, Adam Weiss and wife.
 iii. John-Jacob, b. Sept. 22, 1777 ; bap. Sept. 24, 1777; sponsors, Peter Brechbill and wife.
 iv. John-Daniel, b. Dec. 30, 1779; bap. Jan. 2, 1780; sponsors, Jacob Kramer and wife.
  v. Isaac, b. Sept. 3, 1782; bap. Sept. 29, 1782; sponsors, Jacob Bruner and wife.

NOTES AND QUERIES.—CXVIII.

POTASH.—Messrs. Boyd and Wilson, of Northumberland county, manufacturers of potash, in July, 1789, sent to Philadelphia one ton of potash, for which they were offered £40, but refused the price. What Boyd and Wilson composed this enterprising firm ?

RECORDS OF BINDNAGLE CHURCH.—V.

Family of John Oehrly.

The children of JOHN OEHRLY (EARLY) and his wife Margaret were :
   i. Magdalena, b. Feb. 24, 1778; bap. March 6, 1778; sponsors, George Peters and wife Catharine.
  ii. John-Jacob, b. Dec. 12, 1779; bap. Jan. 20, 1780 ; sponsors, John Oehrly and wife Regina.
 iii. John-William, b. March 5, 1782; bap. March 17, 1782; sponsors, Michael Deininger and Barbara Bindnagle (both single).

iv. Daniel, b. Feb. 9, 1784; bap. March 7, 1784; sponsors, Daniel Wonderly and Regina Deininger.

Family of John Weber.

The children of JOHN WEBER (WEAVER) and his wife Eva Margaret were:

 i. Anna-Christina, b. Feb. 26, 1780; bap. March 29, 1780; sponsors, Andrew Braun and wife Anna Christina

 ii. John, b. Feb. 6, 1781; bap. March 5, 1781; sponsors, Christopher Braun and wife Anna Maria.

 iii. Andrew, b. Sept. 16, 1782; bap. Sept. 29, 1782; sponsors, Andrew Braun and wife Anna Christina.

Family of Martin Lange.

The family of MARTIN LANGE (LONG) and his wife Elizabeth were:

 i. Elizabeth, b. June 6, 1772; bap. June 16, 1772; sponsor, Eve Mueller.

 ii. Eve-Catharine, b. Oct. 5, 1775; bap. Oct. 30, 1775; sponsors, Antony Lange and Eve Catharine Zimmerman (both single).

 iii. Margaret, b. Oct. 11, 1777; bap. Oct. 24, 1777; sponsors, Antony Lange and Margaret Muenich (single).

 iv. Julianna-Barbara, b. Feb. 21, 1780; bap. March 19, 1780; sponsors, Antony Hemperly and wife Julianna.

 v. Christina, b. Nov. 9, 1784; bap. Nov. 21, 1784; sponsors, Michael Boby and wife Veronica.

 vi. Jacob, b. July 17, 1791; bap. August, 1791; sponsors, Jacob Lotz and wife Elizabeth.

Family of Johannes Schaick.

The children of JOHANNES SCHAICK—the first three by his first wife—his second wife being Lena Margaretta:

 i. Eve-Catharine, b. March 18, 1773; bap. March 26, 1773; sponsors, George Henry Ziegler and wife Dorothea.

 ii. Christina, b. Dec. 13, 1775; bap. Dec. 31, 1775; sponsors, George Henry Ziegler and wife Dorothea.

 iii. Dorothea, b. Aug. 14, 1776; bap. Aug. 24, 1776; sponsors, George Henry Ziegler and wife Dorothea.

 iv. John, b. April 24, 1778; bap. May 16, 1778; sponsors, Michael Malvier and wife Maria Elizabeth.

 v. John-Henry, b. Feb. 2, 1780; bap. March 19, 1780; sponsors, John Nicholas Bohr and Catharine Boby (both single).

vi. *Anna-Margaret,* b. March 22, 1782; bap. March 28, 1782; sponsors, Peter Neu and Elizabeth Bohr (both single).
vii. *Mary-Elizabeth,* b. June 19, 1784; bap. Aug. 1, 1784; sponsors, John Anthony Wirth and wife Elizabeth.

Family of Johannes Fuchs (Fox).

The child of JOHN FOX and his wife Maria Elizabeth was:
i. *Lena-Maria,* b. Feb. 13, 1780; bap. March 26, 1780; sponsors, Jacob Fox and wife Anna Mary.

Family of Christopher Ernst.

The child of CHRISTOPHER ERNST (EARNEST) and his wife Lena Margaretta was:
i. *John-Jacob,* b. Sept. 25, 1779; bap. Oct. 2, 1780; sponsors George Peter and wife Catharine.

Family of Jacob Kisner.

The children of JACOB KISNER and his wife Catharine were:
i. *Catharine-Elizabeth,* b. April 3, 1780; bap. May 7, 1780; sponsors, Jacob Baumann and Elizabeth Bindnagle (both single).
ii. *John-Henry,* b. April 26, 1782; bap May 17, 1782; sponsors, Henry Kisner and Barbara Bindnagle.
iii. *John-Jacob,* b. Nov. 7, 1785; bap. Nov. 27, 1785; sponsors, William Erle (Early) and Barbara Bindnagle.
iv. *Eve-Catharine,* b. Dec. 15, 1786; bap. Dec. 26, 1786; sponsors, George Sprecher and wife Eve Catharine.

Family of Michael Bolz.

The children of MICHAEL BOLZ and his wife Veronica were:
i. *John-Michael,* b. Jan. 22, 1758; bap. Feb. 19, 1758; sponsors, Andrew Fehl and wife Barbara.
ii. *Jacob-Frederick,* b. March 2, 1760; bap. March 23, 1760; sponsors, Jacob and Catharine Bolz (both single).
iii. *Catharine-Sophia,* b. Oct. 30, 1761; bap. Nov. 25, 1761; sponsors, Jacob and Catharine Sophia Bolz (both single).
iv. *Mary-Barbara* (twin), b. Oct. 30, 1761; bap. Nov. 25, 1761; sponsors, Michael Hochlaender and Barbara Bolz (both single).
v. *John,* b. Nov. 6, 1763; bap. Dec. 4, 1763; sponsors, Jacob Neff and Catharine Sophia Bolz (both single).

vi. George, b. Nov. 19, 1765; bap. Dec. 8, 1765; sponsors, George and Anna Sabina Fernsler (both single).

vii. John-David, b. March 12, 1768; bap. March 26, 1768; sponsors, Michael Boby and wife Barbara.

viii. John-Frederick, b. Nov. 11, 1769; bap. Nov. 20, 1769; sponsors, Michael Boby and wife Barbara.

ix. John-Peter, b. Oct. 18, 1771; bap. Oct. 28, 1771; sponsors, John Zimmerman and Elizabeth Mueller (both single).

x. Catharine-Elizabeth, b. Dec. 21, 1772; bap. Dec. 24, 1772; sponsors, Michael Hochlaender and wife Catharine.

xi. John-Peter (second), b. June 29, 1775; bap. July 16, 1775; sponsors, Michael Hochlaender and wife Catharine.

THE HISTORY OF THE FLAG.

" The Stars and Stripes became the National flag of the United States of America by virtue of a resolution of the Confederated or Continental Congress, passed June 14, 1777, as follows:

" *Resolved,* That the flag of the thirteen United States be thirteen stripes, alternate red and white; that the Union be thirteen stars, white, in a blue field, representing a new constellation."

This resolution appears in the Journal of Congress, volume 2, page 165. Although passed on the date above given, it was several weeks before it was made public, and not until the month of September following was it noticed in any of the New England newspapers until the 3d of that month when it was copied by the Boston *Gazette.* It is probable that this was due more to design than from ignorance as to its adoption.

The flag seems to have been the result of the work commenced by General Washington, Benjamin Franklin, Mr. Lynch, Benjamin Harrison and Col. Joseph Reed. On the 2d of January, 1776, Washington was in the American camp at Cambridge, organizing the new army which was that day created. The committee of conference, consisting of Franklin, Lynch and Harrison, sent by Congress to arrange with Washington the details of the army, were with him. Colonel Reed, one of the aides-de-camp, was also secretary of the committee of conference. The several designs for flags had long occupied the thoughts of Reed and his associates. The flag in use by the army was a plain red field, with the British union of the crosses of St. Andrew, St. George and St. Patrick on the upper left corner. Several gentlemen of Boston sent to the American camp copies of the king's speech. It was received on the date mentioned above, and the effect is described in the *British Annual Register*, 1776, page 147, thus:

"The arrival of the copy of the king's speech, with an account of the fate of the petition from the Continental Congress, is said to have excited the greatest degree of rage and indignation among them; as a proof of which, the former was publicly burnt in the camp; and they are said, on this occasion, to have changed their colors from a plain red ground, which they had hitherto used, to a flag of thirteen stripes, as a symbol of the number and union of the Colonies."

The use of stripes to mark the number of the States on the flag cannot be clearly traced, but it may be accounted for by a custom of the camp at Cambridge. The army of citizen volunteers comprised all grades of men. Very few were uniformed. It was almost impossible for the sentinels to distinguish general officers from privates. Frequently officers were stopped at the outposts and held for identification until the arrival of the officer of the day. Orders were issued that the different grades of officers should be distinguished by a stripe of colored ribbon worn across the breast. Washington, as commander-in-chief, wore a ribbon of light blue. The stars on the blue field—" a new constellation "—were suggested by the constellation Lyra, time honored as an emblem of union. The thirteen stars of the new constellation were placed as the circumference of a circle, and on a blue field, in accordance with the resolution already given. That was the flag used at Burgoyne's surrender, October 17, 1777. By a resolution of Congress, passed January 13, 1794, to take effect May 1, 1795, the flag was changed to fifteen stars and fifteen stripes. That was the flag of 1812. By a resolution passed April 4, 1818, to take effect on the following July 4th, the flag was again changed to one of thirteen stripes and twenty stars; and a new star, to represent a new State, ordered to be placed on the blue field on the 4th of July following the admission of such State.

GENEALOGICAL NOTES.

BRADLEY.

SAMUEL BRADLEY, of Hanover, d. May, 1785, leaving his estate to his wife Agnes and relatives as follows:

Brother John Bradley and his children Samuel, William, Mary, and John.

Brother James Bradley and his son Samuel.

Brother Matthew Bradley.

Mary and William Shay, children of William Shay.

BRADY.

LUKE BRADY, of Londonderry, d. October, 1787, leaving a wife Eleanor. He devised to his friend, James Welsh, a "certain tract of land in the State of Virginia, due to me for service done in the said State," also "one certificate against the State of Virginia of eighty pounds one shilling."

BARGER.

CHARLES BARGER, of Derry d. June, 1788, leaving a wife Elizabeth, and issue:

 i. Eve.
 ii. Catharine.
 iii. Adam.
 iv. George.

The executors were his son-in-law Valentine Hoofnagle and Daniel Henning.

BOAL.

PETER BOAL, of Paxtang, d. April, 1791, bequeathing his estate to his sisters (not named), and his brothers, John Michael and Henry. Peter Boal was a private in Captain Collier's company, Colonel Elder's battalion, under the command of Col. Thomas Hartley, and severely wounded in the attack on Fort Muncy, in Northumberland county, August 20, 1778.

BOWER.

JOHN GEORGE BOWER, of Derry, d. August, 1792, leaving a wife Eva Margaret, and issue:

 i. Maria-Barbara.
 ii. Anna-Barbara.

BINDNAGLE.

MARTIN BINDNAGLE, of Paxtang, d. September, 1792, leaving a wife Mary Elizabeth, and issue:

 i. Christina, m. ——— Dilman.
 ii. Maria-Barbara.
 iii. Catharine-Dorothea.
 iv. John.

The executors of his estate were the wife and Jacob Zollinger.

BARRETT.

JOHN BARRETT, of Harrisburg, d. September, 1800, leaving his estate to his mother, Elizabeth Barrett, of county Down, Ireland, and his brother, James Barrett, of the same place.

CORBETT.

PETER CORBETT, of Paxtang, d. August, 1785, leaving his estate to his daughter Margaret, who had previously married ——— Sturgeon, whose children were Jean, Peter, Samuel, John, and Thomas Sturgeon.

CARR.

JOHN CARR, of Derry, d. February, 1789, his estate being devised to the following:
Sister Rosanna Campbell.
Sister Mary McMichael, her children John, James, Jean, and Mary.
Brother Joshua.
Sister Susanna, m. ——— Coulter.
Susanna Graham.
Sister's son, Robert Edmiston.
Susanna and Mary Caldwell.
Rosanna Green.
The executors, sister Rosanna and Robert Clark.

CALHOUN.

WILLIAM CALHOUN, of Paxtang, d. September, 1786, leaving wife Agnes, and issue:
    i. Elizabeth, m. Henry McCormick, and had *Isabel,* and
      William.
   ii. William.

NOTES AND QUERIES.—CXIX.

SCOTT—MCCLURE.—Dr. James Scott, of Pennsylvania, son of ——— and ——— (McClure) Scott, of Pennsylvania, m., July 28, 1795, Ann Overton Lewis, of Virginia, and had issue:
    i. John-Thomson, m., Jan. 5, 1832, his cousin, Huldah Lewis, of Virginia.

ii. James McClure, m., Dec. 13, 1832, his cousin, Sarah Travers
Lewis, of Virginia.
iii. Mary-Ann, m. L. A. Boggs, of Virginia.
Who was this Dr. James Scott, whose mother was a McClure.

H. E. H.

GENEALOGICAL NOTES.

CLARK.

BENJAMIN CLARK, of East Hanover, d. March, 1801, leaving issue
    i. Thomas.
    ii. Margaret, dec'd.; m. John Gilichen.
    iii. Mary, m. Richard McClary.
Also a grandson, Benjamin Clark, and granddaughter, Elizabeth,
m. Baltzer Stein, " children of my daughter Jean Clark."

ELLIS.

ANN ELLIS, widow, of Hummelstown, d. in 1788, leaving children :
    i. Christiana, m. Samuel Miller.
    ii. Ann, m. —— Wolfkill.
    iii. [*A dau.*], m. Matthias Hoover, and had *Matthias.*

EBRECHT.

JOHN PHILIP EBRECHT, of Harrisburg, d. October, 1792, leaving
issue :
    i. Rebecca, m. Abraham Miller, and had *John-Philip.*
    ii. Wendelina, m. Martin Battorff, and had *Philip.*

GREENLEE.

JAMES GREENLEE, of Hanover, d. March, 1785, leaving a wife and
following children :
    i. William, m., and had a son *James.*
    ii. James.
    iii. Alexander.
    iv. Robert.

HARRISON.

SARAH HARRISON, widow, of East Hanover, d. Sept., 1806, leaving
children as follows :

  i. Elizabeth. m. ——— Martin.
  ii. Mary, m. ——— Ward.
  iii. Jean.
  iv. Sarah.
  v. James.
  vi. Stephen.

HUNTER.

 I. WILLIAM HUNTER, of Londonderry, d. June, 1786, leaving a wife Martha, and children :
  i. Robert.
  ii. William.
  iii. James.
  iv. Archibald.
 II. DAVID HUNTER, d. September, 1787, bequathing his estate to his grandchildren, Jennet, Mary, and Sarah Hunter.

KEILER.

 PETER KEILER, of Upper Paxtang, d. April, 1801, leaving a wife Gertrude, and children :
  i. John.
  ii. Peter.
  iii. Gerhard.
  iv. Benjamin.
  v. Margaret, m. Jacob Frack.
  vi. Elizabeth, m. John Frey.
  vii. Gertrude, m. Daniel Miller.
  viii. Mary.
  ix. Catharine.
  x. Veronica.

KENNEDY.

 THOMAS KENNEDY, of West Hanover, d. January, 1803, leaving a wife Jean, and children :
  i. Robert.
  ii. Joseph.
  iii. Mary.
  iv. Jean.

LYTLE.

 JOHN LYTLE, of Lytle's Ferry, near Halifax, d. June, 1806. He left his estate to the following :

Son Green.
Sister Jenny Ayres.
Sister Elizabeth Watson.
Sister Mary, wife of John McCleary.
Half brother, Samuel Irvin.

LUTHER.

Dr. JOHN LUTHER, of Harrisburg, d. January, 1811, leaving issue:
    i. Catharine.
    ii. Cornelius.
    iii. Martin.
    iv. John.

LOGAN.

John Logan, of Londonderry, d. February, 1788, leaving a wife Hannah, and children:
    i. Thomas.
    ii. William.
    iii. John.
    iv. Margaret, m.————Willson.
    v. Mary, m. Samuel McCleary.

THE CAMBRIAN SETTLEMENT

ON THE WATERS OF CONEMAUGH AND BLACKLICK CREEK.

[The following advertisement over the name of Morgan J. Rhees, of May, 1797, refers especially to that region now known as Cambria county. As a portion of our State history, it is of value and will no doubt prove interesting not only to the readers of *Notes and Queries* in general, but particularly those who dwell within the limits of the "Cambrian Settlement." But where is Beula? Echo answers, where?]

This settlement, although in its infant state, offers considerable encouragement to Emigrants, and others, who have an enterprising spirit and are willing for a few years to undergo and surmount difficulties in the acquirement of Independence.

Several families are now on the land, and many more have engaged to follow in the Spring, when a town named BEULA, one mile square, will be laid out; 395 acres of which will be given and sold for the sole benefit of the first settlers, viz: for public Buildings, Schools, a Library, the encouragement of Agriculture, and Manufacture, and 200 acres in the settlement for the dissemination of Religious knowledge.

Such institutions, it is presumed, must have a tendency to promote the welfare of the settlement, and be of public utility to the neighborhood in general—a neighborhood which the late John Craig Miller, Esq., did not hesitate to declare, would become in time, "The Garden of Pennsylvania." The situation is certainly healthy, fertile and pleasant. The surveyor, J. Harris, Esq., certifies "that the spot on which the settlement is formed, consisting of 20,000 acres, is in quality good, and in general, sufficiently level for cultivation; that most of the tracts (400 acres each) are altogether tillable, that the whole is proper for pasture and wheat, abounding in meadow, which may be watered by numerous streams, on which are many valuable mill seats, &c.

Colonel Elliott asserts, "that this land is peculiarly adapted to grass and that it is fit for any kind of cultivation."

Patrick Cassady, Esq., testifies, "that at least one-fourth thereof will make meadow; that on an average it is level enough for farming; that the hills are of the richest soil, and that it abounds with durable springs and runs, which are sufficiently large for water works."

Many of the settlers, now on the spot, confirm the above testimonies. The great weight of timber is the principal objection. The trees, however, are of the best quality, and consist of the Sugar tree, Cherry, White Walnut, Hickory, Chestnut, Linn Beech, Poplar, Ash, Oak, Cucumber, Birch, and Hemlock or Spruce.

The distance from navigable streams, according to P. Cassady, is as follows: From the Frankstown branch of the Juniata 13 miles, from the west branch of the Susquehanna 13 miles, from the Clearfield Creek 14 miles, from Chest Creek 8 miles, and lying on the Conemaugh and Blacklick, which empty into the Allegheny river.

The imagination may figure to itself numerous advantages arising from such a situation, but there are real ones to be expected from this spot. It is on the Juniata road from Philadelphia to Pittsburgh, about 230 miles from the former, and near 80 from the latter. This route to the westward is likely to become the most public on account of its being most level and equally near. It avoids the Sideling hills, the Tuscarora, the Shade and the North mountains. The portage from the Juniata to the Conemaugh is likewise the shortest between the Eastern and Western waters. This will of course cause it to be a natural deposit for stores, and it is not out of the scale of probability, but BEULA, being in the center of a new settlement, will in time be a manufacturing town, a seat of justice, and a considerable mart for inland trade.

At present it is supposed that 500 families may be supplied by different proprietors with farms, within a moderate distance of the town. Those who are anxious to have situations in its vicinity may be suited by applying to Morgan J. Rhees on the land, or to W. Griffiths, No. 177 South Second street, Philadelphia, who will either sell or grant improvement leases. Terms of payment will be rendered easy to the purchasers, and every possible encouragement will be given to the industrious labourer and mechanic. Saw and grist mills will be immediately erected; and in the course of next summer public buildings and the cutting of roads will employ a great number of hands, all of whom will have it in their power to become proprietors of part of that soil, which they clear and cultivate.

Every purchaser of a tract or patent of about 400 acres, is entitled to one acre, or four lots, 58 feet by 125 feet each, in the town. Professional men and mechanics, by building a house with a stone or brick chimney, and becoming residents before the first day of October, 1797, shall have the same privilege. No ground rent on the lots will be required from those who purchase in the settlement, or build in the town, previous to that period.

Five hundred lots of the above dimensions are now for sale, at ten dollars per lot, payable in cash or valuable books. The books are to form a public library in the town, for the use of the settlers, and all the money arising from the sale, will be laid out for the purpose above mentioned.

Indisputable titles will be given by the subscriber as soon as the number and situation of the lots are known, which shall be determined by lottery on or before the first day of October next.

RECORDS OF BINDNAGLE CHURCH.—VI.

Family of John Michael Boltz.

The children of JOHN MICHAEL BOLTZ and his wife Eva, were:

   i. John-Peter, b. Dec. 7, 1778; bap. Jan. 15, 1779; sponsors Michael and Fanny Boltz.

   ii. John-Jacob, b. June 23, 1780; bap. July 8, 1780; sponsors, Jacob Boltz and Catharine Messersmith.

   iii. Henry, b. April 2, 1782; bap. May 11, 1782; sponsors, Henry Mueller and Barbara Boltz.

   iv. John-Michael, b. July 17, 1783; bap. Aug. 13, 1783; sponsors, Vallentine and Lena Rug (?).

Family of Andrew Beyer.

The children of ANDREW and MARGARET BEYER were:
   i. John-Jacob, b. April 3, 1780; bap. June 4, 1780; sponsors, Jacob Boltz and Elizabeth Wolf.
   ii. John-Jacob (second), b. Feb. 6, 1785; bap. June 12, 1785; sponsors, Jacob Boltz and Elizabeth Rug.

Family of John Stover.

The children of JOHN and BARBARA STOVER were:
   i. Eve-Elizabeth, b. June 5, 1780; bap. June 25, 1780; sponsors, John William Early and Eve Wolf.
   ii. George, b. March 14, 1783; bap. June 18, 1783; sponsors, George Sprecher and Catharine Wolstein.

Family of John Flueger.

The children of JOHN and ELIZABETH FLUEGER were:
   i. Susan-Mary, b. June 7, 1780; bap. June 25, 1780; sponsors, George and Barbara Wolf.
   ii. Ludwig, b. Feb. 19, 1784; bap. April 16, 1784; sponsors, Michael and Mary Regina Flie (?).
   iii. Anna-Mary, b. May 2, 1786; bap. March 14, 1786; sponsors, Michael and Mary Regina Flie (?).

Family of John Nicholas Nye.

The children of JOHN and EVE CATHARINE NYE were:
   i. Anna-Margaret, b. May 12, 1772; bap. May 26, 1772; sponsors, John Nicholas and Lena Margaret Nye.
   ii. Christina, b. Sept. 22, 1773; bap. Oct. 2, 1773; sponsors, Philip Baier and Mary Elizabeth Nye.
   iii. Mary-Catharine, b. May 28, 1775; bap. June 12, 1775; sponsors, Superiors.
   iv. John, b. July 7, 1776; bap. July 20, 1776; sponsors, John Nye and Margaret Bohr.
   v. John-Philip, b. Nov. 2, 1778; bap. Nov. 16, 1778; sponsors, John Nye and Catharine Schnetz.
   vi. Eve-Catharine, b. Dec. 25, 1780; bap. Jan. 7, 1781; sponsors, John Nye and Catharine Schnetz.
   vii. Christina-Barbara, b. Oct. 12, 1783; bap. Nov. 6, 1783; sponsors, Michael Malvier and Barbara Behm.
   viii. John-Henry, b. Dec. 18, 1785; bap. Feb. 19, 1786; sponsors, John Snoke and wife.

Family of John Christian Weisbach.

The children of JOHN CHRISTIAN WEISBACH and wife Anna Sabina were:

    i. Anna-Mary, b. Feb. 14, 1781; bap. Feb. 25, 1781; sponsors, Christian and Mary Ann Fetter.

    ii. Anna-Catharine, b. June 11, 1782; bap. July 7, 1782; sponsors, Christian and Mary Ann Fetter.

Family of Adam Zimmerman.

The child of ADAM and ELIZABETH ZIMMERMAN was:

    i. John-Michael, b. Jan. 15, 1781; bap. May 25, 1781; sponsors, Michael Brandt and Eve Catharine Zimmerman.

Family of Andrew Kraemer.

The children of ANDREW and EVE MARGARET KRAEMER were:

    i. Elizabeth, b. July 10, 1774; bap. Sept. 11, 1774; sponsors, Jacob Riel and Rosina Kraemer.

    ii. John, b. March 21, 1777; bap. April 4, 1777; sponsors John Zimmerman and Mary Weber.

    iii. Christina, b. Dec. 14, 1778; bap. Jan. 20, 1779; sponsors, Michael Boltz and wife Fanny.

    iv. John-Michael, b. Oct. 28, 1780; bap. Jan. 28, 1781; sponsors, Michael Boltz and wife Fanny.

    v. Eve-Catharine, b. ———, 1782; bap. March 23, 1783; sponsors, Valentine Kros and wife Enis.

Family of Nicholas Alberdahn (Albert).

The child of NICHOLAS and CATHARINE ALBERT was:

    i. Balthazer, b. Dec. 7, 1781; bap. Dec. 30, 1781; sponsors, John and Elizabeth Weber.

JOHN DOWNEY,

EDUCATOR AND ESSAYIST.

[At the dedication of the Downey school house, Harrisburg, the following address was delivered by Dr. William H. Egle.]

It is eminently proper, that in the services of this hour, something should be related concerning the man for whom this school building has been named. For what is a name unless we know somewhat of

the individual. In our court records we read over the names of men
who lived and died prior to the war for Independence; or when this
fair city on the Susquehanna was not yet dreamed of, or ever the
county of Dauphin had existence; or later on, at the beginning of the
present century, people who assisted at the early establishment of the
beautiful place we are so proud of and delight to call our home. No
interest attaches to many of the names we see—from the fact that
they left no record behind—but there are others who made their
mark in their day and generation. Not professional men, doctors,
lawyers and preachers, but real genuine men of mark who left their
impress for good on the history of the town and county, and whose
virtues and merits should not go unrecorded.

Among these noted and honored men was JOHN DOWNEY, and it is
of him and of his services to the community in which he lived almost a hundred years ago, that I propose to interest you in my brief
address. He was born at Germantown, Pa., in 1765, and was the son
of John and Sarah Downey. Among the slain near the Crooked
Billet, on the first of May, 1778, during the most trying hours of the
Revolutionary war, was Capt. John Downey. The *Pennsylvania
Packet*, then published at Lancaster, during the occupancy of Philadelphia by the British troops, in a letter from Plumstead, Bucks
county, under date of May 4th of that year says:

" On Friday, the first instant, fell the gallant Capt. John Downey,
late schoolmaster in Philadelphia, whose worth entitles him to a
place in the annals of America. He took an active and early part in
our struggle for liberty. He went as a volunteer to Jersey, last winter
was a year where he behaved gallantly in the battles of Trenton and
Princeton. He being chosen captain of a company of Philadelphia
militia, served his tour of duty, two months, last summer, at Billings-
port, when on account of his superior knowledge of mathematics, the
Executive Council employed him to make a military survey of the
river Delaware which he performed with great exactness. Since
which time he has performed many very important services to his
country, a love to which prompted him to attempt anything which
promised its welfare. He lately acted as an assistant commissary,
and in this capacity was with our brave militia when attacked last
Friday. From his known readiness to fight and bleed for his country, it is more than probable when the attack began he made the attempt to join his countrymen, when he was shot through the shoulder,
and thus he lay in his blood until the enemy returned, when they
dispatched him in a cruel manner, for his body was found with one
of his hands almost cut off, his head slashed in several places, his

skull cut through, his brains coming out at his nose, and scattered all around.   He was an enlightened patriot, an affectionate friend, a gallant soldier, a fond husband and an intelligent parent.   He had no inheritance to leave, as his little property was left in Philadelphia, but he has left a sorrowful widow, and five helpless children, in very indigent circumstances.   They are worthy the charitable."

The massacre at the Crooked Billet was one of the most inhuman transactions of the war for Independence.   Of the five helpless children left by Captain Downey, was John, then in his thirteenth year. Through the aid of a fond and devoted mother, and the friendship of the survivors of that bloody conflict, the son received an excellent classical education in the old Academy at Germantown, and a few years later opened a Latin and Grammar school at Harrisburg.   His entire energies at the time being devoted to education, he became one of the most successful teachers in the early history of the town.   At this period, in a letter to Gov. Thomas Mifflin, who had then entered upon his third term as Chief Executive of the State, and the limit, under the Constitution of 1790, John Downey proposed a "Plan of Education," remarkably foreshadowing the present school system, and which has placed him in the front rank of early American educators. This letter shows that he had a plain insight into the wants of the community long before they became evident to those in authority. But to the letter:

HARRISBURG, *24th Feb., 1797.*

" HONORABLE SIR :

"As a private member of the same community, over whose concerns you have been so long called to preside, I take the liberty of communicating to you my opinion respecting, what I take to be, some of its dearest interests.   I do so with the more freedom, presuming upon the liberality of your private character, and the sincerity of your public declarations.   I feel myself more peculiarly called upon to do so at this time, as the last period of your administration approaches— your successor in office is unknown, and we can neither appreciate his private or his public character.

"The subject to which I would particularly call your attention is the privation of mind in the mass of the community ; a subject which involves in it a variety of most important discussion, being pregnant with almost every evil from whence we have reason to dread alarm. From this source, finesse, hypocrisy, and property already begin to over-balance the talents and virtues, and society here is again threatened with the return of superstition and tyranny, from whose baneful influence, so long and so severely felt by the human race, we thought we had got free.

"This pestiferous malady I would trace to a radical defect in our Constitution, with whose vital essence an universal system of education ought to have been interwoven, as the heart from whose perennial spring a pure and salubrious stream could alone diffuse immortal energy to the whole system.

"From your public addresses I am already informed that this subject has engaged your serious attention, nor am I to learn that your power in such cases extends only to recommendation and that this recommendation has hitherto met with very inadequate returns. Yet the importance of the subject loudly calls for repeated and more energetic efforts. The object should not only be presented, but the subject traced with a master-hand in a perspicuous and concise system, which may reconcile the present circumstances of our society to the progressive perfectability of mind, which may safely leave the speculative doctrine of religion to the zeal of its numerously varying sectaries, and embrace only those subjects connected with man's interest and happiness as a member of civil society over which alone society has control.

"As a rude outline of such a system :

"Let the mind, as soon as it has gained some knowledge of the rudiments of its native tongue, be entertained with a simple history of such subjects as are daily presented to it through the medium of the senses, and this impressed by such anecdotes as are calculated to awaken its attention. From the history of external objects adapted to its infant powers, it may rise to morals, and universal morality may be inculcated by such interesting examples of individual morality as may fix the heart in the interest of humanity and virtue. The private interest and usefulness of the individual may now be attended to by teaching him writing, arithmetic, book-keeping, mensuration, mathematics, and geography ; and this course finished by showing him his importance to society, with mental powers duly cultivated under the protection of his inherent and inalienable rights, with the baneful consequences of his dereliction of them, and both illustrated by select facts drawn from a general but concise view of history.

"Such a course, it is presumed, may be sufficient to qualify him for the ordinary duties and common occupations of life. But, if the circumstances of any admit of, or their energies require more extensive information, they may pursue it by such means as opportunity or industry may place within their reach.

"To carry such a plan into effect :

"To teach the introductory branches of education as far as reading, writing, arithmetic and book-keeping, two or more schools may be erected in each township, and supported by such an annual tax upon property as may be sufficient as to secure a moderate independence to the teachers. The more advanced paths of science, already noticed, may be taught in one school erected in each township and supported in the same manner with the former. While more liberal science may be cultivated at an academy erected in each county, which a very moderate assessment throughout the county will be sufficient to support. Attendance upon the schools for a sufficient time should be strictly enjoined under an adequate penalty.

" Perhaps the public mind is not ripe for the reception of some such plan. It may, however, be forwarded by a variety of preparatory means.

" From the use which may be made of the influence of office, men of liberal and enlarged minds should be sought after and preferred to public employment. These, though best qualified to fill office with dignity and intelligence, are not found foremost in the race for public favor; while those who beg recommendation are commonly beneath the office they court, soon forget those who befriend them and tyrannize with all the insolence of office over those who are placed within the reach of their influence. The former endeavor to deserve office by embracing every opportunity of bettering the condition of those within their reach. The latter struggle to obtain and strain to hold office by keeping under the public mind and thwarting every plan proposed for its improvement.

" It might, also, not be unworthy the attention of the Legislature to raise agriculture from its present servilly, imitative practice by encouraging scientific pursuits. Individuals, equal to the task, should be encouraged in each county by an adequate fund sufficiently restricted by penalty, to the express purpose of ascertaining by experiment the easiest and best means of preparing our land for rotary crops; the succession of crops best adapted to the demand, soil and climate, and to publish annually a fair statement of the appropriations of the fund, with the success of these experiments.

" But a more arduous task remains for the Legislature.

> "In this rank age,
> Much is the patriot's weeding hand required.
> The toils of law (which dark insidious men
> Have cumbrous added to perplex the truth,
> And lengthen simple justice into trade),
> How glorious were the day that saw these brake
> And every man within the reach of right.

" This philanthropic wish, it is presumed, may be in a great measure accomplished by simplifying the multifarious and perplexed forms of law procedure, reducing them to one common standard throughout the State, and publishing these under its authority as the unerring rule by which every process shall be conducted. This might produce a happy effect upon the public mind by reducing legal business within known boundaries; it will not then elude the grasp of common capacity, but every man may, in a great measure, transact his own business, and thereby banish the chicanery, and fraud, and aristocratic pride which has so long disgraced an otherwise liberal profession.

"Many other topics of reform and improvement might be added, and each of them supported by such a variety of considerations as would carry this greatly beyond the bounds of a letter. But if the subject impresses you with the same idea of its importance, such consideration will be unnecessary. If it does not, it might be presuming too much to think that anything which I might offer would change your opinion.

"My chief reasons for troubling you are that if the subject strikes you with the same idea of its importance is likely to produce much more powerful effects when modeled by your ideas and clothed with your language, and to meet with more attention from your character and influence than it would if it appeared in a more questionable shape. To me it appears that you could not close your presidency with more dignity or utility than by turning the attention of the Legislature to this and other branches of reform and improvement during a short session called expressly for the purpose, should its present be too much crowded with other business, for a full discussion of the merits of this. It will doubtless give me pleasure to find that our ideas meet upon the subject. But if they do not, neither do they lessen the respect with which I am your fellow citizen.

Jno. Downey.

"*To the Hon'ble Thos. Mifflin, Governor of Pennsylvania.*"

It will be seen, by perusing this remarkable letter carefully, that not only the present school system is gracefully outlined, but on more than one subject John Downey was in advance of not only the age in which he lived, but, in reality, of the present era. It will also be observed that "Civil Service Reform" is no new thing. Mr. Downey, as may well be supposed, from his enlightened views, became one of the most prominent men in this section, and for almost one-third of a century was at the head of the leading enterprises of the day. He became the first cashier of the old Harrisburg bank, and was largely instrumental in securing the erection of the bridge over the Susquehanna river. He served as a member of the Legislature in 1817–18, and filled other positions of trust and honor and profit. Shortly after coming to Harrisburg, in addition to his duties as teacher, he filled the office of town clerk for a long period, and served as a justice of the peace from 1807 until his death. His dockets, in the possession of the speaker, are models in their way. "Squire Downey," as he was more frequently called, wrote a great deal for the newspaper press, and his productions are noted for their elegant diction. His series of papers entitled, "Simon the Waggoner," "Simon Slim," and Simon Easy," although mostly of a political character, sparkle with real, genuine wit, well worthy a permanent setting as a valuable contribution to literature. Mr. Downey died at Harrisburg the 21st of July, 1827, in the 62d year of his age, and the *Oracle of Dauphin* writes his epitaph in this one sentence: "A useful magistrate and a pious man." Mr. Downey married Alice Ann Beatty, daughter of Capt. James Beatty, of Harrisburg. She died in Ashland county, Ohio, May 14, 1841, aged sixty-four years. Their daughter, Ellen Downey, married Hon. Daniel Kilgore, of Ohio, and left a large family. Such in brief were the services of a teacher of the "olden time," and for whom you have named this building. He well deserves this recognition at your hands, and it has afforded me great pleasure to relate to you what I have learned concerning him. In his day and generation he was the wisest, for he saw in the future that great system of a free education which I sincerely trust each scholar who hears me this day will take every advantage of. Mr. Downey ninety years ago believed in compulsory education. Let the pupils of this school now, and in the years to come, prove by their regular attendance that their desire for knowledge is the great incentive that actuates them in the pursuit of the liberal education which the Board of School Control of our city are determined to guarantee them without regard to distinction of race or color.

NOTES AND QUERIES.—CXX.

CONTINENTAL CURRENCY.—Many have heard of this term, some have handled the money, but few know the history of it. For the benefit of our readers we give this information. The first issue of bills of credit was made by the Continental Congress under authority of the resolution of June 22d, 1775, for $2,000,000. On the 23d of

July Congress ordered the issue of $1,000,000. From time to time new issues were authorized, so that at the beginning of 1780 the enormous sum of $200,000,000 was afloat. The inevitable result was that the Continental money depreciated. In February, 1777, $100 in specie were worth $107 of currency. In February, 1780, $7,500 were necessary to purchase $100 in specie. After that the currency became utterly worthless. Congress never formally repudiated it, and never took any measures to redeem it.

BOYD AND WILSON was a well-known firm one hundred years ago in the town of Northumberland. Capt. John Boyd belonged to the Third Pennsylvania in the army of the Revolution. He was many years a justice of the peace and died at Northumberland February 13, 1832, aged eighty-two years. One of his daughters married Rev. W. R. Smith, D. D., once a noted preacher at Sunbury; another married Hon. Stephen F. Headly, a very able lawyer and accomplished gentleman, who represented Columbia county in the Senate some forty years ago, I believe. Both these gentlemen are dead, but have descendants. John B. Smith, I think, still lives in Peoria, Ill. Gen. William Wilson (my wife's grandfather), the other partner, was a well known man in his day, and was associate judge of Northumberland county, when he died in 1813. In the fall of 1787 the adoption of the Constitution of the United States met with considerable opposition in Northumberland county; the old officers of the Revolution rallied to its support, and Gen. William Wilson and his partner, John Boyd, became delegates from Northumberland county in the State Convention of Pennsylvania, which met on the 12th of December, 1787, and ratified the Constitution of the United States for our State.   J. B. L.

IN EARLY TIMES.

"PETITION OF THE INHABITANTS OF PAXTANG" IN 1745.

[To the researches of Samuel Evans are we indebted for the following, which is a valuable contribution to our local history. At some other time we propose giving some account of the majority of the signers. The road referred to especially was probably that which commenced at now Paxtang street, from Race street to Paxtang creek, and continued on the low ground through Highspire—the run there being then known as Renick's run—to the Swatara. Most of this road was absorbed by the original incorporators of the Harrisburg and Middletown turnpike. The "back road" is yet in existence. The paper is in the handwriting of Robert Baker, the first signer.]

The Humble Petition of the Inhabitants of Paxtang to the Honourable Court of Quarter Sessions, Sitting in Lanchester ye first tuesday in feb'y in the Year of our Lord own thousand seven hundred & fourtey five.

WHEREAS, We understand that there is application made to your Worships for a Road from John Harrises from the pine fourd upon Swatara to Coume Down on the River Side within the Bottoms which we Luck upon to be an unsupportable Burden that we are unable to Bair, for many Reasons; first, because of the maney Grate Swamps & mudey Runs that is to be Bridged; secondly, when they are Bridged there is no Expectation of them standing one Season, by Reason of the floods; thirdly, because the most of the Way is so soft that a Leetil time Wagons would Cutt it so that we never will be able to make it good nor maintain it, & besides all this, sum years ago John Harris sued for & obtained a Road from his house to the pine fourd: & notwitstanding of all our Labour & pains in Cutting & Bridging of the s'd Road, we acknowledge that it is not Good, nor scarce passable by the Direct Survey; Whereas a small vareyation might have mist those plases that is not passable. We are Bold to assert not six Rod might a mist sum of them. We beg Lave of Your Worships to hear us patiently to Represent our Case fairely as it is; & first, we have briefly shewn sum of the Evils that will attend that Road on the River side within the Bottom; and secondly, that the road already surveyed & Cutt from John Harrises to the pine fourd is not Good; & now we wou'd humbly shew whie this Latter Road is not Good & scarcely can be made Good; & first, because there was contending parties about the farries, to Witt: John Harris & Thomas Renicks; & the s'd Harris having obtained an order of court for this Back Road & all the men that was appointed for they Laying out of it was strangers to these Woods . . . . . owne; & he being Renickses special frind & near kinsman, the worst way he piloted them the Less it answred Harrises intent & the more Renixes; and besides all this the verey same day that this Back Road was laid out the Sherieph held a vandew of Peter Allon's Goods & there was few or none of the near neighbours at home to show them a Better way which we presume sum of your pettisnors can do, and notwithstanding of all the objections that may be made, that we did not varey a small matter when we Cutt the Road in answer to that; so we would had we not been Devided, theye that was for Renickes was punctul for the survey, sum threatening to stop it if we Left the Survey & others affraid

if they left the survey they wo'd have to coume & Cutt it again;
Therefore your petitisnors Humbley begs that there may be a final
stop put to the River side Road, & we acknowledge that it is the
Glorey of a Countrey to have Good Roads; & we promis to be as as-
sistive as possable we can, & Dos purpose a Better Way & as near as
aney yett purpos'd, & we can shew your Worships a Reason for it,
the Distance between Susquehana & Swatara is but a Littel way, &
the Watters 'or Runs falling both wais we can find Champion Drye
ground between the two, not that we are . . . . . own Road by
another, but that, that will be for a publick good.

Your Worships Compliance to our pettision will oblige your Humble
pettisioners Ever for to pray:

Robert Baker,	David Shields,	Samuel McCorkel,
John Shields,	John Barnett,	Thomas Forster,
Richard McClure,	Michael Graham,	Jeremiah Sturgeon,
Oliver Willey,	Andrew Colwell,	John Lowry,
Andrew Hanah,	Alexander Meharg,	James L——,
Thomas Smith,	John Killcreest,	William Chambers,
William Sharp,	James Kern,	James Gilchrist,
Matthew Shields,	William S——,	Jacob S——,
James Morgan,	Thomas Farrell,	William McMullin,
John Gray,	Andrew Scott,	John Willey,
James Polk,	Thomas Elder,	Alexander Culley,
Robert Smith,	Thomas Dugal,	William Barnett,
James Eaken,	James Coler,	John Cavet,
Samuel ——	Robert Gray,	Samuel Sturgeon,
William Chambers,	Timothy Shaw,	Alexander Osborn,
John Johnston,	John Forster,	Thomas Simpson,
Thomas Morrison,	Anthony Sharp,	William Scott,
George Alexander,	Henry McIlroy,	Thomas W——,
Patrick Montgomery,	Robert Armstrong,	Andrew Forster,
Joseph Scott,	John Porience,	Nehemiah Steen.

RECORDS OF BINDNAGLE CHURCH.—VI.

Family of Daniel Mueller.

The children of DANIEL and MARIA CATHARINE MUELLER were:
  i. *Anna-Catharine*, b. Aug. 8, 1781; bap. Aug. 26, 1781;
     sponsors, Emanuel Shuey and Catharine Brunner.
  ii. *Martin*, b. June 4, 1783; bap. June 7, 1783; sponsors,
     Martin Mueller and Eve Catharine Ziegler.

Family of John Adam Weiss.

The child of JOHN ADAM and EVE WEISS was:
  i. *Jacob*, b. Dec. 10, 1781; bap. Dec. 30, 1781; sponsors, John
     Nye and wife Mary Ann.

Family of George Michael Brunner.

The child of GEORGE MICHAEL and EVE MARGARET BRUNNER was:
  i. *Anna-Catharine*, b. Dec. 17, 1781; bap. Dec. 30, 1781; sponsors, Martin Meyer and Catharine Brunner.

Family of Jacob Reisch.

The child of JACOB and MARGARET REISCH was:
  i. *Simon*, b. Jan. 5, 1781; bap. Feb. 20, 1781; sponsors, Valentine and Mary Agnes Sterger.

Family of Jacob Knizel.

The children of JACOB and ELIZABETH KNIZEL were:
  i. *John-Jacob*, b. Feb. 12, 1774; bap. Feb. 27, 1774; sponsors, Jacob and Ann Mary Hedderich.
  ii. *Christian*, b. Nov. 23, 1778; bap. Nov. 29, 1778; sponsors, Michael and Anna Mary Ely.
  iii. *John*, b. Sept. 13, 1781; bap. Oct. 7, 1781; sponsors, Joseph and Eve Carmony.

Family of Michael Meyer.

The children of MICHAEL and CATHARINE MEYER were:
  i. *John*, b. Jan. 13, 1782; bap. Feb. 17, 1782; sponsors, Adam and Eve Weiss.
  ii. *Elizabeth*, b. ——; bap. Jan. 27, 1784; sponsors, Eberhardt and Elizabeth Weiss.

Family of John Gerberich.

The children of JOHN and CATHARINE GERBERICH were:
  i. *Eve-Catharine*, b. Feb. 10, 1782; bap. June 7, 1782; sponsors, Henry and Eve Catharine Schreiber.
  ii. *Henry*, b. Oct. 22, 1783; bap. Aug. 1, 1784; sponsors, Henry and Eve Catharine Schreiber.

Family of Jacob Stober.

The children of JACOB and EVE STOBER were:
  i. *Jacob*, b. Oct. 26, 1769; bap. Nov. 11, 1769; sponsor, Mathias Hess.
  ii. *Anna-Mary*, b. June 28, 1771; bap. July 10, 1771; sponsors, John Snoke and Anna Mary Weber.
  iii. *Adam*, b. Feb. 23, 1773; bap. June 9, 1773; sponsors, Adam Stober and Mary Weber.

    iv. Christina, b. Nov. 26, 1774; bap. Dec. 3, 1774; sponsors, John and Christina Stober.

    v. John, b. Sept. 25, 1776; bap. Oct. 5, 1776; sponsors, John and Christina Stober.

    vi. Margaret, b. Nov. 2, 1778; bap. Nov. 18, 1778; sponsors, George and Mary Gestweid.

    vii. Valentine, b. April 16, 1780; bap. May 4, 1780; sponsors, George Adam and wife Enis Stober.

    viii. Margaret, b. March 14, 1782; bap. April 5, 1782; sponsors, George Adam and wife Enis Stober.

Family of Jacob Bauman (Bowman).

The children of JACOB and CATHARINE BOWMAN were:

    i. Catharine, b. June 28, 1782; bap. July 2, 1782; sponsors, Adam Deininger and Mary Hemperly.

    ii. John, b. Feb. 6, 1784; bap. April 3, 1784; sponsors, Antony Hemperly and wife Julia.

Family of George Wolf.

The children of GEORGE and BARBARA WOLF were:

    i. Anna-Mary, b. July 29, 1780; bap. Aug. 17, 1780; sponsors, Christina Sponsler and Jacob Kissner and wife Catharine.

    ii. Magdalene (twin), b. July 29, 1780; bap. Aug, 17, 1780; sponsors, Christina Sponsler and Jacob Kissner and wife Catharine.

Family of Andrew Kiefer.

The children of ANDREW and MARY ELIZABETH KIEFER were:

    i. Mary-Eve, b. July 26, 1780; bap. Aug. 20, 1780; sponsors, John Adam and Mary Eve Weiss.

    ii. Andrew, b. July 6, 1783; bap. Aug. 13, 1783; sponsors, Andrew and Lena Braun.

    iii. John-William, b. Aug. 20, 1785; sponsors, John William Early and Barbara Bindnagle.

    iv. Susanna, b. Dec. 7, 1788; bap. Jan. 11, 1789; sponsor, Jacob Tichley.

Family of Christian Early.

The children of CHRISTIAN and ELIZABETH EARLY were:

    i. Christian, b. Aug. 23, 1780; bap. Sept. 3, 1780; sponsors, John Early and wife Regina.

ii. *John,* b. Feb. 18, 1783; bap. March 23, 1783; sponsors, Jacob Sieple and wife Enis.

iii. *Anna-Catharine,* b. May 13, 1784; bap. June 27, 1784; sponsors, Michael Killian and wife Catharine.

Family of Andrew Braun.

The children of ANDREW and CHRISTINA (the 2d wife) BRAUN were:

i. *John,* b. Nov. 5, 1780; bap. Nov. 12, 1780; sponsors, John and Eve Margaret Weber.

ii. *Andrew,* b. ——, 1782; bap. March 23, 1782; sponsors, Frederick and Enis Lenert.

NOTES AND QUERIES.—CXXI.

IN THE FRENCH AND INDIAN WAR.

[The following correspondence relating to the Indian maraudings subsequent to the defeat of General Braddock's army, is herewith given for the purpose of future reference. It will give our readers not familiar with the events of that era the dangers which beset our ancestors in the early days of their settlement.]

[Declaration of Adam Torrance.]

I, and Thomas Forster, Esq., Mr. Harris and Mr. McKee, with upwards of forty men, went up the 2d inst., [October, 1755,] to Captain McKee, at New Providence, in order to bury the dead, lately murdered on Mahahony creek; but understanding the corpse were buried, we then determined to return immediately home. But being urged by John Shekalamy, and the Old Belt, to go up to see the Indians at Shamokin, and know their minds, we went on the 24th, and staid there all night—and in the night I heard some Delawares talking—about twelve in number—to this purpose: "What are the English come here for?" Says another: "To kill us, I suppose; can we then send off some of our nimble young men to give our friends notice that can soon be here?" They soon after sang the war song, and four Indians went off, in two canoes, well armed—the one canoe went down the river, and the other across.

On the morning of the 25th we took our leave of the Indians and set off homewards, and were advised to go down the east side of the river, but fearing that a snare might be laid on that side we marched off peaceably, on the west side, having behaved in the most civil and friendly manner towards them while with them ; and when we came to the mouth of the Mahahony creek, we were fired on by a good number of Indians that lay among the bushes; on which we were obliged to retreat, with the loss of several men; the particular number I cannot exactly mention; but I am positive that I saw four fall, and one man struck with a tomahawk on the head in his flight across the river. As I understand the Delaware tongue, I heard several of the Indians that were engaged against us speak a good many words in that tongue during the action. ADAM TORRANCE.

The above declaration was attested by the author's voluntary qualification, no magistrate being present, at Paxtang, this 26th October, 1755, before us—

John Elder, Thomas McArthur, Michael Graham, Alex. McClure, Michael Teass, William Harris, Thomas Black, Samuel Lenes, Samuel Pearson, William McClure.

N. B.—Of all our people that were in the action, there are but nine that are yet returned.

[*John Harris to Secretary Peters.*]

PAXTANG, *October 28, 1755.*

To Richard Peters:

SIR: I received your letter and shall observe the contents. There is melancholy news, concerning which I have written to his Honor, the Governor. If there were encouragements for 1,000 or 1,500 men to meet the enemy and build a fort some place up Susquehanna, I imagine a number of men will go at their own expense to assist.

I am, sir,

your most humble servant,

JOHN HARRIS.

P. S.—I shall endeavor to keep out a few Mohawks, that are here, as spies. The Belt promised to send out some, but it was our River Indians, and some scouts from the French army, attacked us at Mr. Penn's creek. Yours, J. H.

[*James Galbraith to the Provincial Authorities.*]

PAXTANG, *October 31, 1755.*

From John Harris at 12 p. m.

To all his majesty's subjects in the Province of Pennsylvania and elsewhere: Whereas Andrew Mountour, Belt of Wampum, two Mohawks, and other Indians, came down this day from Shamokin, who say the whole body of Indians or greatest part of them in the French interests, is actually encamped on this side of George Gabriel's near Susquehanna; and that we may expect an attack in three days at farthest; and a French fort to be begun at Shamokin in ten days hence. Tho' this be the Indian report, we, the subscribers, do give it as our advice to repair immediately to the frontiers with all our forces to intercept their passage into our country, and to be prepared in the best manner possible for the worst event.

Witness our hands:

James Galbraith, John Allison, Barney Hughes, Robert Wallace, John Harris, James Pollock, James Anderson, William Work, Patrick Henry.

P. S.—They positively affirm that the above-named Indians discovered a party of the enemy at Thomas McKee's upper place on the 30th of October last.

Mona-ca-too-tha, The Belt, and other Indians here, insist upon Mr. Weiser's coming immediately to John Harris' with his men, and to council with the Indians.

Before me, JAMES GALBRAITH.

[*Rev. John Elder to Secretary Peters.*]

PAXTANG, *9th November, 1755.*

Mr. Peters, Esq.:

I have just received an express, informing me that out of the small party on guard last night in Tullyhoes gap of the mountain, five were killed and two wounded. Such shocking accounts we frequently receive, and though we are careful to transmit them to Philadelphia, and remonstrate and petition from time to time, yet to no purpose, so that we seem to be given up into the hands of a merciless enemy.

There are within these few weeks upwards of forty of his majesty's subjects massacred on the frontiers of this and Cumberland counties, besides a great many carried into captivity, and yet nothing but unreasonable debates between the two parties of our legislature, instead of uniting on some probable scheme for the protection of the province. What may be the end of these things, God only knows; but I really fear that unless vigorous methods are speedily used, we in these back settlements will unavoidably fall a sacrifice, and this part of the province be lost.

If I have expressed my sentiments with too much warmth, you will be kind enough to pardon me, as it proceeds from a hearty regard to the public good.

Sir, your obedient servant,

JOHN ELDER.

NOTES AND QUERIES.—CXXII.

ALEXANDER.—In reply to a correspondent the following took out warrants for lands in Pennsylvania:

Hezekiah Alexander, 150 acres in Peters township, Cumberland county, June, 1767.

John Alexander, in Hamilton Ban township, York county, in 1767.

George Alexander, in Hamilton Ban township, York county, as early as 1760.

James or Joseph Alexander, 200 acres at mouth of Buffalo run, in Cumberland county, in 1767.

William Alexander, 150 acres "on main branch of Conecocheague, Cumberland county," in 1767.

Jacob Alexander, 50 acres in Ayr township, Cumberland county, in 1767.

James Alexander, 300 acres in Kishacoquillas Valley, Cumberland county, in 1767.

ANDREW MONTOUR.—The following letter, dated at Paxtang, December 28, 1754, gives us the influence through which this noted member of the Montour family secured a commission in the Provincial service:

"SIR—This week Capt. Andrew Montour has made his interest so good with my brother, Wm. Harris, as to persuade him to go with him to our camp, and he engages that he shall receive a Lieutenant's command under him, upon the strength of which, and the willingness to serve his king and country, he resolves to go. Their company of white men I expect to have completed by Monday next, or the day following; they expect to march for Wills' creek by the way of Aughwick, in order to take a number of Indians with them. Some Indians that are here leave their families, and set off with them with all cheerfulness; and I'll ensure upon my brother's inclining to go; the young men about here enlisted immediately with the small encouragement I gave them, which was but my duty, and I hope that this company will act their part so well as to be a credit to our *River Men*, of which almost the whole consists. It is rumored here that there are now taken prisoners lately at our camp, fifteen French Indians. Upon what I hear our Indians at Aughwick are to go and determine their fate, either death or Liberty. I only mention this, but am not yet certain of the fact. Excuse blunders.

"Your very humble servant,

"*Edwin Shippen, Lancaster.*"   "JOHN HARRIS.

RECORDS OF BINDNAGLE CHURCH.—VII.

Family of John Zimmerman.

The children of JOHN and MARGARET ZIMMERMAN were:
  i. *Elizabeth,* b. May 27, 1781; bap. June 5, 1784; sponsors, Henry Mueller and Elizabeth Muenich.
 ii. *John,* b. Jan. 15, 1783; bap. March 23, 1783; sponsors, Henry Mueller and Barbara Zimmerman.
iii. *Michael,* b. Dec. 9, 1784; bap. Jan. 4, 1785; sponsors, Jacob and Susan Seefle.
 iv. *Margaret,* b. Feb. 8, 1788; bap. Feb. 16, 1788; sponsor, Daniel Hufnagle.
  v. *John-Jacob,* b. Oct. 19, 1790; bap. Oct. 31, 1790; sponsors, Jacob Kraemer.

Family of Andrew Henry.

The child of ANDREW and ELIZABETH HENRY was:
  i. *Jonas,* b. March 2, 1783; bap. March 23, 1783; sponsors—

Family of Jacob Jungmann (?).

The child of JACOB JUNGMANN, and his wife Margaret, was:
  i. *Mary-Elizabeth,* b. Nov. 13, 1782; bap. Nov. 23, 1783; sponsor, Christopher Maurer.

Family of George Bamberger.

The child of GEORGE and MARGARET BAMBERGER was:
  i. *Anna-Margaret,* b. Jan. 29, 1783; bap. March 23, 1783; sponsor, Oscar Stoever.

Family of Peter Schmeltzer.

The child of PETER and CATHARINE SCHMELTZER was:
  i. *John,* b. May 16, 1783; bap. June 12, 1783; sponsors, John and Elizabeth Reifert.

Family of Michael Ely.

The children of MICHAEL ELY were:
  i. *John,* b. July 8, 1773; bap. July 24, 1773; sponsors, Christian Heckedorn and Mary Meyer.
 ii. *Jacob,* b. May 4, 1775; bap. May 26, 1775; sponsor, Jacob Wenrich.

iii. Elizabeth, b. July 23, 1776 ; bap. Aug. 12, 1776 ; sponsors, Michael Daniel and wife.

iv. Mary, b. Aug. 16, 1778; bap. Sept. 6, 1778; sponsor, Jacob Kitzel.

v. Mary-Catharine, b. April 5, 1781; bap. April 12, 1781 ; sponsors, John Meyer and wife.

vi. Mary-Margaretta, b. June 12, 1784; bap. June 27, 1784; sponsor, Elizabeth Betterley.

vii. Christianna, b. March 10, 1786; bap. March 12, 1786; sponsors, John Oehrley and wife.

viii.–ix. Two daughters (twins), b. Oct. 17, 1787 ; bap. Nov. 4, 1787; sponsors, George Illinger and wife, and John Held and wife.

Family of Valentine Knox.

The children of VALENTINE and CATHARINE SOPHIA KNOX were :

i. John-George, b. Oct. 23, 1782 ; bap. Jan. 1, 1783; sponsors, John George Knox and Barbara Boltz.

ii. John-David, b. April 19, 1784 ; bap. May 2, 1784 ; sponsors, Michael Boltz and wife Fanny.

Family of Peter Killinger.

The child of PETER and CHRISTIANA KILLINGER was :

i. John-Michael, b. July 1, 1783 ; bap. July 6, 1783 ; sponsors, Andrew and Elizabeth Killinger.

Family of Valentine Steger.

The child of VALENTINE and AGNES STEGER was :

i. Christina, b. July 17, 1783 ; bap. Aug. 6, 1783 ; sponsor, Jacob Reisch.

Family of Andrew Weber.

The children of ANDREW WEBER were:

i. Mary-Christina, b. Sept. 21, 1783 ; bap. Oct. 17, 1783 ; sponsors, Daniel Hufnagle and Christina Muenich.

ii. Jacob, b. Dec. 27, 1785 ; bap. Feb. 19, 1786 ; sponsors, Stoffel Miller and Rosina Muenich.

Family of Michael Stuckey.

The child of MICHAEL STUCKEY and his wife Elizabeth were :

i. Catharine, b. Jan. 13, 1781 ; bap. Jan. 28, 1781 ; sponsors, Peter Nye and Catharine Fernsler.

iii. John-Michael, b. Sept. 27, 1783 ; sponsors, George Sprecher and Cath. Huber.

Family of Frederick Hetzler.

The child of FREDERICK and BARBARA HETZLER was:
i. *John-Jacob,* b. Sept. 30, 1783; bap. Nov. 16, 1783; sponsors, John Jacob Hertzler and Margaret Sprecher.

NOTES AND QUERIES.—CXXIII.

THE FIRST NEWSPAPER PUBLISHED IN HARRISBURG.

[We are indebted to the courtesy of the editor of the *Pennsylvania Magazine of History* for an advanced copy of the following, which is of much local interest. In the history of the newspapers of Dauphin county it is stated that probably the first newspaper published at Harrisburg was the *Harrisburg Advertiser,* as that was the sub-title of the *Oracle of Dauphin.* The finding of this copy of the first newspaper proves that our assertions were correct as to a previous publication to the *Oracle,* and we were not far from the name—" *The Harrisburg Journal and Weekly Advertiser."* The verses which are quoted were evidently written by Major Eli Lewis, one of the publishers and the author of the poem, "St. Clair's Defeat."]

THE FIRST NEWSPAPER PUBLISHED IN HARRISBURG, PENNSYLVANIA.

The author of the recently published "History of Dauphin County," in the chapter devoted to the " Newspaper Press of Harrisburg and of the County," states that "there are no files of the first newspaper," and " our entire knowledge consists in the fact that it is stated in the *Oracle of Dauphin,* in 1807, when noting the death of Major Lewis, and in the *Chronicle,* in 1827, when referring to the authorship of the ballad on 'St. Clair's Defeat,' that the first newspaper venture at Harrisburg was by Eli Lewis." The first number of *The Oracle of Dauphin and Harrisburg Advertiser* was issued October 20, 1792, by John W. Allen and John Wyeth.

In the collection of the Historical Society of Pennsylvania will be found No. 3 of Vol. I. of *The Harrisburg Journal and the Weekly Advertiser,* published on Wednesday, September 9, 1789, which therefore antedates the publication of *Oracle of Dauphin and Harrisburg Advertiser* somewhat over three years. The journal was "printed by T. Roberts & Co.," who announce in their advertisement at the foot of the fourth page, "Subscriptions at Two Dollars *per annum*, Advertisements in English and German languages, Essays and Letters of Intelligence are thankfully received; and printing in its different Branches is done with care and Expedition."

In size the paper is 4 pages, 10½ by 16½ inches, with twelve columns of printed matter, each three inches wide. The title is printed from two-line Minion old-style type, and is embellished with a wood cut representing a globe supported by the Goddess of Liberty on one side and Gottenberg on the other, surmounted by the American eagle with outspread wings, encircled by thirteen stars. The motto within the scroll beneath we have been unable to decipher. The general typographical appearance of the paper will compare favorably with newspapers of the period.

The advertising patronage of the number is contained in the first column of the first page, and out of five advertisements two were inserted by the publishers. One reads: "To the public. The Gentlemen that were intrusted with Subscription Papers, for the *Harrisburgh Journal and the Weekly Advertiser* are requested to send them in as quick as possible, as the paper is now in circulation, And we remain your Humble Servts. T. Roberts & Co." Following this, Lieut. John Gloninger, of the Troop of Light Dragoons, notifies the members to meet at William Palm's, in Londonderry township, Oct. 1, to elect one Captain, two Lieutenants and one Cornet. Squire John Kean requests the owners of a piece of Green Baize, which had been stolen, to come forward and prove property; and Alexander Graydon, Clerk of the Quarter Sessions, notifies all persons who have been recommended for Tavern Licenses, "that they do not receive an absolute License (as has been erroneously supposed) which is of no avail against the Penalties, on selling Liquors by the small measure without License." Extracts from the Journal of the House of Representatives of August 28th fill the balance of the page.

The second page is made up of "Law of the Union," comprising "An Act to regulate the collection of the Duties imposed by law on the tonnage of ships or vessels, and on Goods, Wares and Merchandizes imported into the United States," and "Foreign Intelligences," from London of May 12th.

The third page contains intelligence from Vienna, May 16th; Constantinople, April 7th; Warsaw, May 2d: Hamburg, June 2d; Stockholm, May 22d; Charleston, August 10th; Halifax, August 1st; New York, August 29th; Philadelphia, September 2d; and a reprint on "Jealousy," from the *Pennsylvania Packet*, which concludes:

"Now all the good he gets of his wife,
She wears the breeches, he the horns for life."

Under an embellished heading, the first column of the fourth page
is devoted to Poetry; and the following lines, which may possibly be
from the pen of Eli Lewis, describes the advantages of Harrisburg,
should it be selected as the site for the Federal town."

"Harrisburgh Explained,

in the following petition.

"Whereas it is of consequence,
Congress should fix its residence—
That seat of honor and renown,
Call'd long since the 'federal town;'
The people now of Harrisburgh,
From a conviction not absurd,
That there's no other situation,
Can equal this in all the nation;
Your honors do most humbly pray,
To make it your abode for aye.

"Nature provideth here so ample,
We only select a sample,
Of what this blessed place affords,
Enough to tempt a House of Lords!
Where'er you turn your wond'ring eyes,
Ten thousand pleasing prospects rise!
The streams meandering thro' the vales,
'Blue Hills,' whose height no skies assails;
The air salubrious, sweet and bracing,
All fogs, and noxious vapors chasing;
And as no mortal man can think,
But what you all must eat and drink,
Our markets give, ye gods, such meat.
As ye, in your own hotels, eat;
We've beef, and veal, and lamb and mutton,
As fine as e'er was table put on;
And dunghill fowls, wild ducks and widgeons,
And snipes, and geese, and quails and pigeons,
Pheasants, and ortolans, be sure,
To please the daintiest Epicure.
Our river gives us fish in plenty;
Of sorts we reckon more than twenty—
As Shad and Salmon, pretty picking,
Without a bone your throat to stick in;
That Susquehanna theme of song
Upon whose waves are borne along
An hundred thousand loads of wheat,
Transported in Tioga fleet—
Tioga fleet! yes, here in peace.
Congress may sit till time shall cease,
Nor ships with horrid broadsides scare 'em,
Nor soldier with a gun come near 'em.

"At present we've two hundred houses,
All filled with loving wives and spouses ;
But timber, shingles, scantling, boards,
The neighborhood great store affords;
We'll give you stones all veined with blue,
And thank you when you take them too ;
But as for bricks, you pay for making,
They cost us time and pains in baking;
We've carpenters and masons good,
As ever work'd in stone or wood ;
Artists in every kind of work,
To build your houses in a jerk.
We've tailors, saddlers and shoemakers,
Printers, Bakers, and good clock makers :
Taverns in plenty too abound,
And liquors of all sorts are found ;
Besides all these, there are ' exteriors,'
We need not mention our superiors,
But for convenience and delight,
To crown the day and 'eke out the night;
Then come good Sirs make this your seat
Where Nature's choicest bounties meet :
The public good prompts this petition,
From yours with reverence and submission.—*Cives.*"

An " Eastern Anecdote," copies of the following Acts of Congress : "An act to Establish an Executive Department, to be denominated the Department of War." "An act to provide for the Government of the Territory Northwest of the river Ohio ;" " An act providing for the Expenses which may attend Negotiations or Treaties with the Indian Tribes, and the appointment of Commissioners for managing the same, approved by " G. Washington, President of the United States ;" with the following "Advertisement Extraordinary," completes the make-up of the paper :

One Thousand Guineas Reward.

Ran away from the Subscriber, within a few years, his *whole estate,* consisting of houses, land, &c. They gradually and almost imperceptably stole away, after being put in motion by the magick art of one *Intemperance,* who then lived in the family. Any person who will put me in the re-possession of said Estate shall be entitled to the above reward.   TOPER.

N. B. All persons are cautioned to beware of said *Intemperance,* who, as I am told, has established several places of rendezvous in almost every town, where numbers of the incautious are daily seduced.

RECORDS OF BINDNAGLE CHURCH.—VIII.

Family of Adam Deininger.

The children of ADAM and ROSINA DEININGER were:
  i. *Christina*, b. Feb. 1755; sponsors at bap., John Early and wife Regina.
  ii. *Margaret*, b. Jan. 4, 1758; sponsors at bap., Michael Heiner (?) and wife Margaret.
  iii. *John-Adam*, b. Oct. 12, 1760; sponsors at bap., Casper Dieler (?) and Hocklander.
  iv. *Michael*, b. Nov. 17, 1763; sponsors at bap., Nicholas Brechbill and wife Julianna.
  v. *Regina*, b. April 26, 1766; sponsors at bap., John Early and wife Regina.
  vi. *Susan*, b. April 5, 1769; sponsors at bap., John Early and wife Regina.
  vii. *John*, b. Jan. 1, 1772; sponsors at bap., John Early and wife Regina.

Family of Nicholas Palm.

The child of NICHOLAS and CATHARINE PALM was:
  i. *John*, b. March 2, ———; bap. April 14, ———; sponsors, John Palm and wife Elizabeth.

Family of Michael Eli.

The children of MICHAEL and MARY REGINA ELI were:
  i. *Susan*, b. Sept. 20, 1789; bap. Sept. 27, 1789; sponsors, Jacob Young and wife Elizabeth.
  ii. *Michael* (twin), b. Sept. 20, 1789; bap. Sept. 27, 1789; sponsor, Thomas Early.

Family of Daniel Hufnagle.

The child of DANIEL and CHRISTINA HUFNAGLE was:
  i. *John-Jacob*, b. Nov. 26, 1784; bap. Jan. 5, 1785; sponsors, John Adam Weber and Elizabeth Muenich.

Family of Peter Nye.

The child of PETER and JULIANNA NYE was:
  i. *Mary-Barbara*, b. Jan. 17, 1785; bap. March 13, 1785; sponsors, Joseph Carmony and wife Eve.

Family of Jacob Kraemer.

The children of JACOB and CATHARINE KRAEMER were:
    i. John-Jacob, b. March 2, 1785; bap. June 12, 1785; sponsors, John Zimmerman and wife Margaret.
    ii. Peter, b. June 18, 1790; bap. Aug. 29, 1790; sponsors, Adam Weber and wife Elizabeth.

Family of George Wolfe.

The child of GEORGE and BARBARA WOLFE was:
    i. John-George, b. Jan. 26, 1785; bap. Sept. 23, 1785; sponsors, John Fluger and wife Elizabeth.

Family of Christopher Fox.

The child of CHRISTOPHER and SUSAN MARGARET FOX was:
    i. Christopher, b. May 30, 1785; bap. Aug., 1785; sponsors, Jacob Kraemer and wife Anna Catharine.

Family of John Wolfe.

The children of JOHN and ELIZABETH WOLFE were:
    i. Catharine-Elizabeth, b. Jan. 6, 1784; bap. Jan. 11, 1784; sponsors, Andrew Braun and wife.
    ii. Catharine, b. Sept. 16, 1785; bap. Sept. 26, 1785; sponsors, Conrad Tielmann and Catharine Wolf.

Family of Peter Nye.

The family of PETER and REBECCA NYE were:
    i. Barbara, b. Oct. 4, 1783; bap. Oct. 18, 1783; sponsor, Barbara Nye.
    ii. John, b. Jan. 27, 1785; bap. March 27, 1785; sponsors, John Nye and wife Catharine.
    iii. John-Peter, b. March 27, 1787; bap. Nov. 18, 1787; sponsors, Michael Nye and Barbara Birhnson (?).
    iv. ——, b. ——, 1791; bap. ——, 1791; sponsors, Adam Biele and wife.

Family of Gottlieb Strumann (?).

The child of GOTTLIEB and JOHANNA AUGUSTA STRUMANN was:
    i. John-Michael, b. Dec. 20, 1783; bap. Dec. 25, 1783; sponsors, Michael Eli and wife.

Family of Jacob Seehale (?).

The children of JACOB and SUSAN SEEHALE were:
  i. *Benjamin,* b. Nov. 21, 1777; bap. March 4, 1778; sponsors, John Zimmerman and Margaret Muenich.
 ii. *Catharine,* b. June 28, 1779; bap. July 4, 1779; sponsors, John Peter and wife.
iii. *Elizabeth,* b. Oct. 7, 1781; bap. Oct. 20, 1781; sponsors, Daniel Wunderly and wife.
 iv. *Magdalena,* b. Nov. 6, 1783; bap. Dec. 11, 1783; sponsor, Catharine Muenich.

Family of John Kraemer.

The child of JOHN and CATHARINE KRAEMER was:
  i. *John-George,* b. Nov. 9, 1787; bap. June 8, 1788; sponsors, John George Muenich and Gretchen Brechbill.

Family of Christian Bamberger.

The children of CHRISTIAN BAMBERGER and his wife Magdalena were:
  i. *Magdalena,* b. Jan. 12, 1769; bap. Jan. 28, 1769.
 ii. *John,* b. Feb. 26, 1772; bap. March 3, 1772.
iii. *Christina,* b. Jan. 8, 1774; bap. Jan. 24, 1774.
 iv. *Michael,* b. Jan. 1, 1776; bap. Jan. 30, 1776.
  v. *Anna,* b. Jan. 2, 1778; bap. Jan. 2, 1778.
 vi. *Catharine,* b. March 17, 1779; bap. March 30, 1779.
vii. *William,* b. Feb. 8, 1783; bap. March 13, 1783.

Family of Adam Berger.

The children of ADAM BERGER and wife were:
  i. *George,* b. May 5, 1790; bap. June 27, 1790; sponsors, George and Catharine Sprecher.
 ii. *Magdalena,* b. Jan. 1, 1792; bap. Jan. 8, 1792; sponsors, John Oehrlie and wife.

Family of Michael Braun.

The child of MICHAEL and CHRISTINA BRAUN was:
  i. *Anna-Catharine,* b. Jan. 14, 1784; bap. March 7, 1784.

Family of Jacob Bolz.

The child of JACOB BOLZ and wife Elizabeth was:
  i. *Elizabeth,* b. Jan. 14, 1784; bap. March 7, 1784; sponsors, John Bolz and Christina Fernsler.

Family of Andrew Killinger.

The child of ANDREW and ELIZABETH KILLINGER was:
  i. *John-Frederick,* b. March 22, 1784; bap. Sept 16, 1784;
     sponsors, Frederick and Dorothea Bickle.

Family of Frederick Schell.

The child of FREDERICK and DOROTHEA SCHELL was:
  i. *John-Henry,* b. March 13, 1784; bap. May 7, 1784; spon-
     sors, Martin and Elizabeth Bindnagle.

Family of Adam Wert.

The child of ADAM and ELIZABETH WERT was:
  i. *Mary-Elizabeth,* b. May 8, 1784; bap. May 29, 1784; spon-
     sors, John and Anna Margaret Snoke. Jr.

Family of Jacob Young.

The child of JACOB and MAGDALENA YOUNG was:
  i. *John,* b. May 15, 1784; bap. June 1, 1784; sponsors, John
     Reichert and wife Elizabeth.

Family of Michael Noland.

The children of MICHAEL and REBECCA NOLAND were:
  i. *Elizabeth,* b. Aug. 30. 1782; bap. Sept 26, 1782.
  ii. *Henry,* b. June 21, 1784; bap. Sept. 26, 1784; sponsors,
     John and Elizabeth Early.

Family of Philip Johns.

The children of PHILIP JOHNS were:
  i. *Jacob,* b. Sept. 25, 1791; bap. Oct. 30, 1791; sponsors,
     Johne Thuhe (?) and wife.
  ii. *Christina,* b. Sept. 27, 1793; bap. Oct. 7, 1793; sponsors,
     Conrad Maeyer and wife.

Family of George Sprecher.

The child of GEORGE SPRECHER was:
  i. *Margaret,* b. Jan. 26, 1791; bap. March 6, 1791; sponsor,
     Margaret Sprecher.

The foregoing completes the baptismal record. Later and other
records ought to be in existence.

NOTES AND QUERIES.—CXXIV.

ORIGINAL LAND WARRANT.—Col. Henry McCormick, of Harrisburg, has the original patent to the land now constituting his fine summer residence on the Yellow Breeches, near Williams' Grove. It bears date 1734, and what is remarkable is that the boundaries of the farm to-day are just what they were at that time. There are not many farms surveyed and patented as early as this one that have preserved their original acres, even in the conservative agricultural element of Cumberland county. One or two in Dauphin and one or two in Lebanon are all we know of in this vicinity.   H.

GENEALOGICAL NOTES.

BOWMAN.

THOMAS BOWMAN, of Derry, d. January, 1763, leaving a wife Mary, who was a daughter of Samuel Campbell, and issue:

    i. Hugh.
    ii. Jean.
    iii. Elizabeth.
    iv. John.

Thomas Hall was a legatee. The witnesses to the will were Hugh Campbell, John Campbell and John Clark.

BOYD.

SAMUEL BOYD, of Drumore township, Lancaster county, d. January, 1770, leaving children:

    i. John, and had a son *Samuel.*
    ii. Samuel, d. prior to his father, and left *Joseph, Samuel. William,* and *Margaret.*
    iii. Margaret, m., and had *Samuel,* and *Matthew.*
    iv. Elizabeth.

The executors were William Richey, Jr., and John Boyd.

BAKER.

JOSHUA BAKER, gunsmith of the town of Lancaster, d. June, 1754, leaving a wife Rebecca, and children:

  i. Mary, m. Rev. John Elder.
  ii. Joshua.
  iii. Ann, m. ―――― Dougherty.
  iv. Eleanor, m. ―――― Woods.
His executors were the wife, Rev. George Craig and Robert Thompson.

―――

BOHRE.
 MATTHEW BOHRE, of Hanover, d. January, 1782, leaving a wife Mary Elizabeth, and six children, besides the following:
  i. Nicholas, was executor of his father's estate.

―――

CUNNINGHAM.
 SAMUEL CUNNINGHAM, of Mount Joy township, Lancaster county, d. July, 1777, leaving a wife Jannett, and children:
  i. Samuel.
  ii. Sarah, m. ―――― Porterfield.
  iii. Martha, m. ―――― Barr.
  iv. James.
  v. [*A dau.*], m. ―――― Campbell, and had *Hannah.*
  vi. Robert.
Robert, the youngest child, was executor.

―――

COULTER.
 JAMES COULTER (resided west of the Susquehanna), d. January, 1735–6, leaving a wife Mary, and children:
  i. Samuel.
  ii. Sarah.
In his will he refers to his brother, Joseph Coulter, " at Bainbridge in the kingdom of Ireland."

―――

CAMPBELL.
 GEORGE CAMPBELL, on March 26, 1759, " sergeant of Captain John Singleton's company, now in the Hospital at Fort Ligonier," made a will, bequeathing his estate to his mother, Eleanor Campbell, of Baltimore. What Campbell family was this?

―――

COOK.
 JAMES COOK, of Donegal township, Lancaster county, d. in October, 1774, leaving a wife Mary, and children:

   i. James.
   ii. John.
   iii. David.
   iv. Dorcas.
   v. Margaret.

The executors were his wife and brother David Cook.

DeHuff.

JOHN DeHuff, of the town of Lancaster, d. August, 1754, leaving a wife Catharine, who was executor of the estate, and children as follows:

   i. John.
   ii. Abraham.
   iii. Susanna.
   iv. Henry.
   v. Matthias.

JOHN BANNISTER GIBSON.

SKETCH OF AN EMINENT PENNSYLVANIA JURIST.

John Bannister Gibson was of Scotch-Irish lineage, one of three sons of George Gibson, of Shermansdale, then in Cumberland and now in Perry county, who was a soldier of the Revolution, and had attained the rank of colonel, when he fell at St. Clair's defeat in 1791. His mother was Ann West, a daughter of Francis West, one of the early Provincial justices of Cumberland county. He was born on the 8th of November, 1780, died on the 2d of May, 1853, and his bones await the resurrection beneath the marble shaft, in the old grave-yard in Carlisle, on which is inscribed the following from the pen of his devoted friend, the late Judge Black:

In the various Knowledge | which forms the perfect Scholar, | He had no Superior. | Independent, upright and able, | He had all the highest qualities | of a great Judge. | In the difficult science of Jurisprudence | He mastered every Department, | Discussed almost every question, and | Touched no subject which he did not | adorn. | He won in early manhood | And retained to the close of a long life, | The Affection of his brethren on the | Bench | The Respect of the Bar, | And the confidence of the people.

His brothers were Gen. George Gibson and Francis West Gibson, Esq., both of whom survived him. The latter was for some years, when quite an aged man, a resident of Carlisle, but returned to the old homestead, where they were all born and reared, and died there. Gen. George Gibson was for many years an officer of the U. S. army. He was an intimate personal friend of President Jackson, with whom he served in the army in the war of 1812. On the 18th of April, 1818, he was appointed Commissary General of Subsistence, with the rank of colonel, and continued at the head of this department until the 20th of September, 1861, when he died with the rank of brevet major general, U. S. army, after having served in it with nonorable distinction for forty-three years.

John Bannister Gibson entered Dickinson College, and graduated from it during the presidency of that distinguished scholar, Charles Nisbet, D. D., studied law with Hon. Thomas Duncan, then an eminent lawyer and afterwards an associate member of the Supreme Court with him, and was admitted to the bar in 1803. After opening an office in Carlisle, he went to Beaver county, and not succeeding as well as he expected, removed to Hagerstown, Md., but being still dissatisfied returned to Carlisle and settled down to the practice of his profession in 1805. In 1810 he was elected to the House of Representatives, and whilst there was a member of a committee that reported an address to Governor Snyder for the removal of Judge Cooper, then president judge of the Eighth Judicial district of this State, but he put on record a strong protest against the doctrines contained in the address, and afterward became an intimate friend of Doctor Cooper, who at a later period was professor of chemistry at Dickinson College, and subsequently at the University of Pennsylvania, and ultimately became president of Columbia College, South Carolina.

In 1812 he was appointed President Judge of the Eleventh Judicial district, and in 1816 an Associate Judge of the Supreme Court, and upon the death of Chief Justice Tilghman, in 1827, he was appointed Chief Justice, which position he held up to 1851, when the judiciary became elective, and the people had wisdom enough to retain him in the place he had filled so well. He was for twenty-four Chief Justice and thirteen years an Associate Justice of the Supreme Court, and thus spent more than half of his life on that bench, his opinions running through seventy volumes of our reports. He was appointed to it originally, and afterwards its Chief Justice by a Democratic Governor of the State. This was under the Constitution of 1790. Under that of 1838 he was reappointed Chief Justice by a Whig Governor, and when the judiciary system was again changed he was elected to the Supreme Bench after a nomination by a Democratic convention, and " it is said he narrowly escaped what might have been a dangerous distinction, a nomination on both of the opposing tickets."

In regard to his personal characteristics very little more is known here than in other portions of the State. His duties kept him most of his time away from Carlisle. His habits were domestic, and the little while he had here was spent with his family, and even then he was generally engaged writing opinions assigned to him at the term that had ended. All that was seen of him here in the latter years of his life outside of his immediate family, and a few personal friends, was witnessed in his passing from his dwelling to the offices of members of the bar, who had books of reference that he wanted to look into.

But he was one to be remembered when seen. He was over six feet in height. His frame was large and his figure ungainly. His gait was slow and he seldom gave heed to what was happening around him or who was passing by. He was careless of his appearance, as the neck handkerchief in the portrait we have, both by its color and tie, will illustrate. But all the same, there was that about him which attracted the immediate attention of any intelligent person that met or passed him on the street. What this was is hard to define, unless there is in our race an intuitive perception of and deference toward great intellect and genius in men, as there certainly is toward beauty and virtue in women.

One who knew him in his prime said of him, "that his face was eminently handsome and full of intellect and benevolence—that his manners were frank and simple, and that he was free from affectation or pretension of any sort." Those who saw him only in advanced life remember his face as strong, rather than handsome, but through the wrinkles discerned traces of the superb complexion which he transmitted to his descendants. That he was free from affectation is hardly reconcilable with the fact that he cut short a full head of dark brown hair and covered it with a wig after he went on the bench, and continued to wear it to the last, although he had beneath it at death a full head of gray hair; and that he was without pretension of any sort, with this, that he commences his will dated the 17th of January, 1852, thus : "I, John Bannister Gibson, the last of the Chief Justices under the Constitution of 1790."

His attainments outside of his profession were varied and considerable. He had a natural talent for music, and cultivated it, and was considered a connoisseur of music and art. He was well read in the British classics, fond of the English drama, and familiar with the dramatists of the Restoration ; but his fame will ever be associated with the highest judicial tribunal of our State, where he reigned supreme.

Judge Black, in response to the motion of Hon. Thaddeus Stevens, at the first meeting of the court after his death, among other things said: "Abroad, he has for many years been thought the great glory of his native State." This is a high enconium, and yet in confirmation of it a distinguished citizen of our State in the lifetime of Judge Gibson stated that he was in Westminster Hall giving attention to an argument when one of the counsel cited an American authority, without giving the name of the volume or case, when the Chief Justice said at once, "That is by Chief Justice Gibson, of Pennsylvania. His opinions are considered of great weight in this court."

Perhaps as fine a portrayal of the characteristics of one great mind by another as can readily be found is that by Black of Gibson in the response above referred to. We have no space for more of it than the following, and it is given not because it is finer than other portions which relate more particularly to his character as a judge, but because it refers to qualities of head and heart, alike admired by lawyer and layman. "He was of all men the most devoted and earnest lover of truth for its own sake. When subsequent reflection convinced him that he had been wrong, he took the first opportunity to acknowledge it. He was often the earliest to discover his own mistakes, as well as the foremost to correct them. He was inflexibly honest. The judicial ermine was as unspotted when he laid it aside for the habilaments of the grave as it was when he first assumed it. I do not mean to award him merely that common place integrity, which is no honor to have, but simply a disgrace to want. He was not only incorruptible, but scrupulously, delicately, conscientiously free from all willful wrong, either in thought, word or deed.

"Next, after his wonderful intellectual endowments, the benevolence of his heart was the most marked feature of his character. He was a most genial spirit, affectionate and kind to his friends, and magnanimous to his enemies. Benefits received by him were engraved on his memory as on a tablet of brass, injuries were written in sand. He never let the sun go down upon his wrath. A little dash of bitterness in his nature would, perhaps, have given a more consistent tone to his character, and greater activity to his mind. He lacked the quality which Dr. Johnson admired. He was not a good hater."

What chance of success he would have in a canvass for the judgeship at the present day, in the way it is now conducted in some localities, it is hard to conjecture. You could hardly conceive of him moving round with 12th Sergeant and Rawle under his arm to prove to a jacobinical democracy that he held that the Supreme Court had no right to pronounce an act of Assembly void although it was a manifest breach of the Constitution, or with 10th Barr to show to another class of constituents, that husbands may make valid conditions in restraint of marriage in devises of real estate; and yet we have not been without candidates for judicial office who were ready to give their opinions on questions that were to be judicially determined by them with the same freedom that a peddlar would his about his wares. He knew little about the primaries. He could not have learned how to run a convention. He was ignorant of the methods to control the floating vote. He was not a man of the people and had no skill in making friends in the popular sense of the word. So great was his want in this respect that he lost the vote of the representatives of his county, when he was nominated for election in 1851, although one of the delegates was a member of the bar of high standing and character, whose instructions were not to favor his nomination. At that time one of those most opposed to him was Judge Black, who had taken a dislike to him because he thought Judge Gibson had failed to give him that recognition which he knew he was entitled to claim. This only tended to endear them to each other when Black learned that he was a man of modesty, absent-minded, and without the ability to remember faces, and forgetful of injustice to himself.

In that old grave-yard, but a few paces from him, sleeps Dr. Nisbet, to whom he was devotedly attached when a young man, whose memory he always revered. He it was who designed and wrote the Latin inscription on the monument erected to the memory of the learned Scotchman that gave Dickinson College its first distinction. Near to him lies Judge Duncan, with whom he studied law, his townsman, kinsman, and for some years his associate on the supreme bench; and nearby also Judge Brackenridge, his immediate predecessor in the same court, who took notice of him when an awkward country boy attending college, invited him to his house, and opened to him the treasures of the finest library here at that day. The delights of this association he mentioned often in his family, and spoke of Brackenridge with tenderness to the end of his days. James Ross lies there, author of the Latin grammar, a fine classical scholar and the instructor of many ingenuous youths; and there, too, lies Doctor Alfred Foster, *facile princeps* of a brilliant circle that has passed away.

In that sacred ground, within a radius of a hundred yards lie David Watts, Samuel Alexander, S. Dunlap Adair, Hugh Gaulagher, Wm. M. Biddle, Hon. John Reed, Hon. James H. Graham, all of whom argued cases before him, and some of them had their opinions passed on by him ; and there, too, are still others distinguished in war and peace, in Church and State, and in every walk in life; but of them all few have left as stainless and none as great a name.

A. BRADY SHARPE.

NOTES AND QUERIES.—CXXV.

BINDNAGLE CHURCH.

Nearly two weeks ago, accompanied by "E. W. S. P.," who has been editing the old records of Bindnagle church, we took in this landmark of the early German settlement in Lebanon county. The location of the church is a beautiful one—on a high rocky bluff on the east bank of the Swatara, five miles north of Palmyra. It overlooks a large tract of charming country—of finely cultivated farms, wood and meadow and orchard—to the Conewago hills on the south and the first range of the Blue mountains on the north.

The building is a plain substantial brick edifice, erected in 1803. It has recently been repainted, both exterior and interior. Inside it presents the same arrangement it did eighty years ago—but the gaudy painting of the walls in attempted imitation of variegated marble proves that this at least was no improvement.

There are three doors, one on the east or front, the south and north sides, respectively. The seats are the old style straight back, and the little pulpit so high that in looking at the minister one would run in danger of dislocating the neck. A gallery runs around three sides.

Over the pulpit is the sounding board, beneath which some traveling artist has painted a portrait of St. John, the Evangelist. Above the pulpit and near it is a painting of what was intended for a picture of the Divine Master. The poet and artist, John Landis, in his palmy days would have been shocked at this artistic triumph. Around it on the same panel are the words—

" Bete und Arbeite."

On either side are two panels with cherubs to the top, and below on the right side the legend—

"Liebe Gott uber Alles."

While to the left is that of—

"Liebe deinen Nachsten."

In the main aisle running from the south to the north door are two large cannon stoves, the pipes of which connect with a huge sheet iron drum almost on a level with the gallery, from the center of which passes the smoke flue.

We next inspected the old relics—and of these there are quite a number, all worth examining as illustrative of a century ago. An elegant copy of "Sterbens-Kunst," printed in Leipsic in 1713, and bound in vellum, containing 1,274 small quarto pages, is one of the treasures. The little bells which were attached to the old collection bags of velvet, and which hang beside the columns supporting the gallery, are shown. In the early times, when a minister thought nothing of an hour and a half and even of a two and three hour sermon, we are not surprised that the collectors of "Peter's pence" deemed it necessary to arouse the sleepers by the tinkling of the bell. The old black gown worn by the minister, riddled with moth-holes, reminds one of the days when the Lutheran ministers followed in the wake of the great Reformer and fully believed in distinctive church furniture and church clothing.

The communion service is of interest. The pieces are all of pewter and exceedingly quaint in design. A small tankard has engraved on it, " M. B. H., 1715." This was evidently an old family relic, brought from the Fatherland by an early settler and presented to the church. There are two large tankards of similar shape, on one of which is the inscription, " *Gest von Mich'l Zimmermann, 1762 ;*" while upon the other is engraved "*Gest von I. W. Kissner, 1762.*" There seems to be only one goblet remaining. It is quite large and inscribed, "*M. Miller, den 20 Decemb'r, 1754.*"

The baptismal bowl is a large pewter dish, which would hold about a gallon of water. Four small pewter platter plates complete this antiquated communion service.

The old coffin cloth is still in existence—although much faded and moth-eaten. On it are worked in large letters, " H. B. N.,1754." This was no doubt the gift of Heinrich Bindnagle. In good preservation is the Bible rest and the cloth covering used in 1753.

To complete these relics of the old times there is in the possession of the church a large box filled with Continental money. We suggested that this ought to be sold and the proceeds turned into the church treasury. Otherwise it may disappear. Of course it is only valuable as a curiosity.

We examined everything about this venerable edifice—even to the wrought iron hinges and locks of almost a century ago, and then turned into the graveyard, where rest the remains of the fathers and mothers of the years which have gone. Even this God's acre has been carefully tended. The briars and weeds which rendered it almost impassable have been recently removed and grass seed sown. It speaks well for the survivors. We hurriedly made transcripts from the stones which mark the resting place of Bindnagle's sleeping children, and as darkness came on apace, bade adieu to this old landmark of early settlement, with feelings of great veneration for Bindnagle church.

LETTERS FROM OLD IRON MASTERS.

[The following transcripts furnished us by John W. Jordan, of the Historical Society of Pennsylvania, may not interest the general reader, but to the iron manufacturers of to-day have a special value.]

DURHAM, *April 12th, 1750.*

Dear Sir : The bearer is one of the company's servants whose arm was bruised by the overset of a cart, beg the favor to recommend him to your doctor, whose charges with the ferryage, two quarts of oats for our creatures, and a pint or quart of beer for the man shall be paid to you. . . . . The furnace will be in blast in June next. We then can cast for you what 56, 28, 14 and 7 lbs. weight you shall want, ...
Your most humble servants,
WILLIAM LOGAN & CO.

GREENWICH IRON WORKS, *July 12th, 1750.*

Sir : This is to desire you please to order something of Dr. Otto to cure persons that is poisoned in mowing grass, and please to order your saddler to make conveniences in my saddle to carry a pistol on each side of the saddle. . . . . . Your humble serv't,
JACOB STARR.

Received of John Brownsfield, twenty-eight pounds in full for one ton bar iron had of me the 18th of January last.
Witness my hand this 7th of May, 1751.
JOHN POTTS.

DURHAM, *23 April, 1752.*

Friend Jasper Payne: There was no agreement made between John Brownfield and me about the price of iron, and I only told him that I could not sell it under £28 per ton, but if William Logan, whom I expect up in a short time, would lower the price, he should know of it. . . . . In behalf of William Logan & Co.
HENRY MITCHELL.

UNION IRON WORKS, *Dec. 19th, 1794.*

Dear Sir : I received your favor with balance of the old account. . . . . . Being confident of the goodness of our new iron have sent you five hundred of it to make a trial, assuring you at the same time you shall have whatever quantity of it you want, 20 shillings per ton less than you can possibly get it for anywhere else. . . . . .
Sir, your most humble servant,
JOHN HACKETT.

UNION IRON WORKS, *20th Dec., 1754.*

Dear Sir : The bearer informs me that you are willing to supply us with shoes as follows: Women's shoes at 5 shillings per pair and men's at 7 shillings; and if there should happen to be any boys' shoes among them you must fix your price accordingly. It is true that I can have them of others 6d. a pair cheaper, but I have reason to think that your shoes are 6d. a pair better. Therefore, if these terms are agreeable to you, I would recommend to you to get a hundred pair made, and send them as soon as it suits your convenience. I am, with great convenience, your very humble servant,

JOHN HACKETT.

———

DURHAM, *6th May, 1757.*

Mr. Oerter : Please send by Peter Christian the four blind-halters I wrote for some time ago, and likewise a skin fit for sewing leather, and if the saddler has any good snaffle bridles, please to send one. All which charge to account of Durham company. I am, sir, your humble servant, GEORGE TAYLOR.

———

GENEALOGICAL NOTES.

———

DIXON.

ROBERT DIXON, of Drumore township, Lancaster county, d. in January, 1767, leaving a wife Ann, and children:

    i. William.

    ii. Robert.

———

DENNY.

MARGERY DENNY, widow of Walter Denny, of Little Britain township, Lancaster county, d. June, 1761, leaving daughters as follows:

    i. Sarah, m. John Evans.

    ii. Ann, m. Robert McQuestion.

    iii. Margery, m. David Dunning.

———

DUFFIELD.

GEORGE DUFFIELD, of Salisbury township, Lancaster county, d. March, 1774, leaving a wife Elizabeth, and children:

    i. William, m., and had *George.*

    ii. Mary, m. ——— McIlvain, and had *George,* and *Andrew.*

    iii. John, m., and had *George, John, Elizabeth, Francina,* and
        Margaret.
    iv. Samuel.
    v. George, m., and had *George,* and *Elizabeth.*

EWING.

  JAMES EWING, of Lebanon township, d. April, 1776, leaving a wife
Sabina, and children :
    i. William.
    ii. John.

EARLEY.

  JACOB EARLEY, of Donegal, d. April, 1777, leaving a wife Christina,
and children :
    i. John.
    ii. Jacob.
    iii. Lutery, m. —— Smith.
    iv. Agnes, m. —— Winagle.
    v. Eva.

ENSMINGER.

  NICHOLAS ENSMINGER, of Lebanon township, d. May, 1781, leaving
a wife Elizabeth, and children, besides others not named :
    i. Peter.
    ii. Daniel.

FLORA.

  JOHN FLORA, of Rapho township, Lancaster county, d. during the
war of the Revolution, leaving a wife Anra, and children :
    i. Elizabeth.
    ii. Rachel.
    iii. John.
    iv. Anna.
    v. Barbara.
    vi. Catharine.
    vii. Mary.
    viii. Magdalena.
    ix. Salome.
    x. Judith.

FULTON.

JOHN FULTON d. April, 1753, and left issue :
   i. Andrew.
   ii. John.
   iii. Elizabeth.
   iv. Margaret.
His brother Samuel was executor.

GROSS.

MICHAEL GROSS, merchant, of Lancaster, d. in March, 1771, leaving his estate to his wife Elizabeth, and family, as follows :
My much honored father in Germany.
My sister's daughter, Lucina Karith, in Germany.
Nephew Martin Gross.
Niece Elizabeth Lauman, wife of Ludwig Lauman.
Adam Zantzinger, son of Paul Zantzinger, brother of my mother.
Mary and Barbara, daughters of Paul Zantzinger.
Paul, son of Paul Zantzinger.
My brother, George Gross, of Paxtang, and his children, Michael George, Christian, and Catharine.
My daughter, Catharine, married to Henry Keppele.
The executors were Henry Keppele, Sr., son-in-law Henry Keppele, and Ludwig Lauman.
[The foregoing is of much genealogical value and interest to many in our county.]

GINGRICH.

CHRISTIAN GINGRICH, of Warwick township, Lancaster county, d. August, 1778, leaving a wife Elizabeth, and children :
   i. John.
   ii. Michael.
   iii. Daniel.
The executors were his son John and Christian Hollinger.

GEIGER.

CHRISTIAN GEIGER, of Warwick township, d. May, 1779, leaving a wife Christiana, and children :
   i. Christian.
   ii. George.
   iii. William, d. prior to his father.

    iv. Elizabeth, m. Peter Leib.
     v. Margaret, m. John Bender.
    vi. Anna-Maria.

GRAY.

MICHAEL GRAY, of Donegal, d. November, 1784, leaving a wife Mary, and children :
     i. William.
    ii. Janet, m. ——— Porter.
    iii. Nelly.
    iv. Joseph.
     v. Rachel.

NOTES AND QUERIES.—CXXVI.

THE SWATARA CAVE was explored in 1773 by Rev. Peter Miller, of Ephrata.

"THE HIVE" was the name of a newspaper published in Lancaster from 1803 to 1805. The following honey was secured therefrom by Squire Evans:

April 19, 1804, Isaac Smith, of Little Brandywine, married Margaret Fleming, sister-in-law of Amos Slaymaker, Esq.

May 17, 1804, Michael Hubley died, aged 83 years. He was a native of Germany and arrived with his father at Philadelphia in the year 1732. In May, 1740, he came to Lancaster. The family took an active part in the Revolution.

On Sunday, September 9, 1804, Henry McCausland was killed at the house of William Tweed in Salisbury, by a son of Philip McGuire, in a drunken frolic.

James Cochran, aged 37, was thrown from his horse and killed while driving team near Greensburg, Pa., Sept. 7, 1804.

Died Sept. 12, 1804, in Mount Joy Township, Brigadier General Mills, who was an officer in the Revolution.

Col. James Mercer died Nov. 18, 1804.

Married, by the Rev. Latta, Charles S. Sewell, of the Eastern Shore, Md., to Miss Catharine Keagy, of Lancaster, January 9, 1804.

Died January, 1805, Chester C. Smith, printer.

Elizabeth Slaymaker, wife of Henry Slaymaker, died January 29, 1805, aged 33 years.

James Ross, Jr., son of Gen. James Ross, was drowned at New York, Feb., 1805.

Feb. 20, 1805, Jacob Slough married Polly Greaff, daughter of Jacob Greaff, Esq.

March 9, 1805, John Long married Polly Hager.

On March 15, 1805, Rev. Arthur married Edward Mott, Jr., to Miss Faithful Slaymaker, daughter of Amos Slaymaker, Esq.

Samuel Evans died April 21, 1805, aged 45.

FISHING ON THE LEHIGH.

[For the following notes in relation to the catching of fish over a century ago, we are indebted to Mr. John W. Jordan, of the State Historical Society.]

Before the beginning of white settlements in the valley of the Lechauweeki (Lehigh), that river had a great reputation among the Delaware Indians for the variety and abundance of its fish, particularly shad, which were caught in large numbers and dried. The means adopted to secure this excellent article of food, and subsequently followed by the Moravians and their Indian converts, was in this wise: A dam of stones was built across the river, the walls converging into a pool. About one mile to the rear of this a cable of grape vines was twisted, on which, at intervals, brush was secured. This barrier stretched from shore to shore, being held in position by the Indians in canoes, and was towed down towards the the dam. The frightened fish driven before it, were forced into the pool, where they were captured by men stationed on the walls of the dam for that purpose. This was called bush-net fishing, and was superceded by the gill net and seine, until the improvements made in the bed of the river, by the Lehigh Coal and Navigation Company, prevented the shad from resorting to its waters to spawn.

In March, of 1701, the Assembly passed an act for "the preservation of fish in the rivers Delaware, Susquehanna, and the Lehigh, commonly called the West Branch of the Delaware," and prohibited any person "building, repairing, or maintaining, or aid, assist, or abet the building of any wear, rack, basket, fishing dam, pond or other device for the taking of fish in said rivers, by which fish may be obstructed from going *up* the said rivers . . . . . . or shall destroy or spoil any spawn, fry or brood of fish, &c.," under penalty of

£20 for every offense or six months' imprisonment. Between March 1st and December 1st it was unlawful for any person to offer for sale " any rock fish which shall not measure twelve inches at least from the eye to the fork of tail."

Now we do know that the Moravians, before the "running season," always opened their dams for all fish to go *up* stream, but they also closed them as the time approached for them to come *down* stream, and as they were always a law-abiding people we can assert that no rock-fish were offered for sale contrary to the prescribed size as provided by the act.

While Governor John Penn, with his wife, brother and suite were visiting Bethlehem in April of 1768 they watched the single men fish. According to appointment, Capt. Nicholas Garrison and Mr. John Arboe escorted them from the Sun Inn to the Congregation House, where they were joined by Bishop Seidel and wife. Proceeding to the wash house by the Lehigh, they found ferryman Fuehrer waiting with his batteaux, into which the Governor, the Bishop, and Mr. Arboe got, and were rowed to the rear of the fish net, and afterwards into the pool, where the process of fishing was viewed. The ladies and suite looked on from the high ground overlooking the dam. Six hundred and forty shad were caught on the occasion. A few days later Lord Charles Montague, Governor of South Carolina, with his wife, visited the town and also the fishery.

The following statement of some of the catches of the fishermen, gathered from official records, is of interest:

1744, May 25,	150	shad.
June 12,	250	"
1749, May 6,	1,002	"
1754, May 8,	300	"
1756, April 27,	600	"
1757, May 10,	2,200	"
1763, May 9–13,	3,100	"
1764, May 10–19,	4,290	"
1768, April 29,	640	"
July 2,	50	rockfish.
1773, June 19,	40	"
1776, June 29,	80	"
1777, June 28,	38	"
1778, April 27–May 12,	8,077	shad.
1780, May 10,	2,150	"
1784, May 6,	1,200	"
1785, May 18,	900	"

GENEALOGICAL NOTES.

GRUBB.

THOMAS GRUBB, of Little Britain, Lancaster county, d. Aug., 1779, leaving a wife Isabel, and children as follows :

    i. *Ann,* m. Joseph McCreary.
    ii. *Charity,* m. Alexander Laughlin.
    iii. *Prudence.*
    iv. *Joseph.*
    v. *Jean,* m. John Evans.
    vi. *John.*
    vii. *Thomas.*
    viii. *James.*
    ix. *William.*
    x. *Benjamin.*

GIBBONS.

JAMES GIBBONS, of Londonderry township, d. March, 1781, leaving his estate to—

Eliza Beatty, wife of Hugh Beatty, of Northumberland county.

My cousin Hugh Beatty.

[Who was this family of Beatty. Information is requested regarding them.]

GILCHRIST.

JAMES GILCHRIST, of Little Britain township, Lancaster county, d. May, 1782, leaving a wife Sarah, and children :

    i. *Margaret,* m. Charles Harrow, and had *James G.* and *Alexander.*
    ii. *Sarah,* m. James Robertson.
    iii. *Robert.*

GINTER.

CHRISTIAN GINTER, of Lebanon, d. in March, 1785. He commences his will "In namen Pater, Filius et Spiritus Sanctus, Amen." He left a wife Dorothy, and child, as follows :

    i. *Dorothy,* m. George Welsh, deceased. His executor was his "good friend, Rudolph Kelcker, of the Town of Lebanon, Taylor."

HAYES.

DAVID HAYES, of Rapho, d. in May, 1780, leaving a wife Jean, and children as follows:

i. [*A dau.*], m. Alexander Scott.
ii. *John,*
iii. *Robert.*
iv. *Patrick.*
v. *David,* m. Jean ———, and had *Elizabeth.*

He left a legacy to his nephew David Kerr. The executors were Robert and Patrick Hayes and Alexander Scott.

———

HUSTON.

ANDREW HUSTON, of Paxtang, d. in May, 1782, leaving a wife, whose maiden name was Park. The legatees were:

Brother James, and his sons Andrew, James, William. and John.
Sister Margaret, wife of Thomas Mayes.
Niece Jean Hilton.
Niece Mary Smith.
Brother John and his son John.
Niece Margaret Stewart.
Nephew Robert Thome.
The children of John Rutherford, Thomas, Samuel, John, William, Jean, Martha, and Mary.
Sister-in-law Margaret Rutherford.

The executors were John Rutherford, William Thome, and Samuel Hutchinson.

———

HUTCHINSON.

JAMES HUTCHINSON, of Donegal township, Lancaster county, d. prior to 1795, leaving issue:

i. *Samuel.*
ii. *James.*
iii. *Thomas.*
iv. *John.*
v. *Elizabeth.*
vi. *Robert.*
vii. *Jane.*

———

HENDRICKS.

TOBIAS HENDRICKS, Sr., of East Pennsboro' township, then Lancaster, subsequently Cumberland county, d. in November, 1739, leaving a wife Catharine, and children:

  i. Henry.
  ii. Rebecca.
  iii. Tobias.
  iv. David.
  v. Peter.
  vi. Abraham.
  vii. Isaac.

HOGE.

JOHN HOGE, of East Pennsboro' township, Lancaster, now Cumberland county, d. October, 1754, leaving a wife Gweenthleen, and children:
  i. John.
  ii. Jonathan.
  iii. David.
  iv. Benjamin.
  v. Mary.
  vi. Elizabeth, m., and had *Rachel.*
  vii. Sarah.
  viii. Rebecca.
  ix. Abigail.

HOWARD.

GORDON HOWARD, of Donegal township, Lancaster county, d. in March, 1754, leaving a wife Rachel, and children:
  i. Thomas.
  ii. Joseph.
  iii. John.
  iv. William.
  v. Robert.
  vi. [*A dau.*], m. James Allison.
  vii. [*A dau.*], m. Samuel Allison.
  viii. Martha.

HALL.

I. HUGH HALL, of Derry, d. February, 1758, leaving a wife Sarah, and children:
  i. Thomas.
  ii. John.
  iii. George.
  iv. James.
  v. Hugh.
The executors were the wife, and Joseph Candour.

II. THOMAS HALL d. March, 1759, leaving a wife Isabella, and children :

  i. Mary.
  ii. Sarah.
  iii. Hugh.
  iv. Elizabeth.
  v. John.

III. SARAH HALL, of Londonderry, d. April, 1783, leaving her estate to :

  Granddaughter Sarah Hall.
  Son-in-law, Jacob Cooke, and his daughter Sarah.
  Daughter Rose Cooke.
  Son William.
  Son Samuel.

NOTES AND QUERIES.—CXXVII.

EARLY EDUCATION within the bounds of Carlisle Presbytery was the subject of a very interesting address by Rev. Mr. Vance at the recent Centennial of that venerable body. There are some facts, however, which it were well to incorporate with his sketch, the principal of which is that the Rev. John Roan had a school for the especial training of ministers. There were at least three eminent divines of the Presbyterian Church whose early education was intrusted to that faithful servant of the Gospel—William Graham, Joseph Montgomery and Samuel Eusebius McCorkle. We have before us the account of the first named, who was afterwards the founder of the now celebrated Washington and Lee University of Virginia. Mr. Roan's account book gives us the following :

" William Graham entered September 23, 1767.
" January 23d to 31st, 1768, absent.
" April 2d to 25th, absent.
" May 1st, absent some days.
" June 13th. Returned 8th mo., 2d.
" Dec. 24th. Some days absent.
" Went away Feb'y 2, 1769.

"In all here near 9 months. I told his father, June 10,
    1769, that it should be charged at about £8 per annum,
    viz: . . . . 6. 00. 0.
"Recd Dec'r. 21, 1769, of ye above, ... 4. 10. 0.
"Again, May, 1771, ... 0. 07. 6.
"Jan. 20, 1773, ... 1. 10. 0.
"Lent to Mrs. Graham, Nov. 25, 1773, ... 0. 10. 0.
"Jan. 14, 1774, ... 1. 05. 0."

TRADE-BOATS ON THE DELAWARE IN 1754.—The early population
of the settlement at Bethlehem, in this State, was increased yearly by
immigration from the Old World and by accessions from the neighboring counties, and with it, too, its traffic. In order to keep a goodly
stock of store goods always on hand to meet the demand, and for the
hauling of machinery and material for their manufactories, the
wagon service had been largely augmented. With a view to lessen
this expensive mode of carriage, the Moravians, in July of 1754, decided to build a boat, suitable for the transportation of the products
of their farms and mills to the capital, and for store and other goods
on the return trip. Work was at once commenced, and the " Little
Irene" was launched on September 27th. She was rigged with two
masts and sails, and when loaded at her wharf with fifty-six bags of
wheat, drew but eleven inches of water. Captain Shaute, Chief Mate
Brinck, and a crew of two negroes set sail a few days later down the
Lehigh and into the Delaware to Trenton, making soundings, buoy-
ing channels, and marking rocks and sand bars for future voyages.
On the 14th of October this expedition returned, and on the 6th of
November following the "Little Irene" with a cargo of linseed oil
set sail for Philadelphia, and made that port in less than five days.
With a miscellaneous cargo she set sail on her return voyage, but on
reaching the Falls of the Delaware, and being unable to sail around
or be hauled over them, she was unloaded and sold at Trenton. This
early attempt to establish a line of river boats to trade between
Bethlehem and the capital of the Province was thereupon abandoned.

CREDITORS A HUNDRED YEARS AGO.

The writer of the following letter, Henry Keppele, Sr., was a
prominent merchant of Philadelphia prior to and during the Revolution. He was the owner of considerable property in the towns of
Lancaster, Lebanon and Reading, as his correspondence with his attorney, Jasper Yeates, of Lancaster, to whom this letter was written,

go to show. He may seem to be exacting, but no owner of property to-day will allow his house to be occupied upwards of five years without attempting to collect the rent:

PHILADELPHIA, *Dec. 6th, 1775.*

"SIR: By this opportunity would desire you immediately to issue against ——— Bucher (Presbyterian minister) living in Lebanon for a debt of £48.15, being 5 years & 5 months house rent at £6 a year; the agreement was made between him & Mr. Dehaas for the same; he is now moved out of my house into another. Have also sent a Bond of John Sibbach, who now lives in Middletown, for which you will please to sue and lay the execution upon his effects. Please to lett me know how my affairs stand with Stiegle; he is now in our Goal & likely to remain there some time; if you can possibly find out any way to secure me, no doubt but you will do it; perhaps if you Issue an execution & let it remain in the sheriff's hands, he may possibly some time or other find out to secure part, if not all my debt.

"The money, per Mr. John Hubley, have rec'd, for which have given him a receipt, part of the money rec'd of Gartner & Kuntz (£24.12.4); and some time ago, when you was in Town paid me part of the debt; as I cannot now recollect how much it was, should be obliged to you to let me know the sum that I may enter it regular. I suppose the £24.12.4 is full of their first Bond. Their other Bond has been due some time, and I don't mean to favor them, as I don't think that I'm very secure; must therefore desire you to take such steps as will get me my money soonest. I have still another bond from them in my hands, besides the one now in yours, which is not yet become due. I expected to have rec'd George Fry's Debt before now, but am in hopes you have it secured for,

"Sir, your obedient servant,

"HENRY KEPPELE.

"*To Jasper Yeates, Esq., in Lanc'r.*"

The "Presbyterian minister Bucher," was the Rev. John Conrad Bucher, pastor of the Reformed church at Lebanon. In early days this denomination was called German Presbyterian or German Calvinist. The trouble was not with the Rev. Mr. Bucher, but with his congregation, who were to pay the rent to Mr. Keppele, but failed to do so. It was, however, paid in full shortly after this date.

"Mr. Dehaas" was Col. John Philip DeHaas, of the Revolution, who resided at Lebanon many years. He died in Philadelphia on the 3d of June, 1786.

John Sibbach kept a store at Middletown prior to the Revolution, coming there from Lebanon. Nothing further is known of him.

"Stiegle." This is the celebrated Baron Steigle who, through certain parties, became financially ruined. An interesting notice of him is to be found in the "History of Lebanon County," page 295.

" Gartner & Kuntz" were probably merchants of Lancaster.

"George Fry," the owner of the Frey estate, and the founder of the " Emaus Institute," of Middletown, was one of the worthies of Dauphin county. Unfortunately little is known of his early history, birth, and parentage, but he left a bequest, which, if conducted as it now is, will perpetuate his name for generations to come as one of the benefactors of mankind.

COL. JOHN STEELE.

[The first burial in the Harrisburg cemetery was Gen. James Steele, a brother of Col. John Steele, of whom we have this interesting sketch by a valued correspondent.]

John Steele, son of William Steele, was born in Drumore township, Lancaster county, in the year 1758. His father sent him to Rev. James Latta's academy at Chestnut Level, and while pursuing his studies he formed an attachment for Abigail Bailey, which was reciprocated by her. Her father hoped to see her marry a son of a wealthy neighbor, and was very much opposed to his daughter marrying young Steele, whom he thought did not have estate enough to support her befitting her position in society. He was therefore forbidden to pay his addresses to Miss Abigail, who in a very spirited manner told her father that she loved Mr. Steele and that if she did not marry him she never would wed another. Mr. Steele's father sent him to the academy to be educated with a view of entering the ministry; but while at school he heard the call of his country to arms, and he told the venerable Dr. Latta that until his country was free, he would relinquish his studies for the duties of the camp. His three brothers, Archibald, James and William, enlisted on the same day.

John Steele entered the army as a volunteer, and although but eighteen years of age his soldierly bearing soon won for him the command of a company, which he led into battle at Brandywine, where he received a British ball through his shoulder. From loss of blood from the wound which he received, he was reduced to the point of death. Six faithful soldiers carried him upon a sheet several miles to a house occupied by two elderly maiden ladies, who nursed him faithfully until he was able to be removed. He never forgot their kindness to him. Before he could return to active military duty his father heard that he had been wounded, and after much search found him in Bucks county, whither he had been carried, after many removals, to a place of safety.

He returned to his home before he had been entirely recovered from his wound, and while there an unskillful surgeon thought it necessary to probe the wound, and in so doing divided an artery, and he had no means of tying it; to prevent him from bleeding to death his sister held the orifice with her fingers until a messenger was dispatched to Lancaster, a distance of sixteen miles, for a physician, who came, and when he arrived he discovered that he left his case of instruments in Lancaster, to which place he returned for them, and during this time his faithful sister never took her fingers from the wound, an example of patience and heroic courage seldom seen anywhere.

As soon as Captain Steele recovered, he returned to his companions in arms, and followed General Washington through many battles, and participated in the capture of Cornwallis at Yorktown. When in New Jersey he was a member of General Washington's staff. At the conclusion of the war he returned to his home with an arm disabled, poor and penniless, but with the consciousness that he had served his country faithfully. In 1780, when he arrived in sight of his father's mansion on leave of absence, he observed a large number of carriages and horses surrounding his home, he knew that it meant a funeral procession. His heart was filled with agony, not having the remotest idea as to which member of his honored family was about to be consigned to the grave. It was his father, the noble sire who sent forth every son of his to the war. This was a sad affliction to the young soldier.

Miss Bailey, who had waited seven long years for the return of Captain Steele, remained true to her pledge, and they were married in the year 1784. For several years prior to her marriage this remarkable lady had been living with her brother, Francis, in Lancaster and kept house for him. She frequently took her needle and work with her to the printing office of her brother, and watched him with great interest when setting type. She said, one day, "Brother, I think I can help you," and she immediately commenced to set up the form from which was printed the first *Pocket Almanack* ever published in Pennsylvania. The knowledge of printing thus obtained was of great value to her husband in after life.

Captain, subsequently General, Steele, soon after his marriage removed from Lancaster to Philadelphia and embarked in printing and publishing. His business was successful and his restless and ambitious spirit prompted him to embark in other branches and more extensive business. He built a paper mill along the Octorara in connection with his brother-in-law, Col. James Thompson, and his nephew, Col. James Steele. To this place he removed from Philadelphia with his family. While there he multiplied copies from his standing type, from which many editions of standard works were printed. The late Matthew Carey purchased these forms to prevent rivalry in the publication of the same works. He was a person of undoubted genius, that could not be tied down to a particular avocation. Agriculture was a favorite pursuit, and he retired from his printing and paper manufacturing to his farm at Octorora. He did not remain long in retirement. Being one of the most ardent and ablest Jeffersonian Democrats in the State, he was not permitted to live in retirement, his friends insisted upon electing him to the Lower House, and afterwards to the State Senate in 1801—a year of bitter partisan warfare, in which the Federal and anti-Federal parties were nearly evenly divided. General Steele's election was contested in the Legislature, for the reason that he held an office supposed to be incompatible with that of Senator, and after a bitter fight the Federalists ousted him from his seat in the Senate. He was re-elected in 1803, and was admitted to his seat, and was Speaker of the Senate in 1805.

Governor McKean caused William Dixon, the publisher of the Lancaster *Journal*, to be thrown into prison for libel, which was published in the heat of a political campaign. When he was released from prison the Democrats made all the political capital they could out of the affair, and got up a grand demonstration in Lancaster. General Steele was made chief marshal, and he made an eloquent, but inflammatory speech upon the occasion. In 1806 he was the candidate of his party for United States Senator, and tied Andrew Gregg on several ballots, but was finally defeated by a few votes.

In the year 1808 he was appointed Collector of the Port in Philadelphia, a position he held until 1826, when he resigned on account of declining health, and died February 27, 1827. His wife died on the 13th of March following.

In all the years General Steele held the office of Collector he never suffered a dollar of the Government money to remain in his hands, but deposited every cent in bank, and the Government never lost a penny of the moneys collected by him. He was a strong advocate of domestic manufactures and the system of internal improvements by the State. In religious circles he was a trustee of the Third Presbyterian church, in Philadelphia, for many years.

Capt. John Steele, son of the above, died at his home near Gordonville, Lancaster county, October 27, 1853. He had been a member of Lodge No. 51, of Ancient York Masons of Philadelphia, and Past Master. Appropriate ceremonies were held by the Masons, in memory of their distinguished deceased brother. Captain Steele commanded a company in the war of 1812, and subsequently was appointed Collector of the Port of Philadelphia, a position he held for some years, a trust he executed with the strictest integrity. He was also controller of the public schools of Philadelphia. For more than thirty-four years he served in the capacity of Secretary and Treasurer, Warden and Master in Lodge No. 51, and filled the chair of the Right Worshipful Grand Master in the Grand Lodge of Masons.

Captain Steele married Jane Porter (1791–1867). Their daughter Abiann married Col. Reah Frazer, a distinguished member of the Lancaster bar, and their children (surname Frazer) were:

   i. Susan-Carpenter.
   ii. Henry-Carpenter, of Pittsburg.
   iii. Reah, paymaster in the U. S. A.
   iv. J.-P.-Wilson, a merchant of Philadelphia.

Captain Steele's second daughter, Dolly, married Henry E. Slaymaker, Esq., a prominent citizen of Lancaster.

It may be related in this connection that James Buchannan was always esteemed a valued friend of the family, but for some reason, best known to himself, declined to support Captain Steele for appointment as Collector of the Port of Philadelphia. Captain Steele, his friends, and especially his son-in-law, Colonel Frazer, became very much angered at him, and opposed him politically with great spirit thereafter.

A daughter of Gen. John Steele, No. 1, married the Rev. Doctor Milldollar.   SAMUEL EVANS.

THE COUNTY OF FRANKLIN.

A RESUMÉ OF EVENTS CONNECTED WITH ITS FORMATION.

The county of Cumberland, the sixth county formed in the Province of Pennsylvania, was erected in 1750. It embraced "all and singular the lands lying within the said Province to the westward of Susquehanna, and northward and westward of the county of York" (organized the year previous). It was "bounded northward and westward with the line of the Province." From this vast area and ample limits were subsequently constructed Bedford in 1771; a portion of

Northumberland in 1772; Westmoreland from Bedford in 1773; Washington in 1781, and Fayette in 1783 from Westmoreland. Originally comprising two-thirds of the area of Pennsylvania, the county of Cumberland is well deserving the name "Old Mother Cumberland."

We first hear of efforts for the formation of the county of Franklin during the closing years of the struggle for independence in petitions therefor in 1780; but remonstrances were poured in upon the Assembly to postpone the subject until the Revolutionary War was over. No sooner was the prospect of peace heightened than renewed efforts were made by the inhabitants of the western parts of the county of Cumberland for a division, representing "the inconveniences and hardships which they suffer by the large extent of the said county . . . . . the great distance at which the said petitioners dwell from the town of Carlisle, where the courts of justice and the public offices of the same county are held and kept." On the 25th of March, 1782, the petitions therefor were ordered by the General Assembly to be referred to Moses Maclean, Mr. Agnew and Mr. Maclay, with directions to bring in a bill. A bill was subsequently reported and passed second reading, but the inhabitants of "New Town" township petitioning to have Shippensburg included in the new county, while the inhabitants of Lurgan township remonstrated forcibly against a division—the whole subject was dropped until the following Assembly. The next Assembly were not favorable to the new county project, and the matter was referred by them to their successors. The new Assembly had scarcely organized when a petition was received from John Clark for the appointment of register for the probate of wills for the new county to be erected out of Cumberland. This was Col. John Clark, of the town of York, a brave officer of the Revolution. His application was premature. Numerous petitions for the division of the county of Cumberland poured in upon the legislative body, while not a few remonstrances against the same. The latter were chiefly from Shippensburg and Lurgan township, a portion of whose inhabitants preferred, since the former place was not considered eligible for the county seat, to remain with the old county. On the 16th of March, 1784, the committee to whom the petitions and remonstrances were referred reported the following:

"*Resolved*, That a new county be granted and laid out, to begin on the York county line on the South Mountain; thence by a square line to be run from the said beginning on the North or Blue Ridge, leaving Shippensburg to the east of said line; thence from the summit of the said North Mountain by the ridges dividing the waters of

Shearman's Valley from the waters of the Path Valley, to the Gap, near the heads of the said Path Valley joining Bedford county; thence by the Bedford county line to the Maryland line; thence by said line to the line of York county; thence by said county line to the place of beginning; to be called ———— county; and that the said new county town shall be established by law, at the well-known place called Chambers Town, and not elsewhere; and that a committee be appointed to bring in a bill accordingly."

On the 18th of March the resolution was read the second time, and Messrs. Rush, Coleman and McPherson were appointed a committee to bring in a bill. As yet it will be seen no name was mentioned in connection with the new county project. The committee appointed were: Jacob Rush, of Philadelphia, subsequently president judge of the courts of that city; Robert Coleman, of Lancaster, the great ironmaster, and the head of that family so intimately connected with the iron trade of Pennsylvania; and Col. Robert McPherson, of York county, the brave soldier of the Revolution and the grandfather of Hon. Edward McPherson, of Gettysburg; a remarkable committee —gentlemen of culture, and eminent in public affairs. To them must the credit be given of naming the county FRANKLIN for that patriot, sage and philosopher, whose reputation was even then worldwide. It was a deserving honor, and the first in successive ones which next to the immortal Washington has given name to more towns and counties than any other in the American Union.

On the 25th of March the bill was reported and read the first time. Four days after it was read the second time and ordered to be printed. Then followed a flood of petitions, for and against not only the division of the county, but the location of the county seat. For the latter Green Castle and Shippensburg were anxious to be selected— although the latter was unwilling to be included within the limits of the new county unless it was thus honored. Green Castle contended that it was equal as centrally as Chambers Town, and much better situated with reference to the back counties and to Maryland.

On the 25th of August, the Assembly took up the bill and debated it at length, which was continued on the 30th. On the 6th of September a clause was adopted to the effect "that the inhabitants of the new county of Franklin should have their full proportion or share of what moneys were raised for Cumberland county uses, after all just demands against said county of Cumberland, before passing this act, are paid."

On the 9th of September, 1784, the bill "was enacted, and signed by the speaker," and thus was erected the County of Franklin with Chambers Town as the seat of justice "and not elsewhere."

NOTES AND QUERIES.—CXXVIII.

HOLLINGER.—Daniel Hollinger m., first, April 29, 1788, Catharine Stauffer, who d. January 24, 1793. Their children were:
  i. Anna, b. February 13, 1789.
  ii. Barbara, b. January 22, 1791.
  iii. John, b. January 11, 1793; d. in infancy.
Daniel Hollinger m,. secondly, June 23, 1793, Barbara Groff, b. December 18, 1775, in Rapho township, Lancaster county ; d. September 15, 1857. Their children were:
  iv. Daniel, b. August 31, 1794.
  v. Jacob, b. April 9, 1797.
  vi. John (second), b. March 30, 1799.
  vii. Christian, b. February 2, 1801.

BAD INDIANS IN 1776.

In 1776, owing to British intrigue with the Indians west of the Ohio, Congress sent commissioners to Pittsburgh to enter into a treaty with the savages, so as to preserve peace on the frontiers. Numerous outrages had been committed by marauding bands, especially from the Wyandot towns on Lake Erie. All complaints by the settlers were laid before the commissioners, who were Col. John Montgomery, of Carlisle, and Judge Yeates, of Lancaster. One of these is before us, and we give it from the fact that it refers to several Indians more or less prominent in the Border wars on our frontiers. It is as follows :

To the Honorable Commissioners of Indian Affairs, the petition of Nicholas Haggerty humbly sheweth :

That Impsayprasetha, a Half Mingo & half Shawanese Indian, Couzin to Keyashuta, did, about the middle of last July, take a Horse of your Petitioner's from the Common near Pittsburgh and rode him him to Cochocking, where he sold the said horse to Ahinos, a Delaware Indian, who hired him to Mr. Willson, and was rode to the Lake by John Montour, who knew the Horse and told Mr. Willson where he had seen him. Your Petitioner, therefore, prays you will be pleased to take such steps as you shall think proper to assist him in the recovery of His Horse, and your Petitioner will ever pray, &c.

NICHOLAS HAGGERTY.

Pittsburgh, October the 21st, 1776.

GENEALOGICAL NOTES.

HUTCHINSON.

ROBERT HUTCHINSON d. January, 1774, leaving a wife Mary. It is not known if he had any children. His executors were his brothers-in-law, Joseph Hutchinson and William Cathcart.

HAYES.

HUGH HAYES, of Londonderry, d. April, 1779, leaving a wife Mary, and legatees as follows:
Daughter *Margaret.*
Brother Patrick.
Sister married ——— Buchanan.
Sister married ——— Morrison.
The executors were his wife and John Gilchrist, Sr.

HOUSER.

MARTIN HOUSER, of Lancaster, d. July, 1779, leaving a wife Catharine, and children :
    i. Martha, m. David Lanuth.
    ii. Margaret. m. Christian Wirtz.
    iii. Dorothea.
    iv. Hannah, m. Richard White.
    v. Mary, m. Henry Zihler.
    vi. Barbara, m. Martin Lowman.

A legacy was left to his grandchildren, Christopher and Magdalena Houser.

HALL.

CHARLES HALL, of Lancaster, d. June, 1783, leaving a wife Salome, and children :
    i. David.
    ii. Charles.
    iii. Anna-Maria.
    iv. Mary-Ann-Elizabeth.
    v. Salome.
    vi. Ann.

HALDEMAN.

JACOB HALDEMAN, of Rapho township, Lancaster county, d. in April, 1783, leaving a wife Maria, and children :

    i. Abraham.
   ii. Peter.
  iii. Elizabeth, m. Samuel Stauffer.
   iv. John.
    v. Jacob.

IRELAND.

JAMES IRELAND, of Derry township, d. September, 1767, leaving a wife Ann, and child:
    i. Mary, m. ——— McFarland.
He left a legacy to his cousin Hannah Ireland. His executors were Robert Wallace and Matthew Laird.

JOHNSTON.

I. JAMES JOHNSTON, of Hanover, died in January, 1763, leaving issue:
    i. Robert.
   ii. William.
  iii. Mary.

II. JAMES JOHNSTON, of Paxtang, d. September, 1783, leaving his estate to the following:
Son James.
Daughter Jean, m. John Forster.
Stepdaughter Elin McClain.
Stepdaughter Mary McClain.
Granddaughter Martha Wilson.
Son-in-law Thomas Means.

JAMISON.

I. MARGARET JAMISON, of Donegal, d. in April, 1783, leaving her estate to:
Brother James, and his son John.
Brother John, and his children Margaret, Mary, Agnes, and John Fleming.

II. JOHN JAMISON, of Donegal, d. in July, 1783, leaving a wife Rosanna, and children:
    i. Agnes.
   ii. Mary.
  iii. Margaret.
   iv. John-Fleming.

KEAGY.

JACOB KEAGY, of Lancaster. d. December, 1783, leaving a wife Catharine. His estate was divided between her and the following: Children of George Ziegler's second wife.

Cousin Mary Ziegler, dau. of George Ziegler, dec'd.

Cousin Jacob Ziegler, at present in Europe.

Son John.

Father John Keagy.

Brother John Keagy.

Brother Isaac Keagy.

Sister Anna, married to Isaac Neaff, and their sons John and Isaac.

KOONTZ.

LUDWIG KOONTZ, of Middletown, d. March, 1776, leaving his estate to—

Brother Henry, and his daughters Mary Elizabeth and Anna Margaret.

Christopher Heppick or his heirs.

LYTLE.

EPHRIAM LYTLE, or LITTLE, of Mount Joy, Lancaster county, d. January, 1776, leaving a wife Jennett, and children:

 i. Joseph.
 ii. Nathaniel.
 iii. Ruth.
 iv. Jean.
 v. Rebecca.
 vi. Priscilla.
 vii. Ephriam.
 viii. Elizabeth.

POSTAL FACILITIES OVER A CENTURY AGO.

The early records of the Moravian Church, in Philadelphia, contain frequent notices of the arrival of vessels at that port from Europe and the West Indies, with letters for the settlements of the church in Northampton county. If it so happened that the Bethlehem wagon or the post rider was not in the city, a "brother" was at once dispatched with them to Bethlehem. Such journeys were performed either on foot or on horseback, and not unfrequently the streams to be forded, swollen by an early thaw or high water, or covered with ice too thin to bear a horse, caused delays or compelled a return.

In July of 1742, a regular weekly post and express was established between Bethlehem and Philadelphia, four postilions were appointed, and Revs. John C. Pyrlæus and George Neiser commissioned agents at the former, and John Stephen Benezet at the latter place. The service was to start from Bethlehem every Monday and go to Falckner's Swamp (now Montgomery county); thence to Germantown by Tuesday evening; on Wednesday to Philadelphia and return by night to Germantown; thence to Falckner's Swamp on Thursday, and reach Bethlehem by Friday night. In 1747 a daily mail was established between Bethlehem and Nazareth. One of the mail bags used in this route is preserved in the Moravian Historical Society's collection. This is a well authenticated tradition, that one of the postilions happening to be in the city when the Declaration of Independence was passed by Congress, hastened to the stables, mounted and hurried on to Bethlehem with the news. On reaching his destination he first discovered that in his excitement he had saddled and ridden the wrong animal.

It was not until September of 1763 that the first public conveyance was run between the capital of the Province and Bethlehem. The enterprise was started by George Klein; every Monday morning a stage wagon left the Sun Inn of Bethlehem, and the return trip was made every Thursday.   J. W. J.

IN THE CUMBERLAND VALLEY.

[The following document came into our possession through the Yeates papers. It gives some facts which may be valuable for genealogical reference. It refers to lands in possession of Robert Callender, of whom we gave an interesting sketch in our old series of *Notes and Queries.*]

No. 1. 500 acres in the name of James Silvers, mortgaged to the Academy for £1,000.

2 & 3. Adjoining the above tract in the name of R. Callender, containing 539½ acres. On this place there are many valuable improvements (to wit) two large Stone Houses, one Built within this three or four years, One Stone Merchant & 1 Saw Mill, also One other Stone Country Mill, with Barns, Stables and Out Houses, suitable for the wintering & foddering a very considerable number of Cattle. One of the above Messuages with Merchant Mill lets for the yearly rent of £120, now in the Tenure of Eph'm Blaire, sheriff of the Cumberland ; the Residue or Remaining Part in the Hands of Dutch Men on the Shares with myself, from whence I receive £150 annually.

2. The Plantation on the mouth of Letort Springs, whereon I dwell, originally granted by Sam'l Blumstead (impower'd so to do by the Proprietarys) to Randle Chambers (being part of a 1000a. grant) from Randle the original purchaser to his son James Chambers in ffee; from the s'd James to Ezekiel Smith, who conveys to myself and from I hold, containing 455a., on which place there are erected the following improvements, One very large stone Merchant mill, one Stone fulling mill, Saw mill, two frame dwelling Houses, with large and convenient Out Houses for the accommodation of cattle, a large stone Barn 110 ft. by 44, built this last Summer.

3. One other Plantation being ab' a ½ mile from the Last mention'd Plantation & part of the 1000a. there mention'd granted to Randle Chambers, the Elder, by Blumstead, & from him by Devise to his son John, from the said John by Devise to Randle Chambers, who by Deed convey'd to myself. Containing 212a.; there are on this place 40a. of valuable water'd Medow, which I keep for my own use. The residue of the Place Rents for £35 yearly with frame dwelling House, Barn, Stable and Out House.

No. 138, '39, 167, 212. Four Lots of Ground in the town of Carlisle, 2 of which there are valuable improvements thereon and which Let for the yearly Rent of £25 each.

The Above Described Plantations & lots of Ground I do not intend disposing of, or I might have for the Place whereon Mr. Blaine lives £6000, but which I think not near the real value thereof, & the others, if Disposed to Sell, Equally Valuable.   ROBT. CALLENDER.

Philada., Octob'r 24th, 1772.

NOTES AND QUERIES—CXXIX.

SOME OLD CORRESPONDENCE.

[*The Indian Commissioners to Robert Hanna.*]

PITTSBURGH, *Oct. 27, 1776.*

SIR: The Congress have directed the Commissioners for India affairs in this Department to invite some of the Indian chiefs t Phila'da. Mr. Lockrey was kind enough to mention to us that som of the Light Horse men wou'd accompany us part of the way dow the Road. As the carrying down some Indians will be productiv of the happiest effects to this country, by Preventing any Indian Wa we have no Doubt but that part of y'r Company would willingly g some Distance with us in case we could bring the Savages to consent to the Journey. The very appearance of an Escort may be of good service to the Public Interest. We apprehend that about a Dozen men with an officer would answer every purpose. We do not know whether we shall be able to carry our Point with the Savages; but will do our utmost Endeavors for this End. If we succeed we shall acquaint you in due time of it, of the day when we expect to leave this place. In the mean time, it might be well to consult the Inclinations of your men, whether they would approve of the business; that in case of their willingness they might Hold themselves in readiness. We beg you will communicate this Letter to Mr. Lockrey; and are sir,

Your most Humb. Servants,

JOHN MONTGOMERY,
JASPER YEATES.

To Robt. Hanna, Esq.

[*Col. John Montgomery to Judge Yeates.*]
CARLISLE, *3d April, 1777.*

DEAR SIR : Inclosed you have Sundrie papers from Mr. Deveraux Smith, which informs that the Indians have done Damage in this Province, and that an Indian War seems near at Hand. I trimble for the Poor Inhabitants who are almost unprovid'd with arms, and indeed too many of their men is order'd away. I fear Congress will see their Error when too late in ordering Col. McCay's Batt'n from Kitaning. I think immediate assistance ought to be sent, and I hope you write to Mr. Wilson to urge it in the warmest manner. Sepose some of the Malitia were ordered from Virginia, and some from Bedford county and some from Maryland, to continue there for a few months until Regular troops could be sent up. These are a few crude thoughts, as the Bearer waits. I have the above acct. from William Lockrey, and believe it's too true. Mrs. Montgomery Joyns in compliments to you & Mrs. Yeates.

I am, Dear Sir, Your Very Humble Servant,

JOHN MONTGOMERY.

[*Col. John Montgomery to Jasper Yeates.*]
CARLISLE, *7 March, 1777.*

DEAR SIR : Your letter of the 20th Feb., covering the abstracts of the pay Rolls of the Westmoreland Militia is now before me. Col. Proctor is at camp. Shall pay him on his return, the others shall send to Mr. Deveraux Smith, with proper receipts, who, I doubt not will take the trouble of paying the money.

A few weeks ago 4 Indians came opposite Kitaning and called for a canno. Andrew McFarline went over, and as soon as he landed the Indians seized him and turned the canno adrift and carried Mc-Farline prisoner, it is thought to Neagra or Detroit. Capt. Morehead is gone with a party to Take care of the Stores at Kitaning; it is evident that the Indians meant only to take a prisoner, as there was no soldiers at Kitaning, and only McFarline and a man or two of Mr. Spear.

I am, Dear Sir, Your very humble servant,

JOHN MONTGOMERY.

Capt. Jasper Yeates.

EARLY SETTLERS OF THE "UPPER END."

[The following information came to us when preparing the history of the county, but like much more data was necessarily omitted by the publishers from the work. As a portion of the history of that section we herewith preserve them in *Notes and Queries.*]

BUFFINGTON.

BENJAMIN BUFFINGTON, the first of the name who located in Lykens Valley, was an early settler there. He came from Berks county, died in 1814, and was buried in the grave-yard at Short mountain by request. His sons were *Eli, George, Levi,* and *John.* Eli settled near Gratz, where his grandson Jeremiah now resides. He married Elizabeth Kissinger and their sons were *Abraham* and *John-E.* The latter, b. 1799; d. 1867; m. Susanna Artz, and had sons *Elias, Jeremiah,* and *Daniel.* The other sons of the elder Benjamin Buffington inter-married into the Hoffman family, lived to be old men, and had large families. Jacob Buffington, Sr., b. 1800; d. 1878; was by occupation a mechanic, and one of the most expert hunters in his day. He married Mary Guntryman; and his sons were *Isaac, Jonas, Jacob, Emanuel,* and *Levi.* Solomon Buffington, b. 1819; d. Jan. 1, 1878; was a mechanic and farmer. He was a prominent member of the U. B. Church for many years, and took an active part during the war of the Rebellion. Two of his sons were in the Union army. His wife was Margaret Matter, and their sons were *Moses-C., Edward,* and *Uriah.*

REIGLE.

ANDREW REIGLE resided on and owned the farm near the end of Short mountain, afterwards owned by his son Jacob. He was a soldier of the Revolution. He married in 1770 Catharine Hoffman.

Their oldest son, John Reigle, was a justice of the peace many years and followed farming. He married Susan Sheetz, and of their children *Simon* resided at Harrisburg, and *Obed-J.* in Williamstown. Daniel, son of Andrew Reigle, married Catharine Harman. Their son Daniel was a county commissioner in 1852, serving three years. Jacob, son of Andrew married Nancy Hartman. Andrew, Jr, was a farmer, and served in the war of 1812–14. He married a Miss Stine. Elizabeth Reigle, a daughter of Andrew, Sr, married Daniel Sheesly, and they were the grandparents of Sheriff Sheesly of this city. (See *Notes and Queries, No. lxxix.*)

FRECK.

MATHIAS FRECK was a native of Baden, Germany, from whence he emigrated in 1815. In 1821 he married Eliza Penrose, daughter of Col. Joseph Penrose, of the Revolutionary army, and the year after settled in Lykens Valley, locating first at Gratztown. Of their children Joseph M. Freck was a large coal operator, and resides at Pottsville, this State. Roland Freck was recently postmaster at Millersburg. John L. and Newton C. Freck are heavily engaged in the lumber business in Millersburg.

HOFFMAN.

JOHN B. HOFFMAN, b. in 1792; d. 1875. He was a blacksmith by occupation; had been a military captain and promoted to a lieutenant colonelcy, and served in the war of 1812–14. He was a prominent member of the German Reformed Church, holding the offices of deacon, elder and trustee. Politically he was a staunch Democrat. Colonel Hoffman married Margaret Bowman, and his sons were *George, John, Christian. Josiah, James,* and *Peter-A.*

BRETZ.

BENJAMIN BRETZ was born in Lykens Valley in 1796 and died in 1878. He was probably a grandson of Ludwig Bretz, who was one of the first settlers in that region, a soldier of the Revolution, and wounded at the battle of Long Island in 1776. Benjamin carried on farming; filled the office of supervisor several terms and was prominently identified with the military. He was a member of the German Reformed Church, and much honored and respected. He married Margaret Paul, and they had sons, *John,* and *Anthony.*

RUNK.

PHILIP RUNK was born in Lykens Valley, September 16, 1805, and died in January, 1873. His father came to the valley after the Revolution, and was one of the first settlers in Jefferson township. The son was a farmer, served in the military in early life, and a prominent member of the U. B. Church. He married Elizabeth Smith, and their sons were *Jacob, Michael,* and *Adam.* Jacob was at one time a presiding elder in the U. B. Church.

COOPER.

ADAM COOPER came to Lykens Valley during the Revolutionary war, and was a private in Capt. Martin Weaver's company of Upper Paxtang, which marched to the relief of the settlers on the West Branch in the spring of 1781. He was a farmer and a great deer hunter. He married a daughter of Ludwig Shott, an early settler, and they had a large family. The late John Cooper, who represented Dauphin county in the Legislature in 1850, and who recently deceased, was a son. Connected by marriage to the Cooper family are the descendants of Jacob Schwab, or Swab, as now written. He was a native of Berks county, and died in 1866, at the age of seventy-five years. He married Catharine Metz, and of their children, Eli Swab filled the office of county commissioner two terms.

ETZWEILER.

DANIEL ETZWEILER, Sr., was born April 12, 1800, and died September 15, 1878. He was a farmer, filled the office of supervisor two terms, served five years in a volunteer militia company, and was one of the founders of St. James' Lutheran and Reformed church near Carsonville. He was a great hunter, and excelled in deer shooting and the trapping of bear on the mountains. Mr. Etzweiler married Christiana Smith, of Northumberland county, and their sons were *Jonathan, Daniel, Michael, Elias, Peter, Adam,* and *Henry.*

IN ARMSTRONG AND POWELL'S VALLEYS.—I.

Boarding the 11.25 a. m. train north, found us after a short ride at Halifax, where we left the cars for a six miles' drive up Armstrong Valley to Jacksonville. Thence to the hospitable home of a friend, located on the top of the "dividing ridge" overlooking Powell's and Armstrong Valleys. After an enjoyable dinner our host drove us to Enterline post office, named for a family which settled there at an early day. Our objective point was the Lutheran and Reformed church, commonly known as "Bauerman's." The edifice is a one-story frame, built some fifty years ago. In the grave-yard we transcribed the following as the oldest persons buried therein:

Bowerman, Michael, b. Nov. 27, 1804; d. March 20, 1865.
Bowerman, Mary, *wf.* of M., b. Feb. 18, 1804; d. Feb. 29, 1868.
Bowerman, Sarah, *wf.* of John, b. June 22, 1787; d. Dec. 23, 1862.
Baker, John, b. May 19, 1804; d. April 13, 1876.
Bessler, Abraham, b. June 19, 1793; d. July 8, 1861.
Bessler, Susannah, b. Sept. 10, 1794; d. March 24, 1859.
Clark, Elizabeth, *wf.* of George R., and relict of Michael Faber, b. 1806; d. at Shamokin, June 10, 1872.
Dornsley, Margaret, b. Jan. 18, 1765; d. Dec. 19, 1838.
Enterline, Peter, b. Dec. 11, 1795; d. April 29, 1853.
Enterline, Susannah, *wf.* of P., b. Jan. 5, 1795; d. March 21, 1868.
Enders, Phillip, b. May 23, 1805; d. Dec. 14, 1859.
Faber, Michael, b. Aug. 8, 1808; d. July 7, 1855.
Fawver, M. Magdalena, *wf.* of John. b. May 6, 1784; d. Jan. 16, 1845.
Hoover, John, b. Aug. 7, 1808; d. Dec. 25, 1878.
Hare, Catharine, d. April 13, 1834, aged 19 years.
Hoffman, John B., b. Sept. 17, 1793; d. April 30, 1875.
Hoffman, Barbara, *wf.* of J., b, May 19, 1795; d. Oct. 12, 1861.
Kitzman, Catharine, *wf.* of John, b. Oct. 9, 1800; d. Aug. 12, 1852.
Lehr, John, d. May 4, 1883, aged 78 years, 20 days.
Lehr, Johanna, *wf.* of J., b. Nov. 23, 1807; d. Feb. 16, 1877.
Long, J. Leonard, b. Dec. 13, 1803; d. Dec. 27, 1862.
Lenker, Adam, b. June 8, 1807; d. Feb. 23, 1857.
Lebo, Jonas, b. Dec. 20, 1811; d. Feb. 15, 1852.
Paul, John, b. Sept. 7, 1807; d. July 10, 1863.
Paul, Catharine, *wf.* of J., b. July 24, 1811; d. Jan. 18, 1873.
Richard, Joseph, b. Feb. 20, 1779; d. Jan. 8, 1856.
Richard, Catharine, *wf.* of J., b. Feb. 16, 1772; d. May 11, 1854.
Sheets, William, b. May 20, 1805; d. April 19, 1879.
Sheetz, Maria, *wf.* of George, b. Jan. 30, 1778; d. ———.
Sheesly, Elizabeth, *wf.* of Michael, b. Jan. 31, 1820; d. April 15, 1862.
Sheesly, John, b. June 16, 1779; d. March 13, 1853.
Sheesly, Sarah, *wf.* of J., d. July 8, 1853, aged 86 years.
Sawyer, Samuel, b. Feb. 8, 1813; d. Oct. 24, 1850.
Sweigard, Elizabeth, *wf.* of Christian, and daughter of John and Sarah Sheesly, b. Dec. 29, 1808; d. July 31, 1853.
Sweigard, J. Ludwig, b. Nov. 19, 1772; d. Aug. 28, 1854.
Sweigard, Regina, *wf.* of J. L., b. Oct. 15, 1784; d. March 11, 1841.
Sweigard, Peter, b. Jan. 26, 1795; d. Dec. 29, 1855.
Sweigard, Eve, *wf.* of P., b. Dec. 22, 1793; d. Nov. 11, 1875.
Schott, Catharine, *dau.* of Peter and Elizabeth and *wf.* of Jonas Lebo, b. April 16, 1809; d. Dec. 8, 1859.

Spayd, John, *s.* of Sebastian and Christina, b. April 9, 1803; d. March 18, 1868.
Spayd, Elizabeth, *wf.* of J., b. April 13, 1803; d. July 15, 1885.
Welker, Jacob, b. Aug. 12, 1797; d. Dec. 19, 1865.
Welker, Elizabeth, *wf.* of J., b. May 24, 1798; d. July 4, 1879.
Wilson, William, d. March 14, 1843, aged 81 years.
Wells, Hannah, *wf.* of Samuel, b. March 10, 1786; d. March 30, 1855

NOTES AND QUERIES.—CXXX.

POPULATION OF DAUPHIN COUNTY IN 1800.—In that year Dauphin county included what is now the county of Lebanon. The population by towns and townships according to the census of that date was as follows:

		Slaves.
Harrisburg,	1,462	10
Derry,	1,656	10
Lower Paxtang and Swatara,	3,180	28
Middle Paxtang,	722	5
Upper Paxtang,	2,274	
West Hanover,	1,849	13
Londonderry,	1,570	7
East Hanover,	1,272	10
Bethel,	1,837	3
Annville,	1,485	
Heidelberg,	1,990	
Lebanon,	2,870	8

TOPICS FOR THE HISTORIANS.

MR. EDITOR.—It is exceedingly delightful to former residents of Harrisburg now living at a distance to find in the *Notes and Queries* column of the TELEGRAPH each Saturday the various historical contributions, reminiscences, etc., and it argues well for the interest which you have produced in these things. There are various topics, however, which I think should be written upon—things that would be new to this generation; and by your permission I will enumerate some of them, with the hope that those who are best informed will not delay in recording for preservation and future use whatever may be known at the present day. Many of the topics will awaken memories of "lang syne" in the old borough, and recall persons and things which this faster age has pushed to forgetfulness.

1. Who was "Fitzpatrick?" the insane genius who wrote acrostics; and in tragic attitudes continually moaned for "Mary, O! Mary, Ma-a-ry!"

2. Recollections of "Muster Day" and "Battalion drill."

3. The Dauphin Guards. [Attention! Capt. J. M. Eyster.]

4. The old-time Shad Fisheries on the Susquehanna.

5. Recollections of "Green Bay" tavern—"Governor Schutt."

6. Zeke Carter, the colored property holder; northwest corner Fourth and Market, whose houses burned down in 1838.

7. The old stage lines; the first running of locomotive and trains to Harrisburg; the canal packet boats, with their polite captains and gay teams.

8. The Washingtonian temperance excitement of 1844, and its weekly meetings in the old court house; not forgetting Johnny Alexander, chairman of the " Ex-e-cu-tive Com-me-tay!"

9. The old fashioned political celebrations on 4th of July; the dinners in the woods, toasts, speeches, and songs.

10. The schools of the borough and their teachers; the North Ward "Exhibitions;" the venerable pedagogue "Pappy Mitchell," not forgetting his white hat and blue cloak.

11. The fire engine companies; the old "fire bucket" system— with its auxilliaries of pails, pans, tubs, &c.—and the big fires of yore.

12. The original Harrisburg Brass Band; the singing societies and clubs; the choirs, the prominent singers of different kinds.

13. Cook's circus, which made a great show for some time on State street, introducing scenery in connection with "Mazeppa" and other equestrian spectacles, and disastrously breaking up there, supplied the livery stables with handsome stock.

14. The Sunday-schools of Harrisburg.

15. The prominent colored people: George Chester, Curry Taylor, and Tom Brown, the well-remembered caterers. Dorsey and Nathans and Dorris, the barbers. Jake Smith, the fine violinist. Perry Hooper, the water cart man. Old Toby, the hewer of wood and carrier of water for boats and carts at the depot. Together with the headquarters of the colored population: "Judy's Town," "Bassacove," "Jones' town," "Hardscrabble," "Tanner's alley."

16. The Church Fairs—All held in the upper room of the old court house.

17. The old chestnut tree that stood until the year —— (?) on N. W. corner State and Second streets, where " Black Ben " and others, it was said, had been hung.

18. Jake Wentz and " Pappy " Dubbs," celebrated fifer and drummer of the town. (Was not the latter's father a Revolutionary soldier ?)

To the foregoing list of topics many others could be added, and will doubtless suggest themselves to your older readers. The fact that some are seemingly insignificant should not deter any one from recording their knowledge concerning them, for the trifles of the present make *history* in the future.   G. B. A.

IN ARMSTRONG AND POWELL'S VALLEYS.—II.

Straw's Lutheran and Reformed church is a branch of Miller's church. It is a one-story frame building situate about one and a half miles east of Jacksonville. It is now unused, many of the mem bers having died, others having left with the tide of emigration, while those who remain have gone back to their former church home. In the burial ground we copied the following records:

Jury, Catharine, *wf.* of Daniel, b. May 13, 1792; d. March 2, 1866.
Kumbler, John, b. April 8, 1794; d. April 8, 1868.
Kumbler, Elizabeth, *wf.* of J., b. Jan. 20, 1811; d. April 4, 1885.
Miller, Daniel P., b. May 22, 1810; d. March 1, 1873.
Miller, Maria M., *wf.* of Peter, b. Oct. 25, 1797; d. Nov. 13, 1854.
Ressler, Susanna, *wf.* of George, b. Feb. 5, 1816; d. May 8, 1874.
Schweigert, Johan, b. Dec. 1, 1810; d. Mar. 12, 1849.
Schupp, Johannes, b. Oct. 12, 1769; d. June 11, 1855.
Schupp, Elizabeth, *wf.* of Joseph, b. Feb. 1, 1798; d. Sept. 11, 1858.
Schup, Joseph, b. Mar. 19, 1790; d. Jan. 11, 1852.
Schup, Elizabeth, *wf.* of John, b. April 24, 1784; d. July 15, 1870.
Shoop, John, b. Feb. 8, 1803; d. Jan. 3, 1880.
Shoop, Mary, *wf.* of John, b. May, 1809; d. Mar. 22, 1862.
Straw, Anna Maria, *wf.* of Nicholas, b. Jan. 27, 1775; d. Mar. 16, 1862.
Wittman, Samuel, b. Jan. 13, 1816; d. May 17, 1849.
Zimmerman, Adam, b. Sept. 29, 1802; d. May 19, 1884.

" Miller's " church, Lutheran and Reformed, is situated about three miles east of Jacksonville and about one mile west of Centre View. The church is the second building, the former having been replaced by the present-one about fifty years ago. This is a commodious structure, one story frame, with high steeple in which is a silver-toned bell, whose strains reverberate through this valley to call the staid farmers to their devotional duties. Among the many tomb stones we transcribe the following as the once old inhabitants of this portion of Armstrong Valley:

"Grand Mother Barry"—Flower, Catharine, d. Nov. 16, 1857, aged 62 years.

Fisher, John Philip, b. Sept. 15, 1786; d. Dec. 23, 1858.

Fisher, Ann Catharine, b. July 20, 1792; d. Nov. 13, 1861.

Hoke, Catharine, *wf.* of Isaac, b. Nov. 24, 1824; d. Sept. 2, 1874.

Helt, David, b. Mar. 2, 1817; d. May 30, 1883.

Hecker, Christiana, *wf.* of Simon, b. Sept. 27, 1797; d. Aug. 9, 1838.

Miller, John, b. Nov. 7, 1777; d. July 6, 1861.

Miller, Anna Cath., b. May 5, 1783; d. Aug. 21, 1865.

Miller, Peter, b. May, 1780; d. May 30, 1842.

Miller, John S., b. July 10, 1782; d. Jan. 4, 1860.

Miller, Elizabeth, *wf.* of J. S., b. Aug. 6, 1793; d. Mar. 7, 1871.

Miller, Henry, *s.* of Samuel and Barbara, b. April 2, 1789; d. Dec. 14, 1864.

Miller, Michael, b. Feb. 12, 1805; d. Dec. 27, 1864.

Miller, Barbara, *dau.* of Henry and Elizabeth, and 2d *wf.* of Isaac Collier, b. Mar. 12, 1841; d. Jan. 26, 1863.

Minnich, Geo., b. Sept. 17, 1807; d. Oct. 22, 1875.

Parmer, Abel, b. Oct. 6, 1795; d. April 26, 1879.

Paul, Saiah, *wf.* of Jacob; b. April 13, 1818; d. May 31, 1869.

Sweigert, John, b. Feb. 20, 1786; d. June 26, 1832.

Sweigert, Elizabeth, *wf.* of John, b. June 16, 1792; d. Sept. 30, 1849.

Sweigert, Adam, b. Feb. 22, 1784; d. Mar. 21, 1849.

Sweigert, Elizabeth, *wf.* of A., and *dau.* of Henry and Christiana Werfel, b. Oct. 7, 1788; d. Oct. 7, 1852.

Schneider, Jacob, b. April 16, 1807; d. Jan. 7, 1858.

Schneider, Ann, *wf.* of J., b. June 1, 1805; d. Jan. 2, 1878.

Snyder, Wm., b. June 9, 1779; d. April 23, 1852.

Snyder, Ann Eliz., b. April 26, 1784; d. Jan. 7, 1852.

Snyder, J. C., b. Oct. 17, 1813; d. Oct. 16, 1885.

Schupp, Daniel, b. Oct. 11, 1785; d. April 30, 1845.

"Und zeught mitsenir Ehifrau
9 kinder, 4 Sohne u. 5 T."

Schupp, Susannah, *wf.* of D., b. June 7, 1789; d. Dec. 11, 1863.

Straw, John, b. July 4, 1774; d. Dec. 21, 1847.

Straw, Barbara, *wf.* of J., b. Jan. 26, 1781; d. June 11, 1854.

Trawitz, John, b. July 12, 1810; d. Mar. 1, 1880.

Trawitz, Elizabeth, *wf.* of J., b. Dec. 2, 1803; d. June 23, 1812.

Werfel, Jacob, b. Sept. 10, 1793; d. June 15, 1859.

Werfel, Mary, *wf.* of J., b. Sept. 19, 1794; d. Dec. 30, 1875.

Werfel, John, b. April 15, 1785; d. Nov. 9, 1874.

Werfel, Margaret, *wf.* of John, b. May 25, 1789; d. April 20, 1865.

Werfel, Susanna, *dau.* of Jacob, and *wf.* of Philip Miller, d. Nov. 17, 1842, aged 26 years, 1 m. and 15 days.

[This grave has a brick wall two feet high covered with a marble slab, upon which is the inscription. This is such an unusual occurrence for Germans that we were led to inquire the reason, when we were informed that the husband desired to prevent any one from treading upon his wife's grave, and hence the manner of covering the same.]

Zimmerman, Elizabeth, *wf.* of Adam, b. March 1, 1802; d. March 3, 1868.   E. W. S. P.

RECORDS OF BINDNAGLE CHURCH.—IX.

It is to be regretted that the record of marriages is so meagre as the following proves to be. It is probable the early register was kept at Hummelstown, but unfortunately the "Kirche" book of that charge is lost. In the Bindnagle book after the following, this memorandum is appended: "All those members of this congregation and from the neighborhood and married since 1837 by Rev. William G. Ernst, Evangelical Lutheran minister, have been entered in the church book at Lebanon."

MARRIAGES.

Albright, Andrew, m., December, 1795, Catharine Steiner; witnesses, Henry Oehrley and wife Rebecca.

Baumgartner, John, m., February 25, 1798, Elizabeth Kiefer; witnesses, parents and others.

Bolton, Valentine, m., March 5, 1795, Magdalena Ziegler; witnesses, Henry Ziegler, Godfred Zimmerman, and so forth.

Eisenhouer, Peter, m., August 24, 1795, Anna Early; witnesses, Thomas and Catharine Early.

Goetz, Martin, m., April 17, 1798, Salome Neydig; witnesses, Christian Early, Daniel Miller, and so forth.

Hemperly, Anthony, m. Catharine Vogt; witnesses, George Hemperley, Jacob Kitzmiller, and many others.

Job, John, m., March 7, 1795, Elizabeth Rudy; witnesses, parents, Jacob and Catharine Rudy.

Moyer, Jacob, m. Susan Lentz; witnesses, Jacob Lentz, and many others.

Pew, Benoni, m., February 18, 1798, Margaret Horstick; witnesses, Thomas Early, and many others.

EARLY COMMUNICANTS.

The records pertaining to the persons who partook of the Holy Communion are very complete. We give only the names of those who partook of the Sacrament December 13, 1795, being the second on record. The figure following each name indicates the number from that family who communed:

Catharine Schnae,	1
John Killinger,	1
Frederic Fernsler,	1
Michael Palm,	2
Maria Sens (?),	1
Michael Zimmerman,	2
Adam Deininger,	1
Juliana Jung,	1
John Oehrly,	3
Henry Miller,	2
Adam Bart,	2
Jacob Meunzer,	1
Andrew Holzberg,	2
Anna Mary Muey (?),	2
Henry Ziegler,	1
Jacob Kreamer,	2
Godfried Zimmerman,	2
Dorothea Sprecher,	1
Thomas Oehrly,	2
Peter Eisenhauer,	2
Andrew Brendes (?),	1
Magdalen Elter,	1
John Palm,	2
Catharine Blauch,	1
—— Schmall,	2
Total number,	43

NOTES AND QUERIES.—CXXXI.

JACOB EARLY (*N. & Q. cxxv.*)—His son John m. Margaret ——. In the year 1807 they resided in Rockingham county, Va. His daughter "Lutery," or Lydia, m. Christopher Smith; in 1807 she was a widow residing in Rockingham county, Va. His daughter Agnes m., May 16, 1775, John Mathias, son of Mathias Wentnagle

[Winagle].   The latter b. May 14, 1716; and on Feb. 28, 1786 (his wife was Maria Catharine Ritter), "the Lord of life and death called him out of this troublesome world to a joyous eternity."   His daughter Eva m. John Frederick, a brother of John Mathias Winagle, b.May, 30, 1759.   In 1807 both were living in New York State.   Information of his descendants is wanted.   His son Jacob, b. Oct. 23, 1759; d. March 29, 1806, at what is now the town of Highspire; buried in the Reformed grave-yard, corner of High and Pine streets, Middletown, where, over his grave, is a neat marble tombstone.   He resided in the old house, yet standing to the right, on the turnpike, as you enter Highspire from Middletown, and kept the Cross Keys Inn there, and after his death his widow, whose maiden name was probably Catharine Musser, succeeded him, although on October 10, 1807, the widow and brother and sisters above named conveyed the estate to Conrad Alleman.   The estate consisted of 14¾ acres and 19 perches, bounded as follows: "Beginning at a tree by the river Susquehanna; thence along line of land of John Witmer's heirs, N. 16 deg., E. 63 p. and 6-10 of a p. to a stone on the great road, along line of G. R. Smith, 61 d. and ½ E. 12 p. to a post; thence along the same S. 49¼ deg. E. 39 2-10 p. to a post by Nicholas Bressler's land, S. 36 deg. W. 54 1-11 p. to the Susquehanna river; up said river N. 62 d. W. 3 p. to place of beginning.   This same piece of land Conrad Alleman and Mary his wife conveyed by their deed dated December 23, 1813, to Henry and Carolina Berents, of Marietta, Pa., and Michael and Catharine Dochterman, of Mt. Joy township, which they laid out into town lots in 1814, and named it High Spire.   Almost immediately afterwards they laid out 56 acres adjoining and called it "Highspire *Continued.*"   In this connection we give a reservation in the Early deed, as it is a part answer to No. 4, of "Topics for Historians" in last *Notes and Queries,* subject also to a lease given by Early in his life to George Parthemore and others of "a right to fish for shad on the shore of the premises (which now is above Burd's run), and for said Parthemore to use as much drift wood during the said lease as may be necessary for fires for said fishery," &c., &c.   E. W. S. P.

EARLY PENNSYLVANIA IMMIGRATION SOUTHWARD.

In perusing recent Southern local history, a Pennsylvanian is struck with the records of the early settlers, whether Scotch-Irish or German, especially the former.   Those conversant with the history of our own State know that from the years 1740 to 1770 was the Scotch-Irish exodus, the main cause due to the discrimination by the Proprietaries of Pennsylvania against the settlers from the north of Ireland. The result was the movement southward, first to the Cumberland Valley, thence to the beautiful valleys of Virginia and the Carolinas. The history of the Scotch-Irish, who have furnished more representative men and women than any other class of settlers in America, has yet to be written, but we trust that some one equal to the task will soon undertake it. The German immigration southward was very limited until after the close of the struggle for independence, when they, too, followed their Pennsylvania neighbors, the Scotch-Irish; and to these two classes of early settlers in our State, the Southern States owe much of its thrift, its enterprise and patriotism. We are led to these reflections by reading "The Annals of Augusta county, Virginia," by Joseph A. Waddell, which we have received through the courtesy of R. A. Brock, Esq., of the Virginia Historical Society. It is a work of great value, and to the student of Pennsylvania history of more than ordinary interest. None such should fail to secure a copy. In connection with Col. Peyton's admirable history of Augusta county, published two years ago, a great deal of information can be gathered relating to Pennsylvania families, and if other and adjoining counties in the Virginia Valley could have the same work done for them which Col. Peyton and Mr. Waddell have accomplished for that of Augusta, what a great boon it would be to lovers of history, biography, and genealogy. Mr. Waddell, while giving his entertaining story in the form of annals does not forget in his copious notes to relate to us much concerning individuals and families. From these we give the following, being more particularly of local interest.

John and Andrew Pickens were early settlers in Paxtang. Here a son of the former, Gen. Andrew Pickens, of South Carolina, distinguished in the Revolution, was born, 19th of September, 1739. About two years afterwards they removed to Augusta county, Va., and in 1752 to the Waxhaw settlement in South Carolina.

Robert McClanahan first settled in Paxtang, but went with the Scotch-Irish immigration to Virginia. He was a brother of the celebrated Blair McClanahan, who at the close of the Revolution became a famous politician of Philadelphia. Robert McClanahan married Sarah Breckenridge, daughter of an early settler in the Cumberland Valley. Their three sons, *Alexander, Robert,* and *John* were prominent in the Indian wars, while the first named was a lieutenant colonel in the Revolution. They afterwards drifted to Kentucky. A daughter of Robert McClanahan married Alexander St. Clair, a representative man of Augusta county.

Few persons are aware of the fact that the distinguished family of Breckenridge were early settlers in the Cumberland Valley, from whence they too followed the tide of immigration into Virginia, and subsequently into the "dark and bloody ground." Kentucky's early settlers were almost wholly from Pennsylvania by way of Virginia; and also many of Tennessee's first families.

This volume is certainly replete with much that is valuable to us as Pennsylvanians. Most of the individuals who through the remarkable events of almost a century and a half rose high above the surface were either actual early settlers in this State or descendants thereof; not omiting the author's ancestor, the Rev. James Waddell, to whom Wirt in his excellent but almost forgotten work, "The Spy" pays such a grand tribute—the remarkable eloquence of the "Blind Preacher." At no distant day we hope to take up this subject of early Pennsylvania immigration to the southward, which this most excellent work has prompted us to do.

GENEALOGICAL NOTES.

LAWLOR.

MARY LAWLOR, widow, of Lancaster, d. August, 1778, leaving one child:

  i. Ann, m. George Ross, and their children were *George, James,* and *Mary.*

LEDLIE.

JOHN LEDLIE, of Middletown, d. in July, 1769, leaving issue:
  i. Sampson, m., and had *Aaron, Roger,* and *Mary.*

LAMB.

JOHN LAMB, of Paxtang, d. April, 1770, leaving a wife Jean, and issue:

  i. Martha.
  ii. Margaret.
  iii. Eleanor.

MCNUTT.

JOSEPH MCNUTT, of Hanover, d. March, 1767, leaving issue:
  i. Bernard.
  ii. Joseph.
  iii. William.
  iv. Martha, m. —— Dean.

  v. Jean.
  vi. Mary.
The executors were Hugh Ray and John Rogers.

MARSHALL.

JAMES MARSHALL, of Drumore township, Lancaster county, d. December, 1772, leaving a wife Jean, and children:
  i. Patrick.
  ii. John.
  iii. James.
  iv. William.
  v. Robert.
  vi. Samuel.
  vii. Thomas.
  viii. Mary.
  ix. Martha.
  x. Margaret.

McKINNEY.

JOHN McKINNEY, of Paxtang, d. November, 1749, leaving a wife Jean, daughter of Roger Cunningham, and children:
  i. John.
  ii. Hugh.
  iii. Mary.
The executors were "my brother Matthew McKinney, my brother-in-law Thomas Harris, and my brother Henry McKinney."

MURRAY.

JOHN MURRAY d. in October, 1745, leaving a wife and children as follows:
  i. Bettie.
  ii. Isabel.
  iii. Richard.

McALISTER.

NEAL McALISTER, of Derry, d. in November, 1757, leaving a wife, and children:
  i. John.
  ii. Neal, m., and had a son *Neal.*

McKNIGHT.

JAMES McKNIGHT, of Paxtang, d. November, 1753, leaving a wife Martha, and children:

    i. Francis.
    ii. Samuel.
    iii. John.

The executors were Martha and William McKnight.

———

McCORD.

WILLIAM McCORD d. March, 1761, leaving his estate to:
Son-in-law Thomas McCord.
Son-in-law John Means.
Son-in-law Patrick Montgomery.
Son-in-law George Alexander.

———

MONTGOMERY.

I. ROBERT MONTGOMERY, of Paxtang, d. February 22, 1776, leaving a wife Sarah, who d. October 15, 1784, and had children:

    i. Mary, m. ——— Duncan.
    ii. John.
    iii. Hugh.
    iv. David.
    v. Elizabeth, m. John Gallacher.

II. JAMES MONTGOMERY, of Leacock township, Lancaster county, d. February, 1772, leaving a wife Frances, and children:

    i. William, m., and had *John.*
    ii. James.
    iii. Jean, m. William Ramsey.
    iv. Sarah, m. James Sterrett.

———

NELSON.

JAMES NELSON d. April, 1765, leaving a wife Ann, and children:

    i. Joseph.
    ii. John.
    iii. Robert.
    iv. Samuel.
    v. Isabel [*Betty*], m. ——— Patton, and had *Mary* and *John.*
    vi. James.

NOTES AND QUERIES.—CXXXII.

CRAWFORD FAMILY.—The Hon. Edwin Salter, of New Jersey, sends us the following notes of the Crawford family, of Monmouth county, that State. Information as to the Pennsylvania branch is requested.

JOHN CRAWFORD, gentleman, of Ayrshire, Scotland, in 1678, bought 200 acres of land at Nut Swamp, Middletown, Monmouth county, and other lands. He had a son George Crawford, who describes himself in a deed as "son and heir" of John Crawford. He married Esther Scott, daughter of John Scott, and died 1745. They had issue:

    i. George, died without issue.
    ii. Richard, m. Catharine Shepard, and had issue whose line is preserved; he d. 1798, and his wife d. 1807.
    iii. William, m. Catharine Bowne, and had issue, and line preserved.
    iv. Joshua, went to Pennsylvania.
    v. Job, went to Pennsylvania.
    vi. Lydia.
    vii. Elizabeth.

The sons Joshua and Job Crawford, who went to Pennsylvania, had descendants who subsequently removed to Virginia and thence to Georgia. The late Senator William H. Crawford, of Georgia (Presidential candidate in 1824), was a son of Joel Crawford who went from Pennsylvania to Virginia; it is supposed he was a son of Joshua Crawford.

MARRIAGE LICENSES AT LANCASTER 1791–1799.—I.

[The following list is copied from a book in the Quarter Sessions office in Lancaster, in which are also entered a list of tavern applications. There does not seem to have been a prior record to 1791, nor subsequent to December 17, 1799.—S. E.]

1791.

Sept. 12. David King to Jane Snodgrass.
    20. Thomas Minshall to Rebecca Young.
    29. Matthew Richey to Rachel Chambers.
Oct. 10. Henry Huber to Barbara Huber.

13. James Corbitt to Jane Wilkins.
13. George Rowland to Elizabeth Weidler.
15. Peter Huber to Mary Huber.
17. Abraham Landis to Mary Burkholder.
19. William Hutchison to Mary Clark.
19. John Stockton to Ann Bedford.
28. Daniel Lyman to ―――― Eymany.
29. David Strome to Ann Hare.

Nov. 1. Cornelius Myer to Catharine Kendrick.
8. Jacob Bower to Barbara Stouffer.
10. John Swarr to Margaret Hernley.
12. Abraham Witmer to Anne Stoner.
21. Christian Shaub to Eva Boyer.
22. Christian Nolt to Ann Eshelman.
25. Richard Neagle to Mary Reyley.
29. John Fortney to Elizabeth Miller.
30. Franciscus Curtis to Eva Trumpeter.

1792.

Jan. 3. Andrew Templeton to Rosanna Hart.
14. James Clark to Sarah Boyd.
16. Jacob Mays to Catharine Hogendobler.
23. George Fresher to Elizabeth Holl.
26. George Fisher to Mary Fry.
31. George Maxton to Mary Roth.
31. John Swenck to Christina Lindemuth.
March 1. Thomas Clark to Jane Caldwell.
April 9. Jacob Martin to Magdalena Martin.
11. George Peters to Catharine Zanck.
28. Thomas Grubb to Rachel Ewing.
28. Henry Garber to Elizabeth Bard.
May 2. John Graham to Margaret Moore.
4. Ulrich Shellaberger to Magdalena Zimmerman.
8. Christian Kline to Margaret Sheaffer.
28. John Eresman to Christina Huber.
June 7. Samuel Hindman to Elenor Nesbitt.
12. Abraham Buckwalter to Frena Ginder.
14. Samuel Elliot to Margaret Mabin.
July 5. John Smith to Anna Weston.
22. Martin Ridebach to Rachel Pinkerton.
30. William Mayes to Eleanor Watson.
Aug. 9. David Manning to Frena Kauffman.

21. John Reigel to Maria Hertzler.
30. John Clark to Mary Coile.
Sept. 4. Jacob Wentz to Margaret Lyons.
15. Peter Sands to Susanna Spencer.
24. John McGlaulin to Mary Wells.
Oct. 1. Dan Quinn to Catharine Steen.
2. Martin Martin to Eva Wagoner.
8. James Harrison to Mary Craiger.
9. Henry Clarke to Mary Hovenduder.
18. Jacob Carpenter to Mary Carpenter.
29. Henry Myers to Barbara Furry.
29. Michael Bear to Catharine Sando.
30. Francis Smith to Margaret Scott.
30. Timothy Mealy to Jane McKeon.
Nov. 1. William Kirkpatrick to Elizabeth Hoofnagle.
1. George Trissler to Susanna Baker.
2. David Swartz to Susanna Deeter.
6. Martin Meybery to Elizabeth Buckwalter.
9. Daniel Hare to Esther Hersht.
17. John Herr to Mary Houry.
20. William Baxter to Elizabeth Smith.
27. John Daler to Ann Baker.
Dec. 1. Jacob Lehman to Catharine Eicholtz.
3. Henry Hare to Elizabeth Harnish.
4. Samuel McCullough to Martha Ball.
8. James McCoye to Isabella McEntire.
27. Martin Furry to Catharine Kendrick.

1793.

Jan. 1. Andrew Bitzer to Susanna Sweigert.
1. David Longenecker to Ann Hare.
28. Elab Howard to Anna McCasland.
Feb. 2. John Frileck to Barbara Lowman.
11. Peter Kline to Elizabeth Deeshler.
26. John Cunningham to Margaret Elliot.
28. Casper Snyder to Susanna Kerr.
28. Frederick Mellman to Susanna Charles.
March 1. John Resh to Barbara Hess.
7. Andrew Carter to Mary Redsecker.
13. Joseph Morrison to Elizabeth McCullough.
23. James McGinley to Agnes Sample.
26. Christian Neyswanger to Barbara Martin.
26. Jacob Albright to Susanna Hall.
26. Joseph Johnston to Jane Asking.

27. John Pinkerton to Mary Waggoner.
April 2. William Snodgrass to Eleanor Peggs.
3. John Brown to Mary Atchison.
20. Peter Wilhelm to Elizabeth Beck.
23. Abraham Kling to Susanna Holl.
23. Tobias Kendrick to Mary Bowman.
May 8. William Darrough to Ann Morrison.
14. Christian Sherrer to Ann Shaup.
16. John Bare to Susanna Forry.
18. Hilarius Ehenzeler to Catharine DeHuff.
21. John Hare to Mary Licht.
24. Abraham Henry to Elizabeth Martin.
28. Tobias Kreiter to Mary Thompson.
June 7. Jacob Carrigan to Margaret Rapp.
8. Jacob Foehl to Magdalina Ziegler.
22. John Rose to Catharine Thomas.
25. Christian Kendrick to Barbara Meiley.
July 1. John Bradburn to Mary Churchman.
15. John Sheib to Catharine Bixler.
20. Daniel Hess to Magdalena Ament.
24. Martin Bare to Elizabeth Brubaker.
29. Archibald McNeel to Martha Sheffer.
30. Michael Knight to Barbara Shuereishman.
Aug. 6. Jacob Kepperling to Barbara Huber.
17. John McPherson to Elizabeth McPherson.
31. James Boyd to Mary Jordan.
31. John Sensell to Anna Eyman.
Sept. 3. John Shofe to Anna Hess.
20. Nathaniel Ewing to Ann Breading.
Oct. 15. Conrad Brehmer to Henry Wolf.
15. John Christoph Hoenig to Margaret Miller.
17. John Demith to Catharine Trissler.
19. William Michael to Susanna Weaver.
Nov. 12. Michael Gross to Elizabeth Greybill.
19. Daniel Perkins to Sarah Willson.
28. Samuel Rowland to Mary Bare.
29. Martin Bare to Margaret Burd.
30. John Craig to Margaret Johnson.
30. John Bassler to Catharine Kishey.
Dec. 10. William Thompson to Mary Johnson.
10. Andrew Kauffman to Elizabeth Miller.
17. Adam Werfle to Elizabeth Simonee.
18. Jacob Werfle to Mary Sands.

1794.

Jan. 23. Henry Rutter to Rachel Ferree.
    7. John Pratt to Sabina Stouffer.
    7. Adam Reigart to Susanna Metzgar.
  10. Thomas Thompson to Mary Know.
  16. John Shenk to Ann Bare.
  21. Geo. Yeates to Elizabeth Burns.
Feb. 3. Isaac Graff to Susanna Hamaker.
  12. John Young to Mary Ankrim.
  12. John Fry to Elizabeth Kreeg.
  24. John Kauffman to Barbara Reibley.
  26. Jacob Hoomer to Elizabeth Freymayer.
Mar. 19. Hugh Mayhaffey to Elizabeth Haines.
  22. Alexander Dysart to Eleanor Patterson.
  24. Mathias Haverstick to Elizabeth Maurer.
  25. Benjamin Eshleman to Freonia Steman.
  25. Ludwig Diffenderfer to Anna Maria Shaffer.
April 1. John Eshelman to Maria Eshelman.
  5. David Correl to Susanna Hess.
  5. Adam Holtzworth to Cathrine Flick.

NOTES AND QUERIES.—CXXXIII.

FRENCH EMIGRANTS IN THE WHISKEY INSURRECTION.—By reference to the " Executive Minutes " of Thursday, September 18, 1794, we find that " the Governor instructed the Attorney General not to permit the enrollment for the Western Expedition of any French Emigrants who have sought a temporary asylum in this country, and that he communicate his instructions to the proper officers of the several corps and request their particular attention to them." What was the cause of these instructions?

FREE SCHOOLS.—On the 14th of December, 1792, a petition, numerously signed from the inhabitants of the town of Harrisburg, was presented to the General Assembly praying for the establishment of free schools in said town. This petition was prepared by John Downey, and the principal citizens of the town signed the same. The Legislature then were not liberal enough in their ideas to countenance the measure. That bright day came at last.

ROAD OVER PETER'S MOUNTAIN.—On the 22d of January, 1794, a contract was entered into by the Commonwealth with John Ayres, of the county of Dauphin, for improving the road over Peter's mountain from John Ayres' farm to McCall's tavern. The full compensation was $720. The contractor at once went to work, and the road which heretofore had been considered a dangerous one, was made easy and safe. The contractor did not make any money out of this contract, but imbued with a patriotic spirit, he assumed the duty. The road is the one now used in crossing the mountain, and little repair has ever been made to it.

RECORDS OF BINDNAGLE CHURCH.—X.

TOMBSTONE INSCRIPTIONS.

[The burial ground is located to the northwest and adjoining the church. It is crowded with graves, except the addition of one-half acre which was given by William Early some thirty years ago but held under his control, or that of his descendants. No more charming spot could have been selected for a final resting place than upon this bluff which overlooks the Swatara creek, and upon the back ground the verdant hills. Many of the early graves are marked with sand stones, some of which are almost illegible. The first person buried from which we can gather any record by the tombstone is Jacob Schering, who d. in 1771. The following are most of the transcripts:]

Albert, Elizabeth, *w.* of Thomas Goetz, b. Feb. 6, 1787; d. Nov. 29, 1869.

Boltz, Anna Maria, *w.* of Henry, b. February 10, 1783; d. Sept. 23, 1854.

Boltz, Henrich, b. Oct. 16, 1769; d. June 19, 1847.

Boltz, Simon, b. Nov. 25, 1815; d. Jan. 30, 1864.

Beck, Elizabeth, b. Sept. 12, 1798; d. Feb. 26, 1866.

Beck, Peter, b. Sept. 29, 1788; d. May 2, 1850.

Beck, Michael, b. 1736; d. 1814.

Boyer, Rebecca, *w.* of Peter Snavely, b. Nov. 29, 1809; d. March 24, 1855.

Baumgartner, Catharine, *w.* of John, b. Nov. 7, 1812; d. July 12, 1866.

Baumgartner, John, b. Aug. 7, 1801; d. Aug. 14, 1869.

Balm (Palm), Rebecca, b. Jan. 17, 1792; d. Jan. 7, 1871.

Bechtol, Jacob, b. 1750; d. 1806.

Bechtol, Mary, b. 1760; d. 1806.

Burmann (Poorman), Elizabeth, *w.* of M. Reichert, b. Oct. 5, 1806; d. Oct. 30, 1857.

Burmann (Poorman), Elizabeth, *w.* of John, b. Aug. 12, 1809; d. July 5, 1832.

Bishop, Adam, b. 1797; d. March 15, 1851.

Bolden (Bolton), Anna Maria, *w.* of John, b. Sept., 1781; d. March 13, 1826.

Benson, Alexander, b. Sept. 8, 1819; d. June 12, 1845.

Braun (Brown), Joseph, b. Oct. 29, 1796; d. May 26, 1828.

Braun (Brown), Phillip, b. Dec. 15, 1763; d. Sept. 10, 1833.

Braun (Brown), Catharine, b. Feb. 19, 1770; d. Feb. 2, 1841.

Braun (Brown), Michael, b. Jan. 15, 1724; d. March 13, 1785.

Clark, Sarah, *w.* of Jacob Nye, b. July 27, 1813, d. March 4, 1837.

Crone, John, b. Jan. 1, 1789; d. May 12, 1847.

Deininger, Mary, *w.* of George Walmer, b. March 1, 1792; d. Jan. 1, 1835.

Deininger, Adam, b. Sept. 19, 1764; d. Jan. 3, 1850.

Deininger, Christina, *w.* of A., b. Oct. 12, 1760; d. Oct. 14, 1828.

Deininger, Leonard, b. Jan. 7, 1787; d. Sept. 6, 1852.

Deininger, Henry, b. Nov. 1, 1790; d. April 23, 1798.

Deininger, Benj., b. Feb. 12, 1793; d. March 5, 1824.

Deininger, Michael, b. Nov. 17, 1763; d. Aug. 26, 1805.

Deininger, Mary Magdalena, b. Aug. 6, 1752; d. Aug. 23, 1775.

Deininger, David, b. Feb. 17, 1797; d. May 4, 1798.

Deininger, Barbara, b. at Aicholz, Germany, 1723; d. 1800.

Diffenbaum, Catharine Anna, b. Jan. 6, 1748; d. July 25, 1822.

Darcus, Leah, *w.* of Absolem, b. May 24, 1847; d. Feb. 18, 1870.

Early, Catharine, *nee* Hershey, *w.* of William, b. June, 1780; d. Aug. 1, 1815.

Early, Benjamin, *s.* of William and Catharine, b. Dec. 11, 1803; d. May 5, 1827.

Hier Ruhet | Johannes Ohrle (Early) | War Gebboren den 9ten Janu | A. D. 1724, und starb den 19ten | September, A. D. 1796, | Sein Alter war 72 Jahr, | 8 monath und 10 tay. | In den Estand Gebreden mid | Susana Brubaren, den 10ten April, | 1753, had ein kind Gezeicht | mid Regina Sihleen, in den | Estand gegeben den 10 Mertz, | 1756, had 9 kinder Gezeicht.

Early, Mollie, b. 1822; d. 1846.

Early, William, b. March 5, 1782; d. Dec. 12, 1863.

Early, Christina (*nee* Kreider), *w.* of William, b. Sept. 4, 1784; d. Sept. 28, 1868.

Early, Magdalena (*nee* Snively), *w.* of John, b. April 28, 1813; d. June 25, 1869.

Early, Emma, b. April 27, 1843; d. Oct. 7, 1861.
Early, Maria (*nee* Maulvier), *w.* of Joshua, b. 1816; d. 1852.
Early, Sarah (*nee* Weidner), *w.* of Joshua, b. 1818; d. 1868.
Early, Margaret, b. 1838; d. 1856.
Early, Elizabeth, b. 1844; d. 1854.
Early, William, b. 1874; d. 1879.
Farling, Anna, *w.* of John, b. March 12, 1794; d. March 16, 1874.
Farling, John, b. July 6, 1797; d. Dec. 8, 1875.
Frantz, Susanna (*nee* Wolf), b. Feb. 28, 1811; d. Jan 10, 1865.
Fishborn, Catharine, *w.* of J., b. Oct. 28, 1801; d. Oct. 29, 1821.
Frantz, Barbara (*nee* Wagner), *w.* of Thos., b. Jan. 7, 1812; d. Dec.
    24, 1866.
Fahrney, Susanna, b. 1781; d. 1819.
Getz, John, b. May 24, 1808; d. Mar. 6, 1861.
Goetz, Thomas, b. Dec. 23, 1774; d. Sept. 18, 1814.
Hemperley, George, b. July 15, 1767; d. July 18, 1857.
Hemperley, John, b. Feb. 21, 1804; d. April 24, 1864.
Hemperley, Elizabeth, *w.* of John, b. Aug. 2, 1806; d. May 19, 1850.
Hemperley, Anna Maria (*nee* Yingst), *w.* of George, b. June 7, 1797;
    d. Aug. 27, 1858.
Hemperley, George, b. Sept. 20, 1797; d. April 23, 1850.
Hemperley, Anthony, b. Oct. 20, 1768; d. Aug. 13, 1828.
Hemperley, David, b. Oct. 16, 1836; d. Dec. 3, 1864.
Hemperley, Jacob, b. Sept. 9, 1831; d. Sept. 3, 1863.
Hemperley, David, b. Jan. 31, 1809; d. Mar. 10, 1845.
Hemperley, Jule, b. Feb. 16, 1729; d. Sept. 1, 1802.
Hemperley, Anthony, b. May 9, 1714; d. Feb. 11, 1788.
Hemperley, Rosina (*nee* Palm), b. May 3, 1766; d. June 10, 1799.
Hill, Amos B., b. Mar. 9, 1848; d. Feb. 25, 1870.
Horst, Jacob, b. Nov. 24, 1798; d. Dec. 22, 1874.
Horst, Maria (*nee* Ricker), *w.* of J., b. Nov. 9, 1809; d. Jan. 16, 1870.
Hautz, Johannes, b. May 18, 1782; d. May 18, 1838.
Hautz, Christiana (*nee* Schwanger), b. 1777; d. 1812.
Hautz, Dorety, b. 1776; d. 1815.

MARRIAGE LICENSES AT LANCASTER, 1781–1799.—II.

April 12. Daniel Hackmann to Anna Culp.
   12. Christian Culp to Elizabeth Hagey.
   15. David George to Ann Maria Breemer.
   20. George Brunkhart to Philipena Kleiss.
   22. John Sneider to Margaret Peters.
   26. Jacob Leonard to Sarah Hatton.

April 30. James Brown to Eleanor Winter.
May   3. Daniel Meisner to Mary Martin.
     10. Francis Parks to Mary Plotaberger.
     20. John Shultz to Susanna Frealick.
June 20. George Gingrich to Barbara Meist.
     24. Jacob Steman to Barbara Bare.
     28. Abraham Sweiher to Elizabeth Fordinee.
July 29. Samuel Hinkle to Ann Lightner.
Sept. 2. Jacob Frealick to Frena Fritz.
     21. Richard Jenkins to Catharine Crawford.
     22. Peter Lutz to Elizabeth Parks.
     22. William Ramsey to Jane Thompson.
     25. Jacob Hartman to Elizabeth Bressler.
Oct.   6. John Harnish to Elizabeth Bossler.
     7. Thomas McCreary to Elizabeth Grey.
     10. David Sampson to Catharine Boyer.
     12. Jacob Linton to Margaret Crawford.
     16. Adam Moore to Mary Kuhn.
Nov. 5. Peter Miller to Elizabeth Bare.
     6. James Long to Elizabeth Niel.
     13. John Swisher to Barbara Dulisong.
     16. Frederick Speck to Barbara Musselman.
     21. Henry Hare to Elizabeth Killheffer.
     24. Christian Winter to Anna Palmer.
     27. Joseph Barton to Rebecca Anderson.
Dec.   4. John Shober to Elizabeth Bender.
     7. James Murray to Ann McElhenny.
     11. John McIlvain to Isabella Barton.
     23. Thomas Clark to Elizabeth Price.
     23. John Bower to Catharine Allbright.
     24. Jacob Ehrman to Elizabeth Ganter.
     28. Robert McHaffey to Mary Robinson.

1795.

Jan.   3. John Schenck to Barbara Greider.
     7. Benjamin Fenton to Rebecca Moore.
     13. Robert Ramsey to Elizabeth Milligan.
     27. Samuel Niepser to Martha Whitesides.
     31. Samuel Adams to Esther Ream.
Feb.   7. Daniel Dorraingdan to Elizabeth Graff.
     12. William Elliot to Hannah Ball.
     23. Jacob Fry to Elizabeth Metzgar.
     24. Henry Sheibley to Elizabeth Miller.
     26. John Whelen to Phoebe Meville.

Mar. 23. William Pratt to Elizabeth Huber.
April 2. Leonard Sneider to Elizabeth Rowland.
      10. Thomas Hooper to Eleanor Pratt.
      23. Christian Henry to Elizabeth Goodman.
      23. Arthur Travers to Elizabeth Ferree.
      30. Jacob Steitler to Mary Little.
May 22. Martin Hoober to Mary Miller.
      25. Michael Kapp to Catharine Benton.
      26. Michael Weber to Catharine Stouffer.
June 10. Henry Heistand to Elizabeth Jordan.
      11. William Fulton to Martha Hill.
      12. Abraham Graybill to Christina Roedy.
      12. Jacob Graff to Martha Landes.
      24. David Shultz to Barbara Alder.
      27. Peter Eckman to Elizabeth Kendig.
July   4. Christian Musselman to Susanna Gaesy.
       5. Joseph Showalter to Elizabeth Dritt.
      10. Jacob Hiestand to Elizabeth Stouffer.
      14. George Tire to Maria Gratzer.
      21. Jacob Foutz to Mary Frank.
Aug. 10. John Glen to Eleanor McGowen.
      14. Patrick McCann to Mary Hart.
      14. Edward McBride to Grace Derir.
      18. Henry Resh to Ann Huber.
      20. Joseph Money to Mary Montgomery.
      25. Daniel Keeportz to Feronica Miller.
April 10. David Barton to Catharine Graeff.
      18. Jacob Walter to Ann Stouffer.
      21. Andrew Schmull to Barbara Wigell.
      22. Christian Fisher to Maria Mourer.
      30. Nathan Webster to Rachel Sidwell.
Oct.   8. John Andrews to Catharine Gillian.
      13. Samuel Wright to Susanna Louden.
      17. James Wilcox to Mary Sheffel.

EARLY FAST AND THANKSGIVING DAYS IN PENN-SYLVANIA.

From the Executive Minutes, we learn that under the Constitution of 1776, the following proclamations were issued :

By President Thomas Wharton, Jr., Solemn Fast on Thursday, April 3, 1777, and Wednesday, April 22, 1778.

By Vice-President George Bryan, Thanksgiving, Wednesday, Dec. 30, 1778.

By President Joseph Reed, Thanksgiving, Thursday, Dec. 9, 1779; Solemn Fast, Wednesday, April 26, 1780; Thanksgiving, Thursday, Dec. 7, 1780, and Solemn Fast, Wednesday, May 3, 1781.

By President William Moore, Thanksgiving (surrender of Cornwallis at Yorktown), Thursday, Dec. 13, 1781, and Solemn Fast, Thursday, April 25, 1782.

By Vice-President James Potter, Thanksgiving, Thursday, Nov. 28, 1782.

By President John Dickinson, Thanksgiving, Thursday, December 11, 1783.

By President Benjamin Franklin, Thanksgiving, Thursday, Nov. 29, 1787. It is possible a similar day was appointed by President Franklin the following year, but there is no record of it upon the minutes.

By President Thomas Mifflin, Thanksgiving, Thursday, November 24, 1789.

NOTES AND QUERIES.—CXXXIV.

PAUL'S CREEK AND VALLEY.—When and why was the name changed to Powell's? In looking over some old documents we find that it was uniformly written and printed Paul's.

PAPER MILL IN LEBANON COUNTY.—By an advertisement of John A. Heilman in 1804, we learn that he had been carrying on the manufacture of paper for thirteen years. Where was this mill located, and at what date was the manufacture stopped.

IN THE CUMBERLAND VALLEY.—Carefully and systematically we are going over the records at Carlisle, and although it will be some time before we shall complete our present researches, we have learned much of the early history of the valley. The emigration of the families, their connection with each other, their early settlement in that beautiful country lying between the Susquehanna and the Potomac, and their transit to the lovely valleys southward, we have had a chance to study. We have learned bits of biography and genealogy which many in the near future will appreciate and carefully preserve.

The history of the Cumberland Valley has not been written, but we hope to see the day when some one fascinated by research, and charmed with its lore, will take up the subject, which so many pirates have attempted to do and of course signally failed. To prepare the history of any locality requires years of patient labor and research, and it cannot be expected that much value attaches to hasty information unreliably given and loosely thrown together. In a few weeks we hope to present some contributions to the history of the Valley "west of ye Sasquahannah," and to the southward.

RECORDS OF BINDNAGLE CHURCH.—XI.

Tombstone Inscriptions.

Karmany, John, b. March 22, 1809; d. Oct. 30, 1833.
Karmanin, Eva, b. Oct. 16, 1738; d. May 19, 1805.
Karmany, Anthony, b. Jan. 1, 1787; d. Aug. 25, 1865.
Karmany, Eve Christina, *w.* of A., b. Mar. 12, 1785; d. Aug. 5, 1841.
Karmany, Maria Margaret, b. 1759; d. 1775.
Kratzer, Maria, b. Aug., 1791; d. March 23, 1828.
Keller, George, b. Oct. 19, 1793; d. Oct. 30, 1866.
Keller, Valentine, b. Mar. 6, 1803; d. Oct. 17, 1837.
Kisner, Henry, b. Jan. 27, 1726; d. Dec. 27, 1801.
Killinger, John, b. Dec. 25, 1765; d. Sept. 11, 1810.
Killinger, Susanna, b. Feb., 1769; d. June 21, 1809.
Lehman, Jacob, b. 1744; d. 1805.
Loy, Andrew, b. Feb. 16, 1795; d. Oct. 27, 1863.
Loy, Sarah, *w.* of A., b. Dec. 17, 1813; d. Jan. 15, 1885.
Light, Christian, b. March 16, 1792; d. Oct. 3, 1842.
Light, Catharine, b. Sept. 18, 1793, in Lebanon township; d. Oct. 1874.
Landis, Anna C., b. Aug. 19, 1802; d. March 15, 1849.
Lentz, David, b. June 9, 1803; d. Sept. 30, 1854.
Lentz, Jacob, b. July 17, 1759; d. March 23, 1845.
Lentz, Elizabeth, *nee* Ulrich, *w.* of J., b. 1769; d. 1842.
Lentz, Catharine, *nee* Rauch, *w.* of John, b. Nov. 25, 1818; d. March 20, 1869.
Lentz, David, b. June 9, 1803; d. Sept. 30, 1854.
Laudermilch, John, b. Jan. 24, 1768; d. Oct. 6, 1854.
Miller, David, b. Nov. 30, 1780; d. Sept. 30, 1853.

Miller, Cath., *w.* of D., b. July, 1786; d. Jan. 8, 1844.
Moyer, Cath., *w.* of John, b. 1808; d. Oct. 27, 1856.
Malvier, Michael, b. Oct. 1, 1756; d. March 30, 1803.
Maulfier, Maria, b. April 9, 1763; d. Aug. 9, 1822.
Maulfair, John, b. April 6, 1771; d. May 20, 1856.
Maulfair, Margaret, *w.* of J., b. Oct. 27, 1775; d. Oct. 8, 1859.
Maulfair, Eve, b. Oct. 2, 1736, d. March 16, 1793.
Maulfair, Elizabeth, *nee* Seltzer, *w.* of John, b. Sept. 13, 1807; d. Nov. 27, 1857.
Maulfair, Elizabeth, *w.* of Henry, b. Feb. 5, 1814; d. Feb. 13, 1840.
Maulfair, John Michael, b. 1729; d. 1807.
Moyer, Elizabeth, b. 1784; d. 1813.
Moyer, John, b. Nov. 4, 1800; d. Nov. 30, 1842
Moyer, John, b. July 3, 1799; d. Sept. 11, 1853.
Moyer, Susan E., b. Oct. 29, 1776; d. Oct. 18, 1849.
Moyer, Henry B., b. June 15, 1838; d. Nov. 9, 1858.
Mertz, John, b. July 29, 1780; d. Aug. 28, 1855.
Nye, Adam, b. Oct. 19, 1787; d. Sept. 11, 1859.
Naftsger, Catharine, b. March 19, 1802; d. Oct. 6, 1871.
Nye, Jacob, b. Aug. 31, 1809; d. June 7, 1867.
Phuh, Margaret, *w.* of Benoni, b. Oct. 27, 1767; d. March 27, 1843.
Pue, Benoni, b. 1768; d. June 22, 1834.
Palm, Michael, b. May 21, 1770; d. July 31, 1834.
Palm, Maria Barbara, b. May 26, 1768; d. March 27, 1834.
Palm, William, b. 1754; d. 1806.
Preis (?), David, b. 1748; d. 1774.
Purman (Poorman), Elizabeth, b. 1809; d. 1832.
Rauch, Susan, *w.* of John, d. aged 65 years.
Richtor, Melchior, b. Oct. 12, 1806; d. Jan. 28, 1869.
Rauch, Jacob, b. March 11, 1772; d. Dec. 5, 1834.
Rauch, Anna Margaret, b. March 8, 1776; d. June 1, 1862.
Rauch, Sarah, *d.* of J., b. Dec. 18, 1805; d. Nov. 1, 1860.
Schneider, John, b. 1795; d. 1802.
Snyder, Jacob, b. Nov. 29, 1824; d. Nov. 27, 1857.
Stine, Jacob, b. Sept. 18, 1794; d. April 6, 1840.
Stuckey, Cath., *w.* of M., b. June 14, 1792; d. June 22, 1866.
Stuckey, Michael, b. Sept. 27, 1783; d. Aug. 13, 1856.
Stuckey, M. F., *s.* of Fred. and Susan, b. Sept. 9, 1812; d. Aug. 11, 1863.
Stuckey, Fred., b. Sept. 24, 1815; d. Feb. 27, 1842.
Stuckey, Michael, b. 1753; d. 1821.
Stuckey, Elizabeth, b. 1761; d. 1823.

Schnug (Snoke), John, b. March 14, 1774; d. March 14, 1830.
Schnug (Snoke), Eve, b. Jan. 26, 1794; d. March 16, 1848.
Schnug (Snoke), Christian, b. Oct. 17, 1786; d. Oct. 17, 1851.
Schnug (Snoke), Margaret, b. March 12, 1782; d. Feb. 28, 1852.
Schnug (Snoke), Matthias, b. Dec. 26, 1796; d. May 1, 1852.
Schnug, George, b. 1788; d. Feb. 2, 1864.
Schnug (Snoke), Cath., *nee* Fernsler, *w.* of George, b. Jan. 22, 1801; d. Feb. 18, 1865.
Schnug (Snoke), Margaret, b. Sept. 11, 1776; d. Jan. 30, 1807.
Schnug (Snoke), Johannes, b. April 30, 1750; d. Dec. 15, 1808.
Schenug, Jacob, b. 1725; d. 1771.
Strack, Hannah, b. 1752; d. 1822.
Steahley, Elizabeth, *w.* of D., b. Oct. 10, 1817; d. Aug. 17, 1854.
Schneider, Elizabeth, *w.* of J., b. Aug. 12, 1777; d. Nov 10, 1829.
Schneider, Thomas, b. Jan. 29, 1813; d. Aug. 6, 1832.
Shire, Anna, b. Nov. 21, 1784; d. Aug. 26, 1847.
Schneider, Eliz., b. Dec. 4, 1802; d. Aug. 5, 1835.
Schneider, Julianna, b. July 25, 1798; d. Oct. 7, 1827.
Scherer, Michael, b. April 1, 1800; d. March 31, 1859.
Seebert, Hannah, b. March 2, 1832; d. Aug. 20, 1850.
Shafer, Jacob, b. Jan. 22, 1801; d. May 2, 1869.
Shafer, Elizabeth, b. March 9, 1798; d. April 3, 1859.
Scheirnig (?), Adam, b. Oct. 15, 1826; d. May 27, 1860.
Unger, Jacob, b. Nov. 14, 1792; d. Feb. 19, 1870.
Wolf, Maria, *nee* Frantz, *w.* of D., b. April 24, 1809; d. Feb. 16, 1867.
Withers, Eve, *nee* Horst, *w.* of J., b. May 29, 1819; d. June 8, 1874.
Walheim, Cath. Margaretta, b. 1774; d. 1776.
Weidner, Joseph, b. April 13, 1797; d. Dec. 31, 1858.
Weidner, Cath., *w.* of J., b. July 11, 1788; d. April 2, 1854.
Zeigler, Christian, b. Dec. 1, 1772; d. May 5, 1840.
Zimmerman, John, b. Apr. 11, 1756; d. Mar. 18, 1823.
Zimmerman, Anna Margaret, *w.* of J., b. May 23, 1756; d. Sept. 13, 1839.
Zimmerman, Moses R., b. June 5, 1829; d. Oct. 9, 1848.
Zimmerman, Jacob R., *s.* of J. and E., b. Oct. 18, 1839; d. Jan. 14, 1855.
Zimmerman, John, b. June 5, 1795; d. Dec. 12, 1807.
Zimmerman, Polly, *w.* of H., b. Feb. 7, 1807; d. Sept. 5, 1841.
Zimmerman, Gottfried, b. Dec. 15, 1763; d. Feb. 8, 1853.
Zimmerman, Anna Maria, *w.* of G., b. July 11, 1772; d. Feb. 18, 1849.
Zimmerman, Jacob, b. Nov. 12, 1798; d. April 8, 1842.
Zimmerman, Michael, b. April 5, 1797; d. Dec. 25, 1868.

MARRIAGE LICENSES AT LANCASTER, 1791–1799.—III.

1795.

Oct. 19. Henry Sneider to Mary Bard.
24. Philip Shaum to Mary Lauman.
Nov. 3. Henry Paulus to Elizabeth Eshelman.
7. John Gall to Mary Bender.
18. Henry Downer to Susanna Harvey.
23. Jacob Dubbs to Mary Hill.
26. John Cockey to Elizabeth Zantzinger.
Dec. 26. John Hagey to Eve Snider.

1796.

Jan. 14. James Armstrong to Mary Steman.
16. Andrew Foltz to Elizabeth Wilhelm.
18. Christian Greider to Ann Harnish.
20. David Brubaker to Maria Groff.
26. John Fried to Elizabeth Shirk.
Feb. 11. John Campbell to Margaret Williamson.
March 2. Benjamin Cryder to Ann Diffebach.
14. Adam Arbuckle to Mary Guy.
21. Isaac Stoner to Elizabeth Pfifer.
26. Henry Hartman to Mary Miller.
28. Samuel Sweigart to Catharine Holtzinger.
29. Jacob Johnson to Eve Bechtel.
April 1. Jacob Stake to Mary Barber.
5. John Buck to Dorothea Frey.
11. John Swartz to Anna Maria Snider.
11. Martin Meily to Elizabeth Hare.
12. Ludwig Urban to Martha Kendrick.
16. George Lefever to Susanna Hartman.
22. Joseph Wike to Elizabeth Hoar.
30. John Grove to Martha Wengert.
May 19. George Barber to Catharine Lindenberger.
26. John Logan to Catharine Mundorf.
27. Michael Kauffman to Mary Correll.
June 1. John Bosler to Susanna Greider.
11. John Fetter to Elizabeth Doebler.
13. Andrew Gillespie and Ann Johnston.
13. Daniel Werntz to Christina Snyder.

June 13. Jacob Maynard to Barbara Shenk.
     13. John Swarm to Magdalena Yeager.
     14. Jacob Landis to Ann Brown.
July 10. Jacob Kelker to Rebecca Thome.
     21. Peter Sugar to Elizabeth Eberman.
     26. Jacob Thoman to Margaret Riggebaugh,
Aug. 6. Daniel Furry to Ann Resh.
      6. Christian Kilhefer to Maria Yesler.
      9. Christian Hare, Jr., to Elizabeth Withers.
     10. George Hamilton to Ann Hamilton.
     16. John Dursch to Elizabeth Knisley.
     26. John Seitz to Sarah Hammel.
     27. Christian Shultz to Catharine Withers.
     30. Christian Smith to Elizabeth Curtz.
Sept. 3. John McGlaughlin to Hannah Dougherty.
     27. John Everle to Elizabeth Burd.
Oct. 5. Henry Cryder to Elizabeth Hartman.
      6. Samuel Boyd to Mary Pollock.
     17. John McCara to Jennet Clark. .
     22. John McGlaughlin to Mary Webb.
     25. Andrew Glinn to Ann Steighton.
     30. Peter Keller to Catharine Shaeffer.
Nov. 1. Samuel McClutchen to Ann McClutchen.
      1. Daniel Habecker to Elizabeth Bender.
      3. William Cutshall to Ann Crow.
     22. Michael Laly to Catharine Fetter.
     26. Daniel Herr to Esther Witmer.
     26. Jacob Witmer to Susanna Herr.
     29. John Brecht to Elizabeth Kuntz.
Dec. 3. Christian Hare to Catharine Keiner.
     24. Jacob Reed to Catharine Job.

1797.

Jan. 13. William Robinson to Mary Carter.
     17. John Kohler to Magdalena Kauffman.
     17. Peter Riggebaugh to Ann Riggebaugh.
     17. John Feldeberger to Elizabeth Kneisley.
     23. Henry Rubb to Ann Martin.
     24. John Fisher to Catharine Frey.
     28. Jacob Shenk to Elizabeth Hostetter.
     31. Martin Maurer to Catharine Mengle.

Feb. 2. Joseph Crommell to Catharine Dering.
     15. Patrick McElrone to Ann Gallacher.
March 1. Jacob Hawenstine to Susannah Shaver.
      7. Jacob Good to Barbara Eshelman.
    27. John Temple to Catharine Murray.
    28. William Gray to Elizabeth Light.
Feb. 8. Jacob Harnish to Ann Shenk.
    11. Henry Kline to Maria Sweigart.
    12. John Gardnar to Jane Cooper.
    25. William Forshback to Mary Carver.
May 6. Rudy Herr to Elizabeth Barl.
    13. Samuel Herr to Barbara Kilheffer.
    30. Daniel Kendrick to Margaret Fisher.
June 2. David Herr to Barbara Corley.
    12. Leonard Grimm to Martha Curley.
    12. David Reinehart to Barbara Ohlinger.
    12. Joseph Bartholomew to Susanna Hollingsworth.
    13. George Strong to Mary Fissysy.
July 11. George Beemsderfer to Elizabeth Snitz.
    22. John Lorentz to Ann Hock.
    27. William Kirk to Rachel Parker.
Aug. 8. George Getz to Elizabeth Markley.
    15. Jacob Spickler to Susanna Hoover.
    21. James Fillson to Mary Bohanan.
    22. Jacob Hirsh to Elizabeth Bitner.
    31. James Love to Rachel Henderson.
Sep. 1. Christian Shoffe to Elizabeth Sides.
    13. Daniel Menear to Hannah Clark.
    15. Jacob Rohrer to Elizabeth Bowman.
    16. Martin Eckman to Elizabeth Kercher.
    19. John Shalleberger to Elizabeth Kauffman.
    29. George Wagoner to Margaret Armor.
    30. Michael Hess to Eliza McDannal.
Oct. 4. John Graft to Mary Hockman.
Nov. 30. John Speer to Sarah Love.
    30. Jacob Graybill to Elizabeth Horsht.
    30. Ephraim Ferree to Elizabeth Shultz.
Dec. 6. John Vance to Margaret McCullough.
    9. John Messenkope to Barbara Lauman.
    26. Jacob Warfel to Mary Stoutseberger.
    26. George Nauman to Solomea Hall.

NOTES AND QUERIES.—CXXXV.

"MILLIONS FOR DEFENCE, BUT NOT ONE CENT FOR TRIBUTE," were the utterances of Charles Cotesworth Pinckney when Ambassador to the French Republic in 1796.

EICHOLTZ, THE PAINTER.—What is known of Jacob Eicholtz, the portrait painter, of Lancaster, who had his studio in the residence of his brother George, on Pine street, in 1822. Many of our citizens then had portraits painted by him, and a list of these would be of great interest and value.

THE PENNSYLVANIA NAVY.—In an historical article going the rounds of the newspaper press, a brief reference is made to the British ship Augusta which was blown up by the explosion of her magazine in the Delaware during the Revolution in an engagement between her and the Continental navy. Credit should rest where credit is due. On the 23d of October, 1777, the Pennsylvania navy, under Commodore John Hazelwood, of Philadelphia, resisted the attempt made by the British vessels, Augusta, Roebuck, and Merlin, to pass up the Delaware. It was the Pennsylvania navy which attacked these war vessels, and through its fireships succeeded in setting fire to the Augusta and Merlin, while the Roebuck fortunately, through the rising of the tide, floated off and escaped.

BREVET MILITARY RANK IN THE REVOLUTION.—By the following resolution, which is found in the journal of Congress, volume viii., p. 407, under the date of Thursday, September 30, 1783, it will be seen that our statement in regard to brevet titles in the war of the Revolution was correct:

"*Resolved,* That the Secretary of War issue to all officers in the army, under the rank of major General, who hold the same rank now that they did in 1777, a brevet commission one grade higher than their present rank, having respect to their seniority; and that commissions for full colonels be granted to the lieutenant colonels of 1777—the resolutions of May 27th, 1778, nowithstanding."

FIRST IRON WORKS IN PENNSYLVANIA.—The following may, perchance, satisfy a correspondent: In 1717 Jonathan Dickinson spoke of the great expectations of the iron works, forty miles up the Schuylkill. Where they were situated is not so well settled. It is supposed that the reference was to the Coventry forge, on the French creek, in Chester county, which is said to have been built by a man named Nutt. It is reported to have gone into operation in 1720. But a forge is also mentioned in March, 1719 or 1720, at Manatawney, now in Montgomery county. In 1728 Mr. Logan wrote that there were four furnaces in Pennsylvania in blast. One of these was in Lancaster county—probably built by Kurtz in 1726. These four forges were those at Coventry, Manatawney, Kurtz's (in Lancaster county), and probably works said to have been erected by Sir William Keith, between 1700 and 1726. Which of these four furnaces was the first, or who first made iron in them, is a thing which we presume nobody knows.

THE INDIAN TATAMY.

[The following sketch of the celebrated Tatamy, an Indian of the Delaware tribe, was sent us several years ago by the late Jacob Fatzinger, Esq., of Northampton county.]

Funda Tatamy was born in the Province of New Jersey about the year 1695, but when young moved into the forks of the Delaware. He acted as interpreter and peacemaker for the Proprietaries for a number of years. During the year 1758 he was sent by the Governor of New Jersey with a message to the Minisink Indians. He also served as interpreter to the celebrated missionary, David Brainerd, became a convert to his religion, himself and wife receiving the rite of baptism on the 21st of July, 1745, the former receiving the name of Moses Funda Tatamy. Tatamy made a settlement and had a plantation near a place called the "Orchard" in the vicinity of the present village of Stockerton, in Northampton county, previous to the year 1733. In that year a survey, including the settlement and plantation, was made for him, the tract containing 315 acres and allowance. This tract was warranted to him by patent dated April 28, 1738 (called patent No. 1), "in consideration of the friendship we bear and the regard always expressed for the Indians of this our Province." But since the tract of land granted by this patent was subject to an entailment, a new patent was given to him, *his heirs and assigns*, dated January 22, 1741, upon condition of his paying the sum of £48 8s. 6d. and surrendering patent number one, in order to be canceled. This tract afterwards became the property of William Allen, as the following receipt will show: "Received, Philadelphia, January 8, 1760, of Melchior Stecher £56 in part of interest due from George

Shombach on the tract of land of 315 acres I sold Shombach in Northampton county, 27th December, 1753, who has since sold the same to Melchior Stecher, to whom I am to convey said tract of land in fee, upon his, the said Melchior Stecher, paying the remaining principal of the consideration money, being £222 14s. and £10 13s. 10d., being the balance of interest due thereon the 27th December, 1759. William Allen." It seems that the title from Allen to Stecher was not perfected during the lifetime of the former; for we find that Edward Shippen, as executor of William Allen, deceased, by deed July 24, 1800, conveyed said tract, called "Tatamy's tract," to Henry and Matthias Stecher, devisees of Melchior Stecher, deceased. After careful search among the records of Northampton county we have been unable to find the conveyance to W. Allen or a recital to that effect. The missing deed, if found, would supply a link in the history of Tatamy. Of his death we have no information. Of the descendants of Funda Tatamy we know but little. He had sons, William, and Nicholas. On the 8th day of July, 1757, William was shot by a Scotch-Irish lad while straying from a body of Indians, who were marching from Fort Allen to Easton under escort of Capt. Jacob Arndt, from the effects of which he soon after died. Nicholas died near Easton some time during the year 1784, and left a wife Ann, and a son called Moses. The records of Northampton county show that Ann made her mark, but Moses wrote his own name in a fair handwriting. The personal property of Nicholas Tatamy was appraised by Philip Odenwelder and Johannes D. Walter and amounted to £4 10s. 6d. He at one time owned a tract of land containing 180½ acres, called the Indelamookong, situated on the northeast branch of the Susquehanna river opposite an Indian settlement called Sheshequin, formerly in Northampton county. This tract was granted to him by patent dated December 6, 1773. He afterwards sold it to a certain John Brotsman, of the city of Philadelphia.

MARRIAGE LICENSES AT LANCASTER 1791–1799.—IV.

1798.

Jan. 18. Jacob Ferree to Elizabeth Lefevre.
     20. Jacob Grubb to Elizabeth Shertzer.
Feb. 2. William Camper to Ann Hertzler.
    12. Philip Hoffman to Elizabeth Kehler.
    20. Abraham Herr to Barbara Shaup.
    22. Jacob Finfrock to Ann Montgomery.

Feb. 22. John Montgomery to Mary Finfrock.
Mar. 2. Crosby Phipps to Phœbe Passmore.
      5. James Philips to Catharine Funk.
    21. Charles Thalman to Mary Cooper.
    27. Henry Brechbill to Susanna Eshelman.
    31. Isaac McCullough to Ann Carson.
April 13. Henry Funk to Ann Martin.
    26. James Carson to Ann Porter.
May 5. Wm. McPherson to Margaret McCullough.
    31. Michael Arnolds to Elizabeth Stober.
June 12. Stewart McMullen to Jane Higgins.
    12. George Engle to Magdalena Howerter.
    12. Isaac Kendig to Elizabeth Faulk.
    12. Jacob Haines to Eleanor Allen.
    13. Edward Stapleton to Susanna Hamer.
    13. John Ferguson to Susanna Hooe.
    23. John Leonard to Margaret Kline.
July 9. William Lightner to Esther Brenneman.
    19. Thomas Johnson to Mary Johnson.
    21. Jacob Musser to Ann Hartman.
    24. Theophilus Hartman to Ann Eichelberger.
    28. John Hess to Mary Brua.
    31. Abraham Hess to Mary Shaeffer.
Aug. 4. Joseph Newcomer to Maria Habecker.
    18. Benjamin Miller to Barbara Bowman.
Sept. 11. John Bell to Margaret McEllroy.
    14. Adam Thomas to Ann Eshelman.
    25. Andrew Rees to Frena Eshelman.
Oct. 2. George Carolus to Mary Shaeffer.
    10. John Brenneman to Ann Kilhefer.
    25. John Hess to Margaret Kline.
Nov. 6. Benjamin Weaver to Ann Shultz.
     6. Samuel Ford to Mary Roth.
    12. Moses Findley to Jane Kuntz.
    21. Jacob Stees to Magdalena Fissler.
    27. George Awrey to Barbara Mundorf.
Dec. 3. Christian Miller to Elizabeth Sneedley.
    12. Martin Kendig to Maria Zeigler.
    22. Henry Kauffman to Annie Barr.

1799.

Jan. 22. George Brunner to Mary Markley.
    26. John Binkley to Catharine Kauffman.

Jan. 26. John Ford to Barbara Longenecker.
Feb. 1. John Stone to Ann Taylor.
     27. David Martin to Susanna Eshelman.
Mar. 7. Michael Weidler to Elizabeth Miller.
      8. Peter Heister to Ann Meyers.
      9. Abraham Witmer to Anna Ebersole.
     19. Abraham Hernley to Barbara Stouffer.
     21. John Scott to Jane Cowan.
     30. David Pratt to Mary Clackner.
April 3. George Seibert to Elizabeth Cramer.
     13. George Dobler to Esther Kuntz.
     22. Ernest De Bennet to Hannah Sturgeon.
     23. Martin Light to Ann Herr.
     23. Martin Huber to Maria Eshelman.
May   7. John Shenk to Esther Hess.
     12. Casper Hendle to Catharine Feather.
     16. John Doner to Elizabeth Hertzler.
June 10. Joseph Martin to Elizabeth Miller.
     12. Samuel Summers to Ann Heble.
July 1. David Burkholder to Susanna Greider.
     18. John Kleiss to Margaret Kean.
     20. James Graham to Mary Henderson.
     22. John Herr to Barbara Good.
     22. Casper Henrich Vombohl to Maria Burn.
Aug. 1. Henry Shope to Susannah Greenawalt.
      3. Daniel Keeportz to Barbara Shenk.
     12. Abraham Erisman to Catharine Miller.
     31. David Madden to Magdalena Miller.
Sept. 7. Philip Benedick to Sybella Ent.
     21. John Eshelman to Mary Weaver.
     24. Christian Sauser to Ann Martin.
     24. Abraham Hoffer to Elizabeth Stoner.
Oct. 1. Robert Peoples to Hannah Carson.
      7. Frederick Miller to Mary Beels.
     10. John Rider to Catharine Kauffman.
     11. Matthew Lewallen to Maria Gill.
     15. John Jones to Mary Simms.
Nov. 2. William Boal to Ann Kirk.
     21. Isaac Ralston to Maria Endress.
Dec. 10. Christopher Kline to Ann Eshelman.
     14. Jacob Brunner to Maria Neff.
     16. Daniel Lintner to Elizabeth Binkley.
     17. Martin Herr to Susanna Herr.

NOTES AND QUERIES.—CXXXVI.

THE FIRST STEEL SKATES ON THE SUSQUEHANNA.

Some of the Seneca Indians still live on a small plat of land in the lower part of New York State, near the Pennsylvania border. One of the old men of the tribe was visited by a reporter not long ago, and in telling of the extremely cold winters experienced by him he related a very odd and interesting story of the Susquehanna river. According to the old Seneca's narrative there once lived in a Seneca village of the upper Susquehanna a tall, bright lad named Sau-we-nau. One autumn Sau-we-nau accompanied a number of chiefs to Philadelphia, the object of the visit being to trade as well as to see the sights. While in Philadelphia Sau-we-nau, who at that time was twelve years old, was given a pair of skates—the first skates with steel runners he had ever seen. He prized them very highly and, strapping them together, hid them in the folds of his blanket so that the envy of other Indian lads might not be stirred. But it so happened that some boys of the Nanticoke tribe, which had just migrated from the Chesapeake Bay up the Susquehanna to a point beyond where Harrisburg stands, learned about Sau-we-nau's prize, and on the night of the departure of the Nanticokes Sau-we-nau missed his skates. Without saying a word he slipped away with the expectation of over-taking the Nanticoke lads before morning. In this he was disappointed, for the Nanticoke boys learning that they were pursued, left their elders and pushed on ahead across the country now traversed by the Pennsylvania railroad. Sau-we-nau passed the Nanticoke chiefs and kept on the trail of the boys until about noon the next day. Then he was so faint and hungry that he had to rest and find food. He gathered enough berries to satisfy his appetite, and chewing bits of sweet roots as he ran, he kept on the trail until sundown. Then he saw the waters of the Susquehanna and knew that the Nanticoke boys would soon reach their homes. Spurred by this, Sau-we-nau dashed along the river for an hour or more, when he suddenly came upon the Nanticoke boys sitting at the roots of a riverside tree. Sau-we-nau tapped the soles of his moccasins to tell the Nanticokes what he wanted, but they laughed and tapped their foreheads to indicate that he must be crazy. The Seneca and Nanticoke tongues were so different that Sau-we-nau tried to address the boys in English, of which he had a bare smattering. He told them that the

Senecas and Nanticokes were at peace, and that the latter shouldn't bring a winter war over such a small matter as a pair of skates. He demanded that the skates should be returned at once, and that the Nanticoke boys should give him the broken head of an arrow as an acknowledgment of their submission. Sau-we-nau's speech provoked still louder laughter, and almost before he knew it Sau-we-nau was overpowered and bound. He was taken to the Nanticoke village just above and there kept a prisoner until far into December. The Senecas in Philadelphia had missed Sau-we-nau in the morning, and after a long search had made complaint to the Governor, but no one suspected the cause of his disappearance or his real whereabouts. In November they hastened to return to their village, fifty miles above the present city of Williamsport, giving Sau-we-nau up as lost to the tribe forever.

As a prisoner Sau-we-nau was made to work on arrows, moccasins and pelts, and indeed to do drudgery that no Nanticoke lad would think of doing. He waited for an opportunity to escape, but the Nanticoke boys watched him so closely, night and day, that cold weather came and he was still kept in a tent with old squaws. When ice covered the Susquehanna the Nanticoke boys bound him and led him to the river bank that he might see them use his skates. Sau-we-nau not only was disgusted with his unhappy situation, but it made him doubly miserable to see the poor skating of the Nanticokes. The latter had never been accustomed to skates, because they had come from a milder climate, while Sau-wa-nau had used skates with wooden runners ever since he could walk.

One day when the ice was in fine condition the Nanticokes took Sau-we-nau to the river to torment him. They bound his legs together with thongs and for the first time strapped the skates to his feet. Sau-we-nau couldn't stand, of course, and his ridiculous tumbles and rolls caused all the boys, warriors, women and children in the village to gather around him on the ice and shout with laughter. As the fun continued it grew more and more barbarous, and at last two strong warriors began to play "shinny" with poor Sau-we-nau, tossing him here and there on the ice, in the midst of the most uproarious merriment. But the Seneca boy was patient under the buffeting. He felt better with the skates under his moccasins than he had felt at any time during his imprisonment. Indeed, he thought he saw how a bold stroke could set him free and, while making believe to be unconcerned, he kept his purpose of escape well in hand. The merrymaking Nanticokes completely surrounded him, leaving a circle on the ice just large enough for the two warriors to send him sliding and sprawling from one to the other. The warriors had tossed him so many times that both were almost out of breath. Sau-we-nau saw this and noticed, too, that it took longer for him to pass between the warriors than at first. Could he get a knife? Yes; he thought he saw the point of one sticking beneath the belt of one of his tossers. Could he cut the thong and gain his feet while passing between the warriors? Yes; he thought he could. Anyhow, he would try. So when he was seized for perhaps the twentieth time Sau-we-nau slipped his hand into the tosser's belt and in a twinkling secured the knife. The hundred bystanders saw the movement and yelled the tosser to hold him, but the toss had been given, and while the whole crowd was rushing forward Sau-we-nau was slashing the thongs that bound him and gaining his feet. Oh, how strong he felt when freed from the thongs. He darted here and there between the yelling Nanticokes dodging blows, and striking with his knife until in a few seconds he cleared the crowd and shot away up the Susquehanna. Arrows sped after the flying Sau-we-nau, but he escaped them. Every man and boy in the village ran after him, but in an hour he left them out of sight and leisurely skated toward the camp of the Senecas, near the headwaters. When he reached the camp, two days later, Sau-we-nau told the story of his hardships, and the Senecas declared war against the Nanticokes. The war was waged for two years and many Nanticokes and Senecas were slain.

GENEALOGICAL NOTES.

McGowan.

JOHN McGOWAN, of Martick township, Lancaster county, d. October, 1775, leaving issue:

   i. Thomas.
   ii. John.
   iii. Arthur.
   iv. Ellen.
   v. Jean.
   vi. Mary.

MOORE.

I. WILLIAM MOORE, of Paxtang, son of Adam and Jennett Moore, d. June, 1776, leaving a wife Agnes, and children:

   i. [*A dau.*], m. John Davidson, and had *Elizabeth, Agnes,* and *Robert.*

  ii. Margaret, m., Thos. Mays.
  iii. ⌊*A dau.*], m. James Murdoch, of Rowan county, North
      Carolina.

II. AGNES MOORE, of Paxtang, d. October, 1784, leaving her es-
tate to
  My brother John Forster.
  My sister Sarah Forster.
  To Agnes and Mary, daughters of my brother John Forster.

____

McCLENAHAN.

WILLIAM McCLENAHAN, of Paxtang, d. September, 1783, leaving a
wife Margaret, and issue:
  i. William.
  ii. James.

____

MONTGOMERY.

SARAH MONTGOMERY, widow, of Paxtang, d. October, 1784, leaving
her estate to her children as follows (*see N. & Q. cxxxi.*):
  i. Mary, m. ———— Duncan.
  ii. William, d. prior to 1784.
  iii. Elizabeth, m. John Gallagher, and had *Sarah*, and *Thomas*.
  iv. David.
  v. John.
  vi. Hugh, m., and had *Sarah*, and *Mary*.

O'NEAL.

CHARLES O'NEAL, of Paxtang, and lately of Ireland, d. September,
1770, leaving issue:
  i. William, in 1770 residing in Ireland.
  ii. Elizabeth.
  iii. Prudence.

____

POER.

ALEXANDER POER, of Paxtang, d. in 1739, leaving a wife Margaret
and several children, names not given. His executors were James
Harris, Robert Harris and James Morrison, all of them probably
sons-in-law.

____

PFOUTZ.

MICHAEL PFOUTZ, of Warwick, Lancaster county, d. about the last
of May, 1769, leaving a wife Catharine, and children :

    i. Jacob.
    ii. John.
    iii. Michael.
    iv. Catharine.
He also makes a bequest to his mother, Ursula Pfoutz.

———

REED.

    I. THOMAS REED, of Estuarara, d. July, 1734, leaving a wife Mary, and children :
    i. John.
    ii. Nathan.
    iii. Eleanor.
    iv. Alexander.
    v. Thomas.
    vi. Mary.
    vii. James.

    II. ADAM REED, of Hanover, d. in January, 1769, leaving a wife Mary, and children :
    i. Eleanor, m. Robert Whitehill.
    ii. Mary, m. John Harris.
The witnesses to the will were John Williams, John Young and William Stewart, and the executors, William Hamilton, Esq., and Samuel Holliday.

    III. JOHN REED, of Upper Paxtang, d. May, 1777, leaving a wife Margaret, and children :
    i. Elizabeth.
    ii. William.
He makes a bequest to his brother James. Samuel Cochran and George Clark were his executors.

———

STEWART.

    WILLIAM STEWART, d. May, 1748, leaving a wife, and issue:
    i. Isabel.
He makes bequests to his brother Thomas and sister Ann.

———

STUART.

    JOHN STUART, d. October, 1749, leaving a wife Ann, and children :
    i. George.
    ii. Suit.
    iii. Jean.

SEMPLE.

HUGH SEMPLE, d. in May, 1749, leaving a wife, and issue:

 i. Mary.

He makes bequests to his brothers-in-law, James and Samuel Graham.

———

STURGEON.

SAMUEL STURGEON, of Paxtang, d. in March, 1750, leaving a wife, and children:

 i. Jean.

 ii. Thomas.

 iii. Sarah.

The executors were his brothers Henry and Jeremiah Sturgeon.

NOTES AND QUERIES.—CXXXVII.

McKINNEY—BUCKALEW.—John Buckalew m. Miss McKinney and moved from New Jersey to Northumberland county, Pa., in 1774. He was one of the Committee of Safety for Turbet township in 1776. The settlers were driven to seek refuge in block houses and forts by hostile Indians. J. B. finding himself without employment, he and his family and Mr. McKinney, his father-in-law, moved down to Harris Ferry, and from thence to Rock Run, Maryland, and was there employed by the Continental Congress. Amos Buckalew, John's son, was born at Rock Run, July 5, 1781. After the close of the Revolution John Buckalew and his family returned to Northumberland county, Pa. Amos there married Miss Mary Laird. He and his brother, John M. Buckalew (father of the Hon. Charles R. Buckalew, present member of Congress-elect), purchased several hundred acres of land in Fishing Creek township in 1808. Amos afterwards moved to Marietta, in Lancaster county, where he became a lumber merchant. After remaining there a year or two he removed to Columbia, where he embarked in the lumber business with Daniel Musser in 1811. In the year 1812 they purchased several acres of land south of Union, between Second and Third streets, and Perry street in Columbia, and laid the same out into building lots. It was known as the "Musser and Buckalew Plan." Amos Buckalew seems to have taught school for a time in Columbia also. He died in Columbia in 1816. The late Judge McKinney, of Harrisburg, came from this family.

SAMUEL EVANS.

THE UNDERGROUND RAILROAD.

A Chapter in Its Local History.

The reverberations from Fort Sumpter, on the 12th of April, 1861, proclaimed to the American people several things, one of which was, that the last train on the "Underground Railroad" had reached its destination. This institution had for its object the assistance of runaway slaves to a place of safety, and whilst its lines extended throughout the length and breadth of the land, it cannot be said to have been a regular organized body. That is to say, it worked under no charter granted by any earthly authority; had no officials, not even a treasurer, but was simply composed of those individual men and women whose sense of right and justice was strong enough to enable them to lend a helping hand to the fleeing slave—public sentiment and the laws of the land to the contrary, notwithstanding. And whilst many of the operators were members of the Anti-Slavery Society and subscribers for *The Liberator* and *The Freeman*, deriving inspiration and comfort therefrom, the road which they operated was in good running order before Mr. Garrison began his warfare against that "relic of barbarism," the "peculiar institution."

The work of the "Underground Railroad," as its name imports, was carried on in secret and without records; its transactions, therefore, live only in the memory of the few surviving actors, and unless some modern Herodotus shall search out these survivors, tradition will soon be almost the only source from which to gather information concerning an institution which in the old days of slavery created no small stir.

We are able to contribute, at this time, but a single chapter of its history, noting a few incidents relating to but one of the stations.

A large portion of the colored *men* who sought freedom by flight, traveled either singly or in pairs; pushing forward at night and hiding by day, their pathway was the mountain ranges and their guide the Polar star. These usually succeeded in gaining their object without much assistance from the "Underground Railroad." But when half a dozen or more traveled together, especially if women and children were of the company, their case would have been well nigh hopeless without help by the way.

One of the routes from Western Maryland and Eastern Virginia lay through *Paxtang Valley*, where dwelt a settlement of Abolitionists, prominent among whom for many years was William Rutherford, a philanthropist, who for fifty years sheltered and assisted every poor slave who knocked at his door. His house, which was the principal

station in the valley, stood about a quarter of a mile north of the
turnpike road, and was connected therewith by a private lane, at the
mouth of which, and near the center of the highway, stood until
1857, a large locust tree, the peculiarity of which was its being the
only tree of any kind that grew in the road between Harrisburg and
Hummelstown.   It therefore served as an unmistakable guide post
to Mr. Rutherford's house—and many a forlorn and weary fugitive,
upon reaching that old tree, thanked God and took heart again.

During the summer and fall months, it was no uncommon occurrence for half a dozen negroes to arrive in the night—rest and refresh
themselves in the barn during the day and proceed northward under
the direction of a guide the following night, and no one in the neighborhood knew anything about it.   Slave catchers seldom ventured
this far down the valley, and when they did, almost invariably returned unsuccessful.   Once, however, they stole a march upon a
company at Mr. Rutherford's—completely surprising every one on
the premises.

Sometime in the month of October, about the year 1845—ten runaways were brought to Mr. Rutherford's by some agent, now unknown.   They arrived on Thursday night and were to be kept
secreted until the following Saturday night, by which time arrangements for their further progress would be perfected and conductors
sent to pilot them onward.   The party consisted of an elderly man
and his six sons—all mulattos, the youngest of whom was a youth of
eighteen.   Two brothers of a darker hue, remarkable for their stalwart proportions—and a short thick set black man, so black that, as
one of the wits of the day remarked, " charcoal would make a white
mark on his face."   Mr. Rutherford quartered them in his barn and
supplied them with eatables which were carried to the barn from
time to time in a large basket.

For some reason, now forgotten, the conductors failed to appear at
the appointed time.   Mr. Rutherford could have easily forwarded
the party to some other station, but, not wishing to interfere with
plans already perfected, and no intelligence of pursuit having reached
him, he deemed it safe to allow them to remain over Sunday.   Nothing extraordinary occurred during the day until about five o'clock in
the evening, when the negroes were assembled on the barn floor to
partake of supper.   The basket had been brought in and was about
to be attacked, when some one called attention to a cavalcade, consisting of two carriages preceded by four horsemen, moving slowly
down the turnpike road, like a funeral.   It excited no alarm, however, until it reached the old locust tree, when it suddenly wheeled
in the lane at full gallop.   Mr. S. B. Rutherford, then a boy, was at

the barn, and ran to the house to tell his grandfather, who immediately sent him back to warn the negroes of danger. When he reached the barn, however, not a negro was visible.

By this time two of the horsemen had reached the barn, and dismounting, stationed themselves as outside guards, the other two took up similar positions at the house. The leading carriage, driven by John W. Fitch, a liveryman of Harrisburg, and containing four men, stopped at the house. Mr. Rutherford came out and was introduced by Fitch to Mr. Buchanan, of Maryland, a very courteous gentleman, who, after shaking hands, requested a private interview. The two retired to the front porch and sat down, when Mr. Buchanan explained his errand, showed his authority for searching the premises, and stated that he had brought several officers of the law with him, and would proceed with his search and get away as speedily as possible. Meanwhile, the second carriage, containing four men—one of whom was Mr. Potts, of Maryland, owner of several of the fugitives, had driven to the barn and the men stationed themselves in front of the stable doors.

Mr. Buchanan, having finished his interview, also went to the barn and with one or two others entered the floor, where nothing was visible but the basket of provisions, which in the hurry had been left standing in the middle of the floor, and was looked upon as pretty good evidence that the negroes were not far off. The barn was full of hay and grain, and there was but one way of ascending from the floor to the mows, and that lay through a small opening in the threshing floor loft about four feet square. Messrs. Buchanan and Potts both called their servants by name, but got no answer, and whilst it was by no means certain that the negroes were in the barn at all, not a man of the pursuing party dared venture up to see. Calls and threats and promises were again tried, but to no purpose. While this was going on above, Mr. Rutherford's boys were doing up the chores, closely watched by the detachment of slave hunters stationed about the stable doors—so great was their fear lest some one might slip off and alarm the neighborhood. Among those who guarded the stables was a blustering, big-whiskered Marylander (the owner of one "nigger," and he one of the runaways), whose command of oaths was wonderful, and whose valor in single combat or otherwise was, according to himself, phenomenal. He positively refused to allow the boys to take the horses out to water, and was so troublesome generally that one of the young men was obliged to get a pitch fork and threaten to impale him, whereupon he wilted and had nothing more to say.

An hour passed, and no sound coming from the lofts, it was determined by the party in the floor to ascend and see what was up there.

Upon hearing this the negroes became alarmed, and one of them appeared at the top of the opening and threatened to brain the first man who came within his reach. This satisfied the hunters that the birds had not flown. Additional precautions were now taken to prevent any one from leaving the premises. By this time night had set in, lanterns were procured, and several hours more were spent in the vain endeavor to persuade the negroes to come down. A consultation was now held which resulted in sending a messenger to Harrisburg for reinforcements. Soon after the departure of the messenger, while Messrs. Rutherford and Potts were sitting in the house amicably discussing the slavery question, four strange negroes arrived, two of whom went directly to the barn and the other two entered the house and sat down behind the stove. These were the conductors sent to pilot the fugitives to Pottsville, and until their arrival at Mr. Rutherford's had no knowledge of the betrayal of the hiding place of their company. The two who went to the barn were arrested by the guards. The two men at the house were not molested, but remained quietly behind the stove until an opportunity offered of communicating with Mr. Rutherford, who explained the situation and advised them to slip off and collect a force large enough to intimidate the slave catchers. They soon afterwards disappeared.

About 10.30 p. m. the pro-slavery messenger arrived with two carriages and several men, prominent among whom was a character well known in Harrisburg at that time as "Moll Rockey," who afterwards became a very respectable citizen and often spoke of that night's escapade as one of the things of which he had repented. "Moll Rockey" was a host in himself and proved a valuable acquisition to the slave catchers, for in a short time the negroes surrendered and came down—when lo! instead of ten there were but six. A search with lanterns and pitchforks was made in every part of the barn, but in vain, no more negroes could be found. Among the missing was the "nigger" owned by the blustering big-whiskered man before mentioned.

By midnight the search had ended and the slaveholders hurriedly took their departure. Instead of returning to Harrisburg they crossed the country to Middletown and thence to York.

About an hour after their departure a company of probably forty men, mostly colored, armed with all sorts of weapons, arrived upon the scene. They had come from Harrisburg and vicinity in two divisions over different roads, and their temper was such that had they encountered the slaveholders a bloody battle would have been fought. Of the four slaves who escaped two fled from the barn unobserved on the approach of the pursuers and secreted themselves in a neighboring cornfield until nightfall, when they made their way to Mr. A. Rutherford's barn, where they remained until the following night, when they were sent north in company with a third who had hid himself so deeply in the hay mow that he was overlooked. The fourth, who was the father of the six sons, was in the mow at the time of the surrender—but slipped down the hay hole into the stables and escaped through a cellar window which the besiegers had not observed, and was consequently unguarded. He was never heard of afterwards. So quietly was this affair conducted that the nearest neighbors knew nothing of it until the next day.

The hiding place of this party was betrayed by a mulatto named James Millwood, a waiter in Coverly's Hotel, corner of Second street and Market Square, where Messrs. Buchanan and Potts stopped when they came to Harrisburg.

It is a curious fact that in the majority of cases where slaves were captured and returned to their masters, they owed their betrayal to men of their own color.

This chapter, incomplete as it is, would be still more so if we failed to pay a tribute to the memory of William Jones, late of Harrisburg —better known in his day and generation as "Pap Jones."

"Pap Jones" was a large, well-built man, of pure African descent, and possessed in a large measure that quality known among colored men as "Coon sense," which being interpreted means genius, with a large share of cunning superadded.

For many years Mr. Jones was one of the most efficient men connected with the "Underground Railroad" in this locality. He had acquired a thorough knowledge of the routes leading northward, and was always prepared to furnish competent guides. His large covered wagon, drawn by two horses and driven by himself in the capacity of rag merchant, was frequently to be met with on the roads leading towards Wilkes-Barre or Pottsville.   w. f. r.

A CENTURY OF GOVERNORS.

The Executives of the Commonwealth from 1790 to 1890.

[The inauguration of a new Governor for the State of Pennsylvania, who, should he fill up the term for which he was chosen, will close a century of worthies who, by the voice of the people, occupied the Executive chair of our Commonwealth. From 1681 to 1776 our government was a Proprietary one, or, in other words, Pennsylvania was simply a Province whose deputy governors were appointed by

William Penn or his descendants. With the dawn of the Revolution this feudal system ended, and the State of Pennsylvania organized a government which it placed in the hands of an Executive Council, the presiding officers of which were termed Presidents. With the close of the war for Independence a newer constitution was formed with the present system of Executive authority. Twice since 1790 the fundamental law of the Commonwealth has been modified. Under that of 1790 three terms were allowed—that of 1837–8 limited it to two terms, while under the Constitution of 1873–4, a single term of four years was the requirement. During the Revolution the Presidents were Thomas Wharton, Jr., Joseph Reed, William Moore, John Dickinson, Benjamin Franklin and Thomas Mifflin. The latter held the office when the Constitution of 1790 went into effect, and was elected the first Governor of the Commonwealth.]

I. THOMAS MIFFLIN, 1790–1799.

Thomas Mifflin was born in Philadelphia, in 1744, of Quaker parentage. On the completion of his education in the Philadelphia College he entered a counting house. He visited Europe in 1765, and returning, entered into mercantile pursuits. In 1772 he was chosen to the Assembly from Philadelphia, and in 1774 a delegate to the first Continental Congress. He was appointed major of one of the first Pennsylvania battalions; accompanied Washington to Cambridge as aide-de-camp; in August was made quartermaster general; shortly afterwards adjutant general; brigadier general, March 16, 1776, and major general, February 19, 1777. He commanded the covering party during the retreat from Long Island. After the battle of Germantown he resigned his position in the army. In 1782 he was elected a delegate to Congress, of which body he was president in 1783. He was a member and speaker of the Legislature in 1785; a delegate to the convention to frame the Federal constitution in 1787, president of the Supreme Executive Council from October, 1788, to December, 1790; and Governor of the State from 1790 to 1799. It was during his term of office that the famous, but little understood, so-called Whiskey Insurrection took place. Governor Mifflin died at Lancaster, January 21, 1800, while serving as a member of the Legislature, and lies interred close by the wall of Trinity Lutheran church, in that city.

II. THOMAS McKEAN, 1799–1808.

Thomas McKean, son of William McKean, of Scotch–Irish ancestry, was born in Chester county, March 19, 1734. After an academic and professional course of study he was admitted an attorney, and soon after appointed deputy attorney general for Sussex county,

Delaware. In 1757 he was elected clerk of the Pennsylvania Assembly, and from 1762 to 1769 was member thereof for the county of New Castle. In 1765 he assisted in framing the address of the Colonies to the British House of Commons. In 1771 he was appointed collector of the port of New Castle; was a member of the Continental Congress in 1774, and annually re-elected until February, 1783. In 1778 he was a member of the convention which framed the Articles of Confederation; and 1781 president of Congress. In addition to these duties in 1777 he acted as president of Delaware, and until his election as Governor, from 1777 to 1799, held that office, and also executed the duties of Chief Justice of Pennsylvania. He was a promoter of and signer of the Declaration of Independence; commanded a battalion which served under Washington in the winter of 1776–77. He was elected Governor of Pennsylvania three terms (1799 to 1808) under the Constitution of 1790, of the convention framing which he was a member. He died at Philadelphia on the 24th of June, 1817.

III. Simon Snyder, 1808–1817.

Simon Snyder was born at Lancaster, November 5, 1759. His father, Anthony Snyder, was a native of Oppenheim, in Germany, emigrating to America in 1748. He apprenticed himself at the age of seventeen to the trade of a tanner at York, and during intervals pursued his studies. In 1784 he removed to Selinsgrove, where he entered into mercantile pursuits. He was early elected a justice of the peace, which office he held for twelve years. He was a member of the convention which framed the Constitution of 1790; and in 1797 was elected a member of the House of Representatives, of which he was chosen Speaker in 1802, serving in that position for six successive terms. With him originated the arbitration principle incorporated with other wholesome provisions for the adjustment of controversies brought before justices of the peace, in a law commonly called the "hundred dollar law." In 1808 he was elected Governor of Pennsylvania, and served for three terms. Upon retiring from that office in 1817 he was chosen to the State Senate, but died while a member of that body, November 9, 1819. He was interred at Selinsgrove, and by direction of the Legislature a neat stone marks the last resting place of this first of the German Governors of our State.

IV. William Findlay, 1817–1820.

William Findlay, the son of Samuel Findlay, was born at Mercersburg, Franklin county, June 20, 1768. His ancestors were Scotch-Irish. He received a good English education, and was intended for the law, but owing to the pecuniary embarrassments of his father, who met with a severe loss by fire, a collegiate course, then considered necessary, was denied him.   After marrying, in 1791, he began life as a farmer.   He was appointed a brigade inspector of Franklin county, the first office he held.   In 1797 he was elected a member of the House of Representatives.   In 1803 he was again chosen to that office, and successively until January, 1807, when, having been elected State Treasurer, he resigned his seat in the House.   For ten years he filled the latter position.   In 1817 he was elected Governor over General Joseph Hiester.   He served one term.   At the session of the Legislature, in 1821–22, Governor Findlay was chosen United States Senator for six years.   At the expiration of the Senatorial term, President Jackson appointed him treasurer of the United States Mint. He died at Harrisburg, November 12, 1846; and is there buried. His daughter became the wife of Governor Shunk.

V. Joseph Hiester, 1820–1823.

Joseph Hiester, the son of John Hiester, was born in Bern township, Berks county, November 18, 1752.   In 1775 he raised a company of eighty men, and received his commission as captain.   When the battalion was formed he was appointed major.   He participated in the battle of Long Island, severely wounded, was taken prisoner, and suffered a year's confinement in a British prison-ship.   After his exchange he again joined the army and was wounded at Germantown. He was for many years a member of the Legislature; served in the Pennsylvania convention to ratify the Federal Constitution of 1787; was delegate to the Constitutional Convention of 1790, and was a member of Congress from 1797 to 1805, and again from 1815 to 1821, when he was elected Governor of the State, which station he filled one term.   He died June 10, 1832, and his remains rest in the Charles Evans cemetery at Reading.

VI. John Andrew Shulze, 1823–1829.

John Andrew Shulze, son of the Rev. Christopher Emanuel Shulze, a Lutheran clergyman, was born July 19, 1775, at Tulpehocken, Berks county.   He received a classical education.   He'was ordained in 1796 a Lutheran minister, and for six years officiated as pastor of several congregations in Berks county.   Owing to a rheumatic affection he forsook the church and entered upon mercantile pursuits at Lebanon. In 1806 he was elected to the State Legislature and served three years. In 1813 Governor Snyder appointed him Surveyor General of the State, which office he declined, but accepted the prothonotaryship of the new county of Lebanon, which office he filled eight years.   In 1821 he was again chosen a Representative, and the year following a State Senator. In 1823 he was elected Governor, and in 1826 re-elected by a vote of 72,000, his opponent only receiving 1,000 votes in the whole State. In 1840 he was a member of the Electoral College. In 1846 he removed to Lancaster, where he died November 18, 1852, and there buried. He was a man of superior ability and considerable scholarly attainments.

VII. GEORGE WOLFE, 1829–1835.

George Wolfe, the son of George Wolfe, was a native of Allen township, Northampton county, where he was born, August 12, 1777. He received a classical education. Before his majority he acted as clerk to the prothonotary, at the same time studying law under John Ross. President Jefferson appointed him postmaster at Easton, and shortly after Governor McKean commissioned him as clerk of the Orphans' Court, which office he held until 1809. In 1814 he was chosen a member of the Legislature, and in 1822 representative in Congress, a position he filled for three terms. From 1829 to 1835 he occupied the executive chair and left his mark upon the progress of the State. He was the author of the common school system, though subsequently it was shaped by Governor Ritner into a more effective mold. He was an uncompromising Democrat. He believed in the people and sought their welfare. The only public schools in the State at that date existed under a law passed in 1809. They were intended only for the children of the poor, and were maintained as a charity and not as a right; and he sought to place education upon the basis of citizenship. The period of his executive life was full of striking events. The Pennsylvania canal system was begun during his executive career; while the financial difficulties which followed General Jackson's attack on the United States Bank greatly affected Pennsylvania. In Governor Wolfe's second term the exciting troubles arising from the attempt of South Carolina at nullification made State politics almost as lively and exciting as they became when the Republican party was organized. General Jackson appointed him comptroller of the Treasury in 1836, and President Van Buren collector of the port of Philadelphia in 1838. He died at Philadelphia, March 11, 1840. His remains lie in the cemetery at Harrisburg.

VIII. JOSEPH RITNER, 1835–1839.

Joseph Ritner, the son of John Ritner, an emigrant from Alsace-on-the-Rhine, was born March 25, 1780, in Berks county. He was brought up as a farmer, with little advantages of education. About 1802 he moved to Washington county. Was elected a member of the

Legislature from that county, serving six years, and for two years was Speaker of the House of Representatives. In 1829 he ran against Governor Wolfe, but was defeated. In 1835 he was elected Governor of Pennsylvania, as the Anti-Masonic candidate. He was an earnest advocate of the common school system, so successfully inaugurated during the administration of Governor Wolfe, and it was his fortunate task to maintain the system and perfect it through sagacious legislation. To his services in this direction was added his unquestioned devotion to and bold avowal of sympathy with the anti-slavery movement. In 1848 he was nominated by President Taylor director of the mint, Philadelphia, in which capacity he served for a short term. He died on the 16th day of October, 1869, at his farm near Mount Rock, Cumberland county, and is there buried.

IX. DAVID R. PORTER, 1839–1845.

David Rittenhouse Porter, the son of Gen. Andrew Porter, of the Revolution, was born near Norristown, Montgomery county, October 31, 1788. He received a good classical education. When his father was appointed Surveyor General young Porter went as his assistant. During this period he studied law, but his health becoming impaired, he removed to Huntingdon county, where he engaged in the manufacture of iron. In 1819 he was elected member of the Assembly, serving two years. In 1821 Governor Hiester appointed him prothonotary of Huntington county. In 1836 he was chosen State Senator, and in 1838 was elected Governor under the new organic law which went into effect that year. He was re-elected in 1841. During his term of office the first great discussion over the introduction of railroads occurred in this State. The Governor's course was marked with liberal views and he sagaciously promoted the new power whenever he could. He also proved himself a wise friend and defender of common schools. He was a man of marked ability. He died at Harrisburg August 6, 1867, and there buried.

X. FRANCIS R. SHUNK, 1845–1848.

Francis Rawn Shunk, the son of John Shunk, was born at the Trappe, Montgomery county, August 7, 1788. He became a teacher at the age of fifteen, and in 1812 received the appointment as clerk in the Surveyor General's office under Gen. Andrew Porter. In 1814 he marched as a private soldier to the defense of Baltimore. In September, 1816, he was admitted to the practice of the law. He filled the position of assistant and then principal clerk of the House of Representatives for several years; next became secretary of the Board of Canal Commissioners; and in 1839 Governor Porter appointed him

Secretary of the Commonwealth. In 1842 he removed to Pittsburgh, engaging in his profession. In 1844 he was elected Governor of Pennsylvania and re-elected in 1847. Shortly after he was stricken with a fatal sickness and resigned, leaving the office to be filled by the President of the Senate, William F. Johnston, until a new election could be had. Governor Shunk died on the 30th of July, 1848, and was buried at his request at the Trappe, the place of his birth. It may be here stated of Governor Shunk that he was a man, sincere, honest, and upright, pure in his private morals, and no less so in his public character.

XI. WILLIAM F. JOHNSTON, 1848–1852.

William Freame Johnston, son of Alexander Johnston, an officer of the British army, who emigrated to Pennsylvania in 1796, was born at Greensburg, Westmoreland county, November 29, 1808. With a limited academic education he studied law and was admitted to the bar in May, 1829. Removing to Armstrong county, he was appointed district attorney, a position he held until 1832. He represented Armstrong county for several years in the lower House of the Assembly, and in 1847 was elected a member of the Senate from the district composed of the counties of Armstrong, Indiana, Cambria and Clearfield. At the close of the session of 1848, he was elected Speaker of the Senate for the interim, and on the resignation of Governor Shunk on July 9th following, assumed the gubernatorial functions according to the provisions of the Constitution. At the general election in October, he was elected for the full term, serving until January 20, 1852. Governor Johnston in politics was a Whig, with a decided leaning to anti-slavery views. The compromise measures of 1850 and the fugitive slave law were passed during his tenure of office. In his message to the Legislature he took strong grounds against the latter and helped materially to prepare the way for the political movements against the extension of slavery. His advanced position on these subjects was very naturally followed by a reaction, which placed in power a vigorous representative of the old Democracy. On retiring from office, Governor Johnston entered into active business life. He was appointed by President Johnson collector of the port of Philadelphia, but owing to the hostility of the United States Senate to most of that President's appointments, he was not confirmed. He died at Pittsburgh, October 25, 1872.

XII. WILLIAM BIGLER, 1852–1855.

William Bigler, the son of Jacob Bigler, was born January 1, 1814, in Shearman's Valley, Cumberland, now Perry county. He received a fair school education. Learned printing with his brother from

1830 to 1833, at Bellefonte. In the latter year he established the Clearfield *Democrat*, which he successfully carried on for a number of years. He subsequently disposed of his paper and entered into mercantile pursuits. In 1841 he was elected to the State Senate, chosen Speaker in the spring of 1843, and at the opening of the session of 1844. In October following, he was re-elected to the Senate. In 1849 appointed a revenue commissioner. In 1851, elected Governor of the State, serving for three years. During his term of office he favored and secured the passage of legislation favorable to the great plan of internal improvements which has so largely developed the resources of this State. In January, 1855, he was elected for the term of six years to the United States Senate. Governor Bigler was a prominent delegate to the Constitutional Convention of 1873, and to his labors are we indebted for a number of the beneficial features of that instrument. He was one of the earliest champions of the Centennial Exposition of 1876, and represented Pennsylvania in the Board of Finance, and his efforts ministered greatly to its successful issue. Governor Bigler died at Clearfield, August 9, 1880, and there buried.

XIII. JAMES POLLOCK, 1855–1858.

James Pollock, the son of William Pollock, was born at Milton, Northumberland county, September 11, 1810. His early education was committed to the care of Rev. David Kirkpatrick, who had charge of the classical academy at Milton. He graduated from Princeton in September, 1861; in 1835 he received the degree of A. M., in course, and in 1855 the honorary degree of LL. D. was conferred upon him. Jefferson College conferred a like honor in 1857. In November, 1833, he was admitted to the bar; and in 1835 appointed district attorney for Northumberland county; from 1843 to 1849 served as a member of Congress; in 1850 appointed President Judge of the Eighth Judicial District, and in 1854 elected by the Know Nothings, then in the heighth of political power, Governor of the Commonwealth. After a brilliant term in the executive office, he became an active organizer and leader in the Free Soil movement which gave rise to the Republican party. In the so-called compromise convention, assembled at Washington city in February and March, 1861, Governor Pollock represented Pennsylvania. From 1861 to 1866 he filled the office of Director of the United States Mint, under the appointment of President Lincoln. He resigned when President Johnson entered on his term, and was re-appointed in 1869 by President Grant. [Died at Lock Haven, April 19, 1890.]

XIV. WILLIAM F. PACKER, 1858–1861.

William Fisher Packer, son of James Packer, was born in Howard township, Centre county, April 2, 1807. At the age of thirteen he began to learn the profession of printing in the office of Samuel J. Packer, at Sunbury. Mr. Packer's newspaper being discontinued William F. returned to Centre county, completing his apprenticeship in the office of the *Patriot.* In 1825 he was appointed a clerk in the register's office of Lycoming county. In 1827 he began the study of law, but purchasing an interest shortly after in the *Gazette,* he continued his editorial career with that paper until 1836, when he assisted in establishing the *Keystone* at Harrisburg, remaining connected therewith until 1841. In February, 1839, he was appointed a member of the Board of Canal Commissioners; in 1842, Auditor General of the Commonwealth; in 1847 and 1848, elected member of the Legislature, being chosen the latter year Speaker of the House; in 1849, elected to the Senate; and in 1857, Governor of the Commonwealth, and was undoubtedly one of the strongest executive and administrative Governors that the State has ever had. His term preceded the triumphal advent of the new Republican party, which was marked by all the fierce contentions of the canvass struggle, and by the excitement of the Harper's Ferry raid in Virginia under John Brown. He died in the city of Williamsport September 27, 1870.

XV. ANDREW G. CURTIN, 1861–1867.

Andrew Gregg Curtin, son of Roland Curtin, was born April 23, 1815, in Bellefonte, Centre county. He was educated under Dr. Kirkpatrick, at Milton, studied law at Carlisle and Bellefonte, and was admitted to the bar in April, 1837. In 1840 he took an active part in politics in the Harrison campaign, and in 1844 canvassed the State for Henry Clay. On the 17th of January, 1855, he was appointed Secretary of the Commonwealth by Governor Pollock, and in virtue of his office became Superintendent of the Public Schools. His superintendence has one great landmark, the institution of normal schools. In 1860 he was elected Governor of Pennsylvania. His administration of that office during the war gave him renown throughout the country, and added historic grandeur to the annals of his native Commonwealth. His foresight caused the organization of the Pennsylvania Reserves, and contributed largely to save our National Government, imperilled by the disaster of Bull Run. His ever enduring record, however, in connection with the war, was the establishment of orphan schools for the children of those who fell in the service of their country. In 1869 he was appointed by President

Grant Minister to Russia. He was a member of the Constitutional Convention of 1873, and represented the Twelfth District in the House of Representatives of the United States. [Gov. Curtin died at Bellefonte, October 7, 1894.]

XVI. John W. Geary, 1867–1873.

John White Geary, son of Richard Geary, was born near Salem, Westmoreland county, December 30, 1819. He taught school, became a merchant's clerk in Pittsburgh, afterwards studied at Jefferson College; finally became a civil engineer, and for several years was connected with the Allegheny Portage railroad. He was lieutenant colonel of the Second Pennsylvania regiment in the Mexican war; wounded at Chapultepec, and for meritorious conduct was made first commander of the city of Mexico after its capture and colonel of his regiment. In 1849 was made postmaster of San Francisco, soon after alcalde of that city, and its first mayor. In 1852 returned to Pennsylvania and settled on his farm in Westmoreland county. From July, 1856, to March, 1857, he was Governor of Kansas. Early in 1861 he raised and equipped the 28th Pennsylvania volunteers; was promoted brigadier general of volunteers April 25, 1862; wounded at Cedar Mountain; led the 2d division of the 12th corps at Fredericksburg, Chancellorsville, Gettysburg, Wauhatchie and Lookout Mountain; commanded the 2d division of the 20th corps in Sherman's march to the sea; appointed military governor of Savannah on its capture, December 22, 1864; elected Governor of Pennsylvania, 1866, serving two terms. He died suddenly at Harrisburg on February 8, 1873. His career was certainly an adventurous one, and as useful as it was eventful. In recognition of his valuable services to the State and Nation the General Assembly erected a handsome monument at his grave in the cemetery at Harrisburg.

XVII. John F. Hartranft, 1873–1879.

John Frederick Hartranft, son of Samuel E. Hartranft, was born in New Hanover township, Montgomery county, December 16, 1830. In his seventeenth year he entered the preparatory department of Marshall College, and subsequently was transferred to Union College, Schenectady, where he graduated in 1853; studying law, he was admitted to the bar in 1859. At the outset of the Civil war he raised the Fourth Pennsylvania regiment. At the first Bull Run battle he served on General Franklin's staff, the period of enlistment of his regiment having expired one day previous. Upon the muster out of his "three months'" regiment, Colonel Hartranft organized the Fifty-first. He accompanied General Burnside in his expedition to North Carolina in March, 1862, and with his regiment was in all the engagements of the Ninth corps, including Vicksburg; led the famous charge that carried the stone bridge at Antietam; was made brigadier general May 12, 1864; in command of the Third division, Ninth Army corps, March 25, 1865; gallantly recaptured Fort Steadman in the lines before Richmond, for which he was breveted major general. Was elected Auditor General of Pennsylvania, in 1865, and on August 29, 1866, the President tendered him the position of colonel in the regular army, which he declined. In 1868 General Hartranft was re-elected Auditor General. In 1872 he was chosen Governor of the Commonwealth, and re-elected in 1875 for the term of three years. At the close of his gubernatorial career, he removed to Philadelphia, and filled the offices of collector of the port, and postmaster of that city with marked ability. During that period and until his death, October 17, 1889, at Norristown, he was major general in command of the National Guard of Pennsylvania.

XVIII. HENRY M. HOYT, 1879–1883.

Henry Martyn Hoyt, son of Ziba Hoyt, was born in Kingston, Luzerne county, June 8, 1830. He remained upon his father's farm until his seventeenth year, when, having finished his preparatory studies under the Rev. Dr. Reuben Nelson, he entered Lafayette College. He finished his academic course at Williams College, Mass., where he graduated in 1849. Opened a high school at Towanda, Pa., and was a professor of mathematics at the Wyoming Seminary in the Wyoming conference; read law with Chief Justice George W. Woodward, and admitted to the bar in 1853. At the outbreak of the Civil war he was active in the raising of the 52d regiment, P. V., and was appointed by Governor Curtin lieutenant colonel. Served in Naglee's brigade, army of the Potomac, until January, 1863, when the brigade was sent to join the land forces intended to co-operate with the naval attack upon Fort Sumter under Admiral Dupont. He was engaged in the siege of Morris Island under General Gillmore, and was captured in a night attack in small boats across Charleston Harbor on Fort Johnson. Upon his exchange he rejoined his command, and at the close of the war was mustered out with the rank of brevet brigadier general. In 1867 he held the office of Additional Law Judge of the courts of Luzerne county, under appointment of Governor Geary. He was elected Governor in November, 1878, and was inaugurated in January, 1879. At the close of his official term he resumed the practice of law, and died at Wilkes-Barre, December 1, 1892.

XIX. ROBERT E. PATTISON. 1883-1887.

Robert Emory Pattison, son of Rev. Robert H. Pattison, D. D., of the Methodist Episcopal Church, was born December 8, 1850, t Quantico, Somerset county, Maryland. He was educated in the Grammar school of Philadelphia, and graduated from the Central High School, being the valedictorian of his class. He was registered a law student with Lewis C. Cassidy, of Philadelphia, in December, 1869, and admitted to the bar in 1872. In 1877 he was nominated for City Controller of Philadelphia, and elected; and in 1880 re-elected to the same position by a large majority. In 1882 he was nominated for Governor, elected in November and inaugurated in January, 1883, the youngest person who has ever filled the gubernatorial office, as also the only executive who was not a native of the State. His last message to the General Assembly was an able paper, and credit must be given Governor Pattison for ability, honesty of purpose, and faithfulness to the fundamental law of the State. [Was Governor from 1891 to 1895.]

XX. JAMES A. BEAVER, 1887-1891.

James Addams Beaver, the son of Jacob Beaver, was born October 21, 1837, in Millerstown, Perry county. He was educated at Jefferson College, Cannonsburg, where he graduated in August, 1856. having previously passed two years at the academy at Pine Grove Mills. He studied law in the office of Hugh N. McAllister, Esq., in Bellefonte, and was admitted to the bar in January, 1859. As a member of the Bellefonte Fencibles, a volunteer company of which Governor Curtin was captain, he acquired some knowledge of military tactics. At the outbreak of the war that company tendered its services, of which he was chosen first lieutenant, and was the third company to arrive at the camp of rendezvous at Harrisburg. At the expiration of the three months' service he aided in recruiting the Forty-fifth Pennsylvania regiment, and was chosen its lieutenant colonel. The regiment was ordered to South Carolina, and did good service there. In August, of 1862, a regiment was recruited almost entirely in Centre county, Lieutenant Colonel Beaver was made its colonel, the regiment being the One Hundred and Forty-eighth. The regiment was ordered to join the army just before the battle of Fredericksburg. In the battle of Chancellorsville, Colonel Beaver was shot through the body and severely wounded. As soon as he was able to be moved he was sent north, arriving in Harrisburg while Lee was marching toward the Susquehanna. Though still suffering from his wound, he took a position on Gen. D. N. Couch's staff, and was placed in command of Camp Curtin. He rejoined his regiment in the latter part of July, 1863. At the battle of Auburn Hill, and again at the battle of Bristoe Station he distinguished himself, and did good service in all the battles of the Army of the Potomac. At Cold Harbor, while in command of the brigade, he was wounded in the right hip, and at Petersburg he was blown up by a shell, which exploded almost under his feet, and severely wounded in the left side by a piece of the missile. On recovering, he returned from the north, and reported for duty in time for the battle of Ream's Station, on August 24, 1864. In this battle he was struck in the right leg, which was very badly shattered, and the next day amputated at the hip. This necessitated his retirement from active military service, and he was mustered out in 1865. Upon returning home General Beaver resumed the practice of law at Bellefonte. He was a delegate to the Republican National Convention at Chicago, and was the unanimous choice of the delegation from this State for Vice-President, but peremptorily declined the honor. He was also a candidate for United States Senator in the memorial contest which closed by the election of Senator Mitchell. In 1882 he was nominated by the Republicans for Governor, but through defection was defeated. In 1886 he was unanimously nominated for the same office and chosen by a handsome majority. It may be stated in this connection that General Beaver's distinguishing characteristics are his earnestness in the discharge of duty, and complete mastery of every subject he undertakes.

NOTES AND QUERIES.—CXXXVIII.

PURDY.—Col. James Purdy, of the Revolutionary army, died August 7, 1813, aged eighty years, in Fermanagh township, Mifflin county. His two sons, William and Hugh Purdy, officers in the army, were killed at St. Clair's defeat on the Miami, November 4, 1791.

RODGERS.—Rev. William Rodgers, a chaplain in the Pennsylvania Line of the Revolution, died at Philadelphia, April 7, 1824, in the seventy-third year of his age. He was one of the most eminent of American divines.

IRWIN, COL. JAMES.—This gentleman died at Old Province, September 20, 1818, "formerly a representative in Congress from Pennsylvania. He joined McGregor's standard at Amelia Island, and has since been attached to the command of Colonel Aury." Such is the notice of the *Chronicle.* Who was this James Irwin, and what further is known of his career?

———

AN OLD-TIME NOTE.—The following note of James Logan to the Proprietary of date September 20, 1736, it may be presumed, had some reference to the difficulties then experienced with the Scotch-Irish settlers who had been prevented from locating on Conestoga Manor, which was not denied the German emigrants, or it may have reference to some other trouble:

"If the Propriet'r please to take notice of Ja. Anderson, Minist'r of Donegal, and hold some free conversation with him, it may p'haps be seasonable at this time, when those people ought by all means to be animated to vigorous Resolution. He just called on me when I was much engaged, & I expected to see him again, but could not. I suppose he goes not out of town till to-morrow morning, & that he will then w'thout fail, if not otherwise hindered. E. Shippen accidentally calling here, I thought the hint might be of some importance. Thy faithful fr'd,   J. LOGAN.
"*Stenton, 20th 7ber, at noon.*"

———

GENEALOGICAL NOTES.

———

STECKLEY.

CHRISTIAN STECKLEY, of Derry, d. in October, 1767, leaving a wife Catharine, and children:

  i. John.
  ii. Barbara.
  iii. Chrisly.
  iv. Abraham.
  v. Mary.
  vi. Catharine.

The executors were Jacob and John Lehman, of Derry.

———

STEPHEN.

ANDREW STEPHEN, of Paxtang, d. March, 1770, leaving a wife Ann, and children:

  i. Hugh.
  ii. Ann.
  iii. Andrew.
  iv. Ezekiel.

SIMONS.

MICHAEL SIMONS, of Hanover, d. in May, 1775, leaving a wife Margaret, and children:
- i. *Peter.*
- ii. *John.*
- iii. *Mary,* m. Thomas Hears.
- iv. *Elizabeth,* m. William Weirick.
- v. [*A dau.*] m. Henry Fensler.
- vi. *Catharine,* m. Peter Weirick.

SNODGRASS.

ROBERT SNODGRASS, of Hanover, d. in March, 1777, leaving children:
- i. *Joseph.*
- ii. *James.*
- iii. *Elizabeth.*
- iv. *Margaret.*
- v. *Mary.*
- vi. *Susan.*
- vii. *Isabel.*

The witnessess to the will were John Rogers, William Snodgrass, Jr., and John Kean.

SHAW.

I. DANIEL SHAW, of Hanover, d. in March, 1778, leaving a wife Phebe, and children:
- i. *Robert.*
- ii. *Samuel.*
- iii. *Jane,* m. William Haggerty.

II. ALEXANDER SHAW, of Hanover, son of the foregoing, although not mentioned in his father's will, d. in September, 1778, leaving bequests as follows:
Bro. Robert and his son Samuel.
Sister Jean Haggerty.
£20 to Mr. Elder's congregation.

SHWAB.

JOHN SHWAB, of Leacock township, Lancaster county, d. in December, 1780, leaving children:
- i. *Jacob.*
- ii. *Henry.*

   iii. Daniel.
   iv. Adam.
    v. Julianna, m. Natz Zwicker.
   vi. [*A dau.*] m. John Hook.
  vii. Catharine, m. Ludwig Shott, and had *Julianna.*
 viii. Margaret, m. George Dial.
   ix. George, m. daughter of, Casper Bolzer.
    x. [*A dau.*] m. Peter Shaup, and had *John.*
   xi. Conrad.

          ———

SCOTT.

   PATRICK SCOTT, of Paxtang, d. in May, 1782, leaving a wife Ann, and children :
    i. Robert.
   ii. Jackson.
  iii. Jane, m. ——— Fanagan.
  iv. [*A dau.*], m. ——— Jackson, and had *Alexander, Samuel,*
     and *Violet.*

          ———

SAWYER.

   WILLIAM SAWYER, of Londonderry, d. in October, 1784, leaving his estate to his " dear auld woman Sophia," and children :
    i. William.
   ii. Benjamin.
  iii. John.
  iv. Hannah.

          ———

THOMPSON.

   JOHN THOMPSON, of Hanover, d. September, 1778, leaving children
    i. Andrew.
   ii. William.
  iii. Jean, m. John Robinson.
  iv. John.

          ———

WYLIE.

   OLIVER WYLIE, of Paxtang, d. in October, 1757, leaving a wife Jean sister of Moses Harper, of Paxtang, and children:
    i. Margaret.
   ii. Oliver.
  iii. William.

WILSON.

DAVID WILSON, d. in March, 1766, leaving a wife Margaret and children:

  i. Samuel.
  ii. Robert.
  iii. Elizabeth, m. Samuel Woods, and had *Nathan.*

———

WATSON.

WILLIAM WATSON, of Hanover, d. in October, 1770, leaving a wife Sarah and children:

  i. Samuel.
  ii. William.
  iii. Hugh.
  iv. David.
  v. Patrick.
  vi. [*A dau.*], m. Alexander Kennedy.
  vii. Sarah.
  viii. Eleanor.
  ix. Mary.
  x. Martha.
  xi. Ann.
  xii. Jean.

———

WHITTAKER.

MARY WHITTAKER, widow of Robert Whittaker, d. in January, 1776, leaving children:

  i. Rachel
  ii. Phoebe.
  iii. Ralph.
  iv. Milison, m. Robert Hall.

———

WINGERT.

CHRISTIAN WINGERT, of Bethel township, now Lebanon county, d. in February, 1775, leaving a wife Elizabeth, and children:

  i. John.
  ii. Elizabeth.

His brother John was the executor.

GEORGE CROGHAN.

A Pioneer Worthy of the Cumberland Valley.

[We had nearly completed a sketch of this distinguished personage, when we were favored with the following prepared by Isaac Craig, Esq., of Allegheny City. The article is of more than ordinary interest. The Mrs. Schenley referred to by Mr. Craig at the close of his article is the widow of a captain in the English army, resident in London, and the owner of millions of real estate in Pittsburgh. Mrs. Schenley has five daughters and one son. Her eldest daughter is the widow of a younger son of an English lord. The second daughter married a clergyman of the Church of England, and the third, Agnes, is the wife of a son of Sir Thomas Ridley, who was Under Secretary of State during a former administration of the Marquis of Salisbury. Mrs. S. is about 60 years of age, a great sufferer from asthma, which forbids her residence in Pittsburgh, and in London where she can only spend May, June and July for the same reason. Her recent generous offer of the "Point" at Pittsburgh to the city, filled with tumble-down tenements on leased ground, has caused much excitement in that metropolis of Western Pennsylvania.]

George Croghan was born in Ireland, and educated in Dublin. On emigrating to America, he settled in Pennsboro', west of the Susquehanna river, some five miles from Harris' Ferry, now Harrisburg. He became an Indian trader, in which capacity he is found in 1746, on the shores of Lake Erie, between the mouths of Cuyahoga and Sandusky. While thus engaged, he acquired a thorough knowledge of the Indian languages, and so much influence with the tribes in the Ohio Valley, that the government of Pennsylvania employed him as their agent in those parts; but the incursions of the French, and the seizure and destruction of his property by the Indians, in the interest of the French, reduced Croghan to bankruptcy, and obliged him to retire among the mountains, in what is now Huntingdon county, where he erected a fort at Aughwick; here he had charge of a number of Indians, in the pay of the Province. On the arrival of General Braddock, in 1755, Croghan received a captain's commission, and accompanied the expedition against Fort Duquesne, and remained with that unfortunate officer until his death, when he returned to Aughwick. In 1756 he was employed in raising men for the defense of the Western frontier, along which he erected three stockade posts; but, considering himself ill-used by the Pennsylvania authorities, he threw up his commission, and in July he repaired to Sir William Johnson, whom he accompanied to Onondaga, and by whom he was, in November, appointed Deputy Indian Agent, with charge of the Pennsylvania and Ohio Indians. His time was now taken up in making treaties and assisting in conferences with the Indians, and other official duties.

In May, 1760, he assisted at the meeting which General Monckton held, at Fort Pitt, with the Western Indians; and, afterwards, accompanied Major Rodgers to take possession of Detroit.

In the latter part of 1763 he was sent to England, by Sir William Johnson, to urge on the Ministry the necessity of agreeing with the Indians on a boundary line which was settled afterwards in the treaty of Fort Stanwix, in 1768, and to recommend some arrangements in regard to the Indian trade. On this voyage he was shipwrecked on the coast of France. On his return, in 1765, he was sent to Illinois, to pacify the tribes in that quarter, who were breathing nothing but war. On his way thither, he was attacked, on the 8th of July, by a party of Kickapoos and Mascoutens, who killed five of his men, and wounded and took himself prisoner, and carried him to Vincennes. Through the interposition of some friendly Indians, he and the remainder of his party were released, and he proceeded to Illinois. At Fort Chartres, he succeeded in accommodating matters, and in arranging for the surrender to the English of all the posts the French held in the Western country. Col. Croghan then proceeded to Detroit.

In May, 1766, he returned to Fort Pitt, where, on the left bank of the Allegheny river, about four miles up, he had, for sometime, a settlement, with the consent of the Six Nations.

From Fort Pitt he went to Illinois, and from there to New Orleans, and from thence by sea to New York, where he arrived in January, 1767. In the ensuing summer he was ordered to Detroit for the purpose of restoring, to their respective tribes, some Indians who were prisoners there, and to correct some abuses at that post; and in January, 1768, was examined before the Pennsylvania House of Assembly on the subject of murders committed by the Indians on the Western frontier of Pennsylvania.

At this time the Assembly placed on record its testimony of " the address and fidelity with which Mr. Croghan has always executed his commission, and the eminent service he has rendered the Nation and its Colonies in conciliating the affections of the Indians in the British interest."

In the following March he held another conference with the Indians, at Fort Pitt, where he succeeded in removing, from their minds, much uneasiness, on account of the above mentioned murders.

In October, 1768, he assisted in the conferences, held at Fort Stanwix, with the Six Nations and other tribes, and embraced that opportunity to purchase from the Indians a tract of 100,000 acres of land, lying between the Lake Otsego and the Unadilla river, in New York, for which he obtained a patent the following year, when he secured 18,000 acres additional, in Cherry Valley, N. Y. He returned to his place, above Fort Pitt, where on the 10th of October, 1770, George Washington dined with him when on his way to the Kanawha, Croghan providing him with Indian guides and accompanying him some distance down the Ohio river. Some time after this Virginia set up a claim to that part of Pennsylvania west of Laurel Hill, and exercised jurisdiction over Pittsburgh. In this controversy Colonel Croghan sided with Virginia. He was still residing on his farm, on the Allegheny river, when the news of the battle of Lexington reached him.

A meeting of the inhabitants of Pittsburgh was held on the 16th of May, 1775, to give expression to the feelings and sympathy and indignation that pervaded the community, and resolutions were unanimously passed, in entire consonance with the general feeling throughout the country, and a Committee of Correspondence was appointed to watch over the district—Colonel Croghan's name being the first on the list.

In the following year, however, he was superseded as Indian agent, Congress having appointed Col. George Morgan to that office; and, although Colonel Croghan continued to reside on his farm, his enemies succeeded in creating doubts as to his attachment to the cause of the Revolution, and, in a proclamation issued by the State of Pennsylvania in June, 1778, his name appears among those said to have joined the enemy, and who were summoned to come in and surrender themselves on pain of attainder.

Colonel Croghan evidently purged himself of all these suspicions, for in April, 1780, he was a resident of Lancaster, and the following June, of Passayunk, where he conveyed to Joseph Wharton his then remaining interests in his lands, at Otsego county, N. Y. Colonel Croghan did not long survive these transactions; he died in Passayunk, Pa., in August, 1782. His will was proved at Philadelphia, Sept. 3, of that year.

There prevails a general but erroneous belief that Col. George Croghan, the hero of Fort Stephenson, and William Croghan, the father of Mrs. Schenley, are descended from Colonel Croghan, the Indian agent. The truth is the latter had no son; his daughter Susannah married Lieut. Augustine Prevost, of the 60th or Royal American regiment, afterwards a major general in the British army; she succeeded to her father's property in Cherry Valley, N. Y.

Colonel Croghan had a daughter by an Indian woman who was the third wife of the famous Mohawk chief, Joseph Brant. Several historians give interesting accounts of the marriage. Campbell in his Annals of Tryon County, p. 251; Buchanan in his Sketches, vol. 1, p. 36; Drake in his Indian Nations, p. 591, give the following account of it: "Colonel Brant was married, in the winter of 1779, to a daughter of Colonel Croghan by an Indian woman. He had lived with her some time ad libitum according to the Indian manner, but at this time being present at the wedding of a Miss Moore, at Niagara (one of the captives taken at Cherry Valley), insisted on being married himself; and thus his consort's name was no longer Miss Croghan, but Mrs. Brant. The ceremony was performed by his companion-in-arms, Col. John Butler, who, although he had left his country, yet carried so much of his magistrate's commission with him as to solemnize marriages according to law. They had seven children, viz.: Joseph, Jacob, John, Margaret, Catharine, Mary, and Elizabeth, who married William J. Kerr. Joseph, John, and Mary died previous to 1864.

The rank, baptismal and surname of "the hero of Fort Stephenson" being identical with those of Col. George Croghan, the Indian agent, very naturally lead many persons to suppose that the former was the son of the latter, but there was no relationship.

Maj. William Croghan, who was an officer in the 4th Virginia regiment, commanded by Col. John Neville, married a sister of Gen. George Rodgers Clark, "the Washington of the West," and he named his son "George" after his brother-in-law, General Clark, thus making his name identical with that of the Indian Agent—George Croghan. Another son was named after himself, William, and he, William Croghan, was the father of Mrs. Schenley.

NOTES AND QUERIES.—CXXXIX.

CARSON.—Jane Carson, widow, of Harrisburg, d. in December, 1828, leaving children :

 i. Sarah, m. ——— Chamberlain, and had a daughter *Jane*.
 ii. John.
 iii. William.
 iv. Robert.
 v. Dinah, m. Henry Russell.

Can any of our readers give us any information whatever relating to this family of Carson ?

DEATHS OF REVOLUTIONARY HEROES.—Among our notes we find
the following, which are valuable for biographical reference :

Bower, Gen. Jacob, d. at Womelsdorf, Berks county, August 3, 1818,
  aged 61 years.
Boal, Col. William, formerly of Lancaster county, d. at his residence
  in Franklin county, Dec. 17, 1831, at an advanced age.
Clunn, Col. Joseph, of Bucks county, d. May 17, 1816, aged 71 years,
  "much lamented by his friends and particularly by his surviving
  companions of 1776."
Culbertson, William, of York county, d. July 9, 1824.
Ellis, Francis, d. at Lewistown, October 24, 1818, at an advanced age.
Frailey, Peter, prothonotary of Schuylkill county, d. at Orwigsburg,
  November 16, 1831, " a soldier of the Revolution."
Foster, Ezekiel, of McKean county, " a soldier of the Revolution," d.
  October, 1821.
Gilliard, Mr., a soldier of the Revolution, d. at Middletown, April,
  1824.
Geiger, William, of Middle Paxtang township, Dauphin county, d.
  November 14, 1824, aged 72 years.
George, Henry, d. at Harrisburg, September 7, 1831, aged 87 years.

ON THE JUNIATA IN 1789.

[The Columbia Magazine for 1789 contains the following account
of the Juniata Valley, which after the lapse of almost a century is exceedingly interesting. We have no knowledge as to the author.
Scott in his " Geography of Pennsylvania " made such free use of the
sketch that we are inclined to the belief that it was from his pen.]

A DESCRIPTION OF THE JUNIATA RIVER IN THE STATE OF PENNSYL-
VANIA.

Juniata is one of the branches of the Susquehanna, into which it
empties its waters, about twenty miles above Middletown, on the opposite side.

It flows through an extensive and variegated country, abounding
in wood, mountain, fine vales chiefly of slate and limestone, and
some remarkable precipices. In its course it likewise rceives a considerable number of creeks to augment its waters, some of which are
capable of great improvements in navigation, having few rifts to im-
pede the attempt.

Of these the Raystown branch seems to be of the most note, as for
size it is nearly equal to the Juniata much lower down ; however, in
fact, it is a continuance of that river, while that which is still con-

tinued by that name insensibly loses its size a small way beyond Standing Stone or Huntingdon town, branching out into small creeks and becoming quite inconsiderable.

Raystown branch is remarkable for its crooked courses, bending and turning among the hills and mountains in a sudden and uncommon manner, especially at that part called the " horse shoe," at which place, to cross by land, it is not more than three-fourths of a mile, while to keep the course of the stream, round the whole extent of the tour, will consume near a day's laborious march.

Upon the stream there are many signs of copper and coal, and I have no doubt but that in the mossy surrounding mountains valuable discoveries might be made.

Upon the head waters of the Juniata plenty of lead ore has been found, and an abundance of iron, but owing to its remote situation has been neglected.

After crossing at Miller's Ferry, which lies a few miles from the mouth of the river, and keeping up at midway to Standing Stone, a three-fold junction of the mountains is plainly to be perceived, being the Tuscarora, Shade, and Narrows Mountains.

Through them, at this place, commences what is known by the name of the "Long Narrows," formed by one continued break through the above mentioned hills, and continues, surrounded by astonishing crags, for upwards of eight or nine miles, during which space the traveler has nothing to walk on for either himself or horse (which he is obliged to dismount for better security), than the piled rocks and stones that have from time to time accumulated by their fall from the surrounding parts.

Bounded by these mountains on the one hand and the river upon the other, no choice can remain, but absolute necessity forces such as have business in these remote districts to proceed, making a virtue of performing what is not in their power to avoid.

After passing through this miserable place, immediately upon the other side stands the town or settlement called "Old Town," consisting only of a tavern and a few scattered hovels, and containing nothing worth notice.

Another similar pass is through Jack's mountains, still higher up the river, which is rather worse than the other, but a shorter extent; being of larger and rude masses of rock than at the other pass, and the road oftentimes running under the water, which, added to the difficulties here met with, renders it extremely dangerous.

From a part of the Narrows the view was taken. At this place there are evident signs of a valuable mine of copper, and on the other side, before you reach the Narrows from below, at Drake's Ferry, is an extensive mine of alum and copperas.

OLD-TIME ROAD PETITIONS.

PETITION OF THE INHABITANTS OF THE UPPER PART OF PAXTANG
ABOVE THE NARROWS.

[The names attached to the following, although few in number, were of persons who resided along the Susquehanna above Peter's Mountain, John Hambright and Dr. William Plunket, as far up as Shamokin, now Sunbury.]

To the worshipful, the Justices of the General Court of Quarter Sessions of Peace, held at Lancaster for the County of Lancaster, the first Tuesday in May, 1767.

The Petition of sundry inhabitants of the upper part of Paxtang township, in the county aforesaid, above the Narrows, and others, Humbly Showeth:

That the inhabitants of the upper part of Paxtang aforesaid and others who have Lands or business to transact in the interior parts of the Province above Samuel Hunter's, suffer many inconveniences and difficulties for want of a Publick Road from the said Samuel Hunter's, in the Township aforesaid, to James Reed's, where a Ferry is kept over the River Susquehanna.

That for want of such Road the Inhabitants of that part of the Country are under the necessity of transporting of produce of their Farms to market by Water in small Boats & Canoes, which, at many seasons is impracticable, and by reason of the many Falls and Shoals in the River Susquehanna, is generally attended with great Danger and Difficulty.

That the said Road, if laid out and opened, will also be of great benefit to the Inhabitants of the New Settlements on Juniata and other places on the West side of Susquehanna, and be a great inducement to them to bring the produce of their Farms to the markets in this county & Province.

Your Petitioners therefore pray your Worships to appoint proper persons to view, and if they see cause lay out the said Road by Course and Distance in the best and most convenient manner as and for a publick Road, and to make report of their proceedings to the next Court, and your Petitioners as in Duty bound will ever pray, &c.

James Murray,	John Taylor,	John Murray,
Marcus Hulings,	John Reed,	James Eaken,
John Forster,	Robert McCord,	John Hambright,
James Forster,	Samuel Chambers,	William Plunket.

[On this petition is the following endorsement: "The Court appoints Henry Rennick, Alexander McClure, John Harris, William Kelso, William Dickey, & John Cavatt to view the Premises, and that they or any four of them, if they see Cause, lay out same by Courses & Distances & make Report to next Court." An additional memoranda is made: "No Report made to Augt., 1767." The cause of this is possible due to the following, by which it will be noticed that the names of most of the viewers are attached thereto.]

Pet'n of the Inhabit. of Lower Paxtang for a Division Line between them & Upper Paxtang, August, 1767.

To the Worshipfull, the Justices of the County of Lancaster, to Meet at Lancaster, in August Term, 1767.

The Petition of the Inhabitants of Lower Paxtang humbly sheweth :

That Before the warr broke out Upper Paxtang, above the Narrows, was a separate Township from lower Paxtang, and had their annual officers, James Murray and William Clark, served as Cunstables in said Paxtang, above the Narrows, & they had their own Inspectors, &c.; and whereas, your Petitioners are informed that the Inhabitants of Upper Paxtang above the Narrows Pettioned your Honours for a road from the Narrows to James Reed's, and attained an order for a view of the same as in Lower Paxtang, which Greatly Alarmed your Pettioners. Your Petitioners therefore humbly Prayeth that your Honours would take it under due Consideration and grant your Pettioners relief by Confirming the Division of said Township ; and your Pettioners, as in duty bound, will ever pray, &c.

William Dickey,	John Harris,	James Thorn,
Thomas McArthur,	Francis Lerue,	Jacob Awl,
William Cooke,	Patrick McGranahan,	Robert Fruit,
Henry Renick,	Andrew McCollum,	Wm. Montgomery,
Michael Simpson,	Joseph Hutchison,	Michael Graham,
Stephen Poorman,	John Leadle,	Robert Clark,
Jacob Ruip,	William Sloan,	John Cavet,
Joseph Cook,	William McNight,	John Montgomery,
Hugh McKillip,	John Simpson,	John Chambers,
Thomas Renick,	William Steel,	Andrew Cochran,
John Rutherford,	James Smith,	Thomas Willey,
John Duncan,	James Renick,	John Smith,
David Scott,	James Collier,	Jacob Bomberger,
John Collier,	Samuel Steel,	John Knob,
Samuel Miller,	John Bumbery,	James Carson,
David Purviance,	William Smith,	John Collam,
Edward Sharp,	John Willson,	James Chambers,
Samuel Cochran,	William Kerr,	William Kelso,
James Willson,	Jacob Striker,	Alexander McClure.
Christian Graff,	Andrew Huston,	

[On this we have the endorsement: " The court orders that the Paxtang Line be made from the mouth of the Fishing creek, where it empties into Susquehanna, and from thence along the top of Kittatenia Mountain to Beaver Creek, the said Kittatenia Mountain being that next to Lower Paxtang." This was the first recognition of the existence of Upper Paxtang township. See History of Dauphin county, p. 441.]

NOTES AND QUERIES.—CXL.

HARTTAFEL.—Information is desired of Robert Harttafel, organ-builder, a resident of Lancaster in 1749.

HOPSON.—John Hopson, who, in June, 1761, resided at Lancaster, but prior to that date was a butcher on Long Island, N. Y. Information requested.

MARRIAGE RECORDS, MORAVIAN CONGREGATION, AT LEBANON, PA., 1751–1811.

1751, March 17.—Henry Zander to Mary Pristarju.
1753, January 12.—David Heckadorn to Susanna Kunz.
1754, May 1.—John Eberman to Maria Zander.
1756, February 24.—Philip Meurer to Anna Maria Schasters.
1757, May 24.—Adam Orth to Catharine Kucher.
1758, Aug. 8.—George Wambler to Elizabeth Strahaus.
1759, May 9.—Adam Faber to Elizabeth Spitler.
1761, June 30.—Casper Kieth to Ann M. Stephan.
1762, May 4.—George Heidrick to Elizabeth Ohricks.
1763, April 26.—Balzar Orth to Rosina Kucher.
    April 26.—Jacob Scherzer to Barbara Stoehr.
1765, April 30.—Philip Uhrig to Margaret Hederig.
1767, Nov. 24.—Abraham Frederick to Maria B. Buehler.
1769, Feb. 28.—Philip Faber to Magdalena Stoehr.
1770, Sept. 18.—Ehrhart Heckadorn to Catherine Meylin.
1773, Aug. 3.—J. A. Borroway to Elizabeth Uhrich.
1773, Nov. 2.—John Frederick to Julia Ann Buehler.
1779, April 13.—John Kunzlein to Johanna Buehler.

Nov. 23.—Isaac Borroway to Ann I. Uhrich.
1785, March 31.—Frederick Stohler to Catharine Uhrich.
1786, April 22.—Jacob Lanius to Barbara Frederick.
1789, Nov. 15.—Daniel Brozman to Ann M. Spicker (m. n. **Buehler**).
1793, July 21.—Andrew Kapp to Susanna Shoebel.
1795, Nov. 3.—Gottlieb Orth to Sarah Steiner.
1797, Oct. 8.—Jacob Widmer to Hannah Orth.
1799, March 17.—John F. Williams to Rebecca Flor.
Nov. 13.—Conrad Bremer to Rebecca Kuehner.
Nov. 17.—Peter Gloninger to Elizabeth Zerman.
1800, April 15.—Michael Uhrich to Susanna Kapp (m. n. **Krause**).
Oct. 19.—Nathaniel Koehler to Maria Bruecher.
Dec. 28.—Jacob Kiefer to Dorothea Gilbert.
1801, Dec. 27.—William Weitzel to Elizabeth Rudy.
1802, Jan. 5.—Philip Zander to Catharine Jaeger.
Jan. 24.—Peter Gardi to Ann R. Williams.
June 13.—Jacob Steiner to Sabina Hats.
July 4.—John Kelker to Barbara Zimmerman.
Aug. 11.—Heinrich Seiler to Catharine Feyerabend.
Sept. 4.—George Pfeffer to Margaret Steiner.
1804, May 22.—Simon Schutt to Magdalena Schark.
1805, Aug. 30.—John Tshudy to Maria Schaffner.
Dec. 22.—Nathaniel Koehler to Maria Kauffman.
1809, Jan. 24.—John Stiles to Catharine Benigna Kloz.
1810, May 27.—Jacob Uhrich to Hannah Goldman.
1811, Jan. 20.—John Bucher to Regina Schmidt.

OLD-TIME ROAD PETITIONS.

[The following petition of date May, 1743, contains the following endorsement: "Thos. Mays, Thos. Farrel, Jno. Foster, Alex'r Osborn, Jno Cavit, Jno. Kilcreest, or any four to view and lay out. Ord'r. made out & del'd to Mr. Carson."]

To their worships, the magistrates for the county of Lancaster, to sit in court at Lancaster the 3d day of May, 1743.

The petition of several of the inhabitants of Paxtown, Humbly Sheweth:

That your Petitioners labor under great inconveniences for want of a Road from the place where the Provincial Road crosses Spring Creek through the township to the foot of the Blue Mountains; this would be of singular advantage to the most of the Inhabitants inasmuch as it would lead thro' the middle of the Township both to the Provincial & County Roads.

The path we formerly had is frequently blocked up through people's indiscretion; it being our misfortune oftentimes to consult the Publick good less than our private advantage and by that means frequently to hurt both. So that when we have occasion to travel downward with any carriage we many times have great difficulty to come at the big Road. May it therefore please your Worships to take this our case under consideration and order a Road to be laid out and open'd with all convenient speed from the above mentioned place on Spring Creek the shortest and best way to Mr. Elder's house at the foot of the Blue Mountain, and your Petitioners as in duty bound, shall, &c.

John Elder,	Joseph Chambers,	Thomas Foster,
James Forgeson,	Thomas Armstrong,	John Foster,
Alex. Osburn,	Robert Chambers,	James Kerr,
William Cunningham,	William Forster,	Thos. Foster, Jun'r.,
John Johnson,	Robert Armstrong,	Thomas Mays,
John Carson,	Thomas Gallagher,	Joseph Davies.

By virtue of the Annexed Order of Court, bearing date the February Sessions, 1743–4, We, the subscribers in the s'd order named, Do hereby make our Return & say—That, the Road leading from James Galbreath's mill into Tolpehocken Great Road should begin at the said Galbreath's mill; thence thro' the old road to the Meeting house: from thence to the lowest ford of the Quithopohella; thence on a straight course over the other two fords of the said Creek of Quithopohella; thence by the Lower End of Henry Bostler's plantation, keeping the old road; from thence to a saw mill, and thence into the Tolpehocken old great road. Given under our hands this 7th Aug., 1744.

Robt. Harris,
Ralph Whitsitt,
Peter Fisher.

[The following memorial or remonstrance against the laying out of the road alluded to is valuable so far as it gives us the names of residents of Derry township, the early tax list being of the date of 1751. The majority of the names are in the handwriting of the individuals, some few being written by those who carried the petition.]

To the Honorable Court to Sitt at Lancaster, the Seventh of this instant:

The Petition of the majority of the inhabitants of the township of Derry, humbly sheweth:

That whereas there is an order of Court for the making of a road through said township, Beginning at our present Shirrif's mill and to run a straight Course to Stuffel Summors, and from that to the Great Road at Tulpahakin, which Road, if carried on, will be assuredly to the Great Detriment of the afores'd inhabitants; whereas the said road will run almost parrilele with the Provintial Road through s'd township, which Road will not exceed one mile and quarter apart, within the Bounds of s'd township, the said inhabitants having had three Roads to cut and uphold in said township already, so therefor your Petitioners humbly Desires that the honorable Bench will take under your consideration and confirm nothing to the Detriment of a multitude to answer the sinestor ends of very few; and your petitioners will ever pray.

Aug. ye 1st, 1744.

James Walker,	James Mills,	Robert Chambers,
James Murray,	William White,	Rowland Chambers,
Chas. Milliken,	James Galbraith,	And'w Morrison,
William Tut [Toot],	Patrick Homes,	John Magee,
William Morrison,	James McCalester,	James McDowell,
Mos. Potts,	John McClelland,	Daniel Black,
Thomas Rutherford,	John McQueen,	Thomas Black,
Robert Mordah,	Neal McCalister,	John Laird,
Andrew Bridget,	John Ree,	Hugh Laird,
Anthony Sandford,	James Ree,	Andra Duncan,
William Rea,	Alexander Rodey,	John Duncan,
Thomas Willson,	Thomas Loagan,	John Cooch,
Hugh Hays,	William Vinsont,	Alex. Mebane,
John Dunbar,	Richard Robison,	Andrew McCrery,
Patrick Hays,	Robert Robison,	John McCalon,
Robert Rusk,	John McCallester,	John Tinnen,
John Gibson,	John Hays,	James Tinnen,
John Care,	William Hay,	Charles Clark,
Moses Willson,	David Foster,	David McCord,
Alexander Leckey,	Andrew Moor,	William Caldwell,
William Chaikwod,	Robert Foster,	James Frolad,
William Creag,	John Foster,	James Long,
James Carithers,	David Foster,	Thomas Kinnen,
Hugh Carithers,	James Foster,	Moses White,
Widow Wale,	William Smith,	James Caruthers,
John Douglas,	Samuel Gordan,	John Gurly,
John McCafer,	Patrick Kelly,	Thomas Eacken
Robert Teatt,	James Hays,	John Strean,
Peter Bomgarner,	John McCord,	John Couhran,
James McCord,	Alex. Blackburn,	Jacob Meyars,
William Boyd,	William Blackburn,	Crisly Landis,
David Taler,	Henry Chambers,	John Mebane,
David Johnston,		

[On the petition which follows is this endorsement: " Nov'r, 1744. Peltn for a road from Harris's to Lanc'r. Jas. Armstrong, Andrew

Steen, Thos. Mays, Thos. G———, Sam'l Parks, John ffoster, or any 4 of them." The strangest part of this document is the fact that the signature of John Harris is not attached to it. The original contains the autographs of early settlers remarkable for penmanship.]

To the Worshipful Justices of the Court of Quarter Sessions now sitting in Lancaster:

The Humble Petition of John Harris & several others Inhabitants of Lancaster County, Humbley Sheweth:

That y'r Worp's Hum'le pet'rs, finding a much nearer way to ye Town of Lancaster from s'd Harris' Ferry Than the road now cut & opened, by three miles Distance, betwixt s'd Harris's ferry and Stephen Sisney's, at the Pine ford on Swatara.

And y'r Pet'rs have sufficient reason to say that it is a much nearer & better road. And that there is several very Steep Hills on ye present road, which in Frosty or Rainy Weather is so very Slippery & Dangerous Either for Waggons going up or Down s'd Hills. For going up they have almost Incredible Trouble, and coming down again they run the risque of Damaging their fre't by oversetting, & their lives & their creatures' lives, which would be entirely avoided were there a Road cut as y'r Pet'rs require down the east side of Susquequehanna to Pineford afores'd. All wh'h y'r worp's Pet'rs Humbly submits to y'r worp's better Judgment to act therein as you in y'r Wisdoms shall Think fit.

Geo. Corwin,	James Galbraith.	James Graham,
James Allcorn,	John Wilson,	John Foster,
Wm. White,	Jas. Roddye,	Henry White,
David Willson,	Alexd'r Armstrong,	Rob't Buchanan,
Stephen Cessna,	John Cessna,	James Mitchell,
John Smith,	Robt. Lowrey,	David Campbell,
Geo. Gibson,	Simon Girte,	John Potts,
Henry Smith,	Robert Miller,	William Carnahan,
John Miller,	John Brandon.	Christopher Johnston.
Samuel Smith,	Joseph Chambers,	

NOTES AND QUERIES.—CXLI.

NEVILLE, BURROUGHS, O'BANNON, CAINE.—I desire to know if George and Anne Burroughs Neville (*Pennsylvania Genealogies, by Wm. H. Egle, M. D., Neville and Craig*) had other issue than General John Neville, and if so, their names, marriages, etc. Also the descent of George Neville and of his wife Anne Burroughs—names of father and mother of each, if no more. I am a great-great-grandson of Anne Neville (believed to have been a daughter of George and Anne (Burroughs) (Neville) and her husband Wm. (E.) O'Bannon. The following grants of land are of record in the Virginia Land Registry: James Neville, 1,300 acres in Northampton co. Mch. 26, 1662, Book No. 4, p. 539; John Nevill, 500 acres in Gloucester co. M ch. 6, 1675, No. 6, p. 549; John Nevill and John Marlow, 92 acres in Isle of Wight co. Apl. 20, 1684, No. 7, p. 378; James Nevil, 400 acres in Henrico co. Apl. 27, 1725, No. 12, p. 200; do. 400, and 400 acres, Sept. 29, 1729, No. 13, p. 406, 407; James Nevil, 400 acres, do. Sept. 28, 1732, No. 14, p. 463; James Nevill, 20 acres, do. Mch. 12, 1739, No. 18, p. 552; James Nevill, 400 and 2,550 acres in Goochland co. Sept. 25, 1746, No. 24, p. 501 and 520. I shall be pleased to correspond with any one interested.   PAUL CAINE.

MOSES TATEMY.

[In *N. & Q., cxxv.*, appeared a notice of this noted Indian. The following admirably supplements that article.]

MOSES TATEMY—Written variously *Tattama, Totami, Titamy;* sometimes called *Old Moses*, also *Tundy.* At the conference held in the Great Meeting House at Crosswick's, in February, of 1758, he is registered as a *Mountain Indian.* He was a convert of and for sometimes interpreter to David Brainerd, the missionary. He attended most of the treaties held with Teedyuscung, in the capacity of assistant interpreter. His son William, after he was shot, was attended by Dr. Otto, of Bethlehem, who had him conveyed to the house of John Jones, a farmer living a mile east of Bethlehem. Dr. Otto reported the case to Justice Horsefield as follows:

"BETHLEHEM, *27th July, 1757.*
"MR. HORSEFIELD:

"*Sir*—I yesterday attended William Tatamy twice. His wound looks well, is without inflammation, and discharges its pus regularly. The swelling is also gone. To-day he turned himself alone, which he has not been able to do before, so that I believe, with good nursing and attendance, if nothing unforseen happen, he may, by God's Help, recover. The violent Pain he complains of, at times, I apprehend, proceeds from some of the bones in his Groin being shot thro', or at least the tendinous parts being much lacerated. You may depend upon it, I shall do all in my power to perfect a cure.
         "I am, Sir,
               "Your most humble Servt,
                           "JOHN MATTHEW OTTO."

After lingering for a month, young Tatemy died on the 9th August. Meanwhile he had been visited by the Moravians from Bethlehem, and ministered to spiritually by Rev. Jacob Rogers. Two days later his remains were interred in the old grave-yard, near the Crown Inn, on the south side of the Lehigh opposite to Bethlehem, in the presence of upwards of two hundred Indians, Mr. Rogers reading the funeral service. For a "coffin, digging the grave, and burying him," the Province was charged £2, 2s. Tat's Gap in the Blue Mountains, two and a half miles west of the Delaware Water Gap, perpetuates the name of Tatemy.

It may also be stated that immediately after the interment the missionary, J. J. Schmick, at her urgent request, baptized a Delaware woman, as she was lying under a tree near the Crown Inn in the last stage of consumption. She received the name of Johanna. The following day she died, and on the 13th was buried. An Indian boy, who had also died, was buried by the savages with heathen rites, in a corner of the consecrated ground.   J. W. J.

REMINISCENCES OF AMOS KAPP.

Our venerable friend, Amos Kapp, Esq., of Northumberland, has been interviewed by the newspaper reporter, and the Williamsport *Gazette and Bulletin* of the 7th gives the following among others of Mr. Kapp's reminiscences, colloquially :

On asking him if he was a native of Harrisburg he promptly replied :

"Yes, I'm a Harrisburger by birth. I was born in that place on the 27th of August, 1809, and I'm just rounding off my 78th year. My father and mother lived in a building that adjoined the Bolton House site, in the corner of Market square."

"Did you remain there long?"

"Until I was nearly grown up."

"You became an employe of Calder & Wilson, the famous stage coach firm, did you not?"

"I did. At an early age I was sent to Philadelphia to serve as their agent. We had our office in the Red Lion Hotel, No. 200 Market street, above Sixth. It was kept by Mrs. Yerkes."

"That is a good while ago?"

"Yes, nearly sixty years. I was there during the great cholera scourge, and remember seeing two men fall down and die in the market house!"

"Those were exciting times?"

"Very indeed. I soon after left and went to my home at Harrisburg."

"Your father still lived at the old place?"

"He did. He inherited it from his father. My grandfather's name was Michael. He purchased the property from Harris. My father's name was Michael also. Sister Catharine and myself were the only children. She was the eldest and died about three years ago. 'Aunt Kitty,' as she was called, was the same age as General Cameron, having been born in 1799."

"Did you ever belong to a military company also?"

"When quite a young man I was a member of the Dauphin county cavalry. The company was commanded by Captain McAllister. General Cameron was a member of the company also."

"Have you any relics of the company?"

"I have the old bridle, saddle, holsters and pistols. And what is more interesting still, I have the old sword. Very few can show older military equipments!"

Mr. Kapp said that Calder & Wilson sent him to Northumberland January 1, 1833, to serve as their stage agent at that place. He came and opened an office as per orders.

"How long did you serve in that capacity?"

"Two years. I then purchased sixteen horses and two coaches from my employers and started business for myself."

"How far did you run your coaches?"

"My section of the stage line was from Liverpool to Milton. Above Milton the line was continued by Samuel Lloyd, up the river to Muncy, Williamsport and other points."

"Did you run your part of the line long?"

"Until the canal was built and packet boats were introduced. That was about 1836. I was then interested in the boats until the railroad came. We ran the boats in the summer and our coaches in the winter time."

"You became interested in the railroad?"

"Yes; I was connected with the Northern Central. I owned 500 shares of stock at one time, and was a member of the board of directors for several years."

"Did you run any other stage line than the one up the river?"

"Yes, I had a line from here to Danville and above, and also ran coaches to Pottsville."

"In the busiest stage coaching days you must have had many horses?"

"At one time I had over one hundred head and about twenty drivers. A few of my old drivers are living here yet."

"How many coaches?"

"About ten."

"What kind were they?"

"They were the famous Troy and Concord coaches. And in later years a very good coach was built at Harrisburg."

"Were coaches expensive?"

"They cost $500 each. And the item for repairs was considerable, too."

Mr. Kapp has lived an eventful life, and it is always a pleasure to meet him and listen to his reminiscences of the olden times, particularly when the stage coach rattled over the highways, and the approach to a town was heralded by the blowing of a horn. Those were halcyon days. He is remarkable in another respect, and that is in the number of Governors of Pennsylvania that he has seen inducted into office.

"How many Governors have you seen inaugurated?"

"Seventeen!" he promptly replied.

"I remember seeing Snyder retire from office in 1817. I was then about eight years old. Findlay, who succeeded him, lived on Front street, Harrisburg, between Market and Walnut."

"Where did the first inaugurations take place?"

"Findlay and Hiester were inaugurated in the old court house, which stood where the present one now stands."

"You knew more than half of these Governors personally?"

"I knew them all quite well, from Wolf to Beaver."

"Do you know any other person in the State who has witnessed that many inaugurations?"

"I do not. There are many older men, but they did not take the same interest in these affairs of State and make it a point to attend them."

"Your opportunities were always good to be present?"

"That is true. Being a native of the State capital, and so situated on the line of travel, and having the facilities was a great advantage to me. Had it not been for this, and my inclination to be present on such occasions, perhaps, I could not say that I have seen seventeen governors inducted into office."

OLD-TIME ROAD PETITIONS.

[We conclude our series of old-time road petitions, valuable alike to the local historian and to the genealogist. If we could reproduce from the originals the very excellent autographs, the appreciation would be greater.]

The Court of Quarter Sessions held at Lancaster on the first Tuesday of August, 1751:

The humble Petition of the subscribers, Inhabitants of Hanover township, sheweth:

That y'r Petitioners living at a distance from Market are obliged to keep Wagons to carry on our business, & have now a tollerable Road to Philadelphia. But our Business frequently calling us to travel thro' Paxton to Susquehanna River we find ourselves hamper'd & at a great loss for a Road there. We, therefore, humbly request that we may be granted an Order of Court to lay out & open a Road from Sam'l Robison's to John Harris's Ferry, which we hope will be a damage to none, and will be a considerable Benefit to y'r Petitioners.

William Erwin,	Tho. Robison,	Peter Stewart,
James Finey,	James Stuart,	John Stewart,
Thomas Robinson,	Rich'd Sankey,	James Reed,
Samuel Barnett,	Lazarus Stewart,	Benjamin Clark,
Robt. Kirkwood,	John Cunningham,	Abraham Williams,
John Merten,	Adam Reed,	John McCluer,
Alexander Merten,	Jno. Young,	Thos. McCluer,
Alexander Meklheney,	John Forester,	William McCluer,
Philip Robison,	John Crawford,	Samuel Robinson.

On the foregoing is this endorsement: "Aug't, 1751, Pet'n for Road. Sam'l Simpson, John Young, Adam Reed, Wm. Irwyn, Jno. Montgomery, Jno. Johnston, or any four of them to Lay out Road to Paxtang Meeting House."

[This " Pet'n ag't the Road from Swatara to Chesney's Ferry" of " Nov'r, 1754," is marked " Rejected." Chesney's Ferry was subsequently Chambers' Ferry, now below Steelton.]

The humble petition of the Inhabitance of Paxton to the honerable Court of Quarter Sessions in Lancaster the first of November, 1753.

Your Humble Petititioners Sheweth:

That there is no need for a Road from the Provincial Road to begin at Swatara Creek, for it and the Provincial Road is within Call, the one to the other for about five miles of the road to Chessney's Ferry, and therefore we conceive that it is not necessary and Asures Your

Worships that it is to the Great Dammage of some and the Intolerable burden to all; and therefor wou'd humbly beg that Your Worships May Retract the Orders, and your Petitioners, as in Duty Bound, Shall ever pray.

We do show that the men that was appointed for the Laying out out of the Road was not caled, and they did it privtely to all as that fare as they could.

Henry Ffoster,	James Welsh,	James Williamson,
Thos. Sturgeon,	Hugh McKillip,	Thomas King,
Benja'n Whitley,	Andrew Hannah,	Andrew Cochran,
Joseph Kelso,	James Collier,	Andrew Calwell,
Samuel Parker,	John Cavett,	George Clarke,
Rob't Montgomery,	Timothy Shaw,	William Barnett,
Jas. Willson,	Thomas McArthur,	John Barnett,
Peter Corbay,	Thomas Woods,	John Wilson, Jun,
Jas. Armstrong,	John Montgomery,	John Wilson. Sen'r,
William Bell,	John Shields,	Wm. Wilson,
William Calhoon,	David Shields,	Hendrey McKiney,
John Smith,	Hendrey Sharp,	Wm. Kirkpatrick,
Robert Right,	Thos. Dougan,	Edward Sharp,
John Rooss,	Pat'k Montgomery,	William Sharp,
Josias White,	James Lusk,	James Cahoon.

[The following is thus endorsed: "Nov'r Sess'ns, 1754. Pet. of Sundry Inhabit'ns of Derry, Paxtang & Hanover, for a Road. Order iss'd—Robert Allison, Thomas Logan, Martin Brandt, Robert Murdock, Moses Willson, James Galbreath, or any four of them, to view and lay out s'd Road, &c."]

To the Worshipfull, The Justiss of Lancaster County, to sit the November Term, 1754:

The Petition of Sundry of the Inhabitants of the Townships of Derry, Paxtown and Hanover Humbly Sheweth:

That your Worships were pleased to Order a Road to be Lay'd and Cleared from Robert Allison's mill, on Connewago Creek to Samuel Scott's, on Chickes Creek, Your Petitioners are therefore of opinion if we Had A Road Lay'd out from John Harrises at Swatarow Creek to s'd Road it would be no small advantage to Us in order to Transport our Goods to market and go to our Courts at Lancaster, as well as serve the Publick. Your Petitioners, therefore, Humbly intreats Your Worships wou'd please to grant an order of Court to Lay out s'd Road from John Harrises. at Swatarow, to the Road Lay'd out from Robt. Allison's to Samuel Scott's, and your Petitioners as in Duty Bound will pray.

John Roan,	Andrew Johnston,	Joseph Sherer,
David Shields,	Joseph Heslet,	William Hanna,
Arthur Chambers,	Charles McClure,	Thomas Rutherford,
Robert Chambers,	Oliver Wiley,	Thomas Simpson,
Henry McClure,	George Harris,	Samuel Simpson,
John Harris,	John Gray,	Hendry McElroy,
William Harris,	John Wilson,	John Hutchison,
James McCrea,	John Harris,	John Woods,
John Blackburn,	Moses Dickey,	Andrew Woods,
Jonas Larue,	Andrew Hanny,	James Finney,
Jas. Galbreath,	Joseph Willson,	Thomas Sharp,
William Galbreath,	John Carson,	David Walker,
Robt. Wallace,	Samuel Hunter,	John Shields,
Hugh Willson,	James Armstrong,	Hendrew Mehany,
James Walker,	Robert Smith,	James Polk,
John Fforster,	John Karr,	Thomas Mayd,
Richard McClure,	Joseph Davis,	Thomas Dougan,
Alex'r McClure,	William Sharp,	John Johnson,
John Means,	James Aken,	William Chambers.
Wm. Kirkpatrick,	William Wilson,	

NOTES AND QUERIES.—CXLII.

CARLISLE IN 1806.—Thomas Ashe, Esq., an English traveler in America, published an account of his visit in 1808. His allusion to Carlisle is very funny. "Harrisburg, a handsome Dutch town, stands on the east bank of this river [the Susquehanna.] I did not stop, however, but pursued my course to Carlisle, which has a college, and the reputation of a place of learning. This may be so, but I have the misfortune to dispute it; for though indeed I saw an old brick building called *the University*, in which the scholars had not left a whole pane of glass, I did not meet a man of decent literature in the town. I found a few who had learning enough to be pedantic and impudent in the society of the vulgar, but none who had arrived at that degree of science which could delight and instruct the intelligent." Now, this man probably remained in Carlisle over night—and yet he presumed to give an opinion of the people he knew nothing of.

"JOHN HARRISES AT SWATAROW."—It will have been noticed in the road petition of 1754, that we have the signature of two John Harrises, and it may be considered they were one and the same person. John Harris, of Swatara, and John Harris of Harris' Ferry, were different persons altogether. We are inclined to the belief they were cousius, at least they were related. It is more than probable that the former was the John Harris who was such a prominent personage in the Revolutionary history of Cumberland county, and who laid out the town of Mifflin on the Juniata.

HARRISBURG IN 1820.—From an "E nigrant's Directory," published in London in 1820, we have this account of the Capital City of Pennsylvania: "Harrisburg, the chief town of Dauphin county, and the seat of government for the State ef Pennsylvania, is situated on the northeast bank of the Susquehanna River, ninety-seven miles from Philadelphia, on the road leading to Carlisle and Pittsburgh. It is handsomely laid out on the elegant plan of Philadelphia, having four streets running parallel with the river, named Front, Second, and so on; and these are crossed by others at right angles, called Mulberry, Chestnut, Market, Walnut, Locust, and Pine. The houses are mostly of brick, have a good appearance, and the town is rapidly increasing since it became the seat of government. There is a handsome court house, a German church, a stone jail, and the public edifices for the accommodation of the State Legislature will be the most elegant structure in Pennsylvania. Harrisburg was first planned in the year 1785, and has been progressively improving ever since. From its commanding and central situation it will, in all probability, become one of the largest inland towns in the United States. Town lots sell for more than $2,000; and land in the neighborhood from $80 to $100 per acre."

SIMON GIRTY.

SOME FACTS RELATING TO THE WHITE RENEGADE.

With the rapid flight of time the aged people of the present day, who are the only remaining links of connection between the early frontiersmen and the present generation, are passing away, and with them many an interesting incident of those perilous days when every man carried his life in his hand is lost beyond recovery. It is the duty, therefore, of those who know any unrecorded events in the history of the western portion of the country to preserve them in some permanent form. Hence this article.

In the early frontier history of Pennsylvania and Virginia, few characters stand out more prominently against so dark a background as Simon Girty, "the renegade," and his brothers. The Girtys were of Irish descent, their father having emigrated from Ireland to Pennsylvania about 1740, where he became a licensed Indian trader. Every authority says that the father was a man of bad character and dissolute habits. " The old man was beastly intemperate. A jug of whiskey was the extent of his ambition. ' Grog was his song, and grog would he have.' His sottishness turned his wife's affection." In some drunken revel the old man was murdered, and the widow immediately married, about 1754—and with her husband removed to the extreme frontier.

Simon Girty, Sr., had four sons, Thomas, Simon, George, and James. These were all taken prisoners by the Indians, and, with the exception of Thomas, who subsequently escaped, they were all adopted into different Indian tribes. Thomas, who had been captured at Fort Granville, was rescued by Colonel Armstrong in 1756, when he took Kittanning—*Penna. Archives, ii. 775.* He returned to civilized life and died, it is supposed, in Butler county, Pennsylvania, in 1820. He was one of Brady's spies in the Indian wars after the Revolution.

George was adopted by the Delawares, and grew up with them a thorough savage. He remained with them until his death, which is said to have occurred, while drunk, on the Miami of the Lakes about 1813. He fought with the Indians at the battle of Point Pleasant. James was adopted by the Shawanese, and, like George, became entirely identified with them—proficient in all their bloodthirsty customs, sparing neither age nor sex in his warfare upon the white settlements, and delighting in torturing and practicing new methods of cruelty upon the unfortunate white captives who fell into his hands.

Simon was adopted by the Senecas, but did not remain long with them, returning with his mother to the settlements. He figures more prominently in pioneer history than either of his brothers. He was one of the two scouts whom Lord Dunmore sent to notify General Lewis of the proposed junction of the two armies at the Shawanese towns. And as George was with the Delawares at that time, it is believed that Simon conveyed through him to the Indians the strength and position of the army under Lewis, and so induced them to begin that eventful battle which resulted in the defeat of the Indians at Point Pleasant in 1774. It is said that he was intimate with and frequently enjoyed the hospitality of Colonel Crawford, who was so fiendishly tortured in 1782.

Simon's subsequent history is so deeply enshrouded in the blood of his countrymen, that the only bright spot in his history, the only fact which indicates that one touch of human sympathy still remained in his heart—his treatment of Simon Kenton—is scarcely remembered.

When the war of the Revolution began Simon made an effort to secure a commission in the American Army, but, failing in this, he, in company with Elliott and McKee and a dozen kindred spirits, left Pittsburgh and joined the Indians. Tradition gives him the reputation of great courage and cruelty. All that is certainly known of him represents him as unusually vindictive against the Americans, and his conduct at the death of Colonel Crawford, who had so often befriended him, displayed the grossest inhumanities, although McCutcheon, in the *American Pioneer*, thinks otherwise. It is said, however, that there were times when he manifested a tenderness of feeling and a compassionateness which it is difficult to reconcile with his usually barbarous habits. Albach says he was scrupulously honest in the payment of his debts, on one occasion selling his horse to fulfill a "promise to pay," and that it was when under the influence of liquor that his heart knew no such emotion as mercy. For many years the manner and the place of the death of Simon Girty was unknown. Albach states that it was said he was cut to pieces by Johnson's mounted men at the battle of the Thames. This proves not to be correct.

NOTES AND QUERIES.—CXLIII.

DR. ROBERT HARRIS OF THE REVOLUTION.—While attending the funeral of a relative at the Great Valley Presbyterian church, in Tredyfferin township, Chester county, I observed a small neat headstone on the right hand side, close to the avenue leading from the entrance of the yard, with the following inscription :

"*Doct. Robert Harris,* | *of Paxtang,* | *who departed this life* | *March 4, 1785,* | *aged 29.*"

This marks the grave of Robert Harris, Surgeon's mate, 2d Pennsylvania Continental Line, Nov. 1, 1777, who died at John Phillips' "Blue Ball" Tavern, Tredyfferin township, March 4, 1785, from quinsy, while on his way home from Philadelphia. See "Pennsylvania in the Revolution," vol. 1, p. 401.   JOHN B. LINN.

Bellefonte, March 26, 1887.

DEATH OF A WORTHY COLORED WOMAN.—In a recent Philadelphia newspaper it is stated that " Mrs. Ann Elizabeth Ball died at her residence, No. 830 Auburn street, where she resided for the past forty-six

years. She was born a slave in Lancaster county, Pa., and was owned by Colonel Jesse Ball, of Virginia, who moved into the State about 1797. She suffered very few of the hardships of slavery, being liberated by her master when quite young. After Mrs. Ball removed to this city she took an active part in the Underground Railroad, whence she became widely known throughout the State. She had a record of sixty-three slaves whom she personally aided to freedom, and it was her boast that none were ever taken back whom she aided. She was nearly 80 years old. Gilbert A. Ball, president of the Matthew Stanley Quay club, is her son." I will be grateful to any one who will authenticate this statement about Jesse Ball, of Virginia. HORACE EDWIN HAYDEN.
Wilkes-Barre, Pa.

NEVILLE, BURROUGHS, O'BANNON, CAINE (*N. & Q.*, *cxli*).—Colonel John Neville appears among the membership of the Virginia branch of the Order of the Cincinnati. The following grants to the name Burroughs are of record in the Virginia Land Registry: Christopher Burroughs, Book No. 1, p. 341, 200 acres in Elizabeth City county, May 4, 1636, "Hard Rights," or "Transports," entitling the patentee to fifty acres of land each: Christopher Burroughs (the patentee), Anne Burroughs (probably his wife), Wm. Burroughs (probably his son), and John Phillips. Christopher Burroughs, Book No. 2, p. 347, 150 acres in Lynhaven Parish, Lower Norfolk county, November 7, 1651; Venomy Burroughs, No. 6, p. 378, 944 acres in Lynhaven Parish, Lower Norfolk county, October 3, 1661. Application to the clerk of Norfolk county, Va., as to wills of record of the names Burroughs might prove to be effective in obtaining desired information.
R. A. BROCK.
Richmond, Virginia.

IN THE REVOLUTION.

TWO INTERESTING LETTERS.

[The following is from Mr. Peters, merchant in Philadelphia, to a very prominent personage in Bethlehem. It is sufficiently explanatory.]

PHILADELPHIA, *Aug. 24, 1779.*

DEAR SIR: The blind way of trade puts me at a stand. I cannot purchase any coffee without taking to one bill a tierce Claret & Sour, and at 6£ 8 per gall. Sugar I may purchase at about the limited price, and that is the only article that can be bought. I have been trying day for day, and never could get a grain of coffee so as to sell it at the limited price, these six weeks. It may be bought, but at about 25 s. per ℔. Then it is very dangerous to get it out of town, for the least trifle you must produce your bill and swear that you have given no more and made no presents, whether that you intend to make any presents after you have a permit or certificate. Sometime ago I might have sent wagons out of town and never have been stopped, but that time is over. Should you want sugars, I will buy for you, but I think you had better wait 'till this d——d Committee is broke. It cannot last long, for we must all very soon shut up stores and starve.

I am, Dear Sir,
Your humble servant,
J. PETERS, JR.

To Mr. Francis Oberlin, Merchant at Bethlehem.

[The letter which follows, from General Washington to the Rev. Mr. Ettwein, afterwards a bishop in the church, relates to the proposed occupations of the Moravian settlement at Lititz for hospital purposes. Outside of the city of Philadelphia there were no buildings so adapted for hospitals as those found in the Moravian villages, hence they were always in demand. For this and the former unpublished correspondence we are indebted to John W. Jordan, Esq., of the Pennsylvania Historical Society.]

HEADQUARTERS, *28 March, 1778.*

SIR: I have received your letter of the 25th instant by Mr. Hasse, setting forth the injury that will be done to the inhabitants of Letiz by establishing a General Hospital there—it is needless to explain how essential an establishment of this kind is to the welfare of the army, and you must be sensible that it cannot be made anywhere, without occasioning inconvenience to some set of people or other— at the same time it is ever my wish and aim that the public good be effected with as little sacrifice as possible of individual interests— and I would by no means sanction the imposing any burdens on the people in whose favor you remonstrate, which the public service does not require. The arrangement and distribution of Hospitals depends entirely on Doctor Shippen, and I am persuaded that he will not exert the authority vested in him unnecessary to your prejudice. It would be proper however to represent to him the circumstances of the inhabitants of Letiz; and you may if you choose it, communicate the contents of this letter to him.

I am, Sir,

Your Most Obed't Servt,

GEO. WASHINGTON.

The Reverend Mr. Ettwein, Bethlehem.

NOTES AND QUERIES.—CXLIV.

OLD CONEWAGO CHURCH.—" J. G." writes us in regard to the tombstone inscriptions in the old Conewago Presbyterian church-yard, four miles east of Middletown. We would willingly publish them if we had them; but several years ago we visited the locality, and not a stone was visible. If " J. G." can ascertain where any of the tombstones are which were removed we will be thankful to him. It is greatly to be regretted that we have no list of those whose remains lie in that plowed-over " God's acre."

UNITED STATES TAX IN 1813.

[The following gives the apportionment of the Direct Tax of the United States upon Pennsylvania, July 14, 1813. Of the Three Million Tax, then directed to be raised, the States of Massachusetts, New York, Pennsylvania, Virginia, and North Carolina paid more than one-half. This table is valuable more especially as a historic fact and reference in the study of political economy.]

	Dols.	Cts.
City of Philadelphia,	79,500	
County of Philadelphia,	38,200	
Chester,	18,270	
Delaware,	7,060	
Montgomery,	15,300	
Bucks,	16,600	
Lancaster,	37,400	
York,	11,540	
Adams,	545	
Northampton,	11,140	
Wayne,	2,640	
Berks,	21,550	

Dauphin,	$17,650	
Cumberland,	10,300	
Franklin,	9,000	
Northumberland,	7,580	
Mifflin,	3,500	
Huntingdon,	3,070	
Bedford,	2,060	
Somerset,	2,000	
Cambria,	400	
Fayette,	4,500	
Greene,	2,130	
Washington,	6,920	
Allegheny,	5,210	
Armstrong,	1,450	
Westmoreland,	5,440	
Indiana and Jefferson,	1,320	
Centre,	3,150	
Clearfield, Potter, and McKean,	300	
Luzerne,	2,720	
Lycoming,	2,500	
Tioga,	389	16
Mercer,	1,710	
Butler,	1,500	
Beaver,	2,510	
Crawford,	1,260	
Venango and Warren,	800	
Erie,	780	
Total,	$365,479	16

THE TREASON OF ARNOLD.

Floating through the newspapers several years ago we came upon the following which is important in connection with the treason of Benedict Arnold: Most readers of American history are aware of the fact that the dropping of the British ship *Vulture* down the Hudson from opposite Teller's Point led to Andre's capture. And it is generally known, also, that she thus dropped down the river to avoid the fire from a battery on the Point. The following, written by Cornelius Atherton, of Chenango county, New York, throws some additional light on the subject:

" I was informed by my mother years ago, when I was a young

man, that on his learning the British ship *Vulture* was anchored in
the river below West Point, my father, Cornelius Atherton, with another man (name forgotten) went to a Colonel Livingston, in command of a small battery, five or six miles below West Point, asking
him to send a small detachment up on the Heights, and drive the
Vulture away, but the Colonel dare not weaken his small force. He
finally gave them a twelve (or four) pounder carronade and two gun-
ners, with ammunition a plenty. In a short time they had their
gun in position on the highland banks, within easy range of the
Vulture and perfectly safe from her guns. After trying cold shot for
a few times without effect they improvised a furnace and made the
balls red hot, and at the first fire struck a red hot ball in the deck
of the vessel. A second and third went equally successful. She
cast her cable and took her way down the river, out of the way of
the gun on the heights. This I believe to be a true statement of the
cause of Major Andre's capture, and saving West Point from falling
into the hands of the British.   Cornelius Atherton."

The twelve-pounder here spoken of was probably a much smaller
piece of ordinance, for Lossing says, " Colonel Livingston asked
Arnold for two pieces of heavy cannon for the purpose of destroying
her, but the General eluded the proposal on frivolous pretenses, so
that Livingston's detachment could only bring one four-pounder to
bear upon her. He had obtained some ammunition from Colonel
Lamb at West Point, who sent it rather grudgingly and with the
expressed wish that there might not be a wanton waste of it. ' Firing
at a ship with a four-pounder is in my opinion,' he said, ' a waste of
powder.'

If the gun was a four-pounder, instead of a twelve-pound carronade, it is readily understood how two men could manage it, and
also why cold shot was of no use, and hot shot became necessary.
But it seems odd that a paper throwing light upon an incident so
well investigated as everything connected with Arnold's treason and
Andre's capture was should have turned up at this late day.

IN THE REVOLUTION.

Non-Associators in Londonderry Township—1777.

[The following is the assessment of £3 10s. made in 1777 on the
non-associators. Many of the names upon this list were those of associators in 1775 and 1776, who for some reason were unable to march
in the spring of 1777, hence the assessment. It will be noticed that
the large majority are Germans.]

Allen, David,
Allen, Robert,
Bowman, Henry,
Bowman, Jacob,
Beam, Christly,
Balman, John,
Balman, Jacob,
Bradley, Matthew,
Bishop, Stophle,
Buchtender, John,
Bail, Ludwick,
Bail, John Nicholas,
Buck, John,
Buck, Christy,
Buck, Frederick,
Buck, John, Jr.,
Burkholder, Jacob,
Beam, Peter,
Byers, Andrew,
Bryand, Michael,
Brunan, John,
Carmon, John,
Cook, Jacob,
Cluny, William,
Croun, Conrad,
Carmany, Joseph,
Cooper, John,
Daugherty, Hugh,
Disham, John,
Davis, John,
Dinis, Michael,
Diner, Adam,
Dougherty, James,
Donal, James,
Eyle, Michael,
Eversole, John,
Espy, Thomas,
Erhart, Chrisly,
Early, Chrisly,
Early, John,
Flegar, John,
Foster, David, Jr.,
Franey, Joseph, Jr.,
Franey, Joseph, Sr.,
Farney, John,
Faiget, Joseph,
Fishburn, Ludwick,
Fishburn, Deitrick,
Fishburn, Philip,
Hamel, John,
Hughey, James,
Huntsberger, Jacob,

Huntsberger, Olary,
Horst, Jacob,
Hays, William,
Hays, John,
Henry, Adam,
Hoover, John,
Henry, Vehdal,
Henry, George,
Hershey, Henry,
Hershey, Benjamin,
Haron, John,
Hackert, John Chas.,
Hashbarger, John,
Jones, John,
Kinerigh, Emanuel,
Kelly, Thomas,
Kreiger, Henry,
Keener, Adam,
Katharing, Michael,
Lang, Thomas,
Lernan, Jacob,
Langnecker, Daniel,
Langnecker, Jacob,
Liver, Michael,
Landes, John,
Landes, Felix,
Mackey, John,
Miller, Daniel,
Myer, John,
McGrager, Matthew,
McClintock, Joseph,
Moore, Edward,
Mackey, Jacob,
Null, Chrisly,
Null, George,
Null, John,
Nowland, John,
Nafsker, John,
Nigh, Hanicle,
Nigh, John,
Over, John,
Over, Peter,
Pinagle, Martin,
Poughman, Philip,
Plough, Jacob,
Plough, Daniel,
Pooreman, Peter,
Poor, Daniel,
Petlan, Philip,
Pentar, John,
Remas, Philip,

Rowland, Thomas,
Resar, Peter,
Rice, Jacob,
Resar, John,
Stench, Abraham,
Suster, John,
Sulivan, James,
Sulivan, Jeremiah,
Shaw, Wm., Sr.,
Sayers, William,
Sayers, Benjamin,
Sayers, John,
Sayers, William, Jr.,
Shank, Dewald,
Smith, Michael,
Stewick, John,
Strickley, John,
Shank, John,
Stall, Dinnis,
Soner, Christly,
Stall, Frederick,
Snider, Chrisly,
Stover, Joseph,
Stover, Jacob, Jr.,
Shealy, Michael,
Shier, Jacob,
Shank, Michael,
Spence, David,
Speace, John,
Siner, Christly,
Sanes, William,
Taner, Michael,
Tanner, Christly,
Talibach, John,
Talibough, Jacob,
Talibough, Christly,
Talybough,Peter, Jr.,
Taylor, Francis,
Teets, Philip,
Thomas, Peter,
Wray, David,
Wagler, Jacob,
Warnock, Edward,
Wiltman, Wolery,
Wray, Robert,
Worst, Mark,
Wolf, Michael,
Wallace, James,
Wise, John,
Witmor, Abraham,
Wishan, Conrad.

NOTES AND QUERIES.—CXLV.

BLUNSTON'S LICENSES.—I.

The following is a copy of one of the Blunston licenses. The printed forms were not exactly alike. Some gave the holder when presented to the Land Office, the privilege of taking out a warrant of survey, a preliminary necessary, before a patent for the land was granted. Many of the early settlers were very negligent in this respect. After taking out a warrant of survey they paid their taxes, and sometimes a quit rent also. When their land came to be divided, or sold, their titles were defective; this was doubtless one of the causes which induced Benjamin Chambers to visit England.

Pennsylvania, ss:

By order of the Proprietary: These are to License and allow Benjamin Chambers to take and settle and Improve of four hundred acres of Land at the Falling Spring's mouth and on both sides of the Conegochege Creek for the conveniency of a Grist Mill and plantation. To be hereafter surveyed to the said Benjamin on the common terms other Lands in those parts are sold. Given under my hand this thirtieth day of March, 1734. SAMUEL BLUNSTON.
Lancaster County.

The manors laid out for the Proprietaries were erected for different reasons. I will mention a few by way of illustration. In 1717 the Indians residing at Turkey Hill, near Conestoga Creek, and several miles further up the Susquehanna river, complained that the settlers were encroaching upon their hunting ground, and they expressed a determination to move away. To quiet them the Proprietaries directed Mr. Taylor, their surveyor for Chester county, in 1718, to lay out a manor at Conestogoe, and take in the Indian Towns, &c. A Manor was laid out extending from the mouth of the Conestogoe up to Martin Chartier's trading post (now Haverstick's) and extending back about six miles from the river. This Manor contained about seventeen thousand acres. The Ganawese or Canoy Indians were not satisfied, and they moved up to Canoy Creek and settled upon the farm now owned by John Haldeman. This expedient was successful for about twelve years, when the great influx of settlers became clamorous for the Manor land.

In 1733 and 1734 about twelve thousand acres of the Conestoga

Manor were divided into farms and sold to actual settlers. Three thousand acres along the river front were reserved, and were not sold until after the Revolution, when the tract was purchased by Dr. Parrish, Penn's agent, who divided it into small farms.

In the years 1720 and 1721 it came to the knowledge of the Proprietaries that Lord Baltimorè claimed the land on the west side of the Susquehanna river, and intended to send some of his adherents there to effect a settlement, This movement caused much uneasiness in the Penn family. Half a dozen families who had effected a settlement in Conejohela Valley were ejected. The Indians complained of their ill treatment, &c., and Governor Keith came up to consult and confer with the Indians in the summer of 1722.

As the Indian title to these lands was not then extinguished, and under the policy of the Penns was not open for settlement, the Governor suggested that a Manor be laid out to embrace most of the land in dispute. The Indians readily consented to this arrangement as the best one under the circumstances. The Governor had a patent for five hundred acres. Before he returned to Philadelphia he took his surveyor over the river and located his land at Newberry, which took in a few settlements upon the lands embraced in his survey. On the 18th of June, 1722, he issued his warrant for surveying the Manor of Springetsbury, directed to Col. John French (a member of the Provincial Council and a resident of New Castle), Francis Worley, Esq. (a justice of the peace who resided near the present village of Colemanville in Conestoga township, Lancaster county, some of whose descendants now reside in York, Pa.), and James Mitchell, Esq. (who resided in Donegal, about two miles northeast from the present town of Marietta.) They made their survey on June 21, 1722. The Manor contained over seventy thousand acres. This scheme for a few years was successful, and very few persons ventured to settle upon the Manor. In the spring of 1730 Capt. Thomas Cresap moved from his ferry at Rock Run, Md., and moved to Conejohela Valley, opposite Conestoga Manor, where he built a house and established a ferry. His brothers-in-law, Evans, Cannon, and Low, came with him and took up the adjoining land. In the years 1732, '33, and '34 the German emigrants from the Palatinate came to know the rich land in the valley three miles above where Cresap settled, called Grist Valley, named after John Grist, who settled along the creek also named by him in 1720.

Thomas Penn arrived in Philadelphia August 12, 1732, and in September, 1732, an agreement was made between the Penns and Lord Baltimore to run a temporary line between their respective

Provinces. Captain Cresap was an active and aggressive adherent of Baltimore, and he paid no attention to an imaginary line. He erected a block house, and soon gathered quite a company of Marylanders around him. He raided Grist Valley and abused the Germans, many of whom he induced to renounce their adherence to the Penns and accept under Baltimore. To counteract this movement, and prevent the Germans from vacating their improvements, Thomas Penn came up to see Samuel Blunston at Wright's ferry, and after due deliberation Mr. Blunston was appointed agent to issue licenses to actual settlers on the west side of the river. Proper blanks were printed and sent to Mr. Blunston. Prior to this time John Hendricks, Joshua Minshal and John Wright, Jr., had permission to settle on the west bank of the river.

So far as the Germans were concerned, the licenses failed to hold them; and when the Marylanders made it very hot for them, every one of them fled to the eastern side of the river, and were only saved finally in their possessions by the pluck and determination of the Scotch-Irish settlers of Donegal, who came to the rescue of the Quakers, and virtually prevented the Marylanders from taking up all the land on the west side of the river under Baltimore patents, at least in Conejohela and Grist Valleys. The Scotch-Irish settlers who located in the neighborhood of "Carrol's Manor" and "Diggs' Choice" in the Manor of Maske, and the manors in Cumberland Valley, who held Blunston's licenses, could not be driven off their land, but held against all comers. Blunston's licenses were issued to actual settlers in the hope that they would hold their land against intruders, and at the same time it could not be said that the Proprietaries of Pennsylvania were selling land and issuing patents before purchasing the Indian title. The policy of Maryland was not to purchase land from the Indians, or cajole them with presents, but to drive them by force away, and, I believe, as a Province they did not treat with the Indians as a nation. SAMUEL EVANS.

NOTES AND QUERIES.—CXLVI.

CRAIG—ALLEN.—Mrs. Sarah Allen, relict of David Allen, of Carlisle, "much esteemed and lamented," died March 1, 1794, in the 56th year of her age. Subsequently, August 5, 1794, the executors of her estate publish a notice to John Craig, the brother of the late Sarah Allen, of Carlisle, supposed to be living near Pittsburgh, to make known his residence. What is known of John Craig?

CARMICHAEL, WILLIAM.—This gentleman, who was a native of Maryland, died at Madrid, Spain, February 9, 1795. None of the biographical notes concerning him give the correct date, while Drake states that he died at Paris. The new Encyclopedia of American biography copies Drake and furnishes nothing more.

CHAYNE.—John Chayne married, October 24, 1799, Sidney Moffatt, both of East Pennsboro' township, Cumberland county. Are these the ancestors of the Chayne family of this city?

CONTRIBUTIONS TO PENNSYLVANIA BIOGRAPHY.—I.

EDMONDS, WILLIAM.

Williams Edmonds was born 24th October, 1708, at Colford, Gloucestershire, O. E. His father was a merchant, and the family attached to the Established Church. In his youth he learned skindressing in Monmouth. He emigrated in 1736 to America, established himself in business in New York, and in 1739 married Rebecca de Beauvoise, a French Huguenot. She bore him four children and died in 1749. Having united with the Moravian congregation in New York as early as 1741, after the death of his wife he removed to Bethlehem. On 31st March, 1755, he married Margaret, daughter of Henry and Eve Anthony, of New York, who was born in 1721. In October of that year he was elected to the Assembly from Northampton county. In 1763 he removed to the neighborhood of Nazareth, where he conducted a store, and in 1772 took charge of the store opened in that village. Here he died 15th September, 1786. His wife died in 1773 and left one child, a daughter, *Judith.*   J. W. J.

BROCKDEN, CHARLES.

Charles Brockden's name and autograph are familiar to every student of the early deed history of Pennsylvania, as the former is endorsed on all patents of confirmation that were issued from the Land Office in the interval between 1715 and 1767. He was born 3d April, 1683, in the Parish of St. Andrew, London, O. E., his parents being members of the Established Church. After finishing his education he was entered in an attorney's office, who was disaffected to the reigning monarch, William III. While pursuing his studies he accidentally overheard a conversation between his employer and a number of other persons, in which a plot against the government was broached. At the close of the conference young Brockden was discovered, and a number urged that he be put to death; but upon the representation of his employer, that he was of too feeble intellectual capacity to make use of his knowledge, his life was spared. It was then decided that he should be sent out of the country, but this project was not executed until sometime after, when some circumstances had re-excited the fears of the conspirators. He was sent to Philadelphia in 1706 and placed in the office of Thomas Story, the Penns' first keeper of the Great Seal and Master of the Rolls. On Story retiring from office in 1715, Brockden succeeded him and continued therein until September of 1767, when the infirmities of old age rendered his further incumbency unsatisfactory to Governor John Penn, and he was removed. Official relations with Count Zinzendorff, in 1742, proved the means of his attachment to the Moravians, and in March of 1743 he united with their congregation on Race street. For upwards of twenty years he approved himself an eminently useful as well as devoted member of that body.

From a letter of Bishop J. C. F. Cammerhoff to Zinzendorff, the following anecdote is taken: " Recently while Brother Brockden was visiting Brother Reinke [pastor of the Moravian congregation] Rev. [George] Whitefield came in, and in the course of the conversation Whitefield said to Brockden, ' I perceive you are urging me to unite with the Moravians.' ' You are right,' replied Brockden. ' I wish you were a Moravian, not that I think it would add the weight of one grain to their cause, but you would find some rest and repose, which in your present situation is impossible. I pity you indeed, for you remind me of those birds of the Malacca Islands which being destitute of feet are forced to be always on the wing."

Brockden was twice married. His first wife, Susan Fox, died in May, 1747, and although professedly belonging to the Society of Friends, was, in accordance with her request, buried on her husband's farm. Five of his children by his second wife, Mary Lisle, were baptized by Moravian clergymen—*John*, in August of 1749; he died August, 1756. *Charles*, in September, 1751; *Mary*, in September, 1752; *Richard*, in 1754, he died July, 1756, and *John*, in September, 1756. A daughter by his first wife was married in 1768 to Thomas Patterson. Charles Brockden died 20th October, 1769, at his country seat " Hospitality " near Camden, and was buried in his family burial ground. Charles Brockden Brown, the novelist, (*See Egle's Penn'a Genealogies, p. 326*,) born January, 1771, died February, 1810, was a grandson. J. W. J.

BLUNSTON'S LICENSES.—II.

The Quit Rents paid to the Penns were entirely devoted to the purchase of presents for the Indians. Herewith I have copied a letter written by Benjamin Chambers to James Tilghman, Esq., secretary of the land office, which gives some inside history into the character of its author, and the reason he came into possession of the land at "Falling-water."

Sir—The Service done by Benjamin Chambers for which the Honorable Thomas Penn was pleased to give me that tract of land on Seder Spring in the Manor of Louder on the west side of the Susquehannah, was for my going one of the Principal Persons to turn off Crisop [1] and Lord Baltimore's surveyers, who were chaining up the River Side on John Wright's Land, with a Possey of men not Less than Thirty that Crisop had with him, which Party we ordered to take up their Cumpas and Begon, or we would Breake it and make them Begon to their cost, or word to that Purpose; whereupon they went off on sight. I also went one of a party under the command of Samuel Smith, then high Shiriff of Lancaster County, to take Crisop, and when he had gone privately as near his Home as the Bushes would permit, and daylight being feairly Brook, the Sheriff thought as we seen some of them up that it would not be safe for us to storm his house, least he should shoot some of us before we could get a hold of him, so he ordered us to withdraw at that time, which we did. Some time afterwards Mr. Wright and Mr. Samuel Blunstone had an account that a general muster was appointed at Colonel Rigbey's [2], in order to draught a large number of the Melisha to go up to Cadores and Coneydeuhela Settlement to Disstrain for Levies that the were pleased to charge the Inhabitants there, on which Account I was chosen to go a Spy to Bring an account of their proceedings. I went down the East side of Susquahannah, and crossed at Rock Run Ferrey [3] and went to the muster in quest of my Servent who was seaf at home; but soon after I went into the Company I was told that Crisop had been there that Morning and was gon down to Colonel Hall's to meet the Governor of Maryland, who was to come to the muster that day to give his orders against Pennsylvania. On heairing that Crisop was to com with the Governor, as he knew me well, I knew my doom was to go to Goal for Stoping his Lordship's Surveyers. I allso thought I must be gone before the Governer and Crisop came, and after Enquiering after my Servent I went to my Horse and to Lead him to a pair of Bars before I could mount. Rigbey seeing me about to go sent men to bring me to him; he asked me where I lived, I told

him at the Fawlling Spring [4] on Cannogogige in Lancaster County,
as it was then; he asked me what I was after; I told him my servent
that had Run away. He asked me when I left home, I told this day
eight days; he Replyed you Ride a good Horse why were you so long
on the Rode; I told on my business I had to Inquire at Every one I
met and to Advertise at every public place, which detained me. He
asked me where I lodged the first Night, again the second, which
Learned me that I must mak my Lodgings and the days that I had
taken to come there; again he asked me where I Lodged the last
Knight, I told him the Gentleman's House, and that he came to the
muster with me; he sent for the man to Inquire if I had Lodged
there, he Replyed I had, which was one sentence of truth proved in
my feavour; he asked me if I had a pass, I Replied I had not; he
demanded my Reason, I told him I was aquented with all the Magistrates in Lancaster County and thought that the would Laugh at me
to aske a pass to go a little way into a neighboring province in pur-
sute of my servent and that I thought no man would ofer to take me
up for a servant, but as a Spy, and that as Crisop [5] went down to
meet the Governor; he told that there was two spys sent out of Pennsylvania, and that they were to go down on the one side of Susquahannah and up the other, and according to the way I came here
he thought I must be one of them. I Replyed that I was sorry that
his Honour had such a bad opinion of me, but that I had no land
near the disputed land, and were come after no such thing; he said
he could not be of my opinion, but would keep me 'till the Governer
and Crisop would come, and if Crisop knew anything against me, he
would send me to Anopolas. I told him that Crisop knew nothing
against me; that all my consarn was, that while I was detained there,
my servent was making his Escape; he said that I had no Reason to
complain, that I was in his power to make me pay two Hundred of
Tobacco, for coming into Maryland without a pass; I thanked him
for that favor, but it would be too Tedious to Weight our arguments,
but he told me that I must continue there 'till Crisop came, then I
thought he should give no orders but I would hear them; he mustered the Regiment and Informed them that there was twenty out of
Each company to make their Hundred Men to assist the Shiriff to
collect the Levies in the Settlement of Codores; the Day I heard
apointed that they and their officers were to Rendevouse at Wright's
Ferrey; then I thought I had got my Errent, and if I could Prevail
with the Colonel to let me go, his detaining me had well answer'd the
design I went about. Soon after I went there it began to Reain and
continue very dul, some times hard Reain which gave me high cor-
rage that the Governer would not Ride that day, and that I would

turn a corner on them that night if possibel, but I prevailed on him so that he dismissed me at night as an honest man. I went home with one of the Melisha and told him that Crisop bore such a spite to Pennsylvania that if he should here that any man from there had been at the Muster he would asert that he is a spy and would send a party for me, and give me all the trobel he could; therefore I intend to start by Break of day and go home, and if my servent come amongst them I hoop that the will leay him in goal as they were so sharp on one. He conveyed me about six miles, where I entered the Barrens of Baltimore, and steered my course and got to Wright's Ferrey that night, and on telling how it had happened with me, the told me that here was a great company to be at the Rearing of a House in Donegall, and that I should go and let them know the day appointed that Mearylanders would com to Disposes the Pennsylvanians if the would not submit to their government, which I did, and notice waas sent to Lancaster, and when the three Hundred Marylanders come Headed by Colonel Hall and Rigbey, they seeing what they took to be an over match for them, they thought fit to Retreat. The Honorabel Thomas Penn Being at Samuel Blunston's, Esq., and hearing how I have managed at Rigbey's sent for me to let him hear the apologies I made before Rigbey; the pleased his Honour so well that he told Mr. Blunsten that he would make me a Compliment for my good conduct on that affair; I told Mr. Blunston that if his Honour would be pleased to do so, that I would Rether have it in Land than any other way, and as I was a millright; and that there was a stream called Seder Spring in the Manor of Lowder, that I would build a mill on it, that might accomodete aney one of the Honorable Fameley that might think fitt to make a Contery Seat there. On his Hearing my desire, his Honour was pleased to order his secretary of the Land Office, who was James Steel at that time, and was ordered to Be Recorded for a Corn Mill and plantatior., as may appear by the Records; this was dated in the year of our Lord one thousand Seven Hundred and Thirty-Six. Lord Baltimore tho' he lost all the Land he contended for, gave them that aspoused his side of the quarel desenter Land in Frederick County; that now Crisop's tract given him, tho' he was under pay, would now sell for Five Thousand pounds; Capt. Hickinbottom and many others Received Cleair Patten's for Valuabel Tracts of Land in the Mareyland part of Connigogige Valley, not far from where I live, at the great Falling Spring. It had been better for me to have pay'd the Honourable Proprieators Fifteen pounds Ten per Hundred for Three Hundred acres, and then I would not have the Trouble of going to London and Stock Castell about it.

I am Sir, your Humble Servant,

July 2, 1774.   BENJ'N CHAMBERS.

REFERENCE NOTES TO THE FOREGOING.

1. Capt. Thomas Cresap and ——— Franklyn, one of Baltimore's surveyors, with an armed retinue came up to John Wright, Jr., who had charge of the ferry on the west side of the river, at the termination of the present bridge, May 6, 1736, and commenced to survey the plantations of John Wright, Esq., and John Hendricks (who sold his land, 300 acres, to Samuel Blunston, Esq.)

2. This muster of militia was held at Col. Nathaniel Rigby's, September 2, 1735. On September 5, 1735, three hundred arrived at Captain Cresap's, commanded by Colonel Rigby, Col. Edward Hall, and Capt. Charles Higgenbottom, Aquila Paca and ——— Guest. On the 6th day of same month this warlike party marched up to John Hendricks, in battle array, to the beat of drum. Hendricks' house stood a short distance above John Wright's ferry house, which had been converted into a fort, and defended by two or three dozen of men. Cols. Rigby and Hall were making preparations to storm the fort, when they saw three flat loads of armed Donegallians approach the shore, who evidently intended to offer battle. Captain Cresap wanted to fire some blunderbusses into the crowd in the boats, but was prevented by Colonel Rigby. After making a show of attacking the Pennsylvanians the Marylanders ingloriously retreated to Captain Cresap's fort. Capt. John Wilkins (ancestor of the Pittsburgh family) was decoyed by John Hendricks, who had joined the enemy and captured and bound and sent a prisoner to Annapolis upon this raid.

3. "Rock Run" empties into the Susquehanna river a few miles above Port Deposit.

4. It would seem from this fact that Colonel Chambers was living at Falling Spring prior to his application for a grant for the land and the privilege of erecting a "corn mill." In a deposition made by Mr. Chambers on December 8, 1736, he stated that he was twenty-three years of age and a millwright. He located at Falling Spring late in the spring of 1736. It may be stated in this connection that a few years after the death of Capt. James Patterson, in October, 1735, in Conestogoe Manor, Colonel Chambers married his daughter, by whom he had one child, Col. James Chambers, of Revolutionary memory.

5. Capt. Thomas Cresap moved from Conejohela Valley about the year 1738, and located about two miles from Cumberland, at a place called "Old Town," in Maryland, where he established a trading store and became an Indian trader. Although a carpenter by trade, he acquired a knowledge of Land Surveying, and for many years was one of the most prominent ones in Maryland, and it is said that

he added at least one-third of Lord Baltimore's possessions to his Province by the discovery of the head spring of the Potomac, from which place he ran a line due north to the Pennsylvania line. Captain Cresap raised a company at his own expense, and fought the Indians and French during the Indian wars of 1754–55–58–64. His son, Capt. Michael Cresap, raised a company and marched at their head to Boston in 1775. He died in New York October 23, 1775. Colonel Cresap became a very prominent man and was much respected in the western part of Maryland and Pennsylvania. He did not like the Quakers, nor their peaceable measures; but came to admire his Scotch-Irish neighbors, who could give blows as well as take them. General Ord, of the Pennsylvania Reserves, was a descendant of Colonel Cresap, and there is a lieutenant in the navy now who bears his name and is of his blood, who bids fair to attain distinction in his profession.

The Rigbys, Halls, Pacas and Higgenbottoms were prominent families in Baltimore county, now Hartford county, Md.

SAMUEL EVANS.

NOTES AND QUERIES.—CXLVII.

THE LOSS OF THE LUZERNE.

It is known to but few persons that efforts at ship building were made on the Susquehanna. During the war of 1812 the excitement was at fever heighth, and the patriotism of the people exceeded Revolutionary times, save in a few sections where the war was denounced. "Brittannia ruled the waves" then as now, but her navy was her most vulnerable part. At this juncture large vessels were constructed on the Ohio and Allegheny, floated down the Mississippi to New Orleans, where they were properly equipped and manned ready for sea. We are reminded of these facts in our history by the Reminiscences of Mr. D. Yarrington in a recent number of the Wilkes-Barre *Record of the Times.* Speaking of his early recollections of Wilkes-Barre, he says:

"During the war of 1812 the great ship Luzerne was built on the river bank in front of John W. Robinson's stone house. I saw the launch. A thousand or more people were present. The war spirit was rampart at that time, and the people of our town expected that the noble Luzerne was going to assist in bringing the " Flag of Great

Britain " down.   A few days after the launch a sufficient flood arose and the ship was manned and started down the river towards the ocean, but in passing the Falls of Conewago, she ran on the rocks and lay there till the ice in the river broke up next spring, when she was totally destroyed."

What is known of this vessel's run on the Susquehanna?   There ought to be a record somewhere.   Can any of our readers give us light?

THE WORD "SUSQUEHANNA."

Its Etymology According to Heckewelder.

The *Pennsylvania Magazine* of history and biography for April publishes this note:

Heckewelder, in his " Indian Names of Rivers, Creeks, and other noted places of Pennsylvania, together with their meaning," &c., (original Ms., Hist. Soc. Pa.) states: " The Indian (Lenape) distinguish the river which we call Susquehanna thus: The North Branch they call *M'chwewamisipu*, or to shorten it *M'chwewormink*, from which we have made it Wyoming.   This word implies: *the river on which are extensive clear Flats.*   The Six Nations, according to Pyrlæus [Moravian missionary] call it *Gohonta*, which hath the same meaning.

"The West Branch they call *Quenischachachgekhanne*, but to shorten it they say *Quenischachachki*.   The word implies: *the river which has the long reaches or straight courses in it.*

"From the forks, where now the town of Northumberland stands, *downwards*, they have a name (this word I have lost) which implies: *the Great Bay River.*   The word Susquehanna, properly *Sisquehanne*, from *Sisku* for *mud*, and *hanne* for a *stream*, was probably at an early time of the settling of this county, overheard by some white person while the Indians were at the time of a flood or freshet remarking: *Juh! Achsisquehanne* or *Sisquehanne*, which is *how muddy the stream is*, and therefore taken as the proper name of the river.   Any stream that has become muddy, will at the time it is so, be called *Sisquehanna*."

Recently the etymology of this stream has been the cause of considerable controversy.   Possibly Heckewelder is correct, but his authority has been denied by several who have made Indian names a study.   As the centuries recede, however, our only recourse is to those who like Heckewelder and others have left a record of their studies in aboriginal nomenclature.

DAUPHIN COUNTY SETTLERS ON LAKE ERIE.

[Mr. Russell, of Erie, a few years ago published some interesting scraps of local history. In writing of the early settlement of the " Triangle," as Erie county was then called, he says:]

The New England Yankees, as the Reeds, Colts, Strong, Judson, Marvins, Russells, and the Irish, headed by William Miles, the Blacks, Kings, Smiths, Wilson, Lowrys, and others, were the original founders of Erie county, and made the first settlements and locations. The Germans, always slow, did not dare to go so far into the woods until some one else had gone first. The first Pennsylvania German who penetrated these wilds was Jacob Weis, from Dauphin county, who came under the patronage of Col. Thomas Forster, who was agent for the Harrisburg and Presqu' Isle Land Company, in 1797, to assist erecting and starting a set of mills at the mouth of Walnut creek in Fairview township, which he faithfully did, and got the mills in operation and made them successful. Jacob then, with John McFarland, a brother-in-law of Colonel Forster, selected lands in the southwest corner of Millcreek township, and spent their days there.

In 1800 George Buehler, from Dauphin, now Lebanon county, located in Erie, was a man of business here until 1811, and then removed to Harrisburg, and died there in 1816.

In 1801 Christian and Jacob Ebersole, from Lancaster county, with their families, came here in search of homes. Jacob located in Fairview and resided there until 1810, when he sold out and removed to Ohio. Christian Ebersole located in East Millcreek, made a most excellent farm out of the forests, and died there in 1835, leaving a family of most excellent and industrious citizens, who have ever maintained the reputation of strict integrity. One son still lives with his sons in Harborcreek. For honesty, industry, and all that goes to make good citizens, they have ever been proverbial, and would make property if they were put in a hollow log stopped up at both ends—if you did not set it on fire.

The spring of 1802 had another addition in the person of John Riblet, Sr., and family, and John Zuck and family, from Hagerstown, Md. They selected good lands for themselves and sons near Erie, and they and their descendants have ever maintained good homes on those grounds. Two years later Conrad and George Brown, and families, arrived and located, and have been citizens of Erie county ever since, their families being still among us. All of the above names and people have done much to clear up the forests and to advance the prosperity of the county, and in looking over those names it is a difficult matter to say if any one has ever been guilty of breaking the laws of the land, failed to pay his just debts, or ever troubled the courts or jails. These farmers and their descendants have been a great addition to the wealth and capital of our county, and such people will always be successful. Their industry has been rewarded with the good farms and good homes to this day occupied by them.

The years 1805 and 1806 had another addition in the persons of the Stoughs, Zimmermans and Kreiders, with large families, who all took up lands and made large improvements, but the Kreiders remained but a few years and left; the others spent their lives here. In 1828 new additions were the Shanks, Brennemann, Oxer, Huidlers and Mohrs, and the next two years the Messrs. Charles Kreider, Fickinger, and in 1831 Martin Warfel and family. In 1832 the Wolf family, Hersheys, &c.

All these came here with money, and judiciously invested it in our best farming lands, and made themselves permanent homes. As farmers and citizens they could not be excelled, and they have added vastly to the improvement and wealth of our county. For the past thirty years but very few of that nationality have come in and located here, most having gone to the western prairie country. But those names already given, and the Butts, Gingrichs, Kuhls, Ohlwilers, Freys, Bersts, Ripleys, &c., have made some of our most successful farmers and business men and capitalists in the city and county. The original stock has nearly all passed away, and left their families and successors in good circumstances, with unspotted reputations for honesty, industry and good moral principles. And when we look back to the first settlers, and consider the different nationalities, we must have a great respect for the Pennsylvania-German population of our county.

[In this connection it would be well if those interested in genealogy would, by correspondence, secure what information they can relating to these people of the same surname, who went out from this locality sixty to eighty years ago.]

AN ANTI-MASONIC CALL.

[The following call for an Anti-Masonic Convention in 1835 is well worth reproducing in *Notes and Queries*. It is a portion of the record of that infamous crusade which fifty and more years ago defaced the proud escutcheon of our State founded upon the spirit of tolerance. Of the signers to this call, none survive.]

Democratic Anti-Masonic State Convention. To meet at Harrisburg on Monday, the 14th day of December next, at 10 o'clock A. M.

In obedience to the direction of the Democratic Anti-Masonic State Convention of the 4th of March last, we do hereby respectfully recommend a Democratic Anti-Masonic State Convention to meet in the Court House, at Harrisburg, on Monday, the 14th day of December next, at 10 o'clock a. m., to elect delegates to the National Convention—to select Electors of President and Vice-President of the United States, if deemed advisable, and to propose and concert with the Anti-Masonic party of other States, the time and place of holding a National Convention; and also to adopt such other measures as shall be deemed best for the promotion of the cause of Anti-Masonry and the general welfare.

For the purpose of electing delegates to the State Convention, not exceeding in number the Representatives in both Houses of the General Assembly, the respective Anti-Masonic County Committees are requested to call, at an early day, COUNTY CONVENTIONS, or, if preferred, COUNTY MEETINGS, of the Democratic citizens opposed to Freemasonry and all other Secret Societies.

JOSEPH WALLACE,
SAMUEL SHOCH,
GEORGE W. HARRIS,
FRANCIS PARKE,
WM. W. IRWIN,
ZEPHANIAH McLENEGAN,
SAMUEL SHOUSE,
JOHN H. EWING,
CHESTER BUTLER.

Harrisburg, October 21, 1835.

NOTES AND QUERIES.—CXLVIII.

CUMBERLAND VALLEY WORTHIES.

ADDAMS, ROBERT.

Robert Addams, son of Thomas and Katharine Addams, was born about 1745, in what was subsequently known as Toboyne township, Cumberland county, Pa. He was a soldier during the Bouquet expedition to the westward in 1764, and when the Revolution began he raised a company of Associators. Most of these afterwards formed his company in the Sixth Pennsylvania battalion, Col. William Irvine, his commission bearing date January 9, 1776, and was in the Canada expedition of that year. He was killed June 21, 1776, at Isle aux Noix, by a predatory band of Indians and Canadians.

CULBERTSON, JOSEPH.

Joseph Culbertson, son of Alexander and Margaret Culbertson, was born about 1753 in the Cumberland Valley. His ancestors came from the north of Ireland about the year 1730, subsequently locating about seven miles from what is now Chambersburg, where owing to contiguous farms owned by members of the family went by the name of "Culbertson's Row." Joseph was an early Associator, and when the Sixth Pennsylvania (Col. William Irvine) was formed was commissioned ensign of Capt. James A. Wilson's company January 9, 1776. He was in the Canada campaign and killed at Isle aux Noix, June 21, 1776. His brothers, Robert and Samuel, were officers in the Pennsylvania Line of the Revolution.

WILSON, JAMES ARMSTRONG.

James Armstrong Wilson, son of Thomas Wilson and Jean Armstrong, was born in 1752 in the Cumberland Valley. He came from good fighting stock, his ancestors having served as officers in the French and Indian wars. When the Revolution opened he raised a company which was included in Col. William Irvine's Sixth Pennsylvania battalion, of which he was commissioned captain January 9, 1776. He was in the Canada campaign and taken prisoner at Three Rivers. After his release from captivity he returned to his home near Carlisle, Pa., where he remained until his exchange was effected. He was afterwards promoted to major in one of the new regiments of the Pennsylvania Line, but owing to disability, caused by exposure in the Canada campaign, he was retired from service. He died at his residence March 17, 1788, in the thirty-sixth year of his age. The *Carlisle Gazette*, of a subsequent issue, says: "The many virtues of this good and amiable man endeared him in a particular manner to all who knew him. . . . . . . In him his country has lost a distinguished and inflexible patriot." Major Wilson married Margaret, daughter of Capt. Robert Miller, of the Revolution, who with several children survived him.

THE SHARON HOUSE AT EPHRATA.

AN INTERESTING NOTE IN THE HISTORY OF THE BRETHREN.

A Moravian minister from Bethlehem, while itinerating in Lancaster county in the spring of 1747, called at Ephrata, the seat of the Seventh Day Baptists. He was kindly received by Peter Miller (Brother Jabez), who then ranked second to Beissel. From Miller he learned the following: Some time prior to his visit the largest of the buildings (which we believe is still standing on the banks of the Cocalico) had been completed, and that the withdrawal of the Eckerline brothers had been in consequence of a disagreement respecting its dimensions. There was, it seems, a diversity of opinion among the members of the building committee, a state of things not unusual in similar bodies even in our day. There were those who suggested 66 feet, those who proposed 99 feet, and others who insisted upon 100 feet, as the most desirable length for " Sharon." Each party advocated its preference with the tenacity of purpose and the consciousness of superior judgment, which are always manifested and held by the dissenting members of a building committee. Hence this one was in danger of dissolution, and the erection of the much needed structure likely to be postponed indefinitely. But in this critical juncture, knowledge asserted her supremacy over ignorance, and proved, too, the means of healing the breach, save that the worthy Eckerline brothers, chagrined at their defeat, went out into the wilderness.

The solution of the difficulty was made by those who insisted upon 99 feet. They having one night received a Divine token that there was a cabalistic meaning attached to the component parts or elements of figures, and next night they were instructed, too, in the mysteries of the occult science. It was after this fashion, said Brother Jabez, that the cabalists argued and spoke, " Know ye, Brethren! that 0 is the symbol of God, and 1 the symbol of man. Now is not God greater than man? Was he not *before* him from all eternity, and is he not *above* him in the heaven of heavens? This being so, ye who advocate 100 for the length of Sharon do greatly sin, in that you merely place *man before God*. And ye who advocate 66, how stupendous is your guilt in impiously presuming to place *God below man*. Ye both err! We alone are right; for wherein we select 99 as the length of Sharon, we place *God above man*, detracting naught from the infinite majesty of him who is seated in the heaven of his saints!"

This argument proved irresistible, and the workmen staked off the length of the house for the virgins of Ephrata 99, one foot less than 100 feet.   J. W. J.

NEIDIG'S MEETING-HOUSE.

The historians of this section of Pennsylvania having written and rewritten all that could be gathered of the English (Presbyterian) churches, it was naturally to be expected they would then turn their labor to the history of the German (Reformed, Lutheran, Mennonite, United Brethren and other) churches, but in this we are disappointed. We naturally then turn our labor of love to this new field—to the church of our ancestors. In the past we have given records from the "Kirchbuch" of Shoop's and Bindnagle's, which were of the Lutheran and Reformed, but we now come to the story of one of the first churches in the denomination of the United Brethren in Christ, a denomination which at present has over forty meeting-houses in Dauphin county and equally as strong in the adjacent counties.

Neidig's meeting-house is located about three miles east of Harrisburg in the village of Oberlin, though formerly named after the church in Swatara township. Rev. John Neidig, who was the leader in organizing this church, was born in the Tulpehocken settlement. His father's name was Adam and mother's Christian name Anna Maria. He was raised in the faith of Simon Menno, but on arriving at manhood was not long in renouncing some of their peculiarities, and about 1787 joined Behm and Otterbein in organizing the Church of the United Brethren in Christ.

Mr. Neidig located in Dauphin county on a farm midway between Oberlin and Highspire, where he resided all his life. His remains lie in the cemetery at Highspire, over which is erected a plain marble stone with the following inscription:

In Memory of | John Neidig, | Minister of the Gospel to the United | Brethren in Christ for 53 years, | Born April 10, 1753, and died January | 11, 1844, | Aged 78 years, 9 months and 1 day.

Mr. Neidig m. Mary Bear, of Lancaster county, who was b. May 20, 1771, and d. October, 1842. Their children were:

    i. *Elizabeth*, m. Michael Frantz.
    ii. *Abraham*, m. Nancy Hagey; removed and died in Frederick county, Md.

iii. Daniel.

iv. John, m. Nancy, daughter of Rev. Hershey; they removed
to Linn county, Iowa, where they died.

v. Samuel, m. Elizabeth Miller, whose grandfather was the
founder of Annville, Lebanon county, formerly called
Millerstown (Millerstettle).

vi. Annie.

vii. Jacob, m. Catharine Shoop, of Cumberland county, where
they lived and died.

viii. Benjamin, m. Catharine Snavely; after wife's decease he
married Mary Hershey, of Hagerstown, Md.

ix. Isaac, resides in Muscatine, Iowa.

x. Jonathan, m. a sister of John's wife.

The meeting-house, so called in early days, in which Mr. Neidig
was largely interested in building, was the second built by the U. B.
denomination. This was in 1793. The building was limestone and
was quite large for those primitive times, being about thirty by forty
feet, with a steep combed roof. The interior presented a common appearance, with no pulpit, but a large table at one end of the room.
Around three sides sat the leaders in singing, who were all male persons, and at the other side the "prediger." The large old-fashioned
fire place found its position in one corner of the room, where burned
the oak and hickory cord-wood, which, we are told, often died out
long before the sermon had ended. The seats were rudely constructed
benches, without backs. When they were erecting the church, the
neighbors who were opposed to church-building said derisively that
if they would build the house "about the size of a corn-crib it would
be plenty large enough to accommodate them for all time to come."
But such it did not prove. This house stood fifty-seven years, wherein
gathered the dwellers of old Neidig to hear the Word expounded by
the early and faithful veterans of the cross. Hallowed memories still
cling around the spot where once the old "kirche" stood. The com-
municants of this church have continued on until now it is the mother
of more than forty churches in Dauphin county, and more than thirty
in Lebanon county, and where, by the energy of its membership and
their piety and zeal for the Master, it became too small, so that in 1849
it was replaced by the present frame structure.

The cost of the building and the payers of the same with the price
of materials in those days are interesting information, which we give
from the original German, as follows:

	£	s.	d.
Account of John Neidig—			
Contributed in cash, ...	3	15	0
Hauling stone six and a half days, ...	4	17	0
Breaking stone four days, ...		15	0
Hauling stone two days, ...	1	10	0
Hauling stone and sand one day, ...		10	0
For old lime, 114, ...	5	14	0
Hauling stone and sand one day, ...		15	0
Hauling stone one half day with ox team, ...		7	6
Account of Jacob Gutte (Good)—			
Hauling stone three days, ...	1	5	0
Working at timber one day, ...		3	0
Hauling stone and sand, day and a half, ...	1	2	6
Hauling 18 bushels new lime, ...	1	2	6
Paid cash for boarding, ...	4	11	8
Account of Conrad Lang (Long)—			
Hauling stone one day, ...		15	0
Account of Philip Braun (Brown)—			
Paid in cash, ...	3	15	0
Account of Jacob Stobetz—			
Breaking stone two days, ...		7	6
Account of Ludwig Degen—			
Breaking stone one day, ...		3	9
Account of Jacob Kehr (Keer)—			
Paid in cash, ...	7	10	6
Account of Jacob Eyly (Eli)—			
Jacob Eyly (Eli) and Daniel Bucks (Books) dug the excavation.			
Daniel Books worked three days at the timbers, . .		11	3
Worked at timber one day, ...		3	9
Paid bill for whisky for carpenters, ...		14	0
One gallon of whisky for carpenters, ...		3	9
One quart of oil, ...		2	9
Nine pounds of putty, ...		3	9
Furnishing wooden frames and moldings, ...	1	17	6
Window glass for the house, ...	3	5	0
Gave seventy bushels of lime, ...	4	7	6
Hauling sand one half day, ...		10	0
Paid for framing timber, ...	1	10	0
Paid for twenty-four pounds of nails for the house, .	1	2	0

	£	s.	d.
Gave one gallon of whisky, ...		3	9
Account of Peter Pfanekuche (Pancake)—			
Paid in cash, ...	2	5	0
Account of Leby (Levi) Eberly—			
Paid in cash for the house, ...		7	6
Account of Franz (Frank) Weitmer—			
Paid in cash, ...		15	0
Account of Widow Windnagle (Winagle)—			
Paid in cash, ...	1	10	0

From the foregoing account it is evident that Jacob Eli was the contractor. If any of our readers can locate those whose names are here mentioned we would be glad to know. It is probable that the house when not completed was not paid for, as will appear by the following:

" We, the United Brethren, do hereby promise to pay the respective sums of money placed opposite our names, for the purpose of paying for the meeting-house we have lately constructed, namely:

	£	s.	d.
Johannes Neidig, ...	10	0	0
Felix Landis, ...	10	0	0
Johannes Lichtly (Light), ...	6	0	0
Jacob Kehr, ...	6	0	0
Philip Brawn (Brown), ...	7	10	0
Heinrich Steiner (Stoner), ...	5	0	0
Johannes Stubetz, ...	5	0	0
Jacob Gutte (Good), ...	5	0	0
Ludwig Degan, ...	5	0	0
Christian Ewy (Eby), ...	2	5	0
Heinrich Stentz, ...	2	5	0
Johannes Schnebly (Snavely), ...	2	5	0
Philip Stentz, ...	1	10	0
Peter Pfanekuche (Pancake), ...	2	15	0
Friedrich Pfanekuche (Pancake), ...	1	2	6
Jacob Shultz, ...	1	17	6
Conrad Lang (Long), ...	0	15	0
Widow Windnagle (Winagle), ...	1	10	0
Widow Witmer, ...	1	15	0
Widow Streher (Strayer), ...	0	7	6

E. W. S. P.

THE SOLDIERS' REST.

A Chapter in Our War History.

The full history of the war for the Union and the suppression of the slaveholders' rebellion has never been written. Isolated chapters now and then, prepared by men who participated in that great conflict, have appeared, and the interest seems to be unending. Yet these chiefly refer to the clash of arms and the deadly struggle. Our own Capital City has had an eventful one, from the very hour when the telegraph informed us that Fort Sumter was fired upon down to the funeral march of the martyred Lincoln, as it fell upon the ears of our citizens, and the return of our comrades to the arms of affection which outstretched to welcome the " boys in blue."

And there are other chapters in the history of that Civil war which are not writ in blood, but in the kindly remembrances of soldiers from all portions of the loyal North, of which we shall essay to speak in these brief historic notes.

We often read of charitable deeds done by men of wealth, but I trust I am not wronging these by saying that nine of every ten of such apparently noble acts are done from selfish motives—the desire for honor and praise or popularity. There are grand exceptions, however, and the history of one such I propose to give our readers.

At the outset of the war there were living here two noble men— one of them has passed to his final reward—" Well done, good and faithful servant." The other yet remains with us, beloved and revered by all who know him in this community. Neither of them with a surplus of this world's goods, and yet this which they did is their grandest memorial, and long may they both live in the hearts of the brave men who fought for the Union. I refer to Messrs. Eby Byers and John B. Simon. To them solely belongs the honor which centers around that noble institution, " The Soldier's Rest."

One evening, when the war had been in progress a year, these two gentlemen chanced to meet in the large depot in Harrisburg, when a train arrived from Baltimore, bringing quite a number of sick and wounded soldiers, who were on their way home, some discharged and others on furlough. Some of these soldiers resided east of Harrisburg, some west, and some north. Many of them were obliged to wait many hours for the trains they were to take, while some were so weak and tired as to be scarcely able to proceed on their journey, at all events. There were no places for them to go to, except the hotels, and few of them had money enough to go there, if any at all. A number, therefore, stretched themselves upon the floor of the sitting-room, with their blankets wrapped about them, and passed the time uncomfortably enough, vainly endeavoring to snatch an hour's sleep in the noisy depot.

"Mr. Simon," said Mr. Byers, addressing his friend, "some provision ought to be made for these soldiers. So many of them have to change cars here and wait for trains. The majority, probably, are too ill or too badly wounded to lay on this hard floor with anything like comfort."

"Just what I was thinking," returned Mr. Simon. "I think a hospital, or something of that kind, ought to be instituted near the depot for their temporary repose. How might that be brought about, think you?"

"I scarcely know," rejoined Mr. Byers. "The State or city might do it, if sufficient influence were brought to bear—but then it might be a long time before it could be arranged, and in the meantime these boys would be arriving every day, and suffering for want of some place to rest."

"Were you thinking, then, that we might get up something of the kind?"

"Yes, I think we might. These young men have been fighting our battles for us, and protecting our homes, as it were; and should we spend half we are worth, or even all, we could not do too much for them."

"I perfectly agree, and am ready to co-operate with you," said Mr. Simon. "What do you propose?"

"I will tell you," returned Mr. Byers. "We might, in the first place, by spending much time, and thus delaying the enterprise, get most of the moneyed men of Harrisburg to aid us. But let us lose no time. Suppose we, without ceremony, go to work and put up near the depot a frame building with two or three rooms, and furnish it with comfortable beds, and all necessary articles, and call it a Soldiers' Rest, or something of the kind. Let every soldier passing through stop and make it his home as long as he chooses. The building will not cost very much. Our wives and daughters can spend much of their time there when it is finished, doing the cooking and keeping the place in order. Besides others of Harrisburg will help them. We, too, can spend considerable time there. We will keep plenty for the boys to eat, and there is no doubt others will contribute in that line. I am sure they will. But if they do not we will do all. Are you agreed?"

"Perfectly! I am glad you suggest it. Let us commence the work to-morrow. I will at once superintend the enterprise; and put my men to work. I have window frames and doors, and in a few days a building can be completed."

"Well," said Mr. Byers, "let us divide the expenses equally. I own a lot or two near the other end of the depot; the ground is un-occupied and we can put the building on it. As I do not want to use the ground at all, that will be no expense to me. To-morrow we will go together and get the necessary lumber."

"Very well, I will be ready."

In one week from that time a neat frame building, all finished and painted stood just across the street opposite the south end of the large depot. It was divided into three comfortable rooms. One was a kitchen, another a dining-room, and the third a room containing some twenty or twenty-five beds. Over the door was a board, like that on a guide post, pointing to the weary traveler the way to re-pose, and on it was painted, in large letters,

"SOLDIER'S REST."

Many a weary soldier, faint with his wounds or weak with sick-ness, has spent a few hours or days of delicious repose there. The citizens of Harrisburg were not backward in furnishing various eat-ables, which together with what was provided by the generous founders of the "Soldier's Rest," served as a feast for the worn so-journers, who arrived on almost every train.

There were pleasant faces there, too. Mr. Byers spent most of his time there, as did also Mr. Simon. Mrs. Byers spent two days in the week there, and so did a daughter of Mr. Simon. O, it was cheering to the old soldier, just from the cold and cruel hospitals at Baltimore, Hagerstown, or Washington, to step into such a place as this and find himself surrounded not only with plenty for the hungry stom-ach, not only with the warm stoves in cold weather, not only with snowy beds for the weary limbs to repose on, but also with happy, smiling, cheerful faces, that spoke a silent but eloquent welcome!

One day, among others that arrived by the Baltimore train, there came a pale, wasted, emaciated man, of middle age, whom disease had rendered so weak that he was scarcely able to walk or stand. Mr. Byers and another gentleman carried him into the "Soldier's Rest" and gave him a seat near the stove, for it was a cold day in winter, and they had had rather poor fires in the cars.

"Will you not lie down and take a sleep?" Mr. Byers asked.

"No, no—I'm so cold! Only let me sit here by the fire?"

" What is your name ?"

" My name is Charles Smith. I served in the Eighth Pennsylvania Reserves, and I live in Pittsburgh."

Mr. Byers kept a record of the names of all those entertained at the Soldiers' Rest, and as he wrote poor Smith's name in the register, and glanced at his pale face and wasted, trembling hands, he feared it might become his sad duty to write to his friends in Pittsburgh and announce his death, for it did sometimes happen that soldiers arrived there so prostrated—having through their anxiety to get home started too soon on their journey—that they lingered a day and died.

" I always take down the names, Smith," said Mr. Byers, " in case we may want to hear from each other hereafter. By all means let me hear from you when you get home. What is your residence ?"

The soldier told him the street and number in Pittsburgh.

"Have you a family ?"

" Yes," returned Smith, with his face brightened with a smile at the thought of so soon meeting the loved ones. " I have a wife, and two such dear little children ! O, they will be so glad to see me !"

" They will, indeed," returned Mr. Byers, good humoredly—for he felt that the poor fellow needed cheering—and I'll tell you what would be a pleasure to me, Smith."

" What is that ?"

" I would just like to be standing behind the door, and none of you know I was there, that I might see the happy meeting."

The poor fellow was so pleased with this idea that he actually laughed outright, and the tears were seen starting from his eyes— tears that came from a tender, loving, overflowing heart. He tried to speak, but could not, and turned away his face to hide what some might call his 'weakness.' It was a weakness that God placed within him and nearly all human beings. Weak, and drooping, and neglected as he had been of late in the cheerless hospital, the comfortable room about him, the sight of the pleasant faces of those in attendance, and the kind, cheerful voice of Mr. Byers, as he pictured the home he should so soon reach, were too much for him, and he wept as some poor, lone little boy might have done under similar circumstances.

Smith was now pretty comfortable, and, telling him dinner would soon be ready, Mr. Byers left him for the time, and gave his attention to others. After putting several of the tired boys to bed, he busied himself in the dining room, as usual, helping to prepare the repast.

When dinner was ready, Mr. Byers came out to announce the fact, and to look after Smith. He was surprised to discover that the invalid soldier had got off his chair and was lying upon the floor very close to the warm stove, in a kind of uneasy sleep.

" Come, Smith," said Byers, " are you going to sleep there?   Let me put you in one of the beds; you will be much more comfortable there."

"Oh no," murmured Smith; "only let me lie here—I feel so good."

" But you would feel much better in bed."

" No, no; let me lie here.   I am getting warm now."

" But I will draw a bed to the stove for you, and will be warmer still."

" No, I don't want to go to bed.   I must go home on that evening train."

" No, you must not think of starting this evening.   You are too weak, and it is a long ride to Pittsburgh.   You must stay with us two or three days.   You are welcome, you know.   Come, get into bed, and I will get you something to eat."

" O, I can't eat.   Don't say eat to me."

" But you must.   I will get you something that will tempt you to eat.   Come, here is a bed close to the stove," and Mr. Byers drew one of the beds from the wall and placed it near the stove.   " Let me help you up."

Smith reluctantly allowed himself to be lifted up and assisted into the bed, Mr. Byers first removing his coat and shoes for him.   He then got some delicacies for him, and succeeded in persuading him to eat.   Smith soon grew more lively and cheerful, and seemed determined to go to Pittsburgh on the evening train.   Mr. Byers would not hear of it, and finally persuaded him to remain until the next morning, at least.

By next evening Smith had revived considerably, and his impatience would allow him to remain no longer.   As he was determined to go, Mr. Byers, who spent the next day at the " Soldiers' Rest," helped him to the cars, and bidding him to write and let him know how he was getting along.   He promised to do so, and with many expressions of gratitude for the kind treatment he had received, he bade Mr. Byers farewell.

But his system was too much prostrated by chronic disease, and five days later Mr. Byers received a letter from his wife—now his widow—informing him that Smith had reached home in tolerably good spirits, lingered a few days and died.   She said in her letter that during his last moments he had raved incoherently about the " Soldiers' Rest " in Harrisburg, and imagined himself still there. Before losing his reason he had given Mr. Byers' address, and begged her in case of his death, to write to him, and say that he remembered him with gratitude in his last moments.

This is only one incident and a true one—among many that happened in connection with the "Soldiers' Rest." I give it to illustrate the character of that pleasant little institution, and of those whose kind hearts suggested it. Messrs. Simon and Byers, the noble, generous, and unselfish men who founded it, devoted most of their time to it till the end of the war, and many a weary soldier has tarried in Harrisburg, and enjoyed delicious repose at the "Soldiers' Rest."

Readers, this is no fancy sketch. It is plain truth. I have too poor an opinion of a selfish world to give credit where it is not due. What our neighbors, Messrs. Simon and Byers, did, reflected great credit upon our Capital City. We were charged during the war with being mercenary; but I say it here without fear of contradiction, that no northern town or city did more for the soldiers—sick, wounded and dying—going to or returning from the battle fields of the Republic, than Harrisburg.

NOTES AND QUERIES—CXLIX.

CONNER.—From a notice in the *Carlisle Gazette* in 1788, we learn that David Conner resided prior to June of that year in East Pennsboro' township, Cumberland county, thence removing to Harrisburg. The notice concludes "Enquire of Robert Patterson, tavern-keeper, sign of the 'White Horse.'" This was the father of Commodore David Conner, who was born at Harrisburg.

GILLILAND—BERRYHILL.—James McCreight, of Hanover, in writing to his attorney at Lancaster, Jasper Yeates, November 30, 1771, says: " S'R : These are to inform you that Andrew Berryhill with his Brother-in-law, Hugh Gilliland, came to Robert Wallace & me, & hath agreed with us to pay the costs upon Hugh Gilliland's Bond to you, and to lift his Bond. S'r, I sent your Receipt along with The Bearer, John Killcrease [Gilchrist] & I would Request the favour of you to send me another Receipt for John Gilliland's Bond, that is if you see cause to give Hugh Gilliland's Bond. I understand John Killcrease is Impowered to lift s'd Bond. S'r, these are from your Humble Serv't. JAMES McCREIGHT."

What is known concerning Hugh Gilliland? Did he not remove to Western Pennsylvania after the Revolution?

OUR ABORIGINES.

NAMES OF TREES, SHRUBS, &C., IN THE LANGUAGE OF THE ONON-
DAGA INDIANS.

[The following contribution to our aboriginal history is translated
from the original MS. (German), by John W. Jordan, of the Historical Society of Pennsylvania. It is scarcely necessary to add that for
the original we are indebted to the learned and erudite Moravian
missionary, Rev. John Heckewelder.]

Garontahogo,	Trees
Ochnechta,	White Pine
Ochnechtoja,	Pitch Pine
Anohnta,	Spruce
Awohagarat,	Chestnut
Otgarhatenniato,	Chestnut Oak
Togehha,	White Oak
Gorontatshe,	Black Oak
Garichto,	Spanish Oak
Gannowahoga,	Swamp Oak
Anawaratos,	Upland Hickory
Otshtik,	Bitter Hickory
Annunogara,	(Shellbark) Hickory
Oschqueowane,	Poplar
Iozgarha,	Beech
Ohosir,	Linden
Osochqua,	Black Walnut
Osaquaquenoni,	Black Walnut Wood
Itewa,	Butternut
Gassoquannionta,	Hazel
Tschiorachsar,	Ironwood
Ganneroch,	White Ash
Esshat,	Water Ash
Gechnas,	Water Beech
Onejar,	Box Tree
Onerachto,	Laurel
Ochnegoehsojah,	Birch
Wachta,	Sugar Maple
Awohannequat,	Maple
Anaungwe,	Locust
Ohx,	Red Maple

Ogarannequat, ... White (Silver) Maple
Toscheli, ... Alder
Sajesegoa, ... Mulberry
Ehri, ... Wild Birch
Ganunquaggeracho, ... Fox Grape
Hasirok, ... Thorn
Swannaggeracho, ... Sassafras
Ochjaquenoni, ... Wild Plum
Taraquitit Tgota, ... Sumac
Onatoaoh, ... Currant
Atanochwerhoni, ... Peach Tree
Garhattagehha, ... Blackberry Bush
Wanatquas, ... Red Willow
[used as a substitute for tobacco.]
Orhechsgoa, ... Thistle
Ganeochuntesha, ... Strawberry Vine
Owahecht, ... The Strawberry
Oztokqui, ... Whortleberry
Tothuntacto, ... Raspberry
Rasek, ... Elder
Anahhozte, ... May Apple
Ozzononta, ... Weeds

COL. THOMAS FORSTER.

[The following facts concerning Col. Thomas Forster, a native of Paxtang and grandfather of J. Montgomery Forster, Esq., of this city, are culled from notes relating to the history of Erie county, prepared by Mr. Russell, of Erie. It is known that Colonel Forster went to Erie as the agent of the "Harrisburg and Presqu' Isle Land Company," remaining there until his death.]

The district or port of Presqu' Isle embraces the south coast of Lake Erie, which is within the boundaries of the State of Pennsylvania, and has a shore of about forty-five miles, the principal shipping point of which is Erie. Freeport and Elk Creek have always done a small trade in lumber, timber, &c. This district was organized in 1801, and Col. Thomas Forster was appointed Collector of Customs for the Port of Presqu' Isle by President John Adams. Colonel Forster was continued in the office until his death, in 1836, a period of thirty-five years. He was in politics what was styled a Federalist, and during the various changes of administration to Whig, Anti-Masonry, &c.,

he remained independent of the new parties, but never would permit himself to be called a Democrat. The office was well and faithfully attended to by him or his deputies.

When the Presidential election of 1828 resulted in electing General Jackson to the Presidency, the Democrats thought it would not do to have the old colonel retain the office and not be a Democrat, but none dared to make the attempt to have him displaced. The colonel had for some years as his deputy, Thomas McConkey, a most excellent man, and who faithfully attended to the duties of the office in every respect. He was a Jackson man, and that was satisfactory to the Democratic party, but the old colonel would not come into their ranks, which greatly excited their displeasure. After the re-election of General Jackson, in 1832, D. C. Barrett, who had recently joined the Democratic ranks, was sent on to Harrisburg and Washington to make a clean sweep of every man in office not a Democrat. After being gone some weeks he returned with a commission for himself from Governor Wolf, as State's Attorney, and one for Robert Cochran, as postmaster in place of James Hughes, removed, but it was impossible for him to get a collector appointed in place of Colonel Forster, the influence of Thomas H. Sill and Judge Baldwin was too strong. Mr. Hamot, who considered himself the leader of the Democratic party in this county, was non-plussed, and had no hesitation in asserting that Colonel Forster *must* become a Democrat. He was bail for him on his bond to the United States, and he must come into the party lines. A formal meeting was held by the principal leaders of the party in the back room of the Erie Bank, on Fourth street, east of French, and Colonel Forster was sent for to attend the meeting. After a free interchange of opinion a resolution was offered by one of the faithful that Colonel Forster is and will hereafter be a Democrat.

THE WETZEL FAMILY

Of Pennsylvania and West Virginia.

Martin and Jacob Wetzel came from Switzerland to Pennsylvania about the year 1747. Their mother died on board the vessel a few days after they were at sea, and upon landing at Philadelphia they were deserted by their step-father. Martin, at the age of fourteen, and Jacob at twelve, were sold for their passage. The elder brother afterwards settled in Oley township, Berks county, while the younger, Jacob, located in Hereford township, same county, where they were residing in 1759.

MARTIN WETZEL, born about 1733, died in 1822, and was buried in the graveyard of Zion's Lutheran church, on Fourth and Chestnut streets, Harrisburg. He resided for a long period near the town, on a farm, which he owned and left to his descendants. He served in the war of the Revolution and participated in the battles of Long Island, Brandywine, and Germantown. He was a man of good judgment, of strict integrity and honor. He married about 1772, a Miss Bertolet, of Oley township, daughter of one of the Huguenot settlers of Berks. We have no further record of her. They had one son :

> i. *Abraham,* b. Nov. 15, 1773, in Oley township, Berks county; d. July 9, 1846, in Harrisburg, and there buried. He was twice married; first, to a Miss Deffebaugh, and had issue; and secondly, August 2, 1810, by Rev. F. D. Peterson, Mary Reynard, daughter of Henry and Elizabeth Reynard, born May 16, 1786; died February 16, 1860; leaving the following children :
>> 1. *Elizabeth,* b. Nov., 1811; d. 1864; m. Thomas McCallen, who d. in 1852.
>> 2. *Martin,* b. May 27, 1817; m. Elizabeth Parthemore; resides in Milford Center, O.
>> 3. *Mary,* b. 1825; d. 1828.

JACOB WETZEL, shortly after the Bouquet expedition to the Muskingum in 1764, where terms were dictated to the savage tribes of the Ohio, removed from Berks county to the western country, subsequently to near Wheeling. He was among the earliest settlers in the " backwoods." It is not known how long he lived there, but one day while his eldest son Martin was out hunting, and another son John was on an errand to the nearest fort or block house, a party of Indians surrounded the house, rushed in, and killed, tomahawked, and scalped old Jacob Wetzel, his wife and all his small children. Two of his sons, Lewis and Jacob, being smart, active boys, were spared and made prisoners. Could the Indians have had a prescience of the sad havoc these two youths would have made of their race, instead of carrying them off as prisoners, they would have carried their scalps to their towns. It is not the province of this sketch to give an account of the escape of these boys, nor of their subsequent careers, neither of their brothers, Martin and John. Their frontier life, made up of tragedies—fierce encounters with the red men—reads like a thrilling romance of the dark ages. The times in which they lived—the circumstances surrounding them—their grievances at the hands of the brutal savages—made them the fearful scouts and dare-devils they proved to be. Our object has simply been to connect them with the early settlers of the same name in this locality.   E. W. S. P.

CONEWAGO BURYING GROUND.

One hundred and fifty years ago Conewago Presbyterian church stood in a valley of that name, and not far from Little Conewago creek, the dividing line between Lancaster and Dauphin counties. The location is four or five miles east of Middletown, a quarter of a mile north of the " Harrisburg and Lancaster turnpike," and within the same distance of the little village of Gainsburg.

On visiting this spot a short time ago, in company with Hon. J. B. Rutherford, of Paxtang Valley, we found in a wheat field on the farm now owned and occupied by John Allwine a plot of uncultivated ground, about 27x85 feet. It is not enclosed. This is what remains of

THE CONEWAGO BURYING GROUND.

At one end of the plat there are the remains of a stone foundation—or, perhaps, the walls of a stone building—making an enclosure of about 10x18 feet. The stones are laid in mortar. On the southeast side the wall is still about two feet high—so high as to suggest the idea that the building may have been of stone; and the dimensions are such as to suggest the thought of the old-time " study house."

Within this enclosure stand several wild cherry trees and black haw bushes. The balance of the plat is in sod, with several sassafras trees (eight or ten inches in diameter) growing at the further end. Blackberry bushes are scattered all over it.

A number of small undressed stones are in position as markers of graves. Near the wall, above mentioned, we found lying prostrate two entire headstones containing inscriptions. These are all there are on the ground. Scattered around are fragments of two others.

The older of the headstones is slate, and the inscription is in good state of preservation. In word and form it is as follows:

Here lyeth ye | Body of John | Dunbar, who | Departed.this life | Oct. ye 5th, 1745 | Aged 51 years.

The other is Hummelstown brownstone. Time and the action of the seasons and the elements have told much more severely on it. Some of the letters are very indistinct, but the inscription may be made out by even a less skillful than " Old Mortality," and is as follows:

In Memory of | George Allison, | Late husband of | Frances Allison. | He Decd. March 29, | 1790. Aged 61 years. | Also | Wm. Allison, son of | the said Dec'd. He de- | parted this life July | 18, 1792. Aged | 5 years.

We speak of these as the days of "Woman to the front!" But just think of it—an inscription on a tombstone of a hundred years ago reading, "Late husband of." Suggestive, that!!

About a hundred yards northwest of the burying ground is the spring at which pious men and women, and young men and maidens, a hundred and fifty years ago quenched their thirst, and around which they devoutly discussed topics, sacred and secular, while the pastor was in the study house during intermission. The spring does not look inviting now. Its surface is covered with a repulsive scum of slimy looking moss, and its flow is clogged by rubbish, decaying vegetation and moss. How changed everything.   w. a. w.

NOTES AND QUERIES.—CL.

PATTERSON.—Prior to the close of the Revolution, Robert, James, William and Peter Patterson, brothers, removed from this locality to Western Pennsylvania. Robert settled in Westmoreland county and the others in what is now Fayette county. James Patterson was a captain in the war of 1812 under General Harrison. What is known concerning the ancestry of these Pattersons?

THE NEW JERSEY LOYALISTS.

A Record of the New Jersey Loyalists in the war of the Revolution has been made the subject of a most excellent monograph by Gen. William S. Stryker, Adjutant General of New Jersey, to whom we are indebted for the pamphlet. Few persons would believe that during the struggle for independence New Jersey furnished the King's army with six battalions of volunteers, numbering not far from three thousand men. And yet such was the case. This was only equalled by the Colonies of New York, Virginia and the Carolinas. General Stryker's sketch is a valuable contribution to our Revolutionary history, and the biographical notes of the loyalist officers is of great interest. Although our own State of Pennsylvania cannot boast of organized loyalists, yet there were many prominent persons conspicuous during the Provincial era—who gave "aid and comfort" to the Crown during the struggle for liberty, and a record of these would be an acceptable contribution to her history. The English and Welsh Quakers were non-combatants—while the German and Scotch-Irish were patriotic, and as will be seen by reference to the records of our State swelled the army of Washington. *They could always be relied upon.* The "Revolt of the Pennsylvania Line" has never been properly understood, and never will be if our history of the Revolutionary struggle is continued to be written by those who do not understand our people, or if they do, are determined not to do justice. General Stryker's researches into the history of his State during the struggle for independence deserve all praise. He is careful and faithful, and this last contribution commends itself to all. He is to be congratulated for his continued efforts in preserving from oblivion much of the entertaining history of the Jerseys.

THE AGNEWS OF MARSH CREEK.

Several years since inquiry was made concerning the settlement of the Agnew family. The following paper recently coming into our possession gives the information:

PHILADELPHIA, *6 April, 1762.*

To Richard Peters, Esq.:

The Case of James Agnew as follows, vizt:

In August, 1738, I, the s'd James Agnew, went in search of a Tract of Land to Marsh Creek, then in Lancaster, now in York County; That I viewed a Piece of Land on a Run called Lick Run, which Runs into said Creek, which I marked out in order to apply for a Warrant and pay for the s'd Land.

The Winter following I applied to you for a Warrant to survey the same Land for my use, But you informed me the Office for granting Warrants to survey the said Land was not oppened, But that I might apply to the Honorable the Proprietor, who was then in Phila., which I accordingly did, But the Proprietor directed me to you. That I returned to you from the Proprietor and you told me you could not then grant me a Warrant, But ask me where the Land Lay, and what Quantity I wanted, which I informed you; and then you told me that you would make an Entry of it, and you took up a Bound Book, and wrote in it which I suppose was an Entry concerning my applications as afores'd.

The Summer following I went with my Family to the s'd Land, where I made Considerable Buildings and other Improvements, and Dwelt with my Family ever since. Soon after there arose a Dispute about the Temporary Line, for which reason I thought not to apply for a Warrant until the Dispute was settled. That since the Line has been settled there has been no access to the s'd Office for a Warrant for the s'd Land. That I was always and now am willing to pay for the same Land and leave the Price to your Honour.

James Agnew.

Indorsed: James Agnew, case of his Plantation at Marsh Creek.

THE EARLY BAR OF CUMBERLAND COUNTY.

The Bar of Cumberland county began with the first courts in 1750. This was under George the Second. Many of the early justices who were commissioned by the King (through the Governor of the Province) never appeared upon the bench. Those who presided, prior to the Revolution, were as follows:

Samuel Smith, from July, 1750, to Oct., 1757.

Francis West, from Oct., 1757, to 1759.

John Armstrong, Francis West and Hermanus Alricks, Jan., 1760.

Francis West, July, 1760.

John McKnight, Oct., 1760.

John Armstrong, April, 1761.

James Galbraith, April, 1762.

John Armstrong, July, 1762.

John Byers, March, 1763.

Thomas Wilson, April, 1763.

John Armstrong, from Oct., 1763, to April, 1776.

These presiding justices sat with associates, whom we have not mentioned. The judges rotated irregularly, and without any discoverable rule of regularity, at brief intervals, until Oct., 1763, when John Armstrong, of historic memory, occupied the bench for a period of nearly thirteen years. The justices from the beginning of the Revolution until the adoption of the Constitution of 1790 were:

John Rannalls and Associates, Jan., 1776,—Jan., 1785.

Sam'l Laird and Associates, Jan., 1785,—Jan., 1786.

Thomas Beale and Associates, April, 1786.

John Jordan and Associates, July, 1786,—Oct., 1791.

In Oct., 1791, appeared Thomas Smith, the first of the judges under the Constitution.

PROSECUTING ATTORNEYS FOR THE CROWN.

The " Prosecutors for the Crown " were:

George Ross, afterwards a signer of the Declaration of Independence, 1751 to 1764.

Robert Magaw, 1765–6.

Jasper Yeates, 1770.

Benjamin Chew, who was a member of the Provincial Council and afterwards, during the Revolution a loyalist, was, at this time, 1759–68, Attorney General, and prosecuted many of the criminal cases, from 1759 to 1769, in the courts in Cumberland county.

After 1770 the names of those "who for our Lord the King, in this part prosecuteth" are not mentioned, but only the old form "*Qui Sequiter Dom Rege Similitur*," or "Attorney General similitur."

EARLIEST PRACTITIONERS.

Of the very earliest members of the bar there are no records of admission, the first of which is William Maclay, in 1760. Before this time, however, and after, the names of practitioners occur according to the following dates : George Ross, 1752; James Smith, 1754; Robert Magaw, 1762; Samuel Johnston, 1763; Jasper Yeates, 1763; the name of Wilson, 1763; George Campbell, 1768; James Wilson, 1770; George Stevenson, 1770; Thos. Hartley (once in 1771, frequently years afterwards) ; David Sample, 1770.

It is a surprising fact that three of the above lawyers, who practiced at the bar of Cumberland county at this early date, were afterwards signers of the Declaration of Independence. These were Thomas Smith, of York ; George Ross, of Lancaster, and James Wilson, of Carlisle. George Ross was but twenty-two years of age when he first appeared as the attorney for the Crown in our courts, and it is also an interesting fact that this period of his life seems not to have been known to any of the writers of the signers of the Declaration of Independence. In a letter written by James Smith from Philadelphia to his wife, dated "Congress Chamber, September 4, 1778," he says: "I breakfasted with Mr. Ross at Mrs. House's." . . . . . I am laying my account upon returning about the 10th of next month, to be able to attend Carlisle and York courts." [See Sanderson's Lives of the Signers, vol. vii., p. 232.] The lawyers admitted to the bar from 1760 to the Revolution, were : William Maclay, 1760 ; Thomas Zennens, 1763; Nicholas Waln, 1763; James Sayre, 1765; Willia n Sweeny, 1765; Robert Galbraith, 1766 ; Andrew Ross, 1770 ; John Hubley, 1770; Col. Thomas Hartley appears 1771 ; James Lucans, Col. David Grier, 1771 ; Casper Wetzel, 1771; David Espy, 1771 ; George North, 1771 ; Andrew Scott, 1771; John Reily, 1773; Capt. John Steel, 1773 (son of " Parson " Steel); John Magill, 1773 ; George Ross, Jr., 1773 ; David McMahan, 1774 ; J. T. Armstrong, 1774 ; Lewis Bush, 1776.

Some of these men whom we have mentioned were distinguished in the Indian wars and in the Revolution. No less than three were signers of the Declaration of Independence; others held high political or judicial positions, but the "iniquity of oblivion has blindly scattered her poppy" over the memory of most of them, and of none can it be said, by any man now living: "Alas! poor Yorick! I knew him, Horatio."　　　　　　　　　　　　　　BENNETT BELLMAN.

CONTRIBUTIONS TO PENNSYLVANIA BIOGRAPHY—II.

DAVIDSON, SAMUEL.

Samuel Davidson, son of George Davidson, was born in 1728 in the Cumberland Valley. His father was among the earliest settlers at Carlisle, where he engaged in merchandizing. About the year 1769 Samuel removed to Bedford, where he took a prominent part in public affairs. From 1770 to 1773 he served as treasurer of the county of Bedford, and in 1774 was commissioned one of the Provincial justices. He was chosen a deputy to the Provincial Conference of July 15, 1774, and appointed by the Conference held at Carpenters' Hall in June, 1776, of which he was a member, one of the judges of the election for Bedford county to choose delegates to the first Constitutional Convention of the State. During the Revolutionary struggle he was colonel of one of the associated battalions of the county, and did effective service on the frontiers in protecting the farmers against the wily savages of the Ohio. Scattered through the Provincial Records and Archives are numerous references of this worthy of Revolutionary times. Colonel Davidson was continued in commission as one of the justices by the Supreme Executive Council, November 13, 1778, and served additional terms as treasurer from 1783 to 1795. He was coroner in 1787, and was a member of the Council of Censors in 1783–84. In July 1798, he was appointed one of the Commissioners for the State of Pennsylvania, under the act to provide for the valuation of lands and houses, and an enumeration of slaves, for the Eighth Division. He died at Bedford, June 11, 1803, aged fifty-five years, more than half of his life being spent in public affairs. He left descendants.

HORSFIELD, TIMOTHY.

Timothy Horsfield, whose name so frequently occurs in the records of the Province of Pennsylvania, in connection with the Indian wars and treaties between 1755 and 1765, was born in April of 1708, in

Liverpool, O. E. In 1725 he emigrated to the Province of New York, and joined his brother Israel on Staten Island, with whom he learned the business of butcher. In 1730 they attended the New York markets, and four years later Timothy became a freeholder in the city of New York. He married, in 1731, Mary, daughter of John Doughty, butcher of Brooklyn. The brothers in 1736 leased two stalls in Old Slip Market, corner Old Slip and Pearl streets, where they did a large and profitable business, especially with the Government. Although a member of the Church of England he attended Whitefield's preaching, where he made the acquaintance of Bishop Boehler and Nitschmann, of the Moravian Church, and we find his name enrolled among the members of their congregation in New York as early as 1744. In 1749 he removed with his family to Bethlehem, Pa. On 9th of June, 1752, he was commissioned by Governor Hamilton a justice of the peace, and on 11th of July, 1763, he was commissioned colonel of the forces to be raised in Northampton county for the protection of the frontiers. This latter commission he soon resigned, and was succeeded by Major Clayton, who was commissioned by Governor Penn 14th of November, 1763. In consequence he lost his justiceship after serving twelve years. He died in Bethlehem 9th of March, 1773, and his wife on October 14th following. Five children survived him.   J. W. J.

PARSONS, WILLIAM.

William Parsons' place and date of birth is unknown to the writer, but he was married in 1722, his wife being a native of Saxony, born in 1699, emigrated to America 1717, and died at Bethlehem in March of 1773. We find him residing in Philadelphia prior to 1722, a shoemaker by trade, and a member of Franklin's Junta Club, in which he passed for "a man having a profound knowledge of mathematics." Between 1734 and 1746 he was librarian of the City Library. About 1743 he was appointed by the Penns their Surveyor General. Ill health compelling him to resign this laborious position in June of 1748, he removed to Lancaster. Here in 1749 he was commissioned justice of the peace. Summoned by the Proprietaries to fill the office in the seat of justice in the newly erected county of Northampton, he removed thither. He held the office of prothonotary, clerk of the courts, recorder, clerk of the commissioners, and justice of the peace. December 29, 1755, he was appointed major of all troops to be raised in Northampton county, with Easton as his headquarters. "As I think," writes James Hamilton, from Easton, "it will be for the good of the service in general that the troops raised in Northampton county should be under the care and superintendence of a field officer, I have, with that view, in virtue of the power granted me, appointed William Parsons, Esq., to be major of said troops." His immediate command, however, was a Town Guard of twenty-four men stationed at Easton. He died at Easton in December of 1757. Much of Parsons' correspondence is in the archives of the State, and valuable for its historical information. J. W. J.

NOTES AND QUERIES.—CLI.

GIRTY.—Thomas Girty, on the 3d of January, 1758, was by the court of Cumberland county bound an apprentice to John Armstrong, Esq., for six years. By reference to *Notes and Queries* (No. cxlii) it will be seen that Thomas Girty had been released from Indian captivity by General Armstrong at the Kittanning. He was a brother of the notorious Simon Girty.

WILKINS.—Peter Wilkins, of Cumberland county, died in November, 1752, leaving a wife Rachel, and children as follows:
    i. James, b. 1735.
    ii. William, b. 1737.
    iii. Margaret, b. 1739.
    iv. Peter, b. 1743.
The widow in 1762 had become the wife of John Reynolds; while the daughter, Margaret, had married James Jack. What is known of this family of Wilkins?

AN OLD LAND SUIT.

[From an old paper in the handwriting of Judge Yeates, we quote the following record of a case in the "Dauphin County Circuit Court, November 5, 1804," "Lessee of William Foulke *vs.* Robert Goudy." It was for ejectment from land in Middle Paxtang township. Messrs. Fisher and Duncan were the attorneys for the plaintiff, while Messrs. Montgomery and Smith were the lawyers for Goudy. The evidence in the case is interesting.]

Samuel Cochran testified: That in 1769 Simpson wrought above the Narrows; in 1770 he built a shop on this disputed Land & wrought there for many years; then he built a dwelling house & a stable, and cleared some small quantity of Land; lived 18 or 20 years on the Land; the Land not worth the Improvements. X. I knew one John Smith living above the run a small distance; but he did not live there before Simpson came there; I never heard that Smith & Simpson lived under Wm. Foulke.

John Bell: Simpson settled in 1770. X. No body lived there before Simpson, & I have known it 50 years. Simpson agreed to relinquished the 15 as. and took a new Warr't for the adjoining woodland.

Thomas Forster: Gallaher called "fool Tom" and "mad Tom."

Ann Thomas: Foulke asked Simpson why he did not stand to the judgment of the men; he said he wouldn't stand to the judgment of any men that did not please me; & I told you then it would be 30 years before it would be ended; Mr. Foulke desired me to take notice of what was said; he said he had offered the £40 and he would not take it. X. Sam. Cochran & Mr. Hatfield were by.

Charles Stewart: In 1769 Jno. Smith asked me to help him build a cabin; Foulke helped us; In 1770 Simpson told me he had got Liberty from Foulke to build a cabin there, & told me the terms, but I have forgot it.

John Bell: Smith's was built after Simpson settled there.

Samuel Cochran: Smith's cabin was raised after Simpson settled there; Gallaher had his senses and was honest as any man.

Joshua Elder, Esq.: John Gallaher was a sensible man and an honest man.

CUMBERLAND VALLEY WORTHIES.

Ante-Revolutionary Justices.

SMITH, SAMUEL.

Samuel Smith was born in the north of Ireland about the year 1700. It is not known when he came to Pennsylvania and settled in Hopewell township, Cumberland county. He was the first named in commission as a justice of the peace, the date being March 10, 1749–50, and hence presided at the first court which was held at Shippensburg on the 24th of July, 1750. Little is known of his subsequent history. He died in October, 1780, at the age of four score, leaving a large family.

WEST, FRANCIS.

Francis West, son of Francis West, of English parentage, was born in the north of Ireland about the year 1730. His father emigrated to Pennsylvania in 1738 and settled in Cumberland county. The son received a fair education, and seems to have been a resident of the town of Carlisle shortly after the organization of the county. He was commissioned one of the Provincial justices of the peace July 13, 1757, and from October of that year until 1759 presided over the courts. About 1771 he removed to Shearman's Valley, where he resided until his death, which occurred in December, 1783. His children were *William, Edward, Ann,* who married Col. George Gibson, of the Revolution, and a daughter, who married a Mitchell.

ARMSTRONG, JOHN.

John Armstrong, son of James Armstrong, was born in 1725 in the north of Ireland. His parents came to Pennsylvania prior to 1740, and settled west of the Susquehanna. When the French and Indian war came on John Armstrong was commissioned a captain in the Provincial service in January, 1756, and on May 11, 1756, lieutenant colonel of the Second battalion. He commanded the expedition to the Kittanning on the Allegheny the same year and succeeded in destroying that nest of red savages, in which he was severely wounded. For this service the corporation of Philadelphia gave him a vote of thanks, a medal and a piece of plate. In 1758–1759 he was in command of the First battalion of the Pennsylvania troops, participating in the Forbes expedition, and for which service he shared in the distribution of land by the Proprietaries. When the war of the Revolution began, Congress commissioned him a brigadier general in the Pennsylvania Line March 1, 1776, serving with distinction during the Jersey campaign of that year. Owing to dissatisfaction in regard to rank he resigned April 4, 1777, and returned to his home at Carlisle. He was chosen by the General Assembly November 20, 1778, a member of the Continental Congress, and again November 12, 1779. He is credited with similar service in 1787 and 1788, but that honor was conferred upon his son John. General Armstrong died at Carlisle March 9, 1795, in the 78th year of his age. The *Carlisle Gazette* of March 11, 1795, in an extended obituary held this language: "It may be truly said of this worthy citizen that his life was eminently useful and exemplary. There are but few characters in which so many amiable and shining qualities are found united. His easy and engaging manners, his sympathy for the distressed, and, above all, his unfeigned piety, gained him the love and esteem of all true judges of merit. He was ever the zealous friend of *liberty, learning* and *religion;* the advancement of which in the world seemed to be the grand object of his habitual wishes and prayers. His mind was abundantly stored with useful knowledge, especially of the religious kind. He possessed a very clear and sound judgment; and had acquired the habit of communicating his ideas on every topic, in an easy, flowing and perspicuous manner. . . . . . His talents in the military line have been abundantly conspicuous; and the world has been long acquainted with his spirited enterprises against the savage tribes, at an early period of life; and his exertions and sacrifices in the common cause of American liberty and independence."

ALRICKS, HERMANUS.

Hermanus Alricks, son of Wessels Alricks, was born in Philadelphia about 1727. His ancestor came over with the Dutch settlers on the Delaware in 1658, and was a man of note in the Colony. Hermanus Alricks resided some years in his native city, where he was engaged in mercantile pursuits. Just prior to the organization of the county of Cumberland, he removed thither, and was appointed its first justice March 10, 1750, an office he filled until his death. He was chosen the first member of the Provincial Assembly from that county, and subsequently commissioned clerk of the court, &c. He was a man of influence in the valley west of the Susquehanna. He died at Carlisle on the 14th of December, 1772.

McKNIGHT, JOHN.

John McKnight was born about 1730, in the Province of Ulster, Ireland. He came to America in early life, and settled in what was afterwards Middleton township, Cumberland county. He was a captain in the Forbes expedition of 1758, and again in active service in 1759. He served in the commission as one of the Provincial justices as early as 1757, and in October, 1760, was presiding over the county courts. He was an elder in Middle Spring Presbyterian church. He died in April, 1768, leaving a wife Mary, and children, *John, David, Mary,* and *Jean.* He was a man of unblemished reputation.

GALBRAITH, JAMES.

James Galbraith, son of Andrew Galbraith, was born in Donegal township, now Lancaster county, about the year 1725. He was brought up a farmer, and between 1745 and 1750 settled in the Cumberland Valley, East Pennsboro' township. He was commissioned one of the earliest justices of the peace, and in October, 1761, was presiding over the county courts. He was chosen to the General Assembly in 1762, and afterwards continued as a justice of the peace. He was an active patriot, and April 10, 1777, appointed county lieutenant. He died in 1790.

***

BYERS, JOHN.

John Byers, son of David Byers, came from the north of Ireland, where he was born in 1715, to the Province of Pennsylvania in 1740. He was at first located in Donegal township, Lancaster county, but afterwards settled west of the Susquehanna, where he purchased three hundred acres of land on Prospect Hill, five miles west of Carlisle, near a large spring and stream flowing from it to the Conedoguinet, now known as Alexander's. During the French and Indian war he was commissioned a captain in Col. James Burd's Second Pennsylvania battalion, April 27, 1758, and was in Forbes' expedition of that year. He was treasurer of the county 1758–59, and served as one of the Provincial justices from July 13, 1757, to the Revolution. During the Revolutionary struggle he seems to have been of unusual prominence and influence in aiding the patriot cause. On the 4th of February, 1778, he was appointed to superintend the storing of flour and other provisions on the west of the Susquehanna. He was a member of the Supreme Executive Council from November 30, 1781, to November 3, 1784, and an efficient member of that illustrious body. Colonel Byers died at Carlisle, on Wednesday, February 13, 1788, in the 73d year of his age, and the *Gazette* states "and on Friday his remains were interred in the old burying ground belonging to the Presbyterian church of Carlisle, of which he had long been a very respectable member . . . . . He was a very good and useful member of society, bore his last illness with Christian patience and resignation, and has left this world, in the active scenes of which he was often engaged, with the character of a steady friend to liberty, virtue and religion." He left several daughters; *Mary* died unmarried in 1804, *Jane* married an Alexander, while others married into the families of Carothers and Henderson.

***

WILLSON, THOMAS.

Thomas Willson was a native of Ireland, where he was born in 1725. He came to Pennsylvania with his parents about the year 1740, who settled in what subsequently was Middleton township, Cumberland county. He was a farmer, and for a long period engaged in merchandizing. He was on the first commission of justices, 1749–50, and in April, 1763, was presiding over the county courts. By marriage he was related to the Hoges and other prominent families of the valley, and was a man of influence. He died in October, 1772.

NOTES AND QUERIES.—CLII.

AN INTERESTING LETTER.

"CHRISTOPHER SHOCKLEY'S COMPLAINT CONCERNING MR. JUSTICE RANNELS."

The following "complaint concerning Mr. Justice Rannels," as the letter is endorsed, forms interesting reading taken in connection with the sketches of the early Provincial Justices "West of Sasquahannah." The letter is addressed "To Mr. Attorney General for Cumberland County," whoever he was at the time :]

January 19th, 1771.

Sir—As you are constituted Attorney General for the County of Cumberland, in Pennsylvania, & as all Infractions of the Law properly fall within your Sphere, the Illegal usage & Treatment which I have received at the hands of Justice Reynolds oblige me to lay before you the subsequent Complaint ; and in order to give you a right Idea of the present Case, I was indebted to a certain Store Keeper, of the aforesaid county, in the sum of seventeen pounds six shillings by a balanced Acc't. Y'r Complainant is an Inhabitant of Maryland. My Creditor took the following Method to obtain his Debt, tho' I never refused to pay the same. He procured some evil disposed people to steal two Horses & one Mare out of my Inclosures in Maryland in the dead |time of night, secured the same, and sent for the Constable of the Hundred, in Pennsylvania, and carried them off. Two days after my creatures were thus clandestinely carried away (or rather stolen), word was sent me by the Constable that three creatures of mine were executed by him at the suit of a certain George Mencer. Mr. Reynolds was pleased to Issue Sumons for me to appear before him, which I refused to doe. Now, good S'r, you will please to observe, upon running the Proprietary Line (which is not yet determined), my House and some part of Land fell into Pennsylvania, and as we are still obliged to pay Tax & Rent to the Proprietary & Government of Maryland, I conceived that I was not compellable by any jurisdiction of y'r Province to obey his usurped Authority. My non-compliance, I presume, piqued his Worship, so that he proceeded forthwith to burthen me in the most expensive manner he could devise. The Debt he divided into seven shares, which made the Costs sevenfold. I should have mentioned before, that upon notice given me where my Horses were, I went to the Constable and offered him two good Free-

holders of Maryland as Bail for the Paym't of the Debt if he would
deliver me the Horses, which he refused, tho' I cannot therein blame
the Constable. Being reduced to such hard circumstances, & unable
to seed my Grain for want of Horses, I thought it no Trespass to recover my creatures, which were surreptitiously taken from me, in a
forceable manner, by breaking the Stable Door & taking them there-
out. My son, who was an Accomplice in the act, some time after they
artfully apprehended. After taking, they tyed him with cords &
brought him before Justice Reynolds, who, I conceive, would have
committed him, had I not sent a £40 Bond by way of Releasm't.
Now, Sir, I have given you a particular Relation of all the Matterial
parts of my Complaint, & as you are a gentleman well versed in the
Law, & as those mal Practices may occasion some severe Reflections
on the Hon'r of y'r Governm't, 'tis hoped that you will punish such
unjustifiable strides of Power, that it may be a Caution for the future
to all Magistrates, and to confine them within their due Bounds. I
am, S'r, with all due Defference and Respect, y'r most h'ble & most
obed't serv't,   CHRIS. SHOCKEY.
    P. S.—The Veracity of the above Narrative (If requested thereto) I
will make appear by men of Probity & Character.

THE ASHMAN FAMILY.

[The following genealogical notes are published in the hope of securing additional data from members of the family not only in this
State, but in Maryland.]

GEORGE ASHMAN, the first of the name of whom we have any record, was born in England about 1665. He emigrated to Anne
Arundel county, Md., prior to 1690, receiving a grant from the King
November 30, 1694, of a farm of 500 acres in Gunpowder Neck, then
Baltimore county, that Province, which he called "Ashman's Hope,"
and on which he settled. The name of his wife is unknown, but it
is generally conceded that she was a descendant of Oliver Cromwell,
as there is a tradition in the family that one of the early Ashmans
married a Cromwell. They had a son named *John.*

JOHN ASHMAN was born in Anne Arundel county, Md., about
1690; married November 26, 1713, Constance Hawkins, whose parents resided in Anne Arundel county, just across the river from the
Cromwells, who had come to this country about the same time as the
Ashmans. She was born about 1693. They had among other children a son named *George.*

GEORGE ASHMAN was born November 8, 1714, at "Ashman's Hope," in Cecil county, Md. After reaching manhood he went to England on business for his father, and while there met Miss Jemima Murray, of Edinburg, Scotland, whom he married and brought with him to his home in Maryland. Her father and family accompanied them and settled in Maryland. Their children were:

    i. George was born about 1750 in Cecil county, Md.; married, May 15, 1775, Eleanor Cromwell; in June, 1776, removed from Maryland to Bedford Furnace, now Orbisonia, Pa., and with Thomas Cromwell and Edward Ridgely, about 1785, erected the old Bedford furnace, the first iron establishment west of the Susquehanna. After coming to Pennsylvania he was commissioned colonel of one of the Pennsylvania regiments which took part in the Revolutionary war. In 1794 he built the stone house at Three Springs, Huntingdon county, Pa., on a large tract of valuable limestone land which he had acquired, and moved thence from Bedford Furnace.

    ii. Elizabeth, m. Richard Colgate, of Baltimore county, Md.

    iii. Ellen, m. John Colgate, of Baltimore county, Md.

    iv. Sarah, b. in 1767, in Cecil county, Md. She removed with her brother George in 1776 to Bedford Furnace, Pa.; in 1786 she married Benjamin Elliott. Their children were (surname Elliott):

        1. *Eleanor,* b. 1778; d. February 13, 1865; m., October 6, 1808, William Orbison.

        2. *Harriet,* b. October, 1790; d. September 16, 1869; m., Aug. 20, 1811, Jacob Miller, of Huntingdon. Their children were *Henry-W., Elliott,* and *G.-Ashman.*

        3. *Matilda,* b. 1792; m., March 28, 1816, Dr. James Stewart, of Huntingdon county, who afterwards removed to Indiana county, Pa. They had one son, *William-M.-Stewart,* residing in Philadelphia.

There is in the possession of Richard Ashman, grandson of Col. George Ashman, at Three Springs, Huntingdon county, Pa., an old looking glass said to be two hundred years old, on the frame of which is a double coat of arms, indicating the union of two families. One of these is the Ashman arms and corresponds with the paintings now possessed by the different members of the family. The original painting from which the copies have been made is in possession of George Ashman, of Phillipsburg, Centre county, Pa.

CUMBERLAND VALLEY WORTHIES.

JUSTICES DURING THE REVOLUTIONARY ERA.

REYNOLDS, JOHN.

John Reynolds, son of John Reynolds, was a native of Shippensburg, or that neighborhood, where he was born in 1749. Of the three John Reynolds in the Cumberland Valley he appears to have been the more prominent one, " Justice Rannels," as is generally noted. He was commissioned a justice of the peace prior to the Revolution, and during the struggle for independence was an active partisan. He was continued in commission of the peace by the Supreme Executive Council, June 9, 1777, and by virtue of seniority became one of the judges of the Court of Common Pleas. He was a member of the Pennsylvania convention to ratify the Federal Constitution in 1787, but voted against the ratification. He was an elder, as also was his father, of Middle Spring Presbyterian church, in which grave-yard rest his remains, having deceased on the 20th of October, 1789, aged 40 years. Few men in the valley left a better record of a worthy and honorable life than " Justice Rannels." Descendants reside at Shippensburg.

LAIRD, SAMUEL.

Samuel Laird came from the north of Ireland in his early youth, where he was born in the year 1732. He appears to have received a good English education, and was among the first settlers of the town of Carlisle. He was commissioned coroner of the county of Cumberland October 2, 1771, and served two years. During the Revolution he took an active part, was one of the commissioners for the county in 1778, and appointed a justice of the peace February 6, 1779. The Supreme Executive Council appointed him, March 3, 1781, one of the auditors of the depreciation accounts, and on the 11th of October, 1785, he was commissioned presiding justice of the Courts of Quarter Sessions, and of the Orphans' Court. He was one of the burgesses of Carlisle borough, May 21, 1787, and under the Constitution of 1789–90, commissioned an associate judge in 1791, in which office he continued to his death. Mr. Laird died at Carlisle, September 27, 1806, in his 74th year. The *Gazette* in its brief reference to him said, " One of the associate justices for Cumberland county—for many years an upright magistrate, before as well as since he took his seat on the bench. . . . . . . He was one of the first inhabitants of this town, always

active in promoting its best interests. Society both civil and religious has lost one of its greatest ornaments." Mr. Laird married Mary
Young, daughter of James Young. She was born October 31, 1741,
and died February 4, 1833; and with her husband was interred in
the grave-yard at Meeting House Springs. Their son *Samuel*, who
married a daughter of the Rev. Joseph Montgomery, a member of
the Continental Congress, was a prominent lawyer of his day. He
died and is buried in Harrisburg.

BEALE, THOMAS.

Thomas Beale, the son of William Beale and Mary, his wife, was
born in East Whiteland township, Chester county, Pa., August 6,
1737. His father was a minister in the Society of Friends. About
the year 1763, Thomas Beale, with his brother David, settled in Tuscarora Valley, in Cumberland, now Juniata county, where they took
up extensive tracts of land. In 1776 Thomas commanded a company in one of the associated battalions of Cumberland county.
He was commissioned a justice of the peace July 18, 1781, and became one of the judges of the Court of Common Pleas October 27,
1786. He represented Cumberland county in the General Assembly
from 1786 to 1789, and opposed the calling of the Constitutional Convention of 1789–90, of which body, however, he was chosen a member from Mifflin county. He was commissioned an associate judge
of the latter county August 17, 1791, holding the office until March
7, 1800. He died Sunday, January 30, 1803. He was a man of considerable prominence in public affairs. His son, William Beale, was
a member of the Pennsylvania House of Representatives from 1799
to 1806, and State Senator from the Mifflin and Huntingdon district
1812 to 1816.

JORDAN, JOHN.

John Jordan, only child of John and Catharine Jordan, was born
in the north of Ireland. His father, who came to America in 1740,
settled in Pennsboro' township, Cumberland county, dying in October, 1754, and according to his will, written in 1750, " being arrived
at a good old age." John Jordan, Jr., was probably then thirty
years of age. He received a good education, and when the Revolution came on he was in active business life. He early embarked in
the contest, and served in the capacity of lieutenant and captain in
the war, his title of major being due to his appointment of major of
the militia in 1792. He was twice elected one of the commissioners

for the county. In 1783 he was elected a justice of the peace for the borough of Carlisle, and commissioned judge of the Court of Common Pleas January 3, 1785. Under the Constitution of 1789–90, he was appointed by Governor Mifflin one of the associate judges on the bench in 1791. He died at Carlisle on the 5th of December, 1789. The *Gazette* in alluding to his death says: " He has during his life been a uniform Whig, a lover of order, his country, Constitution, and laws—and in him society has lost a useful member . . . . . . All of which offices he discharged with probity, propriety and punctuality."

———

AGNEW, JOHN.

John Agnew, son of James Agnew, was born March 4, 1732, in Donegal township, Lancaster county, his parents removing west of the Susquehanna prior to 1740. John subsequently located in the town of Carlisle, was commissioned one of the Provincial justices May 23, 1770, and continued in that office under the Constitution of 1776. He was a member of the Committee of Observation in 1774, and was an active Whig during the war; was commissioned clerk of the Court of Quarter Sessions November 5, 1777, and judge of the Court of Common Pleas, October 26, 1784. He died at Carlisle, April 8, 1790, in his fifty-ninth year, and the *Gazelte*, in its brief obituary of him, says: " He long exercised the office of magistrate, both before and since the independence of America, in which office he gave universal satisfaction. In him the community have lost an upright officer, a worthy friend, and an honest man."

———

NOTES AND QUERIES.—CLIII.

———

GEN. WILLIAM THOMPSON.—From an obituary notice, published at the time, of Mrs. Catharine Thompson, who died at Chambersburg, March 24, 1808, we have this information of her distinguished husband: " He had been a captain in the Provincial service during the Indian war. At the commencement of the Revolution he was appointed a colonel in the army that marched to Boston, and after ad- vanced to brigadier general. At the battle of the Three Rivers he was taken prisoner, and was afterwards exchanged and appointed major general, but the peace took place before he took that command."

INDIAN OUTRAGES IN THE CUMBERLAND VALLEY.

[From a small volume, entitled, " French and Indian Cruelty Exemplified, and the Life and Various Vicissitudes of Fortune of Peter Williamson," published at Dublin in 1766, having then reached its seventh edition, we find the following reference to Indian outrages in the Cumberland Valley, of a date prior to any given by the historians. Taken prisoner in 1754, he continues a relation of his journey to the westward, and narrates the miseries and sufferings of a fellow prisoner, an old, gray-headed man.]

One night after he had been thus tormented, whilst he and I were sitting together condoling each other at the misfortunes and miseries we daily suffered, a party arrived bringing twenty scalps and three prisoners, who had unhappily fallen into their hands in Cannocojigge, a small town near the river Susquehanna, chiefly inhabited by the [Scotch] Irish. These prisoners gave us some shocking accounts of the murders and devastations committed in their parts. The various and complicated actions of these barbarians would entirely fill a large volume, but what I have already written, with a few other instances which I shall select from their information, will enable the reader to guess at the horrid treatment the English and Indians in their interest have suffered for many years past. I shall, therefore, only mention in a brief manner those that suffered near the same time as myself. This party who now joined us had it not, I found, in their power to begin their wickedness as soon as those who risked my habitation, the first of their tragedies being on the 25th of October, 1754, when John Lewis with his wife and three small children fell sacrifices to their cruelty and were miserably scalped and murdered, his house, barn, and everything he possessed being burned and destroyed. On the 28th Jacob Miller, with his wife and six of his family, together with everything on his plantation, underwent the same fate. The 30th the house, mill, barn, twenty head of cattle, two teams of horses and everything belonging to the unhappy George Folke met with the like treatment, himself, wife and all his miserable family, consisting of nine in number, being inhumanely scalped, then cut in pieces and given to the swine, which devoured them. I shall give another instance of the numberless and unheard of barbarities they related of these savages, and proceed to their own tragical end. In short, one of the subtantial traders belonging to the Province, having business that called him some miles up the country, fell into the hands of these devils, who not only scalped him, but immediately roasted him before he was dead; then, like cannibals, for want of other food, eat his whole body, and of his head made what they called an Indian pudding.

From these few instances of savage cruelty, the deplorable situation
of the;defenceless inhabitants, and what they hourly suffered in that
part of the globe, must strike utmost horror to a human soul, and
cause in every heart the utmost detestation, not only against the authors of such tragic scenes, but against those who thro' perfidy, in-
attention, or pusillanimous and erroneous principles suffered these
savages at first, unrepelled or even unmolested, to commit such outrages and incredible depredations and murders.   For no torments,
no barbarities that can be exercised on the human sacrifices they get
into their power, are left untried or omitted.

[The relator then gives an account of the diabolical manner in
which the three prisoners were put to death.   Indeed one shudders at
the recital.   Is it a wonder that our frontiersmen took the retributive
work into their own hands, and wiped out the nest of red vipers at
Conestoga?]

WHAT OUR ANCESTORS DRANK.

[From Acrelius' "History of New Sweden," and other historical
works concerning Pennsylvania, we cull the following list of drinka-
bles our good old ancestors enjoyed.   The record is worth preserving.
In doing so, it has been thought useless to give any definition of
names of drinks common in our time.]

*French Wine, Frontignac " Frontenac," Pontac, Port-a-Port, Lisbon
Wine, Phial Wine* (Fayal), *Sherry* and *Maderia Wine,* which is altogether the most used.

Sangaree is made of wine, water, sugar, a dash of nutmeg, with
some leaves of balm put in.

Hot Wine, Warmed Wine, is drunk warm, with sugar, cardamoms
and cinnamon in it.   Sometimes, also, it has in it the yolks of eggs
beaten up together, and grains of allspice, and then it is called
Mulled Wine.

Cherry Wine.   The berries are pressed, the juice strained from
them, Muscavado, or raw sugar put in; then it ferments and after
some months becomes clear.

Cyder Royal is so called, when some quarts of brandy are thrown
into a barrel of cider, along with several pounds of Muscavado sugar,
whereby it becomes stronger and tastes better.   If it is then left alone
for a year or so, or taken over the sea, then thrown off into bottles,
with some raisins put in, it may deserve the name of apple wine.

Cyder Royal of another kind, of which one-half is cider and the
other mead, both freshly fermented together.

Raw Dram, Raw Rum, is a drink of rum unmixed with anything. Egg-Nog, Cherry-Pounce, Punch.

Mumm, Mimm, or *Mimbo,* made of water, sugar, and rum, is the most common drink in the interior of the country, and has set up many a tavern keeper.

Manatham is made of small beer with rum and sugar.

Tiff, or *Flipp,* is made of small beer with rum and sugar, with a slice of bread toasted and buttered.

Hot Rum, warmed with sugar and grains of allspice; customary at funerals.

Mulled Rum, warmed with egg yolks and allspice.

Hotch Pot (Hot Pot?), warmed beer with rum in it.

Sampson is warmed cider with rum in it.

Grog.

Sling, or *Long Sup,* half water and half rum, with sugar in it.

Mintwater, distilled from mint, mixed in the rum, to make a drink for strengthening the stomach.

Egg Punch, of yolks of eggs, rum, sugar, and warm water.

Milk Punch.

Sillibub is made of milk-warm milk, wine and sugar, not unlike our Oelost. It is used in summer time as a cooling beverage. [N. B.—The Swedish *Oelost* is made by mixing warm milk and beer.]

Still Liquor, brandy made of peaches or apples, without the addition of any grain; is not regarded as good as rum.

Whiskey.

Beer is brewed in towns; is brown, thick, and unpalatable. Is drunk by the common people.

Small Beer from molasses. When the water is warmed, the molasses is poured in with a little malt or wheat bran, and is well shaken together. Afterwards a layer of hops and yeast is added, and then it is put in a keg, where it ferments, and the next day is clear and ready for use. It is more wholesome, pleasanter to the taste, and milder to the stomach than any small beer or malt.

Spruce Beer.

Table Beer, made of persimmons. The persimmon is a fruit like our egg plum. When these have been well frosted, they are pounded along with their seeds, mixed up with wheat bran, made into large loaves, and baked in the oven. Then, whenever desired, pieces of this are taken and moistened, and with these the drink is brewed.

Mead is made of honey and water boiled together which ferments of itself in the cask. The stronger it is of honey the longer it takes to ferment. Drunk in this country too soon, it causes sickness of the stomach and headache.

Besides these they also use the liqueurs called cordial, such as anise water, cinnamon water, and others scarcely to be enumerated, as also drops to pour into wine and brandy almost without end.

Tea is a drink very generally used. No one is so high as to despise it, nor any one so low as not to think himself worthy of it. It is not drunk oftener than twice a day. It is always drunk by the common people with sugar in it.

Brandy in tea is called *lese* (lazy).

Coffee comes from Martinico, St. Domingo, and Surinam ; is sold in large quantities and used for breakfast.

Chocolate is in general use for breakfast and supper. It is drunk with a spoon ; sometimes prepared with a little milk, but mostly only with water.

THE AGNEWS OF MARSH CREEK.

Robert Agnew, banker, of Cootehill, Ireland, furnishes the following information derived from his father who is still living:

"Three brothers of Agnews came from Scotland during the persecutions in that country and settled in Ireland, one at Craigmore, near Randallstown, county of Antrim ; another at Donegore, near Antrimtown, and the other somewhere in the county of Tyrone. One or two sons of the one who settled at Craigmore went to America, supposed to be before 1738 or 1739, and settled in Philadelphia, and it appears they were very successful in business there."

It is supposed that Samuel and James Agnew, who moved from Donegal, in Lancaster county, and settled in the "Manor of Masque" in the year 1739, were the sons of the brother who settled near Randallstown, Craigmore.

JAMES AGNEW was born July 31, 1711, and probably came to Donegal (now Rapho) township, Lancaster county, Pa., when it was organized in 1729 with Arthur Patterson, who married Ann Scott, in Ireland, in 1724. Patterson and Agnew were blacksmiths, the latter being a single man. It is well known that Arthur Patterson carried on the business for many years, and was a skilled workman in various other branches in the manufacture of iron and steel into agricultural implements and edge tools. I cannot discover that James Agnew carried on the business in his own name while he resided in Donegel, and I infer that he was journeyman, and probably worked for Mr. Patterson. It would seem from their intimate and close relationship through life that they were friends. James Agnew married a Donegal lass in 1731, whose name is now unknown. By her he had two children, viz:

i. *John,* b. March 4, 1732.
ii. *Jennet,* b. August 22, 1735, and who married Capt. Abraham Scott. (A tradition in the family is that the Abraham Scott, who married Jennet Agnew, was the father of James Agnew's second wife. I cannot discover any of the name old enough to correspond with his age in Donegal, and therefore I conclude that Capt. Abraham Scott was the person. He was a relative of the Chickies Scotts, but not a brother.)

James Agnew married, secondly, Rebecca Scott, daughter of Abraham Scott. She was born December 17, 1707, and was the sister of Mrs. Anne Patterson, wife of Arthur Patterson, Mrs. James Moore, and Samuel Alexander and Josiah Scott, all of whom settled along Big Chickies creek, at and near where the old Paxtang and Conestoga road crossed now the Lancaster and Harrisburg turnpike. From the letter which appeared in *Notes and Queries* (No. cl.) it will be seen that James Agnew removed to Marsh creek in 1739, where he carried on blacksmithing for many years. He died October 2, 1770. Several years after his death his son, Samuel, purchased land in Carolina and removed there. The Agnews in the South are descended from Samuel. The Rev. Samuel A. Agnew, who resides at Bethany, Lee county, Mississippi, is a Presbyterian minister and a direct descendant of James Agnew.

In a future number of *Notes and Queries* I propose giving a sketch of several members of the Scott family, of whom Mrs. James Agnew was one. SAMUEL EVANS.

Columbia, Pa.

NOTES AND QUERIES.—CLIV.

CONNER (*N. & Q. cxlix.*)—In reference to this *Note* of May 28, permit me to state that while it is quite true that my father, the late Commodore David Conner, U. S. N., was born in Harrisburg, and that he was the son of another David Conner, for a time living in that place. It is a mistake to suppose that his father was the David Conner mentioned, The fact is there were two contemporaneous persons of the name in Harrisburg during the latter part of the last century, both of whom, having been confounded together, are spoken of as one and the same person. The David Conner who was *not* the father of Commodore Conner came from Cumberland county, as mentioned in the said *Note;* the David Conner who *was* the father of Commodore Conner came from Chester county. Each one of the two men is shown,

respectively, as resident in his own county, in the year 1785, by the Tax Lists of said counties, while, in 1788, the original notice in the *Carlisle Gazette* shows that it was the Cumberland man who was then settled in Harrisburg; the Chester county Tax List, for the same year, proving Commodore Conner's father to be still a resident of the last mentioned county.   After removing to Harrisburg, *subsequent* to 1788, the father of Commodore Conner died there in the winter of 1792–3, as the letters of administration on his estate, granted to his widow Abigail, prove.   By an entry in my old family Bible, he records that he was married to the said Abigail Rhodes on the 14th of July, 1772. She was the daughter of Barnabas Rhodes, brother to Samuel Rhoads, mayor of Philadelphia, in 1774, and member of the Continental Congress.   Both men were sons of John Roades, of Whitlow, county Derby, England, who emigrated to Darby, then in Chester county, Pennsylvania, in or about the year 1684.   In writing the surname, I give its spelling as found in each man's signature.   P. S. P. C.
Rowlandville, Md.

<hr>

SAMUEL SMITH (*N. & Q. cli.*)—Was born in the north of Ireland, and came to Donegal township, then Chester, now Lancaster county, in the year 1725, and settled along Conewago creek, at the point where the present Elizabethtown and Hummelstown road crosses the same.   He took up three hundred acres of land, which he subsequently patented (*vide* Patent Book A, vol. 10, page 412, Phila.)   This tract laid in Derry and Donegal townships (now Mount Joy township), and upon the eastern side of the Conewago creek he erected a grist and saw mill.   He was an Indian trader also.   In 1749 he moved to the west side of the Susquehanna river, and was appointed one of the first justices of the Court of Common Pleas for Cumberland county in 1750.   He probably settled first in Hopewell township.   After the purchase of land from the Indians by the Penns, along the Juniata in 1754, Samuel Smith, James Lowrey, Daniel Lowrey, James Sterrett and Edward Johnson, Indian traders, who all resided in Donegal township, moved up the Juniata Valley, and located three hundred acres of land each at "Frankstown."   This land was in Cumberland county at the time.   It is probable that Mr. Smith resided near Frankstown after 1754.   October 19,1757, he sold his farm, grist and saw mill along the Conewago to Capt. Thomas Harris (Indian trader), and at that time he gave his place of residence in Cumberland county.   The witnesses to the deed to Harris were Thomas Wilson and John Smith.   John Harris owned the adjoining farm at Conewago, on the Derry side of the creek.   It is probable that this John Harris was a brother of Thomas Harris.   Their signatures resemble each other very much.   S. E.

GENEALOGICAL MEMORANDA.

DAVID BYERS came from the north of Ireland and settled in Donegal in the year 1730, upon the farm now owned by Jacob Mumma, one of the Republican delegates to the State Convention, [1887.] Mr. Byers died May 20, 1743, leaving his wife Mary, and sons:

    i. David.

    ii. John, who married Rebecca, the widow of Robert Galbraith, the son of John Galbraith, who was the brother of Col. James Galbraith, of Hopewell township, Cumberland county. Robert Galbraith died in 1747 and left two children, one of whom, Rebecca, married Col. Ephraim Blaine, the great-grandfather of Hon. James G. Blaine. Capt. John Byers moved to Cumberland county about the year 1754 or '54.

Capt. John Wilkins also moved to Cumberland county from Donegal about the same time Captain Byers went.

John Byers was one of the executors of Nathaniel Little, who died in December, 1748. Mr. Little owned the farm along Donegal Meeting House Run near Marietta, and about a mile southeast from the Byers farm. He married Jennet, the widow of William Wilkins, and it is quite probable that she was a near relative of Mr. Byers.

Mr. Little, commonly called Lytle, had one son, John. The farm upon which he resided belonged to the children of William Wilkins, in which Mrs. Lytle had a life estate. Mr. Lytle, by will, and his widow, attempted to convey in fee the Wilkins farm to their son John. The Wilkins' heirs resisted this claim, which resulted in a litigation which lasted twenty-five years. Finally John Little paid them and took a quit claim deed. The aid of the Legislature was invoked, which gave Mr. Lytle authority to convey the land to Mr. Hershey. A year or two prior to the Revolutionary war Mr. Lytle moved to Middletown, now Dauphin county, and owned a farm in Paxtang township. He entered the mercantile business in Middletown. This John Lytle has been confounded with Capt. John Lytle, of Cumberland county, and "Lytle's ferry" above Harrisburg, who was intermarried with the Ayres family.. So far as I can learn they were not relatives.

Mr. Lytle was the uncle of Capt. Joseph Lytle, of Mount Joy township, who was killed in the Revolutionary war. Samuel Scott Pedan Lytle, of Mount Joy borough, is a direct descendant of Captain Lytle.

The Lytle farm is the same upon which Peter Allen, the Indian trader, settled in the year 1719. In the year 1726 the Rev. James Anderson purchased the farm from Allen, and in the year 1727 Mr.

Anderson traded this farm for one owned by William Wilkins, where Marietta now is, and where a ferry was established.

Mr. Allen moved to the eastern base of the mountain, above Harris' Ferry.

Mr. Anderson died in 1740.   SAMUEL EVANS.
Columbia, Pa.

JOURNAL OF CAPTAIN GIST.—I.

HE ACCOMPANIED MAJOR GEORGE WASHINGTON ON HIS FIRST VISIT
TO THE FRENCH COMMANDER IN 1753.

[The following journal or diary of Christopher Gist, who accompanied Washington when a major in the Virginia service in 1753, in his tour across the Allegheny mountains, on a visit to the French commandant in Western Pennsylvania, is so little known that we have concluded to publish it. The original in 1835 was in the possession of Judge Shippen, of Franklin, Venango county, this State. It is of more than ordinary historic interest.]

Wednesday, 14th November, 1753.—Then Major George Washington came to my house, at Will's Creek, and delivered me a letter from the council in Virginia, requesting me to attend him up to the commandant of the French fort on the Ohio river.

Thursday, 15th.—We set out and at night camped at George's creek, about eight miles, where a messenger came with letters from my son, who was just returning from his people at the Cherokees, and lay sick at the mouth of the Conegocheague. But as I found myself entered again on public business, and Major Washington and all the company unwilling I should return, I wrote and sent medicine to my son, and so continued my journey, and encamped at a big hill in the forks of Youghiogany, about eighteen miles.

Friday, 16th.—The next day set out and got to the big fork of said river, about ten miles there.

Saturday, 17th.—We encamped and rested our horses, and then we set out early in the morning.

Sunday, 18th.—And at night got to my house in the new settlement, about twenty-one miles; snow about ankle deep.

Monday, 19th.—Set out across Big Youghiogany to Jacob's cabin, about twenty miles. Here some of our horses straggled away, and we did not get away until eleven o'clock.

Tuesday, 20th.—Set out; had rain in the afternoon; I killed a deer; traveled about seven miles.

Wednesday, 21st.—It continued to rain; stayed all day.

Thursday, 22d.—We set out and came to the mouth of Turtle creek, about twelve miles, to John Frazier's; and he was very kind to us, and lent us a canoe to carry our baggage to the forks, about ten miles.

Friday, 23d.—Set out; rid to Shannopin's town, and down Alleghany to the mouth of Monongahela, where we met our baggage and swimmed our horses over Alleghany, and there encamped that night.

Saturday, 24th.—Set out; we went to King Shingiss and he and Lowmolach went with us to Logstown, and we spoke to the chiefs this evening and repaired to our camp.

Sunday, 25th.—They sent out for their people to come in. The Half-King came in this afternoon.

Monday, 26th.—We delivered our message to the Half-King and they promised by him that we should set out three nights after.

Tuesday, 27th.—Stayed in our camp. Monacatoocha and Pollatha Wappia gave us some provisions. We stayed until the 29th, when the Indians said they were not ready. They desired us to stay until the next day; and as the warriors were not come the Half-King said he would go with us himself and take care of us.

Friday, 30th.—We set out and the Half-King and two old men and one young warrior with us. At night we encamped at the Murthering town, about fifteen miles, on a branch of Beaver creek. Got some corn and dried meat.

Saturday, 1st December.—Set out, and at night encamped at the crossing of Beaver creek from the Kaskuskies to the Venango, about thirty miles. The next day rain; our Indians went out hunting, they killed two bucks. Had rain all day.

Monday, 3d.—We set out and traveled all day. Encamped at night on one of the head branches of Great Beaver creek, about twenty-two miles.

Tuesday, 5th.—Set out, about fifteen miles, to the town of Venango, where we were kindly and complaisantly received by Monsieur Joncaire, the French interpreter for the Six Nations.

Wednesday, 5th.—Rain all day. Our Indians were in council with the Delawares, who lived under the French colors, and who ordered them to deliver up to the French the belt, with the marks of the four towns, according to the desire of King Shingiss. But the chief of these Delawares said, "It was true King Shingiss was a great man, but he had sent no speech, and," said he, "I cannot pretend to make a speech for a King." So our Indians could not prevail with them to deliver their belt, but the Half-King did deliver his belt, as he had determined. Joncaire did everything he could to prevail on our

Indians to stay behind us, and I took all care to have them along
with us.

Thursday, 6th.—We set out late in the day accompanied by the
French General and four servants or soldiers, and

Friday, 7th.—All encamped at Sugar creek, five miles from Venango. The creek being very high, we were obliged to carry all our
our baggage over on trees and swim our horses. The Major and I
went first over with our boots on.

Saturday, 8th.—We set out and traveled twenty-five miles to Cusse-
wago, an old Indian town.

Sunday, 9th.—We set out, left one of our horses here that could
travel no further. This day we traveled to the Big Crossing, about
fifteen miles, and encamped. Our Indians went out to look out logs
to make a raft; but as the water was high and there were no other
creeks to cross, we concluded to keep up this side the creek.

Monday, 10th.—Set out, traveled about eight miles, and encamped.
Our Indians killed a bear. Here we had a creek to cross, very deep;
we got over on a tree, and got our goods over.

Tuesday, 11th.—We set out, traveled about fifteen miles to the
French fort, the sun being set. Our interpreter gave the commandant notice of our being over the creek, upon which he sent several
officers to conduct us to the fort, and they received us with a great
deal of complaisance.

Wednesday, 12th.—The Major gave the passport, showed his commissions and offered the Governor's letter to the commandant; but
he desired not to receive them, until the other commander from Lake
Erie came, whom he had sent for, and expected next day by twelve
o'clock.

Thursday, 13th.—The other General came. The Major delivered
the letter, and desired a speedy answer; the time of year and business required it. They took our Indians into private council, and
gave them several presents.

Friday, 14th.—When we had done our business, they delayed and
kept our Indians until Sunday; and then we set out with two canoes,
one for our Indians and the other for ourselves. Our horses we had
sent away some days before, to wait at Venango, if ice appeared on
the rivers and creeks.

Sunday, 16th.—We set out by water about sixteen miles, and encamped. Our Indians went before us, passed the little lake, and we
did not come up with them that night.

NOTES AND QUERIES.—CLV.

A PURITAN DESCENDANT.—Few there are amongst the school children of fifty years ago who have not a vivid recollection of the pictures in the school histories of the landing of the Pilgrim Fathers in 1620 amidst the blinding snow and piercing winds of a bleak December. So interested were they in this picture that the mere mention of "Plymouth Rock" revives the memories of the school days of yore. Among those who landed from the Mayflower was John Carver and his family consisting of eight persons. He was elected the first Governor of this pious band and died in a short time afterwards. As late as 1755 he had a grandson residing at Mansfield, Massachusetts, in which year he died at the extreme age of 102 years. In this same year he was seen laboring in the field with his son, grandson, and great-grandson, while an infant of the fifth generation was in the house. It is not known by the people of Central Pennsylvania that a descendant of the first Governor of the Plymouth Colony resided in Perry county, at Duncannon. Recently, while on a short visit to the above place we visited the beautiful cemetery of the Lutheran and United Brethren, and therein we found a recently erected tombstone of Scotch granite with the following inscription :

Reuben W. Carver, | Son of | Jabish Carver, | Who was the son of Jabez, | son of Jonathan, son of | Nathaniel son of Eleazer | son of Gov. John Carver, | who landed at Plymouth Rock, | Dec. 21, 1620, | was born at Taunton, Mass., | Oct. 3, 1807, | and died at Duncannon, Pa., | Oct. 25, 1885, | aged 78 years and 22 days.

Upon inquiry we were informed that he was a nailer by occupation and hence settled at Duncannon, where is located a large nail factory. His widow yet resides there.   E. W. S. P.

JOURNAL OF CAPTAIN GIST.—II.

Monday, 17th.—We set out, came to our Indians' camp. They were out hunting ; they killed three bears. We stayed this day, and

Tuesday, 18th.—One of our Indians did not come to camp, so we, finding the waters lower very fast, were obliged to go and leave our Indians.

Wednesday, 19th.—We set out about seven or eight miles and encamped, and the next day

Thursday, 20th.—About twenty miles, where we were stopped by ice, and worked until night.

Friday, 21st.—The ice was so hard that we could not break our way through, but were obliged to haul our vessels across a point of land and put them in the creek again. The Indians and three French canoes overtook us here, and the people of one French canoe that was lost, with her cargo of powder and lead. This night we encamped about twenty miles above Venango.

Saturday, 22d.—Set out. The creek began to be very low, and we were forced to get out to keep our canoe from upsetting several times, the water freezing to our clothes, and we had the pleasure of seeing the French overset, and the brandy and wine floating in the creek, and run by them, and left them to shift by themselves. Came to Venango and met with our people and horses.

Sunday, 23d.—We set out from Venango, traveled about five miles to Lacomick creek.

Monday, 24th.—Here Major Washington set out on foot in Indian dress. Our horses grew weak, then we were mostly obliged to travel on foot, and had snow all day. Encamped near the barrens.

Tuesday, 25th.—Set out and traveled on foot to branches of Great Beaver creek.

Wednesday, 26th.—The Major desired me to set out on foot, and leave our company, as the creeks were frozen, and our horses could make but little way. Indeed, I was unwilling he should undertake such a travel, who had never been used to walking before this time. But as he insisted on it, I set out with our packs, like Indians, and traveled eighteen miles. That night we lodged at an Indian cabin, and the Major was much fatigued. It was very cold, all the small runs were frozen that we could hardly get water to drink.

Thursday, 27th.—We rose early in the morning and set out about 2 o'clock. Got to the Murthering town, on the southeast fork of Beaver creek. Here we met with an Indian whom I thought I had seen at Joncaire's, at Venango, when on our journey up to the French fort. This fellow called me by an Indian name, and pretended to be glad to see me. He asked us several questions as how we came to travel on foot when we left Venango, where we parted with our horses, and when they would be there, &c. Major Washington insisted on traveling on the nearest way to the forks of the Alleghany. We asked the Indian if he could go with us and show us the nearest way. The Indian seemed very glad and ready to go with us. Upon which we set out, and the Indian took the Major's pack. We traveled very brisk for eight or ten miles, when the Major's feet grew very

sore, and he very weary, and the Indian steered too much northeast-
wardly. The Major desired to encamp, to which the Indian asked to
carry his gun. But he refused that, and when the Indian grew
churlish and pressed us to keep on, telling us that there were Ottawa
Indians in these woods, and they would scalp us if we would lay out;
but go to his cabin, and we should be safe. I thought very ill of the
fellow, but did not care to let the Major know I distrusted him. But
he soon mistrusted him as much as I. He said he could hear a gun
to his cabin, and steered us more northwardly. We grew uneasy,
and then he said two whoops might be heard to his cabin. We
went two miles further; then the major said he would stop at the
next water, and we desired the Indian to stop at the next water.
But before we came to water we came to a clear meadow; it was very
light and snow on the ground. The Indian made a stop, turned
about. The Major saw him point his gun toward us and fire. Said
the Major, "Are you shot?" "No," said I. Upon which the Indian
run forward to a big standing white oak, and to loading his gun;
but we were soon with him. I would have killed him; but the Major
would not suffer me to kill him. We let him charge his gun; we
found he put in a ball; then we took care of him. The Major or I
always stood by the guns; we made him make fire for us by a little
run, as if we intended to sleep there. I said to the Major, "As you
will not have him killed you must get him away, and then we must
travel all night." Upon which I said to the Indian, "I suppose you
were lost and fired your gun." He said, he knew the way to his
cabin, and 'twas but a little way. "Well," said I, "do you go home;
and say we are much tired, we will follow your track in the morning; and here is a cake of bread for you, and you must give us
meat in the morning." He was glad to get away. I followed him,
and listened until he was fairly out of the way, and then set out
about half mile, when we made a fire, set our compass and fixed our
course, and traveled all night, and in the morning we were at the
head of Piney creek.

Friday, 28th.—We traveled all the next day down the said creek
and just at night found some tracks where Indians had been hunting. We parted, and appointed a place a distance off where to meet,
it being dark. We encamped, and thought ourselves safe enough to
sleep.

Saturday, 29th.—We set out early, got to Alleghany, made a raft,
and with much difficulty got over to an island, a little above Shannopin's town. The Major having fallen in from off the raft, and my
fingers frost-bitten, and the sun down, and very cold, we contented

ourselves to encamp upon that island. It was deep water between us and the shore; but the cold did us some service, for in the morning it was frozen hard enough for us to pass over on the ice.

Sunday, 30th.—We set out about ten miles to John Frazier's, at Turtle creek, and rested that evening.

Monday, 31st.—Next day we waited on Queen Alliquippa, who lives now at the mouth of the Youghiogany. She said she would never go down to the river Alleghany to live, except the English built a fort, and then she would go and live there.

Tuesday, 1st January, 1754.—We set out from John Frazier's, and at night encamped at Jacob's cabins.

Wednesday, 2d.—Set out and crossed Youghiogany on the ice. Got to my house in the new settlement.

Thursday, 3d.—Rain.

Friday, 14th.—Set out for Will's creek, where we arrived on Sunday, January 6th.

NOTES AND QUERIES.—CLVI.

AN ANCIENT BURIAL PLACE.—Two or three years ago one of our local contemporaries contained the statement that several hunters came across a deserted burying ground or grave-yard located on a slight eminence in a pasture field about one and one-half miles northeast of Oyster's dam, on the Conedoguinet, and about the same distance from the mountain. There was not a vestige of fencing or wall to be seen around this ancient burial place, which contained about twenty graves, all, or nearly all, of which were covered with long slabs, of stone evidently quarried in the vicinity. There were a number of the slabs engraved, but the work of the elements had almost entirely defaced the inscriptions. On one of the slabs alone was then visible the following imperfect inscription, nearly illegible, and which was originally cut in rude characters: "Born, 1728; died at the age of twenty-eight years, four months and four days"—showing that the remains under that slab had been interred in 1756—131 years ago! As the slabs were nearly alike and the ground was isolated and deserted, the probability was the dust reposing beneath them was once an entire family whose name and history had long since passed away, and left no descendants to keep this deserted rural cemetery in a decent condition. If any of our readers can give us the exact location of this ground we will visit it in the hope of deciphering some of the inscriptions.

WAR HISTORY AS SHE IS WROTE IN 1887.—The New York *Star* contains a history of the Eleventh regiment of that State, and its prowess in war and peace. Part of its war record is a most astonishing one. Here it is, enemy and all, in a skirmish from Fort Washington to the "walls of Gettysburg:" "The next experience of the regiment was in 1863. It was at the time when the Confederates were making a determined attempt to capture Pennsylvania. All the available men were at the front, and in the emergency the Eleventh regiment was again called on and they readily responded. It was on June 16th that the order came for them to proceed to Harrisburg, Pa., to repel the invasion of that State by the rebels. Accordingly the regiment hastened off, arriving at the scene of action on June 20, where they at once went into camp. On June 28th they broke camp, leaving behind all their property, knapsacks, overcoats, blankets and tents in charge of a detachment of twenty men. They marched to Oyster's Point, eight miles south of Harrisburg, where they fell in with the enemy, with whom they had a brisk skirmish. They were then withdrawn into Fort Washington, and after the eventful battle they were in hot pursuit of the retreating foe, and for several days after they were constantly on the move, following closely on the footsteps of the rebels and dislodging them from every position. On through Maryland and up to the very walls of Gettysburg the regiment pursued them. There they arrived July 6th and encamped near that memorable battlefield."

A CURIOUS DOCUMENT.

[The following copy of a document in my possession may be of some interest in the history of the Cumberland Valley. Patrick Jack named in it is Colonel Jack, an officer of the Provincial and Revolutionary wars, sometimes called the " Black Rifle.]

Know all men by these presents that I James Ward of hopewell towenship & Lancaster County in the provence of pensalveniea Yeamen do make over all my Right Intrest and Cleam of a tract of Land laying on back Crike Joning to Matthew Arthors pleas ouperward of ye sed Creek to sad Matthew Arthors of Antrim township & County aforsaid with all itts apertencess there unto belonging to his heirs and assignes for and in Consideration of twienty three pounds Coarrant Laful money of sad provence the Receipt whereof I acknowledge & to be therwith fully satified and I do oblige myselfe my hears Exacators & administerators or a signs to warent and defend ye said traick of Land from all persons Cliaming under me any right thereto, the Proprietor Excepted, & always Excepted to ye performance of the afforsaid bargain. I bind my selfe hears or assigns in the pennall sum of forty-six pounds of the afforsaid Corance. In witness where-unto I sett my hand and seal this, 9 day of Siptember, one thousand sevan hundred & forty Eight, 1748.

JAMES WARD [L. S.].

In the presence of us,
ALEX'R NESMITH,
EDWARD JOHNSTON.

[On the back.]

Cumberland County ss :

Before me, the subscriber, one of his Majesty's Justices, came Edward Johnston, and was duly sworn as the Law Directs, that he was a witness to the within Bill of Sale. EDWARD JOHNSTON.

Sworn and Subscribed this tenth Day of March, 1772, Before

WM. BROWN.

Cumberland County ss :

Entered in the office for Recording of Deeds for Cumberland County aforesaid in Book C, volume first, Page 419, In Testimony Whereof I have hereto Affixed the seal of the Office aforesaid the 23d Day of December, 1773.

For TURBUTT FRANCIS, ESQ'R,
JOHN AGNEW.

I sine over all my right of the within billesale to Patrick Jack for value resead, as witness my hand and Sel this first of November, 1767.

JAMES ARTHER, [Sel.]

THOMAS BEARD.
his
DIVES × BALEF.
mark.

Recording 4 S.

--------●--------

THE SCOTT FAMILY OF DONEGAL.

Samuel Scott settled at Big Chickies creek, at the point where the Paxtang and Conestogoe road was afterwards laid out in 1736–7, about the year 1726 or 1727. When the Paxtang road was completed he erected a tavern, and also built a grist mill, both of which in their time became places of note. Through the influence of Mr. Scott another road was laid out a few years later than the Paxtang road, leading from the Swatara Valley past the mill of Richard Allison on Conewago creek, now Colebrook grist mill, to a point intersecting the Paxtang road near Mr. Scott's dwelling. Mr. Scott became very rich for that period. He married first a sister of James Poake (the father of James K. Polk), and of David Poake, to each of whom he devised by will thirty pounds. There was no issue by this marriage. He married secondly Hannah [Boyd?] who seems to have been a person of great energy and thrift. The family were strict members of the Presbyterian church at Donegal Springs. When Rev. Colin McFarquahr came there, in 1776, he made his home with the family, and after the death of Mr. Scott, in 1777, he remained with the family until the close of the Revolutionary war, when his own family came from Scotland. Mr. Scott devised to his wife Hannah a life estate in one hundred and fifty acres of land and dwelling where he resided. Part of the land was in Hempfield township and part in Rapho township, upon which was a grist mill. She was not to infringe upon the orchard or tavern then in the tenantry of Capt. Hugh Pedan. He also gave her one thousand pounds in money and a yearly sum of fifty pounds. His nephew, Alexander Scott, son of his brother, Josiah Scott, was to receive the mansion farm after the decease of his widow. He disposed of the remainder of his estate as follows:

To his nephew, Capt. Hugh Pedan, his sister's son, he gave three hundred and ninety-six acres of land, and the tavern, which adjoined his mansion farm.

To his nephew, Samuel Patterson, son of Arthur and Anna Patterson, his sister, he gave a farm half a mile further down the creek.

To Samuel Pedan, son of Griselda Pedan, he gave a farm on the Hempfield side of the creek about a mile below the mill.

To his nephew, Samuel Scott, son of his brother, Abraham Scott, he gave two hundred acres of land at the river.

To his brother, Alexander Scott, he gave half of his lands at the river.

To his nephew, Samuel Agnew, son of James Agnew, he gave a farm near Little Chickies creek, about a mile and a half east from the present borough of Mount Joy, subject, however, to the payment of two hundred pounds. Samuel Agnew in 1779 moved from Marsh creek to South Carolina.

Mr. Scott also gave two hundred pounds to the Donegal church. The executors of the estate paid the congregation in Continental money, which was worthless, and did not benefit the church. Not a single foot of ground owned by Mr. Scott or his brothers is now owned by any of the name, or of the blood. This may with truth be said of the hundreds of the Scotch-Irish Presbyterian landholders in Donegal, in Provincial times. They and their descendants abandoned the Donegal nursery and planted colonies elsewhere throughout the extent of the country, which flourished and were constantly extended in the south and west, until theirs was the controlling power which moulded our institutions and gave us the boon of the liberties we enjoy to day.

ABRAHAM SCOTT, who I suppose married Jennet Agnew, resided in Mount Joy township, a mile or two east from Elizabethtown, was one of the most prominent men in the county. He was captain in Col. Alexander Lowrey's battalion in 1777–80, and participated in the battles of Brandywine, Germantown and in the Jersey campaign. In 1783 he was major in Col. Jacob Cook's battalion. He was a member of the General Assembly for the years 1781–82–83–84 and 1785.

According to Rev. Colin McFarquahr, whose catechetical roll of members of Donegal church commenced in 1776, Captain Scott's family was as follows: Captain Abe Scott, Mrs. Scott, Sr., deceased, Mrs. Scott, Jr., Polly Scott, Samuel Scott, Susanna Scott, a child, an infant.

ALEXANDER SCOTT died March 26, 1786, aged 70 years, and left wife Sarah but no children. He gave 202 acres of land to his nephew, Alexander Scott Lowrey. To Capt. Hugh Pedan, his nephew, he gave 130 acres, upon which tract he directed a mill to be built (now owned by Mr. Garber), which is on the east side of the creek. The old mill was above the tavern on west side of the creek. He also remembered his sister Ann, who married Arthur Patterson, and their children, Samuel, James and Eleanor. Also, his sister Elizabeth's children, who married James Moore. To his sister, who married William Carr, who owned in connection with his brother (who lived in Paxtang) the farm at Donegal Springs, now owned by Mr. Hoover, he also gave a bequest.

Alex. Scott was an officer of the French and Indian war and marched with General Forbes' army to the Ohio in 1758, and was in the battle of Loyal Hannon. He was also an officer in the Revolutionary war.

JOSIAH SCOTT died April 13, 1765, and left a wife Mary, and the following issue:
    i. Robert.
    ii. Alexander.
    iii. Ann, who married Col. Bertram Galbraith.
    iv. Esther.
    v. Jean.

He owned several hundred acres of land at Bainbridge, and a large farm at Big Chickies creek where he resided, also a large tract of land on the Juniata above Frankstown at the mouth of Beaver Dams, and a farm he purchased from Thomas McKee in Upper Paxtang.

Upon Rev. Colin McFarquahr's roll in 1776–7 are the following named families, all residing at Big Chickies, in the neighborhood of Samuel and Josiah Scott: Mary Scott, Wm. Scott, Abe Scott, David Scott (dead), Hugh Scott (dead), Peggy Scott, Mrs. Scott (widow), Alex. Scott, Jennett Scott, James Scott, Mary Scott, Alex. Scott, Margaret Scott, Sarah Scott.   SAMUEL EVANS.
Columbia.

NOTES AND QUERIES.—CLVII.

HOUSE, JAMES.—James House was appointed from Penn'a February 22, 1799, lieutenant first artillerists and engineers; district paymaster March 16, 1802; retained, April 2, 1802, as first lieutenant regiment of artilery; promoted captain November 1, 1805; to lieutenant-colonel Third artillery March 3, 1813; transferred to corps artillery May 12, 1814; transferred to Second artillery June 1, 1821; promoted colonel First artillery May 8, 1822; promoted brevet brigadier general for ten years' faithful service in one grade, May 8, 1832; died Nov'r 17, 1834. Information is desired as to ancestry, date and place of birth and place of death.   S. M. C.

OBITUARY OF REV. JOHN ROAN.—From the *Pennsylvania Gazette* of December 18, 1775, we take the following reference to this noted minister of the Gospel: "On Tuesday, the 3d instant, departed this life, in the 59th year of his age, the Rev. Mr. John Roan, of Lancaster county; where he had for a long series of years, with great fidelity and assiduity discharged the trust reposed in him as a minister of the Gospel of Christ; and merited esteem as an active and useful member of civil society, through the calamities of the late Indian wars on our frontiers; and in the present important struggle for American liberty. And on the following day his remains attended by a numerous concourse of the inhabitants in those parts, of various denominations, were interred in the burying ground at the Presbyterian church in Derry congregation, when a sermon suitable to the solemn occasion was delivered by the Rev. Mr. John Woodhull, of Leacock, from Rev. xxi. 7."

IN THE REVOLUTION.—I.

[The following correspondence concerning the marching of the militia to Philadelphia in 1777 is of interest to us. The letters have not as yet appeared in print.]

[President Wharton to Colonel Galbraith.]

PHILADELPHIA, *April 25, 1777.*

SIR: Agreeable to the enclosed resolve of Congress, and with the Advice of the Board of War, I have determined that the Counties of Philadelphia, Bucks, Cumberland, Berks and Northampton, send their Proportion of Militia to Bristol, to form a Camp at or near that Borough. The Counties of Chester, Lancaster, and York, to form a Camp at or near Chester.

'Your County is to furnish six hundred Men, to march immediately to Chester with as many arms and accoutrements as can be had in the County. If the first Class does not amount to that number, the second Class also are to march.

You are to procure by purchase or otherwise a Blanket for each Man (which is to remain the property of the State). Money will be sent you for this purpose. If they cannot be procured by purchase they must be impressed by their value paid; this is to be done in a way that will give the least offense.

You are to exert yourself to the utmost to Comply with this Order with all possible expedition, as the Enemy are preparing to make an immediate attack on this State.

I have the honor to be, with great respect, Your most Obedient, humble Servant, THO. WHARTON, JR., *Prest.*

[Col. Galbraith to Col. John Rodgers.]

May 2d, 1777.

To the Colonel of the Hanover Battalion :

SIR: Annexed hereunder you have the President's requisition for Six Hundred men from this county ; the Irregular order that returns have been made in, Prevents me for calling on you for your exact Quota of men. I desire that as your Companies which form your Battalion have drawn their rank, that you furnish one full Company agreeable to the Militia Act, on the President's requisition without delay. Necessaries that are wanting, you see will be answered.

In haste I am your Humble Servt. BERTRAM GALBRAITH.

[*Col. Joshua Elder to Col. Rodgers.*]

PAXTANG, *11th May 1777.*

DEAR SIR: Yours I rec'd last Night but cannot possibly comply with your Request, as we have too much Divisions in this Department, the five Sub-Divisions laid off in Paxtang met tolerably well except the Germans, who seem chiefly all to stand aloof; three of the Companies chose their officers very well, and the other two neglected. There was no disputes about pay, but one of them seemed all desirous of being officers, and the other all Privates; declining any commissions that were offered. I have promised my attendance in one of these Companies to-Morrow; as to the Dispute about pay, I think if they would have the least Consideration, might be soon removed, it might answer well enough to draw out a few men when there was no compulsion nor Law to put every Man on an equal Ballance in expense of the War, but as the Law is regulated at present, except the whole State in general, or at least the whole Battalion would condescend to that Plan, it would be in vain for one Company to pretend to it, except they would think themselves wiser lawmakers than the Choice of the State, because each Company or Draught is made out of the whole Battalion, and if they should deviate from the Laws of the State they would be a Derision to all the rest. You can inform them that if they don't choose for themselves, the Lieutenants will be under the Necessity of choosing for them. And you will be good enough to consider and inform yourself what Men will be most likely to suit, if that should be the Case, that you can recommend them to us. I had a letter from Col. Galbraith last Night Desiring I would give you Word to bring the Report of your Battalion, Companies, Rank and Draughts to him at Lancaster next Wednesday, and draw for Rank with other Colonels.

In haste I am your H'ble Servant,   JOSHUA ELDER.
Col. John Rodgers.

[*Col. B. Galbraith to Colonel Rodgers.*]

LANCASTER, *May 15, 1777.*

SIR: In consequence of your late Orders from me to hold the first Class of each Company in your Battalion in Readiness, with arms, and properly Equipt with every other Necessary for your Immediate March to Chester on the Delaware, I Desire that such who fall into that Draught, and Conscienciously scruple the bearing of Arms, may be reported to me by you, or your Order Immediately, that I may find Substitutes in their Room and Stead, and at the same Time make to me a list of such who may be willing to serve as Substitutes within your Bounds. Which orders, you'll on all Occasions of the like kind, observe.

I have the Honor, Sir, to be your Humble Servant,

BERTRAM GALBRAITH,

Col. Commandant.

To Col. John Rodgers, of the Sixth Battalion of Lancaster County Militia.

[*Col. Joshua Elder to Colonel Rodgers.*]

PAXTANG, *May 29, 1777.*

SIR: I have just now got Orders from Col. Galbraith to desire you, by the first Opportunity, to hold the first Class in your Battalion under Marching Orders, ready for further Orders, he was this Day to set out for Philad'a, and will give you further Particulars on his Return.　　　　　I am your Humble Servant,

Col. John Rodgers.　　　　　　　　　　　　　　　JOSHUA ELDER.

[*Colonel Galbraith to Col. Joshua Elder.*]

LANCASTER, *June the 18th, 1777.*

SIR: Since my last to the different Colonels (which by this Time I expect you're made acquainted with) on my way to Lancaster met with an Express from the President ordering the March of the second Class, & to hold the 3d in Readiness, of which, By this my order, I hope you'll Notice your Brother as well as Col Roger's Battalion on that head, that 2 Classes must Immediately March & the 3d held in Readiness.　　　　　In haste I'm y'rs &c,

Col. Joshua Elder.　　　　　　　　　　　　　　　B. GALBRAITH.

NOTES AND QUERIES.—CLVIII.

JAMES SAYRE was born in 1745 in the State of Connecticut. He was educated to the law and admitted to practice at New York city in 1771, although he seems to have been in practice in Philadelphia as early as September, 1767. He abandoned his profession and became chaplain of one of DeLancy's Loyalist batteries. Resigned in 1777 and served as rector of the Episcopal church in Brooklyn from 1778 to 1783. On the evacuation of New York went to St. John, New Brunswick, and was one of the grantees of that city. Returned to the United States, and from 1786 to 1788 was rector of the church at

Newport, Rhode Island. He died at his native town, Fairfield, Conn., in 1798. It is not known what was the occasion of his admission to the Cumberland county bar.

***

AN OLD FAMILY REGISTER.

[Some years ago this register of a German family came into our possession. Having it translated we have considered it proper to print it in *Notes and Queries*, in the hope that it may come to the knowledge of those especially interested. It is a valuable register to the descendants, whoever they may be.]

FAMILY REGISTER OF JACOB BOZART [BOSTART],

Wherein all births and deaths are noted until the third generation:

Anno, 1721, upon Michelmas day, I was married to Esther Mellinger in the 25th year of my age and my wife was 18 years of age.

In the year of Christ 1723, August 9, between 8 and 9 o'clock, our Anna was born into this world. In the year 1724, July 29, our daughter Anna departed from time to Eternity.

In the year 1725, May 21, our son, John Jacob Bozart, was born, between 4 and 5 o'clock, in the sign of the Virgin. In the year of Christ 1726, July 27, our little son, John Jacob Bozart, died.

We also left our Fatherland in the year 1726, and betook ourselves upon the journey to Pennsylvania, and through the aid of the Almighty reached our destination on the 8th of November.

In the year 1727, December 8, our Esther was born in the sign of the Scorpion.

In the year of Christ 1729, in October, our Samuel was born, and in the year 1730 he was called to the Lord; he brought his age no higher than 3 months and 3 weeks.

In the year 1730, December 9, our David was born into the world in the sign of the Ram.

In the year of Christ 1734, February 2, our Veronica was born into the world in the sign of the Twins. In the year of Christ 1737, March 10, she was called to the Lord.

In the year of Christ 1737, April 2, our Henry was born into the world in the sign of the Cancer.

In the year of Christ 1739, December 13, our Maria was born into the world in the sign of the Cancer. In the year 1741 both our children, Maria and David, died. David died June 15.

In the year 1743, January 20, our Martin was born into the world, consequently his sign was that of the Ram. In the year 1748, October 27, our Martin was called to the Lord.

Notes and Queries.

In the year 1752, July 13, our daughter, Magdalena, was called to the Saviour. In the year of Christ 1755, August 27, our Henry Bozart died in the afternoon at 4 o'clock. In the year 1757, April 26, Jacob Bozart also went the way of all humanity.

FAMILY REGISTER OF ESTHER BOZART [BOSTART],

A descendant of Jacob Bozart (Bostart), his eldest remaining daughter, who joined in marriage with Jacob Enger in the year 1747, October 20.

Her eldest son, Daniel Enger, was born Anno 1748, September 18, on Sunday at 12 o'clock, old computation.

In the year of Christ 1750, July 1, on Sunday, at 12 o'clock, noon, our Esther was born in the sign of the Scorpion, old reckoning.

Anno 1752, February 10, our daughter Veronica was born in the sign of the Ram, old reckoning.

In the year of Christ 1753, January 29, Jacob Enger died in the 30th year of his age.

In the year of Christ 1754, January 17, I joined myself with, second marriage, Joseph Bastler, an European by birth, of German blood. He was born in the year 1728, March 19. The children born to us were these:

In the year 1755, January 5, our Catharine was born, upon a Sunday evening at 10 o'clock.

In the year 1757, January 31, Monday morning, at 2 o'clock, our son, Jacob Bastler, was born.

In the year of Christ 1758, both our children went to the Saviour; Catharine died September 17 and Jacob September 23.

In the year 1759, September 17, Monday morning, at about 2 o'clock, our daughter, the second Catharine, was born in the sign of the Cancer.

In the year of Christ 1761, April 20, our daughter Maria was born, on Monday morning, at 4 o'clock, in the sign of the Scorpion.

In the year of Christ 1763, August 11, afternoon at 5 o'clock, our daughter Elizabeth was born in the sign of the Virgin.

In the year of Christ 1776, January 26, Sunday evening, at 8 o'clock, our daughter Magdalena was born in the sign of the Lion.

In the year of Christ 1769, April 13, our son, Joseph Bastler, was born upon a Monday, at 1 o'clock, in the sign of the Cancer.

Herein are correctly recorded the births and deaths of the children of the deceased, Esther Bastler, of her first and second marriage.

Following are the marriages, when and with whom celebrated:

Anno 1770, Thursday, June 14, my daughter Esther Enger joined in marriage with Jonathan Schleister, in the sign of the Fish, was aged 19 years, 10 months and 3 days.

In the year of Christ, 1771, Thursday, March 23, my daughter, Veronica Enger, was married to Jonathan Longenaker, in the sign of the Cancer; was aged 19 years, 3 months and 3 days.

In the year 1779, Sunday, November 21, our daughter, Catharine Bastler, married Jonathan Denlinger, in the sign of the Ram; was 20 years, 2 months and 3 days of age.

In the year 1782, Sunday, June 2, our daughter, Maria Bastler, married Abraham Denlinger, in the sign of the Fish; was aged 21 years, 1 month and 13 days.

In the year 1783, Sunday, April 20, our daughter, Elizabeth Bastler, married Jonathan Basher, in the sign of the Fish; was aged 19 years, 8 months and 8 days.

In the year 1785, April 3, Abraham Denlinger died.

In the year 1791, Tuesday, November 22, our daughter, Magdalena Bastler, married, in the 20th year of her age, Peter Andreas (in the sign of the Cancer), an European by birth, of German extraction. He was born of and brought up by the Mennonites, so that it was with difficulty they united upon our instructions in religion, and in the Book of our Faith.

In the year of Christ 1792, January 17, the grandmother of the children here mentioned died also. She had married Jacob Bostart, Anno 1721, deceased. She brought her age in this world to 88 years and nearly 10 months. She died after a brief illness, not suffering as much as our father in his last illness.

In the year 1797, November 7, our son, Joseph Bastler, married Anna Denlinger, in the sign of the Twins. Was aged 27 years, 7 months and 5 days.

In the year 1802, October 12, our daughter Maria married Martin Mellinger. She lived in the bonds of marriage 17 years, 6 months and 9 days and she lived in widowhood 1 year, less 2 weeks. In the year of Christ 1808, October 13, the father died. In the year of Christ 1809, July 12, the mother died.

FAMILY REGISTER OF JOSEPH BASTLER.

In the year of Christ 1797, Tuesday, November 7, I, Joseph Bastler married Anna Denlinger, in the sign of the Twins.

In the year of Christ, 1798, November 16, a son was born to us, Friday morning at 9 o'clock, by name Jacob Bastler, in the sign of the Fish.

In the year of Christ 1801, February 19, a son was born to us

Thursday morning, at 6 o'clock by the name of Joseph Bastler, in the sign of the Bull.

In the year of Christ 1803, September 23, a daughter was born to us, Wednesday evening between 9 and 10 o'clock. by name of Magdalena Bastler, in the sign of the Fish.

In the year of Christ, 1806, February 5, a son was born to us, Wednesday evening at 8 o'clock, by name of Jonathan Bastler, in the sign of the Virgin.

In the year of Christ 1808, September 18, a daughter was born to us Sunday morning at 6 o'clock, by name of Esther Bastler, in the sign of the Twins.

IN THE REVOLUTION.—II.

[Col. Joshua Elder to Colonel Rodgers.]

COL. JOHN ROGERS.

PAXTANG, *20th June, 1777.*

SIR : The above is a copy of a Letter from Col. Galbraith, which I recd late last night, by which you see there's the greatest Necessity for our utmost Exertions. I recd a verbal Message from Major Brown of yr Battallion to attend an Appeal to be held at Hanover next Monday, I would be glad to be informed at what Time I should attend, or if you are to have the Lieutenant, or another Sub-Lieutenant & Magistrate or by the Lieutenant's orders as we must Endeavor to walk in as straight a Line as possible upon these occasions, or if I cou'd be excused, as I shall have enough to do in this Battalion to procure substitutes, there being so many Germans all of whom refuse going. O their Clay cold heads & Luke warm hearts. Sir, by all that's dear & sacred to us, let me entreat you not to spare the least pains to dispatch your Classes, & if you feel the Loss & Trouble of it now, I hope you'll find the Honor & Benefit of it hereafter.

I'm Sir, yr h'ble servant,

JOSHUA ELDER.

[Colonel Galbraith to Colonel Rodgers.]

To COL. RODGERS.

DONEGAL, *16th June, 1777.*

SIR : In consequence of Orders from the President of the Executive Council of the 13th Inst., as well as from Generals Mifflin, Armstrong

& Potter of the 14th at night, requesting the March of Militia, and giving me information of General Howe's army rapidly Marching thro the Jerseys, being at Rocky run, 5 Miles from Princeton, on Saturday last, Do order you, with all expedition to get in readiness (agreeable to former orders), the first Class of your militia to March to Chester on Delaware, and notify the Second Class to hold themselves in readiness to march at a Moment's warning. You must agree with Substitutes in the room of those who deny Marching (notwithstanding my Publication), at such rates as you can, with the advice of the nearest Sub-Lieutenant who's agreement shall be confirmed by me and at the same time take Care that no Substitutes are taken out of the Second Class for the First. The Cityzens of Philad'a have made up all variances & marched Yesterday Morning unanimously in defense of their Country. In a word, Sir, I hope you'l not loose a moment's time in doing the necessary. Everything will be provided for the men at Lanc'r or at the Camp, except Blankets.

I'm in the greatest haste, Sir, your Humble Serv.,

BERTRAM GALBRAITH, *Col.*

———

[*Colonel Galbraith to Colonel Rodgers.*]

To COLONEL RODGERS.

DONEGAL, *20th June, 1777.*

SIR: By a letter from the President in Council of the 25th Inst, rec'd this Morning, Countermands the March of the first Class of the Militia, on the retreat of General How's troops from Summerset & Brunswick to Amboy & Staten Island, yet at the Same time to hold in readiness at a moment's warning, as no doubt they may be soon called, Should How attempt our Capes. I have wrote to the President & expect in a few days his answer, when you'll receive Particular orders from me. Continue Such Substitutes as are already provided for the protection of the civil Authority, but recommend to the Majistrates to proceed only to collecting of the fines for days of exercise, for a few days, until the President's Answer comes to hand. I have sent a few Notices amongst you which I expect you'll Observe. When I was in your Country our people had brush with a number of rioters in which one of our people was killed by the Stroak of the Coalter of a Plough & three of the others wounded, which I hope will be the means of putting a Stopp to other Insurrections of the like kind.

In haste, rest your Humble Serv't.

BERTRAM GALBRAITH, *Lieut'nt.*

[Colonel Galbraith to Colonel Rodgers.]

DONEGAL, *July 15th, 1777.*

SIR: Yours of yesterday came to hand by Captain Hay, which Surprises me no little, to find that uneasiness should be now arising amongst you, at the very time it ought not to subsist.

By Captain Hay I have sent you the rules by which the Continental Army is governed, to which every Officer & Soldier now with you is subject (or ought to be) which you'l cause to be read at the Head of the Company for their Instruction as to that of their duty, that should they offend, or go out of the line of duty it may not be unknown to them, as I'm determined if in my power to preserve good order. You will call or appoint the men to meet twice a week at your house or elsewhere as you shall see meet, to receive their farther Instructions which shall be handed you from me, as the exigency of affairs may require, but at the same time they (the Soldiers) are to take care that no expense is accrued in the State for their mentainance during such Intervals, their hands must clear their teeth. As the President has put it in my power to continue the guard at my pleasure, I do think proper to continue the Substitutes until the civil authority has no further demand for us; it's not the business of this, that, or the other Class, how the present Class serves their tower of duty or yet the people for whom they are Imployed; as the house of Assembly has appointed me the drudge in that respect, for those very mute good People, & have borne the burthen for them, I'm also determined that they shall give me a Liberty to Judge for them, so that if they make use of Language, let it be amongst themselves, as I hope ever to be able to act agreeable to my duty without Partiality to Persons while in my present station. I hope the Substitutes will behave themselves becoming men of candour and probity. I'm their mark for their wages.

In haste, yours &c.,

BERTRAM GALBRAITH, *Lieut.*

[Col. Joshua Elder to Colonel Rodgers.]

PAXTANG, *July 22d 1777.*

COL. JOHN RODGERS, DEAR SIR: I yesterday came from Colonel Galbraith's, where we fixed on having a Day of Appeal in your Battalion: Inclosed I have sent you a copy of an advertisement which you'll be good enough to put up in the most Public Places, & fix the Place of meeting at the most convenient Place as near the Center of the Battalion as possible.

I am in the meantime your most humble servant,

JOSHUA ELDER.

NOTES AND QUERIES.—CLIX.

PostLethwaite.—In reply to a valued correspondent, who some months since made inquiries concerning Col. Samuel Postlethwaite and his children, we find the following notes:

Col. Samuel Postlethwaite died August 24, 1810, at Carlisle, in his 72d year.

Joseph R. Postlethwaite removed from Carlisle to Pittsburgh, where he opened tavern "Sign of the Bear," in September, 1795, " in the house lately occupied by Capt. John McMasters."

Dr. James Postlethwaite married, April 11, 1799, Betsey Smith, daughter of the late Maj. James Smith, of Cumberland county.

Miss Amelia Postlethwaite, daughter of Col. Samuel, married, January, 1801, Henry Coulter, of Greensburg. Mr. Coulter died at Carlisle March 2, 1802, leaving a wife and one child. Mrs. Coulter died Friday, November 4, 1808, about 200 miles above the Natchez, to which place she was going with her brother. Her remains were taken to Natchez.

Lang [Long] Family.—The assessment for Paxtang township, Lancaster, now Dauphin county, for 1780 has the name of Paul Long as a " freeman." Who was he, and was he the ancestor of the following?

 i. Catharine, m. George Parthemore.
 ii. Kate, m. Paul Utz.
 iii. Lizzie, m. ——— Gardner; they resided in Washington,
   D. C.
 iv. Jacob.
 v. Henry.

John Long, b. 1778; d. Feb. 6, 1833, and buried in St. Peter's grave-yard, Middletown, Pa.; he m., first, Christina Musser, who d. in 1817; they had issue:

 i. Catharine, b. April 12, 1811; m. Matthias Parthemore;
   resided in Highspire, Pa.
 ii. Nancy, unm.; resided in Highspire, Pa.
 iii. Elizabeth, b. Aug. 31, 1814; m. John Hoover; resided in
   Union Deposit, Pa.
 iv. John, d. s. p.

John Long m., secondly, by Rev. Geo. Lochman, June 17, 1817, Fannie Musser, sister to his first wife; Fannie d. aged 66 years; they had issue:

    v. [*A dau.*] d. s. p.

    vi. *John.*

    vii. viii. [*Twins.*]

    ix. [*A dau.*]

    x. Daniel, b. Dec. 8, 1818; m. Mary Bowers; resided in Highspire, Pa.; was known to many of the citizens of Dauphin county as the blacksmith who carried on his trade above the village, along the pike, south of the canal bridge, for nearly 40 years.   E. W. S. P.

AN OLD LANCASTER COUNTY FARMER.

[The death of Mrs. Ann Maria Sehner, of Lancaster county, has called forth the following notice, and facts connected with an old Lancaster county family, which has been forwarded to *Notes and Queries* for publication.]

Mrs. Ann Maria Sehner, widow of the late John Sehner. died on the morning of July 26, 1887, at Lancaster. She was born August 12, 1806, the eldest daughter of Adolph Christian Fick and the last survivor of the family. She was baptized September 8, 1806, confirmed in youth by Rev. Dr. Endress, of Trinity Lutheran church, and united in marriage to John Sehner by Rev. P. Wolle, of the Moravian Church, December 15, 1825.

Her father, Adolph C. Pick, was born at Waren, in the Duchy of Mecklenburg, September 17, 1777, served an apprenticeship in Eppendorf, near the free city of Hamburg, receiving at the end of his term an honorable discharge, a strong letter of recommendation. He came to Philadelphia about the year 1799 and settled in Lancaster, where he soon afterwards married Justine M. Ulmer, daughter of Philip Ulmer and wife Barbara (born Hamerich), and started his business of a butcher. Leaving his family and business he marched to Baltimore in the service of his adopted country in the war of 1812–15. Returning, after an honorable discharge, he continued his business on East King street, adjoining the residence of the parents of Col. Wm. B. Fordney, opposite the home of Robert Coleman, where he died in 1825. His widow survived him 43 years, dying in 1868 in her 83d year.

Her husband, the late John Sehner, born January 4, 1798 (1798–1864), carpenter and builder, was the oldest son of John, born October 7, 1765 (Johannis), Sehner and wife Catharine, whose maiden name was Rung, and a grandson of Gottlieb Sœhner, who landed in Philadelphia from off the ship Fane, Captain Hyndman, October 17, 1749, and settled in Lancaster, where he was married by Rev. I. F. Handschuh to Maria Barbara Kline, on Sunday, September 18, 1750, in the old Lutheran church that stood upon the site now occupied by Trinity Lutheran chapel. Pastor Handschuh's text on that day was Psalm xv.

Mrs. Sehner survived her husband 23 years. Never very robust, though a woman of great industry and energy, devoting her strength and many years to her family and the sick and distressed within her reach, she has now gone to her reward at the ripe old age of 80 years, 11 months and 14 days.

Of nine children (eight sons and one daughter) four sons—John R., Henry C., Benjamin F., and Edward A., and one daughter Justine M., wife of George H. Rothermel, survive her. She leaves also two grandsons, Samuel M. Sehner, son of Henry C. Sehner, and John J. Rothermel, and two great-granddaughters, Frances and Gertrude, children of Samuel M. Sehner.

Jacob Sehner, of Carlisle, who celebrated his 95th birthday on July 16, and who also served in the war of 1812–15, and Gottlieb Sehner, of Manor township, Lancaster county, are also grandsons of Gottlieb Sœhner, of 1749.

NOTES AND QUERIES.—CLX.

DEATHS OF PROMINENT PERSONS.

[The following record is of more than ordinary historical value :]

Anderson, Alexander A., attorney, d. at Lewistown, April 28, 1823, aged 37 years.

Agnew, Mary Ann, daughter of Dr. Samuel Agnew, d. August 13, 1829, at the residence of her brother at Brownsville, Fayette county.

Bucher, Henry, formerly of Dauphin county, d. suddenly in Catlin township, Tioga county, N. Y., June, 1829.

Brady, Dennis, of Harrisburg, d. October 13, 1829.

Beader, Henry, register and recorder of Dauphin county, d. August 3, 1816, aged 53 years.

Brandon, Charles, d. at Middletown, Nov. 11, 1813, aged 63 years.

Boyd, Mrs. Margaret, wife of Rev. Alexander Boyd, and daughter of Dr. John Watson, d. at Bedford, Feb. 20, 1816, aged 25 years.

Bower, the Widow, d. at Middletown, July 17, 1818, aged 83 years.

Bower, Gen. Jacob, an officer of the Revolution, d. at Womelsdorf, August 3, 1818, aged 61 years.

Bogner, Tobias, of Middle Paxtang, d. July 20, 1822, aged 92 years.

Brandon, Mrs. Louisa, a native of Charleston, S. C., d. at Harrisburg, November 14, 1822, aged 22 years.

Brisbin, William, formerly treasurer of Mifflin county, d. November 13, 1822.

Chrystie, Col. John, of the 23d regiment, U. S. infantry, one of the Inspectors General of the army, d. at Fort George, July 15, 1813.

Deckert, Peter S., representative from Franklin county, d. at Chambersburg, February 11, 1823, of a pulmonary disease.

Dock, Philip, died at the residence of his son at Newville, July 15, 1830, aged 84 years.

Enders, Rev. Christian Frederick Ludwig, D. D., died at Lancaster, Sunday, October 7, 1827.

Frazer, John, Esq., for many years clerk in the office of Secretary of the Commonwealth, d. March 6, 1824, at the residence of his brother in Harrisburg.

Findlay, Mrs. Nancy Irwin, wife of Governor Findlay, d. at Pittsburgh, July 27, 1821, while on a visit.

Farrelly, Patrick, member of Congress, died at Pittsburgh, July 12, 1826.

Findlay, William Smith, Esq., attorney-at-law, eldest son of the late Governor of Pennsylvania, died at America, Illinois, August 2, 1821, at the age of 27 years.

Goodwin, Edward, attorney-at-law, d. at Lebanon, February 17, 1819, at advanced years.

Hubley, James B., Esq., attorney-at-law, d. at Reading, Tuesday, August 6, 1826, aged 38 years.

Henry, Mrs. Jane, relict of John Joseph Henry, d. Saturday evening April 15, 1826, at the residence of her son-in-law, Thomas Smith, Esq., near Darby.

Irwin, Mrs. Clarissa, wife of Dr. Joseph Irwin and daughter of Alexander Berryhill, of Harrisburg, d. at Woodstock, Va., January 3, 1832, in the 47th year of her age.

Kurtz, John William, Lutheran minister, d. at Jonestown, May 30, 1799, aged 67 years.

Lauer, William, Esq., d. at Hummelstown, February 14, 1826, aged about 51 years.

McKee, John, d. at the residence of his father, James McKee, of Pittsburgh, October 16, 1831, aged 49 years.

MOORES OF DONEGAL AND HEMPFIELD.

Ephraim Moore, the pioneer settler of this family, located near the "Scotts," in Donegal township, afterwards Hempfield, near Big Chickies creek, in the year 1722. He had two sons living with him, and perhaps daughters also, when he came to Chickies. Both sons were grown up, and had attained their majority prior to 1728. In my article upon the Agnews and Scotts, I stated that it was probable that Arthur Patterson and James Moore came to Donegal about the same time; this can hardly be correct. James Moore must have been in Donegal several years before Mr. Patterson came. The descendants of the latter claim that he came as early as 1724. As I cannot find his name upon any of the assessments of Donegal prior to 1730, I must conclude that he settled here after that date.

Ephraim Moore's sons were:

I. JAMES MOORE, who married Elizabeth Scott, sister of Mrs. James Agnew and Mrs. Arthur Patterson. The first authentic notice I have of him is his participation in Cresap's war. It will be remembered that Capt. Samuel Smith, of Donegal, then sheriff, raised a *posse* of his friends and neighbors numbering about forty-eight persons, of whom James Moore was one. They marched to Capt. Cresap's and after skirmishing all day and part of the night, set fire to Cresap's house and took him and several others prisoners. He did not survive that war. He died in 1736, leaving his wife Elizabeth, and but one child, *Ephraim*. His father Ephraim was then living with him. He left a large farm to his son in Hempfield township. He must have been a prominent citizen. Very likely his exposure among the hills of York county brought on premature disease, which caused his early death.

ELIZABETH MOORE (*nee* Scott), widow of James, died June 4, 1745 She made a peculiar will, from which I am enabled to glean some *data* of the Scotts. She owned no real estate. She divided the live stock on the farm, and other personal property among her relatives. She named her sisters, who were then in America, and several of her nieces. She devised to Elizabeth Patterson, daughter of her sister Ann, and Arthur Patterson. These were ancestors of the Hon. David Watson Patterson, judge of the courts in Lancaster, and the wife of the Hon. John Bayard McPherson, judge of the Dauphin and Lebanon courts.

To her sister, Sarah Scott's children, if they come to this country.

To the following named relatives she gave but one shilling each. They were all large landholders and well-to-do families and for that reason they may have been cut off with a shilling:

To Abraham Lowrey's children. He married her sister first and secondly Sarah, daughter of John and Martha Sterrett. To Grace Pedan's children. She was her sister and married Capt. Hugh Pedan. To Ann Patterson's children, wife of Arthur Patterson. To Rebecca Agnew's children. She married James Agnew as before stated. To Jean Wilson's children (sister). To Abraham Scott's children (brother). To Josiah Scott's children (a brother), and to Samuel Scott (a brother) and children. This Samuel Scott died in 1777, and left no children. If he had any at the time of Mrs. Moore's decease, they must have died in their minority.

The witnesses to Mrs. Moore's will were:

ALEXANDER JOHNSON, who married a sister of John Scott's, who died in 1748. He was the pioneer settler of the name in Donegal. In 1727 some of the neighbors who claimed to own the land upon which his cabin was built, raised his house to the ground, and turned his family out without shelter. (*See Dr. Egle's History of Pennsylvania, page 820.*) This was one of the results growing out of the refusal of the early settlers in Donegal to take out patents for their land. The Penns refused to allow their Surveyor General to survey any land before proper application was made for a warrant of survey.

THOMAS SCOTT, brother of the above.

JOHN SCOTT. These Scott brothers must have been relatives of Mrs. Moore, and, perhaps, members of her family. She named so many of her relatives in her will, and for that reason, perhaps, selected others for witnesses. She must have had some motive in giving so many of her relatives but a shilling. Whatever it was, it shows a strong will, and much character.

My impression is that Thomas Scott removed to the Valley of Virginia, and from thence to Washington county, Pa.

EPHRAIM MOORE, son of James, and grandson of Ephraim Moore, married his first cousin, Elenor, daughter of Arthur and Ann Patterson. They resided upon the old homestead in Hempfield. He accumulated several large tracts of land up the Susquehanna, the exact locality of which I am unable to ascertain, as he directed it to be sold. He died in December, 1776, leaving his wife Elenor, and children as follows:

  i. *Anna,* to whom he gave £110.
  ii. *Elizabeth,* to whom he gave £110.
  iii. *James,* to whom he gave £200.
  iv. *Arthur,* to whom he gave £200.
  v. *Samuel,* to whom he gave £200.
  vi. *Ephraim,* to whom he gave £200.
  vii. *William,* the youngest son, he gave £200.

There was a posthumus child, the name of which I do not know. He directed his mansion farm to be sold as soon as his son William became of age. His lands up the Susquehanna were to be sold soon after his death. His brothers-in-law, James Patterson and Samuel Patterson (sons of Arthur Patterson), were his executors. The witnesses to the will were Alexander Scott, Samuel Patterson and Samuel Rankin.

This branch of the Moore family seems to have removed from Lancaster county after they sold their lands, and I am sorry to say that I cannot find any trace of them.

II. ZACHARIAH MOORE, son of Ephraim, purchased a farm in Donegal township adjoining the church Glebe land, and now adjoining the Cameron farm on the west. He died in 1760. Mary Moore and Ephraim Moore were his administrators. Robert Fulton (father of the inventor) and James Carr were bail. He left sons:

> *i. Hugh,* who was then over fourteen years of age, and came into court April 11, 1763, and asked to have Samuel Scott appointed his guardian.
>
> *ii. Zachariah,* was under fourteen years of age. Samuel Scott was appointed his guardian.

Hugh Moore died in July, 1786, leaving a wife Anney and the following children:

> *i. Nancy.*
>
> *ii. Mary.*
>
> *iii. Rebecca.*
>
> *iv. Andrew,* to whom he gave his real estate. He was declared a lunatic. His brother, Zachariah Moore, and his wife Anney, and James Willson he named as executors.

Anna Moore, widow of Hugh Moore, died in 1793 and named in her will:

> *i. Anna.*
>
> *ii. Mary.*
>
> *iii. Rebecca.*

Zachariah Moore, her brother, and James Willson were her executors. At the March term of court, 1794, Samuel Cook, Esq., and John Mitchell, Esq., were appointed guardians over the estate of Mary Moore, Rebecca Moore, and Andrew Moore, minor children of Hugh Moore. It is probable that either Samuel Cook or John Mitchell married Anna, the oldest daughter of Hugh Moore. Col. Bertram Galbraith and his wife Ann, daughter of Josiah Scott, held five hundred and forty-two acres of land in trust for the children of Hugh Moore.

ZACHARIAH MOORE, son of Zachariah and grandson of Ephraim Moore, married Mary Boggs, sister of Capt. Alexander Boggs, who married Ann Alricks, daughter of Hermanus Alricks, prothonotary of Cumberland county in 1750. Zack Moore and his father were carpenters. The former and his uncle, Capt. Hugh Pedan, made the first radical change in old Donegal church in 1772. A door was cut through the walls at each end of the building, and the windows were changed from a circular to a square head, with larger panes of glass. Zack Moore also put a new shingle roof on the church in 1799. He was second lieutenant in Capt. Robert Craig's company, in Col. Alex. Lowrey's battalion, in 1777, and was in the battle of Brandywine. He died June 19, 1803, aged 54 years, leaving a wife Mary and the following named children :

    i. Ephraim, who accepted his father's farm, containing two hundred and seventy-two acres, at the appraisement.

    ii. Ann, who married Capt. John Pedan, son of Capt. Hugh Pedan. John Pedan entered very largely into speculation at Marietta in 1812, and lost a very large estate when the crash came. One or more of his sons moved to Ohio.

    iii. Mary.

    iv. Zachariah.

    v. Andrew.

    vi. Alexander.

    vii. Jane, married· George B. Ferree, who kept tavern and store in Maytown. He became greatly involved through his love for the "turf" and lost a large fortune. He moved to Mobile, thence to St. Louis and Cincinnati, and to Carlisle, where he kept hotel, and died some years ago. His widow died only two or three years ago in Marietta.

Mrs. Moore (*nee* Boggs) came from a remarkably long-lived family, and came to a great age. She died upon her son's farm at Donegal, February 15, 1847, aged 89 years.

I remember Mrs. Moore very distinctly, having on several occasions visited the family with my grandmother, who was a half sister of Mrs. Alex. Boggs. Two of the Pedan boys were schoolmates of mine, although a few years my senior, under the tuition of Mr. Rankin and Rev. Simpson in Marietta. John Pedan was a very tall young man, and remarkably active. Both he and the late James Brice Clark were over six feet in height before they attained their majority. Pedan frequently stood upon the ground and kicked the hat off Mr. Clark's head, and could turn a back or forward somersault. These feats the boys regarded as extraordinary.

Columbia, Pa.   SAMUEL EVANS.

NOTES AND QUERIES.—CLXI.

MILITARY OFFICERS IN 1806 AND 1807.—The following list of military officers may interest the descendants of those named:

1806.

Abraham Doebler, of Lebanon, brigade inspector of Dauphin and Berks counties.

Jacob Wain, of Harrisburg, colonel of 66th regiment.

Frederick Wolfersberger, of Hummelstown, colonel of the 78th regiment.

George Bowman, of Lebanon, colonel of the 3d regiment.

1807.

James Wallace, brigadier general of 1st brigade, 6th division, Pennsylvania militia.

Henry Kelker, lieutenant colonel of 3d regiment.

George Ziegler, lieutenant colonel of 66th regiment.

William Lower, lieutenant colonel of the 78th regiment.

Christian Seltzer, lieutenant colonel of 117th regiment.

Peter Lebengood, lieutenant colonel of 95th regiment.

David Deibler, major of the Upper Paxtang battalion.

James Ingram, major of the 1st battalion.

John Umberger, major of the 2d battalion.

Joseph Allen, of Hanover, major of the 78th regiment.

AT VALLEY FORGE—1778.

[The following memorial recalls the sufferings of the Pennsylvania troops at Valley Forge during the occupancy of Philadelphia by the British army during the winter of 1778. We say Pennsylvania troops from the fact that with the exception of several New Jersey and New York regiments they chiefly endured the severities of that noted cantonment. The officers who signed the memorial had been sent by their respective commands to Lancaster, where the authorities of the State were located. Immediate efforts were taken to ameliorate the condition of the patriots, but history does not inform us how many lives went out amidst the misery and gloom which brooded over the cabins of the soldiers of the Revolution at Valley Forge.]

LANCASTER, *3d February, 1778.*
To his Excellency the President and the Honbl, Members of the Supreme
Executive Council of this State, a memorial:

Captain Thomas Bartholomew Bowen, of the Ninth, and Captain James Chrystie, of the Third Pennsylvania Regiments, beg leave, agreeable to their Instructions, to lay before your Excellency and the Hon'ble Council, the extremely distressed Situation of these Corps for want of every Article of Clothing.

Barefooted, naked and miserable beyond expression—several brave soldiers having nothing more than a piece of old Tent to shield them from the inclemency of the season, and not more than one Blanket to six or perhaps eight men. Very few indeed, are in any wise fit for duty; the Clothing of both Officers and Soldiers having been lost in the course of the Campaign, particularly twice in consequence of General Orders for storing them at Concord and at Wilmington; and their Blankets lost in the several Actions we have had with the Enemy.

That these Corps, with the Sixth and Twelfth Pennsylvania Regiments, are attach'd to a Division composed partly of Jersey Troops, under the command of General Officers not belonging to the State; who, it may naturally be supposed, will be careful to have the Troops of their own State clothed, preferably to those of another, agreeable to the late Regulations.

That ever since General Conway left us we have had no General Officer to make application for us, or to see that justice should be done us in the distribution of the Clothing remitted to the Army; the Brigade to which we are attach'd, having been successively under the temporary command of Colonels belonging to other States.

That General Wayne having procured a Quantity of Clothing and three hundred pairs of Shoes, it is more than probable he will supply the two Brigades under his immediate Command, in preference to the Regiments of this State annexed to other Divisions; and if their wants are equal to ours, the Surplus, if any, will afford us but a very inconsiderable Proportion.

Your Memorialists therefore, in behalf of the before mention'd Regiments, Pray your Excellency and the Hon'ble Council to grant them speedy Relief, by ordering the Receiver General of Clothing for this State, to supply them with a proportion of the necessary Articles now on hand. Your Memorialists are sensible that Congress, in their late resolution, have directed the Clothing to be issued thro' the hands of the Clothier General; but as General Wayne has found means to supply his Troops without the formalities, which in our present miserable Situation, must greatly retard the relieving our distresses, perhaps that Resolution may not be positively determinate.

If so, your Humanity and Justice will induce your Hon'ble Board to immediately supply the other Troops of this State with a Quota of what is now in Possession.

And your Memorialists, &c.,

JA. CHRYSTIE,
Captn. 3d Penn'a.
THOS. B. BOWEN,
Captn. 9th Penn'a.

Captain Bowen, for himself, would now beg leave to inform your Excellency and Council that he has lost all his clothing, to a very considerable value, in two successive campaigns; And prays he may be indulged with an order for some Linen & other necessities to supply his immediate wants, subject to such prices as are or may be charged, agreeable to the late Resolution of Congress.

THE FAMILY OF CLARK.

[Among our notes are the following data concerning the Scotch-Irish family of Clark or Clarke (the name being written with or without the terminal e). If any of our readers can dovetail these records, or give us information relating to them or their descendants, we will consider it a favor.]

I. WILLIAM CLARK, d. September, 1732, leaving a wife Esther, and children:

 i. William, m. Margaret ———.
 ii. Sarah.
 iii. Esther.
 iv. Priscilla.

II. THOMAS CLARK, probably a brother of the preceding, d. December, 1760, leaving a wife Mary, and children:

 i. Thomas.
 ii. Eleanor, m. Isaac Martin.
 iii. Mary.
 iv. Margaret.

III. WILLIAM CLARK, probably the son of the first named, d. May, 1763, leaving wife Margaret, and children:

 i. Peter.
 ii. John.
 iii. [A dau.], m. John Baldridge.
 iv. Thomas.
 v. Joseph.
 iv. Anne.

IV. JAMES CLARK, m. Jean Campbell, daughter of Samuel Campbell, of Derry, and had among other children:
  i. John.
  ii. Samuel.
  iii. Isabella.
  iv. Jean.

V. JOHN CLARK, of Derry, d. 1752, leaving a wife Elizabeth, and children:
  i. James.
  ii. Thomas.
  iii. Robert.

Robert McElhenny and James Marshall were the executors; and Hugh Rippy, Joseph Rippy, and Nathaniel Clark witnesses to the will.

VI. ROBERT CLARK, of Upper Paxtang, d. February, 1771, leaving a wife Jean, and children:
  i. Eleanor, m. [John] Filson, and had *John, Robert,* and *Anne.*
  ii. Jean, m. Thomas Renick.
  iii. John.
  iv. Elizabeth, m. John Means.
  v. Mary, m. William Wallis.

In addition to the foregoing we find that a George Clark married a daughter of Robert and Elizabeth Montgomery, of Paxtang.

BIOGRAPHICAL DATA WANTED.

Biographical data is wanted concerning the following persons, other than here given. If any of our readers can furnish the same we will be glad to receive it.

ALBRIGHT, DR. FREDERICK.—Graduated in medicine in Germany; practiced his profession at Harrisburg and Carlisle, subsequently removing to the western country.

BERGHAUS, DR. CHARLES L.—Son of Henry Berghaus, d. October 6, 1858, aged 52 years.

BELL, WILLIAM.—Was a member of the House of Representatives from Dauphin county in 1842.

BALSBAUGH, HENRY.—Represented Dauphin county in the Legislature in 1842.

DEPUI, JOHN.—Was clerk of the Senate from 1824 to his death in March, 1829; married Louisa Kurtz, daughter of Benjamin Kurtz.

Cox, Dr. John.—Of Philadelphia, laid out Estherton, on the Susquehanna, in 1767; m., first, Mrs. Sarah Edgell, widow of William Edgell, of Philadelphia; secondly, Esther ———, of the same city.

Cox, John B.—Son of Col. Cornelius Cox; educated at Dickinson College; d. December 15, 1831, at Estherton.

Eicholtz, George.—Born in 1774 at Lancaster; d. June 17, 1859, at Harrisburg.

Fridley, Peter.—Born in 1753; d. April 17, 1823, at Harrisburg; was a soldier of the Revolution.

Fox, John, Sr.—Died at an advanced age at Hummelstown, May 11, 1816; ancestor of the Fox family in that locality.

Gilbert, Jacob.—Represented Dauphin county in the Legislature 1835-6.

Hollinger, Rev. Jacob.

Lauer, William.—Born in 1775; d. February 16, 1826, at Hummelstown.

Leidig, Michael.—He died August, 1811, in East Hanover, now Lebanon county; was a soldier in the Revolution; major in the militia.

Lebkicker, Michael.—Died June 17, 1850, in Harrisburg.

McCurdy, Colin.—Died September 18, 1880; a journalist of prominence; his widow lately deceased.

Musgrave, William.—Born January 4, 1747; d. January 7, 1832; was State Librarian.

McCormick, Henry.—Born in 1769; d. February 24, 1828; buried in old Hanover church grave-yard; m. Jane Mitchell, b. 1764; d. August 6, 1844; descendants reside at Clinton, Iowa.

Moody, Robert.—Born in 1752; d. December 13, 1838; buried in Derry church-yard; wife Mary, daughter of Joseph Hutchison, b. 1748; d. May 18, 1825.

McAlister, Capt. Archibald.—Son of Archibald McAlister; b. April 7, 1756; d. January 16, 1831; captain in Col. Thomas Hartley's regiment, com. January 13, 1777.

McKee, Col. Robert.—Died December 12, 1798, at his residence near Middletown.

McKinley, Isaac Gibson.—Died at Harrisburg December 10, 1860; prominent journalist.

MACHESNEY, JOHN.—Captain in Sixteenth U. S. Infantry ; commissioned March 13, 1813.

OTT, NICHOLAS.—Died about ten miles east of Womelsdorf November 5, 1832, aged 50 years.

PRICE, DR. ABRAHAM C.—Born in 1786 ; d. April 9, 1821, at Middletown.

REED, THOMAS C.—Died May 15, 1865, aged 76 years.

RODGERS, COL. JOHN.—Died December 6, 1799, in West Hanover ; commanded one of the battalions of associators in the Revolution.

REYNOLDS, DR. JOHN C.

REIMUTH, PHILIP.

SEYFERT, ANTHONY.—Notary public March 25, 1793, and coroner of the county of Dauphin from January 9, 1794, to December 7, 1795.

SEAL, JACOB.—Born December 16, 1785; died September 3, 1858.

SMITH, THOMAS.—Surveyor and maker of the county map of 1816.

SAWYERS, JAMES.—A captain in the Revolutionary war, and one of the burgesses of the borough of Harrisburg in 1797.

SCHAEFFER, REV. FREDERICK.—Born February 3, 1770; d. September 9, 1821, at Harrisburg.

UMBERGER, JOHN.—A soldier of the Revolution, who d. in 1813; father of Dr. David Umberger, of Linglestown.

WHITESIDE, DR. THOMAS.

WOLFLEY, JACOB.

WOLF, HENRY.—Died in 1831; sheriff of the county of Dauphin from October 19, 1809, to October 19, 1812, and again from October 16, 1815, to October 19, 1818; notary public, September 13, 1828.

WRIGHT, JOHN.—Represented Dauphin county in the Legislature, 1855 to 1856 ; accidentally killed at Halifax.

NOTES AND QUERIES.—CLXII.

THE TAXABLES IN PENNSYLVANIA in 1760 were 31,667. In 1770, 39,765. In 1789, 45,683; and in 1784, 66,925. In 1787 it was calculated that the white population of the State was about 360,000.

ALLISONS OF DERRY.—John Allison, of Derry, d. in 1747, leaving
a wife Janet, and children:

   i. Robert.
   ii. Jean.
   iii. Isabel.
   iv. Margaret.
   v. Janet.
   vi. James.

He owned land in Virginia.

ROBERT ALLISON, of Derry, d. in 1765. In his will he devised the
sum of £100 to the Philadelphia Hospital, and an equal sum to the
Academy at Newark, Del. He mentions his son, James Allison, and
the following:

Patrick Allison, John Allison, and Jane Clark, children of John
Allison, deceased; Margaret, Patrick, and Robert Allison, children of
William Allison; John, William, James, and Robert Smith, sons of
Jane Smith, deceased; and John and William White, children of
Margaret White.

IN THE REVOLUTION.

[As very frequently during the Rebellion, so it was in the Revolution, those having *political* influence were promoted over the heads of
persons of seniority of rank, and whose meritorious conduct in the
field deserved it. But such is the fate of politics in war, and those
who are shoved aside must abide the decision. Sometimes history re-
peats itself, and the following memorial of the subaltern officers of the
Second regiment of the Pennsylvania Line is an exemplification
thereof.]

                PHILADELPHIA, *January 20, 1776.*

To the Honorable Council of Safety for the State of Pennsylvania,
   The Memorial of the Subaltern Officers of the 2nd Pennsylv'a Regt.
   commanded by Jno. Phillip de Haas, Esqr., Respectfully sheweth:
   That your Memorialists understand by the arrangement making
out by the Hon'ble Board, that they will be deprived of that Rank in
the Army which they think themselves justly entitled to.

   They beg leave to acquaint the Board that they have served with
Reputation, & the Approbation of their Commanding Officers during
the last very severe campaign in the Northern Army, and as they are
not sensible what fault they have committed, they cannot but be
much surpriz'd at the unexpected appointment of several strange
Gentlemen to the Command of the vacant Companies in the above
Regiment.

We have risen to our present rank gradually, & have been in the Service considerable time, & now to be deprived of our just promotions we cannot but think is using us extremely hard & very discouraging to the Service.

All that we now want is that the Honorable Council will be pleas'd to appoint us according to our Seniority in the Batt'n, & our present just cause of uneasiness be remov'd.

We have now laid our Grievances before the Board, and hope that your Honors will take the above facts into tender Consideration.

> JOHN BANKSON,
> GEO. JENKINS,
> CHRISTIAN STADDEL,
> JNO. ELLIS,
> SAMUEL TOLBERT,
> JOHN COBEA,
> JNO. IRWIN,
> WM. MOORE,
> ZACH. ASHMEAD,
> JOHN STOY,
> MAJOR WALBRON.

GENEALOGICAL NOTES.

[We are indebted to Samuel Evans, Esq., of Columbia, for the following " Stray Notes " of old Scotch-Irish families, most of whose descendants nearly a century ago migrated southward and westward. Concerning several, we have already given data.]

SEMPLE.

In December, 1758, Thomas Harris was appointed guardian over George Semple, Sarah and Mary Semple, minor children of John Semple, deceased. At this time Captain Harris lived at his mill on Conewago creek in Mount Joy township. The Semples resided in Derry near the same place.

HARRIS.

William Harris, of Paxtang, died prior to 1762, and left children:

    i. James, over 21 years.

    ii. John, 17 years of age.

    iii. Robert, under 14.

    iv. Mary, under 14 years of age.

James Harris, uncle of these children, was appointed guardian of those under age. The farm contained 275 acres. Catharine Harris, the widow, and James Harris, the brother of William, were the administrators of the estate. The following apportionment was made in 1763:

To James, ... £118 13 4
To Sarah, ... 59   6 8
To Mary, ...   59   6 8
To Robert, ...   59   6 8

ROAN.

Andrew Roan, who died in 1768, left the following children, all of whom were above 14 years of age:

    i. Jennett.
    ii. Sarah.
    iii. Archibald.
    iv. William.
    v. Hugh.

TAYLOR.

Robert Taylor owned a farm of one hundred and fifty acres, adjoining the ferry on the Derry side of the Conewago. He died prior to 1762. Charles McCormick married Mary Taylor, his widow. In Orphans' Court proceedings in 1762 Henry Taylor, son of Robert, took the farm at a valuation of two hundred and seventy-one pounds. Charles McCormick and Mary received £23 9 11¾. Robt. Taylor's children were:

    i. Henry.
    ii. Catharine, m. John Sterling.
    iii. William.
    iv. Robert.
    v. Matthew.
    vi. Jane.
    vii. John.
    viii. Elizabeth.
    ix. Ann.

This family have disappeared from the Derry records.

CAMPBELL.

James Campbell, of Derry, d. in 1771, leaving a wife Rosanna. He named the following in his will:

Jean Edmiston, his step-daughter.
James Vernon, son of his step-son, Henry Vernon.
Robert Cross' children.

Sister Martha Cary, who was then in Ireland.

Sister Elizabeth Long, in Ireland.

James Campbell, son of his son Patrick Campbell, and also his sons John and Patrick.

He gave Flavel Roan £20.

Rev. John Roan was a witness to the will.

LAIRD.

John Laird, of Derry, d. in 1777, leaving a wife Agnes, and children:

  i. James, who got 221 acres on the Swatara.

  ii. Hugh, m. and had *John*.

  iii. John.

  iv. Samuel.

  v. William.

  vi. Elizabeth, m. Matthew McKinney, who was the nephew of Mary Harris (*nee* McKinney), wife of Capt. Thomas Harris.

The witnesses to the will were William Laird and John Mc-Farland.

WALKER.

JAMES WALKER, of Paxtang, d. in 1784, leaving a wife Barbara, and children:

  i. Isabel.

  ii. William.

  iii. James.

  iv. Daniel.

  v. Robert.

  vi. Thomas.

  vii. John.

He also mentions his granddaughters, Catharine Galbraith and Beckey Galbraith.

NOTES AND QUERIES.—CLXIII.

"PINE FORD" was at the crossing of the Swatara, at or near the present town of Middletown, in Dauphin county. In the petitions for a road leading from Harris' Ferry to the Conestoga, and from Thomas Harris' mill on Conewago to Pine Ford, mention is made of this ford, and it was probably well known throughout the Province prior to the erection of Middletown.

McARTHUR.—Thomas McArthur, of Paxtang, died in 1785, well advanced in years. By will he devised his estate to his children:

i. Katharine, m. —— Howard.

ii. Barbara, m. James Walker.

iii. Mary, m. William Peacock, and had, among others, *Thomas* and *James.*

iv. Thomas.

v. [A dau.], m. —— Kyle, and had *Rebecca* and *Margaret.*

RENICK, OF PAXTANG.

I. THOMAS RENICK, a native of Ireland, came with his family to America in 1733. On the 27th of March, 1738, he took out a warrant for 326 acres in Paxtang township, where he had first settled. This land adjoined lands of William Ritchey and Thomas Mayes. Of his family we have the record only of one son.

II. WILLIAM RENICK (Thomas), b. about 1704 in Ireland; d. prior to 1763, in Paxtang, for on the 5th of January that year his estate was divided; and the children severally released their claims against the estate of their father to their brother Henry. The family at that date were:

3.   *i. Henry*, b. 1725; m. Martha Wilson.

4.   *ii. Thomas*, b. 1730; m. Jean.

    iii. Margaret, b. 1733; resided in Cumberland county, Pa.

    iv. Alexander, b. 1736; resided in Cumberland county, Pa.

    v. Samuel, b. 1738; resided in Cumberland county, Pa.; m., and had a son *William.*

    vi. William, b. 1740; resided in Frederick county, Md.; m., and had a son *William,*

    vii. James, b. 1742; resided in Trenton, West Jersey.

III. HENRY RENICK (William, Thomas), b. Dec. 2, 1725, in the north of Ireland; m. in 1750, Martha Wilson. They had issue:

    i. William, b. Monday, Oct. 6, 1749; d. March, 1776.

    ii. Sarah, b. Tuesday, October 15, 1751; d. March 12, 1823; m. John Wilson, b. 1750; d. Nov. 11, 1800.

    iii. Mary, b. Saturday, August 24, 1754.

    iv. Martha, b. Saturday, Nov. 30, 1755; m. William Swan.

    v. Esther, b. August 31, 1758; m., Dec. 14, 1784, Robert Foster, b. 1758; d. Jan. 20, 1834, in Buffalo Valley, and left issue.

    vi. Margaret, b. Sept. 12, 1760; d. s. p.

IV. THOMAS RENICK (William, Thomas), b. about 1730, in the north of Ireland; d. in April, 1777, in Paxtang; m. Jean Clark, dau. of Robert and Jean Clark, of Upper Paxtang; d. in May, 1782. They had issue:

    i. Mary, m. Hugh Miller.

    ii. Jean, m. Thomas Brunson.

    iii. John, d. May, 1784; unm.; directing his estate to be divided between his four sisters and his cousin, Esther Renick.

    iv. Margaret.

    v. Ann, m. Robert Boyd.

ADVENTURES OF TWO FRENCHMEN

IN THE VALLEY OF THE OHIO IN 1788.

[Mr. DeWarville published shortly after his return from an extensive tour in the United States in 1788 an interesting account of his travels. One of his letters translated from the French is here given.]

I have had the good fortune to meet here a Frenchman, who is traveling in this country, not in pursuit of wealth, but to gain information. It is Mr. Saugrain from Paris; he is an ardent naturalist; some circumstances first attached him to the king of Spain, who sent him to Spanish America to make discoveries in minerals and natural history. After the death of his protector, Don Galves, he returned to France. In 1787 he formed the project with Mr. Piguet, who had some knowledge in botany, to visit Kentucky and Ohio.

They arrived at Philadelphia, and passed immediately to Pittsburgh. There the winter overtook them, and the Ohio froze over, which rarely happens. They lodged themselves a few miles from Pittsburgh in an open house, where they suffered much from the cold. The thermometer of Reaumur descended to 32 degrees, while at Philadelphia it was only at 16. During their stay here they made many experiments. Mr. Saugrain weighed several kinds of wood in an hydrostatic balance which he carried with him. He discovered, likewise, which species would yield the greatest quantity, and the best kind of potash. Many experiments convinced him that the stalks of Indian corn yielded a greater quantity than wood in proportion to the quantity of matter. He examined the different mines of the country. He found some of iron, of lead, of copper and of silver. He was told of a rich iron mine belonging to Mr. Murray, but he was not suffered to see it.

On the opening of the spring, they descended the Ohio, having been joined by another Frenchman, Mr. Rague, and a Virginian. They landed at Muskingum, where they saw General Harmer and some people who were beginning a settlement there.

At some distance below this place they fell in with a party of savages. M. Piguet was killed; and M. Saugrain wounded and taken prisoner; he fortunately made his escape, rejoined the Virginian, and found the means of returning to Pittsburgh, having lost his money and all his effects. He then returned to Philadelphia, where I have met him, on his way to Europe.

He has communicated to me many observations of the western country. The immense valley washed by the Ohio, appears to him the most fertile that he has ever seen. The strength and rapidity of vegetation in that country are incredible, the size of the trees enormous, and their variety infinite. The inhabitants are obliged to exhaust the first fatness of the land in hemp and tobacco, in order to prepare it for the production of wheat. The crops of Indian corn are prodigious; the cattle acquire an extraordinary size, and keep fat the whole year in the open fields.

The facility of producing grain, rearing cattle, making whiskey, beer, and cider, with a thousand other advantages, attract to this country great numbers of emigrants from other parts of America. A man in this country scarcely works two hours a day for the support of himself and family; he passes most of his time in idleness, hunting or drinking. The women spin and make clothes for their husbands and families. Mr. Saugrain saw very good woolens and linens made there. They have very little money; everything is done by barter.

The active genius of the Americans is always pushing them forward. Mr. Saugrain has no doubt but sooner or later the Spaniards will be forced to quit the Mississippi, and the Americans will pass it, and establish themselves in Louisiana, which he has seen, and considers as one of the finest countries in the universe.

Mr. Saugrain came from Pittsburgh to Philadelphia in seven days on horseback. He could have come in a chaise; but it would have taken him a longer time. It is a post road with good taverns established the whole way.

THE WATER-SHED OF SULLIVAN COUNTY.

Interposed between the two main streams of the Susquehanna river above its bifurcation at Northumberland, the county of Sullivan is one of the most remarkable sections of eastern Pennsylvania. It is in fact an elevated plateau, its highest parts 2,500 feet above the level of the sea, discharging from three of its sides considerable streams of water to the two great divisions of the Susquehanna above mentioned. Of the latter there are two on the west, two on the south, and two on the east, each of which originating on a high level and gradually making deep cuts for itself toward the edge of the plateau, eventually emerge from their mountain gorges into the river valley beyond. In this way the West Branch receives the Loyalsock and Muncy creeks, and the North Branch Fishing creek, with its main territory, and Bowman and Mehoopany creeks. Strong streams are all these, which if found in Europe would be denominated rivers, and the topography of each in its upper and middle courses would well reward attention. The dense forests of the mountain plateau are composed of beech, maple, birch, and hemlock, but a small part of which have been yet removed, and it may be assured that they have a considerable effect upon the climate and rain fall of the general section of the State in which they are found. Only of late have the geological features and mineral resources of Sullivan county undergone investigation, but from what already appears it is evident that the county is not the desert region, which upon imperfect information, many persons formerly supposed it to be. It has been assumed that when the forests were swept off there would be left only a broken surface poorly adapted to the purposes of agriculture and beneath to the profoundest depths only sterile and worthless rocks. But a limited basin of coal intermediate between bituminous and anthracite has been found and developed at Birch Creek, and recent borings south of that locality indicate more extensive formations of the same material, distinct proof has also been obtained of yellow ochre in a valuable deposit in the neighborhood of Ganoga lake, extending northward for several miles, and iron ores also have been detected at several points.

The whole section is rich in timber and the surface is admirably adapted to grazing purposes and to the production of root crops, grasses and summer grain.

Sullivan is dotted by about a dozen interesting lakes, which we have no doubt will furnish favorite points for summer resorts in future times. Toward the east Mehoopany and Bowman's creek each originate in one of these while the outlet flow of the others are contributions to tributaries of Fishing creek on the south. The two west ponds are located near the center of the county, while those two beautiful bodies of water known as Lewis and Hunter's lakes are found upon the western border.

MARRIAGES BY REV. WILLIAM R. DeWITT.

[The following list of marriages by Rev. William R. DeWitt, who for fifty years filled the pulpit of the Presbyterian church in Harrisburg, may interest our readers. This list forms only a small proportion of the marriages consummated by that revered minister.]

1819.

Nov. 25. Samuel Johnson, of Cumberland county, and Jane Gillispie.
Dec. 23. William Bell and Elizabeth Hutman.

1820.

April 18. Richard T. Jacobs and Sallie Hanna.
28. Henry Antes and Catharine M. Forster.
May 23. Jacob Spangler and Catharine Hamilton.
Nov. 30. John Whitehill and Catharine Orth.
Dec. 9. Cornelius Armstrong and Jane Buffington.
14. Jane Findlay and Francis R. Shunk.

1821.

Nov. 9. Eleanor Whitehill and Philip Frazer.
9. Samuel White and Sarah Hills.

1822.

Sept. 12. George W. Harris and Mary Hall.
19. Alex. Graydon and Jane McKinney.
Oct. 24. John Roberts and Mary Chambers.
24. George W. Boyd and Elizabeth Mish.
Nov. 22. N. B. Wood and Catharine Beader.

1824.

April 13. William H. Doll and Sarah Elder.
Feb. 10. Thomas Baird and Eliza Sloan.
June 29. Dr. Joseph Smith and Eleanor Graydon.

1829.

Mar. 25. John A. Weir and Catharine Wiestling.

1830.

Jan. 14. Robert Allen and Ellen Bucher.
26. James Snodgrass and Mary Richie.
May 31. James McCormick and Eliza Buehler.
June 29. Garrick Mallory and Catharine Hall.

1831.

July 14. James Denning and Caroline Burnett.
Oct. 11. Andrew J. Jones and Ann Jones.

1832.

May 8. Henry Cross and Rose Wright.
Nov. 21. Wm. Wilson Rutherford and Eleanor Crain.

1833.

May 25. Charles C. Rawn and Frances P. Clendenin.
Sept. 12. Austin O. Hubbard and Mary T. Graydon.
Dec. 24. Dr. William Elder and Sarah J. McLean.

1834.

Mar. 23. John Sloan and Mary White.
Sept. 10. Daniel Gehr and Harriet Berryhill.

1835.

Sept. 24. James Kennedy and Elizabeth Hanna.
29. James Gillespie and Jane Sturgeon.
Oct. 15. Joel Hinckley and Theodosia Graydon.
June 30. John Harrison and Elizabeth Murray.

1836.

May 17. Samuel Cross and Mary Wright.
Oct. 12. Capt. James Collier and Sarah Mitchell.

1838.

Aug. 23. Daniel Rider and Sophia McAllister.

1839.

Jan. 1. Anthony Blanchard Warford and Eliza Cameron.
Mar. 5. Joseph W. Cottrell and Esther A. Sloan.
Mar. 13. George W. Urban and Mary Green.

1840.

Feb. 20. James Cowden and Ann Chambers.
Mar. 12. William Carson and Lydia Smith.
May —. Robert R. Elder and Elizabeth G. Elder.

1841.

Jan. 7. Charles Thomas and Susan Coble, both of East Pennsboro.
June 15. Henry Buehler and Fanny S. Mahon.

1842.

Apr. 25. David Craighead and Mary Jane Sloan.
May 24. Rev. Matthew Semple and Caroline Wills.

1843.

June 1. Dr. William C. McPherson and Elizabeth Wallace.

1844.

Elisha S. Goodrich, of Bradford county, and Rose Cross.

1845.

May 13. Wallace Kerr and Eliz. E. Harris.
13. William R. Morris and Cath. H. Harris.

1845.

James Clark and Eliz. Buffington.
Nov. 12. Dr. John S. Bobbs and Cath. M. Cameron.

1848.

Sept. 13. James Ross Snowden, of Philadelphia, and Susan E. Patterson.

1849.

Mar. 1. James Todd and Ann M. Espy.
Dec. 8. John A. Weir and Matilda Fahnestock.
Mar. 8. Robert W. McClure and Margaretta Sturgeon.

1850.

Sept. 18. Augustus K. Cornyn and Eliza H. Jacobs.

1851.

Aug. 19. David Espy and Ann Catharine Jackson.

1854.

Mar. 7. James Elder and Rebecca Orth Whitehill.

NOTES AND QUERIES.—CLXIV.

BOYD.—John Boyd, of Paxtang township, d. in 1772, leaving children :

i. *Margaret.*
ii. *Mary.*
iii. *Jean.*
iv. *Martha.*

Jean Means and Sarah McWhorter were grandchildren. The following were mentioned as sons-in-law :

James Miller.
James Means.
James Anderson.
William McWhorter.
James Burd and John Steele were executors of the estate.

CAVET.—John Cavet, of Paxtang township, d. in 1784, leaving a wife Catharine, and children :

    i. John, m. and had a son *Thomas.*
    ii. James.
    iii. Thomas.
    iv. Lydia.
    v. Grizle.
    , *vi. Catharine.*

In his will he mentions his grandsons, sons of John, James, and Thomas, and granddaughters as follows:

Catharine Boggs.
Catharine McNutt.
Catharine Wylie.   S. E.

DEATHS OF PROMINENT PERSONS.

McElwee, Robert, late clerk in the Treasurer's office of the State, d. Friday, July 6, 1821. [He resided on High street near the arsenal.]

Miller, Jacob, Esq., d. in Harrisburg, Saturday, August 25, 1821, aged 69 years.

Mish, Jacob, d. at Harrisburg, Wednesday, August 17, 1825, of typhus fever, in his 29th year.

Mitchell, Thomas, d. at Annville, Sunday, October 31, 1813, aged 83 years.

Mitchell, Mrs., widow, d. at Harrisburg, Wednesday, September 2, 1818, "a distinguished and pious Methodist of that borough."

McAllister, Rev. Richard, youngest son of Archibald McAllister, of Fort Hunter, d. at the residence of his brother near Savannah, Ga., November 9, 1822.

Melish, John, geographer, d. at Harrisburg December 30, 1822, in the 52d year of his age.

Murray, William, merchant, of Harrisburg, d. at Washington, Pa., May 1, 1823.

Myers, Samuel, member of the House of Representatives from Lehigh county, d. at Harrisburg March 20, 1824, in the 35th year of his age.

Mish, Mrs. Sarah, wife of Jacob, and daughter of John Bickel, of Jonestown, d. July 7, 1824, in her 24th year.

Montgomery, Robert, U. S. Consul at Alicant, Spain, d. there in September, 1823. He was an appointee of Washington.

Maginness, James, mathematician, d. at Harrisburg May 31, 1829.

Mitchell, Mrs. Sarah, widow of the late Thomas Mitchell, d. in West Hanover on Thursday, July 19, 1821, in her 79th year.

Mitchell, John, Esq., formerly a resident of Harrisburg, d. at Millersburg, Tuesday, September 11, 1821.

McJimsey, Joseph A., Esq., died at Harrisburg Thursday, September 20, 1821, aged about 40 years.

Montgomery, Mrs. Jane, consort of Rev. William B. Montgomery, formerly of Danville, Pa., d. October, 1821, at Harmony, in the Osage Nation.

Norton, John, carpenter, d. July 6, 1822, aged 73 years, one of the earliest settlers of Harrisburg.

Nelson, Joseph R., assistant engineer of the Juniata Division of the Pennsylvania canal, d. at Mexico, Juniata county, July 12, 1829, aged 26 years.

Neely, Dr. Jonathan, d. February 1, 1827, at the house of John C. McAllister, Fort Hunter.

AMERICA'S OLD WARS.

During the last one hundred and eighty-seven years America has had nine wars (without counting minor Indian wars), and all of these together make fifty odd years of warfare—that is to say—during that long period America has had two years of peace to one year of war.

Their first war took place in the reign of William III., and lasted from 1689 to 1697. William III., the champion of Protestant interests, waged a long war with the magnificent and profligate Louis XIV. of France. Could Puritan New England refrain from sending a helping hand? Two considerable expeditions sailed from Boston against the northern French possessions, both of which ended in sad wreck and loss, and brought on New England the curse of depreciated paper money. This war was always styled by the Colonists " King William's War."

The next war, known as Queen Anne's war, began in 1702, and ended with the peace of Utrecht in 1713. It was in this war that the great Marlborough won his most brilliant victories. The brave and generous sons of Massachusetts again assailed the French in the north, and wrested from them the Province of Nova Scotia, a conquest which the treaty of Utrecht confirmed.

After thirty years of peace the third war broke out, called King George's war, because it occurred in the reign of George II. It lasted from 1744 to 1748. Once more Massachusetts, with the aid of six other Colonies, sent northward a mighty armament, and conquered the stronghold of Louisburg, on the island of Cape Breton, an event that was celebrated in every town, from Boston to Charleston, with bon-fires, fireworks, illuminations, barbecues and thanksgivings. The valiant Yankee who commanded was knighted and made a lieutenant general for his conduct on this occasion. Sir William Pepperell he was thenceforth called.

Next came the long, fierce war, in which Braddock fell, and Wolfe took Quebec, and all Canada and all India fell under the domain of Britain—the war conducted by William Pitt. In Europe this war is called the Seven Years' war; but in America, where it lasted more than ten years, it is commonly styled the old French war. It began in 1753, and ended with the peace of Paris, in 1763. The people of Pennsylvania, seconded by Virginia and New York, bore the brunt of this great contest.

Then came the war of the Revolution, which lasted eight years; then the rupture with France, in 1798; then the war of 1812; then the internecine war with Mexico; and lastly the war for the Union, which lasted four years, 1861 to 1865.

MEETING-HOUSE SPRINGS.

In North Middleton township, Cumberland county, on the Conedoguinet creek, two and a half miles from Carlisle, is the grave-yard of Meeting-House Springs. A correspondent sends us the following record, which for the present we give space to, intending before the cold season prevents to visit that memorable spot and gather up all the records which time and the elements have not defaced:

JANET THOMPSON.—" Here lys ye Body of Jannet Thompson, wife of ye Rev. Samuel Thompson, who deceased Sept. ye 29, 1744, aged 33 years."

"ALEXANDER MCCULLOUGH, who deceased January ye 15, 1746, aged 50 yrs."

JAMES YOUNG.—" Here lys the body of *James Young, seiner,* who parted this life Feb. 22, 1747, aged 79 years."

MARY DONNEL.—" Here lys ye body of Meyr donnel, who departed this life Oct. 15, 1747, aged 64 yrs."

"THOMAS WITHERSPOON, who departed this life Mar. 22, 1759, aged 57."

McKEHAN.—"Here lys the Body of John and Alexander McKehan." [No date.]

PARKER.—"Sacred to the memory of Major Alexander Parker and his two children, Margaret and John." [No date.]

"RONALD CHAMBERS, died Dec. 24, 1746, aged 60."

WILLIAM GRAHAM, died Apr. 24, 1761, aged 67.

JOHN FLEMMING, died Apr. 22, 1761, aged 39.

JAMES McFARLAN, born Dec. 24, 1685; d. Oct. 31, 1770.

JOHN KINKEAD, died Aug. 4, 1772, aged 51.

MARY KINKEAD (daughter), died Aug., 1758, aged 17.

JAMES WEAKLEY, died June 6, 1772, aged 68.

JANE WEAKLEY (wife), died Nov. 30, 1768, aged 53.

JAMES WEAKLEY (infant son of Samuel and Hetty), died Sept. 4, 1777.

SAMUEL LAIRD, ESQ., died Sept., 1806, in the 74th year of his age. On tombstone these lines:

"Of simple manners, pure, and heart upright,
In mild religion's ways he took delight;
As elder, magistrate or judge he still
Studied obedience to his Maker's will.
A husband kind, a friend to the distressed,
He wished that all around him might be blessed.
A patriot in the worst of times approved,
By purest motives were his actions moved."

There are also names of Drenna, Sanderson, Crocket and others of later date.

FEDERAL CONSTITUTION.

THE PART PENNSYLVANIA TOOK IN ITS PROMULGATION AND ADOPTION.

The Articles of Confederation for a perpetual union of the Colonies, although reported to Congress by the committee on the 8th of July, 1776, was never passed finally until the first day of March, 1781. The widely different opinions of the delegates, notwithstanding the frequent changes in that memorable body, were the chief causes of

delay. At last sectional and State views were thrust aside, and patriotism alone continued to exist; and when peace was declared it
was apparent that a stronger and better law was required for the government of the new-born nation. But the Congress was unequal to
the emergency; it was weak and vacillating. As early as 1782 a
general convention of the States had been suggested. Yet it was not
until 1785 that this plan was put into proper shape. In February,
1787, Congress approved of a convention, and on the 14th of May
that year the representatives from the different States began to arrive
in Philadelphia. Each State sent its strongest and ablest men.
Pennsylvania was not behind the others. She was fitly represented
by such brilliant minds as Franklin, Mifflin, Clymer, Fitzsimmons,
James Wilson and the two Morris', Robert and Gouverneur, of all
of whom the Commonwealth is justly proud.

After great deliberation, the sessions having been held under the
ban of secrecy, the veil of which was never lifted until many of the
actors had passed from the stage of life, the fundamental law of the
nation was promulgated. It is stated that when Franklin affixed his
autograph to that famous document he shed tears, but that with other
sentimentalities which find a place in history now pass as myths of
the century. Next to the immortal declaration itself there was a sort
of sublimity in the transaction. It was nevertheless awaiting not
only the approval of the States but the verdict of futurity.

Given to the States for ratification was the signal for attack. If
ever a document was torn into shreds it was the original Constitution. Wise in its framing, yet there is no doubt that a colder reception could not have awaited it. The name of Washington affixed to
it had at first little weight, and in all the States it seemed as if the
document was doomed. But when the first indignant thunderings
of the opposition had died away, sober reasoning, second thought,
and aye, patriotic reflection changed the current of popular opinion.

Nowhere was the opposition so strong as in Pennsylvania, and it is
an undisputed fact that outside of Philadelphia four-fifths of all the
people were opposed to the spirit and letter of the new Constitution.
When the subject of calling a convention for the purpose of ratifying
that paper came before the Assembly of the State, the opposition was
firm and decided. Fortunately the back counties were not fully represented, the allotment of members not being amply made. Gouverneur Morris dreaded the cold and sour temper of the back counties,
and well he might, for they had no voice in the choice of delegates to
the Federal convention, all of the members being from Philadelphia,
notwithstanding there were able men in other sections of the State.
Hence the back counties and their representatives in the General As-

sembly viewed with distrust the frame of government, in the making of which they had no voice. The metropolis, however, controlled then as now all legislation, and thwarted the will of the people.

Finding that they were to be out-generaled when the calling of a convention came up, the minority absented themselves from the Assembly. This legislative body consisted of sixty-four members, two-thirds of which it required for a quorum, including the speaker. When the subject came up for final consideration only forty-three members were present, including the presiding officer, not a quorum. Immediately the sergeant-at-arms was sent after the recusant members, and by force brought in James McCalmont, of Franklin county, and Jacob Miley, of Dauphin county, passing the measure in this compulsory manner. At no period in the history of our State was ever the "gag-law," as now termed, so violently enforced. It was the first time in the history of any legislative body when a quorum was counted whether voting or not.

The excitement throughout Pennsylvania was great—every effort being made by the supporters of the Constitution to carry the convention. The election was far from a quiet one. In the eastern counties the Federalists had their own way, while in the back counties the opponents of the Constitution easily succeeded. It is possible that when first chosen the majority of the convention were antagonistic, but with such champions as Wilson and McKean, the Constitutionalists carried the day, and Pennsylvania was the second to wheel into line for the federal compact. The dissentients, however, did not yield without a struggle, and the "address of the minority" to the people of the State is one of the ablest documents of the day.

The adoption of the Constitution by the majority of the States was the signal for great rejoicing throughout the confederation, and especially so in Pennsylvania, upon whose decision hung the action of other Commonwealths, for as when then stated, "as goes Pennsylvania so goes the entire Union." The anti-federalists were in nowise disheartened, and determined to right whatever might be amiss in the Constitution. with such men as Findley, Smilie and Gallatin in Western Pennsylvania, with Whitehill, Elliott and Bryan east of the mountains, as leaders, the political contest was continued.

A "Conference," such is the term then employed, was called to meet at Harrisburg to adopt measures looking to a revision of the Federal Constitution. The conference met on the 3d of September, 1788, representatives being present from all the counties save Luzerne and Allegheny, and adopted resolutions, with a memorial to the General Assembly, proposing certain amendments to the federal frame of government, twelve in number. This harmonious action of the conference was supplemented by the nomination of candidates for the first Congress and electors for President of the United States.

Judging from the tone of the newspapers in Philadelphia of that era one would infer that the work accomplished by this conference would not amount to anything, although the Federalist editors seemed to be in a perfect rage during the entire campaign. Notwithstanding the influence over the Germans in arraying them against the Scotch-Irish, the Constitutionalists barely escaped defeat, two of their number, Capt. Stephen Chambers, of Lancaster, and Col. John Allison, of Franklin, both soldiers of the Revolution, having been sacrificed by them to cajole the German vote. That fraud was used by the Federalists was then charged, and looking upon the whole transaction in the light of to-day there is little doubt about it. It was the first and last federal victory in the State.

Of the twelve amendments demanded by the Harrisburg conference nine of them subsequently became engrafted upon the fundamental law of the Union. "They built wiser than they knew." A history of the struggle, from 1776 down through the Revolution to the signing of the Articles of Confederation and the Constitution itself is fraught with absorbing interest. In the political upheavels which have followed, although stones have been added, the foundation built by our fathers remains solid, and if after the lapse of a century the strength of that monument is as firm as when our ancestors struggled over its erection with all their differences of opinion, let us pass down the legacy of "The Union and the Constitution, one and inseparable, now and forever."

A HUNDRED YEARS AGO.

INTERESTING FACTS IN CONNECTION WITH THE ADOPTION OF THE FEDERAL CONSTITUTION.

[From the *Pennsylvania Gazette* for Wednesday, March 26, 1788.]

MESSRS. HALL AND SELLERS: The original letters I send you for publication and which will be left in your hands for inspection afford one proof amongst a thousand that the indefatigable number, the *Centinel*, is endued with a zeal and activity in every work of mischief, always commensurate with its extent, for who but himself, to serve any cause whatever, would condescend to a correspondence with one of the sourest, narrowest, and most illiterate creatures in the State.

PHILADELPHIA, *7th March, 1788.*

Dear Sir: Last Tuesday the post from New England brought sad tidings for some folks here. The convention of New Hampshire, it seems by 70 against, and 40 for, have adjourned until 17th June. Had the final adjustment of the new system been put, it would have been rejected by a great majority. The friends of it, therefore, to let it fall easily, proposed the adjournment and the others gave way. This disaster we consider as fatal to the business. So does its advocates here, and they are in the dumps, and some of the members of the general convention are apologizing for their conduct. Before this news came the party was up in the skies, as their behaviour seemed to express. Yet their success at Boston was so moderated by the propositions for amendment, which, however superficial, broke the sanctity of the new Constitution. Besides, the president of the Boston convention, Hancock, has written to our assembly, sending their doings and amendments and desiring that this State should adopt similar amendments. On the whole, as New York is not likely to concur; nor Virginia, tho' General W. lives there; nor Rhode Island; and as N. Carolina convention meets not till 17th July, and will be much swayed by Virginia; as Maryland is much divided, if not in the whole against; I have no doubt there will be another general convention. Georgia acceded to it, because pressed by an Indian war and wanted aid immediately.

Failing, the conspirators against equal liberty will have much conceit and wicked conduct to answer for. They have seduced the post-officers to stop all newspapers from State to State that contained investigations of their plans, so that the dissent of the minority of Pennsylvania did not get to Boston before their convention rose. Every little town furnished a flaming account, like those of Carlisle, Bethlehem, &c., asserting how much the people of their place and neighborhood approved the new plan. These were circulated and reprinted, from Georgia to New Hampshire, with parades. This deceived the people into the notion that there was a general approbation. In Virginia, at this moment, from the suppression of intelligence and by false letters, it is generally supposed that the opposition in Pennsylvania had vanished, and at Boston the news of the disturbances at Carlisle reaching Boston before the convention there rose, the whole was confidently denied. As the convention of Massachusetts was finishing, a vessel is made to arrive at a port fifteen miles off with account that North Carolina had adopted, though that convention sits not till July. Again, as the convention of New Hampshire was near finishing, this falsehood is newly published at Newport, Rhode Island, and another vessel pretended to seduce another adoption. These are but a specimen of these arts and inventions; but a lying tongue is but for a moment. The people everywhere will see and feel their frauds. Yet, these are generally the doings of the first men in many of the

States. I say nothing of the frauds of calling conventions hastily in all the New England States save Rhode Island, which has called none, in New Jersey, in Pennsylvania, and in Delaware. In the Southern States (all except Georgia), the calls of conventions have been deliberate and distant; so in New York I am glad of the prospect we have because it will prevent the danger of confusion and bloodshed. For if nine States had been nominally led into the plan, while the body of the people in many of them were still averse, civil war must have ensued, as the conspirators would have endeavored to set their scheme in motion without funds to support the necessary standing army. This danger now seems to be over, for which we ought to be thankful.

In Cumberland county all are against it, except a small group in Carlisle, and a few scattered in the country. " This small group in October met and censured their county representatives for attempting the breaking up of the late General Assembly, to prevent the calling the people of every county east of Bedford to elect convention in nine or ten days; with other matters favoring the new plan. These were paraded in the Carlisle *Gazette* as the sense of the people and by the party published here and elsewhere. The county resented it, and warned these men not to repeat the artifice. Yet on the 25th December the same people attempted to rejoice on occasion of the adoption by the convention of Pennsylvania. They were hindered; some blows ensued. Next day the same men, armed, made another essay; they were overpowered and the effigies of two leading members of convention were burned in contempt. Upon this, a letter of many affidavits was dispatched to Mr. McKean pressing his warrants for twenty persons charged with riots; among others Justice Jordan. The business being irksome Mr. McKean alleging it was indelicate for him to act where he was ill-used, persuaded Mr. Atlee and labored me to send up our warrant. I represented the danger of risquing insult to our precept, advising delay, and the rather, as no hasty steps had been taken to bring the city rioters to justice. Mr. A. and Mr. Rush sent up their warrant. It lay some time in Carlisle unexecuted, to bring the accused to submit and ask pardon. Nothing being done, however, in this way, about 26th of February the sheriff was sent to work. Eight or nine refusing to give bail they were imprisoned. By the last accounts from Harrisburg large numbers were assembled from York and Dauphin, as well as Cumberland, to set the prisoners at large. This gave much uneasiness to the conspirators here. Even the chief justice 'tis said, had before the news came consented to drop the prosecution, as the members of the council feared the event. But he wrote to Mr. Atlee too late, if he has written. We hope no further mischief will ensue;

tho' the conspirators in Carlisle told Mr. McKean in their letter they feared that their dwellings would be pulled down. Here, in October, we were forced to hold our tongues, lest well-dressed ruffians should fall upon us. At this day the case is otherwise. Yet many are still silent, lest, the new plan being adopted, they might hereafter be ruined for opposing. Since it was commonly safe from immediate attack, some of us have been open and avowed, and risqued all the malice of these men. The common people are latterly too much of our opinions to hurt us. Indeed, none but gentlemen mobs have been active in Philadelphia. In Montgomery the current of the county is against the plan, the friends of it are silent; Berks very few favor it; the same in Dauphin. In the town of Lancaster there is a party, but few elsewhere in the county. In York the opposers are very numerous.

In Franklin there are the great body of the people. In Bedford and in the over-hill counties very few are for it. Of Northumberland I can say little. Our friends in Bucks and Chester are much increased. The Quakers are changed generally. The solid Quakers here greatly dislike it, but they do not intermeddle. Their young people favor it, and in this city, Baltimore, New York, Boston, &c., there is a majority for it; most so in Boston. Shays' insurrection has been made a great engine of terror to dispose people of that country to receive chains if the western counties can be kept down. Shays and his adherents were aroused to what they did by excessive taxes; perhaps contrived to dispose the New England States to receive new system, to which they would otherwise be averse.

Since writing the foregoing we have accounts from Carlisle that about 1,000 armed men appeared there, and demanding of the sheriff to open the prison, set at liberty the persons charged as rioters, and burned the commitment. The inhabitants of the town, in the meanwhile, kept close within their houses, and the armed men soon went away without doing anything further. Mr. James Hanna, a constitutionalist, attorney-at-law at Newtown, was this day very unexpectedly chosen to succeed Colonel Hart as recorder of deeds and register of wills of Bucks county. Mr. Dubois, nephew of Mr. Henry Wynkoop, was a competitor, yet, to the surprise of everybody, and astonishment of Gerardus Wynkoop, Hanna had 36 votes, and Mr. Dubois but 26. Mr. Irwin, son of Arthur Irwin, of Tinicum, in Bucks county, had 5 votes.

The peculiar reason why the party for the new Constitution is large here is the supreme influence of the bank, the weight of Mr. Morris, the bankrupt and dependent state of the trades generally, the hopes that by giving large powers to Congress, no foreign ship will be allowed to carry off the rice, tobacco, flour, etc., but it shall be limited to American bottoms. These, and a vain delusion that present distress, caused by too large use and consumption of foreign goods and the consequent shipping of specie would be relieved. At Boston all ranks have been taught to believe that it would be a cure for every sore, so infatuated are the inhabitants.

The Assembly is not doing much. A short session is talked of. A day has been spent on the subject of Wyoming, but to no purpose. R. Morris is absent in Virginia. He has been there for some months. Our river is yet shut, but this cannot last above a day or two. I am, dear sir, your very humble servant,   GEO. BRYAN.

To Mr. John Ralston, Allen township, Northampton county.

P. S.—We learn by Mr. Ellicott, late a commissioner for Pennsylvania in running the lines between us and Virginia, that beyond doubt Maryland will reject the new Constitution of the general government. He is just come from Baltimore.

PHILADELPHIA, *12th March, 1788.*

Dear Sir : I wrote a letter addressed to you on Saturday, the 8th instant. It contained a state of present intelligence as to the designed Constitution of the United States. But there was a mistake in giving the vote of New Hampshire adjournment till June. Instead of 70 to 40, it was 56 for and 51 against; which shows its advocates nearly escaped a sudden rejection. The other numbers, 70 to 40, were the estimated size and strength of the parties, of the advocates and opposers. Those in favour of the plan cry out that the others came fettered with instructions; yet this base practice was begun by their friends in Pennsylvania. The place the convention of New Hampshire sits on the 17th June is Concord, 100 miles farther inland, as I am told than Exeter, where this body sat, which bodes no good to the federal party, as they falsely call themselves.

Saturday a person arrived by the stage from North Carolina. He assures that there is no doubt that the new plan will be rejected by that State.

The conspirators are fully detected in stopping the transmission of intelligence from State to State by tricks in the postoffices. Being charged with it early in February, they stiffly denied it. It is at length become too palpable to all. Sure no business of a public nature has proceeded upon such base tricks of fraud and surprise.

I am, dear sir, with compliments to all friends,

Your very obedient servant,   GEO. BRYAN.

To Mr. John Ralston, Allen township, Northampton county.

Old Col. Hart is dead. Robert Whitehill has lately married a widow Montgomery, of Upper Octorara, Chester county.

NOTES AND QUERIES.—CLXV.

McCLURES OF PAXTANG AND HANOVER.

I. RICHARD McCLURE, an emigrant from the north of Ireland, set‑tled prior to 1730 in Paxtang township, then Lancaster county, Province of Pennsylvania, where he took up a tract of six hundred acres of land. Of his children, all born in Ireland, we have the following:

2. i. *Thomas.*
3. ii. *Charles.*
4. iii. *John.*
5. iv. *Richard.*

II. THOMAS McCLURE, son of Richard McClure, b. ——, in north of Ireland; d. in 1765, in Paxtang, whence he emigrated; m. Mary ——, who d. April, 1773, in Hanover. They had issue:

    i. *John,* m. Mary ——; in 1773. They resided in Mt. Pleasant township, York county, Pa.

    ii. *William.*

    iii. *Mary,* m., February 6, 1759, Joseph Sherer.

    iv. *Martha,* m. Andrew Wilson.

    v. *Jean,* m. James Burney.

    vi. *Thomas,* m. Mary Harvey.

III. CHARLES McCLURE (Richard), d. prior to 1761, leaving a wife Eleanor, and children as follows:

    i. *Arthur.*

    ii. *Rebecca.*

    iii. *Jennett.*

    iv. *William.*

    v. *John.*

    vi. *Martha.*

    vii. *Eleanor.*

    viii. *Charles.*

    ix. *Margaret.*

IV. JOHN McCLURE (Richard), d. in 1762, in Hanover; m. Mary ——. They had issue:

    i. *James,* b. 1733; d. November 14, 1805, in Hanover; m. Mary Espy.

    ii. *William.*

    iii. *Jane,* m. William Waugh.

    iv. *Ann.*

V. RICHARD McCLURE (Richard), m., and left issue:
  i. Alexander, m. Martha ———.
7. *ii. William,* m. Margaret Wright.
8. *iii. Jonathan,* m. Sarah Hays.
  iv. Andrew, m. Margaret ———.
  v. Roan, removed to White Deer Valley, Northumberland county; d. October 8, 1833; m. Hannah ———; d. August 20, 1828.
  vi. Margaret, m., September 7, 1757, John Steel.
  vii. David, m. Margaret Lecky.
  viii. Katharine, m. Robert Fruit.

VI. THOMAS McCLURE (Thomas, Richard), d. January, 1778, in Hanover; m., in 1761, MARY HARVEY. They had issue:
  i. William, m. Agnes Lewis.
  ii. Thomas.
  iii. Martha, m. Andrew Wilson, and had *Martha.*
  iv. Mary, m. James George.
  v. Sarah, m. Daniel McGuire.
  vi. Jean, m. Samuel Moor.

VII. WILLIAM McCLURE (Richard, Richard), d. April, 1785, in Paxtang; m. MARGARET WRIGHT, daughter of Robert Wright. They had issue:
  i. Robert, b. Dec. 18, 1763; m. Priscilla ———.
  ii. Rebecca, m. Peter Sturgeon.
  iii. Mary, m. Samuel Russell.
  iv. Sarah, m. David Riddle, of York county, Pa.
  v. Margaret.
  vi. Jean, b. 1788; d. December 21, 1876, in Buffalo Valley.

VIII. JONATHAN McCLURE (Richard, Richard), b. 1745, in Paxtang; d. December 11, 1799; m., November 10, 1768, SARAH HAYS, of Derry. They had issue:
  i. Roan, removed to Buffalo Valley.
  ii. Mary.
  iii. Matthew.
  iv. Jonathan.
  v. Sarah.

NOTES AND QUERIES.—CLXVI.

OLD MILLS.—Redsecker's mill at Aberdeen, on the Conewago, was built by Uriah and Barbara Sharer in 1774. Flour was there made for the American army during the Revolution.

Risser's mill, in the southeastern corner of Conewago township and also of Dauphin county, was built by Christian Snyder in 1769.

Goss' mill was built in 1779 by the "Irish Johnsons," so called to distinguish them from another family of Johnsons who lived in the neighborhood, and who ran the distilleries on the premises now owned by Benjamin Longenecker and the estate of the late John Risser.   C. G. S.

HISTORICAL MEMORANDA.

[The following valuable historical excerpts have been contributed by John W. Jordan, of the Historical Society of Pennsylvania.]

During the years of political excitement which followed the adoption of the Constitution of the United States the authorities of the Moravian Church in America dissuaded their members from taking any active part. That their counsel was not heeded by all is evident from the following entry in the minute book of the congregation in Philadelphia under date of 1st March, 1795 :

" A letter was read from the Conference at Bethlehem, setting forth that recently, much to their sorrow and grief, they learned that some of our brethren in Lancaster had joined some of the self-created political body called *Democrats*, and even accepted office therein."

Records of the first birth, baptism, marriage and death, and the first Indian baptism at Bethlehem, Pa. :

Anna, daughter of Paul Daniel and Regina Dorothea Brycelius born July 16, 1742, and baptized by Count Zinzendorf.

John William Zander, missionary to Surinam, S. A., was married to *Johanna Magdalena Muller*, daughter of John Peter Muller, shoemaker, of Germantown, July 8, 1742, by Count Zinzendorf.

John Muller, a single brother from Rhinebeck, died June 26, 1742, and was buried the next day.

David, alias *Wanab*, a Mohican from Checomeco, was baptized September 15, 1742, by Count Zinzendorf.

Joshua, alias *Tashawachamen*, a Mohican from Checomeco, was baptized September 14, 1742, by Gottlob Buttner.

Prior to the removal of the dead from the Moravian grave-yard in Philadelphia the most conspicuous grave stone was that which covered the remains of the well known printer, Zachariah Poulson :

Beneath this Stone | are deposited | the remains of | Zachariah Poulson, Printer. | He was born in Copenhagen, Denmark, | on the sixteenth of June, 1737, | and emigrated with his father | In the year 1749. | From thence to Philadelphia | where he resided | more than half a century. | On the fourteenth of January, 1804 | In the 67th year of his age | he departed this life | with that peace of mind | which the world | can neither give nor take away.

In an obituary note to the record of his death, his pastor has recorded that after being a member of the Society of Friends, and connected with the Presbyterian Church, he joined the Moravians " on conviction."

AN INDIAN GENEALOGY.

I. TEHOWAGH-WENGARAGHKIN, a Mohawk of the Wolf tribe, was one of the Indian sachems who visited England in 1710. Of him we have no further knowledge. One of his sons was named :

II. AROGHYADAGHA, who represented his tribe at the Treaty of Fort Stanwix, on the 24th of October, 1768. His home was at Canajoharie, the central castle of that nation. He died, it is stated, while on a visit to the Ohio country. His children were :

    i. [*A son*], name unknown.
    ii. [*A son*], name unknown.
    iii. Thayendanegea (Joseph Brant).
    iv. Molly, known in history as Miss Molly, and who became the wife of Sir William Johnson, the commandant of His Brittanic Majesty's forces in the Mohawk country, and also Superintendent of Indian Affairs in America.

III. THAYENDANEGEA, known as Joseph Brant. He was born on the banks of the Ohio in 1742; d. November 24, 1807, at Wellington Square, Upper Canada. It is stated that his first appearance as a warrior was in 1759, when he participated in the Niagara campaign of that year, under Sir William Johnson, who, in 1771, sent him to Dr. Wheelock's Indian school at Hanover, where he translated portions of the New Testament into the Mohawk language. In 1763 he was in the war against Pontiac. He was, at the breaking out of the Revolutionary war, secretary to Guy Johnson, superintendent of the Indians, whom he excited to take arms against the Colonists. Returning from a visit to England in 1775–6, he was employed by the British in predatory excursions against the Colonists in connection with the savage Tory refugee, Col. John Butler; served under St. Leger at the investment of Fort Stanwix; was a leader in the severe battle of Oriskany, 6th August, 1777, and, though it is now believed, not present at the Wyoming massacre, was in that at Cherry Valley, and in July, 1779, led the band that destroyed the Minisinks and defeated the party of Colonel Tusten. He held a colonel's commission from the King, and, after the war, prevailed upon the various tribes to make a permanent treaty of peace. In 1786 he again visited England, where he was received with distinction, and collected funds for the erection of the first Indian church built in Upper Canada, and was afterwards employed by Governor Carleton in the public service. He opposed the confederation of the Indians, which led to the expedition of Wayne in 1793, and did his utmost to preserve peace with the Indians and with the United States. He translated the gospel of St. Mark into the Mohawk language, and did much for the welfare of his people. Brant was thrice married. His first wife, Margaret, was the daughter of an Oneida chief. She died in 1771, leaving issue:

    i. Isaac, b. at Canajoharie; d. 1795 at Burlington Heights, Canada, in a drunken brawl. He was partly educated at a school in the Mohawk Valley, and his education was completed at Niagara. He fell into the habit of drinking while at the military post of Niagara after the war of the Revolution. He committed several outrages of a grave nature, although his father made every effort to reclaim his wayward son. In 1795, on the occasion of receiving the annual bounty of the Government, he threatened the life of his father—in a rencontre which ensued Isaac was seriously wounded—although not dangerously. His rage and violence, however, and refusal to have his wound dressed, resulted in his death. Captain Brant surrendered himself to the authorities, who considering the homicide justifiable, dismissed the case. Isaac Brant left a widow and two children:

        1. *Isaac*, who appears to have been a counterpart of his father. He served with some distinction in the war of 1812–14, but was killed in a drunken frolic.

        2. *Christina*, she married a Frenchman who was killed toward the close of the century on the Wabash river. They left children.

Brant m., secondly, in the winter of 1772–3, by a German clergyman, Susanna, half sister to Margaret; d. shortly after marriage without issue.

Brant m., thirdly, by a clergyman at South Niagara, in the winter of 1780, Catharine, sister of his first wife and eldest dau. of the head chief of the Turtle tribe, first in rank in the Mohawk nation, with whom he had been some years living according to the Indian fashion. She was b. in 1759; d. at Brantford November 24, 1837. They had issue:

 iii. Joseph, Jr., b. 1783; d. 1830; educated at Dartmouth College, but did not complete the regular course; m. and had:

  1. *Catharine,* m. Aaron Hill.

 iv. Jacob, d. in 1846; educated at Dartmouth College, but did not complete the regular course; m. and had:

  1. *John.*

  2. *Squire.*

  3. *Christina,* m. John Jones.

  4. *Jacob, Jr.,* m. Mary Jones.

  5. *Peter.*

  6. *Charlotte,* m. Peter Smith.

 v. John (Ahyouwaeghs), b. September 27, 1794, at the Mohawk village on Grand River; d. there September, 1832, of Asiatic cholera. He received a good English education at Ancaster and Niagara under the tuition of Mr. Richard Cockrel; but through life he improved his mind greatly by the study of the best English authors, by associations and by travel. His manners were those of an accomplished gentleman. When the war of 1812–14 broke out, the Mohawks, true to their ancient faith, espoused the cause of England, and the young chief Tekarihogea took the field with his warriors and did important service. After the declaration of peace he settled down at Wellington Square and became noted for his hospitality. He visited England in 1821 to appeal to the Crown in behalf of his people. In 1827 he was appointed captain and superintendent of the Six Nations. In 1832 he was returned a member of the Provincial Parliament, but was deprived of his seat on account of a want of freehold qualifications. He died shortly after.

 vi. Margaret, d. in 1848, m. —— —— Powles, and left issue.

vii. *Catharine*, d. January 31, 1867, at Wellington Square; m.
Peter John.

viii. *Mary*, m. Seth Hill and left one child, living in 1873.

ix. *Elizabeth*, d. April, 1844, at Wellington Square; m., in
1828, at Mohawk church, William Johnson Kerr, Esq.,
son of Dr. Robert Kerr, of Niagara, and a grandson of
Sir William Johnson. They had four children. Upon
their son was conferred the title of Tekarihogea.

LAFAYETTE IN HARRISBURG.

[We copy from the Lewisburg *Chronicle* of September 29th, the
following address to Robert Goodloe Harper Hayes, who was grandfather of the wife of S. H. Orwig Esq. The writer, William Forster,
was a bachelor cousin of Mr. Hayes.]

HARRISBURG, *Jan'y 31, 1824.*

DEAR SIR: General Lafayette arrived at this place on Sunday
evening last very unexpectedly. We were not apprised of his coming until the morning of the same day. He has taken his lodgings
with the Governor. We have had the pleasure of seeing him this
morning in the State House. I was much disappointed in his appearance. He is quite a robust looking man, speaks somewhat quick,
not very plain. He often says, " My hert warms for de ' Merican
beople." He is to leave this place on Wednesday next for Baltimore.

This day another attempt has been made to elect a United States
Senator. After the vote was taken, the convention adjourned until
this day two weeks. The votes were as follows: Marks, 31; Burnside, 19; Sargent, 20; Ingham, 18; Darlington, 19; Rogers, 5;
Todd, 2.

The judge breaking committees are progressing in the examina-
tion of witnesses. What the result may be is uncertain. The great
number of witnesses and the different records of the courts in the
district will make Chapman's case very tedious.

I would be pleased to hear from you. Please to write.

Very truly,

WM. FORSTER.

MR. R. HAYES, *Mifflinburg, Pa.*

CAPTAIN HUNTER OF HUNTER'S FORT.

Little is known of the individual for whom the Fort at Hunters' was named. From the court records at Lancaster we have gleaned the following. It will be seen that he was connected with the Chambers of that locality, the same family who settled at Falling Springs, now Chambersburg.

In 1757, Capt. Samuel Hunter came into court in behalf of himself and Katharine his wife, late Katharine Chambers, widow and administrator of the estate of Joseph Chambers, deceased, and asked to have three of the justices of the court to meet in Paxtang township to settle her account, for the reason that she was in too feeble health to journey to Lancaster. Whereupon at an Orphans' Court held at the house of Samuel Hunter, in Paxtang, March 31, 1757, before John Allison, Esq., Thomas Forster, Esq., and Adam Read, Esq., they found the value of the estate (perhaps the personal only) to be £1,138; Samuel Hunter to enjoy the upper mill at an annual rental of £140. He had the privilege also of renting the lower mill.

Joseph Chambers left one son, Thomas, and three other children. The court in Provincial times was very accommodating, and the records show that frequently one or more of the justices were assigned to distant townships for the purpose of hearing appeals in the valuation of property, &c. As in the Chambers estate, it was perhaps no unusual thing to hold orphans' court in the outlying townships.

Captain Hunter was executor of the estate of Thomas Chambers, deceased, son of his wife's first husband. He was to pay £274 to William Patterson, Esq., and James Potter for the maintenance of Catharine, Thomas, and James Chambers.

THE SPAYD FAMILY.

Our correspondent " P " sends us some memoranda concerning this family, which is herewith given, dove-tailing with information in our possession:

On the first tax list of the town of Middletown, that for 1778, we find the name of Christian Spayd. Of his children we have the following:

> i. *John*, b. January, 1764; d. October 13, 1822, at Reading. He was a lawyer of prominence, was a member of the General Assembly and a judge of the courts of Berks county. He married Catharine Hiester, a daughter of Governor Hiester, and their children were:

1. *Elizabeth,* m. Edward B. Hubley, member of Congress from Schuylkill county.
2. *John,* a graduate of the Medical Department, University of Pennsylvania.
3. *Catharine-B.,* m. John B. Brooke, a prominent merchant of Reading.
4. *Joseph-Hiester,* a member of the Berks county bar.
5. *George-W.,* once chief burgess of Reading.
6. *Henry,* a graduate of medicine, but died young.
7. *Amelia,* m. Dr. Diller Luther, of Reading.

ii. *Catharine,* b. January 25, 1770; m. ——— McMurtrie. What is known of this family?

iii. *Christian,* b. August 16, 1773; d. August 29, 1841; was justice of the peace, brigade inspector and superintendent of the Frey estate. He was twice married. First, October 10, 1806, to Elizabeth (Betsy) Deyarmond, daughter of Joseph Deyarmond, of Columbia, (Palmyra). Their children were:

    1. *Mary,* married at the age of fifty, Martin Peck, of Middletown.
    2. *Elizabeth,* m. ——— Shannon.
    3. *Joseph,* m. a lady of Philadelphia.
    4. *George,* m. in Harrisburg.
    5. *Christian,* printer.

Christian Spayd m., secondly, a Miss Ward, who survived her husband many years, residing in the stone house at Middletown, opposite the old Bank.

In the tombstone records of Old St. Peter's church-yard, at Middletown, is this inscription:

Spayd, Elizabeth (Frazier), wife of Christian, b. Oct. 26, 1787; d. Aug. 27, 1826.

From this we would infer that although a daughter of Joseph Deyarmond, she may nevertheless have been a widow—or was Christian Spayd married three times.

A daughter of the first wife, Susan Louisa, b. February 12, 1808, d. July 1, 1813.

What further information is there?   **P.**

HIGHSPIRE AND ITS POSTMASTERS.

The United States post-office guide contains many offices of the same name—often as many as there are States in the Union—but there is one office (our own Highspire), which stands alone, and none have ever forgotten it who perchance have ever seen or heard of it. In our efforts to find why this peculiar name was given we have discovered that the office was established in December, 1829, with Jeremiah Kirk as the first postmaster, being appointed at that time. Who he was we know not, and desire information of him. On March 23, 1832, Conrad Allerman was appointed, but never qualified. April 30th of the same year Robert Wilson was appointed. He it was who established, ten years prior to his becoming postmaster, the "Highspire Distillery." The 13th of May, 1834, found John Sener occupying the position. He was from Lancaster city, a blacksmith, and one of the first mechanics in the new town. Henry Stoner, Jr., or "Lame Harry," as he was called, who resided all his life in the town and one of the first school teachers under the free school system, received his commission, dated September 9, 1836. John Horning was commissioned October 18, 1838. Who was he? On February 2, 1839, Robert Wilson again became the custodian of the office. January 4, 1842, Jacob Nissley, who kept the store at the red building on the bridge hill crossing the canal at the pike. He was succeeded by Henry Fleisher, February 4, 1847, who now resides in Alliance, O. George Garman, watchmaker, was commissioned December 14, 1848. Where is he? April 9, 1849, Henry Stoner once more became the postmaster and how well he filled the position can be quickly told in a service of fifteen years, when he was succeeded by Uriah P. Banks, a change brought about by the change of administration, "Andy Johnson" occupying the Presidential chair. November 21, 1865, Jacob Hocker was appointed. After a refusal and lapse of forty years Conrad Alleman was appointed March 22, 1870, which office he held until his death, July 4, 1872. On the 30th of August, same year, Milton John, son of Henry Stoner, was appointed, which office he held until "offensive partisanship" removed him and he was succeeded by J. J. Lehman September 8, 1885, a native and merchant of the town.   E. W. S. P.